Volume IV of
THE CATHOLIC UNIVERSITY
PEDAGOGICAL SERIES

HISTORY OF EDUCATION

A Survey of the Development of
Educational Theory and Practice in
Ancient, Medieval, and Modern Times

BY

PATRICK J. McCORMICK, S.T.L., Ph.D.
RECTOR OF THE CATHOLIC UNIVERSITY OF AMERICA

WITH AN INTRODUCTION

BY

EDWARD A. PACE, Ph.D., S.T.D., LL.D.
LATE PROFESSOR OF PHILOSOPHY IN THE
CATHOLIC UNIVERSITY OF AMERICA

REVISED BY

FRANCIS P. CASSIDY, Ph.D.
ASSOCIATE PROFESSOR OF EDUCATION
THE CATHOLIC UNIVERSITY OF AMERICA

1950

THE CATHOLIC EDUCATION PRESS
WASHINGTON, D. C.

2nd Printing—1948
3rd Printing—1949
4th Printing—1950

Dedicated

in

Grateful Memory

to

The Most Reverend

Thomas Joseph Shahan, D.D.

Bishop of Germanicopolis
Rector of
The Catholic University of America
1909—1928

*Who had a profound interest
in historical studies*

TABLE OF CONTENTS

PAGE

AUTHOR'S PREFACE xi
REVISER'S PREFACE xiii
INTRODUCTION. xvii
GENERAL BIBLIOGRAPHY xxii

PART I

ANCIENT EDUCATION

CHAPTER
I. CHINA. 5
II. JAPAN. 18
III. EGYPT. 23
IV. INDIA 35
V. PERSIA 46
VI. SEMITIC PEOPLES. 58
VII. GREEK EDUCATION 83
VIII. ROMAN EDUCATION 135
SUMMARY OF ANCIENT EDUCATION . . . 157

PART II

CHRISTIAN EDUCATION

IX. EARLY CHRISTIAN EDUCATION 164
X. FATHERS OF THE CHURCH. 173
XI. MEDIEVAL EDUCATION 204
From the Patristic Period to the
Carlovingian Revival
XII. MEDIEVAL EDUCATION (*Continued*) . . . 218
From the Carlovingian Revival to
Scholasticism

vii

CHAPTER   PAGE

XIII. MEDIEVAL EDUCATION (*Continued*) . . . 239
     Educators of the Carlovingian Period

XIV. MEDIEVAL EDUCATION (*Continued*) . . . 253
     Scholasticism

XV. MEDIEVAL EDUCATION (*Continued*) . . . 273
     Universities

XVI. MEDIEVAL EDUCATION (*Continued*) . . . 286
     Religious Orders and Educators of the
     Scholastic and University Period

XVII. MEDIEVAL EDUCATION (*Continued*) . . . 299
     Types of Later Medieval Schools
     SUMMARY OF EARLY CHRISTIAN AND
     MEDIEVAL EDUCATION 308

PART III
RENAISSANCE AND REFORMATION

XVIII. THE RENAISSANCE IN ITALY 319
XIX. THE RENAISSANCE IN OTHER COUNTRIES 345
XX. THE REFORMATION 383
XXI. THE CATHOLIC REACTION 407
     SUMMARY OF RENAISSANCE AND REFOR-
     MATION PERIOD 424

PART IV
MODERN EDUCATION

XXII. REALISM 434
     Humanistic Realists
XXIII. REALISM (*Continued*) 449
     Sense Realists
XXIV. REALISTS AND THEORISTS OF THE SEVEN-
     TEENTH CENTURY 469

CHAPTER   PAGE
  XXV. RELIGIOUS ORGANIZATIONS OF THE SEVEN-
             TEENTH CENTURY.   485
 XXVI. THE EIGHTEENTH CENTURY   501
             Naturalism and Education
 XXVII. THE NINETEENTH CENTURY   516
             The Psychologists
XXVIII. THE NINETEENTH CENTURY (*Continued*) .   530
             The Psychologists (*Continued*)
 XXIX. THE NINETEENTH CENTURY (*Continued*)   541
             The Psychologists and Other Theorists
  XXX. RECENT DEVELOPMENTS IN AMERICAN
             EDUCATION.   564
 XXXI. RECENT DEVELOPMENTS IN AMERICAN
             EDUCATION (*Continued*)   581
XXXII. DEVELOPMENT OF MODERN SCHOOL
             SYSTEMS.   595
XXXIII. DEVELOPMENT OF MODERN SCHOOL SYS-
             TEMS (*Continued*)   617
             The United States
             SUMMARY OF MODERN EDUCATION . . .   629
INDEX   631

AUTHOR'S PREFACE

This book aims to present a survey of the development of educational theory and practice from ancient times to the present. It aspires to be a practical textbook in the history of education, and while necessarily brief, it is, the author hopes, sufficiently expansive on important movements and details to afford that general view of educational advance and development which is imperative for an understanding of current problems. Its special aim is to meet the needs of the Catholic teacher or student, to give him along with a knowledge of educational history that sympathy with Christian institutions and men, especially in the Middle Ages, which a common faith and spiritual heritage demand, and which contemporary histories of education in English do not tend to foster, and also to enable him properly to estimate those educators and schools whose theological and philosophical tenets are at variance with the teachings of the Church.

A general bibliography and special bibliographies for each chapter have been provided, so that, in addition to the references accompanying the text, there will be afforded ample material for collateral reading.

In preparing his manuscript the author has gone, whenever possible, to original sources or recognized authorities. He has frequently consulted and drawn from *The Catholic Encyclopedia, The Cyclopedia of Education,* and the histories of education by Davidson, Monroe, Kemp, Graves, Stöckl, Krieg, and Bartholome. He acknowledges his indebtedness to these works and to the histories in particular for many ideas in arrangement and presentation. He is deeply grateful to his colleagues in the Department of Education of the Catholic University of America: the Rev. Dr. Edward A. Pace who has kindly read all the proofs; the Rev. Dr. Thomas E. Shields and the Rev. Dr. William Turner who have generously advised and directed him on many occasions. To Mr. Joseph Schneider, Assistant Librarian of the Catholic University of America, and Dr. John D. Wolcott, Acting Librarian of the United States Bureau of Education, he expresses sincere thanks for their repeated courtesies and services.

PATRICK J. McCORMICK.

Washington, D. C.
January 18, 1915.

REVISER'S PREFACE

The *History of Education* by Right Reverend Monsignor Patrick J. McCormick, published in 1915, was the first work of its kind in English by a Catholic author. The present writer has used it as a basic text in his classroom for over a period of twenty years and has found it in general quite satisfactory. It has served well the purpose for which it was intended. So rapidly have conditions changed in the educational world during the past quarter of a century, however, and research has added so much to our knowledge of educational theory and practice in the past, that it is now felt necessary to expand the treatment of the various topics discussed in this volume and thus bring it up to date.

In the present revision, much new material has been added, but the reader familiar with the original text will find that substantially its content has been preserved. The section dealing with the Ancient Period delves more extensively into the history and civilization of the particular peoples. This has been done in the belief that it is impossible to give the student an adequate approach to a correct view of what constitutes the education of a people without first putting before him the historical background and special characteristics of a nation's life. It may seem at times that this procedure obscures the main purpose of the educational historian, but the writer feels justified in the bringing in of this ancillary matter on the grounds that the history of education is not merely the history of school theories and practices. The school is but one of the many forces which have contributed to the shaping of education in the past and must not be made to stand for the whole of the educational process.

In the treatment of the other three divisions—Christian, Renaissance and Reformation, Modern—the same point of view has been maintained. The preparation for life given in the home and furthered by the numerous other agencies in society that are potent factors in forming the habits of thought and the moral character of individuals has suggested the introduction of certain features into the text which aim to show that the purpose of education is the complete development of the individual and must not be limited to the training and equipment of the mind. Unfortunately, in modern times the educative process has too often been regarded as not extending beyond the confines of the school.

In the discussion of the educational theorists of the nineteenth and twentieth centuries additional space has been devoted to the analysis of the philosophical concepts of these psychologists as a background for a proper understanding of their educational theories and principles. The present-day educational movements are interpreted in the light of this psychological influence and the pertinent history of the period. The chapters dealing with American educational leaders are entirely new. The discussion of the development of modern state systems of education has been carried down to the opening of the second World War.

The present writer has always considered it an honor that he was chosen by Monsignor McCormick to assist him in the teaching of the history of education at The Catholic University and has found his work in the field simplified by having at hand such a useful compendium as the original text has proved to be. He considers it a still greater privilege to be permitted to contribute towards making the text a more serviceable volume for continued classroom use. The educational changes that seem destined to come after the War, what with the shifting of political boundaries and the spread of the spirit of international understanding, will undoubtedly necessitate a further revision in the not too distant future.

It is the agreeable duty of the present writer to acknowledge his debt to Rt. Rev. Monsignor Patrick J. McCormick, Ph.D., Rector of the Catholic University, and to Rt. Rev. Monsignor Edward B. Jordan, S.T.D., Vice-Rector of The Catholic University, who read the manuscript and made valuable suggestions concerning it. He is deeply appreciative of assistance rendered by staff members of the Catholic University Library, the Library of Congress, and the Library of the United States Office of Education who furnished pertinent references and materials. His sincere thanks are due Miss Mary Dixon, Reference Librarian in the library division of the American Red Cross, Washington, D. C., who gave generously of her time in preparing the index. He gladly makes acknowledgment of his indebtedness to publishers for the use of quotations.

Special acknowledgment is made to the Abbey Press, Fort Augustus, Scotland; D. Appleton and Co., New York; Benziger Bros., New York; A. & C. Black, Ltd., London; Boni and Liveright, New York; Burns, Oates and Washbourne, Ltd., London; The Catholic Education Press, Brookland, D. C.; The Clarendon Press, Oxford; A. Constable, Westminster, England; Harper and Brothers, New York; Harvard University Press, Cambridge, Massachusetts; D. C. Heath and Co., Boston; William Heinemann, Ltd. (Loeb), London; J. Hodges, London; Henry Holt and Co., New York; Longmans, Green & Co., New York; The Macmillan Co., New York; Methuen and Co., Ltd., London; Nogent-le-Rotrose, Paris; Charles Poussielgue, Paris; K. Paul, Trench, Trübner and Co., Ltd., London; G. P. Putnam's Sons, New York; Sands and Co., London; Charles Scribner's Sons, New York; Cambridge University Press, Cambridge, England.

FRANCIS P. CASSIDY.

The Catholic University of America
December 8, 1945.

INTRODUCTION

In proportion as the importance of education is more fully understood, a deeper interest is taken in its history. It has not always been the potent factor in life and civilization which it undoubtedly is at present; but in some form and in some measure it has helped to shape the conduct of individuals and the destiny of peoples. It has held a leading place among those agencies which with little pomp or circumstance have swayed the minds of men and which are now receiving more attention from the historian than they did a century ago. If a knowledge of the social, economic, political and religious institutions and movements which have built up the modern world is a part of general culture, a knowledge of the history of education is not of less value.

Usually, however, books on this subject make a special appeal to teachers; and this is quite intelligible, since, as education is the transmission of our spiritual and intellectual heritage, it is only fitting that they who transmit it should know whence it comes and how. They are advised to study each problem in its growth and so to understand its actual meaning. They are induced to trace the development of system and theory and thereby gain a correct perspective. And frequently they are warned that one means of avoiding mistakes is to ponder the rise and fall of meteoric schemes that are no longer known outside the pages of history.

Such an application of the genetic method has obvious advantages: it provides information which every teacher should possess in order to deal effectually with the present situation and to labor intelligently for the future of education. But there is a further utility which should not be overlooked: history is also the source of inspiration, and if there is any calling in which that source should be ever open and flowing, it surely is the teacher's. He who accepts the office of educator should be imbued with the spirit of the pioneers and the reformers and should be able to appreciate at least the enthusiasm of men like Comenius and La Salle and Pestalozzi. The existence of the school with its constantly increasing facilities has come to be such a matter of course that it is hard to realize what the cost has been in thought and effort expended by individuals, by the teaching Orders, the State and the Church. The operation of the school, moreover, tends at times to become mechanical, and there is need of fresh inspiration to preserve that suppleness of mind which should quicken all teaching. The aims of the school are apt to be obscured by multifarious demands or defeated by influences that are anything but educational; and so it is imperative for the teacher to keep alive, in his own soul at least, that idealism which is the very life of his profession. But even without the pressure of these needs, the true teacher will naturally and spontaneously turn to the past and give heed to its lessons.

For the Catholic teacher the history of education has a special significance. It exhibits a phase of the manifold activity of the Church from which the world has derived inestimable benefit in the material order as well as in the spiritual; and it shows how deeply the modern school is indebted to those who first carried Christianity and civilization to the ends of the earth. It does not, on the other hand, prevent a due appreciation of what has been accomplished in recent times; it enables one rather to discern the origin and follow the development of what is best in modern education.

The greatest educational achievement in the world's history was the conversion of Europe. Without that, there could have been no beginning, to say nothing of progress, in the arts and sciences, in social and political organization. The missionaries found little time for the discussion of methods; but they had whole tribes in their schools and they led their pupils from grade to grade of civilization. They did not theorize about manual training; they taught the barbarians to work. And while they were not much concerned about articulation or co-ordination, they took care that what was taught and learned should find its expression in decent living.

While these pioneers strove to eliminate the errors and superstitions of paganism, they preserved and transmitted the finest literary products of the ancient world. The classic texts which made possible the Renaissance and which have played so considerable a part in modern education, would have been lost amid the ruins of the Empire, had they not been treasured by the monks. Without the patient toil of the copyist in the monastery, scholars could not now win fame by preparing critical editions of the Latin and Greek authors, nor would philology have been thought of as a science. Yet, curiously enough, the man who discovers a manuscript in some out of the way corner of a monastery is applauded for the service he renders while the scribe who wrote the manuscript is forgotten.

As regards content, there has been unquestionably a great expansion in modern education beyond the curriculum of the Middle Ages. But in the matter of organization, the framework of the medieval system has been retained. Thus in the structure of our universities we find many elements that date from the twelfth and thirteenth centuries. The grouping of faculties, the gradation of instructors, the conferring of degrees and the authorization to teach which these implied are all inherited from the medieval institutions. What is more essential, the assembling of various branches of learning and the spirit of inquiry which resulted from the contact of many eager minds have come down to us from the same period and the same Catholic sources. Nor is elementary education of more recent origin. It is now well established that schools for the people flourished long before the sixteenth century and that they were often maintained out of the revenues of the Church as they were conducted under its auspices.

What stands out most clearly in the history of education is the fact that the Catholic school has always combined religion, morality and intellectual training. This is not surprising as long as we dwell upon the "ages of faith." But it becomes very conspicuous in the course of the modern period. Although the Church has been in large measure deprived of the material means and of the control which it once enjoyed, it has nevertheless insisted that education, to be complete, must include the discipline of the will in right conduct. While the State whose existence depends upon the morality of its citizens, has refused to give moral training to its pupils, the Church, though so often antagonized by the State, has consistently provided that training in its schools and thus laid the foundation of good citizenship.

The Catholic teacher, then, has every reason to take an interest in the history of education both as a source of information and as a means of quickening his zeal for the work in which he is engaged. The study of this subject will not only furnish him with a key to the complexity of the educational problem at large, but will also enable him to understand the doctrine and the aims of the Catholic Church in regard to the school and its position on many controverted points. He may even be led to the further insight that as religion and education are so closely bound together in all their vicissitudes, the attitude of any institution, whether ecclesiastical or secular, towards the school is a fairly good test of its earnestness in the cause of faith and morality.

In preparing this volume, the author has rendered a service which will be the more highly appreciated because in the English language at least, it has few predecessors if any. While particular phases of the subject have been treated from the Catholic view-point and while excellent monographs on the educational activity of the different teaching orders are available, there has been wanting hitherto a manual which would outline the whole field and place at the teacher's disposal the net results of more detailed research. It is not of course the author's intention that his readers should confine their study to these pages. He has observed in the treatment of the various topics a certain proportion that will open up a correct survey of the field; but the book will attain its chief purpose by suggesting to the student a further inquiry into some of the problems with which the history of education abounds.

EDWARD A. PACE.

Washington, D. C.
January 6, 1915.

GENERAL BIBLIOGRAPHY

ENCYCLOPEDIAS AND DICTIONARIES

Bibliografía Pedagógica, Rufino Blanco y Sánchez, editor. 5 vols.; Madrid: Tipografía de la Revista de archivos, bibliotecas y museos, 1907-12.

Bibliothek der Katholischen Pädagogik, F. X. Kunz, editor. 18 vols.; New York: Herder & Co., 1888-1916.

Catholic Encyclopedia, Charles Herbermann *et al.,* editors. 15 vols.; New York: Robert Appleton Co., 1907-12.

Cyclopedia of Education, H. Kiddle and A. J. Schem, editors. New York: E. Steiger and Co., 1883.

Cyclopedia of Education, Paul Monroe, editor. 5 vols.; New York: The Macmillan Co., 1911-13.

Dictionnaire d'éducation publique et privée, D. Raymond, editor. Paris: J. P. Migne, 1865.

Dictionnaire de pédagogie et d'instruction primaire, F. E. Buisson *et al.,* editors. 2 vols.; Paris: Hachette et Cie, 1879.

Dictionnaire d'archéologie chrétienne et de liturgie, F. Cabrol and H. Leclercq, editors. Paris; Letouzey et Ané 1913-.

Encyclopaedia Britannica, 14th edition, 24 vols.; New York: Encyclopaedia Britannica, Inc., 1939.

Encyclopaedia Sinica, Samuel Couling, editor. Shanghai: Kelley and Walsh, Ltd., 1917.

Encyclopaedie des gesammten Erziehungs und Unterrichtwesens, K. A. Schmid, editor. 10 vols.; Gotha: Borlag von Rudolf Besser, 1876-87.

Encyclopedia and Dictionary of Education, F. Watson, editor. 4 vols.; London: Sir Isaac Pitman and Sons. 1921.

Encyclopedia of Modern Education, Harry N. Rivlin, editor. New York: Philosophical Library, 1943.

Encyklopädisches Handbuch der Erziehungskunde. 2 vols.; Wien und Leipzig: A. Pichlers, Witwe & Sohn, 1906-08.

Encyklopädisches Handbuch der Pädagogik, W. Rein, editor. 10 vols.; Langensalza: H. Beyer and Söhne, 1903-10.

Handbuch der Erziehungswissenschaft. 10 vols.; Regensburg: Joseph Kösel und Friedrich Pustet, 1928.

Jewish Encyclopedia, Adler, Cyrus *et al.,* editors. 12 vols.; New York: Funk and Wagnalls, 1901-06.

Lexikon der Pädagogik, F. Sander, editor. Breslau: Ferdinand Hirt, 1889.

Lexikon der Pädagogik, E. M. Roloff, editor. 5 vols.; Freiburg: Herder and Co., 1913-17.

Lexikon der Pädagogik der Gegenwart, J. Spieler, editor. 2 vols.; Freiburg: Herder and Co , 1932.

Nouveau dictionnaire de pédagogie, F. E. Buisson, editor. Paris: Hachette et Cie., 1911.

Pädagogisches Lexikon, H. Schwartz, editor. Leipzig: Velhagen und Klasing, 1928-.

Sammlung der bedeutendsten Pädagogischen Schriften aus alter und neuer Zeit, Schulz, Gansen, and Keller, editors. Paderborn: F. Schöningh, 1888-1914.

Sonnenschein's Cyclopedia of Education, A. E. Fletcher, editor. New York: The Macmillan Co., 1906.

The Teacher's Encyclopedia, A. P. Laurie, editor. 7 vols.; London: Caxton Publishing Co., 1911-12.

GENERAL HISTORIES OF EDUCATION

Bartholome, F. *Kurze Geschichte der Pädagogik.* Freiburg: Herdersche Verlagshandlung, 1911.

Boyd, William, *The History of Western Education.* London: A. & C. Black, Ltd., 1932.

Cubberly, E. P., *The History of Education.* Boston: Houghton Mifflin Co., 1920.

————, *Readings in the History of Education.* Boston: Houghton Mifflin Co., 1920.

————, *A Brief History of Education.* Boston: Houghton Mifflin Co., 1922.

————. *Public Education in the United States,* revised and enlarged edition. Boston: Houghton Mifflin Co., 1934.

Davidson, Thomas, *A History of Education.* New York: Charles Scribner's Sons, 1900.

Drane, A. T., *Christian Schools and Scholars.* London: Burns Oates and Washburn, Ltd., 1924.

Duggan, Stephen, *A Student's Textbook in the History of Education.* New York: D. Appleton-Century Co., 1936.

Eby, F., and C. F. Arrowood, *The Development of Modern Education.* New York: Prentice-Hall Inc., 1934.

————, *History and Philosophy of Education, Ancient and Medieval.* New York: Prentice-Hall, Inc., 1940.

Graves, F. P., *History of Education.* 3 vols., New York: The Macmillan Co., 1909-13.

————, *A Student's History of Education,* rev. ed. New York: The Macmillan Co., 1936.

Kane, W. T., *An Essay Toward a History of Education.* Chicago: Loyola University Press, 1935.

Kellner, L., *Erziehungsgeschichte in Skizzen und Bildern.* 3 vols., Essen: G. D. Bädeker, 1880.

Knight, E. W., *Twenty Centuries of Education.* Boston: Ginn & Co., 1940.

Marique, P. J., *History of Christian Education.* 3 vols., New York: Fordham University Press, 1924-32.

Monroe, P., *A Textbook in the History of Education.* New York: The Macmillan Co., 1932.

————, *A Brief Course in the History of Education.* New York: The Macmillan Co., 1913.

————, *Founding of the American Public School System.* New York: The Macmillan Co., 1940.

Moore, E. C., *The Story of Instruction.* 2 vols.; New York: The Macmillan Co., 1936-38.

Schiller, H., *Lehrbuch der Geschichte der Pädagogik.* Leipzig: O. R. Reisland, 1904.

Schmid, K. A., *Geschichte der Erziehung vom Anfang an bis auf unsere Zeit.* 5 vols., Stuttgart: J. G. Cotta, 1884-1902.

Stöckl, A., *Lehrbuch der Pädagogik.* Mainz: Kirchheim & Co., 1906.

Wilds, E. H., *Foundations of Modern Education.* New York: Farrar and Rinehart, 1936.

Other Sources of Educational History

Alexander, Carter, *How to Locate Educational Information and Data.* New York: Bureau of Publications, Teachers College, Columbia University, 1935.

Barnard, H., ed., *American Journal of Education.* 31 vols.; Syracuse: C. W. Bardeen, 1902.

Burns, J. A., *The Catholic School System in the United States.* New York: Benziger Bros., 1908.

————, *Growth and Development of the Catholic School System in the United States.* New York: Benziger Bros., 1912.

Burns, J. A. and B. J. Kohlbrenner, *A History of Catholic Education in the United States.* New York: Benziger Bros., 1937.

Education Index. New York: H. W. Wilson Co.

Kandel, I. L., *Comparative Education.* Boston: Houghton Mifflin Co., 1933.

Meyer, A. E., *The Development of Education in the Twentieth Century.* New York: Prentice-Hall, Inc., 1939.

Monroe, W. S., *Bibliography of Education.* New York: D. Appleton and Co., 1897.

Monroe, W. S. and L. Shores, *Bibliographies and Summaries in Education*. New York: H. W. Wilson Co., 1936.

Monroe, W. S., I. H. Hamilton, and V. T. Smith, *Locating Educational Information in Published Sources*. Urbana: University of Illinois, 1930.

Monumenta Germaniae historica.

Monumenta Germaniae paedagogica.

Musée pédagogique et bibliothèque centrale de l'enseignement primaire, begun at Paris in 1884.

Poole's Index to Periodical Literature. Boston: Houghton Mifflin Co., 1881-1907.

Preussische Statistik, begun in 1890.

Reader's Guide to Periodical Literature. New York: H. W. Wilson Co., 1900.

Schmidt, A. G., *Loyola Educational Digest*. Chicago: Loyola University Press, 1924.

Selected References in Education. Chicago: University of Chicago, 1934.

Shea, J. G., *History of the Catholic Church Within the Limits of the United States*. 4 vols.; New York: J. G. Shea, 1886-92.

Smith, H. L., *Comparative Education*. Bloomington, Indiana: Indiana University, 1941.

Smith, H. L., and W. I. Painter, *Bibliography of Literature on Education in Countries other than the United States*. Bloomington, Indiana: Indiana University, 1937.

Special Reports on Educational Subjects, begun by the Education Department of Great Britain in 1897.

Turosienski, S. K., *Foreign and Comparative Education*. Washington, D. C.: Government Printing Office, 1934.

U. S. Bureau of Education, *Bibliography of Current Research Studies in Education*.

————————, *Bulletins and Reports*.

Part I

Ancient Education

SYNOPSIS OF THE ANCIENT PERIOD

ANCIENT MONARCHIES OF THE EAST

China: Its educational system is the oldest in history. It was static and democratic. The method of instruction was that of exact imitation.

Japan: Method of education pursued almost identical with the Chinese. Only the members of the nobility were instructed.

Egypt: It has the oldest civilization known to man. The class system of education which it developed reached its climax in the training of the priests.

India: Organized a rigid caste system in society with educational facilities offered to the members of the higher castes only.

Persia: An example of state education; all educational efforts were directed toward the training of soldiers.

SEMITIC PEOPLES

Babylonians: Invented a system of weights and measures which has been the basis of all modern systems; mapped out the zodiac; arranged names of days of week.

Assyrians: Accredited with a superior genius in architecture, painting, and sculpture.

Phoenicians: To them are attributed the invention of symbols for numbers and the formation of the alphabet for the Western World.

Hebrews: The highest branch of the Semites in point of morality and religion; surpassed the other nations of antiquity in their lofty idea of government, and in their appreciation of the individual in society.

ANCIENT EMPIRES OF THE WEST

Greeks: Education in Sparta was socialistic and military, the training of the soldier. Athenian education was both civic and cultural and aimed at the training of the citizen for all his duties through a harmonious development of mind and body. Theoretically and practically, it was the most advanced of ancient times.

3

social organization + law

Romans: The education of Rome was at first domestic and
civic, and characteristically practical, blended with the
Greek and became Graeco-Roman. In appropriating Greek
culture, Roman education organized elementary, secondary, and higher grades of schools.

CHAPTER I

CHINA

China receives first consideration in the history of education because of the remarkable antiquity of its educational system. It is the oldest in history, and is of interest and importance not only for its influence on the destiny of the most populous nation in the world, for China comprises between an eighth and a fifth of the world's population,[1] but also for its unique character. For two thousand years China has made little progress in education, or in the science of government.

To the ancients China was known as the land of the Seres; to the people of the Middle Ages as the empire of Cathay. The name China probably came to Europe through the Arabs. The Chinese came from the central part of Asia and first settled around the elbow of the Hoang River. They pushed down the course of the river, and made more permanent settlements about its mouth. From the Hoang they spread to the south and occupied the great valley of the Yangtze, conquering or driving into mountain recesses the native inhabitants, thus becoming the predominant race.[2] They gave up a nomadic for an agricultural way of life; they drained the flooded districts, built canals and roads, and constructed wooden buildings modeled on the lines of their primitive tents.

The Great Wall of China, the largest artificial structure on earth, which was erected in the third century B.C., is an evidence of the early civilization, as well as of the great constructive genius of the Chinese. It was built to keep out invaders. Twenty to thirty feet high,

---

[1] Kenneth S. Latourette, *The Development of China* (Boston: Houghton Mifflin Co., 1920), p. xii.
[2] S. Wells Williams, *The Middle Kingdom* (New York: Charles Scribner's Sons, 1900), II, 144.

twelve feet wide at the top, with numerous towers of
defense, faced with granite or hard brick, this wall runs
for fifteen hundred miles along the north border lines
of China and in its course scales precipices and tops
craggy hills. It is, in a sense, indicative of a characteristic trait of the nation, viz., an inability to change. The
Chinese excluded from their land all foreigners and foreign influences. They greatly revered their parents or
ancestors, making it a first duty to carry on the work
of life in exactly the same way as their forefathers had
done. Their social and ethical ideas and their intellectual culture were fashioned upon the wisdom of the
ancients. Their highest ambition was "to walk in the
beaten paths." It is hard to realize that the inventors
of paper, of printing from movable blocks, of gunpowder,
and the first users of the mariner's compass could have
remained in a static condition for so many centuries,
but this failure to advance is a marked characteristic of
the best Mongolians.

Although much of early Chinese history is shrouded
in fable, reliable traditions go back to three thousand
years before Christ.[3] The names of the dynasties are
complete from the third century of the same era. The
form of government, a patriarchal despotism, obtained
for over two thousand years. In the thirteenth century
the famous Marco Polo visited China. He was welcomed to this mysterious land by the Mongol Emperor,
Kublai Khan, who made his capital at Peking. In the
fifteenth century the Chinese drove the last of the Mongol rulers across the Great Wall and Mongolia became
a province of the empire under the Chinese Ming family
which lasted nearly three hundred years. The Ming
dynasty gave way to the Manchu dynasty, descendants
of the Mongolian enemies of China. In 1644 the Man-

---

[3] *Ibid.*, p. 143.

chu line of rulers originated and lasted until February 2, 1912, when China became a republic.

The emperor, "Heaven's Son," was responsible to heaven alone. Heaven is the father of all and the emperor is the father of his people. As the father performed the religious rites for the family, so the emperor performed the religious rites for the nation. In the administration of the empire, the emperor was assisted by four principal ministers, and below them by a number of assessors who formed a council of state. The government business was executed by seven boards designed for special departments of state control. The surveillance over the empire has always been most effective. The people were governed by a fixed body of laws which were greatly respected by all.

The most common religion in ancient China, ancestor-worship, is linked to early family organization. The family is regarded as the first form of civilized society. The family grew into the clan or village community governed by the fathers of the different households. Filial piety and reverence for the head form a great part of the moral and religious life of the Chinese. The higher class now profess a cult based upon the philosophy of Confucius and Lao-tse; the majority of the people are Buddhists. The introduction of Christianity was attempted by the Nestorians in the seventh century with little permanent success. The work of the Jesuits under Father Matteo Ricci in the sixteenth century was the first successful endeavor to propagate the faith there. Father Ricci believed that the Christian religion in North China could be traced back as early as the second century to St. Thomas, "The Apostle of India and the East."[4] The Catholics of China number 3,089,611[5]

[4] S. Couling, editor, *Encyclopaedia Sinica* (Shanghai: Kelly and Walsh, Ltd., 1917), pp. 349; 554.

[5] *Chinese Year Book* 1940-41 (Shanghai: Commerical Press Ltd., 1941), p. 81.

and the Protestant communicants 512,873,[6] a very small proportion of the population which is estimated to be between two hundred and fifty and four hundred millions.

In Chinese literature are preserved some of the world's most ancient historical and philosophical writings. The *Five Classics*,[7] or the King Books, are the oldest records of the nation. Four of them were revised by Confucius who added the fifth, which is a history of his own time. Besides the *Five Classics* there are also the *Four Books* which were written by the disciples of Confucius, chief among whom was Mencius. The *Five Classics* are: (1) *Shu-King*, the history of the dynasties and the laws; (2) *Y-King*, a work on philosophy and magic; (3) *Shi-King*, the ancient odes, consisting of 311 poems which are moral and domestic in character; (4) *Li-King*, an account of national customs and ceremonial observances; (5) *Tshun-tsin*, Spring and Autumn Annals, by Confucius. The *Four Books* are commentaries on the classics. They include (1) The Great Learning; (2) The Doctrine of the Mean, a continuation of the first treatise; (3) The Analects of Confucius; (4) The Works of Mencius, by a pupil of that philosopher. Lao-tsze is author of Lao-teh-King, Book of Reason and Virtue, which treats of philosophy and theology. A work of pedagogical value is the *Little School* by Tschu-li, of the twelfth century.

The Chinese have a most unwieldy language. It is monosyllabic and has no alphabet. Words now have an ideographic and phonetic element. The characters or symbols are divided into six classes, and can be reduced

---

[6] *Chinese Year Book* 1938-39 (Shanghai: Commercial Press Ltd., 1939), p. 74.
[7] James Legge, *The Chinese Classics*, 2nd ed. (Shanghai: Chinese Book Co., 1895). This is the standard edition in English and contains valuable prolegomena.

to 2,425 all of which are to be memorized by students of the language. They are perpendicular in arrangement and are read from top to bottom. The columns are read from right to left. The spoken language on account of a natural development is vastly different from that of the ancient literature.

There are six different types of Chinese handwriting: the ornamental; the official; the literary; the common hand; the running hand; and the angular, similar to printing. Writing was practiced 1740 years B.C., and perhaps as early as 3000 B.C.[8] It is believed that the first written records were engraved with a special knife upon bamboo slips and wooden tablets. When the Chinese began to write books, they made their characters on slips of bamboo and tablets of wood with a bamboo pencil, frayed at one end to carry the colored liquid which took the place of ink. The knife was used then to erase. A brush of hair was later substituted for the bamboo pencil and silk was then used in connection with the delicate brush. The invention of paper in the beginning of the second century of the Christian era did away with the use of silk which was delicate and expensive, although a certain kind of paper made from silk floss was in use before this time. From the first century on the Chinese have been in possession of the same writing materials that they have today.

Printing on paper from wooden blocks was engaged in on a large scale in the tenth century when an encyclopedia and the Confucian classics were edited under the supervision of the emperor. In the fifteenth century an imperial commission was appointed for the production of another encyclopedia. This work was never printed although it was actually transcribed for that purpose.

---

[8] S. S. Laurie, *Historical Survey of Pre-Christian Education* (New York: Longmans, Green, and Co., 1900), p. 100.

Two other copies of it were later made; one with the original was stored in Nanking, the other in Peking. With the fall of the Ming dynasty, the Nanking copies perished; while the copy at Peking was partly destroyed in the Boxer Rebellion in 1900. During the eighteenth century a third encyclopedia was brought out. It is said to be the largest encyclopedia in the world, running to many thousands of volumes. A copy of the first edition is now to be seen in the British Museum.

Confucius, 551-478 B.C., philosopher and statesman, is the inspiration of the Chinese system of education. "Confucius" is the latinized form of K'ung-Fu-Tse, the philosopher, Kung. Having the greatest reverence for the ideas and customs of the past, he made respect for all that was ancient and ancestral among his people a virtue. Reverence for parents living and dead may be said to be the keynote of his teaching. He labored as an administrator and for the interests of the united empire. Suspected at one time of political intrigues he was exiled, but later reinstated. After death he was worshipped among the sacred ancestors and benefactors of the nation. One can see from the subject matter taught in the schools how much his work affected the education of the succeeding ages.

The third of the *Four Books*, which is known as the Confucian Analecta, or sayings of the master, discloses that Confucius taught in a simple way the most important and common duties of life. Some idea of the character of his teachings may be gotten from the following selected sentences:[9]

Governing with equity resembles the north star, which is fixed, and all stars surround it.

Living without reflection will profit nothing; reflection without learning will leave the mind weary and miserable.

---

[9] Williams, *op. cit.*, I, 657.

Without virtue, both riches and honor seem to be like the passing cloud.

The perfect man loves all men; he is not governed by private affection or interest, but only regards the public good or right reason. The wicked man, on the contrary, loves if you give, and likes if you command him.

He that is sedulous and desires to improve in his studies is not ashamed to stoop to ask of others.

Lao-tsze, 604-515 B.C., was likewise a philosopher professing a very exalted doctrine. The story is that he had white hair and eyebrows at his birth whence he was called Lau-tsz', the old boy. His very existence has been questioned.[10] He is said to have held office at the imperial Court of Chow as keeper of the archives. His system of religion, Taoism, is much more philosophical than Confucianism. Because it was less intelligible, it did not take hold with the people. The ideas of Lao-tsze were accepted after his death by a class of his countrymen, but later became confused with Buddhism.

"Tao" means the way and also the wayfarer; it is man and his destiny. It is based on the idea of one perfect, omnipresent Being, who sways all things and expresses Himself in nature and in man. Tao works by contraries. The secret of its strength is its weakness. The Tao-teh-King[11] emphasizes the principle of returning good for evil, advocates a noble and unselfish morality, and teaches the freedom of the will, the perfectibility of man, and a knowledge of a supreme being in three persons.

Tschu-li, who because of his wide learning was called "Prince of Knowledge," was born about 1129 A.D. In a work entitled *The Little School*, he formulated many

---

[10] Latourette, *op. cit.*, p. 22.
[11] Some scholars doubt the authorship of this work. *Cf.* Latourette, *loc. cit.*

sound educational principles far in advance of the
thought of his time. He believed in respecting the
natural powers of children, and employing them to advance the development of the young; he paid particular
attention to their physical capabilities. This early
work, however, in which one can see much of the spirit
of modern education, had little influence on the Chinese
system, for its principles were not adopted.

It has been stated above that in China is to be found
the oldest organized system of education. From earliest
times formal education of some sort has existed there,
and for three thousand years it has been a matter of
national importance. The Great Shun conducted an
examination of his officials as early as 200 B.C. It is
now maintained on legitimate grounds that schools and
colleges existed in China four thousand years ago.[12]
These were not state institutions, for China never had
a system of national schools or, more strictly speaking,
schools supported by the state.

In the second century B.C., a system of competitive
examinations was inaugurated for all candidates for
civil offices, and the highest positions in the state were
thus offered to men of literary attainments. Education
which had previously been the privilege of the sons of
feudal lords then became the pursuit of the ambitious,
as none was barred from the tests. The system was not
thoroughly organized until the eighth century A.D.

Education aimed to prepare for civil service, which
was determined by various grades of competitive examinations set by the state. Its basic studies were
reading, writing, ceremonial etiquette, mathematics,
music, and to a certain degree, dancing. Schools were
established by individual enterprise, although the state
founded and maintained some institutions. The teacher

---

[12] Laurie, *op. cit.*, p. 125.

was shown great respect at all times, and was obsequiously obeyed. His method was dogmatic and absolute. Instruction under private tutors was very common. Only in recent years has education become compulsory for all children.

The schools, broadly speaking, might be divided into three classes, as they prepared for the degrees offered by the state. The elementary were the most common and were usually conducted by men who had obtained the first degree, "Flowering Talent," designated by many as Bachelor. In them the pupils learned reading, writing and elementary arithmetic. The method of instruction was purely a training of the memory and consisted in the mastery of language forms. The language of the school was a dead language, quite unlike that which was used in every day life. Thus the work of the school had little significance for the pupil. It was much the same as if school boys of today studied Latin only and were compelled to memorize certain Latin classics so that they could recite them perfectly without regard for the meaning of the words or the beauty of the literature.[13] There was little relation between reading and writing; at the essay writing stage the two were combined. The *Four Books* and the *Five Classics* supplied the chief textbooks. Three to five years were required to complete this preparatory course for the lowest degree.

Elementary schools were to be found in practically every village, patronized voluntarily, and supported by private tuition. School was held very often in the temple, but it was not unusual to give instruction in a vacant room of a private house, in a shed, covered nook or corner. There were no schools for girls and no education for the vast majority after the age of fifteen. It

[13] W. A. P. Martin, *The Chinese; their Education, Philosophy and Letters* (New York: Harper and Bros., 1881), p. 64.

is estimated that barely one in twenty received more than an elementary education.

Better provision was made for secondary and higher education. On these levels the same works of literature with supplementary studies occupied the candidates for the higher degrees. It became necessary for them to be familiar with Chinese history, law, finance, military affairs, agriculture; to make a thorough study of the sacred texts through innumerable commentaries; and to be skillful in writing poems and essays after the manner of their ancestors. In the colleges maintained at public expense at prefectural cities and provincial capitals an extensive knowledge of the classics might be obtained.

The gradations of the examinations were so regulated that only those who successfully competed for the degrees were given state positions. Of the thousands who tried for the second degree, "Promoted Scholar," or Master, as it would be termed by us, one in a hundred succeeded. While the two lower examinations were held in various parts of the empire, that for the third degree, "Fit for Office," a rank similar to that of Doctor, took place in Peking and lasted thirteen days. The successful candidates in a still higher examination were admitted into the college of Hanlin,[14] "Forest of Pencils," a kind of Imperial Academy, the members of which were recognized as possessing the ripest scholarship and most polished style. They were honored with the highest offices in the country and were often deputed to act as chancellors and examiners in the provinces.

Education on Western lines was given for the first time in China by Roman Catholic missionaries in 1852, when a college for the education of native priests was opened. It was not, however, until after the Chino-Japanese War of 1895 that a reform of the traditional

---

[14] A good description of the Hanlin is found in Martin, *op. cit.,* pp. 1-38.

educational system was strongly advocated. In 1898, the young emperor, favoring a plan of educational reform proposed in a book written by the Viceroy and circulated through the empire, issued an edict calling for the modernization of schools. Unfortunately, this reactionary movement culminated in the Boxer Uprising. Three years later the Empress Dowager became the protagonist of the cause she had opposed and a special commission was appointed to draw up a national public school system. By an imperial decree of September 2, 1905, the first modern system of education was inaugurated, and the following year, by virtue of another, the former program and method of examinations were abolished. The Revolution, which resulted in the establishment of the Republic, led in 1912 to the reorganization of the school plan of 1903. The gradual manifestation of dissatisfaction with the 1912 plan brought about the adoption of the present educational system which extends from the kindergarten to the post-graduate school. The system of 1903 was basically Japanese, while the plan of 1912 was fundamentally German. The latest system is modeled upon the American school organization.[15]

The curriculum of the new system comprises the study of the Chinese language, literature, and composition; history; geography; modern sciences; foreign languages; gymnastics; and, on the higher levels, political economy; civil and international law. It aims to adapt education to a changed and changing society; to promote the spirit of democracy; to develop individuality; to take into consideration the economic status of the average citizen; to adjust pupils to the needs of life; to facilitate the spread

---

[15] C. W. Luh, *China's New System of Education* (Peking: Chinese National Association For the Advancement of Education. 1923), Bulletin 8; II, 9.

of universal education; to make itself flexible to allow for local variations.[16]

Undoubtedly, the Chinese, through experience with the nations of the West, have recognized the shortcomings of their educational system and its unsuitableness to the demands of modern progress. The old system was very serviceable to the state in many respects. The millions of subjects were kept docile and loyal, and the most learned gave their talents to the public service. The effects, however, such as a formal and external morality, a lack of initiative, an unwillingness to change, unsound and unworthy motives for education, are deplored by the advocates of modern education who labor to evolve a successful educational system suited to the needs of China and in keeping with her national ideals.

FOR FURTHER STUDY

Abel, James F., *A Survey of Education in Countries other than the United States. U. S. Office of Education, Bulletin 37, No. 2.* Vol. I, chap. VII, pp. 30-36.

Analects or the Conversations of Confucius with His Disciples and Certain Others. Translated by William E. Sootkill. New York: Humphrey Milford, Oxford University Press, 1941.

Arndt, C. O., *et al., Education in China Today.* Leaflet No. 69. U. S. Office of Education, 1944.

Becker, C. H., *et al., The Reorganization of Education in China.* Paris: League of Nations' Institute of Intellectual Cooperation, 1932.

Chang, Peng Chun, *Education for Modernization in China.* New York: Columbia University, 1923.

Chen, Li-Fu, *Chinese Education during the War,* 1937-42. Reprinted March, 1943. Chinese Embassy, Washington, D. C.

Chiang, Monlin, *A Study in Chinese Principles of Education.* Shanghai: Commercial Press, Ltd., 1918.

Chuang, Chai-Hsuan, *Tendencies Toward a Democratic System of Education.* Shanghai: Commerical Press, Ltd., 1922.

---

[16] *Ibid.,* p. 1.

Hirth, F., *The Ancient History of China.* New York: Columbia University, 1908.

Kuo, Ping Wen, *The Chinese System of Public Education.* New York: Teachers College, Columbia University, 1915.

Latourette, Kenneth S., *The Development of China.* Boston: Houghton Mifflin Co., 1920.

————, *The Chinese; Their History and Culture.* 2nd ed. rev.; 2 vols. in one. New York: The Macmillan Co., 1934.

Laurie, S. S., *Historical Survey of Pre-Christian Education.* New York: Longmans, Green, and Co., 1900.

Martin, W. A. P., *The Chinese; Their Education, Philosophy and Letters.* New York: Harper and Bros., 1881.

Twiss, George R., *Science and Education in China.* Shanghai: Commercial Press, Ltd., 1925.

Wang, Shih-Chieh, *"Education in China," Yearbook of Education, 1937,* pp. 555-601. London: Evans Brothers, Ltd., 1937.

Williams, S. Wells, *The Middle Kingdom,* 2 vols. New York: Charles Scribner's Sons, 1900-01.

CHAPTER II

JAPAN

The early history of Japan, like that of other ancient nations, is obscure and uncertain. The oldest written records, which contain many myths and popular legends, date from the eighth century of our era. Japanese stories tell of the invasion of the islands of Japan but do not make known who the invaders were. The islands, it is certain, were invaded and very probably by Malays, Koreans, Mongols, and perhaps also by Chinese. These invaders subjugated the aboriginal inhabitants who supposedly are the ancestors of the Ainus, a few thousand of whom are to be found today. The ancient Japanese used iron for swords and arrowheads, grew rice, ate with chopsticks, and were skillful hunters, fishermen, and farmers.[1]

Although Japan was unknown to Europeans before the explorations of Marco Polo in the thirteenth century, the history of its education has been traced to the third century of our era.[2] Chinese literature was then introduced, and a method of education pursued almost identical with the Chinese. These differences, however, are to be noted. Only the members of the nobility were instructed, and a knowledge of Japanese history and laws was required.

The opening of the eleventh century marked the rise of the military class and the establishment of feudalism. The series of wars that followed so retarded the progress

---

[1] Kenneth S. Latourette, *The Development of Japan* (New York: The Macmillan Co., 1918), pp. 9-14.
[2] E. W. Clement, *A Short History of Japan* (Tokyo: Christian Literature Society, 1939), p. 15.

of education that during the next six hundred years the
Buddhist temple was the only place where formal instruction was available, even for the sons of officials.[3]
This period of intellectual stagnation continued down
until the beginning of the seventeenth century when
the Tokugawa shogunate came into power and fostered education for the purpose of furthering its plans
of government.

The Tokugawa shoguns prohibited the propagation of
Christianity, proscribed the reading of Western books
that had come into Japan with the Dutch traders, and
encouraged Buddhism and Confucianism whose moral
teaching inculcated ideas of submission and the love of
peace.[4] In the first quarter of the eighteenth century
this ban on foreign learning was removed and the Dutch,
Russian, French, and German languages were introduced together with the study of geography, natural
history, and the sciences. A high type of education was
then given to the children of the upper classes, while a
lower grade of instruction was provided for the children
of the common people in private institutions. The advancement of the general culture of the masses by the
publication of books and the opportunities afforded for
obtaining Western learning eventually led to an intellectual reactionary movement which included an intensive study of ancient Japanese history. The result was
that the rule of the shogunate, which was virtually
independent of the Emperor, came to be resented, and
devotion to the Mikado was revived.[5] In 1867, the last
of the shoguns capitulated to the young and nominal
ruler, Emperor Meiji, who initiated a movement of

---

[3] Baron Dairoku Kikuchi, *Japanese Education* (London: John
Murray, 1909), p. 33.
[4] Okakura-Kakuzo, *The Awakening of Japan* (New York: Japan Society, Inc., 1921), pp. 54 f.
[5] Kikuchi, *op. cit.*, p. 39.

restoration and enlightenment which succeeded in giving to Japan her modern system of education.[6]

The Japanese language which is polysyllabic and possesses an alphabet, contains many words and characters of Chinese origin. Unlike the Chinese, the words are arranged in sentence structure and are read from left to right. Verbs signifying greetings, salutations, apologies, and requests indicate extreme humility on the part of the speaker. There are no articles; case is indicated by separate particles; prepositions follow the words they govern. The Japanese have produced no great literary works.

Shintoism, which literally means "way of the gods," is properly the religion of Japan. It is without foreign admixture; has no dogmas, no moral code, no sacred books. It is a combination of nature worship and veneration of ancestors. There are many branches of Shintoism, but all may be reduced to the simple practice of following the inspiration of one's heart and obeying the emperor.

According to Japanese teaching the emperor is not only high priest, but the representative and direct descendant of divinity. Accordingly, he has no surname and in early times his palace was the temple wherein rites consisted chiefly of ablutions and purifications. The duty devolves upon him of rendering worship to the gods who are his ancestors and of offering to heaven as supreme mediator the prayers and sacrifices of his people.

Buddhism was introduced into Japan in the sixth century. At the solicitation of Buddhist missionaries, skilled Chinese workmen built temples and set up statues in Japan. Although the Japanese borrowed Chinese styles of architecture, sculpture, and the art of

---

[6] Latourette, *op. cit.,* p. 115.

painting, they modified and adapted Chinese arts to their own tastes and needs. Many imposing Buddhist temples with their images and red appurtenances are found throughout the empire, especially in the cities. Buddhism had practically absorbed the national religion, but its disestablishment at the hands of the Meiji government deprived it of a large part of its revenues and it thus lost much of its former magnificence.

Christianity was introduced into Japan in the sixteenth century through the zealous efforts of St. Francis Xavier. The missionary work of this apostle and his associates suffered an interruption for more than two centuries, when in 1614 it was decreed by the shoguns that Catholicism be abolished; yet, Christian missionaries entering the port of Nagasaki about the middle of the nineteenth century were greeted by Christians in the neighborhood who recognized them as the successors of Xavier and his companions. Protestant missionaries have been active in Japan since 1859, but a very small percentage of the population, which is estimated to be over ninety millions, is Christian.

The Japanese, Mongolians like the Chinese, have been remarkable for their spirit of intellectual progress, and their adaptability to the ideas and customs of other nations. Since the revolution of 1868 they have been more closely in touch with Western nations. Their progress as a world power dates from that time. It should be remembered that they are just as exclusive as the Chinese, but they realized sooner that their exclusiveness was a serious hindrance to their advancement among the nations of the world.

A remarkable development of the school system has taken place during the last three quarters of a century. The character of the Japanese people has been transformed largely through formal education. Modern education in Japan is an expression of a new and vigorous national idea; it is, at the present time, a "business" proposition.[7] All classes and both sexes are given at least an elementary education. Their secondary schools and universities have grown in number and effectiveness along with many technical and agricultural schools, and institutes for the pursuit of the fine arts. Many of their youth have frequented European and American seats of learning, and have been, perhaps, most directly responsible for the introduction of Western ideas into Japanese educational life. Interest, then, in Japanese education centers in its present progressive condition rather than in its historical development.

FOR FURTHER STUDY

Brinkley, F., *Japan, Its History, Arts, and Literature.* 8 vols. Boston: J. B. Millet Co., 1901-2.

Clement, E. W., *A Short History of Japan.* 8th ed. Tokyo: Christian Literature Society, 1939.

Gowen, Herbert H., *An Outline History of Japan.* New York: D. Appleton Co., 1927.

Griffis, William E., *The Mikado's Empire,* 12th ed. 2 vols. New York: Harper and Bros., 1913.

Hart, Albert B., *The Obvious Orient.* New York: D. Appleton Co., 1911.

Kikuchi, Baron Dairoku, *Japanese Education.* London: John Murray, 1909.

Latourette, Kenneth, *The Development of Japan.* New York: The Macmillan Co., 1918.

Okakura, Kakuzo, *The Awakening of Japan.* New York: The Japan Society, Inc., 1921.

Tsurumi, Yusuki, *Present Day Japan.* New York: Columbia University Press, 1926.

---

[7] William C. Bagley, *The Educative Process* (New York: The Macmillan Co., 1907), pp. 34 f.; Benjamin Kidd, *The Science of Power* (New York: G. P. Putnam's Sons, 1918), pp. 144, 228.

CHAPTER III

EGYPT

Historical research has located in Egypt the oldest civilization known to man. This civilization antedates that of China and in all antiquity holds preeminence in the development of science and culture.[1] Egypt would be the first subject of study in the history of education if with this early progress in the arts and sciences it had organized a system of education. China, however, as we have seen, enjoyed this distinction.

Up until the nineteenth century the chief sources of our knowledge of the history of Egypt were the Greek historians, especially Herodotus, who visited Egypt in the fifth century B.C., and the Egyptian priest Manetho who lived in the third century B.C. He knew Greek well and wrote for the information of the Greeks a history of the Egyptian kings, giving a list of the various dynasties and rulers, which has come down to us in fragments.[2] Much additional information regarding Egypt has been derived from the inscriptions which have been deciphered on her relics and remains and from the monuments which have been unearthed by archaeologists.

Authorities are not at all agreed concerning the chronology of ancient Egyptian history.[3] The long line of Pharaohs or monarchs can be traced back to 3400 B.C. The Old Kingdom may be said to have been established about that time when Menes conquered the Delta and added the red crown of lower Egypt to his white crown

---

[1] In the *Odyssey* of Homer the Nile as well as the country is called Αἴγυπτος.

[2] George Rawlinson, *History of Ancient Egypt* (London: Longmans, Green & Co., 1881), II, 5 f.

[3] *Ibid.*, pp. 8-22.

of upper Egypt. The capital of the kingdom was at Memphis, but was changed to Thebes when the Middle Kingdom originated about 2400 B.C. This kingdom came to an end four hundred years later with the establishment of the Empire, which lasted until 525 B.C., when Egypt was reduced to a Persian province. About two centuries later, Alexander the Great conquered this ancient land and established a line of rulers known as the Ptolemies. It was under the Ptolemies that the Old Testament was translated from the Hebrew into the Greek at Alexandria. The last great ruler of the line of Ptolemies was the celebrated Cleopatra.

The Egyptian king claimed supreme authority in all civil and religious affairs. His title, Pharaoh, has descended to us through the Hebrews and is derived from Per-o, which is Egyptian for the "Great House." He received effectual support from a large and powerful priesthood, from which he drew many important executive officials. A multitude of courtiers and of servants were in constant attendance at the palace. Wigmakers, sandal-makers, perfumers, and launderers ministered to the needs of the royal family and recorded with pride their titles upon their tombstones. The king, like all oriental monarchs, had a harem with numerous inmates, but his favorite wife was considered queen. There were usually many sons among whom the vast revenues were liberally distributed, but these princes assisted in their father's government, holding some of the most arduous offices in the service of the state.[4]

The people were divided into classes, which although not so rigid as the castes of India remained nevertheless exclusive. The nobles lived in houses of brick and wood with latticed windows, gaily painted and decorated with bright colored hangings. The living rooms were sump-

---

[4] James H. Breasted, *A History of Egypt* (New York: Charles Scribner's Sons, 1912), pp. 74 f.

tuously furnished with chairs, stools, and chests of ebony, artistically carved and inlaid with ivory, while rich vessels of alabaster, copper, gold, and silver were placed upon standards of the finest workmanship. The lord of the house wore a white linen kilt and very often a broad collar of gold and precious stones. His head was usually shaven and he wore a wig on state occasions. His wife and daughters wore longer wigs, and jewelled necklaces and bracelets were usually part of their apparel. They were clothed in a simple, sleeveless, close-fitting garment of fine linen.[5]

Of the lower classes, relatively little is known. The peasants lived in mud-brick, thatched-roof huts, tilled the ground and tended the flocks for their masters. They were serfs, who could be sold with the land from one master to another. In the towns were to be found the merchants, jewellers, scribes, and other craftsmen. They played a minor role as a class in the Old Kingdom, but during the Middle Kingdom assumed greater importance, so that during the Period of the Empire the manufacturers and business men exercised considerable influence on the government. Their sons were sent to school to learn writing and, becoming scribes, rose to the highest positions in the government. Many of the government officials were selected from this class, instead of from the old nobility.

The highest class in Egyptian society was that of the priests, which, with the military or warrior class, constituted the privileged element of the nation. Some maintain that the priestly class was not strictly hereditary, since the scribes were admitted into it; but at any rate its members could not marry into a lower rank of society. The warriors were not so restricted. All below the priestly class, such as the farmers and boatmen,

---

[5] *Ibid.*, pp. 88 f.

the mechanics and tradesmen, the herdsmen and fishermen, enjoyed no privileges, but were protected by laws
and long-standing customs.[6] The social position of
women was higher than in most Oriental nations.
Women of the upper classes were educated under private tutors. A man possessed but one legal wife and
the closest ties of blood were through the mother. It
was the duty of every son to have the greatest respect
and affection for the mother who bore and nourished
him. Women could even ascend the throne, and, as is
commonly known, some actually did.

In the arts and sciences a very high stage of development was reached thousands of years before Christ.
In fact, the predynastic period achieved greater artistic
excellence than the period of recorded history.[7] Some of
the pottery of the Badarian Age (7500 B.C.) is the most
perfect handiwork that is known for its regularity and
thinness. Mere clay was not good enough a material
for the execution of finer vases, and basalt ground to a
fine powder was used as an artificial basis.[8] The Greeks
considered Egypt the best school of learning and wisdom.
Homer, Herodotus, Lycurgus, Plato, Pythagoras, and
Solon went there to complete their studies. Holy
Scripture says: "Moses was instructed in all the wisdom
of the Egyptians; and he was mighty in his words and
in his deeds."[9]

As weavers the Egyptians were unexcelled in antiquity, and their work in coloring glass has never been
surpassed even in modern times. Their pottery was
the first perhaps to be made by men and has influenced

---

[6] S. S. Laurie, *Historical Survey of Pre-Christian Education*,
p. 33.
[7] Thomas Davidson, *A History of Education* (New York:
Charles Scribner's Sons, 1901), p. 38.
[8] Petrie, W. Flinders, *The Making of Egypt* (New York: The
Macmillan Co., 1939), p. 4.
[9] Acts 7:22.

the work of potters in other lands down to the present. Egyptian masons constructed colonnades long before the Greeks and used the arch before the Romans. The sculptors of Egypt made the earliest statues that can be regarded as artistic. To her astronomers the modern world owes the calendar of twelve months and 365 days. The annual inundation of the Nile aroused and developed a notable genius for engineering and irrigation.

All the ordinary operations of arithmetic were well known to the Egyptian. He had a decimal system of numbers with different signs for one, ten, a hundred, and so on; by attaching distinct signs to these fundamental ideas other numbers were expressed by repetition of these characters.[10] For example, if he wished to write 535 he would write five hundreds, three tens, and five ones. Fractions, obviously, caused difficulty. The fraction with *one* as a numerator was easily handled. All other fractions, with the exception of two thirds, which the Egyptian had learned to use readily, were resolved into a series of several, each with *one* as the numerator.

The elements of algebra and geometry were equally well known to the Egyptian scribe. As it never occurred to him to search for truth for its own sake, he limited his interest in mathematics to the solution of the practical problems that confronted him in his daily life. He was obliged to estimate the quantity of grain in a pile or in a granary and so he undertook to compute the contents of cubes, cylinders, and other solids. He determined the areas of triangles and rectangles, speculated on that of the trapezoid, but estimated the area of a circle pretty accurately. Architects and craftsmen possessed a highly developed knowledge of mechanics despite the fact that the pulley was unknown and the roller also.[11]

---

[10] Rawlinson, *op. cit.*, I, 294.
[11] Breasted, *op. cit.*, pp. 100 f.

The wonderful process which the Egyptians developed of embalming human bodies, and the magnificent structures erected as mausoleums for the dead have impressed subsequent generations. The pyramids were the royal tombs; those of Gizeh are the most noteworthy. The greatest of all was the Great Pyramid of Khufu or, as he is sometimes called, Cheops, which, erected of limestone, rose to a height of 481 feet and covered an area of 755 square feet at its base. According to Herodotus, it took a hundred thousand men twenty years to build it.[12] It was built of two million three hundred thousand blocks of granite, weighing on the average two and one half tons.

Near the pyramids were the tombs of officials and nobles connected with the court of the king. Perneb's tomb, which came to light under the spade of the excavator and may be seen in the Metropolitan Museum of Art in New York City, has several chambers. One was for the statue of Perneb carved in cedar. Adjoining it was another, but shut off by a thick wall with a slit through which the family and friends of the deceased could look at the figure. The main chamber was entered through a vestibule. The walls of this main room were covered with painted scenes showing Perneb's interests in life with large numbers of slaves bearing him offerings. At one end of the wall was the false door before which food and other gifts were placed because it was believed that the *ka*, the immortal part of Perneb, had need of bodily nourishment. To the rear of the tomb was the burial chamber with a deep shaft leading down into it. Lesser folks had tombs much more modest in size and construction, while the poor had simple burial places of different kinds.

Extreme care was taken to provide the dead with

---

[12] Petrie agrees with this estimate. Cf. Breasted, *op. cit.*, p. 117.

comforts as the discovery in 1922 of the tomb of Tutankhamen has disclosed. In it were found numerous
articles of artistic value. A picture, in glass and
faïence, of the Pharaoh and his queen adorned a golden
throne. There were beautiful robes, walking sticks of
gold and silver, carved couches, alabaster vases, and
chariots of sheet gold. Gold-covered monsters and
marvelously executed goddesses guarded the remains of
the king which were enclosed in a series of coffins richly
ornamented.

Egyptian literature is remarkable for its great antiquity, its copiousness, and its varied character. History
is occasionally found among the papyri, but is largely
recorded on the monuments. Works on religion and
theology; historical and lyrical poems; accounts of
travels, personal correspondence; military and statistical reports; romantic tales; orations; mathematical,
medical, and moral treatises; books on astronomy,
astrology, geography, rhetoric, and magic; collections of
proverbs, books of receipts; catalogues of libraries are
included in the content of this ancient literature.[13] It
contains the oldest book in the world, viz.: *Ptah-hetep*,
a mine of counsels and maxims, believed to have been
written about 3600 B.C. This abounds in poems, treatises on law, medicine, mathematics, rhetoric, religion
and even has a few novels. It is not remarkable, however, for literary excellence. *The Book of the Dead*,[14]
or Bible of the Egyptians, treats of death and the rites
of sepulture, contains much of religious doctrine, and
was their code of morality. The virtues of justice,
honesty, truthfulness, charity, economy, and obedience
to authority are inculcated by it.

In religious thought the Egyptians were the most ad-

---

[13] Rawlinson, *op. cit.*, I, 135.
[14] Chas. H. Davis, *The Book of the Dead,* English translation
(New York: G. P. Putnam's Sons, 1894).

vanced of all Oriental peoples save the Hebrews. Their highest conceptions were for the most part unknown to the people of the lower classes. The cultured few, and particularly the priests, believed in the existence of God, Creator and Ruler of the universe; the ignorant worshipped local gods according to the devotions of their temples. The Sun and the Nile were adored, and many of the lower animals were venerated as deities or as their symbols. There was, however, a firm belief in the immortality of the soul and rehabilitation of the body after death. The god Osiris rewarded the good in the next world by returning them to the God of light. and punished the wicked according to the evil nature of their lives.[15] The burial of the dead was surrounded with solemn religious rites which could be accorded only to those who had lived virtuously. The bodies underwent the process of embalming that they might endure to the time of their reoccupation after thousands of years. This veneration for the dead inspired the construction of the pyramids and tombs which remain to the present and reflect the glory of this ancient civilization.

No attempt was made by the state to provide a system of education for all. Elementary instruction in reading, writing, and arithmetic could be easily obtained in private schools or by tutoring under special teachers. Ambitious boys of the lower classes were often prepared under these tutors for the occupation of scribe, or copyist. The scribe, besides receiving a good elementary training, became familiar with current commercial and legal formulas, and took an advanced course in mathematics.

How general elementary education was there is no way of knowing. In the days of Plato the children of the masses seemed to have shared in it. If the laboring

---

[15] Rawlinson, *op. cit.*, I, 314-22.

class, save in exceptional cases, received no benefit from
the schools, there was no reason why a clever boy, whose
parents were interested, could not receive elementary
instruction.[16] The demotic or ordinary form of writing
was at first taught; later instruction in the hieratic,
which was used in the sacred writings, and finally in
the hieroglyphic or ideographic, was obtainable in the
higher schools of learning.

Lessons in writing were practiced on tablets with a
reed stylus, then on papyrus (from which name comes
our word "paper"), with a reed pen using black or red
ink. Books were in long rolls, papyri, and were so called
from the material on which they were written. It was
made from the stem or pith of the papyrus plant which
grew in profusion on the banks of the Nile. The
method of reading Egyptian writing was discovered in
the nineteenth century, when a French scientist, Jean
François Champollion, deciphered the Rosetta Stone.
This large slab had been found by Napoleon's soldiers
near the mouth of the Nile. It contained a decree of
the Egyptian priesthood written in the hieroglyphic and
demotic forms of writing and also in Greek. Knowing
the meaning of the Greek words and a few of the hieroglyphs, this young Frenchman learned after patient
study to read the inscription and in this way made
known the secret of Egyptian writing. It was found
in part that an eagle stood for the letter *a*, a leg and
foot for *b*, an owl for *m*, a chicken for *u*, while a man
with his hands lifted up meant the word *prayer*.

The central temple schools and those attached to the
provincial courts conducted the higher education for
the professions. The teachers were priests, and usually
high officials. From the temple schools came the mag-
istrates, judges, and priests. The scribes frequently en-

---

[16] Laurie, *op. cit.*, p. 41.

tered to become physicians and architects. In these higher schools geometry, elementary trigonometry, astronomy were studied. Mathematics, however, being chiefly practical, was not a science with the Egyptians in the Greek sense. It remained for the Greeks to put this practical knowledge in logical systematic form and transmit it to us as a study of rational principles. Medicine and geography, law and theology were also taught in the Egyptian higher schools. Treatises on geography and astronomy compiled in the second century A.D., by Ptolemy, a mathematician of Egyptian birth, show that the sources of his material were Egyptian as well as Grecian. Drawing and painting were given considerable attention, as is evidenced from the illustrations in the papyrus rolls.

The education of the Egyptians reached its climax in the training of the priests. Naturally their chief study embraced everything connected with their religion: its doctrine and moral teaching; its rites and ceremonies. Their training demanded all the usual learning of the upper class as well as acquaintance with special studies. As mentioned above, they prepared for the professions, were also the architects, physicians, administrators, and, for centuries, leaders of every phase of development in Egyptian civilization.

Although the Egyptians, as already stated, attained to a high degree of civilization and culture and far surpassed the other nations of antiquity in this respect, there was no universal education, no systematic effort made by the state to instruct the lower classes of society. A certain education in the broad sense was provided by the great works in art and architecture, and by the state religion. But their religion, purely spiritual as it may have been among the priests and cultured classes, amounted among the illiterate to a base superstition, a worship of animals and idols. There is no doubt, however, that the learning for which the Egyptians were justly famed perceptibly affected the culture and science of the Hebrews and the great nations of the classic period.

FOR FURTHER STUDY

Abel, James F., *A Survey of Education in Countries other than the United States. U. S. Office of Education, Bulletin 1937, No 2.* Vol I, Chap. VII, pp. 53-56.

Baikie, James, *History of Egypt.* New York: The Macmillan Co., 1929.

Breasted, James H., *Ancient Records of Egypt: The Historical Documents.* Chicago: Chicago University Press, 1905. 5 vols.

—————, *History of Egypt.* New York: Charles Scribner's Sons, 1912.

Cambridge Ancient History. Vol. II. New York: The Macmillan Co., 1924.

Laurie, S. S., *Historical Survey of Pre-Christian Education.* New York: Longmans, Green, and Co., 1900.

Maspero, G., *Life in Ancient Egypt and Assyria.* New York: D. Appleton and Co., 1892.

—————, *Histoire ancienne.* 8th ed. rev. Paris: Hachette et Cie, 1909.

—————, *L'Archéologie égyptienne.* Paris: A. Picard and Kaan, 1905.

—————, *The Dawn of Civilization; Egypt and Chaldaea.* Edited by A. H. Sayce. Translated by M. L. McClure. Fourth Edition. London: S.P.C.K., 1901.

Petrie, Wm. Flinders, *History of Egypt.* London: Methuen & Co., Ltd., 1898-1905.

—————, *The Arts and Crafts of Ancient Egypt.* London: T. N. Foulis, 1910.

—————, *Social Life in Ancient Egypt.* London: Constable & Co. Ltd., 1923.

—————, *Religion and Conscience in Ancient Egypt.* London: Methuen & Co., Ltd., 1920.

—————, *The Revolutions of Civilization.* New York· P. Smith, 1941.

————, *Prehistoric Egypt.* London: British School of Archeology in Egypt, 1920.

————, *Corpus of prehistoric pottery and palettes.* London: British School of Archeology in Egypt, 1921.

————, *The Making of Egypt.* New York: The Macmillan Co., 1939.

Rawlinson, George, *History of Ancient Egypt.* 2 vols. London: Longmans, Green, and Co., 1881.

————, *The Five Great Monarchies of the Ancient Eastern World.* 4 Vols. London: J. Murray, 1862-67.

Wiedemann, Alfred, *Die unterhaltungs Litteratur der alter Aegypter.* Leipzig: Hinrichs, 1902.

Wolf, W., *Individuum und Gemeinschaft in der ägyptischen Kultur.* Glückstadt: J. J. Augustin, 1935.

CHAPTER IV

INDIA

Since the time of Confucius, education in China has been accessible to all classes. It might therefore be characterized as democratic. Ancient Japanese education was, on the contrary, aristocratic. In Egypt, where the people were divided into social strata, the priestly class was the most highly organized, the most powerful, and the best educated. Class distinctions in India were much more complicated and rigid than elsewhere. Here an elaborate caste system developed and only those of the higher castes received a literary education. Advanced education was the right of the highest caste.

The reason why the civilization of India was different from that of the Mediterranean countries was that India was not in the main stream of progress and of history. Although not wholly isolated, the country was hemmed in by mountains, deserts, forests, and the Indian Ocean. Invaders made their way into the fertile plains of this ancient country and occasionally vessels carried ivory, cotton, rice, and spices to Babylonia and Egypt. Presumably ancient India received the Phoenician alphabet through Mesopotamia.

A group of Aryans migrating from their original home crossed over the mountains into India. Where their homeland was is not known. Some investigators claim that their primitive habitat was in the areas which we now call Hungary, Austria, and Bohemia. It is generally supposed that the Aryans migrated in successive waves. Some of them descended into Italy and Greece, where their language became Latin and Greek, respectively; others became the Celts of the British Isles and

Gaul; some became the ancestors of the Germans and Scandinavians in the north; others became the ancestors of the Slavs in Eastern Europe; still others pushed on into Persia and India.[1]

The Aryan invaders of ancient India warred against the natives who are regarded as the ancestors of the Dravidians, a dark-skinned people found in southern India today. At the time they occupied northern India, but yielded quickly before the advance of the superior white man by whom they were either killed or enslaved or driven southward. The conquerors, entering one fertile valley after another, possessed the land but, as they had few contacts with the West, their progress in the course of civilization was impeded.

These Aryans were herdsmen and farmers. The value of exchange was determined in terms of cattle. Cows furnished milk, meat, and leather, while sheep provided wool for clothing. The Aryans tilled the soil with ploughs drawn by bulls and sowed corn which they reaped with sickles. They engaged in chariot racing, gambled with dice, danced, drank intoxicating soma, and played the flute, the lute, and the drum.[2]

In this early period the caste system gradually developed and, although many subdivisions have appeared during the ages, four ancient and principal castes formed the main divisions in society: (1) Brahmans, the priests and teachers; (2) Kshatriyas, the warriors and rulers; (3) Vaisyas, the merchants and traders; (4) Sudras, the artisans and laborers. As time passed a still lower caste, called pariahs or untouchables, was segregated as being quite inferior to the lowest of the four principal castes. The three upper castes were understood to be descendants from the Aryan conquerors; the

---

[1] *Cambridge History of India*, edited by E. J. Rapson (New York: The Macmillan Co., 1922), pp. 68-72.
[2] *Ibid.*, pp. 99-103.

Sudras and the untouchables were descended from the conquered aboriginal inhabitants. All castes being hereditary, a man was born to his state in society and could not rise above it. He must not marry outside his own caste. If he belonged to the Brahmans, the Kshatriyas, or the Vaisyas, he must not speak to a Sudra or eat food contaminated by the touch of a low-caste person. The humblest member of the lowest caste, however, might attain to union with Brahma, the supreme all-embracing Spirit.

The language of the Aryan Hindu was Sanskrit, the oldest form of Aryan speech. It is strikingly similar to ancient Persian, Greek, Latin, Gothic, Celtic, and the modern Teutonic, Romance, and Slavic languages of Europe. The people who speak these languages are known as Indo-European because all their languages are derived from the same ancient tongue, Sanskrit, which spread over India and Europe. The languages differ in many respects, of course, but fundamentally they have the same origin. For instance, the common word "man" in the Sanskrit is *vira* and the same in ancient Persian. The Latin word for man is *vir;* the Greek 'ήρως is allied to it, as is also the Anglo-Saxon *wer.* The English words *virile* and *virtue* are derived from the same source. Manuscripts in Sanskrit are preserved which are of incalculable value to the student of ethnology, ancient history, and Scripture.

Ancient India has been a land of contention among powerful nations. Since the conquest of Alexander the Great, Greeks, Scythians, Portuguese, Dutch, and British have ruled it; and, like the Mohammedans, conquerors of northern India in the fourteenth century, all have left their impress upon it. In the sixth century B.C., Cyrus, King of Persia, sent an expedition into India but with little success. Later, Darius formed a Persian satrapy in northwest India. Alexander the Great, the greatest of invaders, undertook to hellenize this country. Greek culture and ideas were then introduced and influenced its subsequent history.

After Alexander's death, one of his generals, Seleucus, became involved in war with Chandragupta, a Maurya prince, who defeated the Macedonian and made himself emperor of all northern India. This Maurya Empire reached its climax under Asoka, the grandson of Chandragupta, who was a devoted patron of Buddhism. He was a great propagator of the Buddhist faith and morals and a lavish founder of monasteries and shrines of Buddha. He sent bands of missionaries into the adjacent countries and islands and thereby established contact between India and the Hellenistic world.[3] After his death the Maurya dynasty began to decline and gradually crumbled.

From the sixth century A.D. to the fourteenth, Indian history is a series of political disturbances and chronic wars. The various petty princes strove for leadership and one kingdom after another lost supremacy. The jealousies and ambitions of the rulers ultimately prepared the way for the Mohammedan conquests in the fourteenth century.

A way to India by water was known to Europe through the voyage of the Portuguese explorer, Vasco da Gama, who sailed around the Cape of Good Hope and landed on the Malabar Coast towards the close of the fifteenth century. In the following century, the Dutch, who were not on friendly terms with the Portuguese and were obliged to look for eastern produce elsewhere, travelled this same route around the tip of Africa and on to India.[4] In the seventeenth century the Danes successfully established Indian colonies which

---

[3] *Ibid.*, pp. 498-501.
[4] *The Cambridge Shorter History of India,* edited by H. H. Dodwell (New York: The Macmillan Co., 1934), p. 500.

subsequently were sold to England. Towards the close of the century the French found that their only rival in the new country was the English, who had established the East India Company in 1600. The struggle for supremacy which followed ended in British predominance over the French. By an act of the English Parliament the government of India was transferred from the East India Company to the Crown.[5] In 1877 Queen Victoria was proclaimed Empress of India.

India has been divided into British territory and independent native states. Indian states are governed by native princes, ministers, and councils with the advice of the supreme government which is represented by a governor-general or viceroy. The rulers of states are known as maharajas and rajahs according to their rank. They keep their own courts within their territories, administer justice, and have a limited number of standing troops.

British domination in India has always met with opposition, which has crystallized in recent years. The leader of the Nationalists in India today is Mahatma Ghandi. He recognizes the four traditional castes and has labored to abolish the many subcastes and do away with the social ostracism of the untouchables. He advocates among his people non-cooperation with the English government. He urges them to refuse all government and military service and to withdraw their children from British schools and institutions. His program encourages a series of boycotts which aim to drive out English manufacturers and merchants in the hope of gaining for India her autonomy.

Among the Hindus religion pervades and informs the whole of education, just as it largely determines everything else in their national life. Two thirds of the

---

[5] *Ibid.*, pp. 758 ff.

people practice Brahmanism; about one fourth are Mohammedans, and the rest are Buddhists or Christians.
Brahmanism dates from 1200 B.C. It was affected by
the nature worship of the Vedic period when the powers
of nature were personified and worshipped. Brahma
is the Universal God and Creator, with Vishnu, the
Preserver, and Siva, the Destroyer, as other forms of
the deity. With lofty philosophical ideas go many pantheistic conceptions which encourage a base superstition
among the illiterate. God is seen and worshipped in the
heavenly bodies, in the earth, and in living creatures,
such as the cow, the ape, and the parrot.

Brahma is an impersonal existence and the soul of
the universe. All things emanate from this Supreme
Spirit as rays emanate from the sun. The souls of the
worthy return to Brahma after death; the unworthy
must resume life in some of the lower forms. They are
doomed to this process until they acquire a perfection
necessary for absorption in Brahma.

Intimately connected with this idea of transmigration
of souls is the development of the caste system and the
belief that all creatures are sacred. If a man's spirit
is born again in the body of a Brahman, or of a Sudra,
its present habitation is in accordance with its merits.
Each person enjoys the station in life that he has merited
by his past lives. In so far as a person led a life of
virtue or crime he is to be reborn in a higher caste, a
lower animal, or even a plant. The important matter
is that the individual in society be content with his
social status and, by fulfilling his duties, strive to merit
a better position in his next life.[6]

The way to absorption in Brahma is by penance and
prayer and not by the use of external means. Since
God is a quiescent and inactive being, the highest prep-

---

[6] Henry O. Taylor, *Ancient Ideals* (New York: The Macmillan
Co., 1900), I, 81 f.

aration for absorption in him is a life of contemplation
and prayer. In consequence, monasteries for the ascetics and contemplatives have always been in operation
in all parts of India. The belief that sins committed in
a pre-existent state if not expiated before death are
punished in a future birth has led to inhuman practices
of penance and self-torture.

Buddhism was introduced into India in the sixth century B.C. The founder of this religious doctrine was a
young Hindu noble by the name of Gautama. His disciples hailed him as the "Buddha"—the "enlightened
one." While contemplating the thought that all men
must suffer and some time die, he gave up the luxury
of his palace, left behind his wife and child, and set out
as a beggar to achieve peace of soul. Gathering a group
of ascetics around him, he wandered up and down the
Ganges Valley with them, clad in yellow robes, teaching
and spreading the new belief.

Buddha accepted much that the Brahmans taught,
but he rejected the caste system and taught that all men
are equal. He differed widely from them in his plan
of salvation. To obtain deliverance from reincarnation
man must suppress all desire, both lawful and unlawful.
A person who dies with unsatisfied desires is condemned
to be born anew, for another round of sorrow and pain.
When he has completely stifled all craving for pleasure,
all desire for the present as well as for the future life,
he will attain Nirvana, a state of security where in
reality the soul ceases to exist.

The teachings of Buddha were oral discourses and
were not written down until two or three generations
after his death. Meanwhile they were carefully memorized by his disciples. The "Four Noble Truths" which
constitute the essence of Buddhistic belief are: (1) life
is full of pain and sorrow; (2) the cause of pain and
sorrow is desire; (3) pain and sorrow can be escaped

by the attainment of Nirvana; (4) Nirvana can be
achieved through an "Eightfold Path: right belief, right
behavior, right contemplation, right concentration, right
endeavor, right occupation, right resolve, right speech."[7]

Brahmanism led to the growth of Hindu science;
Buddhism led to the development of Hindu architecture.
The monastic system of the Buddhists required extensive buildings made of stone. Temples were dug out
of the solid rock and gave rise to many artistic features
in the form of columns and sculptural designs. As time
passed, Buddhism was superseded by Brahmanism.
Buddha was the object of worship after his death, but,
because his system of religion ignored the deities, the
masses gradually clamored for the worship of their gods.
Buddhism consequently was exiled to certain areas of
North India, to Ceylon, Burma, Thibet, China, and
Japan.

The Vedas, or sacred writings of the Hindus, consist
of the Rig Veda, the Sama Veda, the Yagur Veda, and
the Atharva Veda. Veda means knowledge or lore and
the Rig Veda is the lore of hymns. It is a collection
of more than one thousand hymns, some of the most
beautiful of which were written by women. These
hymns are addressed to the dawn, the sun, the wind,
and other gods of nature. The oldest of these hymns
were composed about 1200 B.C. The Sama Veda is the
lore of chants; it is a résumé of the Rig Veda and presents the hymns and invocations in sacrificial order.
The Yagur Veda is the lore of prayers, popularly known
as the Sacrificial Veda, based upon the Rig Veda and
containing original formulas orderly arranged for use
at particular sacrifices. The Atharva Veda is the lore
of spells; it deals with incantations against evil spirits
and is the private prayer book of the people.

The Code of Manu is the earliest and most important

---

[7] *Ibid.*, pp. 91 f.

law book of India. It embodies the ancient legal practices of the Hindus and presents the traditional customs of a social and domestic character as well as penitential exercises. It also contains many excellent moral precepts. The highest literary expression of the Hindu mind is found in the two great epics, the Ramayana and the Mahabharata. Both these poems relate the deeds of heroes; the latter is said to be seven times the length of the combined *Iliad* and *Odyssey*.

In the elementary school the Vedas were learned from oral teaching. Writing and arithmetic also entered into the curriculum which was taught to all classes except the lowest. Writing was first practiced in the sand. When the pupil had attained facility he then wrote upon palm leaves with an iron point; finally upon leaves of the plane tree with ink.[8] The Hindus were in possession of the so-called Arabic system of numeration before the Arabs themselves. Our decimal system of notation, not with our present characters, but in all its essential features, is derived from India also through the Arabs.

The earliest schools were attached to the court. The Brahmans there taught the sacred hymns, the practices of religion, and their national tradition. Later schools were conducted in the open air, beneath shady trees, except in bad weather when shelter was necessary. The Parishads, or collegiate institutions of learning, have been in existence since 1000 B.C.[9] The method of teaching was the authoritative imparting of the subject matter by the teacher. The Brahmans trained older pupils to teach the younger ones what they had been taught. It was this custom that suggested to Dr. Andrew Bell the idea of the monitorial system which was introduced into England toward the close of the nineteenth century.

---

[8] S. S. Laurie, *Historical Survey of Pre-Christian Education* (New York: Longmans, Green, and Co., 1900), p. 176.

[9] *Ibid.*, p. 168.

The military and ruling class received training in martial discipline, the laws, traditions, and customs, and frequently attended the advanced schools with the Brahmans. The merchants and members of the third class learned what pertained to the commercial interests of the time; they were able to read, write, and calculate and, it is believed, were instructed in legendary lore.

The higher schools, attended chiefly by the Brahmans, but also by the second caste, were far advanced in the sciences. In them astronomy, history, law, mathematics, medicine, philosophy, poetry, and theology were taught. The teachers were not only learned in their own extensive literature, but they wrote much on mathematics and astronomy. Because the Hindus educated for the ideal and not for the practical, the culture of India developed more along the lines of philosophy and religion and less in the direction of science, art, and commerce.

Since 1859 the British have established government schools for the instruction of all classes and both sexes. The educational system ranges from the primary school to the professional school and university. There are normal schools for the professional training of teachers. India has eighteen universities in all. Osmania University is the only one in which the medium of instruction is an Indian vernacular, namely Urdu.[10]

The spirit of the leading religion, Brahmanism, which sees nothing good in life, and rather teaches its passive endurance as a necessary evil to prepare for annihilation after death, thwarts all energy to advancement in science and in life. Hindu education has not changed much in centuries. It is of interest to the student of educational history because of its exemplification of the caste system, as informed and largely determined by the state religion.

[10] Som Nath Chib, *Language, Universities and Nationalism in India* (London: H. Milford, Oxford University Press, 1936), p. 46

FOR FURTHER STUDY

Abel, James F., *A Survey of Education in Countries other than the United States. U. S. Office of Education, Bulletin 1937, No. 2.* Vol. I, Chap. VII, pp. 36-40.

Cambridge History of India, edited by E. J. Rapson. Vol. I. New York: The Macmillan Co., 1922.

Chib, Som Nath, *Language, Universities, and Nationalism in India.* London: H. Milford, Oxford University Press, 1936.

Dasgupta Surendranath, *A History of Indian Philosophy.* Cambridge: Cambridge University Press, 1932-40. 3 vols.

Dutt, R. C., *Civilization of India.* New York: E. P. Dutton and Co., 1900.

Dutt, Shoshee, *India, Past and Present.* London: Chatto and Windus, 1880.

History of India, edited by A. V. Williams Jackson. 9 vols. London: Grolier Society, 1906-7.

Keay, F. E., *Ancient Indian Education; an inquiry into its origin, development and ideals.* Oxford: University Press, 1918.

Laurie, S. S., *Historical Survey of Pre-Christian Education.* New York: Longmans, Green, and Co., 1900.

La Vallée-Poussin, L. de, *L'Inde jusque vers 300 av. J. C.* Tome VI. Histoire du monde. Paris: E. de Boccard, 1924.

Legacy of India, edited by G. T. Garrat. Oxford: Clarendon Press, 1937.

Masson-Oursel, Paul, *Ancient India and Indian Civilization.* Translated from the French by M. R. Dobé. London: K. Paul Trench, Trübner and Co., Ltd., 1934.

Macdonell, A. A., *India's Past.* Oxford; Clarendon Press, 1927.

Noronha, George E., *Backgrounds in the Education of Indian Girls.* Washington, D. C.: Catholic University, 1939.

Rawlinson, Hugh George E., *India, A Short Cultural History.* London: D. Appleton Century, 1938.

————, *Indian Historical Studies.* London: Longmans, Green and Co., 1913.

Smith, Vincent A., *The Oxford History of India, from the Earliest Times to the end of 1911.* Revised and continued to 1921 by S. M. Edwards. Oxford: Clarendon Press, 1923.

Taylor, Henry O., *Ancient Ideals.* Vol. I. New York: The Macmillan Co., 1900.

CHAPTER V

PERSIA

Early in the migration of the Aryan people, one of the finest types, which was to develop into a more active and warlike nation than the Hindus, settled in Media and Persia. What is known of the history of the Persians and of Persian education is derived largely from the Greek historians, Herodotus and Xenophon, and from the sacred writings called *Avesta* and *Zend-Avesta*. The origin of the name Persia is not known. In the strict sense it denotes the territory designated in antiquity as Persis, but the name later was extended to the whole Iranian plateau. In ancient times the greater part of Iran was inhabited by people of Indo-European origin who termed themselves Aryans. The whole country was called Ariana,[1] the land of the Aryans. The people who lived in the northwestern part of the plateau were called Medes and their district, Media; the group in the southern part were known as Persians.

The Medes were established as a ruling power about 500 B.C. Under the command of their king, Cyaxares (B.C. 625-585), they marched, against the Assyrians with the aid of the Babylonians and Scythians, dealt the death blow to the Assyrian empire, and extended their sway as far as Egypt. About a half century later the Medes were conquered by the Persians under Cyrus the Great, who brought all Asia Minor under Persian domination. The Persians and the Medes were now blended into one people and the decree of the king once passed was law for the Medes as well as for the Persians.

---

[1] The Middle Persian is Eran and the Modern, Iran.

Other Persian conquerors after Cyrus, like Cambyses, Darius, and Xerxes, subjected Lydia, Babylonia, Scythia, Egypt, and some of the Greek possessions, building an empire which lasted until the invasion of Alexander the Great. From Mesopotamia Persia inherited the cuneiform[2] system of Babylonian writing, the Assyrian style of architecture, the Assyrian plan of organizing the army, and the Assyrian method of imperial government. From Egypt also the Persians borrowed many ideas. Like the Pharaohs, the Persian kings had rock sepulchres constructed for their tombs. Like the Egyptians and also the Greeks, the Persians used many columns in their buildings, rather slender, however, and set further apart. Persian civilization, therefore, like Greek civilization, was a combination of the older cultures.

After the death of Cyrus, his son Cambyses invaded Egypt, and had himself crowned Pharaoh. Cambyses has been called the mad son of Cyrus whose misrule lasted for eight years ending in death by his own hand on his way back from Egypt to recover his crown which had been seized by a Magian priest, Gaumata, called Smerdis, the Usurper, because he impersonated the king's dead brother.[3] After the imposture was discovered, the false Smerdis was slain by Darius Hystaspes, an ambitious prince who set himself up as king.

Next to Cyrus, Darius was the greatest king of Persia. His empire comprised the whole of the then civilized world except India and China in the far East and Greece and Carthage in the West. While he laid plans to make himself absolute master of the world, he realized that he must settle the problem of hostile Athens beyond the Aegean. About this time the Athenians were putting

---

[2] So called from the Latin *cuneus* meaning wedge. The characters were wedge-shaped.
[3] A. V. Williams Jackson, *Persia Past and Present* (New York: The Macmillan Co., 1906), p. 26.

into effect the democratic reforms of Cleisthenes. They were liberty-loving people and disliked an absolute monarchy. They had helped their fellow countrymen across the sea and refused to yield in any way to the Persian king. Darius, eager to send an expedition against Greece, commanded an attendant that he should remind him of this contemplated project by saying three times when dinner was set before the king, "Master, remember the Athenians."

In the plan of the first Persian invasion there was an assault both by land and by sea; the land forces came by way of the Hellespont, while a large fleet sailed for the Greek coast. But the Greeks of Thrace and Macedonia resisted strongly and the rough seas wrecked most of the ships. Darius with his great wealth fitted out another expedition which landed near Athens. Ten times as many Persians as Greeks fought in the battle of Marathon which followed, yet the Greeks won the day and the defeated forces of Darius sailed back to Asia. While devising further plans for the destruction of Athens, Darius died and was succeeded by his son Xerxes.

Xerxes made preparations against the Greeks on a vast scale. From all parts of his empire he gathered an immense army. As many as forty-six nations sent their best soldiers, men of all colors. These soldiers came on foot, on horseback, on elephants, on camels, and in ships. At the pass of Thermopylae was fought one of the bravest defenses in history. A few Greeks stubbornly held the pass until Ephialtes revealed to Xerxes a secret path over the mountains, and so the Persian king reached Athens. At the battle of Plataea, the Persian army was nearly annihilated. On the same day at Salimas the Grecian fleet was victorious over the Persian forces.

Signs of decadence in the Persian empire became more

and more manifest in the reign of Darius II when Persia
lost Egypt which it had held for a hundred years. The
two sons of Darius struggled for control of the tottering
throne. Cyrus, the younger, hired thirteen thousand
Asiatic Greeks to come and help him against his brother
Artaxerxes. Cyrus was slain in battle near Babylon
and his generals were put to death. The Greeks, reduced to ten thousand, fought their way back to the
coast under the command of Xenophon, the historian.
The "March of the Ten Thousand" recorded by Xenophon himself revealed the decline of Persian supremacy
and the rise of Greek domination.

Persia made valiant attempts to regain her former
glory under a strong king, Artaxerxes III, but these efforts were shortlived. The kingdom passed to Darius
III, a weak and unfortunate ruler, who was compelled
to face one of the greatest of all generals, Alexander
the Great. When Alexander marched across Asia to
India, the Persian empire fell a victim to him at the
battle of Arbela, 331 B.C.

After Alexander's death, the Greek general Seleucus
founded an empire in Western Asia which included the
country of Persia. When that broke up, invaders of the
same stock as Persians, called Parthians, took control
and ruled Persia for the next four hundred years. The
Persians eventually succeeded in throwing off the yoke
of the Parthians and a Persian ruler of the old royal
line, Artaxerxes, founded the dynasty of Sassanian
kings. The magi or wise men who taught the ancient
faith of Zoroaster were then assembled at Persepolis and
the sacred works of the Persians called *Zend-Avesta*
were written. The Sassanid empire came to an end in
639 when the Mohammedans overthrew the Persian
power. A number of faithful Zoroastrians, because of
the change of the national religion to Islam by the
Moslem rulers, emigrated to India and settled at Bom-

bay where they are known today as Parsees and are faithful to their ancient beliefs and practices.

The centuries that followed were marked by invasion and misrule. Persia was invaded from central Asia by the Turks and afterwards by the Mongols. In the year 1500, a new ruler, Ismail, taking the old title of Shah, formed a national government in Persia and reduced the Mongols to submission. He is regarded as the founder of modern Persia. The power of the Shah remained autocratic down until recent times when the throne consented to a constitutional form of government with a parliament. The Shah claims succession in the long line of ancient monarchs who have been rulers in Persia for more than three thousand years. He is the inheritor of the rule of her legendary kings as well as the scepter of the Median dynasty and the crown of Cyrus the Great.[4] Of all the countries in the East that came into contact with Greece and Rome, Persia alone has preserved her independence.

The Persians displayed a great genius for government and control of conquered peoples. They were not interested in spreading their religion or language, but in receiving tribute. The Great King was represented in the foreign possessions by the satraps, who collected the taxes and recruited auxiliaries in time of war. In the administration of the empire, the territory was divided into twenty satrapies or provinces, each under a provincial governor or satrap appointed by the king. The revenues of the empire in actual silver talents would represent in modern terms about one hundred thirty million dollars a year.[5] There were also tributes in the form of horses, sheep, camels, ivory, and incense. The provinces were obliged to furnish grain and other food-

---

[4] Jackson, *op. cit.*, p. 25.
[5] Robert W. Rogers, *A History of Ancient Persia* (New York: Charles Scribner's Sons, 1929), p. 110.

stuffs for the armies quartered upon them. Each satrapy supplied its quota of troops in time of war. The finest troops came from Persia itself and the generals were usually Persian noblemen.

Although the rule of the Great King was a rigid despotism, the tributary nations enjoyed real autonomy and freedom in the administration of home affairs. The provinces were subject to the satraps and the satraps subject to the king. The person of the king was exalted above that of all other officials. He wore garments of richest silk and sat upon a throne of gold, silver, and ivory. To serve him was a mark of noble distinction. Close to him was an official known as the "King's Eye," often his son or brother, who supervised the services of the governors whom the king did not always trust.

To facilitate the control of the empire, great attention was paid to the roads. The king's road led from Susa, the capital, at the center of the empire to Sardis in Asia Minor. The whole network of roads was divided into post routes with horsemen stationed at regular intervals. By a system of road houses, fresh horses, and messengers, reports were relayed from the king to the satrap and from the satrap to the king with great dispatch. Over these roads travelled the king's inspectors, the tribute-bearers, and the royal armies.

The education of Persian youth reflects the warlike spirit of the nation, just as it portrays the religious life during the period of Persian supremacy. The national religion was Zoroastrianism, so called from its first exponent Zoroaster.[6] Some scholars have been inclined to regard this religious reformer a mythical person, but the historical reality of Zoroaster has been firmly established.[7] He lived some time before the reign of

---

[6] The Iranian is Zarathustra. The original meaning of the name is not clear. The latter part *ushtra* means camel suggesting that he lived a simple pastoral life. *Cf.* Rogers, *op. cit.*, p. 17.

[7] *Ibid.*, p. 18.

Cyrus and, while a young man, claimed to have had seven miraculous visions in which he had conversations with the god, Ahura Mazda. These revelations were handed down from one generation to another along with various religious compositions. The religious literature of Zoroastrianism is called *Avesta* which is interpreted as wisdom or knowledge and constitutes the Bible of the ancient Persians. Which of the *Avesta* were composed by Zoroaster and which are the work of his followers it is impossible to determine.

The fundamental belief is in the existence of one Supreme God, Ahura Mazda, creator and sustainer of the universe, to whom all good in the physical and in the spiritual order is attributed. Evil is the work of Ahriman, the spirit of wickedness, who arose out of the conflict of the forces of good and evil at creation. He is inferior to Ahura Mazda and will be finally subdued. Man contending against evil in the world and all spiritual and physical ills, is in constant conflict with Ahriman. Ahura Mazda rewards with immortality his faithful warriors. The good Persian speaks the truth, struggles against his evil inclinations, exterminates beasts of prey, and promotes fertility of the land by the reclamation of arid places. After death, each man's immortal soul will be judged. If good deeds outweigh his sins he will enter into Paradise; otherwise he is handed over to Ahriman. In practice, Zoroastrianism was free from idolatry, and encouraged the virtues that befitted the farmer, warrior, and ruler.

This dualistic conception of the universe was already prevalent before Zoroaster taught the antithesis between good and evil. The early religion of the Persians was very probably like the religion of the Hindus of the Vedic period. Gradually a tendency towards dualism became more marked. Certain gods came to be recognized as evil deities, and others as divinities friendly

to man.[8] The struggle between night and day, between
the storm and the clear sky, of which the Vedic poets
sang, assumed a moral form and was transformed into
a conflict between good and evil.[9]

The *Avesta* is a combined Bible and prayer book. It
consists of five *Gathas* or hymns written in an older dialect than that of the rest of the collection, the *Vendidad*,
or compilation of religious laws and mythical tales, and
the *Zend*, or commentary. In addition to the *Avesta-
Zend*, there was also the *Khordan Avesta* or Small Avesta
which was a collection of prayers. The word *Zend* sig-
nifies explanation and is applied to the exegetical matters
in the text. The Parsee priests use the word Zend to
denote the Pahlavi[10] version and commentary but not
the original scriptures.

In its present form the *Avesta* is fragmentary. The
original text consisted of twenty-one books, only one
of which, the *Vendidad*, has been completely preserved.
Due to the invasion of Alexander some of the sacred
books were lost, while others remained in a scattered
condition, much of their teaching being handed on by
memory. Little was known of their contents until the
eighteenth century when the manuscripts were brought
to Europe and translated into French. Previous to that
time all that was known of them was that such a body
of scriptures existed, which was concluded from references to them in the Greek, Roman, Arabic, and Syriac
writers. In 1762, a French scholar, Anquetil du Perron,
after several years of assiduous research and study in
India, returned to Paris with one hundred and eighty
Oriental manuscripts which he collated and edited dur-

---

[8] William S. Turner, *History of Philosophy* (Boston: Ginn and
Co., 1903), pp. 26 f.

[9] A. H. Sayre, *The Ancient Empires of the East* (London: The
Macmillan Co., 1883), p. 447.

[10] Pahlavi language and literature is of the Middle Persian
Period extending from the 3rd to the 9th or 10th century A.D.

ing the next nine years.[11] His scholarly work resulted in
the Western World receiving in three volumes his *Zend
Avesta*, the first translation ever made.[12] The attacks
made by English and German scholars on the scientific
value of the materials used in making this translation
were refuted by philologists who through the study of
Sanskrit and comparative philology established the
genuineness of the Zoroastrian scriptures held by modern
Parsee priests.

The Persian system of writing may have developed
from the Babylonian and Elamitic or Median forms of
script. It is probable that the Babylonian signs which
consist of hundreds of characters were reduced to one
hundred and thirteen for Elamite and to forty-one
characters for Persian. The writing was originally picture writing with lines and curves; but when records
were made on soft clay by indentation the curved lines
developed into wedge-shape characters.[13] This complex
system of writing was a puzzle to modern scholars until
Sir Henry Rawlinson deciphered the inscription of
Darius carved upon a rock of the Behistan Mountain
in three languages: Persian, Elamitic, and Babylonian.
While a young military officer in Persia he had learned
to decipher the cuneiform characters[14] and working on
the Persian inscription, he was able to translate the
parallel versions of it in Elamitic and Babylonian.

Persian education was of and for the Persian state.
It was practical and warlike and aimed at training de-

---

[11] Rogers, *op. cit.*, p. 30.
[12] The best English translation is by Darmstetter and Mills,
Zend-Avesta, 3 vols., in the *Sacred Books of the East*, Oxford,
1880-97. There are French translations by Darmstetter and by de
Harley, a German one by Spiegel. Most of the Pahlavi books
have been translated into English or summarized by West, *Pahlavi Texts*, 5 vols., in the *Sacred Books of the East.*
[13] Rogers, *op. cit.*, pp. 14f.
[14] The German schoolmaster and philologist Grotefend was the
pioneer in cuneiform decipherment.

voted sons, and able warriors. In accordance with the Persian conception of man's destiny and individual responsibility, it would seem that nothing was neglected that would aid in the formation of the dutiful soldier. The virtues of obedience, truthfulness, justice, and gratitude were considered his noblest adornments and must be accompanied by fortitude, skill, and martial bravery.

Xenophon in his *Cyropaedia,* or *Education of Cyrus,*[15] states that the Persian boys were sent to school to learn justice. Cyrus was taught a keen sense of justice by his teacher who punished him severely because he did not decide "the case of the tunics" properly. A big boy with a little tunic coming upon a small boy wearing a big tunic, exchanged garments with him. Cyrus said this was right. The master flogged him because it was his duty to decide, not whom the tunics best fitted, but whose title was the rightful one.[16]

Elementary education began in the fifth year, when the boy was placed under the tutelage of a member of the court, usually a man of tried reputation, who could be trusted to teach not less by example than by precept. A ten-year training, mostly physical, but which also included religious instruction given by the priest, prepared the boy for a life of usefulness as a servant of the state. He was habituated to martial exercises and to the management of horses. In the company of his king, he hunted wild animals because the training in this sport was the best preparation for war itself. At the capital the place of instruction was in the open court before the king's residence. In other cities the

---

[15] This title is misleading. The first book has to do with his education; the remaining seven deal with his campaigns and his training of others as soldiers and citizens in his empire. The work is more romantic perhaps than historical.

[16] *Xenophon Cyropaedia,* translated into English by Walter Miller in the Loeb Classical Library (New York: The Macmillan Co., 1914), I, 41-43.

training was given in the open squares or on the porticoes of public buildings.

The higher education, confined to the nobles and hereditary priests, embraced astronomy, mathematics, philosophy, and religious literature. Much is written of the learning of the priestly class, the Magi, and undoubtedly what is attributed to them in regard to their accomplishments in mathematics, astronomy, medicine, and finance is substantially true. Judging from the body of sacred writings, with which they were supposedly familiar, their literary knowledge was extensive.

The educational system made no provision for the training of women save domestic, although Persian society gave woman a much higher standing than she had in most Oriental nations.[17] It produced the intrepid warrior, physically able to endure all the hardships of war, having also a careful moral training in the natural virtues of obedience, gratitude, and truthfulness. The masses of the people were not educated. The ruling classes, clerical and lay, were well prepared for their special functions; but, with civil rulers lacking in literary culture or tastes, Persia was unable to sustain "the ravages of peace." Like all warlike nations, she was "nourished in war and wasted in peace." In the time of triumph the immense wealth acquired by conquest and expansion brought luxury, sensuality, and indolence, and sapped the strength of the warrior class.

Persia has furnished an example of state education, a system capable of promoting the growth and expansion of a conquering people, but incapable of building up an intellectually strong race, or giving permanence and vigor to the institutions it had fostered.

---

[17] S. S. Laurie, *Historical Survey of Pre-Christian Education* (New York: Longmans, Green, and Co., 1900), p. 193.

FOR FURTHER STUDY

Abel, James F., *A Survey of Education in Countries other than the United States. U. S. Office of Education, Bulletin 1937, No. 2.* Vol. I, Chap. VII, pp. 40-42.

Botsford, G. W., *Source of Ancient History.* New York: The Macmillan Co., 1934.

Cambridge Ancient History, Vol. IV. New York: The Macmillan Co., 1926.

Jackson, A. V. Williams, *Persia Past and Present.* New York: The Macmillan Co., 1906.

——————, *Zoroaster, the Prophet of Ancient Iran.* New York: The Macmillan Co., 1934.

Justi, Ferdinand, *Empire of the Persians.* In History of All Nations, vol. 2. New York: Lea Bros. & Co., 1905.

Laurie, S. S., *Survey of Pre-Christian Education.* New York: Longmans, Green, and Co., 1900.

Rawlinson, George, *Five Great Monarchies of the Ancient Eastern World.* 4 vols. London: J. Murray, 1862-67.

——————, *The Sixth Great Oriental Monarchy.* London: Longmans and Co., 1873.

——————, *The Seventh Great Oriental Monarchy.* London: Longmans and Co., 1876.

Rogers, Robert W., *A History of Ancient Persia.* New York: Charles Scribner's Sons, 1929.

Sayce, A. H., *The Ancient Empires of the East.* London: The Macmillan Co., 1883.

Spiegel, Friedrich, *Eranische Altertumskunde.* 3 vols. Leipzig: W. Engelmann, 1871-78.

Sykes, P. M., *A History of Persia.* 2 vols. London: The Macmillan Co., 1930.

CHAPTER VI

SEMITIC PEOPLES

The people of Israel have many claims to a prominent place in the history of education before the time of Christ. They were the highest branch of the Semites in point of morality and religion, and they surpassed the other nations of antiquity in their lofty idea of government and in the appreciation of the role of the individual in society.

Their many vicissitudes as a nation brought them under the influence of surrounding peoples, and these contacts left deep impressions on their culture and civilization. Their servitude under the Egyptian Pharaohs lasted over a period of four hundred years. It is necessary now to indicate some salient characteristics of the Babylonians, Assyrians, and Phoenicians, other historical representatives of the Semites, in order to obtain a fuller view of Hebrew learning and education.

Babylonians

It was in the fertile valley of Mesopotamia[1] that the civilization of western Asia first developed. Within this alluvial plain formed by the Tigris and Euphrates Rivers there arose the kingdoms of Babylonia and Assyria. Until the decipherment of the cuneiform inscriptions on the monumental remains of these two great ancient civilizations, the history of Mesopotamia was obtained chiefly from the writings of Herodotus who visited the country and from the Chaldean priest, Berosus. The information of Herodotus is scanty and of

---

[1] Derived from Greek words μεσος middle and ποταμος meaning the middle of the rivers or between the rivers.

doubtful value, but not so the work of Berosus.[2] He was a priest of the temple of Bel[3] at Babylonia and a contemporary of Alexander the Great. Using the archives of the temple, he had made a careful study of the history of his country, the main events of which he set down in Greek. His original work in three books, which was probably entitled *Babyloniaca,* has perished and is known today through quotations at second and third hand.[4] Other important sources for Babylonian and Assyrian history are historical portions of the Old Testament, especially 2 Kings, while equally informative are the prophets Isaiah, Nahum, Jeremiah, and Ezekiel. From the mounds that cover the ancient cities of Babylonia and Assyria have come primary monumental sources in the form of stones, slabs, cylinders, and tablets, thousands of which are found in the various museums and libraries of the world.

The lower part of Mesopotamia is called Chaldea in the Bible. For that reason it is customary to designate the early Babylonian Monarchy as the "Chaldean." Very old names for southern Babylonian are Sumer and Akkad. Sumer was in the extreme south and Akkad just north of Sumer. The Sumerians are regarded as the earliest people in history to settle in Mesopotamia. They developed learning, practiced agriculture, and built temples. These temples were erected in the form of terraces with a succession of stories of diminishing size, using stage upon stage like a tower heavenward.

The land of the Sumerians was invaded by Semitic tribes who were attracted to the agricultural plains of Mesopotamia and spread over the valley. The races

---

[2] A. H. Sayce, *The Ancient Empires of the East,* pp. 326 f.

[3] One of the chief gods of the Babylonians. Identified with Zeus by Herodotus.

[4] Robert W. Rogers, *A History of Babylonia and Assyria* (New York: Eaton and Mains, 1900), I, 259.

mixed together and ultimately established a government, first at Ur and then at Babylon, which became the capital of the Babylonian empire. The Sumerian picture writing which developed into wedge-shaped characters was adopted by the Babylonians and Assyrians and used by many of the neighboring nations. The invaders gradually absorbed much of the higher culture of the Sumerians so that in time they became Sumerianized Semites.

The most famous ruler of ancient Mesopotamia was Hammurabi (2123-2081 B.C.).[5] During his reign the whole country bordering on the Persian Gulf, including Assyria as well as Babylonia, was subject to him. He was a great builder and lawgiver. A copy of his world-famous Code of Laws was unearthed forty centuries after it was compiled, carved on a block of black stone, which was discovered in three pieces on the acropolis of Susa in the course of De Morgan's Persian excavations during the winter of 1901-1902.

The Code contains 285 laws and begins with directions for proper legal procedures. Penalties for dishonest judges, unjust accusations, and false testimonies are prescribed. Decision by ordeal is admitted when there is insufficient evidence against the accused. When a man was charged with sorcery, if he had no witnesses to testify in his behalf, he might leap into the river, and if he came out alive his innocence was established. There were laws concerning family rights, property rights, loans, deposits, and debts; also laws dealing with injuries and damages suffered through neglect in the various trades. The code determined the fees of professional men and fixed the wages for mechanics and tradesmen. It distinguished between real and personal property and went into great detail in regard to the in-

---

[5] *Cambridge Ancient History* (New York: The Macmillan Co., 1923), I, 254.

heritance of children by different wives. Women were allowed to own and sell property, and even enter into business. From the Code we learn that ancient Babylonian society was undemocratic. There were three social classes: nobles, commoners, slaves. The nobles were very likely the descendants of the Semitic conquerors; the commoners included merchants and tradesmen generally; while below them were the slaves who were bought, sold, branded, and mortgaged.[6]

The last of Hammurabi's successors was overthrown in 1926 B.C. Babylonia was then ruled by invaders for over six centuries when it was conquered by Assyria and subjected to it. Frequently the Babylonians revolted against the Assyrian monarch and finally, with the aid of the Medes and Scythians, overthrew him and destroyed the city of Nineveh. Under the cruel and aggressive ruler, Nabuchodonosor,[7] Babylon was made for a short time the center of Eastern civilization. He surrounded the city with massive walls, adorned it with a sumptuous palace, and built for his Persian queen the famous hanging gardens in the form of artificial terraces covered with flowers and shrubs. It was this same king who burned Jerusalem, ordered the Hebrew king's son to be slain before his father's eyes, blinded the king himself and carried off the blind king and thousands of his subjects as captives to Babylon.[8]

---

[6] *Ibid.*, pp. 512-28.

[7] Nebuchadnezzar, Nebuchadrezzar are other forms of the same name. Nabuchodonosor appears to be nearer to the original Babylonian. Nebo was the god of wisdom among the Babylonians and the planet Mercury was sacred to him. Nabuchodonosor is variously interpreted as meaning O Nebo, defend my crown, empire, or work.

[8] The prophet Daniel tells us Nabuchodonosor lost his mind and was for a time a beast of the field. ". . . he was driven away from among men, and did eat grass like an ox, and his body was wet with the dew of heaven: till his hairs grew like the feathers of eagles, and his nails like bird's claws." *Cf.* Daniel, 4:30.

The fall of Babylon, according to Daniel the Prophet, took place during the reign of Baltasar.[9] At a banquet the king and his nobles drank from the vessels of gold and silver that had been taken from the temple in Jerusalem and praised their gods of gold, of silver, of brass, of iron, of wood, and of stone. Meanwhile there appeared fingers as it were of the hand of a man writing upon the surface of the wall of the king's palace three words: Mane, Thecel, Phares, which meant number, weight, and division respectively. Daniel interpreted the meaning of these words for the king in the sense that God had numbered his kingdom and had finished it; the king had been weighed in the balance and found wanting; his kingdom is divided and given to the Medes and Persians. That same night Baltasar was slain and Babylonia was conquered by Persia.[10]

The Chaldeans worshipped the Moon-god and the Sun-god. It was from this worship that Abraham fled when he was called from his birthplace, Ur in Chaldea, about 2100 B.C., to be the father of the Hebrews as a nation which was entrusted with the knowledge of the one true God. The Chaldean priests believed that celestial bodies exercised an important influence upon human affairs. Consequently the temples were observatories as well as sanctuaries where the priests studied the planets and their apparent relations to human events. Unaided by optical instruments,[11] they made marked progress in the science of astronomy with the naked eye and ascertained certain astronomical facts more accurately than was done in India.

---

[9] Baltasar is the Greek and Latin name for Belshazzar, the Hebrew equivalent of the Babylonian, which is interpreted to mean, May Bel protect the king.

[10] Daniel 5:1-30.

[11] The discovery of a crystal lens on the site of Nineveh sugguests that a rude kind of telescope may have been employed for astronomical observations. Cf. Sayce, op. cit., p. 403.

The interest of the Babylonians in astronomy led to a considerable advance in mathematics. Their canals and embankments show great evidence of engineering skill while their architecture reveals a creditable knowledge of the mechanical arts. They adapted to practical use their mathematical and astronomical learning, invented a system of weights and measures which has been the basis of all modern systems, mapped out the zodiac, and arranged the names of the days of the week. In their large cities they had immense libraries which were frequented by a large reading public.[12]

Education was restricted to the priestly class and the higher laity. The scribe, a character similar in training and occupation to the Egyptian scribe, is found there also. He did not hold so high a position either in the state or in society. He learned the art of writing, of calculating accurately, and of making out bills correctly. The scribes wrote with a stylus on plastic clay tablets and cylinders which were baked in ovens of their own or sent to the potter to be baked. Public events of importance, judicial decisions, and business contracts were often recorded on hollow cylinders.[13]

The youth of the highest or noble class received their education at the royal palace under the direction of the king. No literary education for all classes was provided by the state, but in a country which erected monuments with inscriptions for all to read, it is safe to conclude that not a few of the population were given individual instruction in reading and writing by the priests and scribes.[14] Little is known at present of the exact nature of their schools, teachers, or methods of instruction; but of the superior attainments of the learned class in art, literature, and science, and of the

---

[12] Sayce, *op. cit.*, p. 400.
[13] S. S. Laurie, *Survey of Pre-Christian Education,* p. 60.
[14] *Ibid.*, p. 61.

high order of their technical instruction there can be no
doubt.

Assyrians

The Assyrians were a people of purer Semitic stock
than the early Babylonians.[1] They adopted the civilization of the Chaldeans to the south of them but added
to it many cultural features of their own. They never
advanced further than the Babylonians in education or
in science, since the Chaldean philosophers were also
the most learned class in ancient Assyria. The services
of the Assyrians to ancient culture lie not in the development of thought but in the arranging and systematizing
of it. They maintained and spread the arts of Babylonian civilization and made them the common property
of the ancient eastern world.[2] Under various monarchs,
the most distinguished of whom were Shalmaneser, Sennacherib, and Ashurbanipal, the Assyrians built up a
powerful empire which included Mesopotamia, Palestine,
Syria, and Egypt.

The secret of Assyrian supremacy was the imperial
idea which made the king the center of national unity.
He was absolute ruler and commander-in-chief of the
army. Conquered lands were at first left under their
own rulers and compelled to pay tribute. Later the
subjugated provinces were administered by Assyrian
governors who obliged the people under their control to
furnish troops for the royal army and taxes for the royal
treasury. Rebellion was crushed by the authorities with
the utmost severity. It was not unusual to deport the
rebellious to other parts of the empire. In this system of
deportation, however, the new inhabitants did not differ

---

[1] Robert W. Rogers, *A History of Babylonia and Assyria* (New
York: Eaton and Mains, 1900), p. 15.
[2] *Cambridge Ancient History* (New York: The Macmillan
Company, 1925), III, 101 f.

markedly in speech and customs from the peoples amongst whom they were settled. It was a political advantage for the local governors to be spared the difficulties of administration which would have arisen had foreigners been permitted to dwell in their districts and agitate disorder.[3] The Assyrians seem to have been the first great people to develop a system of good roads for the purpose of holding their empire together. They had a network of highways over which the royal armies could be marched and along these roads they organized a messenger service for the quick delivery of government orders.

The imperial idea is revealed in the architecture, painting, and sculpture of the Assyrians in which they are credited with a superior talent. Assyrian architecture was secular in character. While the temple was the most important building in Babylonia, it was in the sister kingdom a mere appendage of the palace. Unlike the temple, which was still erected in the form of a tower, the royal palace was built on a platform which was raised to the level of the palace foundation and extended over a large area commanding a view of a plain or river. It was never more than two or three stories high; the upper stories were lightly constructed. Stone was quarried in the hills and used to form the colonnades or rows of pillars around the building. The stone columns were sometimes surmounted with capitals of artistic design and rested on the backs of lions, dogs, and winged bulls.[4] Wood and brick often took the place of stone; and, although the Assyrians used the arch in the construction of sewers, the roof of the palace was generally supported by wooden beams placed upon massive brick walls. The royal palace had many

---

[3] *Ibid.,* pp. 41 f.
[4] A. H. Sayce, *The Ancient Empires of the East* (London: The Macmillan Co., 1883), p. 395.

courts, corridors, and galleries. Skylights were provided in the roof and the supporting pillars were at times covered with bands of shining silver and copper to reflect the light into the windowless rooms.[5]

The art of sculpture was employed by the Assyrians in the way of ornamentation for the royal palace. Massive winged bulls or lions with human heads were placed before the portals of the palace to guard it from the intrusion of evil spirits. They were known as "Guardians of the footsteps of the King." They were grotesque figures symbolizing, perhaps, strength, swiftness, and intelligence. These usually had five legs because they were to be viewed from the front or the side. The front view must have two legs and the side view, four. In the interior of the royal palace were the bas-reliefs representing scenes of wars and events in the life of the king. Although drawn in profile and with little attention to perspective some of the scenes are full of action and are good specimens of ancient drawing before the time of the Greeks. To heighten the effect of the sculpture in relief the figures were picked out with red, blue, black, and white colors.[6] Of the same characteristic style as the reliefs is the colored-tempera painting with a covering of thin glaze. The painting shows great care in matters of detail, is delicate and tasteful with a design that is good and strong.[7]

The superior skill of the Assyrians is best seen in the very fine cylinder seals which were used by the king. The seals consisted of inscriptions or symbolic designs cut in precious stones which revolved upon a metallic axis. These intaglios were made from onyx, jasper, chalcedony, and feldspar and served to make impressions upon clay. The very earliest of these are clean

[5] *Cambridge Ancient History,* III, 76.
[6] Sayce, *op. cit.,* pp. 395 ff.
[7] *Cambridge Ancient History,* III, 331.

and vigorous. In fact, so extremely fine is the work sometimes that it seems certain emery must have been used in their manufacture.[8]

The libraries established by the Assyrian kings were modeled upon those of Babylonia. The most noted of these was the library in the royal palace of the last great king of Assyria, Ashurbanipal,[9] who has been styled the "Augustus of Assyria." He learned to read the ancient Sumerian by means of a dictionary prepared for him by one of his scribes while he was crown prince.[10] He collected many thousands of books dealing with grammar, lexicography, poetry, history, science, and religion. A host of librarians, copyists, and compilers assisted the king in searching out the old Babylonian clay books in the libraries and temples of the ancient cities to be copied and catalogued. Scholars at his court were also engaged in the production of new books on all the range of learning of the day as well as in the writing of new annals.[11] The preservation of the history, religion, and literature of ancient Mesopotamia was due largely to the aesthetic tastes and cultured interests of this zealous patron of literature. When the city of Nineveh was destroyed by fire in 612 B.C., by the Babylonians who had rebelled against Assyrian domination, the wooden shelves of the royal library were burned and the clay tabets on which traditions and records were inscribed in cuneiform characters fell in heaps in the ruins.

Because the Assyrians were a warlike people, their almost innumerable conflicts are thought to have prevented their advance in learning. In fact their enthusi-

---

[8] Sayce, *op. cit.,* p. 397.

[9] Ashur was the supreme god of the Assyrians. Ashurbanipal means "Ashur has created a son as heir."

[10] A. T. Olmstead, *History of Assyria* (New York: Charles Scribner's Sons, 1923), p. 489.

[11] Rogers, *op. cit.,* II, 279.

asm for war and conquest changed their country from
one of small farms into a land of large estates owned by
the nobility and cultivated by slaves. The freeman belonged to one of three classes: patricians, craftsmen, and
proletariat. From the class of patricians the kings selected their governors, chief priests, and generals. In
times of great stress, it was not uncommon for the king to
appoint women of the patrician class as governors.[12] In
theory, every able-bodied male was subject to a term
of military service, but in practice the wealthy secured
exception by paying a bounty or sending slaves to serve
for them.

In general, the training of youth consisted of practical instruction in military tactics and in such arts and
sciences as were required for their great engineering and
industrial works. Higher education was restricted to
the members of the royal court, the priesthood, and the
scribes.[13] In times of peace the Assyrians cultivated the
fine arts and their really wonderful libraries encouraged
devotion to their god of letters.

Phoenicians

Another Semitic people whose history is connected
with the Hebrews, and who were the foremost traders
and colonizers of antiquity, were the Phoenicians. They
occupied a narrow but fertile strip of land on the western coast of Asia, about one hundred and fifty miles
long and from ten to fifteen miles wide, situated between
the lofty mountains of Lebanon on the east and the
Mediterranean Sea on the west. The Israelites were
their neighbors, closely allied to them by racial affinity.
Despite their limited territory, or perhaps because of it,
they had no desire for political dominion. The advan-

---

[12] *Cambridge Ancient History,* III, 96.
[13] S. S. Laurie, *Historical Survey of Pre-Christian Education,*
p. 62.

tages of the Mediterranean which stretched out before them and the plentiful supply of timber from the cedars of Lebanon led them to establish an empire upon the sea. They controlled the world's trade between the eleventh and sixth centuries B.C.

Their chief cities, Tyre, Sidon, and Byblus, carried on an extensive sea trade in glass and metal work, pottery, textile fabrics, embroidery, and purple dyes, while caravans took merchandise to and from the surrounding nations. Tyre gave its name to Tyrian purple which, extracted from a species of shellfish, was used to color the robes of emperors and kings. It was the royal purple by means of which the Phoenicians had first become prosperous. Byblus was the center of trade in Egyptian papyrus, so much so that its name became a synonym for book. Our word "Bible" is derived from the name of this ancient city. The separate city-states were ruled at first by a king who seems to have been the chief among a commercial autocracy; later the monarchy disappeared altogether and the rule of judges was established.[1] Compared with the powerful monarchies of the east and south, the cities of Tyre and Sidon were politically insignificant; but the mariners and merchants from these two important seaports became the intermediaries between East and West and brought the different parts of the world into relations with one another.

Colonies were established by them on the coasts and islands of the Mediterranean Sea as far west as Spain. Greatest of all their colonies was Carthage, on the coast of what is now Tunisia. Their trading vessels sailed even to Great Britain; in fact, they traded by sea and land with all parts of the known world. They were also manufacturers, notable workers in wood and metals, miners, and shipbuilders. Scripture mentions them as

---

[1] Sayce, *op. cit.*, pp. 421 f.

workers on the Temple of Jerusalem. To them are attributed the invention of symbols for numbers and the devising of the alphabet which came to be used universally in the western world.

Through what channels of historic association or literary influence the Phoenicians obtained their alphabetic characters is still an unsettled question. It is most likely that the Hebrews should have adopted from the Phoenicians their alphabet because of the confidence placed by the people of Israel in the superiority of Phoenician handiwork and their dependence upon Phoenicians in many matters of trade and commerce.[2] Attempts have been made to show that the Phoenician alphabet was derived from cuneiform, from Cretan, and from various other Mediterranean systems of writing; but there is no conclusive proof that it was based on the script of any foreign people. Even if it could be proved that the Semitic alphabet was evolved from Egyptian hieroglyphs, it does not follow that our alphabet is of Egyptian origin.

By the ninth century B.C., the Phoenicians and also the other Semitic peoples of Syria were using an alphabet of twenty-two letters.[3] The oldest Semitic inscription of any extent known thus far has been assigned to the thirteenth century B.C. It is evident, then, that the invention of the alphabet itself must be placed at a much earlier date. The year 2000 B.C. is regarded as being not at all too early.[4] Probably through the Phoenician traders the Greeks learned the alphabet, although there is a theory that the Greek alphabet was not borrowed directly from the Phoenicians themselves, but

---

[2] William A. Mason, *A History of the Art of Writing* (New York: The Macmillan Co., 1920), p. 289.

[3] *Ibid.,* p. 295.

[4] B. L. Ullman, *Ancient Writing and Its Influence* (New York: Longmans, Green, and Co., 1932), p. 16.

from Cyprus. Through the Greeks and the Romans the alphabet has come down to us.

The Greek names of the letters were derived from the Semitic. These names have a significance in Semitic, but in Greek they have none. The Greeks called *b* beta because the Semites called it *beth,* meaning house. The picture of the house was first used as an ideogram to signify the house itself, then as a phonogram to represent its name, and finally, variously modified, it was employed to denote simply the initial sound *b* because that is the first letter of the Semitic word for house, *beth.* The third letter *gimel* (camel) in the Semitic alphabet became *gamma* in the Greek. In Semite *d* was *daleth,* meaning door; in Greek it is *delta.*

The Semites, as the real inventors of the alphabet, had no symbols for vowels. The various characters represented consonants with or without following vowels, so that the reader had to supply the vowel that suited the context. The great contribution of the Greeks to the alphabet was the addition of vowels. The very first letter, *aleph,* was a weak consonant unknown in Greek. In pronouncing the name, the Greeks, much as the Cockney drops an *h,* omitted the consonant, thereby exposing the vowel sound, which happened to be *a,* and in this originated the name and value of alpha. In like manner, the Semitic *he,* a kind of aspirate, when pronounced by the Greeks lost its initial sound and received the value of the vowel sound which followed it, namely epsilon or *e.*[5] The order of the letters is the same in Greek and Semitic. Since the Greeks, like the Semites, used the letters of the alphabet for numerals as well as for spelling words, the order of letters in the alphabet had to be kept always the same. A stood for 1, B for 2, and so on. The order itself seems to be one of chance.[6]

[5] *Ibid.,* p. 23.
[6] *Ibid.,* p. 20.

The use of capitals by the side of small letters was a gradual evolution out of practices originating in antiquity. It is obvious that the alphabet went through various stages of improvement as it was adapted for use by new peoples and under new conditions. While we credit the alphabet to the Semites and the vowels to the Greeks, we recognize that the letter forms as well as the transmission of the alphabet are due to the Romans.

The literature of the Phoenicians has mostly perished. All that remains are scanty quotations from the native annals. Their religion was a nature worship, the adoration of the sun, moon, and other celestial bodies, rivers and mountains, and in practice admitted the basest abuses. Their chief god was Baal or Moloch, the sun-god to whom sometimes human sacrifices were offered. By the side of him there was the moon goddess Ashtoreth whose worship was accompanied by ceremonies that reflected the sensualism of nature.[7]

An immoral and cruel people, the Phoenicians possessed no religious or intellectual safeguards against the dangers to their national life which commercial success had brought. Their training of youth for a career in practical affairs, with the sole aim of accumulating wealth and earthly power without other ennobling and elevating influences, while receiving notice in the history of education, deserves little commendation. Its shortcomings are apparent to all.

Hebrews

The Hebrews[1] lived under a theocratic form of government, recognizing God as King, Lawgiver, and Preserver of their nation. Although they were ruled by

---

[7] Sayce, *op. cit.,* pp. 414-19.
[1] This is the general name of this people. The inhabitants of Judea are properly called Jews.

men at various epochs in their history, Jehovah ever remained their Supreme and Almighty King. Their judges, kings, priests, and prophets were only His visible representatives on earth.

As their main religious belief in the existence of one God, the Creator and Conserver of the universe, inspired their form of government, so it dominated everything else in their national and domestic life. It was so closely associated with their national spirit that to be patriotic meant also to be devoutly religious, the two ideas of religion and patriotism being inseparable. No nation in ancient times had so exalted an idea of temporal government; none gave women so high a position in the family or the family so important a place in the state; none had the means they employed to cultivate the spirit of individualism either in public or in private life.

Jewish history before the time of Christ may be divided into four periods corresponding to the most important political changes: (1) The Patriarchal Period, from the call of Abraham, the first known ancestor of the Jews as a nation, to Moses, the Lawgiver; (2) the Tribal Period, from Moses to the monarchy; (3) the Royal Period, from the institution of the monarchy under Saul to the Babylonian Captivity; (4) the Restoration, from the Babylonian Captivity to the time of Christ. These four periods are of about equal duration.[2]

At the opening of the Patriarchal age, the family of Thare under the leadership of Abraham came out of Ur of the Chaldees and went as far as Haran, the frontier town of Babylonia, and dwelt there. After the death of Thare, the Lord appeared to his son, Abraham, and told him to go into the land of Chanaan and promised him that He would make his descendants a great nation.[3]

---

[2] Francis E. Gigot, *Outlines of Jewish History* (New York: Benziger Bros., 1910), p. 5.

[3] Genesis 12:1-2.

Abraham obeyed and with his wife Sarai and his nephew Lot came into the country now called Palestine.

Abraham was promised a son. The son was born and was named Isaac. Isaac had two sons, Esau and Jacob, the latter of whom was later called Israel.[4] Jacob had twelve sons. One of them, Joseph, his father's favorite, due to envy and jealousy towards him on the part of his brothers, was sold as a slave by them to Ismaelite merchants on their way back to Egypt. The clear interpretation of the dreams of Pharaoh by Joseph aroused the admiration of the king and led him to make Joseph his prime minister.

After a time Jacob and his sons and their families because of famine moved down into Egypt where land was given them. Up until then they had lived a nomadic life, maintaining themselves by flocks and herds. During the four hundred years[5] that they lived in the country of Gessen, a district east of the Delta of the Nile, they learned to cultivate the land and made remarkable progress in the raising of crops. The wonderful prosperity of the Israelites and their marked increase in number led to their oppression by the Egyptions who inflicted hardships upon them, forced them to make bricks from stubble, and would not permit them to go out of the land.

Probably in the reign of the Egyptian Pharaoh Meneptah, the Israelites who numbered about two millions[6] left Egypt under the guidance of Moses and Aaron for the land promised to Abraham. For forty years they wandered in the wilderness of the Sinai Peninsula, between Egypt and Palestine, where the Lord appeared several times to Moses and gave him the Ten Commandments for the people. After the death of Moses, they

---

[4] *Ibid.*, 32:28.
[5] Gizot, *op. cit.*, p. 66.
[6] *Loc. cit.*

circled around to the east of Palestine, led by the warlike Joshua, crossed the river Jordan, captured Jericho, conquered the surrounding country in Palestine and established a system of government by judges, the last of whom was Samuel.

Becoming dissatisfied with the rule of judges, the Hebrews formed a united kingdom with its capital at Jerusalem. Saul was chosen king. He carried on war with the neighboring tribes, the Ammonites, the Philistines, and others. One of Saul's lieutenants was a young man, David, who while a shepherd boy succeeded in killing with a sling and stone the great champion of the Philistines, Goliath. Saul became jealous of David and several times sought his life. Saul, however, and his sons were slain in battle and David became king. The third and last ruler of the united monarchy was Solomon, the fame of whose wisdom was so widespread that faraway kings came to consult with him. He beautified the city of Jerusalem and built a splendid temple on Mount Moriah. He married an Egyptian princess and his court had all the magnificence of an Oriental kingdom. He disregarded the laws of Moses, laid heavy burdens upon his subjects, and impoverished his people.

After Solomon's death, the nation was split by dissensions and divided into two kingdoms. The kingdom of Israel to the north included an area of about nine thousand square miles with a population of four or five millions. The kingdom of Juda to the south embraced about thirty-four hundred square miles and had a population of somewhat less than two millions.[7] The northern kingdom was conquered by the Assyrian king Sargon who captured Samaria, its capital, in 721 B.C., and carried the people of the kingdom away into captivity, where they were "lost" as a separate nation. The

---

[7] *Ibid.,* pp. 238 f.

southern kingdom lasted for more than a hundred years longer, when Jerusalem was pillaged by Nabuchadonosor in 588 B.C. Many of the inhabitants were taken captive to Babylon, while a little remnant of Jews fled into Egypt whither the Prophet, Jeremias, accompanied them.[8]

A half century later, a comparatively small number of Babylonian exiles returned to Judea by permission of Cyrus, the new ruler of Babylonia. The temple was rebuilt and dedicated in 515 B.C. The national life at Jerusalem was reorganized and continued until the Greek domination which began under Alexander the Great and lasted for over one hundred and fifty years. After the death of Alexander, Judea was a cause of conflict between Egypt and Syria for more than a century. It was for the numerous Jews, who had settled in Egypt and had ceased to be familiar with the Hebrew language, that a Greek translation, first of the Law and ultimately of the remaining books of the Old Testament, was made for public reading in the synagogues. The whole collection came to be known as the Septuagint, so called because of the legend that the Pentateuch was translated by seventy-two emissaries from Jerusalem.

Antiochus of Syria undertook to Hellenize the Hebrew nation by means of cruel and systematic persecution, but the Jewish population resisted strongly. Under the patriotic rebellion of the Maccabees the Jews maintained their national spirit and religion. With the advent of Pompey, Judea was made a tributary to Rome; and when, in 70 A.D., the Jews made a last effort for freedom, their rebellion was put down under Titus who captured and destroyed the city of Jerusalem. This marked the end of their nation and they were driven into a final dispersion throughout the world.

---

[8] Jeremias 43:5-7.

During the first and second periods of Jewish history education principally consisted in oral instruction given in the home. Parents were obliged to instruct their children in the divine law.[9] They taught them reading and writing and gave them a religious and moral formation from their earliest years. The education of the child was centered upon the knowledge and observance of the Law. The girls received instruction from their mothers in household duties, while the father taught the boy his trade. Formal schools during these periods were apparently unknown. The training given in family life and through public worship impressed upon the child the ideals that should govern the conduct of his life. Higher education was then confined to the priests. Their studies embraced astronomy, national history, and the divine law.

The Schools of the Prophets, in which young men prepared for the prophetical mission, came into existence about the time of Samuel. They were a kind of monastic school in which teachers were trained to be instructors of the mass of the people. They flourished in many places during the royal period. An elderly prophet, who acted as a president or master, ruled these institutions somewhat after the manner of our religious communities. The students, who were not necessarily levites, lived together and were known as "sons of the prophets." Their first studies were sacred theology, law, and tradition. They also learned astronomy, math-

---

[9] Thou shalt love the Lord thy God with thy whole heart, and with thy whole soul, and with thy whole strength. And these words which I command thee this day, shall be in thy heart. And thou shalt tell them to thy children, and thou shalt meditate upon them sitting in thy house, and walking on thy journey, sleeping and rising. And thou shalt bind them as a sign on thy hand, and they shall be and shall move between thy eyes. And thou shalt write them in the entry, and on the doors of thy house. Deuteronomy 6:5-9.

ematics, Jewish history, music, and poetry. Much time was devoted to prayer and recollection in the way of preparation for the call and inspiration which were necessary for a divine mission in the prophetical ministry.[10]

While the elementary training of the masses still continued to be domestic, the work of these "sons of the prophets" suggests that the audiences they addressed had a good knowledge of their religion and sacred tradition; and the existence of written prophecies indicates also that many besides the priests could read them. The fact, too, that the candidates for the office of prophet were often taken from the ranks of the people evidences a fairly wide extent of literary education.

The successors of the "sons of the prophets" as teachers were the scribes, who originally were copyists, but later became interpreters of the law and the prophets and added to them by their commentaries. Their collected works are known as the Talmud.[11] They arose during the period of the Babylonian Captivity. Although they constituted a lay order, priests and levites were not excluded from them. Esdras was both priest and scribe. They taught the people on the porches of the Temple, and in the synagogues. In later times they established academies for the training of other scribes. The directors of these schools were the Rabbins, or masters. They taught, besides the Hebrew language, law and religion, a considerable amount of astronomy and higher mathematics, and in the third century before Christ offered courses in Greek literature and philosophy. This contact with the mind of the Greeks developed

---

[10] Gigot, *op. cit.*, p. 276.

[11] The Talmud consists of the *Mishna,* or codification of Jewish religious and legal ordinances, and the *Gemara,* or collection of interpretations and discussions concerning the *Mishna.* There are the Palestinian and the Babylonian Talmuds differing in minor respects and so called after the place of their compilation.

subtlety of reasoning among the scribes regarding the Torah [Law] and Jewish traditions and resulted in the formation of two parties, the Pharisees and the Saducees, the former of whom stood for a narrow interpretation of the law while the latter were doctrinally in favor of Greek thought and influence.

The synagogue was instituted under Esdras during the Babylonian Captivity. Although essentially a religious institution for the people in exile, it also served educational purposes. Every considerable community of Jews had one, and in the second century B.C. synagogues were set up even in the villages. Here the scribe was the official teacher. Here the Law was read and expounded on the Sabbath, and religious exercises of prayer conducted. An attendant of the synagogue taught the children during the week, there being two divisions for their accommodation: one for those under ten years of age, and a higher for those between the ages of ten and fifteen.

In addition to reading and writing, the children were instructed in the Talmud, and in oral tradition. Boys who prepared for the office of scribe learned mathematics, law, history, music, and poetry. That the teacher was accorded great authority appears from the maxim: "The voice of the Rabbi, the voice of God." Teachers who could afford to do so taught without pay. Teaching was regarded as a religious duty and teachers who did not have private means supported themselves through some trade or craft. No teacher was permitted to accept more pay than he would have earned at some other work during the hours he devoted to teaching.[12] Instruction was free with the exception of the academies of higher learning which for a time charged tuition fees. The discipline of the classroom was severe, the method

---

[12] Nathan Drazin, *History of Jewish Education* (Baltimore: The Johns Hopkins Press, 1940), p. 60.

principally catechetical, and with the older pupils dis-
putatory. In the absence of books, the memory was of
necessity heavily burdened.

The Hebrew language is regarded as the richest of all
Semitic tongues, due to the value and antiquity of its
literary remains. The Bible is the gift of the Hebrews
to mankind. Inestimable for its worth in respect to the
history of the Hebrews and all Oriental nations, abounding in literary treasures, it is for Christians the inspired
account of God's dealings with men and cherished as the
greatest book of all time. The superior literary genius
of the Hebrews is apparent in the Psalms of David, the
Book of Job, and the Prophecy of Isaiah, which considered merely as literary compositions are unsurpassed
in the literature of any people. The Talmud, or the
Law with its interpretation and commentary, has obviously been of real educational value not only to the
Hebrews who taught it in their schools, but to all students of the Scriptures.

In the organization of the Jewish school system, the
academies for higher learning were established first; later
the secondary schools for adolescents; and finally the
elementary schools. Through the ordinance of Joshua b.
Gamala, the High Priest, about the year 64 A.D., elementary schools were founded in every town and in
every province where Jews resided in large numbers.
Elementary education was hence made available for all
boys without distinction from the age of six or seven.
Parents were exhorted to send their children to these
elementary schools to be taught the Torah by qualified
and competent teachers. Synagogues that were not then
used for school purposes were required by this decree
to be converted during daytime into schoolhouses for
boys. From that time on "synagogue" meant a "school"
whenever reference was made to the buildings.[13]   Girls

---

[13] *Ibid.,* pp. 60 f.

were excluded from the school system, receiving their education from their parents. The education of girls was entirely optional, since the Law did not demand it. Jewish education was essentially character training and from experience it was felt that girls could obtain in the home all that was essential.[14]

History commends the Hebrews more for the content than for the method of their education. While they held the most sublime of religious truths, and were directed by them in their public and private life, they became too much attached to the form and letter, to the written law and the external rite, and in their system of government and in their education lost sight of the spirit of the truths confided to them. They produced no great works of art or science, and their achievements as a nation were insignificant. However, with all their shortcomings and narrowness, with their formalism and externalism in religion, and their failures as a nation, they have been the benefactors of all ages in demonstrating the marked influence on a people of theocratic form of government, and in preserving and conveying to posterity the deposit of moral and spiritual truth which in the form of Christianity was to leaven the world.

FOR FURTHER STUDY

Barton, G. A., *Sketch of Semitic Origins*. New York: The Macmillan Co., 1902.

————, *The Religion of Israel*. New York: The Macmillan Co., 1918.

————, *Cambridge Ancient History*. New York: The Macmillan Co., 1923; 1925. Vols. I; III.

Cornill, Carl H., *History of the People of Israel*. Fourth edition. Chicago: The Open Court Publishing Company, 1909.

————, *The Culture of Ancient Israel*. Chicago: The Open Court Publishing Company, 1914.

Drazin, Nathan, *History of Jewish Education*. Baltimore: The Johns Hopkins Press, 1940.

---

[14] *Ibid.*, pp. 128-33.

Gigot, Francis E., *Outlines of Jewish History*. New York: Benziger Bros., 1910.

Graetz, H. H., *Geschichte der Juden von den ältesten zeiten bis auf die Gegenwart*. 11 vols. New edition. Leipzig: D. Leiner, 1911.

————, *History of the Jews from the Earliest Times to 1870*. Abridged edition, 6 vols. Translation by B. Löwy. Philadelphia: The Jewish Publication Society of America, 1891-98.

Laurie, S. S., *Historical Survey of Pre-Christian Education*. New York: Longmans, Green, & Co., 1900.

Leipziger, H. M., *The Education of the Jews*. New York: T. Laurie, 1890.

Marcus, Samuel, *Die Pädagogik des Israelitischen Volkes: Part I, Die Biebel ein Buch der Erziehung; Part II, Zur Schulpädagogik des Talmud*. 2 vols. Vienna: Brüder Winter, 1877.

Mason, William A., *A History of the Art of Writing*. New York: The Macmillan Co., 1920.

Old and New Testaments.

Olmstead, A. T., *History of Assyria*. New York: Charles Scribner's Sons, 1923.

Petrie, Wm. F., *The Formation of the Alphabet*. London: The Macmillan Co., 1912.

Rogers, Robt. W., *A History of Babylonia and Assyria*. 2 vols. New York: Eaton and Mains, 1900.

Sayce, A. H., *The Ancient Empires of the East*. London: The Macmillan Co., 1883.

————, *Babylonians and Assyrians; Life and Customs*. London: J. C. Nimmo, 1900.

Simon, Joseph, *L'Education et l'instruction des enfants chez les anciens Juifs d'après la Bible et la Talmud*. Third edition. Leipzig: O. Schulze, 1879.

Spiers, B., *The School System of the Talmud*. London: E. Stock, 1898.

Swift, Fletcher H., *Educators in Ancient Israel from Earliest Times to A.D. 70*. Chicago: The Open Court Publishing Co., 1919.

Taylor, Henry O., *Ancient Ideals*. Vol. II. New York: The Macmillan Co., 1900.

CHAPTER VII

GREEK EDUCATION

Of the origins of the Greek people research studies have revealed little. From very ancient times, say 1600 B.C., archaeological evidence shows the existence of peoples of culture in the island of Crete as well as in the other islands and along the coasts of the Aegean Sea. The Greeks are the Hellenic branch of the Indo-Europeans. It is assumed that Aryan people came into Thrace, whence some of them crossed the Hellespont and passing along the eastern shore of the Aegean Sea settled upon its bays and islands. Others moved to the west, occupying the western shore and establishing themselves eventually in Thessaly. Boeotia, Attica, the Peloponnesus, and the other Greek provinces.

The people of ancient Greece styled themselvs Hellenes and called their country Hellas. The name Greece comes to us from the Romans and was almost unknown to the people we call Greeks. Hellas included not merely the Grecian peninsula in Europe, but all the colonies situated on the islands and the Asiatic coast of the Aegean as well as those in the neighboring islands of the Mediterranean. It is evident, then, that the home of Greek civilization was the Aegean Sea, whose geographical position indicates the close relation of Greece to Asia. The Greeks are the heirs of the Orient, but at the same time it is largely due to their influence that European civilization differs from that of Asia because they developed a culture of their own higher than any achieved among Oriental peoples.[1]

---

[1] William C. Morey, *Outlines of Greek History.* (New York: American Book Co., 1903), pp. 69 f.

Due to migrations, considerable displacements of population took place on the mainland of Greece in prehistoric times. One of the most important of these migrations was the coming of the Dorians into Sparta, which resulted in a general shifting of the Greek population affecting nearly all the tribes of Greece. Just when the Dorians were dislodged from Thessaly and succeeded in displacing the Achaeans as the leading people in the Peloponnesus is difficult to say. Their successive migrations covered perhaps several generations, and some time after the Trojan War they became the masters of Laconia. In fact, the first sure date in Greek history is regarded as 776 B.C., the beginning of the Olympic games from which the Greeks reckoned time in cycles of four years. The first Olympiad, so called because the Olympic games took place at Olympia, a city of the Peloponnesus, in honor of Jupiter Olympius, was in that year, and this date is considered as convenient and trustworthy as any other to mark the beginning of the historic period.

Our knowledge of Greek civilization during the prehistoric age is derived largely from legends, from monuments or material relics, and from the epic poems of Homer. The early legends have little historical significance if regarded as accounts of actual events, but they are quite significant inasmuch as they indicate the ideas and beliefs of the people. Among these legends are those dealing with the founders of cities, with Grecian heroes, and with national exploits.

The traditions regarding the founders of cities show that the Greeks were aware of their dependence on the older civilizations. Athens was believed to have been founded by Cecrops, a native of Egypt. He introduced into Attica the arts of civilized life and from him the Acropolis was first called Cecropia. Argos was founded by an Egyptian also, named Danaüs, who fled to Greece with his fifty daughters. He was elected king by the people who received the named of Danaï. Thebes, in Boeotia, was said to have been founded by Cadmus, a Phoenician, who brought into Greece the art of writing. The citadel of Thebes was named Cadmea after him. The Peloponnesus was settled by Pelops, a Phrygian, who became king of Mycenae. He was the grandfather of Agamemnon and Menelaus, chieftains in the Trojan War.[2]

In the legends of their heroes, the Greeks show their admiration for deeds of superhuman courage and for romantic adventures. Perseus slew the Gorgon Medusa whose locks were coiling serpents and whose looks turned every object to stone. Bellerophon was the slayer of the horrible Chimaera with a lion's head, a goat's body, and the tail of a dragon. He also captured the winged steed, Pegasus, mounting which he tried to ascend to the heavens. Minos, king of Crete, drove the pirates from the sea and gave his subjects a code of laws received from Zeus. Theseus freed the land from robbers and delivered Athens from the terrible tribute imposed by the king of Crete. This tribute required the periodical sacrifice of seven youths and seven maidens to the monster, Minotaur. Hercules, the greatest of heroes, performed twelve labors imposed upon him by the king of Mycenae with the consent of Zeus.[3]

The legends of national exploits have for their subjects momentous deeds demanding great courage and fortitude, which appealed to the national pride of every true Greek. The story of the Argonautic expedition narrated the adventurous voyage of fifty heroes who set sail from Boeotia under the leadership of Jason in the ship Argo for the purpose of recovering the golden fleece of the ram Chrysomallus which was carried away to

[2] *Ibid.*, p. 84.
[3] *Ibid.*, p. 84.

Colchis on the shores of the Euxine. The "Seven Against Thebes" was the tragic story of Oedipus and his faithful daughter Antigone, which was afterwards dramatized by Sophocles. The best known of the legendary stories is the Trojan War in which the Greeks united against the Trojans in their effort to rescue Helen, the beautiful wife of Menelaus, the king of Sparta, who had been borne away by Paris, son of the Trojan king. The details of the story which describe the wrath of Achilles, the exploits of Hector and Paris, the deeds of Ulysses, the destruction of Troy and the return of the heroes are the subjects of the *Iliad* and the *Odyssey* of Homer.[4]

Although much of the story of the Trojan War is pure fiction, there is some truth in it, too. Towards the close of the nineteenth century the excavations made by Dr. Schliemann and his colleague Dr. Dörpfeld revealed that the hill of Hissarlik, near the Asiatic shore of the Dardanelles, contained the ruins of the city of Troy. No fewer than nine cities had been built on the site, each rising on the ruins of its predecessor. The sixth city answered to Homer's description.[5] It was surrounded by a stone wall fifteen feet thick, with strong gates and towers. Historians feel fairly certain that this was the Troy destroyed by the Greeks and that the Trojan War occurred about the year 1200 B.C. The war may have been fought, not on account of Helen, but because the Achaeans wished to gain control of the Strait of the Dardanelles so that their ships could enter the Black Sea.

The richest source of information on the prehistoric period we have in the Homeric poems, the *Iliad* and *Odyssey*, which are supposed to have been written in

---

[4] *Ibid.*, p. 86.
[5] *Ibid.*, pp. 87 f.

the ninth century B.C. These poems presume a high civilization and therefore educational history must antedate their composition. The historical value of the poems consists in the numerous allusions made to society and government, education and religion, industry and art, life and customs of the early Greek people. Homer based his story on the romantic lays which minstrels had sung to the accompaniment of the lyre in the palaces of Greek princes for three centuries previous to his time. When later bards recited Homer's poems from memory, naturally mistakes crept into the narrative. With certain reservations, then, the *Iliad* and the *Odyssey* unfold the story of Greek life in the twelfth century B.C.

During this prehistoric age, the government was that of a hereditary kingdom, and education was of a domestic nature. Society consisted of an aristocracy, a middle class, and a slave population. The aristocracy embraced the landowners and proprietors; the second class included the artisans, surgeons, and workmen. Children were educated according to their status in society. Naturally those of the highest ranks received the best education, which then meant training in music and the arts of war. Female education, however, was strictly domestic in character—the girls receiving in the home their preparation for the duties of housewife and mother. The position of woman was much better than in later epochs. Polygamy, for instance, was not tolerated.

At the beginning of their authentic history, the Hellenes were divided into four distinct branches: the Dorians, the Aeolians, the Ionians, and the Achaeans. They were not politically united and frequently engaged in war even before the rise of the city states. The same marked differences in character and civilization and the same antagonism that are so prominent in their later history were then noticeable. Yet, these differences in culture did not prevent their being considered by the outside world as a single people.

The first peoples of historic Greece to attain political distinction were the Dorians and the Ionians. All the other Dorian cities were overshadowed by Sparta, the typical city state of the Dorian race in the Peloponnesus. The chief seats of the Ionian race were Attica and the colonies of Asia Minor. Of all the Ionian city states, Athens was the most typical. The spirit of Athens was democratic, while that of Sparta was totalitarian.

Sparta changed little in government or in culture. The political life of Athens was often unsettled. In the beginning of the sixth century B.C., definite reforms were instituted under the leadership of Solon and towards the close of the same century under Cleisthenes I, Athens became a democracy. It was a limited democracy, however, because all Greek civilization was based on slavery. The Persian wars which took place between 500 and 479 B.C. resulted in the temporary supremacy of Athens. After the Persian wars the Greeks made rapid educational strides at home. Aristotle in his *Politics* says that they "were inspired by what they had achieved and ventured still farther; they sought all forms of knowledge and set themselves to ever new inquiries." During the Age of Pericles (461-430 B.C.) Athens reached its highest power and glory. Pericles aimed to secure the imperial supremacy of Athens and to make it the foremost city of the world. This imperial policy aroused the jealousy of the Peloponnesian states under the lead of Sparta and resulted in an internecine struggle between Athens and Sparta during the years 431 to 404 B.C. at the close of which the leadership passed for a short time to Sparta. After the brief political ascendancy of Thebes, Philip of Macedon began to extend his influence in Greece. In 146 B.C. the Romans conquered the Greeks and made the Greek world a part of the Roman Empire.

The two broad types of culture, the Spartan and the Athenian, represent the most characteristic forms of Greek life and education. The educational practices of Sparta and Athens will be recounted here as the types of national education for the early historic period, and as the highest concrete forms which the Greek theory of education achieved. For the theory, the ideal in its loftiest conception, which never attained its full realization in ancient times, the views of Grecian philosophers and educational theorists will be investigated.

Sparta

The Spartans were conquerors of Laconia and lived in Sparta, the chief city. The original inhabitants, the Periocci and Helots (both old Achaean inhabitants), they held in subjection under a rigid military regime. The Perioeci, meaning "those who dwell around," lived in the outskirts of the country in about a hundred towns and formed a sort of buffer people separating the Helot population from the outside world. The Helots were the serfs who tilled the land allotted to the citizens. Only the Spartans were given the rights of citizenship. The Perioeci, while they were freemen, landowners, traders, and artisans, were obliged to pay a heavy tax to the Spartans. Whatever education they had they procured for themselves. The slaves or Helots had no rights; they were the drudges of their conquerors, and were often subjected to the direst cruelties, even death, by their rulers. Sparta was a country of about four hundred thousand inhabitants, in which twenty-five thousand citizens were maintained by a slave population ten times more numerous, while agriculture, manufacturing and commerce gave a livelihood to nearly one hundred thousand free men.[6]

---

[6] Gustave Glotz, *Ancient Greece at Work*. Translated by M. R. Dobie (New York: Alfred A. Knopf, 1926), p. 90.

The Spartans, while living in a sort of democracy among themselves, constituted an aristocratic class in relation to their subjects. The government assumed the form of a republic from one point of view and of a monarchy from another. There were two kings, and two assemblies of citizens, and in the assemblies lay the chief ruling power of the nation. The higher assembly, or senate, had twenty-eight members all of whom were over sixty years of age and occupied their seats for life. The popular body, to which any citizen over thirty years of age was eligible for election, actually delegated its power to five overseers or Ephors. The Spartan policy was to maintain military supremacy over the subject population.

The system of education is said to date from Lycurgus, the Lawgiver, who flourished about 820 B.C. Its aim at all times was to prepare children for their place in the state, the boy for citizenship and military service, and the girl for her office as wife and mother in the family. The state owned the child from the moment of its birth. It claimed and exercised the right of determining whether infants should live or die. A council of elders decided the fate of the weak and delicate, usually condemning them to death by starvation and exposure.

Seven years were allowed for the home training of the boys under the direction of the mother. They were then sent to the state institution where a superintendent of education, known as the *Paidonomos*, watched over their training. Here they became children of the larger family, the state; they lived together, shared the same food and sleeping apartments, dressed alike; in short, they had all things in common, for everything belonged to the state. They were scantily clothed, and were allowed only a limited amount of food. Their beds consisted of the tops of weeds gathered from the fields. They were organized into packs of sixty-four, a boy of

courage and good sense being selected as pack leader.
He commanded and even punished the rest. Over each
school was placed a young man, at least twenty years
of age, who was called the eiren. Nothing that did not
conduce to the formation of the hardy warrior could be
admitted into their preparation.[7]

The life of the Spartan was a perpetual training for
war. Until he was thirty he slept in barracks; until he
was sixty he ate his chief meal in the community mess.
He was assessed a definite amount in kind and money
for the maintenance of the collective meals and for the
support of his sons in the state institution. The law,
which assigned to each Spartan citizen his allotment of
land, to be tilled by his Helots, also laid down the quota
of provisions and money which he must supply monthly.
The individual who failed to subscribe was excluded
from the messes and lost his citizenship. Wealthier
citizens often gave extra quotas for the education of
sons of foreigners and even of Helots. The usual assessment was two bushels of barley meal, eight gallons
of wine, six or seven pounds of cheese, four pounds of
dried figs; and, for the meat, ten obols, between forty
and fifty cents in our money.[8]

There was little intellectual training for the Spartan
boy. The literary side of his education was overshadowed by the prominence accorded to military and
physical training. Reading and writing could not be
learned at the state schools except by private instruction. Selections from the Homeric poems, the national
songs, were committed to memory, but the motive in
learning them was rather patriotism than appreciation
of the beauties of literature and music. Although most

---

[7]Xenophon, *Constitution of the Lacedemonians*. Translated
selections cited in Botsford and Sihler, *Hellenic Civilization* (New
York: Columbia University Press, 1920), pp. 132 f.
[8] Glotz, *op. cit.*, p. 90.

Spartans could not read, Plato maintains that, while a Spartan at first seems stupid, at the right moment, his pithy speech reveals that those about him are like children compared to him. Music served only as a means of arousing and strengthening the martial spirit. At table where the elders presided, or on the street, the conversation was directed to a discussion of warlike affairs, and questions were proposed to test and train the boys in judgment and appreciation of the problems that would confront the general on the field. The Laconian spoke briefly and to the point; hence the origin of the phrase, "to speak laconically."

A great part of Spartan education was physical. The boys rode horseback and swam daily in the Eurotas. They spent a great deal of their time in gymnastics which served to develop healthy and flexible bodies. Periodically the physical condition of the boys was inspected by the ephors. Everything that could promote bodily strength and endurance, such as exercises in running, jumping, wrestling, dancing, and singing, exposure to heat and cold, privation of food and clothing, in short all that would prepare the boy to endure the hardships of a soldier in actual service, the experienced warriors included in the process of physical training.

A certain moral training accompanied these exercises. Respect and reverence for superiors, obedience, and truthfulness were taught in a very practical way. Modesty and self-restraint were emphasized as most desirable virtues. On the streets the boys were compelled to keep their hands within the folds of their cloak, and walk in silence with their eyes fixed upon the ground before them.[9] It was not deemed improper, however, to lie to others who were not Spartans, and boys were permitted to steal when not satisfied with their food.

---

[9]Xenophon, *Constitution of the Lacedemonians*, p. 135.

Indeed, they were often encouraged to pilfer; if detected, however, they were punished for their want of deftness or cunning. This training was intended to make the boys crafty and to cultivate their warlike instincts.[10] To show the baseness of drunkenness, the slaves were often made drunk. They provided a means for training in cruelty also, for when it was considered necessary to keep down their numbers the youth were allowed to murder them.

The discipline, as we can well suppose, was severe. Punishment by blows and flogging was frequently inflicted by the elders at all stages of the boy's training, even after his eighteenth year when he entered the class of Ephebi or youths. During his special military training, when he acted as instructor of the younger boys, the discipline was also rigid. When the young boys were examined about warfare and failed to answer concisely, the monitors of these boys were flogged, whereupon they in turn flogged the boys who had failed. For about two years the Ephebi were given active training in skirmishing and the use of arms. They then entered the class of Melleirens, or older youth, and for ten years guarded some border fortress. At thirty, a man became a Spartan citizen or warrior, was now obliged to marry, but could visit his wife only clandestinely, because he was forced to live in common with the boys and assist in their training.

The women lived and ate at home. They were responsible for the training of the girls. Like the boys, the girls were organized into packs, went barefoot, and wore only a single garment. They lived an outdoor life and followed a program of physical exercises. They were trained in wrestling, swimming, running, throwing the discus and javelin. Until their marriage, they

---

[10] *Ibid.*, p. 134.

mingled freely with the boys and like them aimed to develop strength of body. After marriage they wore veils in public and stayed at home for the most part. They had an excellent reputation for chastity and were famed for heroic patriotism. The story is related of one Spartan mother who told her son to return from battle with his shield or upon it. Another mother is said to have exclaimed upon hearing that her son died in battle, "I brought him into the world for no other end."

The Spartan system of education was socialistic and utilitarian, designed solely for the benefit of the state and not for the individual. The boy was systematically trained for his place as the defender of the nation, and the girl for the office of mother to give new warriors to her country. The dominant educational agency was the state; it dictated and controlled all family life. Such a despotic system was successful in achieving its purpose, for it produced a nation of warriors able to defend the home and ready for conquest abroad. But it could not go further, and when that rigor of training ceased, and the conqueror appeared, it was bound to disappear with the nation itself. It incorporated no religious teaching, no sound moral training, and it made no provision for the pursuit of the arts and sciences. The all-absorbing and all-pervading spirit of patriotism and devotion to the state, which dominated everything, could not supply for the elements in training that develop character and strength of mind in the individual, and in the social body, and upon which the real stability of a nation depends.

Athens

The Athenians were not only the flower of the Ionians culturally but the most notable of the Greek people for political progress and educational achievement. They gave the world the first example of a democracy, and they surpassed both in theory and practice the best educational efforts that had till then been made.

They were at first ruled by a king, whose title was changed in the tenth century B.C. to that of Archon (Ruler), although the office still remained in the same family. His power had passed, however, to a general assembly which was controlled by the nobles. Later the Archon was elected by the general assembly for a period of ten years, and later still, when the number of Archons had increased to nine, the period of office was reduced to one year. The constitution of Solon gave to all the citizens certain political privileges according to the degree of their wealth. After the reign of the tyrants, about 507 B.C., Athens became under Cleisthenes a well-organized democracy and rose to be the chief of the Ionian states.[11]

The limited nature of the Athenian democracy, however, is revealed by looking at the different classes of people who formed the population of the Athenian citystate. These comprised the citizens, the resident foreigners, and the slaves. It is estimated that according to a census of the population of Attica taken under Demetrius of Phalerum towards the close of the fourth century B.C., the number of citizens was twenty-one thousand; of resident aliens, ten thousand; and of slaves, four hundred thousand.[12] The slave had no political or civil rights, although he might be protected from the cruelty of his master. The resident alien had no share in the government. He could not hold land in Attica, engaged mostly in trade, and was obliged to pay a yearly

[11] H. R. James, *Our Hellenic Heritage* (London: The Macmillan Co., 1921), I, 250 f.
[12] *Becker's Charicles or Illustrations of the Private Life of the Ancient Greeks*, translated from the German by F. Metcalfe (London: Longmans, Green, and Co., 1889), p. 361.

tax and sometimes to serve in the army or navy. The policy of admitting foreigners to citizenship was changed by Pericles who limited citizenship to those who were born of an Athenian father and an Athenian mother. The majority of slaves were employed as artisans, either for their master, or on their own account, paying him a daily sum.[13] The artisan slaves were naturally more independent than those employed in domestic service. The state sometimes employed slaves as executioners, accountants, and secretaries.[14]

The worst effect of slavery was to throw a kind of reproach upon manual labor. All forms of handicraft were regarded as unworthy the dignity of a gentleman. Because slave labor disposed of all the drudgery of life, the Athenian was free to devote his time to his duties as a citizen. These duties included functions as different as generalship or archonship, attendance at the public assembly or at the law courts, or even mere gossip about public officials and public policy.[15] At all events, the Athenian gentleman spent most of his time at the Agora (market place) and other public places. His home was for him chiefly a place where he could sleep and eat and its management was left almost entirely to his wife and slaves.

The Athenian believed that the proper place of woman was in the home. Girls were strictly guarded by their parents within doors and were sometimes married at fifteen or younger.[16] Marriage in general was in accordance with a prearranged contract. Usually the young man in Attica did not marry until he was thirty or over. A wife who belonged to the upper class did not

[13] *Ibid.*, pp. 362-65.
[14] Charles B. Gulick, *The Life of the Ancient Greeks* (New York: D. Appleton and Co., 1902), p. 69.
[15] *Ibid.*, p. 188.
[16] *Ibid.*, p. 122.

leave the house without permission of her husband. A slave always accompanied her when on the street.[17] Only at festivals could she appear in public as a matter of right. Mothers were busily engaged, however, in dispensing household stores, exercising general oversight over their children, and training their daughters in domestic work. Girls were taught to spin, weave, sew, embroider, nurse the sick, and cultivate their personal charms.[18] The only formally-schooled women in Athens were the heterae or courtesans.

Throughout Greece fashion in clothes was simple, determined mostly by the climate. The taste of the Greeks in dress, as in other things, demanded moderation and was in strong contrast to the gaudy apparel of the Orientals. The dress of men and women was quite similar. It consisted usually of two garments, a tunic and a cloak. The tunic worn by the woman extended to the feet, whereas that worn by the man, particularly the warrior, hunter, farmer, or artisan, usually did not reach below the knees.[19] Clasps and girdles were used to keep the clothes in position. The feet were sometimes protected by sandals which a guest removed before taking his place at the table. The veil was always worn in public by young girls and brides. Women of the masses often drew up the cloak like a shawl over the head and face. Fillets for confining the hair, earrings of various sorts, bracelets and anklets were also worn, while fans and parasols were carried for use or ornament.[20] The Athenian gentleman, dressed in tunic and cloak, with sandals, a ring upon his finger, and a walking stick in his hand, left his house early in the

---

[17]Becker, *op. cit.*, p. 169.
[18] Gulick, *op. cit.*, pp. 124 f.
[19] *Ibid.*, p. 155.
[20] *Ibid.*, pp. 168-70.

morning to spend the greater part of the day conversing with his friends or advising his clients.

The city house of the Athenian was an unpretentious structure, as compared with the luxurious apartments of public buildings in Athens. His country house was of a more rambling style, much more spacious, because uncramped by neighbors' dwellings. From the street the city house presented a dead wall with a heavy solid door in the middle, upon which was hung a metal knocker. The normal type of house was of only one story and consisted of two courts. The first, called the andronitis, was entered directly from the street; the second, called the gunaikonitis, was entered by a door at the further end of the andronitis. The house was simply a series of rooms surrounding a court which was open to the sky. The roof was flat and covered with clay tiles. The charm of the house was due to the beauty of perspective especially in the case of the larger houses which had a second court and garden. The furniture was of a refined character. It consisted of couches, chairs, folding stools, and tables of ornamental woodwork, lamps of metal or terracotta, bronze or marble statuettes, vases of precious metals, rugs and cushions. The open courtyard lighted the surrounding rooms and such heating as was required was obtained by means of portable braziers supported on tripods or basins filled with glowing charcoal.[21]

Attractive as the Greek house was in its simple open arrangement, the Athenian boy once he started to school was, like his father, at home only for meals and for sleep. The schools of Athens were not boarding schools as in Sparta, but the school day was long, beginning before breakfast and continuing until almost sunset.

---

[21] Bertha C. Rider, *The Greek House* (Cambridge: The University Press, 1916), pp. 210-18.

Moreover, unlike the rigid state system of Sparta, education in Athens was conducted by individuals. The state had some general regulations affecting education, but in no way undertook to provide a system of instruction. Since the time of Solon, the Lawgiver, 594 B.C., a certain supervision and control had been exercised, although the state did not own the schools. Solon had decreed that every boy should be taught a useful occupation; he regulated the hours of the school day, the requirements of the teacher, his age, etc., the number of children under his care, and introduced the study of Homer into the schools.

The Athenian ideal of education was the aesthetic— a cultured soul in a graceful and symmetrical body. Through a harmonious physical, intellectual, and moral development was to be produced the perfect man: the soldier, prepared to defend the state in time of war, and the citizen, able to add to the culture of the nation by the pursuit of the beautiful in time of peace. It was a training for elegant leisure which was to be used for a well-balanced development and proper enjoyment of one's own powers, of body, of mind, and of soul. The obligation of providing the child with this training rested upon the parents.[22]

Those undergoing elementary training divided the day between the Palaestra, or gymnasium, and the Didaskaleion, or music school. In the former, boys were drilled in all kinds of athletic exercises, including throwing the discus and casting the javelin, wrestling, running, dancing, swimming; all of which, combined with frequent bathing and anointing the body, produced that grace and beauty of form for which the Greeks have never been surpassed. Music, a term of much wider

---

[22] Thomas Davidson, *Aristotle and Ancient Educational Ideals* (New York: Charles Scribner's Sons, 1899), pp. 63 f.

significance with the Greeks than with the modern world, included literary and moral instruction. In this elementary school, reading, writing, and arithmetic were taught besides the patriotic songs and the great epic poems. The pedagogue, or slave, who accompanied the boy to school and was his mentor outside of school hours, placed his charge under the care of the special teachers at different schools. He was not a teacher, nor a tutor in our sense, but rather a guardian. The gymnastic drill, the lessons in music and in letters were conducted by special teachers or instructors.

As the teachers were supported by the fees from their pupils, only the well-paid could furnish schoolrooms for their classes. The teachers of the poor held their sessions in the open air, usually in the shelter of public buildings, such as the temples, or in quiet streets. The calling of teachers of the rudiments was held in no great repute. Often such teachers were freedmen or citizens who had no other means of livelihood. The schoolmaster's income depended on the voluntary donations of parents rendered very often in kind instead of in cash, on the last day of the month. A deduction was made by the parent proportionate to the time that his son was absent from school. The children of wealthy parents were taught by teachers who were often highly respected, as for instance, was the father of Aeschines.[23]

It is interesting to note that in teaching reading the Greeks followed the synthetic method which has been the traditional one even in modern times. The letters of the alphabet were first taught, then the syllables, and finally the words. In the absence of printed books, dictation by the teacher became, of necessity, a frequent practice. Writing exercises first began in the sand and continued on wax tablets. Boys who had acquired some

---

[23] Becker, *op. cit.*, pp. 229 f.

skill wrote on parchments with a reed pen and ink made from gum and lampblack. The abacus was used in teaching the first steps in numeration. Letters were the symbols used to designate numbers, and for this reason the early work in arithmetic was rendered difficult. As much arithmetic was learned as was necessary for the market place. The fingers were ordinarily used, not only in school, but in everyday life to reckon and were also used to express numbers by placing them in different positions.[24] Some knowledge of geography was obtained from the study of the *Iliad* and other historical poems. Selected poems were committed to memory and recited with musical accompaniment. They served as models of composition and as sources of lessons in morality and in patriotism. Besides Homer were also studied Hesiod, Theognis, Aesop, and anthologies.

Secondary schools began to take definite form about the middle of the fourth century B.C. In these schools the sons of the rich continued to study and to spend more time in physical training. Primary education occupied about eight or nine years, but since only the elementary training in letters was compulsory, a poor boy might have little formal schooling. As a rule, Athenians were anxious to send their sons to school until their reception as ephebi, but boys whose fathers could not afford to give them an education beyond the elementary level took to farm work or became apprentices to the artisans. In the secondary schools, drawing, geometry, geography, and grammar in more extended courses were provided in conjunction with a more elaborate training in gymnastics. These schools were originally higher institutions on the same plan as the Palaestra, but they developed into advanced schools of music, mathematics, and philosophy. Two of them, the Academy and the

---

[24] *Ibid.*, pp. 232 f.

Lyceum, have been immortalized because of the association with them of two of the world's greatest teachers,
Plato and Aristotle respectively.

In the higher schools physical exercises were of a
severer nature than in the Palaestra. State officials were
the instructors and the institutions were at times owned
by the state. Their purpose appears to have been to
adapt the physical education more thoroughly to the
final period of preparation of the youth for citizenship.
At the annual festival in honor of Hermes the boys were
given an opportunity to display their progress; and at
the national games boys were frequently entered as con-
testants and their victories were celebrated by the lyric
poets.

Every human ideal was deified by the Athenian. The
god of power, creator of all, was called Zeus or Jupiter.
Below him were the gods and the goddesses of love, of
wisdom, of music, of beauty, and of every perfection and
every passion also that the mind could conceive. A
knowledge of the gods, as well as their cult, entered into
education even from the beginning. Boys paid homage
to the special patrons of the Palaestra, and to the Muses
in the Didaskaleion. There does not appear to have
been any course of instruction in religion during the
primary or the secondary period. The literary studies,
however, abounding in reference to the gods, would seem
to have required some sort of religious instruction.

Moral training was to begin in the home and to continue throughout the whole school period. Seeking the
beautiful intellectually and striving for perfection physically were believed to have a moral effect on the child.
The duties of the pedagogue lay chiefly in supervising
the conduct and guarding the morals of his charge. All
of the teachers, in fact, were charged with the special
care of forming the virtuous man by precept and example. Yet, the moral atmosphere of Athens was dis-

tinctly bad. Plato regarded the whole matter of marital
fidelity as a lost cause.[25]

At eighteen the young man finished his secondary education. He was now known as an ephebe, or youth,
and for two years was engaged in light military duties,
during which he was instructed in the art of fighting
in heavy armor, in throwing the spear, and in tactics.
He also served the state, by which he was maintained,
as a patrol on the frontier and was under a rigid military discipline. At the end of his two years of preliminary training he was presented to the Assembly, received from the state a spear and shield and was enrolled
as a citizen. In the presence of the elders he solemnly
swore to be faithful to the laws and traditions of the
state, never to be a deserter, to be ever ready to fight
for Attica, and to promote the national interest by personal culture and private enterprise. He was now given
the privileges of full citizenship, attended the meetings
of the popular assembly, served on juries, and like the
modern club man enjoyed the pleasant social life of the
city. His training continued throughout the rest of his
life by means of the architecture, sculpture, painting,
drama, and art in general that were all about him.
Under the shade of plane trees, on porches and porticoes,
he exchanged with friends ideas on government, literature, philosophy, and current topics. Much of his intellectual culture was derived through this kind of social
intercourse which may be properly regarded as the education of the market place.

In the domain of art, Athens has been without a peer.
Artists beautified the city with buildings, statues, and
other works of art, while poets and philosophers glorified
it intellectually and spiritually. The best artistic crea-
tions in architecture and sculpture were to be found dur-

---

[25] Becker, op. cit., p. 241.

ing the Periclean Age in the buildings which crowned the Acropolis. The most beautiful of these were the Parthenon, the Propylaea, and the Erectheum. The Parthenon, the finest example of classic architecture, was built entirely of Pentelic marble in the Doric style, and was richly decorated with sculptures by several of the leading artists of the day.[26] The Propylaea was constructed also of the same white marble and formed the magnificent entrance to the Acropolis. One of its charming features was the happy combination of the Doric and Ionic columns.[27] The Erectheum was a temple erected on the spot where rested the honored bones of Erectheus, the hero king of Athens, whose name was joined with that of Poseidon. It had two side porches, the one facing to the north and supported by Ionic columns, the other facing to the south and supported by artistically carved female figures and called the porch of the Maidens.[28]

Phidias was the most renowned of the Greek sculptors. He made three great statues of Athena. His colossal bronze statue of Athena, the Protector, stood between the Parthenon and the Propylaea and, according to Pausanias, the head of the spear and the crest of the helmet could be seen by mariners from the sea.[29] The ivory and gold statue of Athena Parthenos which stood in the great hall of the Parthenon rose forty feet above the base. The shield alone would have been enough to immortalize its author. The gold and ivory could easily be taken off and weighed, as Pericles reminded the court when Phidias was accused of peculation.[30] The third

---

[26] Charles H. Weller, *Athens and Its Monuments* (New York: The Macmillan Co., 1913), pp. 270-77.
[27] *Ibid.*, pp. 229-33.
[28] *Ibid.*, pp. 322 f.
[29] *Ibid.*, p. 343.
[30] *Ibid.*, pp. 295 ff.

statue was known as the Lemnian Athena, so called because it was a gift from the people of Lemnos. It was made of bronze and showed the goddess holding a spear in her left hand while she gazed at a helmet held in her right.[31]

Famous painters of ancient Athens were Polygnotus, Apollodorus, Zeuxis, Parrhasius, and Timanthes. Polygnotus was the first to paint women with transparent garments and to give them headdresses of various colors. He decorated temples, stoas (porches) and in particular the (Stoa Poecile) Painted Porch at Athens. Apollodorus was a true luminary of art who first gave his figures the appearance of reality. He taught Zeuxis who met a successful rival in Parrhasius. The story is told that Zeuxis and Parrhasius presented themselves as candidates for a prize in painting. The former represented grapes in so natural a manner that when he exposed his work to public view, birds, deceived by the likeness, picked at the grapes. Parrhasius produced a picture covered to all appearance with a thin veil. Zeuxis demanded that his rival draw the curtain and show the picture. On discovering his mistake, he surrendered the prize to Parrhasius. Afterwards, in a public competition with Timanthes in which the subject proposed was Ajax, the famous warrior, Parrhasius was defeated. He endeavored to console himself with the remark that he pitied the fate of his hero who was conquered a second time by an unworthy rival.[32]

In the field of drama, Aeschylus was the foremost of tragedians and perhaps the foremost of poets. Of his plays there are recorded seventy-two titles, but only seven actual pieces remain.[33] He introduced the second

---

[31] *Ibid.*, pp. 346 ff.

[32] Botsford and Sihler, *op. cit.*, pp. 554-62.

[33] J. P. Mahaffy, *A History of Greek Classical Literature* (London: The Macmillan Co., 1903), I, Part II, 25.

actor into the play, making the dialogue the principal feature, while the chorus echoed the emotions produced by the play. *Prometheus Bound* is probably his greatest work[34] in which a god is chained to a rock by command of Zeus and made to suffer because of his benevolence to men. Sophocles, when he was but twenty-seven years old, defeated Aeschylus for the first place in tragedy. The titles of more than one hundred of his compositions are known, but only seven are extant in complete form. He introduced a third actor upon the stage and gave less prominence to the chorus. Among his tragedies are *Antigone, Electra, King Oedipus, Oedipus at Colonus, Ajax, Philoctetes,* and the *Trachiniae.* Aeschylus and Sophocles are both pious and reverential to the gods, but the chief interest of the latter is in human beings. For that reason, Sophocles is regarded as the first of the humanists after Homer.[35] Euripides, the last of the great Athenian tragedians, was the author of perhaps ninety-two plays, eighteen of which have come down to us. He displays a lack of reverence for the gods; his characters are men and his choruses wraiths and voices. He was the first to employ the prologue and epilogue which deal with a plot complicated through the medium of love. He is a modernist whose compositions inspired the Roman and Renaissance plays and through them the English and French classical drama.[36] Of his extant plays the *Medea, Hippolytus, Bacchae,* and *Iphigenia Taurica* are considered the best.

Comedy reached its most astonishing development at Athens through the genius of Aristophanes. Eleven of his forty-three comedies have been preserved.[37] He

---

[34] *Ibid.,* p. 34.
[35] Ernest C. Morre, *The Story of Instruction* (New York: The Macmillan Co., 1936), I, 118.
[36] *Ibid.,* p. 119.
[37] J. P. Mahaffy, *op. cit.,* p. 218.

belonged to the old school of thought; ridiculed with freedom and wit the new order of things; burlesqued the politicians of his day and poked fun at the teachings of the Sophists. While some of his plays are not without ribaldry, he was a poet of great versatility. Among his best known works are the *Lysistrata*, the *Clouds*, the *Knights*, the *Wasps*, the *Birds*, and the *Frogs*.

In Greece, as elsewhere, prose literature was not developed until after the epic, the elegy, the lyric, and the drama had been cultivated; even philosophy was at first written in the form of poetry. The first great work of prose to be written in the Greek language was the history of the wars between the Greeks and the Persians by Herodotus, a native of Halicarnassus, born a little before the Persian wars. The subject of his history is that great conflict which consisted of a series of Eastern aggressions upon the Greeks down to the expulsion of the Persians from Europe. He was a great traveler and through careful observations and investigations he became acquainted with the traditions, institutions, and customs of many countries. Much of this information was incorporated in his history, so much so that Herodotus gives us more information about the educational development and culture of ancient nations than all the other Greek historians put together.[38] Herodotus came to Athens during the age of Pericles whom he admired greatly; he was also well known to Sophocles. The general character of his writing is like that of a charming conversationalist and, although he has merited the title "Father of History," his critical judgment has in certain instances been found unreliable.[39]

The greatest of the Greek historians is Thucydides who is rightly claimed to be the father of scientific his-

---

[38] J. P. Mahaffy, *op. cit.*, II, Part I, 23.
[39] *Ibid.*, pp. 28-33.

tory. His subject was the Peloponnesian war which marked the fall of the Athenian empire. The subject, however, is not nearly so important to civilization as the record of it as written by Thucydides. In his hands the art of writing history reached a perfection which no subsequent Hellenic writer, and few modern writers, have attained.[40] The trustworthiness of Thucydides, as a historian, has been universally accepted. "In acuteness of observation, in intellectual force and breadth, in calmness of judgment, in dignity of language, there has never been a historian greater than Thucydides."[41]

Xenophon as a historian cannot be compared with Herodotus and Thucydides. Although many indications of ability and wide experience are apparent in his writings, critics have assigned him to a second rank because he lacked genius.[42] His works fall under four heads: historical books, Socratic books, essays on political philosophy, and technical treatises dealing with varied subjects, such as horses, management of cavalry, and hunting.[43] As a writer of good, clean Attic Greek, Xenophon deserves no small meed of praise.[44] Later Greek historians are Polybius, who wrote a general history in forty books; Diodorus of Sicily, the author of a universal history, also in forty books; Dionysius of Halicarnassus, whose most valuable work is his *Archaeologia*; Plutarch, a Boeotian, who is the encyclopedist of antiquity; and Arrian, a native of Bithynia, who was the chief authority on the expeditions of Alexander the Great.

Another art which exercised even still greater influence in the liberal training of the Athenian was that of oratory. Of the many Athenian orators who attained

---

[40] *Ibid.*, p. 119.
[41] *Ibid.*, p. 123.
[42] *Ibid.*, Part II, 79.
[43] *Ibid.*, p. 51.
[44] *Ibid.*, p. 79.

distinction, the most representative are Lysias, Isocrates, Demosthenes, and Aeschines. Like other orators of his day, Lysias wrote speeches for those who were obliged to plead their own cause in the courts. His orations were written in a simple, direct style, and deal with the characters of the parties to the trial and their socio-economic conditions.[45]

Isocrates was primarily a schoolmaster. The orations which he wrote reveal him as a stylist rather than a thinker. He exercised a wide influence on Hellenic opinion through his pupils who came from all over Hellas to acquire from him the ethical and political knowledge that was deemed essential to statesmanship. His writings, which are mostly political, indicate that he was an eminent publicist.[46]

The greatest of all the orators of Greece was Demosthenes. He possessed a power of diction and a force of persuasion which made him superior to any of his rivals and have given him a place among the world's greatest orators. The first cause which he pleaded was his own case against his unfaithful guardians from whom he recovered a portion of his patrimony. Because of certain defects in his voice and delivery his first addresses to the people were unsuccessful.[47]

It is reported of him that, in an effort to correct a natural impediment in his speech, he placed pebbles in his mouth and in this manner pronounced several verses without interruption while walking in steep and difficult places.[48] He used to declaim on the seashore in the midst of the roaring of the waves in order to accustom

---

[45] Botsford and Sihler, *op. cit.*, p. 45.

[46] *Ibid.*, p. 46.

[47] Plutarch's Lives, *Demosthenes*, translated by B. Perrin. The Loeb Classical Library (New York: G. P. Putnam's Sons, 1919). VII, 15.

[48] *Ibid.*, p. 27.

himself to the milling of people in the assemblies. It
is also reported of him that he had a small chamber
built underground and shaved half of his head that he
might confine himself there and direct all his attention
to the study of his orations.[49] It is believed that he
studied under Plato who assisted him greatly in preparing to speak in public.

The greatest opportunity for a display of eloquence
came to Demosthenes when he undertook the defense of
Grecian liberty against the encroachments of Philip of
Macedon. In these orations he gave to the world a
new word, philippic, which is used to describe a personal, vigorous attack. Philip was assassinated soon
afterward, but Demosthenes refused to believe it, saying
that if it were true the whole earth would be filled with
the smell of his carcass.

Demosthenes found a great rival in Aeschines who,
pretending to accuse Ctesiphon who asked that a crown
of gold be awarded Demosthenes for his patriotism,
manifestly directed his charge against Demosthenes.
The reply of Demosthenes was his masterful speech *On
the Crown*. Eventually Aeschines retired to Rhodes
where he established a school of eloquence. He opened
his lectures with the two speeches that had occasioned
his banishment. His students received the orations with
great applause but when they heard the harangue of
Demosthenes their plaudits were redoubled. Then it
was that Aeschines is supposed to have reminded them
that their acclamations would be yet greater if they had
heard Demosthenes himself deliver his oration.

Although Athenian education was the highest type
of formal training the world had yet seen, and was to
become the inspiration and, in many things, the basis of
schooling in all succeeding ages, it was not complete.

---

[49] *Ibid.*, p. 17.

It lacked certain requirements for a lasting system even from a national viewpoint, since it emphasized and glorified the individual without defining sufficiently his relation to the state. Greek individualism ultimately shaped itself into democracy, but democracy requires a moral bond, whereas the Athenian state, which failed to provide a solid foundation for the teaching and practice of morality, had only a material one.[50]

Until about the middle of the fifth century B.C., Athens may be said to have adhered to the old education according to which the individual was subordinated to the good of the social whole. This early period of Greek education was followed by one of transition and readjustment and the new education which developed gradually lost sight of the civic aim, which was worth,[51] and tended toward extreme individualism which reduced the state to the status of a mere servant to the citizen. Successful in the Persian wars, and enjoying leadership in the Delian League (477 B.C.) over the Ionian states in Asia Minor and the islands of the Aegean Sea, the city-state of Athens took on a newer and broader educational life at home. The changes in the political and social order offered many rich opportunities for personal advancement in the service of the state. Although the old education did not adequately prepare for this new condition of affairs, the change had hardly taken place when a new class of teachers arose to deal with the situation. They engaged to prepare the ambitious for the callings of public life—holding out to them not the old motive of devotion to the state, but the inducement of personal advancement and success.

The Sophists, or wise men, as they were called, were at first wandering teachers, not attached to any institu-

---

[50] Thomas Davidson, *The Education of the Greek People,* p. 82.
[51] *Ibid.,* p. 88.

tion, but going from place to place wherever they found pupils willing to pay for instruction. Many of them, like Protagoras and Gorgias, early Sophists, were men of talent who had traveled widely and were thus able to discuss competently the literary, political, and scientific questions of the time. Some also were capable instructors in science, philosophy, mathematics, rhetoric, and grammar. In fact, the formulation of the principles of Greek grammar and rhetoric is attributed to them.[52] Many others, however, were merely charlatans with some powers of argumentation and oratory and inclined to affect a show of learning.

In philosophy and religion they rank as the first sceptics of Greece.[53] "Man is the measure of all things," said Protagoras. Truth was subjective and was ultimately reduced to individual opinion. Individualism characterized their ethical and political doctrines as well. In dialectics, they aimed to equip their students with the facility to argue on both sides of a question, and to make the weaker appear the stronger reason, thus sacrificing truth to argumentative skill, and giving justification to the use in subsequent ages of the term "sophism" to designate a fallacious or specious argument.

The most famous of the Sophists were Protagoras, Gorgias, Hippias, and Prodicus. It is well to note that some historians consider them a much misrepresented and abused class, and maintain that their work has not been properly appreciated.[54] They regard the Sophists

---

[52] Paul Monroe, *Text-Book in the History of Education* (New York: The Macmillan Co., 1921), p. 116.

[53] Turner, *History of Philosophy*, p. 70.

[54] *Cf.* George Groote, *A History of Greece* (New York: United States Book Co., [*n. d.*]), III, 415; B. A. G. Fuller, *History of Philosophy* (New York: Henry Holt and Co., 1938), pp. 46-51; S. S. Laurie. *Historical Survey of Pre-Christian Education,* pp. 284-87.

as the logical teachers of the transitional period who did a real service in popularizing the learning which was to be taken up later by the great Greek philosophers, Socrates, Plato, and Aristotle. Their apologists, however, cannot deny the pernicious influence of the Sophists on the subsequent civil and educational life of the Athenian people.[55]

Meanwhile the conservative element in society undertook to offset this disorganizing tendency of rationalism, which discredited the old Greek social and moral order. Interestingly enough, the first to oppose this influence were not Athenians. Just as philosophy had its origin in the Ionian cities of Asia Minor, so the efforts to counteract the effects of philosophy were first made in those regions.[56] Long before the Sophists had come into prominence, various reactionary schemes had been advanced to rebuild the traditional social and ethical structure of Greece. Among the plans proposed, the most significant was that of Pythagoras which envisaged the establishment of a social order on a philosophic basis in which every individual would have his appointed place. His school at Crotona, in southern Italy, then a Greek colony, resembled the Spartan system in its organization and the Athenian in its general culture and method of study. Its influence was felt long after the death of its founder, for the Pythagoreans numbered many adherents, and both by teaching and writing widely disseminated their doctrine.

Pythagoras (580-510 B.C.), a native of the island of Samos, was not entirely the product of Greek education. He had traveled and studied, it is said, in Persia, India, and Egypt, and never overcame the influence of Oriental and Egyptian learning. He left no writings; all that is

---

[55] Thomas Davidson, *Aristotle and Ancient Educational Ideals*, pp. 102 ff.

[56] Thomas Davidson, *The Education of the Greek People*, p. 98.

known of him comes to posterity from his disciples.
Many modern scholars believe that the views of these
disciples and their successors have been erroneously attributed to Pythagoras.[57]   It has been asserted that
about no other philosopher or philosophical school has
there been associated more tradition of a legendary nature. Pythagoras was always held in the highest reverence by his followers and his word for any doctrine gave
it indisputable authority. Discourses or written themes
were constantly prefaced by a quotation from the master
—the *Ipse dixit* (He himself said it), which was sufficient to lend weight and support in a time when it was
difficult to prove the authenticity of a statement, or the
veracity of an author.

The higher concepts of the existence of God, the immortality of the soul, retribution in the future life,
and the doctrine of metempsychosis, or transmigration
of souls into the lower animals, are attributed to him.[58]
At any rate it can be seen that he found in religion a
solid sanction for the excellent moral principles he inculcated. For him, God was the ruler of the universe
to whom all nature paid the homage of obedience by
harmonious activity. The "harmony of the spheres"
was the inspiring keynote of his teaching, and discovering nature's harmony he strove to bring men into harmony with truth. The means he adopted were knowledge, music, gymnastics, and the practice of asceticism.

It was the principle of the Pythagoreans that number
is the essence and basis of all things.[59]   They applied
this theory to the study of nature, philosophy, and music,
and in consequence advanced the scientific and mathematical knowledge of the time. As a result of the num-

---

[57] Henry O. Taylor, *Ancient Ideals*, I, 308.
[58] *Ibid.*, p. 309.
[59] William Turner, *op. cit.*, p. 40.

ber theory, so it is believed, they invented the musical scale.

The school at Crotona was in constitution an aristocratic society with Pythagoras as the head. Only those judged by Pythagoras as competent to profit by this higher education were admitted. The pupils came usually from the ranks of the aristocracy. They lived together in small houses surrounding a lecture hall and, like the Spartans, they had all things in common. A fund, which was made up from the fees of the students upon their entrance to the school, defrayed the living expenses. It was managed by the students under the direction of the master who regarded it as a training in economy.

The students were divided into two general classes, viz., the novices and the elect. Pythagoras lectured to all, but gave only part of the doctrine to the beginners during their period of preparation which lasted several years. He was concealed by a curtain during the lecture. The students listened attentively to his discourse, which usually consisted of his dicta, or sayings, never asking a question about the things they could not understand. They were expected to reflect upon these thoughts during the hours of study and silence. Writing was recommended as an aid to memory, and also to reflection. The advanced students received the fullness of doctrine, and were allowed to share in all the mysteries and secrets of their society.

Harmony, as stated above, was the aim in all instruction—harmony of the soul in all its faculties, and with truth; harmony of the body with the mind, which meant the subjection of the lower to the higher element. Indeed the physical exercises were designed to promote health and vigor, another aspect of harmony. In morals, harmony is virtue, and this is obtained by study and religion. Thus, as they proceeded in practice to acquire this manifold harmony for the soul by study, reflection, and music, and for the body, by gymnastics, so they endeavored to realize perfect harmony in the moral order by regular practices of religion and virtue.[60] Three times a day public exercises took place. The master constantly exacted obedience and fidelity, examples of temperance and abnegation; and, it is conceded, he did more to raise the moral consciousness of the Greeks than had ever been achieved before.

The school came to an abrupt close during a popular uprising in Crotona. As it was aristocratic in its tendencies, and perhaps had some influence in the government of the colony, the people in a revolt against the aristocracy burned it. Pythagoras escaped to Metapontum, where he died about 507 B.C.

When the Sophists undertook to educate the Athenians, their chief attention was directed to the adolescents of Athens in the gymnasium stage of education and to the younger citizens who were looking forward to a public career or to a life of pleasure. With the Palaestra and the Didaskaleion, the Sophists had comparatively little to do.[61] In consideration of a substantial fee they offered to teach the young men of Athens any subject and to impart any ability, particularly power in argumentation. Groups of Athenian youths sought them out in the streets, the market place, the gymnasia, and the taverns, so eager were they to learn how the individual might assert himself successfully on all occasions.

Old ideas in philosophy, ethics, and religion were shattered by the Sophists. The inadequacy of the old education to meet the new demands upon it was apparent, yet the new learning needed a solid basis in order to preserve the best elements of the older Athenian

---

[60] Thomas Davidson, *The Education of the Greek People*, pp. 99 ff.

[61] *Ibid.*, p. 89.

culture and to insure the stability of the national life already placed in danger of disintegration. Socrates and his immediate successors endeavored to rid the newer education of its dangerous superficiality and to give it a solid foundation. To counteract the rising spirit of individualism they sought also to restore the ancient ideal of service and devotion to the state. In the first period of reconstruction, the elementary and secondary education remained unchanged, while the higher passed through many remarkable phases of development under the influence of some of the world's greatest philosophers and teachers.

Socrates (469-399 B.C.) was born at Athens, the son of a sculptor. He learned his father's art and practiced it for a considerable portion of his early life. He applied himself meanwhile to the study of the other fine arts as well as of rhetoric and the exact sciences. As a soldier in the Peloponnesian war he gave evidence of unusual hardiness and endurance, and also of that courageous spirit which distinguished his service later as a citizen and as a senator. During the reign of the Thirty Tyrants he risked his life by refusing to further measures which he felt were not for the best interest of the state. He manifested much of that older Athenian patriotism which placed public service above private interest or advancement. In personal appearance, he was far from attractive. He sadly lacked that beauty of countenance and form and that elegance of manner and dress which the Athenians admired so much, and in consequence he fell a frequent victim to the gibes of his rivals for popular favor, the Sophists, poets, and satirists. But while his appearance repelled, his wonderfully sweet voice could attract and hold his hearers. It was one indication at least, of the great and lovable soul within so unattractive a frame, for "never did outward semblance more belie the inward spirit of the man." Of his kindness, piety, and honesty his biographer, Xenophon, leaves no doubt. He makes him the ideal man.[62]   His patience in dealing with a shrewish wife is proverbial; his courage as he faced death on the charge of atheism and corrupting the youth of the city, as described by Plato in *Phaedo*, is equally well known.[63]

Socrates was not a professional teacher like the Sophists, working for pay. He was a seeker after truth. Early in the morning he went to the public promenades and training grounds and talked to anyone who might listen; in the forenoon he walked in the market place questioning and teaching the youth of Athens; and the rest of the day he passed where he was most likely to meet people who were eager to learn from him.[64]   Socrates was naturally influenced by the doctrines of Pythagoras and the Sophists. He expressly took up the principle of Protagoras, i.e., "Man is the measure of all things," but he directed his inquiry first to man himself rather than to nature, taking as his initial principle and the guiding idea of his teaching the maxim, γνῶθι σεαυτόν, "Know thyself." Later the Romans expressed this principle in Latin: "Cognosce teipsum"; and still later Shakespeare wrote: "To thine ownself be true; and it must follow as the night the day thou canst not then be false to any man."[65]

With the Sophists, knowledge was subjective, if any certain knowledge were at all attainable, and this in most cases resolved itself into individual opinion. With Socrates, knowledge is something real, objective, a guide to right conduct, and in fact, virtue; education, the means to obtain it, is to give the individual not the

---

[62] Xenophon, *Memorabilia*, translated in Loeb Classical Library (London: William Heinemann, Ltd., 1923), IV, 359.

[63] Plato, *Phaedo*, translated in Loeb Classical Library (London: William Heinemann, 1913), pp. 391-403.

[64] Xenophon, *op. cit.*, I, 7.

[65] *Hamlet*, I, iii, 78-80.

existing content of knowledge or information but the power of investigating the basis of his ideas. With this power of analysis and reduction of ideas to their basic principles, man can come into possession of the body of truth and eventually virtue, for virtue is living by knowledge.

Unlike the Sophists, with their formal lecture in appointed places, Socrates' plan of teaching was by personal discussion or dialogue. This he took up in different ways according to the needs of his pupils. One method has been called the ironic, and the other the maieutic or birth-giving process. Examples of both have been preserved in the writings of Plato and Xenophon, for Socrates left no written work.

In applying the ironic method, usually with the Sophists and the arrogant whom he set out to confound, he ascertained their views on some interesting subject, and assuming them to be true, or pretending ignorance on his part, he proceeded by further questions to push their ideas to their logical conclusions, or in most instances, to their logical absurdities. In this manner he brought them to confusion, showing either the weakness of their reasoning, the shallowness of their knowledge, or the serious consequences of their erroneous views.

By the maieutic or birth-giving process, he intended to develop a broad and universal knowledge from the limited information already in the mind of his hearer. At first he learned by questions the extent of this mental content, and by it determined a series of questions with which to lead the mind into fields of thought hitherto unexplored. He strove to test the source of all information, to get at the reason or essence of things, and if possible to reach a definition of them. The method was inductive throughout.

Socrates then endeavored to make one's knowledge secure and personal. An idea was not to be accepted on authority until by induction from experience or observation its truth or universal application could be attested. What was found to be conformable to experience, true when tested by logical reasoning, and of universal application was to be accepted. Since he was concerned with ethical questions, his conclusions had moral value and served as a directive influence in the way of virtue.

It is well attested by Xenophon[66] that Socrates believed in the existence of God and the immortality of the soul. While he taught that there was one supreme God, he accepted the inferior and false gods of his countrymen and agreed that worship should be rendered them. He believed learning would make men better individually and as a civic body. Consequently, he labored to teach men how to think in order that he might teach them how to live. He erred seriously in making virtue identical with knowledge, maintaining that no man can knowingly do wrong.[67] The acceptance of this ethical doctrine would do away with free will and accountability.

From his life and teachings it is clear that Socrates believed the supreme good for man to consist in attaining the most complete knowledge of virtue. Herein was to be found man's happiness. He had the distinction of beginning a great educational movement, of developing a method of teaching which was not only effective in overcoming the pernicious influence of the Sophists but succeeded in giving a foundation to knowledge, and a basis for the first system of ethics the pagan world had known.

Plato (427-347 B.C.), the great disciple of Socrates, was born of an aristocratic Athenian family. Endowed with brilliant natural gifts he likely would have entered

[66] Xenophon, *op. cit.*, pp. 54-59.
[67] Cf. Taylor, *Ancient Ideals,* pp. 318 f.; Turner, *History of Philosophy,* p. 83.

into the political life of Athens, had not Socrates turned his attention to the pursuit of wisdom. After the death of his master, he left Greece, spending the next ten or twelve years traveling and studying, principally in Egypt and in the Greek colonies of Italy and Sicily. The sublime truths contained in his teachings are attributed to the influence of the inspired writings of the Hebrews with which he had probably become acquainted during his travels in the East. About the age of forty he returned to Athens and founded there his famous school of philosophy, the Academy, where for thirty-six years he was actually engaged in teaching. To him we are largely indebted for a knowledge of the educational ideas of Socrates, which he adopted and elaborated, and for the most comprehensive educational theory the Greek world had so far formulated.

Socrates had hoped to overcome the individualism of the Sophists, restore stability to society, and at the same time give liberty and scope to the individual, by means of knowledge, a knowledge based on universal concepts or ideas by which man was to live virtuously. Plato accepted the universal idea as the basis of knowledge and taught that the idea was the only reality. Goodness was to be attained by means of virtue, which is the harmony or order of the faculties under the light of reason. The true spiritual life consists in contemplation, in reaching up to see the spiritual beauty of the universe—in communion with God.[68]

The purpose of the state is the cultivation of virtue in individuals. In his ideal state there were three classes: the rulers or philosophers; the defenders or warriors; and the providers, a class including peasants, artisans, and merchants. The philosophers alone are capable of abstract thinking and so possess real knowl-

---

[68] Henry O. Taylor, *Ancient Ideals,* p. 328.

edge or universal truth. The other classes possess only opinion.[69] The three classes he compared to the virtues of wisdom, courage, and thrift in the individual.

The writings of Plato are in the form of dialogues in which Socrates is often represented as the chief speaker. For that reason it is difficult at times to know whether the thoughts expressed are those of Socrates or of Plato himself. The dialogues often are named after some person: The *Protagoras*, in which the nature of virtue is discussed; the *Phaedo*, which presents arguments in favor of immortality; the *Theaetetus*, which is a treatise on the theory of knowledge. The *Republic* and the *Laws* set forth his theory of education. The former is a product of his middle life and the latter is one of the last of his works.

The *Republic* is really a treatise on government. Education of necessity receives careful consideration in it because it is the one means by which the relations of the inhabitants to the model state may be determined. It represents the ideal state or a socialistic body to which all things belong. Its chief concern is education, for by it society is able to differentiate the body politic until a special class is set aside to rule. While the existing form of education is not changed by this dialogue, many valuable suggestions are offered in regard to the current studies, especially music and gymnastics.[70]

The differentiation of classes in the ideal state is made on the basis of ability. At the close of the primary period those who were not adapted by nature for higher studies were to form the industrial class and then take up the pursuit of their crafts. Those of military capabilities were to receive higher training for the preparation as soldiers, and this was usually from the twenti-

---

[69] Plato, *Republic*, translated in Loeb Classical Library (London: William Heinemann, Ltd., 1935), II, vi, 43 ff. *et passim*.

[70] *Ibid.*, I, iii, 261-69 *et passim*.

eth to the thirtieth year. Finally, the most promising of the ephebes after a ten-year course of study were to be selected for a course in philosophy extending over five years and intended to prepare them for the office of ruler, whose term of service would last fifteen years.

In the course of training preliminary to the study of dialectics, the quadrivium of the seven liberal arts is advocated. Arithmetic, plane and solid geometry, music, and astronomy are to be studied not for practical reasons but because they develop a general capacity for abstract thought.[71] Consequently, it is claimed that the whole conception of "liberal" studies and the theory of "formal discipline" may be traced back to Plato's views concerning the value of the mathematical subjects in the training of philosophers.[72]

The *Laws* embodies the maturer views of Plato and marks many changes in his political and educational theories. In it he returns to the older Athenian ideas of government and education, advocating also many features of the Spartan system, such as the common life of the youth under the supervision of the elders, strict military discipline, and the education of both sexes.[73] The philosophers, however, are not now to be the rulers, but rather the priests, and in place of philosophy in education a scientific religion is introduced. More attention is given to the moral benefits of music and poetry.[74]

The philosophical teachings of Plato reveal a noble mind striving to solve the complex problems of life. He rejected the popular mythology of his countrymen and recognized the unity of God and His sovereignty over

---

[71] *Ibid.*, II, vii, pp. 165-95.
[72] Frank P. Graves, *A Student's History of Education* (New York: The Macmillan Co., 1936), p. 41.
[73] Plato, *Laws*, translated in the Loeb Classical Library (London: William Heinemann, Ltd., 1926), II, vii, 67-89.
[74] *Ibid.*, pp. 39-57.

the world. He was convinced that the soul was spiritual
and immortal[75] and that good was rewarded and evil
punished in a future life. He had some knowledge of
the tradition of man's fall from grace and the existence
of angels, creatures mediating between God and man.
The limitations of his gifted mind are apparent in the
errors that are found in his metaphysical and psychological doctrines.

The Platonic theory of education as formulated in
the *Republic* or the *Laws* was never adopted by the
Greeks. It is of value in the history of education for
the many sound principles it embodies. Plato insisted,
for example, on respecting the needs and interests of
the child even in primary training, on the value of play,
the education of woman, and the judicious use of music
and poetry to incite to reverence and virtue. He denied,
however, the rights of the parents over the education of
the young, and made the preparation for citizenship,
or service to the state, the end of education.

Aristotle (384-322 B.C.), the most famous of Plato's
disciples, was a native of Stagira, a city in Macedonia.
His early education he probably received from his father,
court physician to King Amyntas of Macedonia, and to
him he likewise was indebted for his interest in natural
science. From the age of seventeen to thirty-seven he
studied under Plato, ranking as the most brilliant pupil
of the Academy. Upon the death of Plato, he left
Athens. Four years later, while continuing his studies
and investigations, he was called to be tutor of the young
Alexander of Macedon, an office which he held for three
years. He did not return to Athens until about 355 B.C.,
when he founded the Lyceum as a rival of the Academy.
The school received its name, Peripatetic, meaning

---

[75] Plato held that the rational part of the soul alone is produced by God and is immortal. *Cf.* William Turner, *History of
Philosophy,* p. 113.

"walking about," from Peripatos, the covered walk, where the lectures were given, and his followers were called the Peripatetics, perhaps, too, because Aristotle lectured while walking leisurely about with them under the porticos. Aristotle presided over the Lyceum until a year before his death.

Those of Aristotle's works which have been preserved are his lectures, and even these are not wholly authentic. Some appear to be the amplified notes of his pupils. His dialogues are preserved only in fragmentary form. As they exist at present the works embrace treatises on biology, ethics, logic, metaphysics, physics, poetry, politics, psychology, and rhetoric. In the preparation of these treatises he was evidently assisted by his pupils who collected the facts which were classified by the master and reduced to rational principles. For an exposition of his educational theory recourse must be had to the *Politics,* the *Ethics,* and the *Poetics.*

Aristotle's educational scheme is substantially the same as Plato's, in that education is one of the chief functions of the state, a branch of the science of politics. He believed that of the three approved forms of government, namely, monarchy, aristocracy, and democracy, the first was theoretically the best, but since it was the most easily perverted, the last, or republican form, was to be accepted.[76] Like Plato he ventured upon a theory of the state, but because of his scientific spirit, his method of investigation is inductive and before setting forth his views on the ideal commonwealth, he read the constitutional histories of over two hundred and fifty different states.[77] Aristotle had in mind, and this is important, the government of the city-state. Not all were to enjoy the rights of citizenship; he excluded merchants,

---

[76] Aristotle, *Politics,* translated in Loeb Classical Library (London: William Heinemann, Ltd., 1923), IV, x, 339.
[77] Davidson, *Aristotle and Ancient Educational Ideals,* pp. 168 f.

artisans, and slaves. The character of education is determined by the character of the state. Only the prospective citizen is to be educated. The citizen should be moulded to suit the form of government under which he lives.
"And inasmuch as the end for the whole state is one, it
is manifest that education also must necessarily be one
and the same for all and that the superintendence of this
must be public, and not on private lines. . . ."[78]

The end of the state is the happiness of its citizens;
happiness consists in the practice of virtue.

> . . . the best life, whether separately for an individual
> or collectively for states, is the life conjoined with virtue
> furnished with sufficient means for taking part in virtuous
> actions; . . . and if anybody accepts the individual as happy
> on account of virtue, he will also say that the state which is
> the better morally is the happier.[79]

With Aristotle, the highest virtue is intellectual and
its full realization is found in contemplation. A con-
templative existence is nobler than the life of action.[80]
The end of education, as of life itself, is the attainment
of intellectual and moral virtue which bring the greatest
happiness of which man is capable. Moral virtue is
acquired by habit, intellectual virtue by instruction.

In his treatment of the order of training he took it for
granted that the physical should first be attended to, the
moral next, and the intellectual last. Physical training
must begin even before birth; the state should see that
only persons who are well and strong marry. Children
who are born defective must be exposed or put to death.
From birth to seven, children should receive in the home
a good physical and moral training. Instruction really
begins at the age of seven and this is under public

---

[78] Aristotle, *Politics*, VIII, i, 635.
[79] *Ibid.*, VII, i-ii, 539.
[80] *Ibid.*, VII, iii, 551.

supervision. From seven to the advent of puberty, education continues to be largely physical in character with special attention to the training of the emotions. From puberty up to the age of twenty-one the youth is impressed with the importance of civic duties while his intellectual studies are chiefly theoretic—arithmetic, geometry, and astronomy. Aristotle agreed with Plato that the especially gifted should continue to study in comparatively cultured leisure devoting their lives to speculative philosophy and contemplation.[81] The gymnastic exercises which he recommended were to aid physical development and not to produce athletes; consequently they were not to be severe for the growing boy. Proper intellectual training he thought might be obtained through the subjects then in use in the schools if something higher than a mere utilitarian purpose was kept in view. Children should be taught reading, writing, and drawing which included elementary arithmetic, not merely because these subjects serve the purposes of life, but also because many other sorts of knowledge are acquired through them.

And it is also clear that some of the useful subjects as well ought to be studied by the young not only because of their utility, like the study of reading and writing, but also because they may lead on to many other branches of knowledge; and similarly they should study drawing not in order that they may not go wrong in their private purchases and may avoid being cheated in buying and selling furniture, but rather because this study makes a man observant of bodily beauty; and to seek for utility everywhere is entirely unsuited to men that are great-souled and free.[82]

Music is useful as a means of amusement and relaxation; but, more important than that, it enables us

---

[81] Davidson, *Aristotle and Ancient Educational Ideals*, pp. 184-202.

[82] Aristotle, *Politics*, VIII, iii, 645.

"to judge correctly and to delight in virtuous character and noble actions"; it is a worthy part of the child's training then, because of its ethical value. Aristotle attributed certain emotions and wholesome effects to the various melodies and rhythms, and while he held that children should learn to sing and play, he did not sanction their striving after perfection in either respect with a view to making music an art or profession.[83]   From his own method of teaching it is concluded that he considered dialectic or logic the fundamental study for the pursuit of the higher sciences.   It furnished mental exercise and supplied the means of convincing others and of detecting truth and error.   It seems probable that he gave first place to philosophy among the theoretical sciences and to politics among the practical, but we have only his own preferences and those of his disciples to aid us in reaching such a conclusion.

If Socrates may be called honest, Plato spiritual, then Aristotle is rightly judged intellectual.   Plato was idealistic in his metaphysical speculations; Aristotle was realistic.   The former was interested in ideas, the latter in facts.   Plato thought out principles and doctrines through personal reflective thinking; Aristotle first read what others had written on a particular subject before he expressed his views.   Plato wrote in the interest of Athens; Aristotle wrote in the interest of science and for the benefit of the whole world; he searched all the manuscripts he could find for a knowledge of physical things and then undertook to discover the general laws that govern natural phenomena.   For that reason he is regarded as a great scientific pioneer.   His political philosophy, however, is inferior to that of Plato.   Although he opposes the state absolutism of Plato, and maintains the priority of the family in relation to the

---

[83] *Ibid.*, VIII, v-vi, 657-65.

state, he makes happiness or unhappiness in the present life the highest sanction in the enforcement of the laws. Ignoring the personal immortality of the soul,[84] he concludes that beatitude is to be found in the present life.

Aristotle's educational theory was not completed either in the *Politics* or the *Ethics,* in the form in which these two works have come down to us. His influence on contemporary Greek education was slight because his followers were mostly devoted to speculation and research. But, later in the Middle Ages, when his works were introduced in Europe, his great and abiding influence may be said to have begun. The Scholastics accepted his system of thought, and in applying his terminology forever associated it with Christian philosophy and theology. They restored to favor his works on the natural sciences, for Aristotle was the first biologist and natural historian, as well as the founder of the science and art of logic, and they perpetuated both his deductive and inductive methods. "The Master of those who know," as Dante styled him, has not ceased to influence Christian schools.

The later period of Greek education is characterized by no addition to or improvement upon educational theory. It is marked by the spread of Greek culture in the East, following upon the conquests of Alexander the Great. Within a century after Alexander's death the whole of the then known East was Hellenized. The influence of Greek ideas and habits showed itself at first in the opening of Greek schools, palaestras, gymnasia, theatres, and stadia; but in the course of time the deeper elements of Greek culture, namely, art and philosophy, permeated the thought and spirit of the East.[85] In turn, the Oriental influences were bound to modify

---

[84] Turner, *op. cit.,* p. 152.
[85] Davidson, *Education of the Greek People,* pp. 177 f.

the native culture of Greece. Evidences of this are seen in the rise of certain new schools of philosophy which followed Aristotle. These schools not only discredited the old religious idea of the Greeks, but also opposed the foreign superstitions imported into Greece from the Orient.

Almost contemporaneously there arose two schools of philosophy, the Stoics and the Epicureans, both of which had a decided effect on the subsequent life of the Greeks and the Romans. The Stoics took their name from the Stoa Poecile (Painted Porch) or colonnade at the Athenian market place where Zeno (350-258 B.C.), a Semite by birth and founder of this school of philosophy, first taught his doctrines. The Epicureans were the disciples of Epicurus (341-270 B.C.), a native of Samos, who had taught in the cities of Asia Minor before he came to Athens. Both these schools made their objective personal independence. The former maintained that the guide to conduct was the law of the senses, while the latter claimed the law of the spirit. Strangely enough, while the former admitted free will, the latter professed fatalism.[86]

At this same time a large number of rhetorical schools came into existence for the purpose of giving young men a training in oratory and a general knowledge of current questions. They made no claim to teaching anything profound or of forming habits of logical thinking. They were concerned not so much with what was said but with how it was said.[87] From a loose union of the philosophical and rhetorical schools arose the University of Athens. Until almost 300 A.D., Athens remained the intellectual center of civilization. The University of Alexandria, begun after the Greek conquest, became under

---

[86] Davidson, *Aristotle and Ancient Educational Ideals*, p. 211.
[87] Laurie, *Historical Survey of Pre-Christian Education*, p. 293.

the Ptolemies a leading school of Greek culture, continued as such long after the Roman invasion, and finally displaced Athens in importance. Other universities in the Hellenic world were those of Rhodes, Pergamum, and Rome.

There are extremely different opinions concerning the worth of Greek education. Usually it is regarded very highly and praised indiscriminately. All Greeks are looked upon as specimens of superb physical development, whereas the Greek statues which are our chief witnesses to this beauty and perfection of body do not at all represent the general type. The same observation is true when we consider the Greek intellect; Socrates, Plato, Aristotle, and Demosthenes are exceptional men. Based upon slavery, Greek education was obviously snobbish. Mothers and wives were held in very low esteem outside of Sparta. The moral atmosphere of Athens was such that there was little appreciation of the virtue of chastity. It is not to be wondered at that the Athenians were incapable of stable, civic pride.[88]

On the other hand, the Greeks were a vigorous, liberty-loving people whose educational system gave them a freedom of development which made possible the attainment of real excellence in physical beauty, in artistic expression, and in profound thought. The Romans deeply admired the educational achievements of the Greeks. Greek schools of philosophy and rhetoric continued in Rome while Roman youth made up a considerable body of the attendance at the universities of Athens and Alexandria. The Roman emperors felt that they should support and extend the work of education in these schools. With the spread of Greek culture and education throughout the world a broader impulse was given to intellectual and aesthetic progress.

---

[88] *Cf.* W. Kane, *An Essay Toward a History of Education* (Chicago: Loyola University Press, 1935), pp. 48 f.

FOR FURTHER STUDY

Aristotle, *Politics.* Translated by H. Rackham. Loeb Classical Library. London: William Heinemann, Ltd., 1932.

Athenaeus, *Deipnosophists.* Translated by C. B. Gulick, 7 vols. London: William Heinemann, Ltd., 1927-41.

Baumgarten, F. *et al., Die hellenische Kultur.* Leipzig und Berlin: G. B. Teubner, 1913.

Becker, W. A., *Charicles or Illustrations of the Private Life of the Ancient Greeks.* Translated from the German by Frederick Metcalfe. 8th ed. London: Longmans, Green, and Company, 1889.

Bosanquet, B., *The Education of the Young in the Republic of Plato.* Translated into English with notes and introduction. Cambridge: University Press, 1901.

Botsford, G. W. and E. G. Sihler, *Hellenic Civilization.* New York: Columbia University Press, 1920.

Burnet, John, *Aristotle on Education.* Cambridge: University Press, 1903.

Capes, W. W., *University Life in Ancient Athens.* Reprint. New York: G. E. Steckert, 1922.

Davidson, Thomas, *Aristotle and Ancient Educational Ideals.* New York: Charles Scribner's Sons, 1899.

————, *The Education of the Greek People.* New York: D. Appleton and Company, 1906.

Freeman, K. J., *Schools of Hellas.* London: The Macmillan Company, 1922.

Fuller, B. A. G., *A History of Philosophy.* New York: Henry Holt and Company, 1938.

Girard, P. L., *L'Education athènienne au Ve et au IVe siècle avant J. C.* Paris: Hachette et Cie, 1889.

Glotz, G., *Ancient Greece at Work.* Translated by M. R. Dobie. New York: Alfred A. Knopf, 1926.

Gomme, A. W., *Population of Athens in the V and IV centuries B. C.* Oxford: B. Blackwell, 1933.

Grote, G., *History of Greece.* 12 vols. London: J. M. Dent and Sons, Ltd., Vol. I (1934); Vol. II (1930); Vols. III-XII [n. d.].

Gulick, C. B., *The Life of the Ancient Greeks.* New York: D. Appleton and Company, 1902.

Herodotus, *Histories.* 4 vols. Translated by A. D. Godley. London: William Heinemann, Ltd., 1921-24.

Holm, Adolph, *The History of Greece.* 4 vols. Translated from the German. London: The Macmillan Co., 1894-99.

James, H. R., *Our Hellenic Heritage.* London: The Macmillan Co., 1921.

Lane, F. H., *Elementary Greek Education.* Syracuse: Bardeen Co., 1895.

Laurie, S. S., *Historical Survey of Pre-Christian Education.* New York: Longmans, Green, and Co., 1900.

Mahaffy, J. P., *A History of Classical Greek Literature.* 2 vols. London and New York: The Macmillan Co., 1895.

————, *Greek Life and Thought.* New York: The Macmillan Co., 1896.

————, *Old Greek Education.* New York: Harper and Bros., 1882.

————, *Social Life in Greece.* London: The Macmillan Co., 1898.

Monroe, P., *Source Book of the History of Education for the Greek and Roman Period.* New York: The Macmillan Co., 1919.

Morey, William C., *Outlines of Greek History.* New York: American Book Co., 1903.

Murray, G. G. A., *History of Ancient Greek Literature.* New York: D. Appleton and Co., 1897.

Plato, *Laws.* 2 vols. Translated by Paul Shorey. Loeb Classical Library, London: William Heinemann, Ltd., 1936.

————, *Phaedo.* Translated by H. N. Fowler. Loeb Classical Library. London: William Heinemann, Ltd., 1913.

————, *Republic.* 2 vols. Translated by Paul Shorey. Loeb Classical Library. London: William Heinemann, Ltd., 1930-35.

Rider, Bertha C., *The Greek House.* Cambridge: University Press, 1916.

Sandys, J. E., *A History of Classical Scholarship.* Vol. I. Cambridge: University Press, 1903.

Seymour, Thomas D., *Life in the Homeric Age.* New York: The Macmillan Co., 1907.

Stobart, J. C., *The Glory that was Greece: A Survey of Hellenic*

Culture and Civilization. 3rd ed. rev. London: Sidgwick and Jackson Ltd., 1933.

Taylor, Henry O., *Ancient Ideals.* Vol. I. London: The Macmillan Co., 1900.

Thucydides, Vols. I-IV. Translated by C. Forster Smith. Loeb Classical Library. New York: G. P. Putnam's Sons, 1919-23.

Tucker, T. G., *Life in Ancient Athens.* New York: The Macmillan Co., 1922.

Turner, William, *History of Philosophy.* Boston: Ginn and Co., 1903.

Van Hook, La Rue, *Greek Life and Thought.* New York: Columbia University Press, 1930.

Walden, J. W. H., *The Universities of Ancient Greece.* London: George Rutledge and Sons, 1912.

Weller, Charles H., *Athens and its Monuments.* New York: The Macmillan Co., 1913.

Xenophon, *Memorabilia.* Translated by E. C. Marchant. Loeb Classical Library. London: William Heinemann, Ltd., 1923.

CHAPTER VIII

ROMAN EDUCATION

The history of Roman education falls naturally into three general periods which, broadly speaking, are determined by the introduction of Greek culture: the first, that from the foundation of the Republic down to 250 B.C., the old Roman period, when Roman culture knew no Greek influence; the second, extending from 250 B.C. to 146 B.C., the time of foreign conquest, the transitional period, during which Greek culture was gradually introduced; and the third, from 146 B.C. to the fall of the Empire, when the culture of the nation was actually Graeco-Roman.

The traditional date of the founding of the city of Rome is 753 B.C. According to ancient Roman legends the city was founded by Romulus and Remus, twin brothers born to Rhea Sylvia who was forced to become a vestal virgin. At the order of her uncle, Amulius, the twins were to be drowned in the Tiber, but were exposed on the hillside instead and nursed by a she-wolf. When Romulus and Remus had grown up they resolved to build a city on the same spot in which they had been rescued from death and so to perpetuate the memory of their deliverance.

The details of Rome's history as given by ancient writers are discredited by modern historians.[1] It is certain that for a time Rome was a petty city-state ruled by kings who engaged in frequent wars with their neighbors, and that the Tarquins, the last dynasty of kings, were overthrown in the sixth century B.C. Very probably this dynasty was Etruscan. From the Etruscans the Romans learned to write and by them they were

---

[1] Eustace H. Miles, *A History of Rome* (London: Grant Richards, 1901), pp. 89-99.

taught to build temples for their gods in the Etruscan style. The majority of Rome's citizens were farmers who, forced to defend the city and the fertile plain of Latium against the attacks of less civilized neighbors, became schooled in the art of war.

In 509 B.C., Rome became a republic. The government was in the hands of an aristocratic senate because, like all other ancient peoples, the Romans were divided into classes. The patricians held all the privileges of public office until the Laws of the Twelve Tables were drawn up which gave the plebeians the right of intermarriage with the patricians and also the right to hold the highest offices in the state. The social distinction, however, between patrician and plebeian continued; and later, when emancipated slaves became freedmen and were given the rights of citizens, they and their descendants were looked down upon because of the taint of slavery.

The city proper was built on seven hills, among which in the course of time the Palatine, the Aventine, and the Capitoline were the most important. The Aventine, however, was not embraced in the city walls until the fourth century B.C. The Palatine became the home of the aristocrats; the Aventine of the plebeians; and the Capitoline, similar in importance to the Acropolis at Athens, was the center of government and the sacred precinct of the city. The other hills were the Quirinal, the Viminal, the Esquiline, and the Caelian.

In the beginning, Rome was a small republic, but gradually through conquest it dominated the whole of Italy, the lands immediately around and Asia Minor. The main reason for the extension of Roman rule was that war became a most respectable occupation for a Roman when farming failed; war in those days was identified with the extension of territories. When the boundaries of the republic had been extended, then new occupations were provided by means of new colonies and governorships.[2] So rapidly did the power of Rome develop after the second century B.C. that in reality the republic was an empire. It was inevitable then that the Romans should have adopted an imperial form of government in 31 B.C. From that date down to 476 A.D. is the period of the Empire.

The causes of the fall of the Roman Empire are many. The wonder is, not that the Empire fell, but that it was so slow in falling. Greek civilization has been compared to the beautiful cut rose that has quickly withered away, while Roman civilization has all the characteristics of the hardy oak.[3] The fall of the Empire was the culmination of many factors which had been slowly maturing for at least three centuries. The Empire had been built upon the natural virtues which characterized the old Roman citizen, but eventually the evils of bureaucracy and overtaxation weakened the whole structure. By the middle of the fifth century, German mercenaries took the place of Roman citizens in the army. The disunion between the East and the West gave the invader an opportunity to establish himself within the Roman boundaries and the government of the West passed into his hands.[4]

The Roman citizen in the early days of the republic presented a strong contrast to the Greek. Practical rather than aesthetic, he confined his interests chiefly to

---

[2] *Ibid.,* p. 293.

[3] W. Kane, *An Essay Toward a History of Education,* p. 69.

[4] Roman history is the history of the world for many centuries afterward. On Christmas Day, 800 A. D., the Pope crowned Charles the Great, Emperor of the Romans. This empire in the twelfth century came to be called the Holy Roman Empire. In 1453, the Mohammedans captured Constantinople and put an end to the Eastern Roman Empire. The Holy Roman Empire continued down until the time of Napoleon when, in 1806, the last of the emperors, the Austrian, Francis II, gave up the venerable title.

the home, the family, the welfare of the city; and his virtues were a certain constancy, rugged honesty, and devotion to family and state. The Greek was imaginative and impulsive in action; the Roman was matter-of-fact and judged all things by their usefulness. Passing from Athens to Rome is like passing from poetry to prose; from an artist's picnic to a business house.[5]

The Romans specialized in social organization and law. The Roman genius for organization showed itself in the great world empire that Rome achieved. This empire embraced southern and western Europe, western Asia, and the northern portion of Africa; and included the most diverse peoples and races. Its citizens paid taxes into the same treasury, were tried by the same law, and looked to the same armies for protection. The body of civil law organized by the Romans is even today the basis of the legal systems of most of the Western world.

The Roman ideal in education was the formation of the good citizen. The good citizen was a good soldier and a good warrior. Education was primarily the concern of the family. The family was sacred; it was the important social element and could not be, as in Sparta, subordinate to the state. The father enjoyed supreme authority in the family. He could expose his children or sell them into slavery. The law made him the arbiter of their lives and training.

The education given the child in the old Roman period was supplied by the home. The mother cared for the boy until he was old enough to learn from his father the simple and practical duties of the farmer and the soldier. Every male in early Rome performed military service, and while the father had absolute authority over his child he was held to the duty of preparing him for citi-

[5] Thomas Davidson, *A History of Education* (New York: Charles Scribner's Sons, 1901), p. 106.

zenship. There were then apparently few schools and these were conducted by slaves and freedmen. The only literary instruction seems to have been based on the Laws of the Twelve Tables which were compiled for the government of the city by the decemvirs about 451-450 B.C. The laws defined crimes and penalties and treated of property rights, personal rights, and legal procedures. Boys learned these laws by heart, and if, as is thought, they also understood them, they gained considerable culture, for these were the basis of the magnificent code later given by Rome to the world.

It seems probable that when reading and writing were taught, they were taught in the family and by the father. As Laurie says:

This is the only explanation of the wide diffusion of these elementary arts. In any case, whether by domestic teaching or otherwise, reading and writing, so far as required for purposes of utility, were, at least from the fourth century B.C., widely known among certain classes of Roman citizens . . .[5]

The boy assumed the toga virilis at the age of sixteen, entering then upon the responsibilities of manhood. He was thenceforth more in the company of his father and received his education in the forum and on the military field. At the public festivals the youths chanted the national hymns, so it may be assumed that they had some knowledge of music and poetry.

The chief education, in brief, which the Roman boy received was the moral and religious training of home, and free intercourse with his father and mother. The religion of the hearth was the center-point of the religion of the Roman, and the education was the education of the hearth. In religion a high standard of observance was maintained. Pietas, the ethical basis of the family, extended to the gens, and thus a reflected

---

[5] S. S. Laurie, *Historical Survey of Pre-Christian Education* (New York: Longmans, Green, & Co., 1900), p. 323.

influence on home training was felt . . . What Sparta aimed at giving through its public system and compulsorily, the Roman aimed at giving through the parents, and freely, that is to say, he was content with this, because we cannot say that there was any *conscious* aim. The result was that the Roman had a more genuine and personal morality than the Spartan.[6]

There seems to be no doubt that in this domestic and civic education the virtues we associate with the Roman citizen of the early period were successfully inculcated. The young were religious, reverent, obedient, with a sense of duty toward and an attachment for the family and the state.

In the transitional period, while an occasional school is referred to, domestic education largely prevailed. Through the extension of their political and military power, the Romans came in contact with other civilizations, notably the Greek. Consequently, the Greek language became more current in Rome and the patricians often had their children instructed in it. The first notable evidence of the use of Greek educationally is furnished by the translation of the *Odyssey* into Latin and its adoption as a text in the schools. This took place about 233 B.C. Cultured Greeks who were brought to Rome as slaves, upon obtaining their freedom, opened schools in which to teach the Greek language to Roman youths. One of these, Livius Andronicus, undertook to supply the want of a literature by translating the *Odyssey* into Latin. This translation served to train the young Roman to a better knowledge of his mother tongue and prepared the way for the first beginnings of Latin literature. It seems reasonable to conclude that schools from this time on were more numerous and their instruction more advanced on the literary side.

One of the strongest indications of the rising Greek influence may be seen in the opposition of the conserva-

---

[6] *Ibid.*, p. 322.

tive Romans to it and notably that of Cato. His work, *De liberis educandis*, spoken of by Quintilian as the first Latin treatise on education, was written as a protest against the Hellenic idea of culture and aimed to counteract the growing tendency to preserve studies made popular by the Greeks, especially music and literature. Cato believed the Greek influence to be pernicious and claimed that a dissemination of Greek literature among the Romans would ruin the traditional fabric of Roman society. Through his efforts, the senate in 161 B.C. ordered the expulsion of all philosophers and rhetoricians from Rome. Before Cato died, however, he realized the Greek influence had come into Rome to stay and in the end he himself studied Greek.[7]

In the *De liberis educandis*, the practical character of Roman education is illustrated. The requisites for the young Roman who wished to be an orator, physician, husbandman, warrior, or jurist were outlined. Knowledge for its own sake was condemned. The orator should be a man of sound understanding and uprightness of life. Only a noble man can be a good orator. Cato's counsel for the improvement of young men in oratory has been preserved: *"Rem tene, verba sequentur,"* that is, get a good grasp on your matter and the words will follow. A collection of Cato's sayings was long current in the literature in use in Roman schools and of these many have been preserved in Plutarch.

Two years after the death of Cato, Greece became a Roman possession, in 146 B.C. Greek art treasures, Greek scholars, and even complete libraries were transported to Rome by the conquerors. Along with this culture came the educational ideas basic to it. From this period onward Greek culture is fused with Roman, and

---

[7] Aubrey Gwynn, *Roman Education From Cicero To Quintilian* (Oxford: The Clarendon Press. 1926), p. 40.

the Greek language forms an essential element in a liberal education. Rome had conquered Greece, yet Greece in turn conquered Rome according to the oft-quoted words of Horace: *Graecia capta ferum victorem cepit*. From this time also dates the rise of the schools of the grammarians and rhetoricians, at first considered a menace to society, later flourishing and conducted by Latin scholars. The older education disappeared, but in the adoption of the newer the Romans retained the same practical purpose of an earlier time. They did not cultivate literature for its own sake. Success in public life demanded forensic ability, and oratory became the practical end to which the study of grammar, rhetoric, dialectic, and philosophy led. This fusion of Greek culture with Roman is best seen in the system of schools which the Romans developed in the Graeco-Roman era.

In this period three types of schools may be distinguished corresponding to the stages in a boy's training. The elementary school, which was known by the name "ludus," meaning sport or play, could be entered at about the age of six or seven. Why the elementary school was so called cannot be answered satisfactorily. It might very well be that the term was carefully chosen, lest some other name might act as a deterrent and discourage attendance.[8] There could be learned reading, writing, and the simple operations in arithmetic. The first reading book was the *Odyssey* in Latin. Since the memory was cultivated from the beginning of the child's course, many maxims and poetical selections were, as in later times, copied in writing and learned by heart. Until the first century B.C. the custom of learning the Laws of the Twelve Tables continued. We know from Cicero

---

[8] A. S. Wilkins, *Roman Education* (Cambridge: University Press, 1914), p. 43.

that in his time it was no longer in practice. The alphabet and all kinds of combinations of syllables were taught before words were learned. The pupil wrote on wax tablets with the stylus; and the teacher guided his hand in his first efforts to trace the letters. The fingers and pebbles were used in learning how to count; further steps in numeration were taught by means of the abacus; and sums were worked on the tablets. The discipline of the schools was severe and the rod was in frequent use. A favorite form of punishment was to have the boy held on the shoulders of another while the master beat him upon the bare back.[9] The Romans employed the pedagogus to accompany the boy to and from school. He was often a Greek or Syrian and was engaged to teach the boy conversational Greek.

The elementary school was taught by the litterator. He had to take what he could get in the way of fees and provide his own schoolroom. Any serviceable place was used for elementary instruction. School was held in the open air, in some quiet corner of a street or market place. Instruction was also given on a veranda or in a lean-to attached to a shop or to a house. The litterator was in business the same as any other shopkeeper; his shop was a place where elementary instruction could be purchased.[10] As no real qualifications were required of him, his position in society was of course very humble.

Two forms of grammar schools appear in the Graeco-Roman period, viz., the Greek and the Latin. These furnished the secondary education and might be entered about the age of twelve. The instruction was given by the grammaticus and developed out of the increasing literary work of the ludus. The Greek grammar school,

---

[9] Frank P. Graves, *History of Education* (New York: The Macmillan Company, 1909), I, 247ff.

[10] H. Leclerq, "Ecole," *Dictionnaire d'archéologie chrétienne et de liturgie*, 4, 2, 1732 f.

the first in origin, was usually attended first according to Quintilian, because, as he said, the boy "ought first to be instructed in Greek learning, from which ours is derived." The Latin grammar school came into favor with the rise of Latin literature in the first century before Christ. The curriculum was dominated by grammar, but this embraced, besides the technical study of language as we understand it, a course in literature. With no textbooks, the master taught by dictation and oral explanation of the poets read. While Homer was the first of the Greek poets used, others like Hesiod and the dramatists were later introduced. In the Latin schools Vergil, and later Horace, Lucan, and Statius were regularly studied. Great importance was attached to purity of diction and good expression.[11] For this reason drill was given in the parts of speech and syntax. The best authors were paraphrased and exercises in verse writing were common.

In the course of time the quadrivium or mathematical subjects—arithmetic, music, geometry, astronomy—were taught. These subjects were pursued with that same practical purpose which everywhere differentiates the Roman from the Greek schools. Arithmetic did not go beyond practical calculations, nor geometry further than mensuration. Astronomy, as later in the Middle Ages, enabled one to determine the calendar. Music as a study of rhythm aided in the understanding of poetry and the acquisition of a good oratorical style. The motive for gymnastic exercises continued to be military training. The period of secondary instruction was usually completed when the boy assumed the toga. He could then take up military service, make an immediate preparation for his calling as a farmer, or enter the rhetorical school with a view to a career as lawyer or statesman.

---

[11] Laurie, *op. cit.,* p. 338.

Although until imperial times the social standing of the grammaticus was not very high, he was held in greater esteem than the litterator. The accommodations in his school were far superior to those of the elementary school. The grammar school was provided with benches for the pupils and a high seat for the master, while the assistant sat on a stool. The schoolroom was very often quite pleasant and adorned with mural art pieces. The pupils wrote with pen and ink on parchment placed on their knees.[12]

The rhetorical school, which provided a course of study of two or three years, developed out of the practice of debate which had gradually grown up in the grammar schools. In this school, the rhetor gave the youth that special training in oratory and rhetoric which was designed to produce the finished public speaker. No study appealed more strongly to the ambitious young Roman, whose success in law or public life depended so much upon his oratorical power. Eulogies and pleas for plaintiffs and defendants were delivered by the student and criticized by the master. Special attention was paid to intonation, articulation, and other elements of delivery. While immediately concerned with the techniques of oratory, the student was required to read widely, to learn the rules of rhetoric and to become familiar with the essentials of mathematics, science, law, and philosophy in order that his training might be truly liberal. Although law and oratory were the leading studies in this course, the rhetorical schools of imperial times usually provided instruction in the seven liberal arts.

Still more advanced courses were obtainable in the universities, and it was not unusual for young Romans to take advantage of the opportunities for higher learning offered in such centers as Athens, Alexandria, Apol-

---

[12] *Ibid.*, p. 346.

Ionia, Constantinople, Ephesus, Marseilles, Mitylene, Pergamum, Rhodes, Smyrna, and Tarsus. The distinguished philosophical and rhetorical schools were mainly in the East where the instruction consisted largely of philosophic speculation and scientific investigation. The Roman university was the outgrowth of libraries taken as spoils from the Greek; after the development of Latin literature many more manuscripts were added. The curriculum of the universities of Rome emphasized practical studies just as the three other levels of instruction had done. Although courses in the liberal arts were offered, more attention was given to professional work in law, medicine, architecture, and mechanics. [13]

There was no higher institution of learning beyond the school of the rhetor in Rome until 75 A.D. when Vespasian established a library there made up of manuscripts brought to Rome as part of war plunder. Under the patronage of Hadrian and the later emperors, professors were subsidized, appurtenances were multiplied and the institution, though resembling very much the university at Alexandria, became known as the Athenaeum. [14] In the cities, where libraries had been collected and endowed by the emperors, were to be found the most distinguished rhetoricians of the Empire. During the imperial period, when the government began to give grants of money to all grades of schools, many of them lost their private character and a state system of public schools was inaugurated.

Under the prevailing educational system were produced the great Latin authors of the "Golden Age"—the prose writers: Cicero, Caesar, Sallust, Livy; and the poets: Lucretius, Catullus, Vergil, Horace, and Ovid. In comparison, the succeeding age is called "Silver," al-

[13] Graves, op. cit., p. 264.
[14] Paul Monroe, Text-Book in the History of Education (New York: The Macmillan Co., 1921), pp. 203f.

though it yielded great classic names like Seneca, the philosopher; Quintilian, the educator; Tacitus, the historian; Juvenal, the satirist; and Pliny, the letter-writer. [15] The debt of these poets and prose writers to the varied literature of Greece is obvious, yet as Romans they borrowed in a Roman way and made their borrowings their own and their country's.[16] In the field of art Rome did not produce a single artist of world-wide fame like Phidias or Praxiteles. In architecture the Romans never created a distinctive style of their own like the Doric, Ionic, and Corinthian styles of Greece. Though they borrowed from the Etruscans and from the Greeks, they erected in the course of time magnificent monuments—public buildings, aqueducts, roads and bridges, arches and commemorative columns. In imperial times Roman law reached its highest development. During the reign of Justinian (527-565), through the labors of Tribonian, the Roman law was organized and perfected.

The best exposition of the Roman theory of education is to be found in Quintilian's *Institutes of Oratory* (*De institutione oratoria*). Important elements of the theory may also be had in the *De oratore* and *Brutus* of Cicero, the *Oratorum et rhetorum sententiae, divisiones, colores,* of Seneca, the *De grammaticis* and *De rhetoricis,* of Suetonius, and the *Dialogus de oratoribus,* of Tacitus. [17] As the orator is the highest type of the educated Roman, all of these writers regard the orator as the ideally educated man. All maintain that the orator should be ac-

---

[15] J. Wight Duff, *The Writers of Rome* (London: Oxford University Press, 1923), p. 29.

[16] *Ibid.*, p. 9.

[17] Paul Monroe, *Source Book of the History of Education for the Greek and Roman Period* (New York: The Macmillan Co., 1919), pp. 327-509; *cf.* E. C. Moore, *The Story of Instruction,* I, 336.

quainted with practically the entire realm of knowledge and that he should be primarily a good man.

Quintilian (c.35-c.118) was born in Calagurris, Spain, and came to Rome as a boy apparently to complete his studies. He married a young girl who died at the age of nineteen, leaving him two sons, who also died young. At about the age of thirty he gained distinction in the capital as a lawyer. He taught rhetoric for about twenty years and was the tutor of the grandnephews of Domitian.

The *Institutes of Oratory* treats of the complete training of the orator. It does not deal merely with the professional training in rhetoric, but with education in all its stages from infancy onward. In its twelve books, consequently, it can be considered an exposition of the Roman idea of a complete education.

Quintilian's views, especially those on the physical and moral care of the child and his earliest instruction, were significant for his own time and afterward. He believed in the use of ivory letters as playthings so that learning the alphabet would be pleasant, and recommended the tracing and copying of the forms of the letters for the first steps in writing.[18] He laid great stress on the cultivation of the memory, considering a good memory one of nature's best gifts on the mental side.[19] For this reason he urged the extensive memorizing of passages from the poets, of proverbs and adages. He encouraged emulation on the ground that the child will strive to imitate his fellow-pupils more readily than his teacher. He also treated of imitation and regarded it as a favorable sign in a pupil that he imitate the good deeds of others.[20] He disapproved of corporal punish-

---

[18] Quintilian, *Institutio Oratoria*. Translated in the Loeb Classical Library (New York: G. P. Putnam's Sons, 1921), I, 1, 33ff.

[19] *Ibid.*, p. 55.

[20] *Ibid.*, p. 51.

ment, objecting to it because he believed it as fit only for slaves.

I disapprove of flogging, although it is a regular custom and meets with the acquiescence of Chrysippus, because in the first place it is a disgraceful form of punishment and fit only for slaves, and is in any case an insult, as you realize if you imagine its infliction at a later age. Secondly if a boy is so insensible to instruction that reproof is useless, he will, like the worst type of slave, merely become hardened to blows.[21]

Quintilian directed the teacher to study the different dispositions of his pupils and to respect their tastes and mental capacities.[22] He had a high opinion of the average ability of boys. He maintained that among boys good promise is evident in the greater number; and if in the course of time that promise disappears it is due not to the want of native ability but to lack of skill and intelligent care on the part of the teacher. All pupils need relaxation and for that reason they should be permitted to relieve the strain of study by means of play and games. Study after all depends on the good will of the student and if his mind is refreshed he will bring greater energy to his learning. There are certain games which have a decidedly educational value for boys and at the same time reveal character in the most natural way.[23]

In the choice of books none save those of the best authors should be read and such as "have stood the test of time." Of the ten remarkable orators produced by Athens, the student should first read Demosthenes who is by far the greatest and may be regarded almost as the sole model of oratory. Of the Roman orators, Cicero is the most eloquent. The excellencies of these two ora-

---

[21] *Ibid.*, pp. 59f.
[22] *Ibid.*, I, ii, 265.
[23] *Ibid.*, I, iii, 57f.

tors are for the most part similar, but in their actual
style there is some difference. "Nothing can be taken
from the former, nor added to the latter; the Greek reveals a more studied, the Roman a more natural art."[24]
Of the poets, Homer holds first place among the Greek
authors, while of the Romans, Vergil most nearly ap-
proaches Homer.[25] These poets and orators should first
be read and then those authors who also have a high
standard of literature. All reading should be accompanied with attentive consideration and critical discern-
ment "as if we were actually transcribing what we
read."[26]

Quintilian discusses the question of the relation between the schools of the grammarians and those of the
rhetoricians. Evidently there was contention between
the *grammatici* and the *rhetores* as to when the youth
should pass from the grammar school to the school of
rhetoric. Quintilian defends the claims of the rhetoricians.[27] In a lengthy discussion he also champions the
superiority of classroom instruction over private education at home. He asserts that there are two principal
objections heard against public education: public schools
corrupt morals; and one master can give more attention
to one or a very few pupils. To the first objection, he
answers that morals may be corrupted at home as well
and especially by the bad example of parents. He re-
futes the second objection by stating that the greater
part of the learner's time is devoted to private study.
The master cannot stand over the pupil while he is
memorizing or thinking or writing; and there are moreover certain subjects in which it is desirable that in-

---

[24] *Ibid.,* IV, x, 61.
[25] *Ibid.,* p. 49.
[26] *Ibid.,* p. 15.
[27] *Ibid.,* I, ii, 205 ff.

struction should be given to all the pupils simultaneously.[28]

A strong ethical purpose appears in all phases of Quintilian's scheme of training. He placed upon parents the responsibility of securing for the child from his earliest school days the services of a morally good man as teacher, and upon the teacher, a similar responsibility in caring for the boy's moral formation by the observation of his habits and correction of his faults, and the judicious selection of his studies. His ideal teacher is "free from vice himself and refuses to tolerate it in others." He is endowed with self-control, dignified yet always approachable, judicious in exercising authority, clean of speech and genuinely interested in the duties of his calling.[29]

His perfect orator must be the *vir bonus* as well as *vir peritus dicendi*.

The orator then, whom I am concerned to form, shall be the orator as defined by Marcus Cato, "a good man, skilled in speaking." But above all he must possess the quality which Cato places first and which is in the very nature of things the greatest and most important, that is, he must be a good man.[30]

Finally he would have the orator through the study of philosophy become a man of noble character. "For I do not merely assert that the ideal orator should be a good man, but I affirm that no man can be an orator unless he is a good man."[31] Quintilian's treatise has a significant relation to modern education for it was assiduously read and its ideals reproduced by Renaissance educators during the revival of classical culture.

For a just valuation of Roman education it must be

---

[28] *Ibid.*, I, i, 39-47.
[29] *Ibid.*, I, ii, 211-15.
[30] *Ibid.*, IV, xii, 355.
[31] *Ibid.*, p. 357.

borne in mind that the Roman ideal of education was quite different from that of the Greek. It is customary to belittle the aims of Roman education in comparison with the aesthetic ideals of the Greeks. The significant fact in the history of Roman education is that previous to the time of Graeco-Roman culture the majority of the people received a more purposeful and intelligent sort of training.[32] When Greek models and Greek ideals came to be dominant in Roman education, the influence was that of a decaying Greek civilization and the schools were attended by those whose means and leisure would allow it.

From the beginning, slavery was a part of the Roman social system, but in the early days the number of slaves at Rome was much smaller than in later times when vast hordes of captives after victorious campaigns were carried off to Rome to be treated little better than brute beasts. The serious minded Roman lamented the dire results of an extensive system of domestic slavery which tended to demoralize the children of the masters. In the early republic the slaves were reared in the house and were often the foster brothers of the Roman youths; and sometimes they were citizens who had been compelled by debt to sacrifice their freedom. Consequently, it was far easier to train children to a virtuous life under such circumstances than later when the households became luxurious and extravagant.[33] On the basis of the census of 70 B.C. it has been estimated that the slave population of Italy was twice as large as that of free men.[34]

The position of the Roman woman in society was decidedly higher than that of the Greek; in fact it com-

[32] W. Kane, *An Essay Toward a History of Education*, p. 56.
[33] Wilkins, *op. cit.*, pp. 7f.
[34] T. Mommsen, *The History of Rome*. Translated into English by Dickson (New York: Scribner, Armstrong & Co., 1874), III, 494.

pares very favorably with that of the Hebrew woman.
The Roman mother was highly respected and invariably
was found in the company of her husband. She shared
equal rights with him as is clear from the pertinent
maxim: "Ubi tu Caius, ego Caia." Girls were trained
by their mothers in conduct and in the domestic arts.
The instruction in the way of reading and writing given
to boys was doubtless shared equally by the girls.
Whether the ordinary schools were attended by girls
as well as boys is difficult to determine. Coeducation
may have been the practice in country places, but it
was quite the exception in the capital. Even in the
country, parents who wished to give their daughters a
higher education would be able to provide this, at least
in its earlier stages, by employing slaves who were often
persons of learning and culture.[35]

Religion was an important part of Roman education.
The Roman was serious and devout and felt very deeply
the need of religious and moral training in the formation
of character. He acknowledged the voice of conscience
and made an effort to be guided by it. The child learned
his religious duties in the home. The family hearth
was the center of devotions in each household where
prayers were offered to Vesta, goddess of the fire, to the
Penates, the deities who guarded the house, and to the
Lares, tutelary spirits of the family estate.[36] So intimate was the relation of religion to private and public
conduct that every activity of life, such as birth, marriage, ploughing, harvesting, and war, was under the
auspices of a particular deity who was to be propitiated
by sacrifices or ceremonies. What was best in the Roman religion was due to the common traditional morality taught in the homes of the people. This deep reli-

---

[35] Wilkins, *op. cit.*, pp. 14f; 42f.
[36] *Ibid.*, pp. 10ff.

gious feeling was manifest not only in the old Roman
period, but practically throughout the whole history of
Roman society. That society held together as it did for
so many centuries because the Roman drew strength
from his past history and a religion of patriotism may
be said to have survived.[37]

It is not historically correct to connect the decline of
Roman education with the decadence of Roman society
during the Empire, for the school remained the last
stronghold of pagan life and culture. Grammatical and
rhetorical schools became more numerous then in the
provinces and flourished especially in Gaul, Spain, and
Africa. Many of these schools were supported by the
municipalities. Some of them outlived the Empire itself. The emperors substantially encouraged the foundation of libraries, and endowed some of them. They
conferred distinctions on rhetoricians and grammarians.
Antoninus Pius made the higher teachers a privileged
class, exempting them from taxes, service in the army,
and the obligation of holding municipal office. Some
idea of their number may be seen from the restrictions
he placed upon them. He permitted only three rhetoricians and three grammarians in the smaller towns, and
four rhetoricians and four grammarians in the larger,
and five each in the capitals of provinces.[38]

While schools were multiplied and facilities for education were more extensive, the aim and spirit of Roman
culture had nevertheless declined. With corruption in
the highest offices of the Empire, even in the judiciary,
with a privileged and profligate aristocracy, a heavily
taxed middle class, and a nation wholly lacking in morality, the career of the orator no longer offered political
promise to the young. Education without practical pur-

---

[37] Laurie, *op. cit.*, pp. 308f.
[38] *Ibid.*, p. 395.

pose then became formal and artificial. Only the wealthy attended the higher schools. Attempts were made to restore and rehabilitate ancient culture, notably by Julian the Apostate, but these were as futile as they were short-lived. The schools of the grammarians and rhetoricians were superseded by the episcopal and monastic schools of the early Middle Ages.

FOR FURTHER STUDY

Abbott, F. F., *The Common People of Ancient Rome, Studies of Roman Life and Literature*. New York: Charles Scribner's Sons, 1911.

Cicero, *Brutus*. Translated by G. I. Hendrickson in the Loeb Classical Library. London: Wm. Heinemann, Ltd., 1939.

————, *De oratore*. Translated by Sutton and Rackman in the Loeb Classical Library. London: Wm. Heinemann, Ltd., 1942.

Clarke, G., *Education of Children at Rome*. New York: The Macmillan Company, 1896.

Dill, S., *Roman Society from Nero to Marcus Aurelius*. London: The Macmillan Company, 1904.

Dobson, J. F., *Ancient Education*. New York: Longmans, Green, & Co., 1932.

Duff, J. W., *A Literary History of Rome to the close of the Golden Age*. New York: Charles Scribner's Sons, 1928.

————, *A Literary History of Rome in the Silver Age*. New York: Charles Scribner's Sons, 1927.

————, *The Writers of Rome*. London: Oxford University Press, 1923.

Fowler, W. W., *Social Life at Rome*. New York: The Macmillan Company, 1922.

Friedlander, L., *Roman Life and Manners under the Early Empire*. Translated from the German by Magnus, Freese and Gough. New York: E. P. Dutton and Co., 1928-36. 4 vols.

Gwynn, Aubrey, *Roman Education from Cicero to Quintilian*. Oxford: The Clarendon Press, 1926.

Johnston, Harold W., *The Private Life of the Romans*. Chicago: Scott, Foresman and Co., 1932.

Laurie, S. S., *Historical Survey of Pre-Christian Education*. New York: Longmans, Green, and Co., 1900.

Lodge, G., *Greek Influence on Roman Literature*. New York: Columbia University Press, 1912.

Miles, Eustace, *A History of Rome*. London: Grant Richards, 1901.

Mommsen, Theodor, *The History of Rome*. Translated from the German by William P. Dickson. New York: Scribner, Armstrong and Co., 1874. 4 vols.

Monroe, Paul, *Source Book of the History of Education for the Greek and Roman Period*. New York: The Macmillan Company, 1919.

Moore, Ernest C., *The Story of Instruction*. Vol. I. New York: The Macmillan Company, 1936.

Quintilian, *Institutio oratoria*. Translated by H. E. Butler in the Loeb Classical Library. New York: G. P. Putnam's Sons, 1921-22. 4 vols.

Sandys, J. E., *A History of Classical Scholarship*. Vol. I. Cambridge: University Press, 1921.

Suetonius, *De grammaticis*. Translated by J. C. Rolfe in the Loeb Classical Library. New York: The Macmillan Company 1914.

————, *De rhetoricis*. Translated by J. C. Rolfe in the Loeb Classical Library. New York: The Macmillan Company, 1914.

Tacitus, *Dialogus de oratoribus*. Translated by William Peterson in the Loeb Classical Library. New York: The Macmillan Co., 1914.

Taylor, Henry O., *Ancient Ideals*. Vol. I. New York: The Macmillan Co., 1900.

Walters, H. B., *Art of the Romans*. London: Methuen and Co., Ltd., 1928.

Wilkins, A. S., *Roman Education*. Cambridge: University Press, 1914.

SUMMARY OF ANCIENT EDUCATION

The oldest educational system in history, that of China, inspired by the idea of worship of ancestors and reverence for antiquity, showed no advance for centuries. The Chinese, however, profiting by their contacts with the nations of the West, have recently established schools in accordance with European and American ideas. Japanese education down until 1868 was wholly Chinese in type, but since then the educational practices of Japan have been widely modified as a result of occidental influence. The Egyptians attained to a high degree of civilization and culture, and far surpassed the other nations of antiquity; yet they gave general education no direct recognition. Higher education in Egypt received the chief encouragement and reached its climax in the training of the priests. The rigid caste system of India, with its underlying pantheistic philosophy, tended to stifle all endeavor toward national advancement in science and culture. Hindu education has remained for centuries nonprogressive. In Persia the state directed all educational efforts for its own purposes, chiefly the training of soldiers. The Hebrews, who were affected by the culture of the Babylonians, Assyrians, Phoenicians, and Egyptians, had a most exalted idea of government and education. The education of the Jews was primarily religious and moral and bequeathed to posterity a lofty conception of divine and human relations which prepared for the advent of Christianity.

Greek education, as seen in Sparta, a despotic socialistic state, succeeded in producing a nation of warriors, but failed to develop the elements in training which make for the highest manhood and upon which the real stability of a nation depends. Athenian education was a training for elegant leisure. It aimed to produce the perfect citizen through a harmonious physical, intellectual, and moral development. It lacked stability for a lasting system even from a national viewpoint, since it made foremost the individual without defining sufficiently his relation to the state. The ideals of Athenian education became markedly individualistic and the Sophists particularly indoctrinated the young men of Athens with their views of extreme individualism. Socrates and his immediate successors, Plato and Aristotle, undertook to insure the stability of the national life now placed in danger of disintegration by giving the newer education a solid

157

foundation. The influence of Plato and Aristotle on Greek education of their own day was slight, but on the content of education in the patristic and medieval periods it was quite marked. Greek culture and education have led to some of the most noteworthy intellectual and aesthetic achievements that the world has known. The education of Rome, unlike that of Greece, was decidedly practical in character. Through their absorption of Greek culture, the Romans devised a system of schools consisting of elementary and grammar schools, schools of rhetoric, of philosophy, of law, and also of medicine. Due to their practical bent, the Romans likewise achieved a world empire and perfected a system of law which is the basis of every code in all countries of Western Europe except England.

Part II

Christian Education

SYNOPSIS OF CHRISTIAN PERIOD

1. Early Christian Education

    (a) The teaching of Christ
    (b) The teaching Church

    (1) Catechumenal school   } Catechumenate — fullest
    (2) Catechetical school   } development in fourth
                                and fifth centuries.

2. The Patristic Period: The Educational Activities of the Fathers of the Church

    (a) Fathers of the East

        St. Justin Martyr
        Clement of Alexandria
        Origen
        St. Cyril of Jerusalem
        St. Basil the Great
        St. Gregory of Nyssa
        St. Gregory of Nazianzus
        St. John Chrysostom

    (b) Fathers of the West

        Tertullian
        Lactantius
        St. Ambrose
        St. Jerome
        St. Augustine

3. Connecting Link between Patristic and Early Medieval Periods

    (a) Boethius (480-524)
    (b) Cassiodorus (490-583)
    (c) St. Isidore of Seville (560-636)

The

period

from

the

6th

to

the

10th

centuries

has been

called

the

"Dark Ages"

4. Types of Schools at the Beginning of the Medieval Period.
   - (a) Episcopal or Cathedral
   - (b) Song
   - (c) Parish
   - (d) Monastic
5. Carlovingian Revival (8th and 9th centuries)
   - (a) Alcuin of the Cathedral School of York
   - (b) Capitularies
   - (c) Special instructors from Rome
6. Educational Revival in England under Alfred The Great (9th century)
7. The Seven Liberal Arts
8. Education of Women
9. Chivalry
10. Educators of the Carlovingian Period
    - (a) Alcuin
    - (b) Rhabanus Maurus
    - (c) John the Scot
    - (d) Gerbert—Pope Sylvester II

11. Mohammedan Or Saracen Learning
    - (a) Influence on medieval education
    - (b) 10th to 13th centuries
    - (c) Noteworthy in mathematics, natural sciences, medicine and philosophy
12. The Scholastic Movement
    - (a) The period of glory (12th-14th centuries)
      Hugh of St. Victor
      Abelard
      Vincent of Beauvais
      St. Albertus Magnus
      St. Bonaventure
      St. Thomas Aquinas
      Roger Bacon
      Duns Scotus
      William of Occam
13. The University Movement
14. Religious Orders and Educators of the Scholastic and University Period

15. Types of Later Medieval Schools
    (a) cathedral
    (b) monastic
    (c) parish
    (d) song
    (e) town
    (f) venture
    (g) chantry
    (h) guild

CHAPTER IX

EARLY CHRISTIAN EDUCATION

With the teaching of Jesus Christ a new era began in the history of education. The loftiest truths of religion and the highest form of morality were made known by Him, and not merely to a chosen group of philosophers, or to a single nation, but to all mankind. As the Redeemer, He came to restore fallen man to a lost birthright—the friendship of God—and His sublime message of hope and salvation was extended to all. As the Man-God, He raised man to a new dignity, to the dignity of a son of God by adoption and an heir to the heavenly kingdom. All men became His brethren, rejoicing in a sonship under a common Father, and bound by the ties of love for one another. There were to be no castes or classes among them, for God is no respecter of persons.

For His followers, earthly life took on a new significance. This world could not be regarded as a lasting home, but a temporary dwelling place in which the soul prepared for a perfect existence in a future, eternal life. Consequently, its hardships and sorrows were made endurable, and even sweet, since they afforded opportunities for increasing virtue and greater attachment to the things of the spirit. Man learned to seek the things that are above and not the things that are upon the earth, and, with a certain knowledge of the nature of this destiny, there came an appreciation of the individual and his place in society that the world had never before known. The condition of woman was thereby immeasurably elevated over her state in pagan civilization. She was no longer the chattel or slave of man, but his companion who shared an equal dignity with him before the Creator. Marriage became a holy union, a sacrament; motherhood

164

was blessed; and children were held to be the gifts of God. They were the objects of Christ's special dilection, and were held up by Him as the embodiments of that innocence and purity He desired to see in His followers. For their training in the knowledge and fear of the Lord the parents were directly responsible.

With the Christian conception of life came distinctly new ideals in culture and education, and when we consider the subsequent influence of these ideals in shaping educational theory and practice for two thousand years, we realize how fittingly Jesus Christ is called the Great Teacher of Mankind, and how justly His Church is regarded as the greatest educational institution in history.

The Teaching of Christ

The Divine Master possessed all the qualifications of the perfect teacher and, in His infinite wisdom, a complete mastery of the truths He taught. His method of teaching consequently must have reflected this perfection; it must have been perfectly suited to the nature of His doctrine, and to the character of those whom He sought to instruct. Hence the study of His life and work from the educational viewpoint is of great historical and practical value. We may here note in brief outline some of the elements observable in His method which are important in the history of education.

Since our Lord taught by oral and personal instruction, the influence of His presence, His voice, and all those indefinable qualities which constitute the teacher's peculiar force, should not be lost sight of. He constantly associated with His immediate followers, gained their confidence, and expounded His doctrine to meet their special needs. He imparted to them the superior knowledge reserved for those who were to teach the mysteries of the Kingdom of God. He encouraged their questions, rebuked them when they did not ask Him of things uppermost in their minds, and, in general, provoked their wonderment and curiosity. They called Him Rabbi—Master.

Not only the Apostles, but the people generally were affected by Christ's teaching power. They declared that He taught with authority, and not as the Scribes and Pharisees, and they showed by their interest in Him, and by their eagerness to hear Him, how attractive both His manner and doctrine were. They proclaimed Him a great teacher.

An invariable practice with our Lord was to prepare the mind for the truths of His message, and the greater the truth the more detailed the preparation. The teaching of the Real Presence had been foreshadowed by the miracle of the multiplication of the loaves and fishes, and according to St. John, it was not given until the most apparent objections to it had been heard and answered. The frequent references of our Lord to the Old Testament, as prefiguring many things He came to teach, are well known. St. Matthew's Gospel abounds in such instances. Of Nicodemus who questioned Him, He asked, "Art thou a master in Israel and knowest not these things?"[1] The teaching of St. John the Baptist was, in the order of divine Providence, a preparation of the Jewish people for the message of Christ, and it was so referred to by Him when St. John's mission was completed.

There is noticeable in the method employed by our Lord a twofold adjustment to the needs and conditions of the time. First, the general adaptation of sublime and abstract truths to the capacity of the human intelligence; second, the particular application of these truths to individual instances, to certain classes of so-

---

[1] John 3:10.

ciety, to the people of certain localities, or of peculiar occupations in life, as e.g., the rich young man, the Pharisees, the townspeople, fishermen, and tillers of the soil. The first adjustment was accomplished by presenting the truths in plain and simple language intelligible to all; the second, by using forms of speech and illustrations which furnished concrete embodiments of His ideas and were entirely within the comprehension of those addressed. Again, He took some familiar thing in the natural or social order and attached his lesson to it. In this way His doctrine was not only expressed but its assimilation was rendered easy. It was inseparably correlated with the previous knowledge of His hearers; it was associated with the truths of nature and experience, and its retention provided for. The farmer could not forget the parable of the sower, the Pharisees that of the husbandman and his wicked servants, and the people generally that of the marriage feast; nor could they fail to see their application. The lilies of the field, the birds of the air, the sheepfold: all had sublime lessons permanently associated with them.

Finally, our Lord was the living model of His teaching. "Learn of Me because I am meek and humble of heart."[2] He gave example as well as precept. "Follow Me," was the first invitation to the Apostles and the first injunction He placed upon them. They were to imitate Him and represent Him before the faithful; like St. Paul they were to say, "Be ye followers of me as I also am of Christ."[3] Furthermore, our Lord insured the perpetual teaching of His doctrine by making His church a teaching body under the guidance of the Spirit of Truth. He empowered her to teach all men and promised He would remain with her to the consummation of the world.

[2] Matthew 11:29.
[3] I Cor. 4:16.

Going therefore, teach ye all nations; baptizing them in the name of the Father, and of the Son, and of the Holy Ghost. Teaching them to observe all things whatsoever I have commanded you: and behold, I am with you all days, even to the consummation of the world.[4]

The Teaching Church

That the Church was fully conscious of the teaching office committed to her, the history of Apostolic times amply testifies. She was naturally in the beginning engaged in moral and religious teaching. Since she was charged with the task of winning the world to Christ, her instruction at first related to the content of the New Dispensation and the moral obligations it implied; but, in consequence of this teaching mission and the circumstances of life in a pagan environment, it was not long before she undertook to teach, or to provide for the teaching of, matters that were not purely religious. In those early days the Church was definitely an educational institution, although the intellectual element which we associate with learning was far overshadowed by the moral and religious aspects of her doctrine. She was teaching her children how to live, and the sphere of her activity embraced the home as well as the Church. In fact, it was only when the discipline of the family began to wane and the home was frequently found incapable of imparting the moral training deemed essential for the young, that the Church took upon herself the responsibility of providing for their complete elementary training.

From the very beginning the Church adopted in her organic teaching many of the principles that are today held as essential in educational procedure. Her ritual, with its appeal to the mind through the senses, with its symbolism, with its demand for cooperation in prayer

---

[4] Matthew 28:19-20.

and ceremony on the part of the faithful, with the sacraments, as the outward or objective signs of interior grace, with the veneration and imitation of the saints, incorporated some of the soundest psychological principles. Furthermore, she demanded a practical manifestation in life and conduct of the doctrine learned.

The first Christian schools arose to meet the practical need of instructing converts from paganism. Those that we know as the *Catechumenal Schools* provided the instruction and training then required as a preparation for the Sacrament of Baptism. The instructors in the earliest of these schools were the bishops, priests, and deacons; but in the later schools minor clerics and laymen held the office of catechist or instructor. The pupils were of two classes: the inquirers, those who came to learn of the Christian religion and were not yet accepted as candidates for Baptism; and those who after a systematic course of instruction were accepted and properly called catechumens. The content of instruction embraced the doctrines of the Church, the ritual, and the observances of the Christian life. The method of testing the knowledge of the catechumens was that of question and answer—the catechetical. The candidates not only received this intellectual formation but they also underwent an ascetical and liturgical training; and only after years of probation, during which they proved their fitness, were they declared worthy to receive Baptism and be numbered among the faithful. When persecutions ceased and there was less danger of apostasy, the time of probation was shortened, and during the reign of Pope Gregory the Great (590-604) it was reduced to forty days.

Some schools offered more advanced instruction in the Christian faith with a view to counteracting the attacks of pagan adversaries. These are known as the *Catechetical Schools*. They were in reality the higher schools or academies of philosophy and theology. Having originated at episcopal sees, they also served as seminaries for the training of the clergy. The most famous of these schools was established at Alexandria about 179 A.D., and some of the most learned Fathers of the early Church were its teachers. Pantaenus, probably its first great teacher, was a converted pagan philosopher. He naturally sought to adjust his instruction to meet the more subtle questions of the Greek schools of thought. In the time of Clement (†217) and Origen (†254), the curriculum was extended and included courses in Greek literature, history, dialectics, and the sciences. In a panegyric on Origen by Gregory Thaumaturgus, his pupil, we have a graphic account of Origen's school at Caesarea. This is considered the best extant description of a Christian school of the third century. A most interesting detail refers to Origen's interest in physics and the natural sciences.

Nor did he confine his efforts merely to that form of the mind which it is the lot of dialectics to regulate; but he also took in hand that humble capacity of mind (which shows itself) in our amazement at the magnitude, and the wondrousness, and the magnificent and absolutely wise construction of the world, and in our marvelling in a reasonless way, and in our being overpowered with fear, and in our knowing not, like the irrational creatures, what conclusion to come to. That, too, he aroused and corrected in other studies in natural science, illustrating and distinguishing the various divisions of created objects, and with admirable clearness reducing them to their pristine elements, taking them all up perspicuously in his discourse, and going over the nature of the whole, and of each several section, and discussing the multiform revolution and mutation of things in the world, until he carried us fully along with him under his clear teaching; and by those reasonings which he had partly learned from others, and partly found out for himself, he filled our minds with a rational instead of an irrational wonder at the sacred economy of the universe and the irreproveable constitution of all things. This is that sublime and heavenly study which is taught by natural philosophy —a science most attractive to all.[5]

Other famous Catechetical schools flourished at Antioch, Caesarea, Edessa, Nisibis, Rhinocorura in Egypt, Jerusalem, and Carthage. The Catechumenate, as the whole institution was called, reached its fullest development in the fourth and fifth centuries and gradually disappeared after the eighth. With the victory of Christianity over paganism, the elaborate preparation for Baptism was no longer necessary. In later centuries, however, the catechumens themselves very often prolonged the period of probation, either because they feared the severity of Christian life or because they desired that their spiritual rebirth take place at the hour of death.[6]

FOR FURTHER STUDY

Ayer, Jr., J. C., *Source Book of Church History for the First Six Centuries.* New York: Charles Scribner's Sons, 1913.

Battifol, Pierre, *Primitive Catholicism.* Translated from the fifth French edition by L. Brianceau. New York: Longmans, Green, and Co., 1911.

Dawson, Christopher, *Progress and Religion.* New York: Sheed and Ward, 1938.

Duchesne, Louis, *The Early History of the Church.* 3 vols. English translation, London: John Murray, 1909-24.

Eby and Arrowood, *History and Philosophy of Education Ancient and Medieval.* New York: Prentice-Hall, Inc., 1940.

Fuerst, A. N., *The Systematic Teaching of Religion.* New York: Benziger Brothers, 1939. Chapter III.

Funk, F. X., *Manual of Church History.* 2 vols. London: Burns and Oates, Ltd., 1914.

---

[5] Gregory Thaumaturgus, *Oration and Panegyric Addressed to Origen*, translated in *The Ante-Nicene Fathers*, A. Roberts and J. Donaldson, editors (New York: Charles Scribner's Sons, 1925), VI, 30.

[6] A. N. Fuerst, *The Systematic Teaching of Religion* (New York: Benziger Brothers, 1939), pp. 29 f.

Goodier, A., *The Public Life of Our Lord Jesus Christ.* London: Oates and Washbourne, 1930.

Harnack, A., *The Mission and Expansion of Christianity in the First Three Centuries.* Translated from the German by James Moffatt. 2 vols. London: Williams and Norgate, 1904-05.

Hummel, Sister Mary Louis, *The Principle of Apperception in the Teaching of Christ.* Washington, D. C.: The Catholic University of America, 1924.

Kidd, B. J., *History of the Church to A. D. 461.* 3 vols. Oxford: The Clarendon Press, 1922.

Lebreton, J., *La vie chrétienne au premier siècle de l'Eglise.* Paris: B. Grasset, 1927.

Magevney, E., *Christian Education in the First Centuries.* New York: The Cathedral Library Association, 1907.

Newman, John H., *The Arians of the Fourth Century.* New York: Longmans, Green, and Co., 1891.

New Testament.

Pace, E. A., "How Christ Taught Religion," *Catholic University Bulletin,* 14:8, December, 1908.

Ramsey, W. M., *The Church in the Roman Empire before A. D. 170.* 6th ed. London: G. Putnam's Sons, 1900.

Shahan, Thomas J., *The Beginnings of Christianity.* New York: Benziger Brothers, 1903.

CHAPTER X

FATHERS OF THE CHURCH

The Fathers of the Church and the early Christian writers very naturally took a deep and practical interest in education. As bishops, they were conscious of their duty to safeguard the faith of those entrusted to their care and to defend the educational rights of Christians; and, as instructors in the Catechetical schools, they were anxious to adopt the most effective methods of teaching the prospective converts. The elaborate system of religious instruction developed in the Catechetical schools is one evidence at least of the fact that the early Christian Fathers were not merely educational theorists but practical educators as well. In the patristic literature of the Eastern and the Western Church are found many treatises of an educational nature. Some of them are of general interest, dealing with the larger questions of the value or excellence of human wisdom, its utility in the exposition and defense of religious truth, while others discuss the practical problems of catechizing the adults and the young.

St. Justin Martyr (c.100-165) was a convert to the Faith from the ranks of the philosophers. Born of heathen Greek parents in the pagan town of Flavia Neapolis, in Palestinian Syria, he became a Christian when he was about thirty years of age and probably at Ephesus. He taught and defended the Christian religion first in Asia Minor and later in Rome where he conducted a Catechetical school and where he was martyred about 165.[1]

Justin was the first of the Church Fathers to essay a philosophy of Christian thought. His three extant

---

[1] A. W. F. Blunt, editor, *The Apologies of Justin Martyr* (Cambridge: The University Press, 1911), p. x, note 1.

works are the two *Apologies* and the *Dialogue*.[2] The two *Apologies* are actually one because the second is a continuation of the first and dependent on it. The aim of the *Apologies* is to show how Christianity can be reconciled with whatever of truth there is in pagan science and in the attempt to do this Justin makes the doctrine of the *Logos* the key of his philosophical position and insists on its excellence and truth.

The *Dialogue* is with Trypho, possibly Rabbi Tarpho, the most celebrated Israelite of that time.[3] The work is in part an account of real discussions between the author and learned Jews and in part an independent study of the claims of Christianity. The value of Justin's writings lies in the historical position of their author in the development of Christian thought and in their record of the early efforts made to justify Christianity to the Graeco-Roman world.[4]

Clement of Alexandria (c.150-215 or 216) has already been noted in connection with the Catechetical School of Alexandria where he was first the colleague and afterwards the successor of Pantaenus. Clement like Justin Martyr undertook to establish Christianity as a philosophy. The educational theories and principles of Clement are best expressed in his *Exhortation to the Greeks*, *The Pedagogue*, and the *Stromata* or *Miscellanies*, all three of which must be read to get a comprehensive view of his educational doctrine.

The *Exhortation to the Greeks* is similar in purpose to the *Apologies* of Justin Martyr. The *Pedagogue* is definitely pedagogical and practical in tone. It emphasizes moral education and cautions the student not to put

---

[2] Otto Bardenhewer, *Patrology*. Translated by Thomas J. Shahan. (St. Louis: B. Herder Co., 1908), p. 52.
[3] *Ibid.*, p. 52.
[4] John E. Sandys, *A History of Classical Scholarship* (Cambridge: Cambridge University Press, 1906), I, 332.

secondary things first. The Instructor or Pedagogue is Christ of whom he says: "Our Instructor is like His Father, God, whose Son He is, sinless, blameless, and with a soul devoid of passion, God in the form of man. Being practical, not theoretical, His aim is to improve the soul, not to teach, and to train up to a virtuous, not to an intellectual life."[5] The *Pedagogue* rightly regards physical training as an integral part of a comprehensive education. Consequently, it treats in detail matters pertaining to physical development, recommending wrestling, ball playing, and walking for boys, active domestic employment for girls, and manual occupations, such as handling the hoe, turning the mill, and cutting wood, for men.

In the *Stromata* are many beautiful reflections on the purpose of education and the benefit of culture for the Christian. With regard to the value of human knowledge Clement writes: "I call him truly learned who brings everything to bear on the truth; so that from geometry, and music, and grammar and philosophy itself, culling what is useful, he guards the faith against assault."[6] There is a chapter on the superiority of right conduct over right speaking.

Origen (185 or 186-254 or 255), whose entire career was spent in teaching and writing, has been mentioned above in connection with the course of instruction in the Catechetical school. From the account of his school left by his pupil Gregory Thaumaturgus we can gain an idea both of the courses and of the methods of instruction. He is the first great scholar among the Church Fathers.[7] His dogmatical and ascetical writings, his

[5] *The Instructor*, translated in *The Ante-Nicene Fathers*. Alexander Roberts and James Donaldson, editors (New York: Charles Scribner's Sons, 1925). II. 209f.

[6] *Miscellanies*, translated in *The Ante-Nicene Fathers*, II, 309f.

[7] Sandys, *op. cit.*, p. 341.

defense of Christianity against the pagans and Jews, his commentaries on the Scriptures, were so numerous that he is considered the most voluminous Christian writer of the Ante-Nicene period. Many of his treatises are reproductions of his discourses. His great work is the *De principiis* in four books. In this treatise Origen christianized Hellenism and constructed out of the elements of the Creed taught the catechumens a synthesis of the Christian Faith which is the first summa of theology ever organized in the Church.[8] The work, however, was not free from error. It reveals traces of Neoplatonism and the influence of Gnosticism which was masquerading as the true Christianity.

As a foundation of his theological studies Origen prepared a monumental critical edition of the Bible containing six parallel columns in fifty large rolls of parchment known as the *Hexapla*. In the first column he placed the Hebrew text; in the second the Hebrew text in Greek. Four other columns followed with the Greek versions of Aquila, Symmachus, the Septuagint, and Theodotion. The work, though not primarily one of textual criticism, served to show the relation of the Septuagint to the Hebrew text and to the other Greek versions.[9]

St. Cyril (c.315-c.386), Bishop of Jerusalem, was appointed a teacher in the Catechetical school of Jerusalem after his ordination to the priesthood. Twenty-four lectures, *Catecheses*, or catechetical instructions, which he delivered to the catechumens, have been preserved. The first eighteen were addressed to the candidates for Baptism and the remainder to the newly baptized. As the Jerusalem of his day was inhabited by men of many different races and degrees of culture, it

---

[8] James M. Campbell, *The Greek Fathers* (New York: Longmans, Green, and Co., 1929), p. 39.

[9] Bardenhewer, *op. cit.*, p. 147.

is very probable that the slave, the soldier, the young man of the world, and the public officer sat next to each other and were instructed in the same group.[10] The *Catecheses* are among the most precious treasures of Christian antiquity. They are a record of what doctrines were taught to these classes of pupils and of the order of treatment, and are of especial importance in the history of catechetics.

Around *St. Basil the Great* (c.331-379) are grouped three great Fathers of the Oriental Church all of whom by their lives and writings affected early Christian education. St. Basil received a literary education at Caesarea, Constantinople, and Athens, where he was a fellow student of St. Gregory Nazianzus. He gained a reputation for learning even in youth. When he retired from the world to lead an ascetic life, St. Gregory of Nissa, his brother, and St. Gregory Nazianzus joined him. In 370, after the death of Eusebius, he became archbishop of Caesarea.

His Rule for Monks, which organized monastic life in the East, has survived in the Greek Church. It was written in two parts—the larger and the shorter rules—but Rufinus combined the two in his Latin translation of them under the title *Regulae sancti Basilii episcopi Cappadociae ad monachos*. By means of questions asked by the disciple and answered by the master, St. Basil lays down principles for the guidance of superiors and subjects in their conduct based upon a verse or several verses of the Bible. The questions deal for the most part with the virtues of poverty, obedience, renunciation, and self-abnegation, which the monks should practice, and the vices they should avoid.

The treatise of St. Basil on the study of pagan litera-

---

[10] Geraldine Hodgson, *Primitive Christian Education* (Edinburgh: T. and T. Clark, 1906), p. 169.

ture, *To Young Men, On How They Might Derive Profit From Pagan Literature*, favored the judicious use of pagan authors in the education of Christian youth. Some famous passages are the following:

Now to that other life the Holy Scriptures lead the way, teaching us through mysteries. Yet so long as, by reason of your age, it is impossible for you to understand the depth of the meaning of these, in the meantime, by means of other analogies which are not entirely different, we give, as it were in shadows and reflections, a preliminary training to the eye of the soul.

.   .   .   .

These same observations I must make concerning the writers of prose also, and especially when they fabricate tales for the entertainment of their hearers. And we shall certainly not imitate the orators in their art of lying. For neither in courts of law nor in other affairs is lying befitting us, who have chosen the right and true way of life, and to whom refraining from litigation has been ordained in commandment. But we shall take rather those passages of theirs in which they have praised virtue or condemned vice. For just as in the case of other beings enjoyment of flowers is limited to their fragrance and colour, but the bees, as we see, possess the power to get honey from them as well, so it is possible here also for those who are pursuing not merely what is sweet and pleasant in such writings to store away from them some benefit also for their souls. It is, therefore, in accordance with the whole similitude of the bees, that we should participate in the pagan literature. For these neither approach all flowers equally, nor in truth do they attempt to carry off entire those upon whom they alight, but taking only so much of them as is suitable for their work, they suffer the rest to go untouched. We ourselves, too, if we are wise having appropriated from this literature what is suitable to us and akin to the truth, will pass over the remainder. And just as in plucking the blooms from a rose-bed we avoid the thorns, so also in garnering from such writings whatever is useful, let us guard against what is harmful. At the very outset, therefore, we should

examine each of the branches of knowledge and adapt it to
our end, according to the Doric proverb, "bringing the stone
to the line." [11]

The views expressed in this treatise influenced not only
monastic education in the East but Christian education
generally in the Middle Ages and especially in the
Renaissance. By the close of the Early Renaissance
period twenty editions of the tract had been published.[12]

St. Basil was responsible for the early education of
his younger brother, *St. Gregory of Nissa* (†394), who
became a professional rhetorician and was for a time,
it is believed, excessively devoted to pagan culture. He
was won back to Christian studies and practices through
the influence of St. Basil. St. Gregory was a prolific
writer on dogmatic and exegetical subjects. His work
on Catechetics in forty chapters, called the *Great Catechism (Oratio catechetica magna)*, is dedicated to Christian teachers, and is a defense of Christianity against
Gentiles, Jews, and Arians. It defines the Christian attitude towards pagan culture and philosophy. The treatise
was intended for catechists and abounds in directions
to teachers regarding the method of instructing different
classes of converts to Christianity. This explains why
the psychological rather than logical approach is in evidence throughout the work because its art and its appeal
are pedagogical.[13]

St. Gregory of Nazianzus (c.330-389 or 390) was
carefully reared by his mother, St. Nonna. His formal
education he received at Caesarea in Cappadocia, Cae-

[11] Basil The Great's *To Young Men, On How They Might
Derive Profit From Pagan Literature.* Translated in the Loeb
Classical Library by Roy J. Deferrari and Martin P. McGuire
(London: William Heinemann, Ltd., 1934), IV, 383; 389-93.

[12] Campbell, *op. cit.*, p. 61.

[13] John J. Hayes, "The Educational Principles in *The Great
Catechism* of St. Gregory of Nyssa" (unpublished Master's dissertation, The Catholic University of America, 1934), pp. 49f.

sarea in Palestine, Alexandria, and Athens. He became one of the greatest orators and poets of Christian antiquity, and was described by St. Basil as "A vessel of election, a deep well, or rather the mouth of Christ." He represents the type of early Christian bishop who brought all the culture and learning of his time to the service of the Church. Like St. Basil, he favored the study of Greek literature. His *Accusations Against Julian* (*Orationes invectivae contra Julianum Imperatorem*) were a strong protest against the Apostate's efforts to deprive Christians of higher education.

The orations were composed after the death of Julian and probably were never delivered publicly. They voice the bitter opposition of Gregory to Julian's law of 362 which excluded Christians from the cultivation of secular literature. Gregory protests strongly against this interdict and calls upon all who share his views concerning the higher education of Christians to join with him in his indignation against the efforts to deprive them of it. Holding that learning is more to be desired than noble birth, he says that, next to the joys of eternal life, he holds literature most dear to him on earth.[14]

St. John Chrysostom (344 or c. 347-407) began public life as a lawyer. He had been carefully trained in rhetoric and philosophy, and was successful in his profession. Renouncing the world, he joined the anchorites near Antioch, but because of illness was obliged to forego his austerities and return to the city. After ordination he was appointed Cathedral preacher at Antioch. He became patriarch of Constantinople in 397. St. John Chrysostom ranks as one of the most voluminous writers of the Eastern Church. Seven hundred twenty-two of his works, 238 of which are letters, have been preserved.

---

[14] C. W. King, *Julian The Emperor*. An English translation of the *Orationes invectivae* (London: George Bell and Sons, 1888), p. 67.

Among those of educational value are a work *On The Priesthood*[15] and *A Defense of Monastic Life*.[16] In his sermons and letters he dwelt especially on the necessity of Christian training for the children, first in the home, then in the school. We learn from many of his writings the reasons why he urged parents to send their children to the monasteries for their education. The public schools were beset with too many dangers for Christian youth.

If you have masters among you who can answer for the virtue of your children, I should be very far from advocating your sending them to the monastery; on the contrary, I should strongly insist on their remaining where they are . . . But if no one can give such a guarantee, we ought not to send children to schools where they will learn vice before they learn science, and where in acquiring learning of relatively small value, they will lose what is far more precious, their integrity of soul . . . Are we then to give up literature? you will exclaim. I do not say that; but I do say that we must not kill souls . . .

When the foundations of a building are sapped we should seek rather for architects to reconstruct the whole edifice, than for artists to adorn the walls . . . In fact, the choice lies between two alternatives; a liberal education which you may get by sending your children to the public schools, or the salvation of their souls which you secure by sending them to the monks. Which is to gain the day, science or the soul? If you can unite both advantages, do so by all means; but if not, choose the more precious.[17]

As a writer on pedagogical matters, Chrysostom surpasses all other ecclesiastical authors of the Patristic

---

[15] Translated in *The Nicene and Post-Nicene Fathers,* Philip Schaff, editor (New York: Charles Scribner's Sons, [*n. d.*]), 1st Series. Vol. IX, 33-83.

[16] Migne, *Patr. Gr.* XLVII, I, 319-86.

[17] Quoted from A. T. Drane, *Christian Schools and Scholars* (London: Burns, Oates and Washbourne Ltd., 1924), p. 20.

Period. His educational theories and principles are best formulated in his treatise *De liberis educandis*. John Evelyn,[18] who translated this treatise into English in 1657, calls it the Golden Book of Saint John Chrysostom. There is scarcely any phase of education in relation to child development that is not touched upon in this work. It points out the importance of the home training of the child, shows a sympathetic understanding of child psychology, touches upon the subject of vocational guidance, and outlines a direct training for citizenship. It also treats of the cultivation of the powers of observation, expounds the principles of imitation and emulation as important incentives to effort, and contains a practical discussion on the education of girls. Throughout the treatise the great concern of Chrysostom is the development of a sound Christian character by means of religious and moral training in the earnest effort to bring up "a philosopher, and a champion, and a citizen of heaven." Even to this day his method of sex instruction is considered superior to any other theory advanced on the subject in the history of education.[19]

As in the East, the early Christian Fathers of the West include professional teachers as well as educational writers. Most famous are, of course, the Churchmen who by their writings and discourses influenced Christian thought and culture. There were among them some public men, converts to Christianity, who devoted their lives to teaching.

Tertullian (160-240) was born at Carthage where he was well instructed in all the branches of learning of his time. Sometime previous to 197, he was baptized a Christian and ordained a priest, whereupon he served

---

[18] William Upcott, *The Miscellaneous Writings of John Evelyn* (London: Henry Colburn, 1825), pp. 113-137.
[19] Eby and Arrowood, *The History of Education Ancient and Medieval* (New York: Prentice-Hall, Inc., 1940), p. 605.

the Church faithfully as a pastor and as a writer for the next five years, after which he joined the sect of the Montanists. He later withdrew from the Montanists and founded a new sect of his own whose members were known as Tertullianists. Ecclesiastical writers do not indicate that he ever repented of his folly. He died unnoticed by his countrymen.[20]

Despite his unsound reputation, the writings of Tertullian were abundantly used by his immediate successors and the authors of later centuries. Foremost among his works in defense of Christian belief and discipline is the *Apologeticum* in which with irresistible logical power he demands for Christians the rights of which unjust laws deprive them. His ideas are presented in such a well connected order that the whole work constitutes a methodically written and eloquent composition.[21] In his treatise *On Idolatry* he maintained that the perpetual handling and teaching of pagan mythology by Christian teachers compromised their consciences.[22] He was not opposed to Christians studying pagan literature, but he looked with disfavor upon their teaching it. His penetration led him to see that without secular studies, divine studies could not be pursued effectively. Accordingly, he advised giving Christian children the ordinary Roman education of the day and made the home responsible for the necessary religious instruction by means of which children would be prepared to ignore the praises of the gods to which they listened.

Lactantius Firmianus (c. 250-?330) was a teacher of

---

[20] Abbé Bardy, *The Christian Latin Literature of the First Six Centuries.* Translated by Mother Mary Reginald, O.P. (London: Sands and Co., 1930), p. 31.

[21] Pierre de Labriolle, *History and Literature of Christianity,* translated from the French by Herbert Wilson (New York: Alfred A. Knopf, 1925), pp. 67-70.

[22] Tertullian, *On Idolatry,* translated in *The Ante-Nicene Fathers,* A. Roberts and J. Donaldson, editors, III, 66f.

rhetoric in Nicomedia at the time of his conversion to Christianity. His reputation as a teacher won for him, it is believed, an appointment from the Emperor Constantine to instruct his son, Crispus, which took him to Trier in Gaul when his young charge was sent to that city. He may have died there, but of the place and time of his death nothing is definitely known.[23]

The seven books of his *Divinae institutiones* constitute not merely an apology, but a manual of theology as well. In fact, it is the first attempt by a Western writer to give a systematic exposition of Christian theology.[24] Despite its errors, which show the author's lack of accurate interpretation of the Scriptures, it became a standard work for following generations.

There is no Christian writer from whom we can get a truer notion of the attitude of the Church toward pagan learning than Lactantius. He maintained that, while pagan belief and pagan morals were contrary to Christian faith, there was much in the literature of the pagans that could be drawn on freely for the furtherance of Christian teachings.[25] The classical author that exercised most influence not only on his style but on his whole manner of thinking is Cicero. For his eloquence and purity of style he has been called the Christian Cicero.

St. Ambrose (340-397), a native of Trier, was a fine Latin and Greek scholar, and by profession a lawyer. He held public office in the service of the empire under Valentinian I, and was governor of Aemilia and Liguria when chosen by the people to be bishop of Milan. A forceful orator, he attracted unbelievers as well as Christians to his discourses in the cathedral of Milan

---

[23] Bardenhewer, *op. cit.*, p. 203.
[24] *Ibid.*, p. 205.
[25] Edward K. Rand, *The Founders of the Middle Ages* (Cambridge: Harvard University Press, 1928), pp. 49-63.

and many of those who, like St. Augustine, went to enjoy his eloquence were drawn into the fold. The writings of St. Ambrose comprise doctrinal, moral, and scriptural treatises; sermons; letters; hymns and poems.

His principal work as a moralist is his *De officiis ministrorum*, a treatise in three books. Based on *De officiis* of Cicero and written to instruct his spiritual sons, the ministers of the Church, in their moral duties, it was also intended as a manual of morality for all Christians. Although Ambrose followed Cicero very closely in the arrangement of his ideas and his expressions, the plan of his argument is a challenge to Cicero and the whole pagan scheme of decent conduct. The merit of the treatise lies in the ability of its author to translate the system of Cicero into contemporary terms.[26] It encouraged the study of ancient literature and was of influence throughout the Middle Ages. Some of the orations and sermons of St. Ambrose are models of Latin composition and as such were used in the schools of the Renaissance. His treatises on virginity and the duties of consecrated virgins exerted, according to St. Jerome, a great influence on Christian women of that time.

St. Jerome (331 or 340-420), a native of Dalmatia, now a part of Yugoslavia, studied at Rome under the grammarians Donatus and Victorinus. The former's grammar was the textbook commonly used in medieval schools. St. Jerome became passionately fond of the ancient classics. He tells us that only when warned in a dream of the danger of his excessive devotion to them did he resolve to use them solely for Christian purposes.[27] He became an indefatigable writer and teacher in the service of Christianity. He prepared a Latin text

---

[26] *Ibid.*, p. 82.
[27] *Epist.* XXII. Translated in *The Nicene and Post-Nicene Fathers*, Philip Schaff and Henry Ware, editors (New York: The Christian Literature Company, 1893), 2nd Series, VI, 35f.

of the Bible from the Hebrew and Greek versions at the request of Pope Damasus. This came to be known as the Latin Vulgate, the official version of the Scriptures approved by the Council of Trent. The *Liber de viris illustribus, seu catalogus de scriptoribus ecclesiasticis,* was the first Christian literary history whose purpose was to show the number of literary men Christianity had produced. St. Jerome is important for his views on the study of Latin and other languages, e.g., Hebrew, Greek, which he knew thoroughly, and on the education of girls. The latter are found in his letters to Laeta,[28] and to Gaudentius.[29] His concern for the early moral formation of the child; for care in the selection of teachers; and advice on the practical preparation for the after duties of housewife and mother are clear from the following excerpts taken from his letter to Laeta:

Of this kind must be the education of a soul which is intended for a temple of the Holy Ghost:—Let her not learn to hear or say anything but what savors of the fear of God. Impure language let her not understand, or know anything of worldly songs; while her tongue is yet tender, let its acquaintance be only with sweet psalms. Keep her away from the wantonness of youth; nay, let even her maidens and attendants be debarred all secular connections, lest what they have learned amiss they should teach worse. Let her have letters made of box and ivory, and learn to call them by their proper names; these will amuse her, and thus amusement will become instruction. And let her not only know the letters in their order, so as to repeat their names by rote, but change the order frequently, mixing the middle with the first, and the last with the middle, till she can recognize them by sight as well as sound. But when her trembling hand begins to hold a pen, let its tender joints be guided by the hand of another, placed over hers; or else let the letters be

---

[28] *Epist.* CVII, Migne, Patr. Lat. XXII, I, 867-78; *Nicene and Post-Nicene Fathers,* 2nd Series; VI, 189-95.

[29] *Epist.* CXXVIII, *ibid.,* pp. 1095-99; *ibid.,* 258-60.

engraved upon a tablet, so that she may trace out their forms without wandering from the lines of the engraving. Induce her to put syllables together by rewards, and encourage her with such little gifts as please the mind of infancy.

. . . Then you must look out for a tutor of approved age, and character, and learning; nor will a man of learning blush to do that for a relation, or for a noble virgin, what Aristotle did for the son of Philip, for whose sake that philosopher condescended to the office of a clerk, and instructed him in the first rudiments of knowledge. Small things must not be despised, when great things cannot come to pass without them. The letters themselves, and the first rules of education, sound very differently from the mouth of the rustic and the learned.

. . . Let her every day repeat a lesson culled from the flowers of Scripture, learning a number of verses in Greek, and immediately afterward being instructed in Latin; for if the tender mouth is not properly moulded from the very commencement, the pronunciation will acquire a foreign accent, the faults of which will pass into her native tongue. *You* must be her governess, and the model of her untutored infancy; take care that she sees nothing in you, or in her father, which she would be wrong in doing. Remember that you are her parents, and that she learns more from your example than your voice. Flowers are soon dead; the violet, and the lily, and the crocus soon fade in an unwholesome air. Never let her go into public unless accompanied by you; nor enter the sanctuaries built over the martyr's tombs, or churches, without her mother.

. . . Teach her also the working of wool, to hold the distaff, to place the basket in her lap, to ply the spindle and draw out the threads. But let her have nothing to do with silk, or golden thread. Let the clothes she makes be such as to keep out the cold, and not a mere compromise with nakedness. Her food should be a few herbs, and so forth, with sometimes a few small fishes. But not to go into details on this subject, of which I have elsewhere spoken more at length, let her always leave off eating with an appetite, so that she may be able to read and sing immediately.

. . . You will answer here, How can a woman living in the world, in the midst of so vast a population as that of Rome, look after all these things? Do not, therefore, undertake a burden which you are unable to bear; but as soon as you have weaned her with Isaac, and clothed her with Samuel, send her to her grandmother and aunt. Restore its most precious jewel to the chamber of Mary, and place her in the cradle of the infant Jesus. Let her be brought up in the convent, in the company of virgins; let her never learn to swear; to regard falsehood a sacrilege; be ignorant of the world; live the life of an angel; be in the flesh, but not of it; believe every human being to be of the like nature with herself . . . . Resign to the care of Eustochium the infant whose very cries are even now a prayer for thine own good. Make her the companion of her holiness, hereafter to be its heiress. From her earliest years let her look to her, love her, admire her, whose very words, and gait, and dress, are a lesson in the virtues.

. . . If you only send Paula, I will undertake the office of her nurse and teacher; I will carry her on my shoulders, as old as I am; I will mold into form her lisping words, much prouder of my office than any worldly philosopher, training up not a Macedonian king to die by Babylonian poison, but a hand-maiden and bride of Christ, a fit offering to an everlasting kingdom.[30]

St. Augustine (354-430) ranks as one of the greatest of early Christian educators. Born at Tagaste, in northern Africa, of a pagan father and a Christian mother, St. Monica, he was educated in his native place and in Carthage. In his youth he embraced the Manichean heresy and became a skeptic. He taught rhetoric in the schools of Tagaste, Carthage, Rome, and Milan. While living at Milan he attended the discourses of St. Ambrose, attracted by the eloquence of the orator. Here, too, he renounced his heresy and accepted the teachings of Christianity, attributing his conversion to the instruc-

[30] *Barnard's American Journal of Education,* V, 594.

tions of St. Ambrose and the prayers of his mother who had followed him to Italy. He retired with her into solitude and was baptized a Christian. After her death, he returned to Africa where for a time he led the life of a hermit until he was chosen to fill the episcopal see of Hippo.

Many of Augustine's literary works are of educational value, as, for instance, his *Retractions*[31] and *Confessions*. The former consists of two books in which he reviews the ninety-three treatises he had written as layman, priest, and bishop. While the *Confessions* are in the mind of the author a hymn of praise and thanksgiving to God, they set forth at the same time a complete psychology of the human soul. They portray the whole nature of man; emphasize the importance of the senses in the acquisition of knowledge; analyze the nature and power of memory; treat of learning and thinking; and insist that all teaching is based on faith and authority.[32]

His *City of God* has remained a book for all time. The occasion of this treatise was the urgent need for an exposition of God's providence which confronted Christianity after the occupation of Rome by the barbarians at the beginning of the fifth century. Augustine's answer to the question of the fugitives before the invading armies "Why does God allow it?" evolves the Christian philosophy of history under the aspect of two rival cities —the eternal city of God and the city of the world. History to him is the vast interval between the foundation of the fleeting universe and the last judgment in which the terrestrial story of man must be interpreted in terms of the eternal will of God.[33]

---

[31] *Retractationum* I, ii Migne, *Patr. Lat.* XXXII, 583-656.

[32] *Confessions*, Migne, *Patr. Lat.*, XXXII, I, 779-95; *Nicene and Post-Nicene Fathers*, Philip Schaff, editor (New York: Charles Scribner's Sons [n. d.]), 1st Series, I, 142-52.

[33] Joseph P. Christopher, *St. Augustine: Founder of the Christian Philosophy of History* (Washington: The Catholic University of America, 1931), pp. 8-14.

For the instruction of catechumens Augustine composed his work on *Catechizing the Uninstructed (De catechizandis rudibus)* which contains specimen discourses and indicates the methods for religious instruction that he advocated. In this work the catechist is urged not to confuse the candidate with too much matter, but to insist on what is important and to explain it clearly; to give, as far as possible, individual instruction; to adapt the instruction to the candidate's intelligence; to keep up interest, stimulate self-activity, and avoid tiring the memory; to attend to the bodily comfort of the candidate; to teach with a view of educating the candidate's heart as well as his mind; to have but one central theme, the love of God.[34]

The educational ideas which according to Augustine underlie the teaching process in general are exemplified in a very practical way in the *De magistro*. The *De magistro* of St. Thomas Aquinas, of which more will be said later, is complementary to the *De magistro* of Augustine. Aquinas, in this instance, knew Augustine through the study of his work bearing the same title. In formulating the scholastic theory and philosophy of education, Aquinas bears witness that the *De magistro* of Augustine is a living document.[35]

Scattered through the works of Augustine are separate treatises on the liberal arts. His treatise on *Christian Doctrine,* which was an introduction to the study of the Scriptures, contains his views on the right use of the various disciplines, especially rhetoric, philosophy, and

---

[34] Louis A. Rongione, "Saint Augustine's Principles On The Teaching of Religion as Presented In His *De Catechizandis Rudibus*" (unpublished Master's dissertation, The Catholic University of America, 1940), p. 5.

[35] John W. Tuohy, "The *De magistro* of St. Augustine and the *De magistro* of St. Thomas Aquinas Compared" (unpublished Master's dissertation, The Catholic University of America, 1937), p. 36.

pagan literature. Like Jerome, he employs an allegorical simile wherein he illustrates the use that may be made of secular learning. Just as the Jewish people in the flight from bondage took from their Egyptian masters vessels of gold and silver and appropriated them to their own use by the command of God, so the Christian must take from pagan literature its gold and silver, liberal instruction and some excellent precepts of morality, and adapt them to Christian use.

Moreover, if those who are called philosophers, and especially the Platonists, have aught that is true and in harmony with our Faith, we are not only not to shrink from it but to claim it for our own use from those who have unlawful possession of it. For, as the Egyptians had not only the idols and heavy burdens which the people of Israel hated and fled from, but also vessels and ornaments of gold and silver, and garments, which the same people when going out of Egypt, appropriated to themselves, designing them for better use, not doing this on their own authority, but by the command of God, the Egyptians themselves, in their ignorance, providing them with things which they themselves were not making good use of; in the same way all branches of heathen learning have not only false and superstitious fancies and heavy burdens of unnecessary toil, which every one of us, when going out under the leadership of Christ from the fellowship of the heathen, ought to abhor and avoid; but they contain also liberal instruction which is better adapted to the use of the truth, and some most excellent precepts of morality; and some truths in regard even to the worship of one God are found among them. Now these are, so to speak, their gold and silver which they did not create themselves, but dug out of the mines of God's Providence, which are everywhere scattered abroad, and are perversely and unlawfully prostituting to the worship of devils. These, therefore, the Christian, when he separates himself from the miserable fellowship of these men, ought to take away from them and devote to their proper use in preaching the Gospel. Their garments, also, that is, human institutions such as are adapted to that intercourse with men which is indispensable in this life, we must take and turn to Christian use.[36]

Three Christian writers form, as it were, the link between the patristic period and the early medieval. Their works had an influence on the schools of their time and throughout the early Middle Ages. *Boethius*, the first of these (c. 480-524), was a Roman patrician and statesman. While in the employ of the Ostrogothic King, Theodoric, who resided during the greater part of his reign at Ravenna,[37] he was falsely accused of treasonable relations against the Arian ruler with the Byzantine court, was imprisoned, and finally put to death. Tradition has regarded him as a martyr to the Faith; he has been venerated at Pavia, where he was cruelly executed,[38] as Saint Severinus Boethius.

After learning Greek at Athens, a knowledge of which in the West was uncommon, Boethius entered upon his philosophical studies which were to exercise a marked influence on the growth of Scholasticism. He translated into Latin with commentaries Aristotle's treatises on logic and Porphyry's *Isagoge*. He composed five essays of his own on various branches of logic and also wrote a long but incomplete commentary on the *Topica* of Cicero. Medieval philosophy is indebted to him for much of its terminology. His works formed to a large extent the source from which the schoolmen of the early medieval period learned how to discourse on the five "universals" and on the ten "categories" and to form syllogisms in accordance with the Aristotelian rules of

---

[36] *De doct. chr.*, Migne, *Pat. Lat.*, XXXIV, 3, 63; *Nicene and Post-Nicene Fathers*, 1st Series, II, 554.

[37] H. M. Barrett, *Boethius: Some Aspects of His Times and Work* (Cambridge: University Press, 1940), p. 44.

[38] Bardenhewer, *op. cit.*, p. 629.

logic; he may, therefore, be regarded as the first of the scholastics.[39]

Boethius likewise provided the schools with theological tracts in which he applies to theology the principles of logic. In his efforts to justify to reason, with the help of philosophy, the doctrines of the Church, he began the work which the great scholastics, Albertus Magnus and Thomas Aquinas, carried to its culmination.[40] His treatises on arithmetic and music were widely used by the students of the Middle Ages. The treatise on music was a textbook in schools and universities until long after the Renaissance. The work on geometry which is attributed to him is regarded as inauthentic.[41] He may have written on astronomy; but if so, the treatise has not survived.

His greatest influence, however, was exerted by the *Consolation of Philosophy*,[42] written while in prison. This treatise is a dialogue between Philosophy and Boethius in which the fallen statesman is consoled by realizing that earthly greatness is transitory and that spiritual values must be sought after rather than riches, power, and glory, which depend upon chance. It is only through God that man can be happy. The wise man who encounters misfortune accepts it as a challenge to make fresh progress in knowledge and wisdom.

Although the discussion is truly idealistic there is no mention in it of Christ or of the Christian religion. The

---

[39] de Labriolle, *op. cit.*, pp. 499f. *Cf.* Martin Grabmann, *Die Geschichte der scholastichen Methode* (Freiburg: Herdersche Verlagshandlung, 1909), I, 148-77.

[40] Barrett, *op. cit.*, p. 145.

[41] Bardenhewer, *op. cit.*, p. 620.

[42] *De consolatione philosophiae* libri quinque. Edidit Adrianus A Forti Scuto, S.T.D. (London: Burns, Oates and Washbourne, Ltd. 1935). English translation by H. R. James, in New Universal Library; and by W. V. Cooper, Temple Classics; also revised English translation by H. F. Stewart in Loeb Classical Library.

work gives indication of a wide reading in the literatures of Greece and Rome and is enriched with stanzas of poetry,[43] with stories and historical references. Besides direct quotations from Plato, Aristotle, Homer, and Euripides, and from Latin writers, such as Cicero, Lucan, Catullus, and Horace, there is manifest an intimate knowledge of Vergil, Seneca, Ovid, Juvenal, and Tibullus. In view of this evidence, the charge has been made against Boethius that he was not a Christian, or that, if he were, he abjured the Faith before his death. His several tractates on Catholic theology discredit this interpretation. Moreover, the treatise is a strictly formal dialogue which adheres to the realm of natural truth. In it, Boethius recognized the propriety, which Augustine had already championed, of offering solutions to the complex problems of life which were purely philosophical, but fully in agreement with revealed truth.[44] In medieval times certainly his Christianity was never questioned and his philosophical treatise was a favorite study within the walls of monasteries and in the world outside.

The *Consolation of Philosophy* gave to the Middle Ages a system of logic of enduring value and a philosophical vocabulary with which to expound it.[45] It was an inspiration to Dante as well as to numerous other medieval scholars. It was translated into Anglo-Saxon by Alfred the Great and into English prose by Chaucer; other versions of it in German, French, Italian, Spanish,

---

[43] This form of composition, consisting of prose sections alternating with verse, is Greek in origin. It appeared for the first time in Latin literature in the satires of Varro. Nearer to Boethius' time it was adopted by Martianus Capella in his fantastic treatise: *Marriage of Mercury and Philology*. Cf. Barrett, *supra*, p. 76; Laistner, *infra*, pp. 61f.

[44] de Labriolle, *op. cit.*, p. 505.

[45] M.L.W. Laistner, *Thought and Letters in Western Europe* (London: Methuen & Co., Ltd., 1931), p. 63.

and Greek were made by the close of the early Renaissance. The four hundred manuscripts of it which are extant together with twenty or more commentaries are indicative of the influence of this treatise on Western thought.[46] It is a masterpiece in which the union of the Christian spirit with the classical tradition is perfectly expressed.[47] It not only proves Boethius to be the last of the Romans; but, in employing philosophy for an understanding of ultimate truth, it reveals him as the founder of medieval scholasticism.[48]

Cassiodorus (c.485-c.580) was born of a Syrian family living in Italy and, like Boethius, became a Roman statesman. He held the office of consul after having been governor of Lucania and Bruttium. In 540, when the Gothic kingdom had virtually come to an end, he retired from public life, became a monk, and founded a monastery on his own estate at Vivarium.[49] In a large sense, he was the instructor of the Gothic conquerors in the traditions of their offices and in Roman government.

The creative literary ability he displayed in the midst of a very busy life at court did not cease with the transfer of his activities to the cloister. His monastic writings include serviceable manuals of exegesis of the Scriptures; *Historia ecclesistica tripartita,* in twelve books, which became the ordinary textbook in ecclesiastical history for the medieval period;[50] a grammatical treatise *De orthographia* completed in his ninety-third year as an aid to his monks in the copying of manu-

---

[46] de Labriolle, *loc. cit.*

[47] Christopher Dawson, *The Making of Europe* (London: Sheed and Ward, 1932), p. 65.

[48] Edward K. Rand. *Founder of the Middle Ages* (Cambridge· Harvard University Press, 1928), pp. 154ff.

[49] Thomas Hodgkin, *The Letters of Cassiodorus* (London: Henry Frowde, 1886), p. 50.

[50] Bardenhewer, *op. cit.,* p. 636.

scripts;[51] and the best known of his literary works, *Institutiones divinarum et secularium litterarum* in two books, one of which is a discussion of Christian learning and in general of monastic life, the other a compendium of secular knowledge such as was regarded indispensable to the study of the Scriptures. The twelve books of the *Variae*, prepared during his prefecture, contain a number of official documents and letters composed by him for his sovereign and for himself during his years of public service.

Cassiodorus has merited the title "the father of literary monasticism."[52] His determination to make the monastery the refuge of learning amid the barbarism of his age has earned for him the eternal gratitude of Europe. He had proposed to Pope Agapetus that a school of theology and Christian literature be founded at Rome in imitation of the schools of Alexandria and Nisibis, but the clash of arms consequent on the invasion of Italy by Belisarius prevented the realization of this project. Cassiodorus, therefore, resolved to make his monastery at Vivarium not merely a retreat, but a theological school and a workshop for the multiplication of manuscripts wherein both sacred and secular learning was to be preserved and transmitted to after ages. He set aside and equipped a room for literary work which was called the *scriptorium*. The activity of the copyist was employed in making copies of the Scriptures, of the writings of the Fathers, and of the classics of pagan antiquity. The library of the monastery had a splendid collection of manuscripts made possible through the wealth of its founder and patron.

Cassiodorus wished the monks to be representatives of learning. Though his idea of making the monastery a

---

[51] de Labriolle, *op. cit.*, p. 508.
[52] Hodgkin, *op. cit.*, p. 57.

place of literary toil and of theological training was not absolutely new, he was the first to develop the project systematically and on an extensive scale.[53] The rule of his monastery was drawn from the writings of Cassian; but it was in harmony with the Rule of St. Benedict which admitted literary work and the copying of manuscripts as an approved occupation of the monastery. The early schools of the Benedictines, undoubtedly influenced by the literary work of the monastery of Vivarium, made genuine contributions to the cause of literature at a time when the light of learning was threatened with extinction, and so the immediate followers of St. Benedict may rightly be regarded as Cassiodorians.[54]

The chief educational treatise of Cassiodorus, the *Institutiones*,[55] was the first work completed by him as monk. This was intended as a manual of instruction for his fellow monks. The treatise makes theology the subject of supreme interest, but at the same time emphasizes the importance of a literary training for the proper understanding and teaching of Christian doctrine. It unites Christian culture with pagan learning and strongly advocates the use of literature in the service of the Church. The second part, *De artibus et disciplinis liberalium litterarum,* is particularly of educational interest. It recommends to every monk the study of the seven liberal arts. The superior position of the language studies in relation to the mathematical group in the mind of Cassiodorus is seen from the length of his discussion on logic and rhetoric. The former receives eighteen pages, the latter six; while the mathematical subjects are treated in one or two pages at most.[56] It is claimed that the use of the phrase "the seven liberal

---

[53] *Ibid.,* p. 59.
[54] *Loc. cit.*
[55] Edited by R. A. B. Mynors (Oxford: Clarendon Press, 1937).
[56] Hodgkin, *op. cit.,* p. 65.

arts" is found for the first time in Christian literature
in this treatise.[57]

The course of study which Cassiodorus planned for his
monks included the mechanical arts as well as the liberal. Under the former, he emphasized in particular
the study of medicine and agriculture. The program of
education outlined by him made further utilization of
the established pagan curriculum and contributed to the
development of schools and the progress of scholarship.
Every monk was obliged to study. Provision was made
for individual differences and each was allowed to select his field, but study was obligatory. The sanction
given to a classical education by Cassiodorus led to the
development of an educated clergy who, salvaging the
best from the past, made it an integral part of Christian
culture to be transmitted to posterity.[58]

St. Isidore (560-636) was educated and trained by his
brother Leander, Bishop of Seville. If we are to judge
from the testimony of his writings and from the available information regarding the clerical schools of the
period, Isidore's course of study embraced the liberal
arts, together with some elements of law, medicine,
chronology, and geography. He also had a thorough
training in Scripture, liturgy, and theology. His vast
erudition was not the outcome of instruction under a
master but rather the achievement of a lifetime of
study.[59] He became a prolific writer, and finally was
elevated to the See of Seville.

Throughout his long tenure of the metropolitan see,

---

[57] Paul Abelson, *The Seven Liberal Arts* (New York: Teachers
College, 1906), p. 9.

[58] Sister M. de Chantel Leis, *Christian Utilization of Pagan Educational Facilities.* University of Pittsburgh Bulletin, October 1,
1934, pp. 240f.

[59] Sister Patrick Jerome Collins, *The Spiritual Life According
to Saint Isidore of Seville* (Washington, D. C.: The Catholic
University of America Press, 1940), p. 12.

Isidore strove to counteract the spreading barbarism of his surroundings by the diffusion of education and learning. He erected many educational institutions, produced voluminous works, improved the organization of the Church of Spain, and played a momentous part as theologian and canonist. The codification of ecclesiastical law which is known under the name of the *collectio Hispana* was carried out under his general supervision.[60]

He is chiefly known in the history of education for his *Etymologics* (*Etymologiarum libri* XX), a compendious encyclopedia of general knowledge, sacred and profane, which was the sourcebook of information for centuries afterwards. This work, finished by Isidore only a short time before his death, was written at the urgent request of his friend and pupil, Braulio, who edited the encyclopedia and divided it into books.[61] The subject matter is described with a fanciful etymology, which circumstance gave the name to the whole work.[62] The first three books of the encyclopedia treat of the seven liberal arts, while the remaining books deal with medicine, law, chronology, the Bible, ecclesiastical offices, God, angels, saints, the Church and different sects, languages, peoples, army, citizens, man, animals, the earth, stones, metals, agriculture, botany, war, games, ships, dress, food, drink, and furniture. The ideas of earlier authors whom Isidore quotes on the different branches of knowledge were known to him from compilations current in his time, but the Christian sources on which he relied and many of the classical works he knew at first hand.[63] The variety of subject matter on which he wrote indicates the richness of the episcopal library at Seville in his time. The

---

[60] Laistner, *op. cit.*, p. 91.

[61] Charles H. Lynch, *Saint Braulio, Bishop of Sargossa* (Washington, D. C.: The Catholic University of America, 1938), p. 49.

[62] Bardenhewer, *op. cit.*, p. 662.

[63] Laistner, *op. cit.*, p. 93.

Etymologies furnished much of the material for all medieval dictionaries.

Isidore also composed other works of the same general character. His *Libri duo differentiarum,* a dictionary of words, synonyms, and theological notions, proved useful to the medieval student. Another important and influential work, *De rerum natura,* was an elementary manual of physics which was compiled from the astronomical writings of his predecessors. His *Rule for Monks* was also of considerable influence and gave proof of his deep concern for the formation of the cleric who was charged with the responsibility of preserving learning and culture.

The influence of Isidore's writings on the European mind during the Middle Ages was tremendous. He was known as "the teacher of Spain."[64] It is true that he made few original contributions, either to theological thought or to secular learning; he is mainly a compiler, but his greatest compilation became a standard work of reference. Every monastery library of any importance claimed a copy of his *Etymologies.* Manuscripts of his works in large numbers were in use in the schools of Ireland and from this source the Irish monk acquired an intellectual training that prepared him for the important role played by him in education during the early medieval period.[65]

FOR FURTHER STUDY

Ambrose, St., *De officiis.* Translated in a *Select Library of Nicene and Post-Nicene Fathers,* Philip Schaff and Henry Wace, editors. New York: The Christian Literature Company, 1896. 2nd Series. Vol. X, 1-89.

Augustine, St., *Confessions; De civitate Dei; De doctrina*

---

[64] V. M. Otto Denk, *Geschichte des gallo-fränkischen Unterrichts und Bildungswesens* (Mainz:Verlag von Franz Kirchheim, 1892), p. 215.

[65] de Labriolle, *op cit.,* p. 518.

christiana. Translated in *The Nicene and Post-Nicene Fathers,*
Philip Schaff, editor. New York: Charles Scribner's Sons, [*n. d.*]
Vol. I, 45-207; Vol. II, 1-511; 515-97.

————, *De catechizandis rudibus.* Translated by Joseph P.
Christopher with a commentary. Washington, D. C.: The Catholic University of America, 1926. 15-121 pp.

————, *De magistro.* Translated, under the title *The Philosophy of Teaching,* by Francis E. Tourscher. Villanova, Penn.:
Villanova College, 1924.

Bardenhewer, Otto, *Patrology.* Freiburg-im-Breisgau, 1910.
Translated from the second German edition by Thomas J. Shahan.
St. Louis: B. Herder Co., 1930.

Bardy, Abbé, *The Christian Latin Literature of the First Six
Centuries.* Translated by Mother Reginald, O.P. St. Louis:
B. Herder Co., [*n. d.*].

Basil, St., *Address to Young Men on the Right Use of Greek
Literature.* Translated, in *Essays On The Study And Use Of
Poetry by Plutarch and Basil the Great,* by Frederick M. Padel-
ford. New York: Henry Holt and Co., 1902. 101-20 pp.;
translated, in the Loeb Classical Library, by Roy J. Deferrari and
Martin R. McGuire. London: William Heinemann, Ltd., 1934.
Vol. IV. 379-435 pp.

Belloc, Hilaire, *Europe and the Faith.* New York: The Paulist
Press, 1920. Chaps. I-VI.

Bigg, Charles, *The Christian Platonists of Alexandria.* New
York: The Macmillan Co., 1886.

Boissier, Gaston, *La Fin du paganisme.* Paris; Hachette et Cie,
1894.

Bright, William, *The Age of the Fathers.* London: Longmans,
Green, and Co., 1903. 2 vols.

Campbell, James M., *The Greek Fathers.* New York: Longmans, Green, and Co., 1929.

Cassidy, Frank P., *Molders of the Medieval Mind.* St. Louis:
B. Herder Book Co., 1944.

Chrysostom, St., *Golden Book of, Concerning Education of
Children.* Translated by John Evelyn in the *Miscellaneous Writings of John Evelyn,* by William Upcott, London: Henry Colburn, 1825.

Cyril, St., *Catecheses.* Translated in *The Nicene and Post-*

Nicene Fathers. Philip Schaff and Henry Wace, editors. New York: The Christian Literature Co., 1894. 2nd Series. Vol. VII, 1-157.

D'Arcy, M. C., *et al., The Life of the Church.* New York: The Dial Press, Inc., 1932. 27-159 pp.

Dawson, Christopher, *The Making of Europe.* London: Sheed and Ward, 1932.

Denk, V. M. Otto, *Geschichte des gallo-fränkischen Unterrichts und Bildungswesens von den ältesten Zeiten bis auf Karl Den Grossen.* Mainz: Verlag Von Franz Kirchheim, 1892.

Duchesne, Louis, *Histoire ancienne de l'Eglise.* Paris: 1906-10. 3 vols. English Translation, London: John Murray, 1909-24.

Dudden, Frederick H., *The Life and Times of St. Ambrose.* Oxford: Clarendon Press, 1935. 2 vols.

Fortescue, Adrian, *The Greek Fathers.* St. Louis: B. Herder Co., 1908.

Grabmann, Martin, *Die Geschichte der Scholastichen Methode.* Freiburg: Herdersche Verlagshandlung, 1909. 2 vols.

Gregory of Nazianzus, St., *Orationes invectivae contra Julianum Imperatorem.* Translated, under the title *Julian The Emperor,* by C. W. King. London: George Bell and Sons, 1888. *Panegyric on St. Basil.* Translated in *The Nicene and Post-Nicene Fathers.* New York: The Christian Literature Company, 1894. 2nd Series. Vol. VIII, 395-422.

Gregory Thaumaturgus, St., *Oration And Panegyric Addressed To Origen.* Translated in *The Ante-Nicene Fathers,* Alexander Roberts and James Donaldson, editors. New York: Charles Scribner's Sons, 1925. Vol. VI, 21-39.

Hodgson, Geraldine, *Primitive Christian Education.* Edinburgh: T. and T. Clark, 1906.

Jerome, St., *On Female Education.* Barnard's American Journal of Education, Vol. V, 593-98.

Justin, St., *Apologies, Dialogue with Trypho.* Translated in *The Ante-Nicene Fathers,* Alexander Roberts and James Donaldson, editors. New York: Charles Scribner's Sons, Vol. I, 163-93; 194-270.

Labriolle, Pierre de, *History and Literature of Christianity.* Translated by Herbert Wilson. New York: Alfred A. Knopf, 1925.

Lactantius, *Divinae institutiones.* Translated in *The Ante-Nicene Fathers.* Alexander Roberts and James Donaldson, editors. New York: Charles Scribner's Sons, 1925. Vol. VII, 9-223.

Laistner, M. L. W., *Thought and Letters in Western Europe.* New York: The Dial Press, 1931.

Lalanne, J. A., *Influence des Pères de l'Eglise sur l'education publique pendant les cinq premières siècles de l'ère chrétienne.* Paris: Sagnier et Bray, 1850.

Leigh-Bennett, E., *Handbook of the Early Christian Fathers.* London: Williams and Norgate, 1920.

Migne, J. P., *Patrologia.*

Origen, *De principiis.* Translated in *The Ante-Nicene Fathers.* Alexander Roberts and James Donaldson, editors. New York: Charles Scribner's Sons, 1925. Vol. IV, 239-382.

Rand, Edward K., *The Founders of the Middle Ages.* Cambridge: Harvard University Press, 1928.

Sandys, John E., *A History of Classical Scholarship.* New York: The Macmillan Company. Vol. I, 3rd ed., 1921.

Swete, Henry B., *Patristic Study.* New York: Longmans, Green, and Company, 1902.

Tertullian, *Apologeticum.* Translated in *The Ante-Nicene Fathers*, Alexander Roberts and James Donaldson, editors. New York: Charles Scribner's Sons, 1925. Vol. III, 17-55.

Ueberweg, Friedrich, *History of Philosophy.* Translated from the 4th German edition by George S. Morris. New York: Charles Scribner's Sons, 1892. Vol. I.

Willmann, Otto, *Didaktik als Bildungslehre nach ihren Beziehungen zur Social-forschung und zur Geschichte der Bildung.* Braunschweig: F. Vieweg und Sohn, 1894-95. 2 vols. Translated, under the title *Science of Education*, by Felix M. Kirsch, O.M. Cap., from the fifth German edition. Beatty, Pa.: Archabbey Press, 1930, 2nd edition. Vol. I.

CHAPTER XI

MEDIEVAL EDUCATION

From the Patristic Period to the Carlovingian Revival

With the collapse of the western division of the great Roman Empire, the Teutonic peoples were destined to reshape Europe. The various groups—the Franks, the Anglo-Saxons, the Alans, the Burgundians, the Visigoths, the Ostrogoths, the Vandals, and the Czechs—one after another set up their petty kingdoms and principalities of feudal medievalism. It was among these disconnected peoples that the Church in the early Middle Ages strove to exercise her educative influence. The conversion of the barbarians into law-abiding Christians was a long and difficult task, which was accomplished only as a result of relentless effort on her part. As Draper says:

In ages of lawlessness and rapine, among people but a step above savages, she vindicated the inviolability of her precincts against the hand of power, and made her temples a refuge and sanctuary for the despairing and the oppressed. Truly she was the shadow of a great rock in many a weary land.[1]

At the beginning of the Middle Ages,[2] central Europe, Scandinavia, and Russia were still pagan. It was not until the close of this era that the last stronghold of paganism was Christianized.[3] The chaotic centuries

---

[1] John W. Draper, *The Intellectual Development of Europe* (New York: Harper and Brothers, 1900), p. 146.

[2] Dates of beginning and end of the Middle Ages are more or less arbitrarily assumed according to point of view adopted. The Middle Ages are herein regarded as extending from Boethius in the sixth century to Erasmus in the sixteenth.

[3] The first nation to be converted to the Christian religion in the West, outside of the Roman world, was Ireland. Christianity was firmly established among the Scots with the death of St. Columba. The first Germanic nation to adopt the Catholic faith was that of the Franks at the beginning of the sixth century. After the invasion of the Anglo-Saxons, most of Britain relapsed

between the age of Constantine and that of Charle-magne witnessed successive waves of barbaric invasion sweeping over Europe. The conquered population suf-fered again and again all the horrors of war at the hands of the conquerors. Amid these destructive inroads which ushered in the so-called "Dark Ages,"[4] the Church made a desperate effort to save civilization and religion. She preserved the traditions of the ancient culture and la-bored to form in the new nations of Western Europe habits of intellectual endeavor. She persuaded them to strive for mastery in living by adopting the Christian conduct of life. These efforts of the Church to improve conditions within the body social and politic are attested by her educational activities in the cathedral, parish, song, and monastic schools which she had established before the close of the Patristic period.

The school which undertook in a specific manner to train young men for the various clerical offices was the *Episcopal* or *Cathedral School,* so called because it was originally maintained in the household of the bishop (*episcopus*), or at the cathedral of the diocese. In the earliest of these schools the bishops personally

---

into heathenism. The work of conversion in England was not completed until the close of the seventh century. The conver-sion of the Germans beyond the Rhine was due mainly to St. Boniface in the first half of the eighth century. The continental Saxons became Christians half a century later. The Slavs of central Europe were converted in the ninth century. Poland re-ceived the Christian religion from Bohemia in the tenth and eleventh centuries; Russia became Christian at about the same time by way of Constantinople. Denmark, Norway, and Sweden accepted Christianity in the eleventh century. The Finns were converted in the twelfth century, the Prussians in the thirteenth, and the Lithuanians in the fourteenth.

[4] The centuries from the sixth to the tenth inclusive are regard-ed as "Dark Ages." During this time European civilization was not as high from the standpoint of intellectual achievement as was that of the Graeco-Roman world; nevertheless, these cen-turies were not without scholars and cultural interests.

instructed and trained the young clerics; but in the fourth or fifth century, with the growth of the Church and the increasing number of her monasteries, the school was enlarged and the work of teaching was delegated by the bishop to a special cleric called the *scholasticus*. It not infrequently happened that converted rhetoricians and grammarians, who had previously been teachers in the public schools, continued their profession in these episcopal schools. With their accession the curriculum was broadened and the institution developed, as in Gaul, into a great public school. It thenceforth served not only as a seminary for clerics but also as a higher school or academy of Christian learning.

Episcopal Schools grew in number with the spread of the Christian faith and the establishment of the new episcopal sees. An idea of their extent can be obtained from the fact that in the year 614 there were 112 bishoprics in Frankland alone and during the Middle Ages each cathedral seat had its school.[5] They were, as a rule, the leading schools of a diocese and the models for schools in smaller communities. Some of the early episcopal schools were those of Rome, Carthage, Arles; and from the sixth century onward, those of Paris, Poitiers, Le Mans, Clermont, Rheims, Orleans, York. Many of these continued throughout the Middle Ages.

Instruction was confined at first to those studies demanded by the preparation of the future priest or cleric for service in the Church and for defending the cause of Christianity against the attacks of pagan adversaries. It embraced the sacred sciences of Scripture and theology; later, literary and philosophical studies were included. In some of the schools of Gaul, besides the Latin and Greek classics, there were advanced studies in Sacred

---

[5] E. P. Cubberly, *Syllabus of Lectures on the History of Education* (New York: The Macmillan Company, 1904), p. 59.

Scripture, philosophy, and mathematics. The school of St. Hilary at Arles was of this standard and from it came learned bishops and churchmen. The school of York, one of the famous cathedral schools of England, offered instruction in the liberal arts and law. The episcopal school was, however, essentially a training school where the virtues necessary to the leaders of the faithful were inculcated, and where the moral and spiritual formation of the student was of paramount importance.

Toward the close of the period under consideration, in the time of Chrodogang, Bishop of Metz (742-766), the canonical life was instituted at the episcopal sees, i.e., the bishop lived in community with his clerics or canons. The school profited by this better organization of clerical life at the diocesan centers. The rule which Chrodogang gave his clergy was based on the rule of St. Benedict. A most important chapter is the one dealing with the training of boys. Through his efforts a mighty impulse was given to the spread of community life among the secular clergy, not only in Frankland, Germany, and Italy, but even in England. The community life was lived in the larger parish churches as well as in the cathedrals. The canons of the cathedral conducted the cathedral school; those of the local church conducted a "canonicate" school. By the end of the eighth century, the influence of Chrodogang was so generally widespread that he was styled "the Lighthouse of Europe." [6]

Parish Schools also were organized in this period. At Edessa as early as the middle of the second century, the priest Protogenes taught the children of his parish reading, writing, singing, and the elements of Christian doctrine. [7]

---

[6] Denk, *op. cit.*, pp. 272-76.
[7] A. Stöckl, *Geschichte der Pädagogik* (Mainz: F. Kirchheim, 1876), p. 78.

The Fathers assembled at the Council of Vaison, Gaul,
529, urged the priests of their jurisdiction to maintain
schools in their houses in imitation of the custom already
prevalent in Italy and there producing good results. We
can see from the language of the council that the chief
aim of the bishops was the preparation of young men
for the offices in the Church, not necessarily for the
priesthood. The students were free to leave and enter
the married state.[8]

The fourth and fifth canons of the Ecumenical Council
of Constantinople decreed that all parish priests should
teach children or establish a school in which they might
be taught. This command to found parish schools is
repeated in synods and local councils. How many parish
schools there were, it is not possible to estimate. The
very repetition of the decrees regarding them would lead
one to conclude that the legislation was not completely
carried out. This is undoubtedly true, but the conditions
of the time are partly to blame for that.[9]

Song Schools were organized to prepare youth for
participation in the services of the Church. Pope Gregory the Great (540-604) had founded the Schola Cantorum at Rome, and bishops wherever possible imitated
his example so that finally the song school came to be
maintained at the cathedral as regularly as the grammar
school. It is noteworthy that in these schools reading,
writing, arithmetic, and religion were taught and not
merely singing; the more promising boys even began
the study of grammar. Song schools were also established in connection with local churches. The cathedral
precentor supervised the work of these schools and sometimes of all parish schools. In the course of time he was
superseded by the scholasticus or headmaster of the

---

[8] G. D. Mansi, *Collectio amplissima Conciliorum* (Paris: H.
Welter, Editeur, 1901), VIII, 726 f.

[9] *Cf.* W. Kane, *An Essay Toward A History of Education,* p.
102.

cathedral school who was designated by the third Lateran Council as the superintendent of all diocesan schools.[10]

The institution which was destined to exert a most profound influence on education during the Middle Ages was the *Monastic School*. Monasticism had arisen in the East and, long before the state schools of the Roman Empire had disappeared, the cenobites and the monks had engaged in educational pursuits. They not only taught those who were to become monks, but received children solely for their Christian education and training. As the Church was only then emerging from the persecutions into freedom, she could not usually maintain schools, and those then existing, that is, the pagan and Jewish schools, offered many dangers to the faith of Christian youth. It is true that many of the early fathers, like St. Basil, St. Gregory Nazianzus, St. Augustine, and St. Ambrose, had attended the public schools and even taught in them; nevertheless, parents were conscious of the dangers and desired to confide their children to the care of religious for their education. This was not, of course, always possible, for the monastery was primarily founded as a house of prayer and retreat and not as a school. Provision was gradually made, however, for the systematic instruction of the young. The Rules of St. Basil and St. Pachomius show how early this was done in the East.[11] For the West we note that bishops like Caesarius of Arles (470-543) and his successors were obliged to determine the age at which children might be received into the cloisters of men and women because of the eagerness of parents to place them there.

The two different forms of monastic life, eremetical and cenobitical, had appeared in Egypt at the close of

[10] *Cf.* Pierre J. Marique, *History of Christian Education* (New York: Fordham University Press, 1924), I, 139 f.
[11] Migne, *Patrologia Gr. XXIX; Patrologia Lat. XXIII*.

the third and the beginning of the fourth century. From Egypt, monasticism spread into Palestine, Asia Minor, Mesopotamia, Persia, India, and the islands of the eastern Mediterranean. St. Athanasius receives the credit for bringing the account of the Egyptian monks to Rome on his first visit to the Papal city in 340 where he was accompanied by two disciples of St. Anthony. Monasticism in the West enjoyed early the support of such men as Ambrose, Jerome, and Augustine, and monastic communities were soon established in Italy and the other provinces of the Western Empire. A few of the early western monasteries of the fourth and fifth centuries were Marmoutier, founded by St. Martin of Tours; Lerins, established by St. Honoratus on a rocky isle off the south coast of France; and the Abbey of St. Victor, at Marseilles, erected over the tomb of St. Victor by the ascetical writer John Cassian.

Monasticism received its great impetus in the West from St. Benedict, who established the order which bears his name at Subiaco, Italy, in 528. When he issued his rule or constitution a few years later, it was almost immediately adopted by the monasteries of Europe. It was carried into Gaul by St. Maur; into Spain by St. Martin of Deume; and into England by St. Augustine. In this rule, called the Constitution of Monasticism, reading, prayer, and labor were the occupation of the monks. Manual labor consumed much of the day, but at stated hours, especially on Sundays, the reading exercise was of obligation. It is interesting to note in the rule the injunctions for sacred reading, and the frequent quotations from Scripture, with which the monks from their reading and psalm singing were necessarily familiar.[12]

St. Benedict wrote his rule about the year 530 and revised it before his death in 543. It provides in its

---

[12] *Rule of St. Benedict.* Edited and translated by D. O. Hunter Blair (Fort Augustus: Abbey Press, 1934), pp. 129-133.

seventy-three chapters for the organization and administration of the monastery, from the election of the abbot to the punishment of offenders. Its many beautiful expressions, its inspiration to the monks for the highest motives in their lives, are unfortunately not as familiar as the provisions for the punishment of delinquents and offenders. That the monk was able to read is presumed by chapter 48 on the daily labor of the monks. Before one could be received or professed as a monk, he must be instructed in the rudiments of knowledge.

Idleness is an enemy of the soul; and hence at certain seasons the brethren ought to occupy themselves in the labour of their hands and at others times in holy reading . . . During Lent, let them apply themselves to reading from morning until the end of the third hour, and then, until the end of the tenth labour at whatever is enjoined of them. And in these days of Lent let each one receive a book from the library, and read it all through in order. . . . On Sunday, let all occupy themselves in reading, except those who have been appointed to the various offices. But if anyone should be so negligent and slothful as to be either unwilling or unable to study or to read, let some task be given him to do that he be not idle.[13]

Some of the early fathers of the monastic life like St. Maur interpreted this provision in favor of wider educational pursuits. Besides the instruction of the novices, which was a necessary function of the monastery, the

---

[13] History can hardly separate the influence of the rule of Benedict from the dynamic force of the Benedictine Pope and statesman, St. Gregory the Great. He urged the celibacy of the clergy and the cloistering of monks; founded seven monasteries; and wrote a treatise, *Regulae pastoralis liber,* which treats of the duties of the clergy. He is the father of the medieval papacy. His writings influenced the course of European education indirectly. His condemnation of pagan letters must be understood in the light of social conditions in his time. *Cf.* Laestner, *supra,* pp. 80 f. He was not a profound scholar, but his theological writings, which summed up the teachings of the earlier Fathers, became a compendium of theology during the Middle Ages.

copying of manuscripts,[14] study, and literary work became approved occupations of the monks. The monastery therefore produced both the scholar, like Venerable
Bede,[15] who throughout his long life never ceased to
study and to write, and the missionary, like St. Boniface,
the Apostle of Germany, zealous for the spread of the
Gospel and the benefits of learning among barbarian
peoples. The latter selected Fulda, which was a wilderness in western Germany, as the site for the erection of
a monastery in the middle of the eighth century; this
foundation sent forth many colonies which became the
nuclei of new civil communities. An Irish monk, St.
Columbanus, founded the monastery of Luxeuil, which
in the seventh century was the religious and intellectual center of Frankland. He also established a monastery at Bobbio, near Genoa, which was distinguished for
learning during the later Middle Ages. His disciple, St.
Gall, inspired the building of an abbey near the Lake
of Constance in Switzerland; it was named after him
and promoted the development of many famous scholars
in central Europe.

---

[14] In every well-appointed monastery the library and the
scriptorium were most important departments. The making of
a single book required the services of a number of monks. The
parchment, which was made from the skins of sheep, goats, and
wild animals, had to be carefully prepared. The black ink
commonly used for the text, the red ink for the titles, and the
gold or silver for further ornamentation had to be manufactured.
The pages of the parchment had to be ruled before the copyist
began the work of transcribing the text. The body of the manuscript was then examined by the proof reader. It was given afterwards to the rubricator; and if it were to be an edition de luxe
it was illuminated by an artist of the monastery. The pages,
arranged in order and sewed together, were bound between two
oaken boards, covered with pigskin and provided with metal
clasps.

[15] An English monk (673-735) of the monastery of Jarrow in
England. He was a most distinguished man of letters. His
ecclesiastical history of the English nation provides most of our
information about early culture in England. He wrote commentaries on the books of the Bible which indicate that he had
a good knowledge of Greek.

Monks in the beginning were mostly laymen. The rule of St. Benedict was written for men who like himself sought escape from society in order to live as fully as possible in conformity with the counsels of the Gospel; they did not wish to be clerics with clerical duties and offices. The Benedictine rule required that the life of a monk should be spent in work. One of the favorite mottoes of the Order was "To work is to pray." It was this practical character of the rule that made the monks the pioneers of a new civilization in the wooded districts of Gaul and Germany, England and Ireland.[16] The conditions which the solitary monk faced when he undertook to clear wild forests and bring to the surrounding population the boon of Christian teachings, have been aptly described by Montalembert.

We must then imagine Gaul and all neighboring countries, the whole extent of France, Switzerland, Belgium, and both banks of the Rhine—that is to say, the richest and most populous countries of modern Europe, covered with forests. . . . We must figure to ourselves those masses of sombre and impenetrable wood, covering hills and valleys, the high tablelands as well as the marshy bottoms, . . . and inhabited by innumerable wild beasts, whose ferocity had scarcely been accustomed to fly before men, and of which many different species have since almost completely disappeared from our country. . . . He [the monk] came out of a desolate, decrepit, and powerless old world, to plunge into the unknown. But he bore with him a strength which nothing has ever surpassed or equalled, the strength conferred by faith in a loving God. . . . He thus advanced, undaunted and serene; and often without thinking what he did, opened a road to all the benefits of agriculture, labor, and Christian civilization.[17]

The monastery was looked upon by the common man

---

[16] Ephraim Emerton, *Introduction to the Middle Ages* (Boston: Ginn and Company, 1888), pp. 138-140.

[17] Count de Montalembert, *The Monks of the West from St. Benedict to St. Bernard* (New York: Longmans, Green, and Company, 1906), II, 189 f.

as a retreat from the violence of the world and became
the refuge for many a troubled soul who sought to
escape from the trials of this life. Every monastery was
a center of social service. The spirit of denial gave to
the monk a kind of sacred character in the eyes of the
world and many a weary Christian sought out the
saintly ascetic for consolation and direction. Convinced
that wordly ties tended to draw the thoughts of men
away from higher things, the humble supplicant often
embraced the monastic life; in this way the spread of
monasticism was rapid and at times unexpected.

Sometimes in the middle of the night, the voluntary exile
who has hid himself in the hope of remaining forever forgotten and unknown, hears someone knock at the door of his
hut. It is at first only a reverential and timid tap; he is
silent. It continues; he opens and asks, "What would you
with me? Why do you pursue me into my solitary dwelling?
Who are you?" He is answered: "A poor sinner, or a young
Christian, or an old priest weary of the world." "But what
would you with me?" "Be saved like you, and with you;
learn from you the way of peace and of the kingdom of God."
This unexpected and undesired guest must be admitted. The
next morning, or the next again, comes another, and they are
followed by others still. The anchorites saw themselves thus
changed into cenobites, and monastic life established itself . . .
unexpectedly amid the most distant forests.[18]

From the very beginning, some type of formal schooling was associated with monasticism. In the monastic
school, which was primarily intended for young monks,
but to which children of the nobility and of the poor
were also admitted, the instruction was at first simple
in character. It embraced reading, writing, arithmetic,
singing, and the elements of Christian doctrine. In certain monasteries, especially those of Gaul and Ireland,
some advanced studies were carried on in the early

---

[18] *Ibid.*, pp. 194 f.

Middle Ages. During the seventh and eighth centuries, students from England and the Continent went in great numbers to the Irish monasteries where they were hospitably welcomed. The Venerable Bede, writing of the English noblemen who went there, says: "The Scots willingly received them all, and took care to supply them with food, as also to furnish them with books to read, and their teaching gratis."[19] Some great Irish monasteries of the early period were those of Armagh and Kildare of the fifth century; Clonard, Clonfert, Clonmacnoise, Bangor, and Glendalough of the sixth; Lismore, Cork, and Ross in the seventh. It is believed that they differed in organization and rule from the Benedictine monasteries, being rather of the order of canons regular.[20]

Eventually the seven liberal arts constituted the curriculum of the fully developed monastic school. Although the controlling aim of education was moral and religious, it was not entirely "otherworldly" as the rules of the monks show. Instruction and discipline were under the direction of the religious especially designated by the abbot or superior. The discipline was, from the modern viewpoint, severe but not harsh. The fuller development of monastic education will be shown later, when it is treated in connection with the work of Charlemagne and his successors. The school of the monastery then included two distinct departments: one for interns, those who intended to be monks, and another for externs, those who were to return to the world upon the completion of their education.

---

[19] Bede, *Ecclesiastical History.* English translation by J. A. Giles (London: George Bell and Sons, 1892), p. 163.
[20] John Healy, *Ireland's Ancient Schools and Scholars* (Dublin: Sealy, Bryers, and Walker, 1893), pp. 111-496. *Cf.* A. Allaria, "Canons and Canonesses Regular," *Catholic Encyclopedia* (New York: The Encyclopedia Press, 1913), III, 291.

Domestic Education

Institutional training by no means embraced all that was contemplated in the educational scheme of the Christian Church. In the home the real beginnings of Christian education were made, and the responsibility of the parents in this respect was constantly emphasized in the early Middle Ages. The Christian mother was exhorted to follow the example of Laeta, whom St. Jerome commended for teaching her children to walk in the truth; or to imitate the holy women: St. Emmelia, mother of St. Basil; St. Nonna, mother of St. Gregory Nazianzus; and St. Anthusa, mother of St. John Chrysostom. The letters of the Fathers and the decrees of the early councils of the Church exhorted parents to be faithful to this duty. The home, then, practically supplied the moral training, when the Church because of persecutions and poverty could not maintain schools. With the decline of fervor and piety in the domestic circle, and the neglect of careful home training, the sending of the children to the monasteries was unhesitatingly recommended by the Fathers of the Church.

FOR FURTHER STUDY

Adams, George A., *Civilization During the Middle Ages.* New York: Charles Scribner's Sons, 1921.

Auchmuty, James J., *Irish Education.* Dublin: Hodges, Figgis and Company, 1937.

Azarias, Brother, *Essays Educational.* Chicago: D. H. McBride and Company, 1896.

Bede, *Historia Ecclesiastica gentis Anglorum.* Edited by C. Plummer. Oxford: The Clarendon Press, 1896. An English translation in the Loeb Classical Library by J. E. King based on the version of Stapleton. London: William Heinemann, Ltd., 1930.

Bouquet, M., *Recueil des historiens des Gaules.* 23 vols. Edited by L. Delisle, 19 vols. Paris: Victor Palmé, 1869-1880.

Butler, C., *Benedictine Monachism*. London: Longmans, Green, and Company, 1919.

Chapman, J., *Saint Benedict and the Sixth Century*. London: Sheed and Ward, 1929.

Denk, V. M. Otto, *Geschichte des gallo-fränkischen Unterrichts und Bildungswesens*. Mainz: Verlag Von Franz Kirchheim, 1892.

Dill, S., *Roman Society in Gaul in the Merovingian Age*. London: The Macmillan Company, 1926.

Draper, John W., *The Intellectual Development of Europe*. New York: Harper and Brothers, 1900. 2 vols.

Dudden, F. H., *Gregory the Great*. London: Longmans, Green, and Company, 1905. 2 vols.

Emerton, Ephraim, *Introduction to the Middle Ages*. Boston: Ginn and Company, 1888.

Gougaud, L., *Gaelic Pioneers of Christianity*. An English translation of part of *Les Chrétientés celtiques*, brought up to date. Dublin: M. H. Gill and Son, Ltd., 1923.

Graham, Hugh, *The Early Irish Monastic Schools*. Dublin: The Talbot Press, 1923.

Gregory of Tours, *Historiae Francorum libri X*, Migne, P. L., Vol. 71. English translation under the title *The History of the Franks by Gregory of Tours*, by O. M. Dalton. Oxford: The Clarendon Press, 1927. 2 vols.

Haarhoff, T., *The Schools of Gaul*. Oxford: Oxford University Press, 1920.

Healy, John, *Ireland's Ancient Schools and Scholars*. Dublin: Sealy, Bryers, and Walker, 1893.

Joyce, P. W., *A Social History of Ancient Ireland*. London: Longmans, Green, and Company, 1920.

Laistner, M. L. W., *Thought and Letters in Western Europe*: A. D. 500-900. London: Methuen and Company, Ltd., 1931.

Magevney, E., *Christian Education in the Dark Ages*. New York: Catholic Library Association, 1900.

Montalembert, Count de, *Monks of the West*. New York: Longmans, Green, and Company, 1906. 6 vols.

Zimmer, H., *The Irish Element in Medieval Culture*. English translation, by J. L. Edmands, of *Ueber die Bedeutung des irischen Elements für die mittelalterliche Kultur*. New York: G. P. Putnam's Sons, 1891.

CHAPTER XII

MEDIEVAL EDUCATION (Continued)

From the Carlovingian Revival to Scholasticism

European culture at the opening of the Middle Ages was a chaotic mixture of barbarian and Roman elements. It was the Church through monasticism that brought about the union of Teutonic initiative and Latin order, which made possible the whole medieval development of culture. This synthesis was achieved in the Carlovingian dynasty. Hitherto the barbarians had lived passively on the Graeco-Roman inheritance with which they had come into contact through conquest; now they began to utilize it actively in the work of political organization. Consequently, the center of medieval civilization shifted from the shores of the Mediterranean to the heart of the Frankish dominions. It was in this territory, extending from the Loire to the Rhine, that the ideal of the medieval empire was realized and the fundamental institutions of medieval society, ecclesiastical and political, took form.[1]

Charlemagne was truly a man of genius and one of the greatest leaders of all time. He was a conqueror, an organizer, a founder of governmental institutions, and a promoter of culture and enlightenment. The work he accomplished laid the foundation for all the subsequent history of Europe.[2] The son of Pepin the Short, who deposed Childeric, the last of the Merovingian rulers, and the grandson of Charles Martel, who broke the wave of Arab invasion at the famous battle of Tours in 732, Charlemagne was a typical Teuton in origin, speech, and

---

[1] Christopher Dawson, *The Making of Europe* (New York: Sheed and Ward, 1939), p. 214.
[2] Emerton, *Introduction to the Middle Ages,* p. 180.

appearance.[3]   He had an active mind, spoke colloquial
Latin as well as his native German, and understood
Greek. He tried to learn to write but his efforts were attended with little success.[4] When at dinner he had someone to read to him; he was very fond of history and de-
lighted especially in St. Augustine's *City of God*. He
was not a learned man, but he was an educated man.

The most famous event in the life of Charlemagne
was his establishment of the Western Empire in the
year 800.   On Christmas day of that year, Pope St.
Leo III placed the imperial crown on the head of the
king of the Franks and the Lombards and presented him
to the world as the successor of the ancient Roman emperors of the West.   The coronation of Charlemagne
was a proper recognition of the real political situation
because through conquest he had extended his dominions east and south until he was the recognized ruler
of the continental Germano-Roman world.   With the
restoration of the imperial office in the West, there
began that intimate relationship between church and
state which led to the foundation of the Holy Roman
Empire.[5]

It was Charlemagne's ardent hope to bring all the
German peoples together into one great Christian empire; this was to be accomplished by means of education.
He took advantage of the learning of scholarly men,
called them to his court, reestablished a regular system
of public instruction and thereby greatly improved the
educational conditions of Europe in the eighth and ninth

---

[3] Charlemagne is the French form for the Latin, Carolus
Magnus, Charles the Great.   In German Charlemagne is known
as Karl der Grosse.
[4] J. B. Mullinger, *The Schools of Charles the Great* (London:
Longmans, Green and Company, 1877), p. 70.
[5] The Western Empire which came to be called the Holy Roman
Empire in the twelfth century endured for over one thousand
years.

centuries. He desired that schools be multiplied for all his people so that their intellectual and religious development should go on apace. In the work of this educational revival he had a very efficient agent in Alcuin, the former scholasticus of the cathedral school of York, whom he secured in 782 to conduct his palace school at Aachen.

Alcuin brought teachers with him from York and with their assistance organized the academy. Charlemagne, the queen, his sister and his children, the courtiers, and sons of noblemen were the first pupils. The academy was not an innovation; it had functioned under the Merovingian kings, but it was much more advanced in its instruction than the palace school of the Merovingian period.[6] The liberal arts, as taught in the cathedral school of York, were introduced there, but under serious difficulties on account of the widely differing qualifications of the students. Alcuin and his assistants succeeded with the school, and in a short time extended their influence over the Empire, for Alcuin was appointed by Charlemagne to act in the capacity of a state minister of education. He was responsible in great measure for the success of the educational revival.

In 787 Charlemagne issued a capitulary to all of the abbots and bishops of Frankland, urging them to promote study and the work of teaching in their respective communities. This was the first of the imperial orders, and the beginning of a real movement in the interests of learning. In the capitulary he deplored the decline of letters and literary studies, and urged that measures be taken for the better preparation of teachers. He said in part:

During recent years we have often received letters from

---

[6] The date of foundation of the court school under the Merovingian kings is uncertain. It may have been established in the late sixth or early seventh century. Most probably it was organized by the Irish monks in Gaul, especially Columbanus.

different monasteries, informing us that at their sacred services
the brethren offered up prayers on our behalf, and we have
observed that the thoughts contained in these letters, though
in themselves most just, were expressed in uncouth language,
and while pious devotion dictated the sentiments, the
unlettered tongue was unable to express them aright. Hence
there has arisen in our minds the fear lest, if the skill to
write correctly were thus lacking, so too would the power of
rightly comprehending the Sacred Scriptures be far from
fitting, and we all know that if verbal errors be dangerous,
errors of the understanding are much more so. We exhort
you, therefore, not only not to neglect the study of letters,
but to apply yourselves thereto with perseverance and with
that humility which is well pleasing to God, so that you may
be able to penetrate with greater ease and certainty the
mysteries of the Holy Scriptures. For, as these contain images,
tropes, and similar figures, it is impossible to doubt that the
reader will arrive far more readily at the spiritual sense,
according as he is better instructed in learning. Let therefore, there be chosen for this work men who are both able
and willing to learn, and who are desirous of instructing others,
and let them apply themselves to the work with a zeal
equalling the earnestness with which we recommend it to
them. It is our wish that you may be what it behooves the
soldiers of the Church to be—religious in heart, learned in
discourse and eloquent in speech. . . .[7]

This capitulary was followed in 789 by others of a
practical nature, dealing with the preparation of monks
and clerics, and ordering the establishment of a school
for boys in every monastery and episcopal see, where
they would be taught reading, singing, arithmetic, and
grammar.[8] A capitulary of 802 enjoined that "Everyone

---

[7] Migne, *Pat. Lat.* xcviii, 895. *Monumenta Germaniae historica,*
leges ii, capitul. i, 79.

[8] Et ut scolae legentium puerorum fiant; psalmos, notas, cantus,
compotum, grammaticam per singula monasteria vel episcopias
et libros Catholicos bene emendate (emendatos) ; quia saepe dum
bene aliquid Deum rogare cupiunt, sed per inemendatos libros
male rogant. Migne, *Pat. Lat.* xcvii, 517.

should send his son to study letters, and that the child should remain at school with all diligence, until he should become well instructed in learning."[9]

Charlemagne also obtained special instructors from Rome, whom he sent to different monasteries to assist in carrying out the reform. His measures met with the hearty cooperation of the bishops in many of the important sees and of the abbots in the large monasteries. Bishop Theodulf [10] of Orleans had an excellent episcopal school. A scholar and poet, this bishop extended his efforts beyond his own episcopal see, for he ruled that all the priests of his diocese should keep schools in their parishes. His decree is famous in the history of education, including as it does, a plea in behalf of free elementary education for the poor. It reappears in church councils throughout the Middle Ages. It is as follows:

Let the priests keep schools in the villages and towns, and if any of the faithful wish to give his little ones to learning they ought willingly to receive them and teach them gratuitously, remembering what has been written: "They that are learned shall shine as the brightness of the firmament; and they that instruct many to justice, as stars for all eternity." And let them exact no price from the children for their teaching, nor receive anything from them save what the parents may offer voluntarily and from affection.[11]

When Alcuin retired to Tours in 796, the reform was well advanced. What he accomplished at Tours in mak-

---

[9] "Ut unusquisque filium suum litteras ad discendum mittat, et ibi cum omni solicitudine permaneat usque dum bene instructus perveniat." Capitula examinationis generalis, 12. Mon. Ger. *hist.*, leges ii, cap. i, 235.

[10] Succeeded Alcuin in the office of state minister of education. Alcuin became abbot of Tours in 796. The following year Theodulf issued his decree in behalf of free elementary education.

[11] Migne, *Pat. Lat.* cv, 196.

ing the monastery a famous school is a good example of the success of the educational revival he had directed. Louis the Pious continued the revival of his father Charlemagne, with the assistance of Rhabanus Maurus and St. Benedict of Aniane. During his reign the law was passed (817) directing the maintenance at each monastery of the school for interns, *schola interior,* and the school for externs, *schola exterior;* the first for those who were to become monks, and the second for those studying for the secular priesthood and the laity. Until then, all the students had lived together, much to the annoyance of the monks, who desired that the cloister be free of noise and distractions. The law provided that no school should be maintained in the cloister unless for those who were oblates, i.e., those offering themselves as candidates for the religious life. "Ut schola in monasterio non habeatur nisi eorum qui oblati sunt."[12] Provision had to be made for those excluded from the inner monastery and this was done by opening schools which were placed outside of the enclosure and called schools for externs. In the architects' plan for the monastery of St. Gall, Switzerland, designed in the ninth century, the exact location of this school can be seen.[13]

The Cathedral schools also opened inner and outer departments as a result of ecclesiastical legislation. It was decided at the Council of Aachen, 816 (817?), that separate schools were necessary for the students of the canonicate, and in a short time after the law was passed, schools for externs, i.e., for those not preparing for the canonical life of the cathedral, were established. An excellent example of this arrangement was that of the cathedral of Rheims, where in the ninth century Arch-

---

[12] *Mon. Ger. hist.,* leges ii, capitul. i, 346.
[13] F. Keller, *Bauriss des Klosters St. Gallen* (Zurich: Meyer u. Zeller, 1844), p. 23. *Cf.* F. A. Specht, *Geschichte des Unterrichtswesens in Deutschland* (Stuttgart: J. G. Cotta, 1885), p. 37.

bishop Fulk restored the two schools to their former prestige.[14]

The abbots and bishops cooperated with the civil authorities in behalf of the schools throughout the entire ninth century. In the monastery was the free school, where board and clothing were gratuitously given as, for instance, in the monastery of St. Peter in Salzburg; and in the cathedral was found another type of the public school, as for example at Langres, where Bishop Betto founded his free school. This bishop established other free schools in his episcopal city and diocese. Certain large cities had both the monastic and the cathedral schools. Some of the notable schools in France were Orleans, Arles, Lyons, Tours, Rheims, Soissons, Metz,[15] Verdun, Liège; in Germany, Hildesheim, Speyer, Cologne, Mainz; in England, York and Canterbury. Famous monastic schools were Tours,[16] St. Germain d'Auxerre, St. Germain-des-Prés, St. Denis at Paris,[17] St. Benedict on the Loire,[18] St. Liffard in the diocese of Orleans, St. Riquier, St. Martin at Metz, St. Bertin in the diocese of Cambrai, St. Benedict of Aniane in the

---

[14] *Mon. Ger. hist.*, scriptores xiii. Hist. Remen. iv. 9.

[15] Designated by Charlemagne in the capitulary of 806 as the first Song school of the Empire, a monopoly which it still retained in the eleventh century. *Cf.* Leon Maître, *Les écoles éspiscopales et monastiques en Occident* (Paris: A. Picard et Fils, editeurs, 1924), p. 79.

[16] The school was styled "école calligraphique" because of the attention it gave to calligraphy in the copying of manuscripts. To it we are indebted for the Carolingian type which is of historical importance. *Cf. ibid.*, p. 41.

[17] Merited the honor of educating children of the nobility. Pepin the Short and Charles the Bald received an elementary education here. In the eleventh century, one of its monks, Baldwin, was a distinguished medical practitioner. *Cf. ibid.*, p. 67.

[18] Especially noted for its library facilities. Each student was required to donate two manuscripts to the school. When Gerbert needed a rare book, it is claimed that he usually found it there. *Cf. ibid.*, p. 53.

diocese of Montpellier, Fulda,[19] St. Alban near Mainz, Seligenstadt, Hirschau, St. Gall,[20] Reichenau, and Corbie and New Corbie[21] in Saxony.

An evidence of this widespread movement in the dioceses of the Empire is seen in the canons of councils and other ecclesiastical laws passed during that century. Many bishops followed the example of Theodulf of Orleans and obliged the clergy to open schools in their parishes. They enjoined the priests either to act as teachers themselves or to employ a cleric for that office. When Archbishop Hincmar in the ninth century gave directions to the inspectors of his diocese, he made especial mention of the school. They were to see whether the parish had a cleric who could keep school and participate in the church services by reading the epistle or singing when necessary.[22] Similar laws were made in Orleans and Tours; and at a Council of Rome, called by Pope Eugenius II in 853, the establishment of schools in all of the episcopal sees and subject cities was ordered —schools for the study of letters and the liberal arts as well as theology.[23]

In England an educational revival was also undertaken by *King Alfred the Great* (840-900). Due to the ravages of the Danes, into whose hands nearly the whole

---

[19] The prominence of this school in the ninth century was due to an exceptionally gifted monk, Rhabanus Maurus. His pupils were called to fill important posts in church and state. *Cf. ibid.*, p. 36.

[20] It was modeled on the school of Fulda. Greek, Arabic, and Hebrew were taught. In the ninth century, the library could boast of four hundred catalogued MSS. *Cf. ibid.*, pp. 37 f.

[21] Founded by monks from Corbie in Northern France. It had an uninterrupted line of headmasters and scholars from the ninth to the eleventh century. *Cf. ibid.*, p. 45.

[22] "Si habeat clericum, qui posset tenere scholam, aut legere epistolam, aut canere valeat, prout necessarium videtur." Capitula presbyteris data, xi, Mansi, *Coll. Con.* xv, 480.

[23] Canon xxxiv.

of the east of England had fallen by the year 870, English learning had greatly declined since the time of Alcuin. Alfred stood alone between Christian England and paganism; but for him England might have been lost for centuries to Christianity.[24] The Danes had plundered the monasteries, and the general condition of the Church was deplorable. Many sees were vacant, and some were permanently extinct because of the continuous barbarian invasions. Alfred made a gallant attempt to revive monastic life in England by establishing new monastic foundations and by importing foreign monks of outstanding ability and learning. He was also a liberal contributor to monasteries in Ireland and on the continent.[25]

Solicitous for the spread of culture, Alfred established a palace school which he entrusted to learned masters such as Grimbald of St. Omer, and John, a monk of Corbie. He also secured the services of other monks from the continent and commissioned them to improve the monastic schools of his realm. At his court he saw to it that study was encouraged, and one of his sons, according to the historian Asser, "He entrusted to the school of literary training (Grammar School), with the children of almost all of the nobility of the country and many also who were not noble, under the diligent care of masters. In that school books in both languages, Latin and Saxon, were diligently read."[26] Many of the nobility who had neglected the liberal arts were urged by his example to study and acquire skill in reading. Some found it necessary to do so in order to obtain the royal favor.

---

[24] Charles Plummer, *The Life and Times of Alfred the Great* (Oxford: Clarendon Press, 1902), p. 199.
[25] *Ibid.*, pp. 128 f.
[26] Asserius, *De rebus gestis Alfredi.* Edited by W. H. Stevenson (Oxford: Clarendon Press, 1904), p. 75.

Alfred endeavored to raise the cultural level of his people by encouraging the practice of reading through translation of Latin works into English. In this way he placed within reach of his people many useful works in various fields of learning. He himself translated Boethius' *Consolation of Philosophy;* the *Regulae pastoralis liber* of Pope St. Gregory the Great; Orosius' *Universal History;* and Venerable Bede's *Ecclesiastical History of the English Nation.* Tradition also credits him with a translation of Aesop's *Fables.* He inspired the Anglo-Saxon martyrology and may have dictated parts of the Anglo-Saxon Chronicle. He was also the author of a collection of proverbs and of a treatise on falconry.[27]

In the ecclesiastical law of England during the ninth and tenth centuries priests were enjoined to keep parish schools and, furthermore, to keep schools for school teachers.

Priests ought always to have schools for school teachers in their houses, and if any of the faithful wish to give his little ones to learning they ought willingly to receive them and teach them gratuitously, remembering what has been written: "They that are learned shall shine as the brightness of the firmament, and they that instruct many to justice, as stars for all eternity." But they ought not to expect anything from their relatives except what they wish to do of their own accord.[28]

During King Edgar's reign (957-975) the priests were also urged to teach the boys of their parishes the manual arts or crafts. Two important ecclesiastical canons read: "And that the priest do moreover teach manual arts with diligence"; "And that the priest diligently instruct

---

[27] Plummer, *op. cit.,* pp. 139-157.
[28] D. Wilkins, *Concilia magnae Brittaniae et Hiberniae* (London: R. Gosling, F. Gyles, T. Woodward, C. Davis, 1737), I, 270. *Cf.* A, F. Leach, *Educational Charters and Documents* (Cambridge: The University Press, 1911), p. 37.

youth and dispose them to trades that they may have a support to the Church."[29]   St. Dunstan (924-988), Bishop successively of Worcester, London, and Canterbury, was a skilled craftsman in metal, wood, and ivory, and was always deeply interested in the schools. So much beloved was he by the pupils of his schools that he is often spoken of as the patron of English schoolboys.

In this period of the Middle Ages the monastic school rose to a higher plane than at any previous time and entered upon that stage which immediately prepared for the universities. A better idea consequently can be obtained of its organization and studies than in the time before Charlemagne. With its development, a staff of teachers, instead of one or two, was employed, and the curriculum, especially in the large monasteries, embraced a wide range of studies. It comprised the seven liberal arts and, in many of the large schools, it included law, medicine, the fine arts, and the industrial arts.

The Seven Liberal Arts, or those studies which formed the elements of a liberal education, consisted of the trivium[30] or language subjects, i.e., grammar, dialectic, and rhetoric; and the quadrivium[31] or the mathematical subjects, i.e., arithmetic, music, geometry, and astronomy. All the liberal arts were looked upon as handmaids to theology. Grammar included a study of the elements of language and Latin literature. After three or four years, the student became proficient in the use of Latin which was the language of daily intercourse in a scholar's environment. Prior to the university era

---

[29] J. Johnson, *A Collection of the Laws and Canons of the Church of England* (Oxford: John Henry Parker, 1850-51), I, Canons of 960, Nos. 11 and 51. *Cf.* Mansi, *Coll. Con.* XV a, 513, 517.

[30] Trivium in Latin means a place where three ways or roads meet. It is the assemblage of the three language subjects.

[31] Quadrivium means a place where four ways or roads meet. It is the assemblage of the four mathematical sciences.

the method of teaching grammar consisted in the reading
of authors, pointing out the beauties in the text, asking
the pupils to judge and criticize, making them memorize
passages and write original exercises in prose and verse.
In the later Middle Ages, the character of the instruction
changed and took on more of the dialectical aspect.[32]

There were many textbooks on grammar, Donatus and
Priscian leading in popularity; they were the basis of
many later works. Donatus was an elementary work
dealing with the eight parts of speech; Priscian was a
more advanced treatise. The treatises on the seven liberal arts contained special sections on grammar, i.e.,
those of Capella, Augustine, Boethius, Cassiodorus, Isidore of Seville, Alcuin, Rhabanus Maurus, and Remigius
of Auxerre. The most famous of the later texts in grammar was the *Doctrinale* of Alexander of Villedieu, a work
in verse written in 1199. It was used in Germany,
France, England, Spain, Italy, and Poland.

The classics, especially Vergil, were studied; also the
works of Christian writers. The association of grammar
with literature constantly aimed at and, indeed, realized,
in the older texts lends support to the well established
view that the Latin classics never ceased to be read in
the Middle Ages. Priscian, for example, quotes Vergil's
Aeneid seven hundred times; no one could use such a
grammar or Donatus and be ignorant of the literature
on which they were based.

Dialectic embraced the art of reasoning or logic. It
became a most attractive subject to pupils even before
the university period. Rhabanus Maurus regarded it as
the science of sciences; through it truth was distinguished
from falsehood and valid conclusions were reached. It
was studied largely in Boethius' translation of the *Categories* and *De interpretatione* of Aristotle. Porphyry's

---

[32] Paul Abelson, *The Seven Liberal Arts* (New York: Teachers'
College, Columbia University, 1906), pp. 15-33.

Isagoge was also an important treatise. By the twelfth century, logic became the major subject of the trivium in the schools. The remaining subject of the language group, rhetoric, dealt with the art of expression, and later embraced history and law. Boethius was a favorite text. The typical textbook of technical rhetoric was the *Artis rhetoricae* of Fortunatianus. Sometimes Cicero's and Quintilian's treatises were read as excellent illustrations of Latin rhetorical style. From the Carlovingian period on, the study of rhetoric became the study of prose composition. It included letter and legal document writing. The materials which the teacher gathered for this form of instruction led to the development of the study of canon and civil law in the medieval school.[33]

The subjects of the quadrivium were taught in all secondary schools and were pursued extensively throughout the Middle Ages. The Church urged mathematical instruction and in England no one was ordained to the priesthood who was unable to compute the date of Easter, according to the writings of Venerable Bede.[34] Arithmetic or computation dealt with the qualities of numbers and operations and was considerably advanced in the tenth century owing to the introduction of Arabic notation into Europe. The text for arithmetic and music was also Boethius. Of the science courses, the most extensive at first was that in music which was cultivated essentially to serve the purposes of Christian worship. The early use of the organ in medieval churches and the compositions of Christian musicians naturally promoted interest in the subject. Music included notation and singing, also the theory and history of music. Geometry was very generally taught and the scope of the instruction expanded with a further increase of geometrical

---

[33] *Ibid.*, pp. 54-71.
[34] *Ibid.*, p. 91.

knowledge.[35] Up to the tenth century, the age of Gerbert, the medieval knowledge of geometry was somewhat scanty. It dealt with geometrical and geographical elements used in surveying, architecture, and map making. After Gerbert found a copy of Boethius' treatise on the subject, he compiled a text of his own from the material in it. In the university period the complete works of Euclid reached Western Europe through translations from the Arabic into Latin.[36] In connection with geometry, geography was taught which was based on Ptolemy's works and gave some instruction in mineralogy, zoology, and botany. Astronomy was associated to some degree with astrology and included higher mathematical calculations and physics. Astronomy was studied to determine the Church calendar and the proper time for planting and harvesting crops. The texts used in this subject were adaptations of the treatises of Aristotle and Ptolemy.

The account of the scholastic movement will later show what detailed studies in the natural sciences and philosophy were offered in the monastic schools even before the establishment of the universities. The monks were also practitioners as well as teachers of the arts and sciences, serving their fellow men as skilled physicians, lawyers, architects, sculptors, and craftsmen. With the rise of great schools like Salerno and Bologna, which became universities, law and medicine declined as studies in the cloister; but the monks were still identified with the study of both sciences and for a considerable time with the practice of them.

Education of Women

The education of women was provided for in the convent and parish schools. For those who were to become

---

[35] *Ibid.,* p. 113.
[36] *Loc. cit.*

nuns there was a definite training in reading and writing. In the rule of St. Caesarius of Arles (501-573), the nuns were ordered to learn reading and writing and choir-singing. These arts were taught in classes, while domestic occupations, such as cooking and housekeeping, were performed in turns. The nuns also wove church hangings and spun wool which was woven into material with which they made garments for their own use.[37] They were skilled copyists also.

Wattenback, a student of manuscripts and the medieval art of writing, has collected a number of names of women whom he has found mentioned as scribes. He gives them, adding the remark that other books no doubt were written by nuns where mention of the fact is omitted.[38]

The rules for nuns compiled by St. Aurelian, St. Donatus, and St. Leander contain similar regulations urging women to devote themselves to learning and the cultivation of the arts.[39] The schools conducted by the nuns were very early open for instruction to those not intending to take the vows. In the cloisters of women there were different departments for interns and externs, i.e., for the novices and the laity. It is noteworthy that young girls were there instructed in the useful and household arts.

In some departments of art industry, especially in weaving church hangings, and embroidering altar cloths and church vestments, nuns greatly distinguished themselves. In his comprehensive work on church furniture Bock is eloquent on the industry of nuns. He first praises their early proficiency in the art of weaving and passes on to the art of embroidery. "This art also," he says, "was chiefly cultivated in religious houses by pious nuns up to the twelfth century. The inmates of women's establishments were especially devoted to working

---

[37] Lina Eckenstein, *Women Under Monasticism* (Cambridge: University Press, 1896), p. 49.

[38] *Ibid.*, p. 223.

[39] Specht, *op. cit.*, p. 259.

decorations for the altar. Their peaceful seclusion was spent in prayer and in doing embroidery. What work could seem worthier and nobler than artistic work intended for the decoration of the altar? It is in the nunnery that the art of design as well as the technique of weaving were brought to their highest perfection."[40]

The nuns conducted schools for the young boys and girls of the villages and cities where they were located. It is certain that young girls were received as pupils, because the Bishop of Soissons in 889 ordered them to be kept apart from the boys. The nuns taught the children reading, writing, and singing, and gave them religious instruction and training in manners. They also engaged in higher instruction in the seven liberal arts. Their convents were equally as important as the monasteries of men in their devotion to education.

Some of the houses ruled by women, like so many of those ruled by men, became important centers of culture where the industrial arts were taught and where books were prized, stored, and multiplied. Nuns as well as monks were busy transcribing manuscripts, a task as absorbing as it was laborious, for the difficulties in the way of learning to write can hardly be overestimated, considering the awkwardness of writing materials and the labor involved in fabricating parchment, ink, and pigment; but as the old writer with a play on the words *Armarium,* bookcase, and *Armatorium,* armoury, remarks, "A monastery without its bookcase is what a castle is without its armoury." And all houses, whether for monks or nuns, take rank as centers of culture in proportion to their wealth in books.[41]

Learned women of this period were St. Dodana of the ninth century, who wrote a manual on education for her son; St. Odilia, who founded a school for girls in Hohenburg; St. Hildegard, the adviser of men and

---

[40] Eckenstein, *op. cit.,* p. 224.
[41] *Ibid.,* p. 223.

women of note in church and state; the Abbess Herrad, reputed authoress of *Hortus deliciarum* (Garden of Delights), an encyclopedic work containing much of the knowledge of her time; Gisla, sister of Charlemagne; Gundrade, Charlemagne's cousin, who was interested in astronomy and philosophy; Judith, wife of Louis the Pious; Irmindrud, wife of Charles the Bald; Queen Matilda, who taught all her household, including the servants; Queen Adelheid, the patroness of Gerbert, a deeply learned woman, and others of noble rank whose names have often been preserved to us in books or writings which were dedicated to them.

Chivalry

From the time of Charlemagne, when cavalry supplanted infantry in warfare and the feudal lords depended upon their freemen for supporters and defenders, the chivalric movement gradually developed until in the tenth and eleventh centuries the career of a knight was the leading calling of a layman.[42] Chivalry had two general periods, viz., the heroic or golden age, extending to the period of the Crusades; and the age of courtesy extending to the fifteenth century. The ideal knight was the crusader.

Before the first crusade, knighthood was undisciplined. Military Orders had not yet set a pattern of knightly perfection; heraldry and ceremonial of all kinds were undeveloped; literature of romance was in its infancy; gallantry was no necessary qualification of a knight . . . . feudal obligations were not yet softened by the courtesies enjoined by chivalry. The soldiers of the first crusade were brave, violent, cruel, enthusiastic and devout. . . . By the end of the last crusade, chivalry had ceased to advance. Its rules were fixed and standards of conduct settled.[43]

---

[42] Chivalry denotes the ideas and customs which prevailed among the knights, while knighthood refers to the estate itself.
[43] F. W. Cornish, *Chivalry* (New York: The Macmillan Co., 1901), pp. 109 f.

A very definite training was devised for the preparation of young men for knighthood, in order that in the
development of the skill and competency of the warrior,
the virtues of the Christian general should also be acquired. The dignity of knighthood was not hereditary,
but only the sons of knights were admitted to the training. The sovereign also could create a knight when the
condition of birth was lacking. The Church participated
in the conferring of knighthood by an elaborate ceremony of blessing and prayer, that the motives of the
knight in the use of arms might be the highest and
purest.

The boy intended for knighthood was entrusted to a
feudal lord or prince for his training. He entered the
palace at the age of seven or eight as a page, and was
there made an attendant to the mistress and the ladies
of the household. He learned obedience and courtesy
by actual service, and was taught in the meantime how
to read, sing, and play chess. He was well acquainted
with the stable, the armory, the kennels, hawkpens, and
halls; a great part of his time was spent in running,
jumping, swimming, wrestling, boxing, riding, and bear
hunting.[44]

At about the age of fourteen he became a squire or
attendant of the knight and while he continued his services in the household, at the table, etc., his principal
duty was to accompany his master in the field as shield
bearer or *scutarius*. His duty was to serve the knight
in everything—to groom his horse; to arm him for the
tournament and the battle; and to see that his weapons
and accoutrements were in perfect condition.[45] He was
taught the use of arms, the sword and lance, the management of horses and the virtues becoming the warrior.
He discharged these offices until the age of twenty-one,
learning the value of service and obedience, practicing

[44] *Ibid.*, p. 64.
[45] *Ibid.*, p. 66.

loyalty and fidelity to his lord, always manifesting politeness, respect for women, and reverence for sacred things. Meanwhile he very often learned to speak French. Sometimes Latin, more rarely Greek, was also studied. Poems commemorating the lofty deeds of the knight in arms were memorized and served to foster the knightly spirit.

The ceremony of knighting was designed to impress the young candidate with the solemnity of his vow and his responsibility before God as a Christian soldier. He was required to prepare for it by prayer, fasting, and confession; after receiving Communion at Mass, he pronounced his solemn vow, "to defend the Church, to attack the wicked, to respect the priesthood, to protect women and the poor, to preserve the country in tranquility and to shed his blood, even to its last drop, in behalf of his brethren." He was given a slight tap on the shoulder with the sword (the dubbing) in the name of God and St. George, the patron of Chivalry.[46]

The education of the knight involved much that was physical as a preparation for a military career, and much that was external in politeness and good manners, but character training also played an important role. The knights were bound by their vows to loyalty and honor and the practice of virtue. That there were many of this type, the history of the Crusades makes certain; some like St. Louis attained sanctity. The age of courtesy, in which chivalry declined, saw changes in the ideals of the order; the substantial virtues of the earlier knight were supplanted by the manners and decorum of the courtier. The inspiration that chivalry afforded to modern literatures, its elevating and refining influence on the uncultured warriors of the North, its cultivation of the vernacular in song and poetry, its effect in elevating the position and estimation of women, are points to be noted in the history of European civilization and culture.

---

[46] *Ibid.*, pp. 186 f.

FOR FURTHER STUDY

Abelsen, Paul, *The Seven Liberal Arts.* New York: Teachers College, 1906.

Asserius, *De rebus gestis Alfredi.* Edited by W. H. Stevenson. Oxford: Clarendon Press, 1904.

Besant, Walter, *The Story of King Alfred.* New York: D. Appleton-Century Co., 1924.

Clark, J. M., *The Abbey of St. Gall.* Cambridge: Harvard University Press, 1926.

Clark, J. W., *The Care of Books, An Essay on the Development of Libraries from the Earliest Times.* Cambridge: University Press, 1901.

Cornish, F. W., *Chivalry.* New York: The Macmillan Company, 1901.

Davis, H. W. C., *Charlemagne: The Hero of Two Nations.* New York: G. P. Putnam's Sons, 1899.

Dawson, Christopher, *The Making of Europe.* New York: Sheed and Ward, 1939.

Eckenstein, Lina, *Women Under Monasticism.* Cambridge: University Press, 1896.

Einhard, *Life of Charlemagne.* Translated by Samuel Epes Turner. New York: Harper and Brothers, 1880.

Emerton, Ephraim, *Introduction to the Middle Ages.* Boston: Ginn and Co., 1888.

Gautier, L., *La Chevalerie.* Paris: Librairies-Imprimeries Réunies, 1883.

Hentsch, A. A., *De la litterature didactique de Moyen Age s'addressant specialement aux femmes.* Cahors: A. Coueslant, 1903.

Histoire litteraire de la France. Begun by the Benedictines of St. Maur, Paris, 1733.

Jourdain, C., *Memoires sur l'education des femmes au Moyen Age.* Paris: Impr. nationale, 1874.

Joynt, Maud., *Life of St. Gall.* London: Society for Promoting Christian Knowledge, 1927.

Keller, F., *Bauriss des Klosters St. Gallen.* Zurich: Meyer u. Zeller, 1844.

Ker, W. P., *The Dark Ages.* New York: C. Scribner's Sons, 1904.

Kilgour, Raymond L., *The Decline of Chivalry*. Cambridge: Harvard University Press, 1937.

Leach, Arthur F., *Educational Charters and Documents, 598-1909*. Cambridge: University Press, 1911.

Maitland, S. R., *The Dark Ages*. London: John Hodges, 1890.

Maître, Leon, *Les écoles épiscopales et monastiques en Occident*. Paris: A. Picard et Fils, editeurs, 1924.

Mombert, J. J., *A History of Charles the Great*. New York: D. Appleton and Co., 1888.

Monumenta Germaniae historica.

Mullinger, J. B., *The Schools of Charles the Great*. London: Longmans, Green, and Company, 1877.

Plummer, Charles, *The Life and Times of Alfred the Great*. Oxford: Clarendon Press, 1902.

Putman, G. H., *Books and Their Makers during the Middle Ages*. New York: G. P. Putnam's Sons, 1896-97, 2 vols.

Roger, M., *L'enseignement des lettres classiques d'Ausone à Alcuin*. Paris: A. Picard et Fils, 1905.

Sellery, George C., and A. C. Krey, *Medieval Foundations of Western Civilization*. New York: Harper and Brothers, 1925.

Specht, F. A., *Geschichte des Unterrichtswesens in Deutschland*. Stuttgart: J. G. Cotta, 1885.

Thompson, James W., *The Medieval Library*. Chicago: University of Chicago Press, 1939.

CHAPTER XIII

MEDIEVAL EDUCATION (Continued)

Educators of the Carlovingian Period

In this period there appeared not only a multitude of capable teachers for the various schools, but some educators of rare qualifications. Those most distinguished as scholars and educational writers are here briefly treated. Chronologically the first was Alcuin, whose connection with the school of Charlemagne has already been noted. *Alcuin Flaccus Albinus* (735-804) was a deacon when brought from England to the continent by Charlemagne. Signalizing his cultivation of ancient classical literature, Alcuin assumed the Latin surname Albinus, to which, in recognition of his spiritual kinship with the poet Horace, he prefixed the name Flaccus.[1] In his poem, *On the Bishops and Saints of the Church of York*,[2] he has given a description of the studies pursued in the famous cathedral school of that city and the books in the library. In the list of prose writers he mentions Ambrose, Athanasius, Jerome, Hilary, Orosius, Victorinus, Boethius, Gregory, Leo, Basil, Chrysostom, Cassiodorus, Fulgentius, Aldhelm, Bede; among earlier writers, in prose or verse, Pompeius, Pliny, Aristotle, Cicero, Vergil, Lucan, and Statius; among late poets, Sedulius and Juvencus; among grammarians, Donatus and Priscian. His enumeration of these and other authors indicates that, in the last quarter of the eighth century, the library at York was far superior to any, even in the twelfth century, in England or France.[3]

---

[1] Wilbur, S. Howell, *The Rhetoric of Alcuin and Charlemagne* (Princeton: Princeton University Press, 1941), p. 3.
[2] *Carmen de pontificibus et sanctis ecclesiae Eboracensis* Migne, *Pat. Lat.* CI, 841.
[3] Sandys, *A History of Classical Scholarship*, I, 472.

Amongst his contemporaries Alcuin was regarded as one of the outstanding poets of his age. Laistner makes the following observation on his efforts as a poet:

His diction is fluent, affording ample proof of his wide reading. His lines flow with a certain grace, although they are by no means free from metrical errors. He had an enviable gift for saying the appropriate thing in verse on any occasion. . . . Real inspiration, on the other hand, is rare; and when it does appear, Alcuin fails to maintain a consistently high level throughout.[4]

His writings *On Grammar, On Orthography, On Rhetoric and the Virtues, On Dialectics, A Disputation of the Royal and Most Noble Youth Pippin with Albinus the Scholastic,* and *On the Calculation of Easter,* although following the lines of earlier writers and contributing little that is new, are important as descriptive of the curriculum actually in use. From these treatises and his poems we derive our views on the teaching of certain subjects, like law, in the cathedral schools. In his work *On the Nature of the Soul,* a psychological treatise, he expounds the views of St. Augustine. He also wrote on theological, liturgical, and scriptural subjects. The *Disputatio puerorum per interrogationes et responses,* which is regarded by some critics of doubtful authenticity, can most probably, from both external and internal evidence, be truly attributed to Alcuin.[5] A study of this interesting catechism, the first in the history of catechetics,[6] reveals the pedagogical methods employed during the famous educational revival of the Carlovingian period.

Alcuin was essentially a schoolmaster, and it was just

---

[4] Laistner, *Thought and Letters in Western Europe,* pp. 280 f.
[5] Cornelius Maloney, "The Disputatio Puerorum Per Interrogationes et Responses of Alcuin" (unpublished Master's dissertation, The Catholic University, Washington, D. C., 1943), pp. 19 f.
[6] J. Baierl, R. Bandas and J. Collins, *Religious Instruction and Education* (New York: Joseph Wagner, Inc., 1938), p. 7.

such a schoolmaster that the age required.[7] As an administrator and teacher he "stimulated the interest and industry of pupils, men and women of every rank and age."[8] With his appointment in 796 as abbot of the monastery of Tours this institution assumed a commanding position among the schools in the West. He made it his special duty, by personally supervising the copying of manuscripts in the scriptorium of the monastery, to transmit to future ages the precious treasure of knowledge.

Thus, in every way that lay within his power, he endeavored to put the fortunes of learning for the times that should succeed him in a position of advantage, safeguarded by an abundance of truthfully transcribed books, interpreted by teachers of his own training, sheltered within the Church and defended by the civil power.[9]

As a teacher Alcuin's main concern was not books or studies. He vigorously defended the Faith; and amid the lax morals of the court he bore witness to its elevating influence with the testimony of a blameless life. It is true that he was not an original thinker, but he was an unusual scholar. In this regard De Wulf's evaluation of him is significant.

But if Alcuin lacked originality, he was an organizer of learned institutions and a sower of ideas. . . . The schools which sprang up as a result of the impulse he gave to study continued to be philosophical centers up to the foundation of the University of Paris.[10]

---

[7] Dawson, *The Making of Europe,* p. 224.

[8] Paul Monroe, editor, *A Cyclopedia of Education* (New York: The Macmillan Company, 1911), I, 85. *Cf.* P. Gabriel Meier, *Bibliothek der katholischen Pädagogik* (Freiburg: Herdersche Verlagshandlung, 1890), III, 20-51.

[9] Andrew F. West, *Alcuin and the Rise of the Christian Schools* (New York: Charles Scribner's Sons, 1920), pp. 122 f.

[10] Maurice De Wulf, *History of Medieval Philosophy* (London: Longmans, Green, and Company, 1935), I, 118.

Rhabanus Maurus (776-856), the disciple of Alcuin, ranks higher as an educational writer than his master. Rhabanus, who was a monk of Fulda, was sent by his abbot to complete his education under Alcuin in the monastery of Tours. There he pursued the study of letters and the interpretation of the Scriptures and so endeared himself to his teacher that Alcuin gave him the surname of Maurus in honor of the beloved disciple of St. Benedict. In his treatment of the seven liberal arts he showed a more vigorous mind and much greater independence than Alcuin. He had a broader view of the study of classical literature and a far deeper penetration of the art of logic. From his treatise, *De magicis artibus*, it is evident that he also possessed a more scientific mind. He clearly comprehended that so-called ghosts and other strange manifestations came from a deception of the senses under the influence of overwrought mental faculties; and forcibly challenged the superstitions of astrology and fortune telling.[11]

Upon his return to Fulda, Rhabanus was placed in charge of the school. He eventually became abbot of the monastery and exercised control over some of the largest monasteries and schools in Europe; thus Fulda under his administration became as famous and powerful as Tours had been under the guidance of Alcuin.

At the time of his elevation as abbot, no less than 16 monasteries and nunneries, either founded by former abbots or affiliated at their own desire, already looked up to Fulda as

their parent house. To these Rhabanus added six more—those at Corvey, Solenhofen, Celle, Hersfeld, Petersburg and Hirschau; we may accordingly reckon twenty-two societies wherein his authority would be regarded as law, and his teaching be faithfully preserved.[12]

---

[11] Mullinger, *The Schools of Charles the Great,* pp. 143 ff.
[12] *Ibid.,* p. 151.

Rhabanus composed for the direction of the clergy and his students a work entitled *De institutione clericorum* (On the Education of the Clergy) which

has more than once been justly appealed to, as evidence that strongly contravenes the exaggerated representations of certain writers with respect to the ignorance of the clergy in these times. The mere fact that it was compiled to meet a recognized want, and at the request of many of the community of Fulda, is alone sufficient proof that the prevailing tone was far from being one of vulgar and illiterate contempt for learning.[13]

This remarkable treatise deals with the organization and ritual of the Church, the ecclesiastical calendar, the orders of clergy and their duties. The third book treats of study and learning. Rhabanus adopts the views of St. Augustine in regard to pagan literature and discusses at length the seven liberal arts. The first actual use of the numeral seven in connection with the liberal arts is said to occur in this treatise.[14]

Another work, *De universo*, an encyclopedia in twenty-two books, is based on the etymologies of St. Isidore. It deals with everything then known and has been aptly called "A book on everything." It aimed to give the sum of knowledge and was the kind of book needed in the ninth century for the preservation of what knowledge past ages had produced. The influence of Rhabanus was great as a teacher and churchman. He was appointed in later life to the Archbishopric of Mainz, at that time one of the most important sees in Europe. His students were distinguished in church and state, and because of their great number he has been called the *"Primus praeceptor Germaniae."* It is maintained by one of his biographers that

---

[13] *Ibid.*, p. 143.
[14] Thomas Davidson, "The Seven Liberal Arts," *Educational Review*, II, 467-72.

Wherever, be it in peace or in war, in Church or in State, a prominent actor appears at this period, we may almost predict beforehand that he will prove to have been a scholar of this great teacher.[15]

Some of his pupils well known for their labors on behalf of learning and religion and others who were influenced at least indirectly by him were Lupus Servatus, abbot of Ferrières and devoted student of the Latin classics, whose writings abound with reference to nearly every classical author known at that time;[16] Walafrid Strabo, abbot of Reichenau, poet and author; Otfried, poet and monk, author of *Der Krist* in old High German dialect; Rudolphus, teacher of Fulda, the continuator of the annals of Fulda, begun by Einhard, and the biographer of Rhabanus whom he succeeded as head of the school of Fulda; Werembert and Notker of St. Gall; Eric of Auxerre, a famous teacher in the school of St. Germain d'Auxerre, who afterwards went to Paris where he founded a school which is regarded as the first cradle of the University of Paris; and Odo, the distinguished pupil of Remy at Paris and later abbot of the monastery of Cluny which became the great training center for scholars who did much to make possible the renaissance of the twelfth century.

Probably the greatest thinker of this age was a representative of the Irish school, *John Scotus Eriugena*,[17] John the Scot (815-?), the details of whose life are very obscure. He assumed charge about 845 of the palace school of Charles the Bald who admired greatly the astronomical and dialectic ability of the Irish monks.

---

[15] Th. Spengler, *Leben des heiligen Rhabanus Maurus* (Regensburg: Manz, 1856), p. iv.
[16] Mullinger, *op. cit.*, p. 165.
[17] Eriugena means a native of Ireland.

He was perhaps a priest. Interested chiefly in philosophy and theology, he became identified with the great controversy of the ninth century on predestination. In his treatise on this subject he used logic as his weapon, but his skill and learning did not prevent him from exceeding the bounds of orthodoxy. Because of his bold use of logic and of his efforts to make dialectic a universal study, he is considered by some the first of the schoolmen.[18] He seems rather to be the link connecting early medieval with later scholastic learning.

Eriugena was well versed in Greek philosophy, which he had learned in Ireland. He revived the learned traditions of the Irish, and, as a teacher, made the palace school, which had declined under Louis the Pious, as famous as it had been during the reign of Charlemagne. He translated into Latin the works of the "Pseudo-Dionysius" which were thought in the Middle Ages to have been written by Dionysius the Areopagite.[19] Some of his views expressed in *De divisione naturae* and other writings have been condemned by the Church as heretical. He wrote commentaries on the Gospel and also on Martianus Capella. He exemplified in a very marked degree the Celtic penchant for speculation;[20] his influence lay in the revival of philosophical interest and the study of the Greek Fathers. Despite his many philosophical errors, Eriugena was the most constructive genius of the century, and as "Anastasius the Roman librarian described him 'vir per omnia sanctus.' "[21]

---

[18] Turner, *History of Philosophy*, p. 246.

[19] Critical scholarship has determined that the character of the writings indicates that the author belongs at the very earliest to the latter half of the fifth century and that he was in all probability a native of Syria.

[20] Mullinger, *op. cit.*, p. 175.

[21] Turner, *op. cit.*, p. 257.

Gerbert [22] (c950-1003), a monk of humble origin of
the tenth century, was the greatest teacher and the most
scholarly man of his time.[23] His early education was received in the Benedictine monastery at Aurillac where he
grew to love the classics. As a student he had journeyed
to Barcelona, Cordova, and Seville, in which cities he
learned the mathematics and sciences taught in the Arabian schools. He was, however, a product of Latin
Christian, not of Moslem, scholarship.[24]

Visiting Rome with the Spanish bishop, Hatto, he was
persuaded by Pope John XIII and by the emperor, Otto
I, not to return to Spain. He took charge of the cathedral school of Rheims. Like Eriugena, he was well
versed in Greek philosophy and was especially in favor
of classical studies. In his teaching, Gerbert used as
textbooks Aristotle's *Categories*, Cicero's *Topics*, Porphyry's *Isagoge*, and the commentaries of Boethius. He
taught the Latin poets and dramatists and was most
energetic in founding at Rheims a library of the Latin
authors.[25] His quotations from them and references to
them in his letters are most frequent. While he was
head of the episcopal school, his reputation as teacher
and scholar was brilliant.[26]

In the province of mathematics, Gerbert was regarded
as a man of extraordinary learning. As a mathematician, he did not exhaust the knowledge possessed by men
before him; but he drew intelligently upon the available

---

[22] Richer's *Histories* which give valuable information on the
life and character of Gerbert are published by Migne (juxta
Perz), *Pat. Lat.*, Vol. CXXXVIII, 17-170.
[23] Henry O. Taylor, *The Medieval Mind* (London: The Macmillan Co., 1930), p. 286.
[24] Eby and Arrowood, *History and Philosophy of Education
Ancient and Medieval*, p. 712.
[25] *Loc. cit.*
[26] Maitre, *Les écoles episcopales et monastiques en Occident*,
p. 43.

sources and then taught with understanding.[27] He advanced the current methods of computation in arithmetic and used a special form of abacus, which is thought to have been invented by him. He was a student of geometry; and in teaching astronomy he constructed spheres and other instruments by means of which he showed the movements of the planets and marked the constellations of the heavens.

Gerbert also taught successfully music and medicine and was the tutor of the young Emperor, Otto III. He became abbot of Bobbio and later was chosen Archbishop of Rheims, but his election was declared to be illegal. In 998 he was appointed to the see of Ravenna. The following year he was raised to the pontificate as the first French pope, taking the name of Sylvester II.

The various works of Gerbert on philosophical and mathematical subjects, together with his numerous letters, are of educational value. He has often been credited with having been the first to introduce Arabic numerals in Europe but it now appears that he only helped to popularize their use. He is also believed to have invented the pendulum clock. Because of his inventions and remarkable skill in the use of mechanical devices, accusations of necromancy were brought against him by the ignorant. In the scholastic movement he is in the tenth century what Eriugena was in the ninth and what Abelard will be in the twelfth.[28] He and his disciples examined the enormous mass of theology, philosophy, and science, and undertook to consider problems of classification and method as a task essential to its mastery.[29] His career as a scholar, teacher, and churchman makes clear that the age in which he lived, sup-

---

[27] Taylor, *op. cit.*, p. 290.
[28] Turner, *op. cit.*, p. 261.
[29] Taylor, *op. cit.*, p. 294.

posed to be the darkest in history, was not without its scholars and cultural interests.

Mohammedan or Saracen Learning

The influence of Mohammedan learning on medieval education, which is especially noteworthy in the studies of the scholastics, was exerted chiefly through the followers of Mohammed in the West, that is the Saracens, or as they were called in Spain, the Moors. It began about the time of Gerbert in the tenth century and was pronounced in mathematics, natural sciences, medicine, and philosophy.

Up until the time of Mohammed (c.570-632), the Arabs played no great part in the development of world history. The different tribes warred against one another; but once these peoples of the Arabian desert accepted Mohammed as their religious leader, they became a powerful force in their efforts to disseminate his teachings and in their attempts to subjugate the world. Within ten years of the death of their prophet, the Saracens had destroyed the new Persian Empire and captured Syria and Egypt from the Greeks; less than a century after the establishment of Mohammedanism they had pushed eastward into Asia as far as India and westward across the northern coast of Africa into Spain. In their contact with the more highly cultured people whom they conquered, they soon developed a rather remarkable and brilliant civilization.

In the ninth century, through conquest of the Christians of Syria whom they endeavored to convert, Greek learning, especially philosophy, was taken up by the Mohammedans and Greek texts were translated into Arabic.[30] Their caliphs, religious leaders, were patrons of learning. Elementary and higher schools were established in the countries ruled by them in the Orient and

---

[30] De Wulf, *op. cit.*, pp. 291 f.

in the West. Some of their famous higher schools were those of Bagdad, Cairo, Cordova, Granada, Toledo, and Seville. The kingdom of Granada is estimated to have had seventy public libraries, seventeen colleges, and two hundred primary schools.[31]

Arabian scholars were the translators of Greek mathematical, medical, and philosophical works, and were the first to introduce them to Europe. Alkendi, who is considered the father of philosophy among the Arabs, taught Aristotelian philosophy in the school of Bagdad during the ninth century. Alfarabi taught in the same school in the following century and was the author of a number of commentaries on the philosophy of Aristotle. Several of their leading philosophers, like Avicenna and Averroës, also wrote commentaries on the works of Galen.

In their practical applications of scientific knowledge, the Arabs made original and noteworthy contributions. Their achievements in astronomy and geography were marvelous. They successfully measured a degree of the earth's surface on the shores of the Red Sea and therefore learned of the size of the earth, used the pendulum in the measurement of time, and determined the length of the year. They had observatories, and, it is said, employed the globe for teaching geography in the schools. They adopted the Hindu system of notation and algebra which they perfected for the modern world; and they advanced the science of trigonometry. In chemistry and physics, their discoveries were of importance. They are awarded the distinction of discovering nitric acid in the ninth century and sulphuric acid and alcohol in the tenth century. Their chemists laid the basis of modern chemistry. In medicine and surgery, they were also far

---

[31] Ameer Ali, *History of the Saracens.* Reprinted with corrections. (New York: The Macmillan Company, 1924), p. 570.

advanced. The Jewish scholars of their schools were famous practitioners; they knew the properties of many drugs then unknown to the Christian world, and performed remarkable operations in obstetrics and surgery. The Jews were their firm collaborators in philosophy as well; in the Jewish schools the philosophical works of the Greeks and of the Arabians were preserved, translated into Hebrew, and given over to the Christian scholars, who in turn translated them into Latin.[32]

The Arabs taught the West the art of distillation, the use of alcohol, mercury, syrups, and camphor. From them Europe also received many of its vegetables, useful plants, and orchard fruits: the mulberry, cotton, rice, rhubarb, sugar, asparagus, artichoke, apricot, and peach. They supplied the markets of the West with superior merchandise; morocco leather, silk goods of Granada, arms of Toledo, Cordova harnesses, Cuenca cloth were some of their high-class manufactured products. The Moslem cities were distinguished for their material splendor and excellent sanitary conditions; they had splendid aqueducts, market places, mosques, palaces, and public baths, paved roadways and street lights.[33]

The scholastics were chiefly indebted to the Mohammedans for the translation of Greek philosophers and especially Aristotle. Avicenna (980-1037) in the East, although a physician, wrote many philosophical works and followed the doctrines of Aristotle. The Emperor Frederick II had them translated from Arabic into Latin. Avicenna was studied by the great schoolmen as a representative pagan philosopher and authority in Aristotle. Averroës (1126-1198), one of the chief philosophers of the schools in the West, a physician like Avicenna, was a native of Cordova. His works embrace treatises on

---

[32] Turner, *op. cit.*, p. 318.
[33] *Cf.* Marique, *History of Christian Education*, pp. 112 f.; Charles Seignobos, *History of Medieval and of Modern Civilization* (New York: Charles Scribner's Sons, 1907), p. 117.

medicine, astronomy, and philosophy. He "was regarded as greatest of all Arabian commentators of Aristotle." [34]

The first Latin translations of the physical and metaphysical treatises of Aristotle were made from the Arabic, probably through the medium of the Hebrew.[35] These redactions were not very accurate, but in the course of the thirteenth century translations were made directly from the Greek.[36] The influence of Moslem scholars on the development of philosophy in Europe was only indirect; because of their opposition to Catholic doctrine they provoked discussion and controversy. It was the Christian mind that gave expression to the tenets of Scholasticism.[37]

FOR FURTHER STUDY

Adams, George B., *Civilization During the Middle Ages*. New York: Charles Scribner's Sons, 1924.

Ali, Ameer, *History of the Saracens*. New York: The Macmillan Company, 1924.

Campbell, Donald, *Arabian Medicine*. London: Kegan Paul, French, Trübner and Company, Ltd., 1926.

Dawson, Christopher, *The Making of Europe*. New York: Sheed and Ward, 1939.

De Wulf, Maurice, *History of Medieval Philosophy*. English translation by E. C. Messenger. London: Longmans, Green, and Company, 1935. 2 vols.

Drane, Augusta Theodosia, *Christian Schools and Scholars*. London: Burns, Oates and Washbourne, Ltd., 1924.

Eby and Arrowood, *History and Philosophy of Education, Ancient and Medieval*. New York: Prentice-Hall, Inc., 1940.

---

[34] Turner, *op. cit.*, p. 313.

[35] *Ibid.*, p. 320.

[36] William of Moerbeka translated the complete works of Aristotle into Latin about 1260 at the request of St. Thomas and Urban IV. This version was known as the "translatio nova." It was regarded as the authoritative translation of Aristotle down until the age of the Renaissance, although others were in use.

[37] Turner, *op. cit.*, p. 318.

Gaskoin, C. J. B., *Alcuin: His Life and His Work*. London: C. J. Clay and Sons, 1907.

Hitti, Philip K., *History of the Arabs*. London: The Macmillan Company, 1937.

Howell, Wilbur, S., *The Rhetoric of Alcuin and Charlemagne*. Princeton: Princeton University Press, 1941.

Hurgronje, C. Snoadk, *Mohammedanism*. New York: G. P. Putnam's Sons, 1916.

Laistner, M. L. W., *Thought and Letters in Western Europe: 500-900*. London: Methuen and Company, Ltd., 1931.

MacDonald, D. B., *Aspects of Islam*. New York: The Macmillan Company, 1911.

Mabillon, J., *Tractatus de studiis monasticis*. Viennae: A. Poleti, 1730.

Maître, Leon, *Les écoles épiscopales et monastiques en Occident*. Paris: A. Picard et Fils, editeurs, 1924.

Marique, Pierre J., *History of Christian Education*. New York: Fordham University Press, 1924.

Mullinger, J. B., *The Schools of Charles the Great*. London: Longmans, Green, and Company, 1877.

Ryan, John J., *John Scotus Erigena*. Unpublished Doctor's dissertion, New York University, 1931.

Sandys, J. E., *A History of Classical Scholarship*. Cambridge: University Press, 1921.

Scott, S. P., *History of the Moorish Empire in Europe*. Philadelphia: J. B. Lippincott, 1904. 3 vols.

Seignobos, Charles, *History of Medieval and of Modern Civilization*. New York: Charles Scribner's Sons, 1907.

Taylor, Henry O., *The Medieval Mind*. London: The Macmillan Company, 1930. Vol. 1.

Thorndike, Lynn, *The History of Medieval Europe*. Boston: Houghton Mifflin Company, 1928.

Townsend, W. J., *The Great Schoolmen of the Middle Ages*. London: Hodder and Stoughton, 1881.

Turner, W., *History of Philosophy*. Boston: Ginn and Company, 1903.

————, "Irish Teachers in the Carolingian Revival." *Catholic University Bulletin*, 13:382; 567.

West, Andrew F., *Alcuin and the Rise of Christian Schools*. New York: Charles Scribner's Sons, 1920.

CHAPTER XIV

MEDIEVAL EDUCATION (Continued)

Scholasticism

Scholasticism as a movement in the history of education has been most frequently studied and evaluated in the years of its decline rather than in the period of its greatness, and the estimate of it has been in consequence far from correct. It has been most familiarly known to English readers for the abuses connected with it rather than for its merits and points of excellence, and the magnificent service which it rendered to science and education has been almost entirely ignored. It is safe to say that no movement has been more harshly dealt with by the historians of education, and yet for many reasons it deserved sympathetic treatment from them.

As its name implies, it was in the first place a movement of the schools, and its leaders, schoolmen. It extended over the entire Middle Ages from Boethius to Erasmus, from the sixth to the sixteenth century, including the whole educational theory produced in that wide range of time, and all of the educational institutions, some of which have never been surpassed, and surviving in its effects to the present time; it produced a library of educational literature, and an army of educators who, while differing widely in the various stages of the movements, were united by a common name and profession. Its leaders were teachers, not merely theorists; and, according to the empirical standard of modern times which tries everything in the fire of the educational laboratory, the schoolroom, the scholastics [1]

---

[1] Scholastic is an old term which comes from *Scholasticus,* a title given to headmasters generally in the Middle Ages, and eventually to their system of teaching, e.g., scholastic method, philosophy, theology, etc.

253

should stand high in favor. Its representatives were the administrators of educational institutions, writers on educational theory and practice, patrons of a well-defined system of schools. To obtain a fair idea of the general movement, it seems proper to view scholasticism in the period of its glory, when its brilliant lights illumined the academic world, and its institutions dominated the educational field—in the period from St. Bernard in the twelfth century to William of Occam in the fourteenth.

The twelfth century was the golden age of monasticism, and also the golden age of the schools.[2] It left its imprint very deeply on higher education and, in particular, on scholastic philosophy. The monastery of Cluny and its priories were largely responsible for the training of the scholars who made possible this renaissance of the twelfth century. In the tenth and eleventh centuries the Cluniac monks founded many important houses of studies; by the beginning of the eleventh century Cluny was looked up to as the intellectual, artistic, and religious center of Europe. The reading of books was a part of the cultural tradition of the monastery; the library encouraged not only theological studies but classical learning as well. Many of the monks were well versed in profane literature and profited from the study of the classics.[3] The central location of Cluny led to extensive travel and communication and consequently to the exchange of books and ideas and types of art.[4] Already, however, the cultural supremacy of Cluny was waning and its leadership took a new turn in the asceticism of St. Bernard.

---

[2] De Wulf, *History of Medieval Philosophy*, p. 50.
[3] J. Evans, *Monastic Life at Cluny* (Oxford: University Press, 1931), pp. 98 ff.
[4] Charles H. Haskins, *The Renaissance of the Twelfth Century* (Cambridge: Harvard University Press, 1933), p. 43.

By the early twelfth century, the school at Bec was famous throughout Europe. It owed its intellectual eminence to *Lanfranc* (1005-1089), and to his successor, *Anselm of Canterbury* (1033-1109), who is regarded as the "Father of Scholasticism." Lanfranc was learned in letters and the law; he developed in his school men of prominence who went forth to carry through Europe the new enthusiasm for study. Anselm was a thinker of extraordinary speculative ability and a genuine scholastic. The formula of scholasticism *Intelligo ut credam* has for its complement the motto of Anselm: *Credo ut intelligam*. Anselm adheres closely to the doctrines of St. Augustine. Through him, Augustine became for the scholastics more than a mere authority; he became a representative of reason, a defender of truth.[5] It is especially as a theologian that Anselm is remembered. His works testify to his thorough understanding of the respective roles of faith and reason, the two vital factors in the investigation of revealed truth.[6]

In the twelfth century, the scholastics were of two distinct classes: the rationalists and the mystics or contemplatives, represented in education respectively by Peter Abelard and Hugh of St. Victor. The former gave an undue importance to logic in education and depreciated the utility of other studies in the liberal arts. The mystics, as represented by Hugh, maintained the necessity of a fuller educational scheme; they opposed the narrow educational views of the disciples of Abelard and contended that the arts course by its content and training would give a proper preparation for the study of logic.

Peter Abelard (1079-1142) was the foremost dialecti-

---

[5] Grabmann, *Die Geschichte der scholastichen Methode,* I, 269 ff.
[6] *Ibid.,* pp. 263 f.

cian of the age. He was the brilliant pupil of William of Champeaux. He entered vigorously into the philosophical disputations of the time on the subject of "Universals"; and by his subtle questions and scholarly attainments he attracted disciples from all parts of Europe. The best known of his philosophical works is his *Sic et non* (*Yes and No*) in which the principal theses of theology are formulated and the opinions of the Fathers presented *pro and contra*.[7] This idea of philosophic method was afterwards brought to more definite form by Alexander of Hales and St. Thomas Aquinas.

Abelard's influence on his immediate successors was not very great owing to his conflict with St. Bernard and other ecclesiastical authorities who reproved him, not because he advocated the rights of reason but because of the extravagant claims that he urged on behalf of reason.[8] His influence on the philosophers and theologians of the thirteenth century, however, is apparent; it was exercised through Peter Lombard, his pupil, and other framers of the "Sentences." Abelard has been designated the greatest luminary of the twelfth century [9] who made the University of Paris the intellectual capital of the educational world of that time.[10] He seems rather, as Turner has expressed it, to be like a brilliant comet which dazzled for a moment, but failed to shed permanent light.[11]

The rationalists, like all ardent advocates, in championing the claims of reason, exaggerated the importance

---

[7] This method had been used before, as in the *Sentences* of Anselm of Laon. Abelard popularized it and, like everything he did, it was well advertised. *Cf.* Haskins, *op. cit.*, pp. 353f.

[8] Turner, *op. cit.*, p. 291.

[9] W. J. Townsend, *The Great Schoolmen of the Middle Ages* (London: Hodder and Stoughton, 1881), p. 99.

[10] F. Funk-Brentano, *The Middle Ages* (New York: G. P. Putnam's Sons, 1923), p. 692.

[11] Turner, *op. cit.*, p. 291.

of dialectics and often applied them imprudently. The mystics, who were conservatives, tended to discredit reason in favor of contemplation. An intelligent compromise between the two schools of thought was not reached until the end of the twelfth century. It was rationalism that, having modified its original position regarding the rationalistic element of scholasticism, eventually prevailed in the schools. Meanwhile the mystics added to the *Credo ut intelligam* and the *Intelligo ut Credam* a third principle, *Amo ut intelligam*, and contributed differently yet definitely to the final triumph of the method of dialectics which was to achieve such brilliant results in the hands of the great schoolmen of the thirteenth century.

Medieval chroniclers praise highly the moral uprightness and the scientific achievements of *Hugh of St. Victor* (c. 1096-1141), a teacher and canon regular of the school of St. Victor, Paris. They extol his piety and humility, and stress his familiarity with profane learning as well as with theological studies. In his writings there is exemplified the union of speculative, practical, and mystic theology; in his spiritual life he exhibits the qualities of Augustine and Gregory the Great.[12]

His *Eruditionis didascalicae libri septem*[13] is a unique student's manual. Intended to develop in students orderly habits of study, it is an instructive source of information on the didactics of the Middle Ages. In it are treated all the subjects of the curriculum, together with a discussion of the methods of study. In the pedagogical phraseology of the present time we would say Hugh pointed out the unity and correlation of all knowledge, the mutual relationship of all the studies, discussed the utility of analysis and synthesis in the art of study,

---

[12] Grabmann, *op. cit.*, II, 230-33.
[13] Migne, *Pat. Lat.*, CLXXVI.

emphasized the principle that learning proceeds from the known to the unknown, and, in short, while producing a book helpful as a guide to students, discussed educational theory and method. For this reason he has been spoken of as the only educational theorist excepting Gerson in the Middle Ages, an inaccuracy, it is true, but one containing a tribute to his preeminence in this early period. Another work attributed to him, *On the Vanity of the World,* contains a description of a school in which the students are engaged in copying manuscripts and in studying herbs, physiology, and anatomy; and while we know that he belittles many of these studies in comparison with the divine sciences, his testimony to their existence in the schools is very valuable.[14]

Vincent of Beauvais (†1264), a Dominican friar, contemporary and friend of St. Thomas, is a representative of the scholastic educators in another sense. He also wrote for the benefit of students, but in a manner quite different from that of Hugh of St. Victor. The friend of King Louis IX, he was a member of the royal household and, if not the tutor, at least the director of the education of the king's children. He conceived the plan of presenting the student world with a trustworthy compendium of learning. He deplored the condition of books, which through the ignorance and carelessness of copyists were incorrect and unreliable, particularly in regard to the wisdom inherited from the past. He contemplated producing not only a book of universal knowledge, an encyclopedia, but one whose information would be accurate, taken from original sources and carefully transcribed. King Louis supported him in the project and gave him every opportunity to procure books and copyists for his working library. The work appeared after several years of patient labor, bearing the title of

---

[14] *De vanitate mundi.* Migne, *Pat. Lat.,* CLXXVI.

Speculum majus,[15] the *Great Mirror,* a truly great work of its kind, and which, with another notable treatise, should insure a place for Vincent among the leading educators of the period.

The *Speculum majus* is representative of that class of scholastic educators who, while as orthodox as Hugh of St. Victor, were interested in all science and learning, in all that referred to God, to His creatures, and to nature, and who believed that by learning and education God was glorified. Vincent believed in the unification of knowledge. Although his work incorporated information on thousands of subjects taken from a multitude of authors, ancient and modern, he believed there was one body of knowledge, as there was one system of philosophy. His purpose in the work was to make God better known, both in Himself and in His creatures, visible and invisible, and thereby inflame the sacred fire of love for Him in all hearts; and also to help the preacher, lecturer, controversialist, and student in the explanation of practically all the philosophical, moral, and scientific problems of the time. This was to be done by placing before them the wisdom of the great doctors, poets, philosophers, Christian and pagan, making accessible to all what the past had thought and written.

One can see from the introduction that Vincent was obliged to prove the value and the necessity of his work. He had many critics who distrusted his plan or objected to many of its features. Some thought it too new, others inadequate for the purpose in view, while others disapproved of his extensive treatment of the natural sciences. He answered them in the preface, and it would seem that he forever silenced criticism by the excellence and the usefulness of the book.

---

[15] A complete *Speculum majus* is in the Library of Congress.

The *Speculum majus* has three parts, the *Speculum naturale, Speculum doctrinale,* and *Speculum historiale,* which altogether contain eighty books in 9,885 chapters. It may be interesting to point out some of the topics treated in each part, and especially those with which the medieval student is seldom thought to have been concerned. The *Speculum naturale,* or *Mirror of Nature,* treats of theology, psychology, physiology, zoology, botany, cosmography, mineralogy, physics, and agriculture. One is astounded at the number and variety of subjects included under natural science, on all of which Vincent had gathered information. It is curious perhaps to find theology there, but nature is treated as the work of God's creation; in fact, the very method of treatment is based on the order of creation. For instance, on the fourth day, when the sun and moon were created, he considers all of the heavenly bodies, eclipses, seasons, etc.; and on the sixth day, when God created animals and man, he discusses the types and species of animals then known, down to reptiles and insects, and man both as to body and soul, his faculties, reason, ideas, emotions, etc.; he also gives a detailed description of the human body.

If we recall that he compiled these data when Albertus Magnus was lecturing and writing on studies in physics and the natural order and Roger Bacon was absorbed in his experiments, we realize how incorrect is the assertion that the scholastics abandoned everything else for the study of philosophy and theology. The knowledge of nature which the scholastics had, and the method they advocated for the study, are not well enough known. They did not collectively embrace the study of the natural sciences, nor did they learn as fruitfully of them as later generations of scholars; but they were deeply interested in natural phenomena, and they studied nature by observation, by experiment, and by the inductive method. Albertus Magnus has said in his *De vegetalibus et plantis,* wherein he describes and catalogues all the trees, plants, and herbs known in his time:

All that is here set down is the result of our own experience, or has been borrowed from authors, whom we know to have written what their personal experience has confirmed; for in these matters experience alone can give certainty.[16]

Albert was a great botanist and geographer, and a fine example of the medieval scholar who sought scientific explanations of natural phenomena and who, in more than one instance, surprises us with real anticipations of modern discoveries. Chesterton regards him as the "Founder of Modern Science."[17] His conclusions regarding the natural sciences may be called deductions or speculations, but they were remarkable for their sagacity and conformity with the facts of later experience. All that was known then of natural science Vincent of Beauvais included with natural philosophy under the title of the *Mirror of Nature.*

The second part, *Speculum doctrinale* or *Mirror of Doctrine,* treats of logic, rhetoric, poetry, geometry, astronomy, the instincts, the passions, education, the industrial and mechanical arts, anatomy, surgery, medicine, jurisprudence, and the administration of justice;

---

[16] Earum autem quas ponemus, quasdam quidem nos experimento probamus. Quasdam autem referimus ex dictis eorum, quos comperimus non de facili aliqua dicere nisi probata per experimentum. Experimentum enim solum certificat in talibus, eo quod tam de particularibus naturis simile haberi non potest. D. Alberti Magni *Opera omnia,* vol. X; *De vegetalibus et plantis,* vi, i, I. (Parisiis: Borgnet, 1891). *Cf.* Drane, *Christian Schools and Scholars,* p. 417.

[17] G. K. Chesterton, *St. Thomas Aquinas* (New York: Sheed and Ward, 1933), p. 67.

in short, it is a collection of brief chapters on the subjects of the curriculum of the Middle Ages, i.e., on the
seven liberal arts, and also on the faculties of man concerned in education, the senses, the emotions, the intellect. It is a thesaurus of information for the increas-
ingly popular studies of law and medicine, which were
then contending for supremacy in the schools. One
notes that many questions of an educational nature are
treated there and views expressed which refer to heated
discussions of that great century. To meet some of the
criticisms against the manner and plan of his work, he
defends, like Hugh of St. Victor, the study of literature,
philosophy, the liberal arts, the sciences, as necessary
and useful for theology and for all the purposes of Christian society and the Church; he pleads in behalf of a
liberal education, which in his judgment is one of the
divinely appointed means for the regeneration of fallen
man. He, therefore, treats of the subjects it includes,
and offers many valuable recommendations as to methods and study plans.

The *Speculum historiale,* or *Mirror of History,* forms
the third part and is a history of the world from creation down to A.D. 1250. The author wanted to do for
historical knowledge what he proposed to do for all the
other sciences, i.e., to give the student in a compendious
form the important facts of the past—an indication that
history was then a more real and profitable study than
later, in the Renaissance, when historians were often read
less for their content than for their literary style. The
Speculum majus consequently constitutes for its day the
sum of knowledge. It was for the student what an encyclopedia and textbook would be today, and its influence was considerable.

In another treatise, *De eruditione filiorum nobili-*

um (On the Instruction of Princes),[18] more of the educator's theory is to be found. This was addressed to Louis IX, King of France, and Thibaut, King of Navarre, both of whom had urged Vincent to write on the subject. Like the other numerous treatises on the training of princes, *De regimine principum,* it was intended for wider reading. It embodies Vincent's views and the result of his experience in private teaching. Like the similar treatises of Colonna, Denis the Carthusian, Pope Pius II, and many others of the later Middle Ages, it provides an example of an important form of educational literature, in which the old Roman type of training, as sanctioned by the Christian Fathers, received its exposition and defense. It aspired to make the prince a leader in learning and culture, as he was in power. The writings of Denis and those of the later period are especially important for the truly Christian spirit which the scholastics as well as the humanists desired in every phase of education.

Among the writings of the great schoolmen, Albertus Magnus, St. Thomas, St. Bonaventure, Duns Scotus, and Occam, are to be found many treatises of educational value, as, for instance, those of Albertus on geography, cosmography, plants, and animals, of which some were contributions to their respective sciences, while others would more properly rank as textbooks rather than educational treatises. They were the practical books needed by the schools, and even the manuals of the students. The writers aimed in them to extend the field of science and especially to make knowledge accessible. Erudition

---

[18] *Cf.* Raphael L. Schoof, "The Educational Contents of the *De eruditione filiorum nobilium* by Vincent of Beauvais" (unpublished Master's dissertation, The Catholic University of America, Washington, D. C., 1942). A critical text of this treatise has been edited by Arpad Steiner: *Vincent of Beauvais De Eruditione Filiorum Nobilium* (Cambridge: The Medieval Academy of America, 1938).

being the ideal in education, works appeared aiming to give the sum of knowledge, just as among institutions there arose the school of learning in which the whole range of the sciences was to be taught, viz., the university.

Some did, however, like Hugh of St. Victor, examine the theoretical side of education. In the *Quaestiones disputatae* of *St. Thomas* is a treatise entitled *De magistro (On The Teacher)*, which may be cited as an excellent example of the scholastic theory and philosophy of education. In it questions fundamental to the process of learning are treated, not so much in relation to method as to the psychological processes involved. St. Thomas bases the work of education upon the principles which serve as the foundation for his system of philosophy. His theory on the acquisition of knowledge, the origin of ideas, is applied to the deepest aspects of the educative process. The divine influence in the acquisition of knowledge—for all knowledge comes from God and its first elements are deposited in man as *rationes seminales* —and in the whole process of learning, is scientifically expressed by St. Thomas in regard to both the teacher and the pupil. The teacher's office in cooperating with God in the process is consequently of the highest dignity.

St. Thomas, like all medieval educators, is concerned with the qualifications of the teacher, but he exacts a finer intellectual equipment than most others. His teacher must have not only the moral qualifications always insisted upon by the Christian educational writers, but he must have an intimate knowledge of mental processes, the functions of the senses, emotions, etc., for his work is to assist in the development of the pupil's capacities, in the unfolding of the youthful powers. He did not emphasize self-activity on the part of the pupil; his system everywhere assumes that, for with him the process of learning is "growth in self-activity."

While these are only indications of the principles expressed in *De magistro*, it may be stated here that the work is an excellent embodiment of scholastic philosophy applied to education. As to the process of education, it is interesting to learn that according to St. Thomas education is a matter of developing the inborn capacities of children.

Education is no mere imparting or infusion; it is rather a solicitation, suggestion, and direction, by which the mind is prompted to exert its natural power in normal ways. . . . While chief stress is laid upon the development of intellectual functions, due notice is taken of the subordinate faculties. Sense, imagination, and memory cooperate both in the acquisition of knowledge and its retention. Their importance is clearly shown by St. Thomas when he declares that they account for individual differences in mental capacity.[19]

The physical side of man deserved attention for this reason and also because "Vigor of mind corresponds to soundness of body, so that the healthier organism insures superior intellectual atainment." [20]

On such philosophical theory is based the scholastic science of education; on these principles their methods rested. If we supplement the above treatises with the many writings of the great schoolmen on the mind, the soul, the functions of the emotions, and on psychology generally, we have no mean body of educational thought; and since all of these scholars were teachers it is proper to assume that their theories were applied concretely. They were daily expounding their views in accordance with their principles, and eventually developed the method associated with their name, the **scholastic** method.

---

[19] E. A. Pace, "St. Thomas' Theory of Education," *Catholic University Bulletin*, 8:302, July, 1902.
[20] *Loc. cit.*

The scholastics sought to establish harmony between philosophy and revelation, between the principles of logic and the truths of faith. Philosophy and theology came to be their leading studies when the "Master of Reason," Aristotle, was made the servant of Christian Truth, and his logic adopted as the means for establish‧ing the reconciliation between reason and faith. The method when fully developed, although it differed slightly in many authors, embodied certain elements of procedure. There was always the thesis, or proposition; its discussion and proof; the citation of objections to it; and their solution. The method submitted everything to the canons of reasoning, gave room for the presentation of all sides of the question under discussion, was flexible in the hands of different authors, and succeeded admirably in the exposition and defense of the Christian religion and the clear definition of many points of doctrine. What was its success can best be shown by the scientific spirit it generated, the habit of precise thinking and of accurate expression, and the number of great men and institutions it produced.

The scholastics set about to learn all that was knowable. From the zenith of the movement to its decay and decline men are identified with it who amaze the modern world by their erudition. To Albertus Magnus it was said "Scisti omne scibile," and judging from his writings and the tributes paid to him there is little doubt as to the truth of the statement. Consider the splendid array of doctors in the scholastic movement: *Doctor Universalis*, Albertus Magnus; *Doctor Angelicus*, St. Thomas; *Doctor Seraphicus*, St. Bonaventure; *Doctor Subtilis*, Duns Scotus; and *Doctor Singularis et Invincibilis*, William of Occam; and these titles are but slight indications of the calibre and influence of the leaders. In the fourteenth and fifteenth centuries appear the universal geniuses, such as Pico della Mirandola,[21] the young paragon of learning famous for his challenge to defend nine hundred theses on everything known, and whose erudition is one of the marvels of history; and the other wits of the Academy of Florence, men who had, it is true, outgrown the schools, but who owed it to the scholastics that they had been educated at all.

While scholasticism gave most attention to philosophy, it is erroneous to think that the other branches of knowledge were neglected, or that medicine, law, and letters disappeared from the course of study. To speak only of the latter—for there is no difficulty with the history of the others—let it be noted that the very forerunners of the movement for the revival of letters, Dante and Petrarch, were the pupils of the schoolmen. Where were they taught their Italian and Latin and philosophy, if not in the system developed under scholasticism? On this point of the liberal studies it is well to recall that some of the scholastics themselves were poets and mystics, and that the greatest thinker and scholar of all, St. Thomas, was the author of the sublime poem *Pange lingua,* which includes the *Tantum ergo;* the *Verbum Supernum,* which includes the *O Salutaris Hostia;* and the sublime office of the feast of Corpus Christi.

In their educational scheme the scholastics did not allow the new studies, however absorbing or attractive they were, to supplant the old. The ancient writers were still taught in connection with grammar and to a greater

---

[21] Spent seven years at the chief universities of Italy and France, studying Latin, Greek, Hebrew, Syriac, Arabic, philosophy and theology. Returned to Rome in 1486 and offered to pay the expenses of these who came from a distance to engage with him in public disputation. Thirteen of his theses were condemned by Innocent VIII and the proposed disputation prohibited. Spent latter part of his life in defense of Christianity against astrologers, Jews and Mohammedans. *Cf.* J. Lejay, *Catholic Encyclopedia,* Vol. X; P. Kibre, *The Library of Pico della Mirandola* (New York: Columbia University Press, 1936).

extent than is usually thought possible. They were over-shadowed by theology and philosophy, by law and medicine, because the dominant interests of the time made this inevitable, just as in modern times the natural sciences have competed with the humanities for favor in the schools. To the credit of the schoolmen it should be observed that, when the great revival of literature and art took place in the Renaissance, the scholastic institutions of Italy, the universities, became centers of the movement and furthered its advance even as they had prepared the world for its coming.

In the educational scheme, the various subjects of learning had a definite relationship and showed a co-ordination that is sadly lacking in education today. Whatever studies had been added by the scholastics to the curriculum did not crowd out the older nor take from their importance. There always remained the Temple of Learning, or the Tower of Wisdom, with all the subjects in their respective places. A story could be added to it without disturbing the order. This Temple of Learning is, by the way, a fine example of the coordination in studies dear to the popular imagination of the Middle Ages. It is found in the allegories and poems typifying ascent or advance in learning, just as in the spiritual works the Ladder of Perfection typified ascent in virtue. In the Temple of Learning are represented the unity and the coordination of knowledge. The boy is admitted to it by Wisdom, when his letters have been learned; through grammar on the first and second floors; through logic and rhetoric, or the rest of the trivium on the third; through music, geometry, astronomy on the fourth; through philosophy and physics on the fifth, until finally at the summit, or in the tower, he learns theology, the truth which tells of God.

Some have compared the scholastic system of education to the medieval Gothic cathedral. Centuries in the building, it incorporated all human art and science, unified in purpose and cause to represent the unity and solidarity of Christian learning, pointing upward and lifting thought and inspiration to the divine. As the cathedral surmounted by the Cross is the monument of Christian art and faith, so scholastic education dominated by the science of God is the monument of medieval learning. It represents the work of Christian genius, flowering in the "Mistress of the Sciences," persisting to the present and, unlike the monuments of stone, destined to remain forever.

Scholasticism, like all great movements, saw its period of decay and decline. The elaborate system of reasoning and discussion, which had wrought the solution of the gravest problems in philosophy and theology, suffered when applied to unworthy and even frivolous questions.[22] Scholasticism had served its purpose, and, as in thought so too in education, it gave way to a newer movement. The Renaissance sprang up suddenly, but not as a movement unrelated to its predecessor. It found an educational world ready for its new gospel, a university system everywhere and magnificently established, centers of learned men and societies, an academic world sated with speculation and philosophy and hungry for the culture and the beauty which, it was felt, the revival of a glorious past would bring. The educational aspect of the Renaissance shows effectively how much it owed to scholasticism for the impetus it promptly re-

---

[22] Graves maintains that while scholasticism carried its abstractions and oversubtle distinctions to an extreme, many of the scholastic discussions were not as purposeless or absurd as it is claimed. The celebrated inquiry as to the number of angels that could stand on the point of a needle was an attempt on the part of reasoning beings to present the nature of the Infinite in concrete form. *Cf.* Frank P. Graves, *A Student's History of Education* (New York: The Macmillan Company, 1932), p. 86.

ceived, and how much of an intellectual inheritance it enjoyed particularly by means of the universities, the institutions in which scholasticism had produced its most brilliant results.

However much the present is indebted to the Renaissance, which supplanted scholasticism, it is well to observe that had not the substantial and fundamental subjects of education been retained, i.e., philosophy, theology, the exact sciences, besides letters—for all of which scholasticism stood—and had not the great institution, the university, been able to outlive and survive the college or the product of humanism, the literary movement would have died of its own limitations. What has survived today in university or higher education, and largely in secondary, is the direct bequest of the scholastic teachers, who not only preserved the literature of antiquity, and stamped education with the mark of Christian principles, but who in their works, in spite of the ridicule of a Rabelais, or the bitter attack of a De la Ramée,[23] or the narrow jibe of a reformer, and a literature of abuse and contumely, laid the basis of the education of a considerable portion of modern society.

FOR FURTHER STUDY

Chesterton, G. K., *St. Thomas Aquinas*. New York: Sheed and Ward, 1933.

Conway, Placid, *St. Thomas Aquinas*. New York: Longmans, Green, and Co., 1911.

De Wulf, Maurice, *History of Medieval Philosophy*. English

---

[23] In the treatises *Aristotelicae animadversiones* and *Dialecticae institutiones* written in 1543, he railed against the wooden Aristotelian dialectic of the University of Paris and championed the new studies of the Renaissance. In his own day, the new learning was fast becoming a change from Aristotelianism to an even more mechanical system known as Ciceronianism. *Cf.* W. Kane, *An Essay Toward a History of Education* (Chicago: Loyola University Press, 1935), p. 212.

translation by E. C. Messenger. London: Longmans, Green, and Company, 1935. 2 vols.

—————, *Scholasticism Old and New.* Translated by P. Coffey. New York: Benziger Brothers, 1907.

Drane, Augusta Theodosia, *Christian Schools and Scholars.* London: Burns, Oates and Washbourne, Ltd., 1924.

Eby and Arrowood, *History and Philosophy of Education, Ancient and Medieval.* New York: Prentice-Hall, Inc., 1940.

Evans, Joan, *Monastic Life at Cluny.* London: Humphrey Milford, 1931.

Funk-Brentano, F., *The Middle Ages.* G. P. Putnam's Sons, 1923.

Gilson, Etienne H., *The Philosophy of St. Bonaventure.* London: Sheed and Ward, 1938.

Grabmann, Maurice, *Die Geschichte der scholastichen Methode.* Freiburg: Herder Company, 1909-11. 2 vols.

Haskins, Charles H., *The Renaissance of the Twelfth Century.* Cambridge: Harvard University Press, 1927.

—————, *Studies in the History of Medieval Science.* Second edition. Cambridge: Harvard University Press, 1927.

Hulme, Edward M., *The Middle Ages.* New York: Henry Holt and Co., 1929.

Kane, W. T., *An Essay Toward a History of Education.* Chicago: Loyola University Press, 1935.

Maritain, Jacques, *The Angelic Doctor.* New York: The Dial Press, 1931.

Martindale, C. C., *Catholic Thought and Thinkers.* New York: P. J. Kenedy and Sons, 1920.

McKeon, Richard, *Selections from Medieval Philosophers.* New York: Charles Scribner's Sons, 1930.

O'Donnell, Clement M., *Psychology of St. Bonaventure and St. Thomas.* Washington, D. C.: The Catholic University of America, 1937.

Pace, Edward A., "St. Thomas' Theory of Education," *Catholic University Bulletin,* 8:290-303.

Reilly, George C., *The Psychology of St. Albert the Great.* Washington, D. C.: The Catholic University of America, 1934.

Sackur, E., *Die Cluniacenser in ihrer kirchlichen und allge-*

meingeschichtlichen Wirksamkeit bis zur Mitte des elften Jahrhunderts. Halle: Max Niemeyer, 1892-94.

Schwertner, Thomas M., *Albertus Magnus.* Milwaukee: The Bruce Co., 1932.

Smith, L. M., *The Early History of the Monastery of Cluny.* London: Oxford University Press, 1920.

——————, *Cluny in the Eleventh and Twelfth Centuries.* London: Philip Allan and Co., Ltd., 1930.

Stöckl, A., *Lehrbuch der Geschichte der Philosophie.* Mainz: Franz Kirchheim, 1888. 2 vols.

Taylor, Henry O., *The Medieval Mind.* London: The Macmillan Co., 1930. Vol. II.

Thorndike, Lynn, *A History of Magic and Experimental Science.* New York: The Macmillan Company, 1911. Vol. II.

Townsend, W. J., *The Great Schoolmen of the Middle Ages.* London: Hodder and Stoughton, 1881.

Turner, W., *History of Philosophy.* Boston: Ginn and Company, 1903.

Walsh, James, J., *The Thirteenth, the Greatest of Centuries.* New York: Catholic Summer School Press, 1913.

Weber, A., *History of Philosophy.* Translated by F. Thilly. New York: C. Scribner's Sons, 1912.

Wilms, Hieronymus, *Albert the Great.* London: Burns, Oates and Washbourne, 1933.

CHAPTER XV

MEDIEVAL EDUCATION—(Continued)

Universities

The renaissance of the twelfth century began with the monastic and cathedral schools and ended with the earliest universities. The intellectual life of the age was more marked in the town than in the countryside. The monastery was no longer the important center of learning; the growing importance of the cathedral is reflected in the flourishing condition of its school. The twelfth century expanded the courses of study in the curriculum of the Seven Liberal Arts which furnished the basis of university studies and led to the development of the professional faculties of law, medicine, and theology.[1] Naturally, with this expansion of knowledge and the interaction of masters and students, the universities came into existence. The intellectual revival institutionalized higher learning by producing the earliest universities and fixing their form of organization for succeeding ages.[2]

The earliest universities arose from a variety of causes in cities where famous schools were already established. As they had no charters, it is difficult, if not impossible, to tell precisely when they began to function as universities. It has been said that each of the early universities had its own peculiar origin. However true this may be, it is certain that the universities of Italy, for example, came into existence under conditions quite different from those that gave rise to them in England. Some general causes can be assigned for the rise and spread of the university movement. They were: the

---

[1] Stephen D'Irsay, *Histoire des universités françaises et étrangères* (Paris: Auguste Picard, 1933), I, 99.

[2] Haskins, *The Renaissance of the Twelfth Century*, pp. 368 f.

popularity of the study of law and medicine and the need
of their specialization; the introduction into Europe of
Saracen studies; the growing favor of scholastic philosophy and the reputation of individual teachers; the
growth of free and enterprising cities; the unrest and
the facility for travel resulting from the Crusades; the
action of the imperial and papal power in patronizing
and founding schools.

Each of the earliest universities was famous as the
center for a special study and, as they served as the
models for the subsequent universities, it is well to view
briefly the details of their foundations. The origin of
the University of Salerno is most obscure; medicine was
practiced here as early as the ninth century and the place
was famous for the skill of its physicians in the tenth.[3]
In the eleventh century, Constantine the African (Con-
stantinus Africanus), a translator of Greek medical
works, attracted great numbers of students to the city by
his lectures on medicine. He afterward became a monk
in Monte Cassino. The fame of the school grew when
the crusaders returning to Europe spread broadcast the
news of the skill of the Salerno scholars and physicians.
Rashdall is of the opinion that Salerno was purely a
medical school;[4] unlike the universities which follow it
did not exert any great influence on university organization. In the field of scholarship it made a notable contribution by furnishing to Paris, Bologna, and Montpellier the early textbooks and professors of medicine.[5]

Bologna[6] sprang into fame as a center for the study of
law. Early in the twelfth century Irnerius (†1138) lec-

---

[3] Hastings Rashdall, *The Universities of Europe in the Middle
Ages.* F. M. Powicke and A. B. Emden, editors (Oxford: The
Clarendon Press, 1936), I, 76.

[4] *Ibid.,* p. 77.

[5] D'Irsay, *op. cit.,* I, 109.

[6] Bologna was not the earliest law school. It was preceded by
law schools at Rome, Paris, and Ravenna, but none of these
developed into a university. *Cf.* Rashdall, *op. cit.,* pp. 105-107.

tured on Roman law and jurisprudence and revived the influence of the ancient code. The profession of law offered new attractions, and many clerics and laymen took it up. At about the same time Gratian, a priest, gave new impetus to the study of canon law. His codification of the law of the Church (known as the *Decretum Gratiani*) was one of the most important in the development of the study, and was the only textbook on canon law for centuries. Bologna, through the influence of these two famous teachers, developed rapidly into a great legal center, and became the model of an important type of medieval university, especially for southern Europe, i.e., the democratic or student university as distinguished from the aristocratic or master type.

Modern scholarship favors the view that the *University of Paris* originated chiefly from the cathedral school of Notre Dame, although the influence of the school of St. Victor and that of St. Geneviève du Mont in making Paris a great theological center is generally recognized. In the twelfth century the scholars, Roscelin, William of Champeaux, and Abelard, attracted multitudes to their lectures. Abelard is said to have had thousands in attendance at his courses, and to have included twenty cardinals and fifty bishops among his students. In Paris, interest centered in philosophy and theology. The university was throughout the Middle Ages the greatest theological school. In organization, Paris holds equal importance with Bologna; for it, too, was the model and type of great universities, notably those of the North.

The term university, *universitas,* signified in the eleventh and twelfth centuries a corporation and, applied to schools, meant the society or corporation of students and masters. It referred to the corporation aggregate by which the school was maintained: *universitas magistrorum et scholarium,* not to any group of buildings or material equipment. It came to be applied to the institution where the sciences were taught, and was used synonymously with *studium generale* or general school.[7] In Bologna, where the term was first used, the students constituted the corporation, elected the rector, engaged the professors, and conducted the affairs of the school. This was the model of the "student or scholar universities," upon which the universities of the South of Europe were organized. Paris presented another type, that of the "master university," where the teachers were the controlling power in the corporation. There in the twelfth century the professors formed a corporate teaching body and, although the students were organized into "nations" as in the University of Bologna, they did not administer the affairs of the institution. The "nations" of Paris, composed of the students from the different countries and designated as the nations of France, Picardy, Normandy, and England, elected the rector, who was in the beginning only the representative of the student body. The chief administrative official was the chancellor who (as in all Catholic universities) represented the Holy See. The University of Oxford and those generally in the North of Europe followed the organization of Paris and were the "master universities."

Much uncertainty surrounds the origin of the *University of Oxford*. Some historians have dated its beginning from the time of Alfred the Great, others even earlier. In the twelfth century schools were flourishing there, and in 1167 occurred a migration of students from

---

[7] *Studium* designated a place of higher education, e.g., in theology, law, medicine; *Studium generale* indicated a place of general resort for learning where students from other countries were receiving instruction. The schools were *studia;* the associated masters were a corporation or university of masters. If the corporation was made up of students, it was a university of students. A corporation of masters and students constituted a *universitas magistrorum et scholarium. Cf.* Ernest C. Moore, *The Story of Instruction* (New York: The Macmillan Company, 1938), p. 334.

Paris to Oxford.[8] In 1209, it is recorded, over three thousand left on account of difficulties with the town. Through this dispersion, the *University of Cambridge* originated. In much the same way the *Universities of Vicenza* (1204), *Arezzo* (1215), and *Padua* (1222) took their rise from the student body of Bologna.

The university movement spread to Spain and three universities were opened there in the thirteenth century— *Palencia, Salamanca,* and *Valladolid.* The *University of Lisbon* was also founded in the same century. The *University of Toulouse,* established by Pope Gregory IX in 1233, and the *University of Naples,* set up by Emperor Frederick II in 1244, afford examples of the most significant kind of foundation for the whole university movement. They were created by papal and imperial decrees respectively. All subsequent universities received their charters from either or both of these sources, the majority from the former. During the Middle Ages, before the Reformation, eighty-one universities were established throughout all Europe. Of these, thirteen had no charters, so far as modern research can determine; fifteen were founded by the imperial power; twenty by the papal and imperial powers combined; and thirty-three by the papal power alone.[9] Kings, noblemen, and bishops were the organizers of many universities, but the charter came from a higher and more widely recognized authority. The papal recognition was most coveted, for the Church, established throughout the world and enjoying universal jurisdiction, was held competent above all other powers to authorize great teaching institutions.

The privileges conferred on the universities by the Emperor and Pope aided considerably in their develop-

---

[8] Rashdall, *op. cit.,* III, 29.
[9] Edward A. Pace, "Universities," *Catholic Encyclopedia* (New York: Encyclopedia Press, 1913), XV, 191.

ment. Frederick I (Barbarossa) granted the students of Naples, and eventually of the empire, the privilege of special courts, in which their cases were adjudicated by the bishop of the city or by one of the professors of the university. The students were guaranteed safe conduct or passage like pilgrims, and were exempted from military service and various forms of taxation. On the university was conferred the privilege to grant the license to teach; on the student receiving it exemption from further examination by other universities. He had the right to teach everywhere—*jus ubique docendi*.[10] Another privilege of the university was the "cessatio," i.e., the right to suspend lectures when grievances with the town or municipality could not be otherwise settled. Such a privilege was granted by Pope Gregory IX to the University of Paris in 1231, when he authorized the masters to suspend lectures if redress for their wrongs were not made by the city in fifteen days. These privileges protected the student bodies and enabled the university to safeguard its interest in dealing with cities. Many of the concessions obtained by the universities from the imperial and papal power and through long-standing custom were perpetuated in the charters of the later universities, which stated that the new institution was to have all the rights and privileges enjoyed by the masters and students of the Universities of Paris and Bologna.

The university consisted of the several faculties of theology, law, medicine, and arts, each of which was empowered to confer degrees. The term "faculty" at first meant a subject of study and gradually came to designate the corporate body of masters teaching a given

---

[10] Oxford degrees were not recognized at Paris; the authorities there demanded an examination for the license. Oxford retaliated by refusing admission to Parisian masters. *Cf.* Rashdall, *op. cit.*, I, 14.

subject. Practically all universities offered the course in arts which was preparatory to the courses in the superior faculties. None of the universities in the beginning had all four higher faculties. The teaching at Paris until the close of the thirteenth century was limited to arts and theology, with some instruction in canon law. Montpellier began as a school of medicine in the twelfth century; law, theology, and arts were added in the thirteenth century.[11] In ancient Bologna there was no constitutional connection between the faculty of law and the faculties of arts and medicine, except the fact that the students of all faculties obtained their degrees from the same chancellor; the theological faculty of Bologna was not inaugurated until after the middle of the fourteenth century.[12]

The only academic requirement for admission to the arts course was a reading knowledge of Latin. Boys began arts at twelve or fifteen years of age and were graduated at twenty or twenty-one. The students of the superior faculties were, of course, older men. Women did not matriculate at the university, but there were learned women in university centers holding recognized teaching positions. Each faculty regulated the subjects of study and the length of the courses. The academic career of the student was very much like the preparation required for full membership in a trade guild. The student was first an apprentice in arts, then a journeyman, and finally a master. The chief degree, that of Doctor, or Master, was conferred at the completion of the course after satisfactory examination and defense of a thesis. It indicated the fitness of the recipient to teach, and was designed to determine the qualifications of those aspiring to the teaching profession. In theology, the degree of *Licentiate* arose later to designate one

---

[11] Rashdall, *op. cit.*, II, 129-34.
[12] *Ibid.*, I, 233; 251.

licensed to teach, who had not yet obtained but was preparing for the doctorate. It shows how the time from taking the examination for the license and the actual conferring of the doctorate or the "inceptio" had been lengthened. The grade of *Bachelor,* not at first recognized as a degree, entitled the student to pursue higher courses leading to the doctorate. It was given upon completion of the art studies and signified the apprentice in teaching.[13] It came from *bachelier,* old French for apprentice. The degree *Master of Arts (Artium Magister),* which then really meant the teacher of arts, was the equivalent of doctor of arts. The term *Master* was more commonly used in Paris and the universities of the North; the term *Doctor* in Bologna and the universities of the South. In Oxford and Cambridge, *Master* came to be adopted for the degree in arts and *Doctor* for the degree in law, medicine, and theology.[14]

The method of teaching was chiefly that of lectures and disputations. The professor lectured on the text of the author studied, as for instance in theology, on the *Sentences* of Peter Lombard, or in Law, on the *Corpus juris civilis* (civil law), interpreting it and commenting on it, while the students followed the text and took down the professor's observations. The ordinary lecture was given by the doctor of the course; the extraordinary by the bachelor, the latter course being often for the purpose of repetition or review.[15] The method was not that of mere dictation by the professor and slavish copying by the student—although in the absence

---

[13] From the evidence of university registers only half of the students who matriculated in the faculty of arts received the B.A. degree; fewer than half of these went on to the M.A. *Cf.* Rashdall, *op. cit.,* I, pp. 468 f.

[14] Rashdall, *op. cit.,* I, pp. 19 f.

[15] Charles H. Haskins, *The Rise of Universities* (New York: Henry Holt and Company, 1923), p. 61.

of books the students had to rely chiefly on their notes—
but a learned exposition of the theological, philosophical,
or scientific question under study. The disputation then
afforded opportunity for discussion. This resembled in
some respects our formal debate. A question or thesis
being proposed and its answer or proof given, objections
were raised and treated in an orderly and logical manner. Disputations took place weekly, and solemn disputes, in which the masters and distinguished visitors
assisted and often took part, were held yearly. They
afforded the widest range for proposing difficulties and
objections and freedom for discussing a question from
many viewpoints. In the scholastic period every con-
ceivable subject having a philosophical interest was
discussed.

The content of the studies offered in the university
has been already referred to in connection with scholasticism. While a limited body of knowledge was taught,
it is no longer permissible to hold the view that, apart
from the professional subjects like theology, law, and
medicine, the whole time of the student was engaged
in the study of logic and that the arts were neglected,
especially grammar and rhetoric. In this connection it
should be noted that the faculty of arts, although subordinate to the other three faculties, and offering the
training in logic and disputation preparatory to the
others, had its own important chairs, and had a special
rank in certain universities. The texts for the trivium
still remained: in grammar, Donatus, Priscian, and Alexander of Villedieu; for rhetoric and dialectic, Boethius;
for the quadrivium, in geometry, Euclid; in astronomy,
Ptolemy; and in music and arithmetic, Boethius. As
early as the thirteenth century, there were many manuals
and general works containing extensive information on
all the arts, and these were used in the schools. Such
an encyclopedic work as that of the *Etymologies* of Isi-

dore of Seville was succeeded by the *Speculum majus* of Vincent of Beauvais.

In theology the *Holy Scriptures,* the *Sentences* of Peter Lombard, and the *Summa Theologica* of St. Thomas were the texts used. The treatises of the scholastics abound in scriptural quotations which they adduced in support of their theological teachings. The usual texts for civil and canon law were, respectively, the *Corpus juris civilis* and *Decretum Gratiani;* but where law was the principal study, as in Bologna, other texts, like the *Decretals* of Gregory IX and the *Clementines,* were in use. The medical course followed the works of the Greek writers Hippocrates (†375 B.C.) and Galen (†200 A.D.) and those of the Saracen and Jewish physicians, as of Avicenna and Isaac Judaeus. The professors of Salerno occasionally supplied their own texts; and there gradually grew up a literature on anatomy and general medicine both in special texts and in the current encyclopedic works.

The universities wielded a potent influence on medieval culture and education and in many respects have affected our modern institutions. They were great centers in an academic world where a common and universal language, Latin, was used, and where the most scholarly teachers and students congregated. They were cosmopolitan and democratic in character, having men of all countries in the faculties and among the students, as the nations of Paris and Bologna so well show. Paris has been credited with an attendance of between twenty thousand and forty thousand; Bologna in the twelfth century with ten thousand; Oxford in the opinion of a fourteenth century writer with thirty thousand. Modern estimates place the figures much lower, as e.g., Paris and Bologna at six thousand or seven thousand and Oxford between fifteen hundred and three thousand. Toulouse may have had as many as two thousand students, while most of the German universities during the fifteenth century varied between eighty and one thousand.[16]

Modern education has inherited much from the administrative and academic arrangements of the medieval university especially in regard to the faculties; from its system of degrees; from the provisions made by the university for the qualifications of its teachers; from its training for the professions; from its courses of study, modified in subsequent times, but surviving in one form or another today

The *College* is another and significant contribution of the medieval university to modern education. University Colleges, which became so numerous at Paris and Oxford, were originally the "hospicia," hostels, halls, or boarding places of the students. They were democratic in government, the students electing their own principal, or regent, who was responsible for the rent, board, and expenses. Pious benefactors frequently founded or endowed these "hospicia" for poor students, as, for instance, in the twelfth century, the modest endowment of beds in the Hotel Dieu, Paris, known as the *Collège des Dix-Huit*, for the support of eighteen poor scholars. The convents of religious orders were designated as university colleges. The students from the beginning attended the lectures of the university. Gradually, however, instruction of a lower and higher grade was given in the colleges. In the College of the Sorbonne, founded 1257 by Robert de Sorbonne, Chaplain of Louis IX, for students preparing for the doctorate in theology, the work required was of university grade. Gradually, too, the universities obtained control of the colleges and supervised the private life of the students. With this control there also resulted more generous provision for

---

[16] Rashdall, *op. cit.*, III, 335.

the support of poor scholars. In Paris alone over sixty-seven colleges were founded before the year 1500 according to the list published by Rashdall. The list is very probably incomplete for "more than one college mentioned in it is revealed to us only by a single accidental allusion."[17]

Although Paris was the home of the colleges, the whole collegiate system of the university disappeared at the Revolution and was never revived. It was different in Oxford, for "of all the secular foundations which medieval piety bequeathed to Oxford she has lost not one."[18] Baliol College, founded 1261 for the maintenance of poor scholars, and Merton Hall, founded 1263 by Walter de Merton, a priest, for needy theological students, reproduced many features of the Parisian organization, and the early Cambridge colleges were in turn imitations of Oxford.

The universities constitute the great achievement of the Middle Ages in the intellectual sphere. "Their organization and their traditions," says Rashdall, "their studies and their exercises affected the progress and intellectual development of Europe more powerfully, or (perhaps it should be said) more exclusively, than any schools in all likelihood will ever do again."[19] The university was the institutional embodiment of the medieval educational ideal just as the Church and the Empire were the concrete embodiments of that ideal in religion and government. It was a distinctly medieval creation; ancient civilization had produced no such institution; for, as Rashdall well says, "It is entirely misleading to apply the name to the schools of ancient Athens and Alexandria."[20] Modern education, as we have said, owes much

---

[17] *Ibid.*, I, 532.
[18] *Ibid.*, p. 533.
[19] *Ibid.*, p. 3.
[20] *Ibid.*, III, 459.

to them, for if we have today teaching corporations, courses of study, a system of examinations, degrees, it is as a direct inheritance from the medieval universities.

FOR FURTHER STUDY

Anniversary Essays in Medieval History by the Students of Charles Homer Haskins. Boston: Houghton-Mifflin Company, 1929.

Azarias, Brother, *Essays Educational.* Chicago: D. H. McBride and Co., 1896.

Coulton, G. G., *Life in the Middle Ages.* New York: The Macmillan Co., 1921.

Denifle, P., *Die Entstehung der Universitäten des Mittelalters bis 1400.* Berlin: Weidmannsche Buchhdlg, 1885. Vol. I.

D'Irsay, Stephen, *Histoire des universités françaises et étrangères.* Paris: Auguste Picard, 1933. Vol. I.

Drane, Augusta Theodosia, *Christian Schools and Scholars.* London: Burns Oates and Washbourne, Ltd., 1924.

Eby and Arrowood, *History and Philosophy of Education, Ancient and Medieval.* New York: Prentice-Hall, Inc., 1940.

Haskins, Charles H., *The Rise of Universities.* New York: Henry Holt and Company, 1923.

————, *Studies in Medieval Culture.* Oxford: Clarendon Press, 1929.

Laurie, S. S., *Rise and Early Constitutions of Universities.* New York: D. Appleton and Co., 1891.

Moore, Ernest C., *The Story of Instruction.* New York: The Macmillan Company, 1938. Vol. II.

Norton, Arthur O., *Readings in the History of Education: Medieval Universities.* Cambridge: Harvard University Press, 1909.

Rait, Robert S., *Life in a Medieval University.* Cambridge: Harvard University Press, 1912.

Rashdall, Hastings, *The Universities of Europe in the Middle Ages.* New edition edited by F. M. Powicke and A. B. Emden. Oxford: The Clarendon Press, 1936. 3 vols.

Schachner, Nathan, *The Medieval Universities.* London: George Allen and Unwin, Ltd., 1938.

Seybolt, Robert F., *The Manuale scholarium.* Cambridge: Harvard University Press, 1921.

CHAPTER XVI

MEDIEVAL EDUCATION (Continued)

Religious Orders and Educators of the Scholastic and University Period

Before mentioning some of the leading educators of the scholastic and university period, we must deal, however briefly, with the work of the great religious orders, whose influence educationally was at that time significant and far-reaching. The Benedictine inspiration declined in this later period, but other orders had meanwhile sprung up independently or developed from the old and were in various ways associated with educational activities. Some profoundly affected the universities.

The *Canons Regular*, or communities of clerics leading a common life, wielded a greater influence than in the earlier period of the Middle Ages. It has already been noted how Chrodogang, Bishop of Metz, organized the clerics of his cathedral into a community and gave them a rule based on that of St. Augustine for similar communities. The Bishop of Hippo was regarded throughout the Middle Ages as the lawgiver of the Canons, hence the name Canons Regular of the Order of St. Augustine. It was a common practice for clerics desirous of organizing themselves into communities and of leading a common life to accept this rule rather than the Benedictine, and to devote themselves to works not sanctioned nor encouraged by the older rule. Education was one of their chief activities, both in the cathedral canonicates for the instruction of the future clergy, and in the colleges connected with their churches which were often endowed establishments as collegiate churches, where admission was not restricted to prospective mem-

bers of the order. Some of these are numbered among
the most celebrated schools at the beginning of the university period, e.g., the School of St. Victor, Paris,
founded by William of Champeaux in 1110 and made
famous by Hugh of St. Victor, the scholastic and mystic,
his successor Richard, and the poet, Adam of St. Victor.

The Canons Regular, also called *Clerici Regulares*, or
Regular Clerics, often were given their name from the
place where their institution was located, and this community is commonly spoken of as the *Canons of St. Victor* or the *Victorines*. There were Canons Regular in all
the countries of Europe. It is believed by many that the
monasteries of Ireland were founded by them.[1] Certainly, the Canons were numerous there, and in England
and Scotland in the later Middle Ages. They were engaged in the general parochial works of the clergy and
also the educational, their institutions being open to
secular students as well as to aspirants to the order.

In a similar manner, the *Canonesses Regular* or communities of women following the rule of St. Augustine,
rapidly expanded their activities after their reorganization in accordance with the laws of the Council of
Aachen, 817. Their rule granted privileges and permitted occupations not sanctioned by the Benedictine,
and their institutions were very widely spread in the
eleventh and twelfth centuries, the members devoting
themselves not infrequently to the education of girls and
also of boys. They were usually established where
congregations of men were already located. In Ireland,
during the early period, St. Bridget was the first of the
Canonesses Regular. During the later period, we note
that, with the English establishment of the Canons
Regular at Sempringham by St. Gilbert in 1148, a community of women was also formed. In this case, how-

[1] A. Allaria, "Canons and Canonesses Regular," *Catholic Encyclopedia*, III, 291.

ever, the nuns were given the rule of St. Benedict with
an elaborate constitution and modification drawn up by
St. Gilbert. A large number of congregations of women
were founded in this way, i.e., in connection with the
Canons Regular, in the later Middle Ages, and they
flourished in Great Britain until the Reformation.

In the early thirteenth century, two new orders arose
to meet the urgent religious needs of the time—the
Franciscans and the *Dominicans*. The former were
called the Order of Friars Minor, or Grey Friars, and
the latter, the Order of Preachers, or Black Friars; and,
although neither was founded expressly for educational
pursuits, they were destined to further the cause of
learning both by their patronage and use of the schools
—for their members were academically trained—and
by the services of the distinguished educators numbered
among them.

St. Francis of Assisi obtained the approval of the Holy
See in 1208 for the movement he had already projected
for the regeneration of society. His humble friars, in
some instances men who were formerly wealthy merchants of Assisi, gave all they possessed to the poor, assumed a rough habit, and moved among the people
preaching penance and giving an example of the virtues
of sacrifice and self-denial they had vowed to practice.
Owning nothing, they begged their food, and in the beginning had no monasteries, not even places of shelter.
Their cloister was the world and their mission to win by
example the hearts of men to peace and charity. Their
preaching to the people of all classes, usually in the busy
thoroughfares and marts of trade, from the steps of the
churches, had a wide social effect and was in a broad
sense educational. There were so many people desirous
of association with the friars and yet unable to leave
their homes and occupations, that the Third Order of St.
Francis was organized for them. They participated in

the benefits of the Order and pledged themselves to promote peace and charity among their fellowmen. The Friars within a few years had spread to all of the countries of Europe, as their general chapters held in St. Francis' lifetime show. At the chapter of 1221, five thousand Friars and five hundred candidates for admission attended.

The field of Franciscan activity soon extended beyond missionary works to the conduct of large monasteries and to literary and educational undertakings. They were before long in possesion of houses at the great universities and were represented on the university faculties. Their first establishments in England were in London and Oxford in 1224. By 1230, Ireland was a separate province. In the scholastic revival, the Order produced many distinguished professors in the universities of Paris, Oxford, Cambridge, Bologna, and those of Spain and Germany. Among them were the great schoolmen: Alexander of Hales (†1245), John Duns Scotus (†1308), William of Occam (†1349), and the mystic and philosopher, St. Bonaventure (†1272). The preacher and popular writer on education questions, Berthold of Ratisbon (†1272), the scientist Roger Bacon (†1294), and the poet Giacomino of Verona (†1300), the precursor of Dante, might be mentioned among a host of celebrated friars of the later Middle Ages.

Bacon is of special educational interest because of his efforts to improve ecclesiastical studies by directing the schools to give less time to philosophy and more to the languages, Latin, Greek, Hebrew, and Arabic, to the furtherance of Scriptural studies, and also to mathematics and the natural sciences. A real discoverer in the field of natural science, his merits have been recognized only in modern times. His ideas and proposals on the reform of studies were outlined in his great work, prepared at the request of Pope Clement IV, the *Opus majus,* an encyclopedia of the learning of the time.[2] This was followed by the *Opus minus,* a recapitulation of the *Opus majus,* and the *Opus tertium*[3] which added matters omitted from the other two. Although his reforms failed of realization because of the untimely death of his friend and patron, Pope Clement IV (1268), his textbooks on philosophy[4] and theology,[5] Greek and Hebrew grammars, continued to be used in England down to the Reformation.

The *Order of Preachers* had for its object the salvation of souls, especially by means of preaching. Founded by St. Dominic in 1216, it, too, like the Franciscan Order, spread rapidly. It is estimated that there were seven thousand members in the middle of the thirteenth century; and before the middle of the fourteenth the Order had establishments all over Europe. Every convent had its "doctor" or teacher, who lectured daily to the friars on theology and also to other students, members of the secular clergy. This was the conventual school and in many instances it provided higher courses in theology and the sacred sciences. As in Paris, chairs were at times incorporated with the university, and in this way constituted the faculty of theology for a university. Study was a regular duty of a young friar. Besides his course in the sacred sciences, he pursued the natural sciences; and, when the needs of the missions required, he learned Greek, Hebrew, and Arabic. The

---

[2] English translation, based on Bridges' edition, by Robert B. Burke (Philadelphia: University Press, 1928).

[3] *Cf.* Ephrem O. Wukitsch, "The Educational Contents and Implications of Roger Bacon's *Opus Tertium*" (unpublished Master's dissertation, The Catholic University of America, Washington, D. C., 1942).

[4] *Compendium philosophiae.*

[5] *Compendium theologiae. Cf.,* H. Rashdall, *Fratris Rogeri Bacon Compendium studii theologiae* (Aberdoniae: Typis Academicis, 1911).

Protestant historian Molinier has said of the Dominican schools:

They were not content with professing in their convents all the divisions of science, as it was then understood; they added an entire order of studies which no other Christian schools of the time seem to have taught, and in which they had no other rivals, than the rabbis of Languedoc and Spain.[6]

The Dominicans had, so to speak, an academic mission, and their scholastic activity is especially seen in the development of philosophy and theology. The work begun by Albertus Magnus and completed by his disciple, St. Thomas Aquinas, resulted in a system of theology and philosophy at once "the most complete, the most original, and the most profound, which Christian thought has elaborated." As already noted, both these representatives of the Order were prolific writers, and the latter is of special interest for his treatment of the scholastic educational theory, and his designation by Pope Leo XIII to be the patron of scholars and Angel of the schools.[7]

To the Order of Preachers, the schools were indebted for valuable manuals in theology and philosophy. Vincent of Bauvais produced in his *Speculum majus* the great encyclopedia of the Middle Ages; William of Tournai composed a treatise *De modo docendi pueros* (*On the Manner of Teaching Boys*), and a treatise on Confession for children. In the Renaissance, the Order was admirably represented by Cardinal John Dominici, author of *Lucula noctis*, and a work on the government of the family which contained a chapter on the education of children.[8]

The official work of the Dominicans was preaching, and

[6] C. Molinier, *Guillem Bernard de Gaillac et l'enseignement chez les Dominicains* (Paris: Nogent-le-Rotrose, 1884), p. 30.

[7] *Cf. ante*, p. 264.

[8] *Cf. post*, p. 329.

in the Middle Ages the pulpit was an educational agency. They were the preachers of the Crusades, of the courts, the champions of truth against heresy. In the words of an early Master General of the Order, Humbert of Romans, "they taught the people, the prelates, the wise and unwise, religious and seculars, clerics and laymen, nobles and peasants, lowly and great." They were as a body the leading preachers of the thirteenth century and maintained their supremacy throughout the Middle Ages. Their activities in this line, combined with their systematic teaching in convent schools and in the universities, made of the Order a great educational power.

Among the members of other religious orders and the secular clergy some individual educators may be noted, in order to show the general interest in education and the state of the schools. Distinguished representatives of their orders were, for example, *Thomas of Cantimpré* (†1272), the Augustinian abbot and later Dominican preacher and author, to whom is attributed the treatise *De disciplina scholarium* (*On the Discipline of Scholars*); and *Aegidius Colonna* (Aegidius Romanus, or Giles of Rome), (†1316) of the Hermits of St. Augustine, known by the title, "Doctor Fundatissimus," professor of the University of Paris, who was tutor of Philip IV ("The Fair") of France, and afterward archbishop of Bourges. He wrote for the instruction of his former pupil the treatise *De regimine principum* (*On the Training of Princes*), a work which went through many editions and was translated into French, Italian, Spanish, Portuguese, German, English, and even Hebrew.[9] It consists of three books: the first treats of the government of self—the character and conduct of the prince, the nature of his happiness, the acquisition of virtue and

---

[9] Michael Kaufmann, *Von der Sorge der Eltern für die Erziehung ihrer Kinder, von Agidius Romanus de Colonna* (Freiburg: Herder, 1904), p. 21.

control of his passions; the second treats of the government of his family—his relations with the queen, the children and the servants; and the third of the government of the State—in time of peace and in time of war. Colonna's educational views are chiefly contained in the second part of the second book—on the care and education of children. While addressed to the prince, every chapter is intended for wider application; the prince should be the model father in this matter, and all other parents are urged to follow his example, especially in regard to the choice of teachers, the religious and moral training of his sons and daughters, which will embrace details of upbringing from infancy to the seventh year, from the seventh to the fourteenth, and from the fourteenth onward, and in regard to mental and physical welfare. The special needs of girls in household duties and training for their peculiar virtues are treated in three chapters.[10]

A similar work, *De regimine principum*, interesting for its political as well as pedagogical views, was written by Engelbert (†1331), the Benedictine abbot of Admont in Styria. The work deals especially with political science, but its suggestions on education are sound and practical. Engelbert also produced a treatise on music, *De musica tractatus*, along with works on theology, philosophy, history, and the natural sciences.[11]

Jean Gerson (1364-1429), Chancellor of the Church of Notre Dame and the University of Paris, is a splendid type of the medieval churchman and educator. His office as chancellor of the University made him responsible to the Holy See for the condition of education in all of the

[10] *Cf.* Ezra J. Fenton, "Educational Theories in the *De Regimine Principum* of Aegidius Colonna" (unpublished Master's dissertation, Washington, D. C.: The Catholic University, 1939).

[11] J. Wiechner, *Kloster Admont und seine Beziehungen zur Wissenschaft und zum Unterricht* (Wien: Academie der Wissenschaften, 1892).

schools of Paris, from the University down to those of elementary grade. Nature and training had admirably equipped him to champion the immense interests represented by the University, and to fulfill his peculiar duty of maintaining a high standard of moral and religious education throughout his jurisdiction. He was a successful administrator of a student body numbered by thousands and a writer of educational treatises of value for his own and subsequent generations.

The problem which most interested Gerson was that of religious training. It was his effort to combine the intellectual and the moral, while maintaining a high standard of both, that caused him to exercise his power of supervision, and inspired those of his educational writings which are today of pedagogical significance. He wrote extensively on doctrinal, moral, and ascetical subjects; and, as his treatises were meant for the clergy and laity, they assumed a didactic character. Some of his moral treatises are essentially instructive in form and substance; and, according to Dupin, the editor of his works, he gained a wider reputation in his own and succeeding generations than any other ecclesiastical writer since St. Bernard.[12]

His educational tracts show a remarkably versatility of style and treatment. They were called forth by the circumstances of the time and were not academic addresses prepared for the students of the University. A good illustration is his protest to the municipal authorities against the lascivious pictures and images exhibited in the public places, which were a source of temptation to the young.[13] When the protest was fiercely assailed, he replied with a short treatise on *The Innocence of Children*.[14] He frequently treated the question

---

[12] *Joannis Gersonii Opera omnia.* Edited by M. L. E. Dupin (Antwerpiae: Sumptibus Societatis, 1706), 5 vols.
[13] *Expostulatio ad potestates publicas. Opera,* III, 291 f.
[14] *De innocentia puerili. Opera,* III, 293-96.

of reading. In a tract addressed to the instructor and confessor of the young Charles VII, he has a chapter on reading, its excellence and usefulness, and another on the formation of a portable library. The Bible is the first of books from both the historical and the moral viewpoint, and although spiritual works predominate in the list, one finds Aristotle, Valerius Maximus, Boethius, Seneca, Suetonius, and Livy recommended as suitable authors to be read or studied by the future king.[15]

Gerson combatted the reading of the *Romance of the Rose* by Christian youth in an allegorical treatise—*Contra romantium de rosa*. He draws a round indictment against Christians who praised and defended the work, finding it more polluted than its pagan sources. Ovid had been condemned and banished by a pagan emperor for his too popular teaching of the *ars amandi;* yet the pagan poet had more regard for the ties of matrimony than his modern successor in the *Romance of the Rose.*[16]

Other treatises of educational value are an Instruction for the teachers and pupils of the Cathedral School of Notre Dame;[17] a letter to the students of the College of Navarre on the study of theology;[18] but the tract most familiarly associated with his name deals with the religious training of children and is entitled *Leading the Little Children to Christ.* It was written most probably at Lyons, where Gerson spent the last ten years of his life in exile, unable to return to Paris because of the hostility of the Duke of Burgundy towards him. There, at the collegiate church of St. Paul, he was accustomed to gather the children of the poor about him and instruct

---

[15] *De considerationibus quas debet habere Princeps. Opera,* III, 226-35.

[16] *Contra romantium de Rosa. Opera,* III, 297-308.

[17] *Doctrina pro pueris Ecclesiae Parisiensis. Opera,* IV, 717-20.

[18] *Quid et qualiter studere debeat novus Theologiae auditor. Opera,* I, 106-109.

them in the rudiments of learning and chiefly Christian Doctrine. What he had long counseled and recommended in regard to the religious formation of the young he now undertook as a personal occupation. His course was ridiculed by his enemies and unfavorably criticized by his friends. The principles that supported him, however, were beyond refutation. They are beautifully set forth, with the fruits of his successful experience, in this short treatise which, for its antiquity and excellence, must rank as one of the most precious documents on religious training in Christian literature.

Its text and dominant thought is "Suffer the little children to come to me, and forbid them not, for of such is the kingdom of God." The great and perfect Teacher, Christ, desired the children to come to Him and was much displeased with the disciples who forbade them. Gerson sees reason to rebuke those of his contemporaries who neglect to bring the children to Christ, but he puts aside all bitter reprehension and pleads for their co-operation. He contends that the reformation of the Church must be accomplished through the children, by their systematic training and instruction. The work contains four chapters: the first treats of the children, how necessary for them and for the Church that they come to Christ; the second, of those who scandalize them and thwart their coming to Christ; the third, of the praiseworthy zeal of those who guide them on the way which leads to Christ; and the last gives a justification of his views and a defence of his methods. It concludes with a touching appeal to the children to accept his invitation to be led to Christ by him.[19]

---

[19] *De parvulis trahendis ad Christum. Opera*, III, 277. This treatise has appeared in many Latin editions; also in many French and German translations. *Cf.* F. X. Kunz, *Bibliothek der Katholischen Pädagogik* (Freiburg: Herdesche Verlagshandlung, 1904), XV, 114.

Denis, the Carthusian (1402-1471), born at Rykel, Belgium, the last of the schoolmen, is so called because he is the last of the great scholastic writers. His works form a complete summary of the scholastic teaching of the Middle Ages. They have come down to posterity in forty folio volumes,[20] including treatises on Scripture, theology, canon law, philosophy, polemics, liturgy, asceticism, religious life, and education. Some of his best educational tracts were chapters in works of spiritual direction, e.g., for all Christians, *De doctrina et regulis vitae Christianorum;*[21] for princes, *De vita et regimine principium;*[22] for the nobility, *Directorium vitae nobilium;*[23] for parents, *De laudabili vita conjugatorum.*[24] In the first of these works are chapters on the duty of parents towards their children and vice versa; also on the good and bad qualities of children. *The Dialogue of Jesus and the Boy*[25] was to be read by the students before beginning the study of philosophy. *De doctrina scholarium*[26] resembles the treatise of the earlier scholastic, Hugh of St. Victor, in form and content. It treats mostly of the moral and spiritual aspects of education and was intended for teachers as well as students. The writings of Denis contribute little to educational science, but they represent the ideal of the later scholastic educators, for whom the spiritual and the ascetic took precedence over all other interests.

---

[20] *D. Dionysii Cartusiani Opera omnia* (Monstrolii et Tornaci: Typis Cartusiae S. M. De Pratis, 1896-1911), 40 vols.
[21] *De doctrina, et regulis vitae Christianorum. Opera,* XXXIX, 499-572.
[22] *De vita et regimine principium. Opera,* XXXVII, 375-497.
[23] *Directorium vitae nobilium. Opera,* XXXVII, 524-563.
[24] *De laudabili vita conjugatorum. Opera,* XXXVIII, 57-117.
[25] *Inter Jesum et puerum dialogus. Opera,* XXXVIII, 187-207.
[26] *De doctrina scholarium. Opera,* XXXVII, 339-71. *Cf.* Heinrich Keiser, *Dionys des Kartaüsers Leben und pädagogische Schriften* (Freiburg: Herder Company, 1904); contains translations of principal treatises.

FOR FURTHER STUDY

de Celano, Fr. Thomas, *S. Francisci Assisiensis*. Romae: Desclée, Lefebvre et Soc., 1906.

Drane, Augusta Theodosia, *Christian Schools and Scholars*. London: Burns, Oates and Washbourne, Ltd., 1924.

Heimbucher, M., *Die Orden und Kongregationen der Katholischen Kirche*. Paderborn: Ferdinand Schöningh, 1907.

Jorgensen, Johannes, *Saint Francis of Assisi*. Translated from the Danish by T. O'Connor Sloane. New York: Longmans, Green, and Company, 1912.

Kaufmann, Michael, *Von der Sorge der Eltern für die Erziehung ihrer Kinder, von Agidius Romanus de Colonna*. Freiburg: Herder, 1904.

Keiser, Henrich, *Dionys des Kartaüsers Leben und pädagogische Schriften*. Freiburg: Herder, 1904.

Mandonnet, Pierre, *Saint Dominique: l'idée l'homme et l'oeuvre*. Paris: Desclée de Brouwer et Cie, 1937. 2 vols.

Molinier, C., *Guillem Bernard de Gaillac et l'enseignement chez les Dominicains*. Paris: Nogent-le-Rotrose, 1884.

Wadding, Luke, *Annales Minorum*. Lyons and Rome, 1625-54. 8 vols. Second edition in 16 vols. (Rome, 1731-36). Several continuations (Rome, Naples, Quaracchi, 1740-1886) bring the history up to 1622 in 25 vols.

Wiechner, J., *Kloster Admont und seine Beziehungen zur Wissenschaft und zum Unterricht*. Wein: Academie der Wissenschaften, 1892.

Woodruff, Francis W., *Roger Bacon*. New York: James J. Clarke Co., 1938.

CHAPTER XVII

MEDIEVAL EDUCATION (Continued)

Types of Later Medieval Schools

In addition to the cathedral and monastic institutions, other types of elementary schools flourished in the countries of Europe in the later Middle Ages. Chief among them were the parish, chantry, town, and guild schools; and these were so numerous that we must conclude elementary education was then well provided for in cities and rural districts, not only for boys but also for girls. The Church was solicitous for the education of all. This is clear from the decrees of councils, and the general legislative actions of her officials. As in the earlier Middle Ages, there is notable provision of free schools for the poor.

The Third Council of the Lateran, held in 1179, decreed as follows:

The Church of God, being, like a good and tender mother, obliged to provide for the spiritual and corporal wants of the poor, is desirous of procuring for children destitute of pecuniary resources the means of learning to read and of advancing in the study of letters, and ordains that every cathedral church shall have a master who will instruct gratis the ecclesiastical students of that church and the poor scholars, and that a grant be assigned him which, by sufficing for his maintenance, will thus open the door of the school to studious youths. A free school shall be reopened in the other churches and monasteries, where there formerly existed funds for this purpose. . . . Nobody shall exact any remuneration, either for the license to teach, or for the exercise of teaching even if his right be based on custom; and the license to keep a school shall not be refused to any person who can justify his capacity for it. Offenders shall be deprived of their ecclesiastical living, for

it is meet that, in the Church of God, he who hinders the
progress of the churches by selling, from cupidity, the permission to teach, should be himself deprived of the fruit of
his labor.[1]

The Fourth Council of the Lateran, held in 1215, renewed these decrees, and we have evidence that they were
followed wherever possible. The wars, pestilence, and
consequent impoverishment of churches and abbeys made
it frequently impossible to maintain schools and other
public works of the Church; but from this time onward
until the sixteenth and seventeenth centuries, there are
unmistakable proofs of general activity in behalf of
schools, especially on the elementary level.

For France, our most trustworthy and complete information has come from the history of the schools in
the different dioceses, and in great measure also from
documents not dealing directly with schools. It is difficult to present an exact account of education there in
the twelfth century, because many documents, from
which accurate statistics might be drawn up, have been
destroyed. Recent research has made clear, however,
that primary instruction was the object of anxious care
on the part of the Church and faithful in France then
and throughout the later medieval period. According to
Delisle, "rural schools were multiplied throughout Normandy during the thirteenth century and those following
it," [2] and this is known chiefly from the claims made
by contending parties for the right to appoint the schoolmaster. Another writer says:

We can prove similar facts all over France; at Château-
briant, at Château-Thierry in 1222, at Evreux in 1292, at
Flavigny in 1272, at Jaligny and Nailly in 1256, at Orange in
1208, at Pont-sur-Yonne, at Quimper in 1260, at Saint-Appol-

---

[1] G. D. Mansi, *Collectio amplissima Conciliorum* Vol. XXII,
227 f.

[2] Leopold-Victor Delisle, *Études sur la condition de la classe
agricole en Normandie* (Évreux: A. Herissey, 1851), p. 176.

linaire in 1216, at Tonnerre in 1220, at Troyes, at Villeneuve-l'Archeveque, at Villeneuve-la-Guyard in 1276, at Villeneuve-le-Roi.[3]

Tradesmen and artisans of Limousin often specified in their wills that their children should be sent to school; the preachers of the period make frequent allusion, as to a fact of daily occurrence, to little boys going to school with their alphabet swung over their shoulders; and there is an occasional anecdote referring to the schoolmistress for little girls.

In the fourteenth century documentary evidence is more weighty, fully supporting the view that schools existed in the cities and in the majority at least of large villages. The historian of the diocese of Rouen states that there was in every parish a clerk charged with the management of the school and the drawing up of contracts, and capable of teaching reading, writing, and Latin to children.[4] The treatise of Gerson written about 1400 would have the bishops enquire "if every parish has a school, and how the children are taught, and to open a school there if there be not one already."[5] Recent studies have also shown the wide extent of schools in France in the fifteenth century. The scholarly work of the Abbé Allain concisely presents the evidence for the important dioceses of France, and he concludes that in the provinces of France, where any school records remain, the benefits of education reached down to the working and rural classes.[6] It is interesting to note that in Clermont in 1490, "schools" for little girls were sepa-

---

[3] A. Ravelet, *Blessed John Baptist de la Salle* (Paris: Charles Poussielgue, 1888), p. 19.

[4] C. Beaurepaire, *Recherches sur l'instruction publique, dans le diocèse de Rouen, avant 1789* (Evreux: P. Huet, 1872), p. 53.

[5] *Tractatus de visitatione praelatorum et curatorum. Opera,* II, 560 f.

[6] L'Abbé Allain, *L'instruction primaire en France avant la Révolution* (Paris: La Société Bibliographique, 1887), p. 38.

rated from those of boys and that at Lyons and Troyes there were mistresses for girls.[7]

In the case of Paris the data are more complete. For the thirteenth century, we can even get an idea of the number of teachers. For instance, there were then eleven schoolmasters and one schoolmistress on the roll of the land tax levied by Philip the Fair, and of these only two were ecclesiastics, the others lay teachers. In the next century, on the occasion of a meeting called by the precentor, there were assembled sixty-three: forty-one masters and twenty-two mistresses. In the fifteenth century, the number of schools is estimated at one hundred, the scholars at one thousand; and at the close of the sixteenth century, Claude Joly, precentor of Paris, estimated the teachers at five hundred. The precentor had jurisdiction over the primary schools, gave licenses to teachers, and made necessary regulations. In 1357, school statutes were issued which even in the seventeenth century formed a basis for the school laws of France. In them it is stated that schoolmasters may not teach girls, and schoolmistresses may not teach boys—a prohibition which clearly implies the attendance of both sexes at school.[8]

These schools in France were parochial in organization. Similar types were to be found in Germany and England, but in these countries there were also other types of schools to be mentioned later. In Scotland, the burgh schools "had their origin in connection with the Church, or were called into existence by the people themselves; but in whatever way they were founded, undoubtedly, toward the end of the fifteenth century, schools were planted in every considerable town in Scotland."[9] The town schools, especially in Germany, seem

---

[7] *Ibid.*, p. 23.
[8] Ravelet. *op. cit.*, p. 28.
[9] James Grant, *History of Burgh and Parish Schools of Scotland* (London: W. Collins, Sons and Co., 1876), p. 25.

to have taken their origin from the older established parish schools. The passing of control from the ecclesiastical to the municipal power was not always accompanied by strife, and did not mean, as is so often stated, a revolt against the authority of the Church. As Paulsen says:

Such struggles were never animated by a spirit of hostility to the Church or its doctrines; they were directed exclusively against local educational authority. It is significant that the higher ecclesiastical authority always sided with the cities —a policy quite in accordance with the benevolent interest which the Church evinced, throughout the Middle Ages, in the advancement of education and educational institutions in any shape or form. There seems to be little doubt that, towards the end of the fifteenth century, nearly every city had a school of its own, and that even in small market towns and villages schools were by no means rare. Knepper's survey of Alsatian schools affords an instance; and many a school must have existed besides, whose name has not been handed down to posterity.[10]

Then there were the private elementary schools in which reading, writing, and general elements of education were taught. These were to be found in all large towns and often in considerable number. Called at times *Venture Schools*, they were usually private undertakings, maintained by individual lay teachers or communities of Sisters, or by an association of writers or notaries. Since they taught the vernacular and no Latin, they are regarded as the forerunners of the modern elementary schools. Typical schools for girls were those of Mainz, Frankfurt, Speier, and Brussels.[11]

In the fourteenth and fifteenth centuries some of the Venture schools were conducted by the Wandering Schol-

[10] Friedrich Paulsen, *German Education, Past and Present.* Translated by T. Lorenz (New York: Charles Scribner's Sons, 1908), pp. 29 f.

[11] F. Bartholome, *Kurze Geschichte der Pädagogik* (Freiburg: B. Herder Verlagshdlg, 1911), p. 30.

ars (*Scholares vagantes,* called also *bacchantes*). Former university students, or teachers in town schools, these men moved from place to place and gathered about them small boys whom they instructed. The latter were the A B C shooters, often mere servants of the teachers, who begged and sometimes stole for their masters. In the fifteenth century they were occasionally controlled in their operations, such as begging, by city ordinances. The prevalence of schools of this kind, along with the cathedral schools, chantry schools and parish schools (*Küsterschulen*), widely established in cities and villages, would seem to justify the conclusion of Paulsen who says:

It seems safe to assume that, at the end of the Middle Ages, the entire population of the towns, with the exception of the lowest classes, was able to read and to write. No statistics are available, but the most convincing evidence that could be desired is afforded by the rapid development of the art of printing into an important industry. This would have been impossible without a universal demand for books. If we wish to realize how much the spread of the great intellectual and religious movements at the beginning of the sixteenth century was encouraged by the printing-press, we have only to think of Luther and Hutten and their pamphlets. Speeding on from town to town as if upon the wings of the wind, the new ideas took hold of the masses in a manner only possible amongst a population which was able and eager to read.[12]

To England we look for an example of the development to a high degree of another type, called *Chantry Schools.* This school differed from the parish school in that it was conducted by a priest in charge of a chantry, i.e., an endowment for masses. The donor of the foundation or endowment stipulated that in the chapel built for the purpose, or at a special altar in the cathedral or parish church, masses were offered daily, or at stated times, for the repose of his soul or of others mentioned

---

[12] Paulsen. *op. cit.,* pp. 30 f.

by him; and he often further required that the priest should perform certain charitable works, as, for instance, the care and attendance of the sick in the hospitals, the aged, etc., and, not infrequently, that he maintain a school, "teaching gratis the poor who asked it humbly for the love of God." Ten per cent of the chantries in England, it is estimated, were educational, and that would represent fully three hundred at the Reformation, when they were suppressed.

The chantry school was often housed in the chapel building or in the residence of the priest. The instruction given was usually elementary in scope, but it was often modeled on that of the grammar school of the period, which prepared for entrance into the university.

The *Medieval Guild* is responsible for a kind of education, and consequently a type of school, which was of real significance in this period, and especially in Northern Europe. The guild, which may be regarded as a voluntary association for religious, social, and commercial purposes, formed one of the most important elements in the social life of the later Middle Ages. Although differing in origin and nature in the various countries of Europe, it usually arose as a society for the performance of religious or pious works; later the economic rather than the religious became the dominant purpose. The institution seemed to meet the aspiration of the medieval man for federation and association; and, with the growth of commerce and manufactures in the eleventh and twelfth centuries, the guilds became very numerous, embracing the merchants, traders, etc., under the merchant guild, and the artisans, and the skilled workmen, under the craft guilds. In controlling trade, in organizing and protecting labor, the guild strengthened into solidarity the middle class, and was a factor in the rise of the city states. In fact, the guild officers were at times identical with the municipal government. The student guilds, originally associations of foreign

students at the universities, had a similar influence on
the rise and organization of the universities, especially
Bologna and those of the student type. From them
came in all probability the degrees.[13]

The guild attended to the spiritual as well as the temporal wants of the members. The sick, the aged, and the
orphans were cared for; altars and chapels were maintained for the services of guilds; and masses were said
for the deceased members. A large guild not infrequently had its chaplain and maintained its church and
school. The children of the craftsmen were then given
elementary education in which the vernacular was chiefly
taught, and at times a more advanced course; for these
schools occasionally expanded into the Latin grammar
schools, as for instance in England. A notable example
was the Merchant Taylors', London.

The guild itself, especially the artisans', was an educational institution. It provided a systematic industrial
training by regulating all conditions for the learning of
a trade or craft. For instance, it was specified that only
a master could teach the trade or craft; that apprenticeship should embrace a definite number of years, from
three years to ten according to the character of the craft;
that the journeyman, as the tradesman was called when
he had completed apprenticeship, should work under a
master and not alone; and that he should only be declared a master when he had completed an independent
piece of craftsmanship, a "masterpiece."

The apprentice lived with his master while learning
the craft, and the latter was required by the regulations
of the guild to treat the boy as one of his own children.
He was also required to testify not only to his ability
as a mechanic or craftsman, but to his moral character,
before the rank of journeyman could be granted. The
education, therefore, given by the guild, or directed by

---

[13] *Cf. ante,* p. 280.

its requirements, was twofold, viz.: that of the elementary school and that of the workshop. The boy was trained so as to prepare him for his calling, and society was insured of an intelligent, skilled laboring class. His education, whether provided entirely by the guild in its own schools or not, can be attributed to the guilds; it is an early example of systematic industrial and vocational training.

FOR FURTHER STUDY

Allain, L'Abbé, *L'Instruction primaire en France avant la Révolution*. Paris: La Société Bibliographique, 1881.

Beaurepaire, Charles, *Recherches sur l'instruction publique, dans la diocèse de Rouen, avant 1789*. Evreux: P. Huet, 1872.

Cramer, Friedrich, *Geschichte der Erziehung und des Unterrichtes in den Niederlanden während bis Mittelalters*. Stralsund: C. Hingst, 1843.

Delisle, Leopold-Victor, *Études sur la condition de la classe agricole en Normandie*. Evreux: A. Herissey, 1851.

Eby and Arrowood, *History and Philosophy of Education Ancient and Medieval*. New York: Prentice-Hall, Inc., 1940.

Edgar, John, *History of Early Scottish Education*. Edinburgh: James Thin, 1893.

Leach, A. F., *The Schools of Medieval England*. New York: The Macmillan Company, 1918.

Parry, A. W., *Education in England During the Middle Ages*. London: University Tutorial Press, 1920.

Paulsen, F., *German Education, Past and Present*. Translated by T. Lorenz. New York: Charles Scribner's Sons, 1908.

Ravelet, A., *Blessed John Baptist de la Salle*. Paris: Charles Poussielque, 1888.

Schmitt, Lorenz, *Volkserziehung und Volksunterricht im späteren Mittelalter*. Paderborn: F. Schöningh, 1887.

Thorndike, Lynn, *The History of Medieval Europe*. Boston: Houghton, Mifflin Co., 1917.

Unwin, George, *The Guilds and Companies of London*. London: Methuen and Company, 1908.

Weber, Adalbert, *Die Geschichte der Volksschulpädagogik und der Kleinkindererziehung*. Eisenach: Bacmeister, 1878.

SUMMARY OF EARLY CHRISTIAN AND MEDIEVAL EDUCATION

Schools for religious instruction, catechumenal and catechetical, represent the first educational movements inaugurated by the Church. The Fathers, men of culture and learning, engaged chiefly in the work of apologetics, defending the doctrines of the Church and combating paganism. They stressed the undesirability of having Christian children attend the pagan schools; urged attendance at the monastic schools, and insisted upon the necessity of sound Christian home training. Before the close of the Patristic period, the monastic, episcopal, and parish schools had been already opened.

At the episcopal sees, episcopal or cathedral schools for training the clergy were widely established, also song schools. Parishes maintained elementary schools. Monasticism, having spread rapidly in the West, became a great educational force. Besides bringing civilization and the light of faith, the monks were the veritable teachers of the nations. They taught agriculture and the industrial arts, kept schools for the young, and founded libraries in which the treasures of the ancient literatures were preserved for posterity.

The educational revival under Charlemagne was felt throughout the dioceses of the Empire. Alfred the Great revivified learning in England. As the monastic school developed, more provision was made for the systematic education of the laity as well as of the clergy. A definite curriculum consisting of the Seven Liberal Arts was pursued. The episcopal and monastic schools then became the academies of higher learning, and in their libraries the ancient manuscripts were preserved and reproduced. Women were educated in the palaces and convent schools, many of them becoming celebrated copyists and writers.

Chivalry, which evolved out of the system of feudalism, produced a higher type of soldier in the Christian knight and deeply influenced society.

Many treatises on the content of education appeared during the Middle Ages; and also encyclopedic works aiming to preserve the learning of the past. Christian scholars were influenced by the Moors from whom they obtained Greek mathematical,

308

medical, and philosophical works. Cathedral schools became
especially distinguished during the scholastic period. Interest in
philosophy, which embraced theology, characterized scholasticism;
all other branches were pursued by the scholastics as their writings and the wide range of studies in the universities show.

The university, the great educational achievement of the
medieval period, established in all countries of Christendom,
created an academic world, and profoundly affected the culture
of Europe and all subsequent education. Bologna was the model
and type of great universities, especially for southern Europe.
In organization, Paris held equal importance with Bologna and
became the pattern for numerous universities in the North.

The Canons Regular and the religious orders of men and women
extended their activity to the schools; their members were administrators, teachers, and educational writers. Parish, chantry,
town, and guild schools were common in the late Middle Ages;
consequently there were many free schools providing an elementary education in the vernacular and in the useful arts.

Part III

Renaissance And Reformation

SYNOPSIS OF THE RENAISSANCE PERIOD

Italy

1. REVIVAL OF LETTERS
2. THE FORERUNNERS
   - (a) Dante
   - (b) Petrarch
3. RENAISSANCE FIRMLY ROOTED IN ITALY IN THE FIFTEENTH CENTURY
   - (a) Letters raised to first place in the curriculum of studies by universities and schools
   - (b) Towns of Italy force the universities into giving Letters first place
   - (c) Positions in the state service require courses in Letters
   - (d) Minor lords search out famous humanists for their service
   - (e) Papal court becomes a center for humanistic gatherings; the popes are among the most liberal patrons of the scholars
   - (f) Renaissance opens a wider field for the educated, creates new offices for scholars, and brings honors and emoluments
   - (g) Through the influence of churchmen and schoolmen who visited Italy, schools of Western Europe gradually make Latin and Greek the basis of a liberal education
4. SOME FAMOUS HUMANISTS
   Boccacio, Pier Paolo Vergerio, Giovanni Conversino da Ravenna, Gasparino Barzizza, Guarino da Verona, Vittorino da Feltre, Francesco Filelfo, Emmanuel Chrysoloras, Braccolini Poggio, Battista Guarino, Lorenzo Valla, Giovanni Aurispa, Leonardo Bruni d'Arezzo, Nicholas V, Pius II, Leo X, Maffeo Vegio, Giannozzo Manetti, Niccolo Perotti, Cardinal John Dominici
5. RENAISSANCE EDUCATIONAL THEORY
   - (a) *De ingenuis moribus (On Noble Character)* by Pier Paolo Vergerio

(b) This treatise is representative of the Catholic aims of humanistic scholars who sought to draw from the study of classic literature its cultural elements without detriment to Christian principles

6. RENAISSANCE EDUCATIONAL PRACTICE
    (a) Vittorino da Feltre's school at Mantua

France

1. EARLY HUMANISTIC INFLUENCES
    (a) Petrarch's visit to France in 1361
    (b) Nicholas Oresme, chaplain to Charles V, translated into French some works of Aristotle
    (c) Laurent de Premierfait translated the *De senectute* and *De amicitia* of Cicero and parts of writings of Boccaccio
2. JEAN DE MONTREUIL — FIRST HUMANIST OF NOTE
    (a) Nicholas de Clemanges, his friend, knew some classics then imperfectly known in Italy
3. INFLUENCE OF THE UNIVERSITY OF PARIS
    (a) Textbooks prescribed for the academic course
    (b) Gerson, chancellor of University, familiar with classical authors
4. GUILLAUME BUDÉ (GULIELMUS BUDAEUS, 1467-1540)
    (a) Most distinguished of French humanists
    (b) *De asse et partibus eius*—nine years in preparation—won for him universal reputation for learning
    (c) *Commentarii linguae graecae* established his fame as the first Greek scholar in Europe
    (d) *De l'institution du prince,* his chief educational treatise
5. MATHURIN CORDIER (1479-1564)
    (a) *De corrupti sermonis emendatione libellus,* a work on Latin inflections
    (b) *Colloquia,* a work on Latin conversation
    (c) Advocated classical curriculum in the Collège de Guyenne, at Bordeaux

Spain

1. ANTONIO OF LEBRIJA (ANTONIUS NEBRISSENSIS, 1444-1522)
    (a) First notable humanist
    (b) *Introductiones Latinae,* first Latin grammar of note in Spain
2. CARDINAL XIMÉNEZ
    (a) Distinguished patron of letters
    (b) Founder of College at Alcalá

Portugal

1. RESENDE—humanist, historian and poet
2. BISHOP OSORIO—Cicero of Portugal
3. ALVAREZ—author of a Latin grammar long used in the schools of the Jesuits

Northern Europe

1. BRETHREN OF THE COMMON LIFE
    (a) Embraced the humanistic movement and became influential agents in the spread of classical studies in the Netherlands and Germany
    (b) Classical training given in their secondary schools

Germany

1. JOHN WESSEL (1420-1489)
    (a) Shared the honor of introducing humanism into Germany and of expanding the curriculum of the schools of the Brethren
2. RUDOLPH AGRICOLA (1443-1485)
    (a) Influenced German education and especially the schools of the Brethren
    (b) *De studio formando (On the Regulation of Study)* most famous pedagogical work
3. ALEXANDER HEGIUS (1433-1498)
    (a) Practical schoolmaster and thoroughly in sympathy with the new studies
    (b) Conducted schools of St. Lebuin at Deventer and trained some of the early humanistic educators— Rudolf von Langen, Murmellius, Dringenberg, Erasmus

4. JACOB WIMPHELING (1450-1528)
   (a) Preceptor Germaniae
   (b) *A Guide to German Youth*—the earliest systematic treatise on education by a German scholar
5. JOHANN REUCHLIN (1455-1522)
   (a) Foremost German layman who took an interest in the classics
   (b) Introduced into Germany the study of Hebrew as one of the learned languages; published a Hebrew grammar and dictionary; collected many Greek and Hebrew manuscripts; compiled a Latin lexicon and Greek textbooks some of which were long in use in Germany
6. DESIDERIUS ERASMUS (1466-1536)
   (a) Leading man of letters of his time
   (b) *Moriae encomium, Adagia, and Colloquiorum formulae* attacked medieval learning, the religious orders, Catholic doctrines and practices
   (c) *De pueris statim ac liberaliter instituendis, (On the Liberal Education of Children from their earliest years),* his best known educational treatise
   (d) Represents the Renaissance literary spirit in its good and bad aspects
7. JUAN LUIS VIVES (1492-1540)
   (a) Catholic scholar of the Renaissance and real reformer of the Reformation period
   (b) *De institutione feminae christianae, (On the Instruction of a Christian Woman), De ratione studii, (On the Method of Study), and De officio mariti, (On the Duty and Office of a Husband);* Chapter III contain his views on the education of women
   (c) *De disciplinis tradendis, (On the Transmision of Learning),* his great educational work
   (d) Educational treatises real bequests to modern pedagogy, but he remained unknown until his memory was revived in Spain, Germany, and England in the twentieth century

England

1. EARLY HUMANISTIC INFLUENCES
   (a) Chaucer visited Italy and was familiar with the works of Petrarch and Boccaccio
   (b) Chrysoloras and Poggio both in England early in fifteenth century
   (c) Many Englishmen attended Council of Basle coming into immediate contact with the Italian leaders of the Revival
2. ENGLISHMEN WHO ESPOUSED THE CAUSE OF THE NEW LEARNING
   (a) Humphrey, Duke of Gloucester
   (b) John Tiptoft, Earl of Worcester
   (c) Andrew Holes
   (d) Reynold Chicheley
   (e) William Grey
   (f) John Free
   (g) John Flemming
   (h) John Gunthorpe
   (i) William Selling
3. THOMAS LINACRE (1460-1524)
   (a) Resigned position as royal physician to Henry VIII to become priest
   (b) Notable patron of learning; endowed chairs of Greek and medicine at Oxford and Cambridge
   (c) Translated from the Greek medical treatises of Galen; works on Latin grammar of service in the schools
   (d) Associates of Linacre at Oxford were the ecclesiastics, Grocyn and Latimer, teachers of Greek
4. JOHN COLET (1467-1519)
   (a) A thorough humanist; founder of St. Paul's, London, and dean of the school
   (b) Statutes of St. Paul's curricular organization and organization of teaching staff give him notable place among promoters of humanism in England
   (c) William Lily, headmaster under Colet
5. ST. THOMAS MORE (1478-1535)
   (a) Friend of scholars and humanists

    (b) His house in Chelsea the true center of humanism in England

    (c) Letters to his children and their instructors best express his educational views

6. SIR THOMAS ELYOT (1490-1546)

    (a) Author of the *Governour*—earliest humanistic treatise in English

    (b) Compiled Latin-English dictionary—first of its kind published

    (c) Author of significant but little known treatise—*Defence of Good Women*

7. ROGER ASCHAM (1515-1568)

    (a) Most of life devoted to teaching; taught Greek at Oxford; tutor of Princess Elizabeth

    (b) *Scholemaster*, published after his death, his leading educational work

    (c) Advocated double translation and use of notebooks in teaching Latin and Greek

    (d) *Toxophilus* treats of physical exercises and recreation.

    (e) Bitter against monks and Catholic Italy

CHAPTER XVIII

THE RENAISSANCE IN ITALY

The Renaissance was a dynamic movement of cultural developments which began in the fourteenth century and continued into the sixteenth. It was not merely a revival of learning; it was a general reawakening throughout Western Europe which profoundly affected every phase of thought and life and set at work many social and educational forces the influence of which persists to our day. This new era initiated a revolt against the medieval system of education, brought about a radical change in attitude toward the human body, gave rise to an excessive individualism, and fostered open disregard for Christian teaching.[1] The Renaissance had already gotten under way when the Revival of Learning began in Italy. Essentially an imitation or recapitulation, the revival of letters there was an enthusiastic return to antiquity, a rebirth of ancient Greek and Latin literature. Education profited by it and suffered from it both in theory and in practice.

The Revival of Learning began in Italy in a period notable for its great men, its universal geniuses, whose

---

[1] A decay of the religious spirit of the various European peoples was apparent in the fourteenth century. This was due partly to a lack of confidence in ecclesiastical leaders. The "Captivity of Avignon," as it is called, which lasted from 1305 to 1377, made the Papacy subservient to the French crown. The struggle for the control of the papacy among the French, Italian, and Spanish powers led to the Great Western Schism, which began in 1378 and lasted forty years. This decay was also partly due to the Black Death, a virulent form of bubonic plague, which destroyed within a few years nearly one half of the total population of Europe. This disaster caused not only a decided loss in the quality of educational leaders but of the clergy as well. *Cf.* A. M. Campbell, *The Black Death and Men of Learning* (New York: Columbia University, 1932).

vocation was to "resuscitate antiquity, to gather up afresh the products of the classic past and so to blend them with the medieval spirit as to generate what is specifically modern." [2] The Italians had always looked to the past as the period of their national greatness; in literature they considered classic antiquity as their golden age. Their reverting to it in the fifteenth century, with an enthusiasm which became almost a passion, was the climax of a tendency clearly discernible in Dante and Petrarch and only needing the thirteenth century and the progressive movements of the later Middle Ages to call it forth. Dante and Petrarch are quite properly looked upon as forerunners of the Renaissance.

Dante Alighieri (1264-1321), whose interest in learning was that of a man of the world, was born at Florence. He was first and foremost a poet and is often ranked with Homer, Vergil, and Shakespeare. He was the first literary layman of renown since Boethius and had mastered all the learning of his day. His influence in the Renaissance is not attributed to any treatise on the Revival, but to the spirit of his later writings, in which he yearns for a new and broader culture than was afforded by the scholars of the period. In *Il Convito (The Banquet)* he upholds the medieval idea of erudition, but its purpose is culture and refinement of soul.

Dante did not favor the exclusive use of Latin for literary purposes and for that reason chose the mother tongue for his great poem, *Divina Comedia (The Divine Comedy)*. Although this poem was medieval in spirit and glorified scholastic learning, it revived in intensified form an interest in the writings of classic antiquity. In it Aristotle is regarded as "the Philosopher" and a profound admiration is shown for the other cele-

---

[2] John A. Symonds, *The Revival of Learning* (New York: Charles Scribner's Sons, 1912), p. 8.

brated authors of Greece and Rome. When in a vision
Dante visits the lower world, Vergil is his guide. There,
in the region inhabited by the spirits of virtuous pagans,
he is introduced to Homer, the sovereign poet, Horace,
and Ovid; and he is overcome by the honor of sitting
among them, together with Socrates, Plato, Cicero,
Caesar, Livy, Seneca, and many other classical worthies.
Dante's poems abound in references to ancient authors,
both pagan and Christian; he was so devoted to Vergil
that he quotes him about two hundred times.[3]

Petrarch (1304-1374) was the prime mover of the
Renaissance; he was the first humanist[4] to desert the
medieval system of studies and make classical Latin
literature the basis of a liberal education. As a consequence he has been aptly called "the first modern man."
As a diligent student of Cicero, he succeeded in making
the classics better known and more widely read. So
deep was his veneration for the ancient writers, and in
particular for Cicero, that he wrote letters to him and
cried over them, lamenting the fact that the works of
Cicero had been neglected. An indefatigable scholar
himself, he stimulated by his example the intellectual
ambitions of his pupils and rendered the study of the
Latin classics popular among cultivated persons. He
pointed out their natural beauties to the humanists in
the University of Padua and secured the establishment
of the humanistic studies there. He did not know Greek
but earnestly endeavored to obtain teachers who might
instruct him. His chief influence on the Renaissance lay
in the service he rendered by collecting manuscripts

---

[3] J. E. Sandys, *A History of Classical Scholarship* (Cambridge:
Cambridge University Press, 1921), I, C14.

[4] Scholars who devoted themselves to the study and imitation
first of Latin and later of Greek literature are called "humanists,"
a name derived from the Latin word, *humanitas,* which means
culture, especially in the sense of literary appreciation. The
Greek and Latin classics are still called "the humanities."

from all parts of Europe, in introducing the new learning into the University of Padua, and in his writings, *De viris illustribus* and the *Epistolae*. His *Epistola ad posteros* [5] in particular is a remarkable account of his life and studies and is indicative of his particular form of vanity for fame and honor. Although he did not share Dante's confidence in the dignity of the mother tongue, and preferred to compose in Latin, Petrarch's abiding fame is based upon his Italian verse.

Boccaccio (1313-1375) was more fortunate than Petrarch in endeavoring to master Greek. He supported at his house a teacher of Greek with whom he read the poems of Homer. At this time it is doubtful whether there were in Italy a dozen men who could read the works of the Greek authors in the original. Like Petrarch and particularly every other humanist, Boccaccio was a collector of manuscripts. He aided humanism by collecting and editing manuscripts, especially Greek, and by his zeal for establishing the new studies at the universities. He founded the chair of Greek in Florence in 1350. The Latin works of Boccaccio gave him the only title to fame for two centuries after his death; that on mythology, *De genealogiis deorum gentilium*, very naturally influenced the early humanists and continued to be an authority in later centuries for the student of classical antiquity. The work with which Boccaccio's name is most commonly associated is the *Decameron*, which exerted a profound influence on all literature for three hundred years.[6] Boccaccio was a scholar of the first rank for his time, but his spirit was corrupted by a slavish imitation of the pagan ethics of

---

[5] *Cf.* James H. Robinson and Henry W. Rolfe, *Petrarch: The First Modern Scholar and Man of Letters* (New York: G. P. Putnam's Sons, 1909), pp. 59-76.

[6] Edward Hutton, *Giovanni Boccaccio* (New York: John Lane Company, 1910), p. 311.

the classics; naturalism asserted itself both in his writings and in his life.

The University of Padua wielded a potent influence at the beginning of the Renaissance through the humanistic activities of Giovanni Conversino da Ravenna (†1405?) and Gasparino Barzizza (†1431), both of whom were professors of rhetoric and Latin letters. The former, a pupil of Petrarch, by his excellent lectures on Latin attracted as students many professors of the University, and taught two of the best known humanistic educators, Vittorino da Feltre and Guarino da Verona. Barzizza ranks as the first Latinist of his time. None made a deeper study of Cicero, or used him better for educational purposes. He labored for years in search of the best texts of Cicero, annotated and edited them. Some of his pupils were distinguished humanists, e.g., George of Trebizond and Francesco Filelfo.

Emmanuel Chrysoloras (1350-1413), a Greek of Constantinople, who came to Italy on diplomatic business, accepted the chair of Greek in the University of Florence in 1397 and became the leading professor of Greek in the West. His advent marks the real beginning of the revival of Greek in Italy. He attracted great numbers of students to Florence, among whom were Guarino da Verona and Pier Paolo Vergerio who gave up his professorship in the University of Padua to become a student under him. Guarino afterward published the lectures of Chrysoloras on Greek grammar. This was the only available text for the study of Greek for many years. The humanists, who spared none in their criticisms, refer in the most respectful terms to Chrysoloras as a teacher and scholar. They had a high opinion of his character and showed him more than usual honor during his residence in Italy. He seems to have been an attractive personality and an exemplary man both in public and private life. He became a communicant of the Catholic Church while in Italy, and sought to bring about the union of the Greeks with Rome.

At the beginning of the fifteenth century the Renaissance was firmly rooted in Italy. Universities and schools raised letters to the first place in the curriculum of studies. This was especially true of Pavia and Padua. Even when the universities did not follow this course, the towns forced them into it. Florence received Chrysoloras through the invitation of the citizens and not at the initiative of the University. Venice proceeded to establish chairs at Padua, and made all candidates for positions in the state service take courses in letters at the University. The new spirit invaded the courts of the nobility and the imperial chamber. The emperor would employ only a humanist as secretary, and the minor lords vied with one another to secure a famous follower of the new studies in their service. The papal court throughout the century was a center for humanistic gatherings and the rendezvous of the leaders. The popes were among the most liberal patrons of the scholars.

Nicholas V (1447-1455) invited a large body of scholars to Rome, where he founded chairs of rhetoric for them, and designated many as textual critics and translators, rewarding them munificently. The Vatican Library came into existence during his pontificate, and the work of collecting and translating the ancient classics continued until his death. The library stands as evidence of his patronage as well as of the era of scholarship, for in the last five years of his pontificate more of the Greek classics were done into Latin than in five hundred years which have since lapsed. It is the greatest depositary of ancient classic manuscripts in the world. Other popes who were identified with the Renaissance were *Pius II* [Aeneas Sylvius], (1458-1464), author of the educational treatise, *De liberorum educatione,* and *Leo X* (1513-21), who has been called the Maecenas of the Renaissance. The latter openly spoke of his appreciation of literature as a study, and declared that next to religion it gave the greatest satisfaction to the soul. The condition of the Roman University during his pontificate shows how favorably the new studies were received in the center of Christendom. Its chairs at that time were as follows: three of theology; eleven of canon law; twenty of civil law; fifteen of medicine; one of botany (the first in Italy); five of philosophy; two of mathematics; one of astrology; three of Greek; and eighteen of rhetoric (Latin letters).

The Renaissance created new offices for scholars, and opened a wider field for the educated; in consequence, there was no little strife and rivalry for honors and emoluments. Despite this and the bitter enmities which existed among the ambitious, a real spirit of study was manifested by the early humanists, and a willingness to undergo hardships and suffering to master the new studies. Many, like Verona, journeyed to Constantinople and remained there for years in order to obtain a perfect knowledge of Greek. The lofty purpose of the humanist educator is undeniable. It can be seen in the excellent treatises produced at that time and in the systems inaugurated in the Renaissance schools.

The age of the Renaissance in Italy was prolific in treatises on education. The treatises of Pier Paolo Vergerio, of Leonardo Bruni d'Arezzo, of Blessed Cardinal Giovanni Dominici, of Pius II, of Maffeo Vegio, and of Battista Guarino are the most important that remain to us, while those of Gianozzo Manetti, Nicholas Perotti, and Secco Polentone have since been lost. Francesco Barbaro's tract on *Marriage (De re uxoria),* and the books of Matteo Palmieri and Leon Battista Alberti, though not wholly concerned with education, have each an important section on education.

The first and most significant of all these treatises of the Revival of Letters was the admirable work of *Pier Paolo Vergerio* (1370-1445), *De ingenuis moribus et studiis liberalibus (On Noble Character and Liberal Studies)*. Vergerio is a Catholic humanist of strong religious principle. He was a statesman and a canonist and, though probably in minor orders, he was not a priest. His educational aims are the recognized Catholic aims. Combining as he does the high standard of learning with the inculcation of sound Christian principles, he set the ideal which Renaissance educators were to strive after. This treatise was written about 1392 and was addressed to Ubertino, son of Francesco Carrara, lord of Padua. It outlines a complete training for the young prince, the aim of which is character formation. "The work," says Woodward, "which has been too much overlooked by later students of the Renaissance, was for a century and a half after its appearance amongst the most widely read of all the productions of the Revival of Letters." [7]

In setting forth the value of a liberal education, Vergerio stresses the importance of moral discipline.

We call those studies liberal which are worthy of a free man; those studies by which we attain and practice virtue and wisdom; that education liberal which calls forth, trains and develops these highest gifts of body and mind which ennoble men, and which are rightly judged to rank next in dignity to virtue only. For to the vulgar temper, gain and pleasure are the one aim of existence; to a lofty nature, moral worth and fame.

A virtuous character is the only basis on which to build the humanistic training, for learning is not the antidote to vice and national wickedness. It may be

---

[7] *Cf.* W. H. Woodward, *Vittorino da Feltre and Other Humanist Educators* (Cambridge: The University Press, 1897). Contains translations of treatises by Vergerio, d'Arezzo, Pope Pius II, and Battista Guarino.

used as the means to greater evil in a Claudius or a Nero. There remains no doubt of its supreme advantage to the virtuous, whether in the affairs of state, or in the enjoyment of recreation and leisure.

Literature is memory immortalized, shielding from death and oblivion the thoughts of great men in a noble form of expression. The subjects of liberal studies are history, the first and most important because of its attractiveness and utility to the man of affairs; moral philosophy, which in connection with history teaches truth, the secret of freedom; eloquence, which refines the truth learned in philosophy; all three tend to form the essentials of a liberal education, viz., sound judgment, wisdom of speech, and integrity of conduct.

Literature or letters is the basis of all learning, which in turn assumes as a foundation a thorough knowledge of grammar, composition, and logic, the science and art of reasoning, that which enables the student to detect sophisms and fallacies in the arguments of others. Vergerio is reluctant to discard a subject which, however much abused by scholastics, had a necessary place in the curriculum. Poetry was to be chosen judiciously, and only that which would prompt the finest feelings was to be read. The older subjects of the seven liberal arts, e.g., the mathematical, are retained, and a study of nature recommended, for in the investigation of the laws and causes of natural phenomena Vergerio believed much valuable information was to be found.

In the treatment of the manner of study, the author's long teaching experience is evident. He writes as one expressing the ideas and methods then accepted by the best educators—an implicit tribute to the pedagogical thought of the time. Some notable features of Vergerio's treatise are his views on the training of children in reverence to parents and elders and in courtesy to all; the psychological analysis of the motives prompting the boy to study; attention given to natural endowments, tastes, and capabilities; the treatment and correction of defects in the backward, unwilling, lazy; the aids to progress, such as rewards, emulation, encouragement; the consideration of the individual in everything, in study, recreation, and physical exercise.

Vergerio's treatise had a profound influence on the educational career of one of the world's great teachers, the distinguished Catholic layman and humanistic schoolmaster, Vittorino da Feltre, whose unique court school at Mantua is of paramount interest in the consideration of the aims and methods of Renaissance education and will be discussed later in this chapter. Vittorino's system of education was fundamentally the practical application of the humanistic theory as expressed in the educational treatise of Vergerio.

The excellent treatise of *Leonardo Bruni* (1369-1444), often called Aretino from his birthplace, Arezzo, is thoroughly Catholic. Although he was a friend of the pagan humanist Poggio, he himself was a good Christian scholar. His essay on the study of literature, *De studiis et litteris (On Studies and Letters)*, is in the form of a letter addressed to Baptista Malatesta, one of the earliest of the learned women of the Renaissance. In the education of the Christian lady, Bruni insists that religion and morals hold first place. He presumes that the Christian lady will be acquainted first with the Christian writers of whom Lactantius, Ambrose, Jerome, Augustine, and Cyprian are specially recommended. It is not expected, however, that she will confine her reading to ecclesiastical writers, as morals have been treated by the noblest intellects of Greece and Rome and what they have had to say upon continence, temperance, modesty, justice, courage, greatness of soul commands our respect. Bruni would have her read in particular the classical poets with whom the Fathers of the Church reveal a scholarly acquaintance. In conclusion, he desires that while learning be full and varied ·it should be usable. "But to enable us to make effectual use of what we know, we must add to our knowledge the power of expression." In this letter Bruni expresses the best that the humanists had to say on the study of literature.

Of all the treatises of the early Renaissance, the *Regola del governo di cura familiare* [8] *(Rule for the Government of the Family)* of *Blessed Cardinal John Dominici* (1356-1420) is perhaps the most detailed. This is a valuable pedagogical work which treats in four books of the faculties of the soul, the powers and senses of the body, the uses of earthly goods, and the education of children. It was written to instruct the wife of Antonio Alberti in the government of her family and gives minute details for her guidance. In his instruction, the author holds up a lofty standard of conduct and displays good practical common sense. Dominici was conscious of the irreparable harm that the Classic Renaissance was doing to Christian civilization by tending to establish pagan ideals in the minds of the young; and in this treatise and likewise in his *Lucula noctis,* a work on the study of classical authors, he opposes the pagan tendencies of the new learning. In the treatise on family life he insists that children be brought up as Christians and not as pagans, and denounces a system of training which would have them learn the names of Jupiter, Saturn, and Venus rather that those of the Holy Trinity.

Aeneas Sylvius Piccolomini (1405-1464), later Pope Pius II, is the author of the educational treatise *De liberorum educatione* [9] *(On the Education of Children).* This tractate is a letter to Ladislas, the youthful king

---

[8] *Cf.* A. B. Cote, *Cardinal Dominici as an Educator* (Washington, D. C.: Catholic University of America, 1927).

[9] *Cf.* Brother Joel Stanislaus Nelson, F.S.C., *Aeneae Silvii De Liberorum Educatione* (Washington, D. C.: The Catholic University of America, 1940).

of Bohemia and Hungary. Piccolomini's ideas on the new learning coincide with much of the thought expressed in the first book of Quintilian. The treatise recommends in particular the study of history, advocating the reading of the chief historians. From such study, the author holds, practical wisdom may be gleaned. Pius II expresses the aim of a liberal education in terms of character, which is "our one sure possession." "The place and fortune of men change," he states, "it may be suddenly, profoundly; nor may we by taking thought, cunningly hedge ourselves round against all the chances of life." Character is to be obtained by religious training and through the study of philosophy and letters.

The *De educatione liberorum*[10] of *Maffeo Vegio* (1406-1458) is most comprehensive and most Christian in spirit. During his life as an Augustinian, Vegio kept up his interest in the classics and recommended their study. His treatise is in six books, the first three of which treat of the duties of parents and teachers in education; the last three of the duties of the young to God, their fellow men, and themselves. Vegio reflects in his work much of the educational thought of Vergerio, but prescribes profounder moral and religious instruction. He likewise treats of conduct and manners more fully. In dealing with the respect due to others, he includes the poor and unfortunate. He would have children ruled by love and encouraged judiciously by praise. Punishment, he believes, makes "servile charac-

---

[10] *Cf.* Sister M. Dorothea McCants, D. C., "The Educational Contents of Books I-VI of the De Educatione Liberorum by Maffeo Vegio" (unpublished Master's dissertation, Washington, D. C.: The Catholic University of America, 1941). A critical text of books I-III has been edited by Sister Maria Walburg Fanning (Washington, D. C.: The Catholic University of America, 1933). Books IV-VI have been edited by Sister Anne Stanislaus Sullivan (Washington, D. C.: The Catholic University of America, 1936).

ters." He advocates a practical training for girls in household duties, such as housekeeping, spinning, and embroidery. For Vegio, the supreme end of education is the formation of a sound moral and Christian character.

The *Libro della famiglia (A Book on the Family)*, written by *Alberti* (1404-1472), consists of four books, of which the first deals with the duties of parents to children and of children to parents. In infancy and early childhood the mother holds the first place, but as the children grow older the father is the head. Children are to be brought up in the fear of God and are to be trained in the practices of religion. The home is the great educational force and the character of the home is dependent on the character of the parents. The study of letters rightly imparted should induce interest in noble thoughts and words and deeds. According to Alberti, a useful life consists in the fulfillment of one's duty to family, country and God.

About the same time, *Palmieri* (1406-1475), who was a close friend of Alberti, produced his work, *Della vita civili (On Civil Life)*. Palmieri treats of education as regards the ideal Florentine citizen. His ideas on the training of children in the home, though in no way new, are profoundly Christian. His advice concerning the use of money and his praise of liberality are noteworthy. He favors the building of beautiful churches and the furnishing of costly ornaments for divine worship.

The books of Alberti and Palmieri were written in dialogue form. They are illuminating for the light which they throw on the attributes that were looked for in the Florentine woman. Though it was expected that the women of Florence cultivate culture and learning, they were to possess at the same time the homelier virtues of the good housewife, skilled in the domestic arts of dairying, spinning, weaving, and needlework. Their education was to be characterized by a training in the sense of duty and responsibility so that they might become domestic and businesslike.

Barbaro (1398-1454), who was a pupil of Guarino da Verona, wrote his work on *Marriage* when he was seventeen years of age. In the chapter on education, *"De liberorum educatione,"* Barbaro reproduces much of the current opinion regarding the training of children.

The period draws to a close in Italy with the remarkable treatise of *Battista Guarino* (1443-1513), *De ordine docendi et studendi (On the Method of Teaching and Studying)*. Battista was the son of Guarino da Verona, the only one of Guarino's large family who showed any taste for scholarship. He followed in his father's footsteps and finally occupied his place as professor in the University of Ferrara. The younger Guarino was associated with his father as an expert in textual emendation in the latter's school at Ferrara. The plan of education here was much the same as that adopted by Vittorino. Probably at his father's suggestion, Battista wrote this treatise upon the method of teaching and reading the classical authors. The tract represents the educational plan and method pursued by his father.

In these early Renaissance educational treatises one notes ideas common to all of them. The duties of a mother, the choice of a nurse, the selection of a tutor, and the effects of environment on early training are all taken up for discussion and every writer has something to say on each of these important topics. The role of the mother in the child's early formation and direction is emphasized. Noble Roman women are cited who have been famous in history for their conscientious performance of the duties of motherhood. Vegio, however, who has great admiration for St. Monica, prefers to hold her up as "the model of all teaching mothers." The home training is to be a religious training. Children are to be brought up in the love of God, their country, and their home. The child will have his prayers by heart, the Our Father, the Hail Mary, the Creed, the Commandments, and portions of the Gospels. Respect for parents and elders is to be taught from the earliest years, and courtesy to all is to be inculcated. In the child's physical training, a certain hardiness is to be cultivated. Soft beds and artificial heat are prohibited; while fresh air, suitable dress, plain diet and moderation in eating and drinking are prescribed.

Not all are agreed at what age the child should enter upon a definite and systematic course of instruction, but all insist that actual instruction should be made pleasant and attractive. Lessons are to be alternated with games and bodily exercises which serve to build up the body physically and strengthen the limbs. Swimming, fencing, gymnastics and military exercises, music and singing are recommended. The choice of the teacher should be made only after much forethought. The teacher stands in a quasi-parental relation to his pupils and they should be united by mutual affection, with veneration on the part of the pupil and deep personal interest on the part of the teacher. The course of study is based on Latin and Greek letters, with history and philosophy holding a dominant place, while mathematics, the study of nature, and astronomy hold a subordinate position. The curriculum for girls is substantially the same as that proposed for the boys. More stress, however, is laid on religious reading and less instruction is advocated in rhetoric. Corporal punishment is condemned. Children are to be ruled not by fear but by love.

The similarity of subject matter in these early Renaissance educational treatises shows a dependence on the same materials out of which these humanists built up their ideal of education. As the whole history of the Renaissance was rooted in antiquity, it was natural that

the Italian humanist scholars and educators of the fourteenth and fifteenth centuries should likewise find in
the writings of the ancients many of those ideas which
they were to carry out educationally. While Cicero's
De oratore (On the Orator) and Plutarch's *De liberis
educandis (On the Education of Children)* proved helpful in shaping Renaissance educational practice, Quintilian's educational treatise, *De institutione oratoria
(The Institutes of Oratory)*, in particular influenced the
pedagogy of Renaissance educators during the revival
of classical culture. Vergerio's *De ingenuis moribus* reproduced many of the educational ideas of Quintilian
and gave an impetus to the production of subsequent
educational treatises of the early Renaissance.

The *De institutione oratoria* of Quintilian treats of
more important pedagogic topics than any other ancient
educational treatise. It appears that the teachers in the
monastic schools of the Middle Ages followed many of
its suggestions. During the later Middle Ages it was
apparently forgotten, but in the fourteenth century the
rediscovery of the lost Quintilian was an occasion of
great rejoicing among the humanists. A part of this
great treatise was known to Petrarch, while the first
modern introduction to the study of Quintilian was produced by Vergerio. A complete copy of Quintilian was
discovered in the early part of the fifteenth century by
Poggio in the monastery of St. Gall, Switzerland, and
was copied by him in fifty-three days. About the same
time Cicero's *De oratore* was found, which previously
had been known only in a mutilated form; and a little
earlier Guarino had rendered into Latin Plutarch's
treatise on education.

The outstanding feature of these early Renaissance
treatises on education is the Catholic spirit that pervades
them. Their authors were completely Catholic in character and influence. The religion of Christ was for them

the central fact of life. They gloried in the golden age of classical culture, but their devotion to the ancient classics was tempered by their adherence to the unchanging Catholic faith. Schooled in the scholastic institutions of medieval learning and with Vergerio as their preceptor, they undertook to draw from the study of ancient literature its cultural elements without detriment to Christian principles and Catholic tradition. These noble scholars combined their enthusiasm for the classics with genuine love for the teachings of Christianity. As Symonds has so well said, "They received their earliest education in the religion of the Middle Ages, their second in the schools of Greece and Rome."

The new studies in the Early Renaissance made their home not so much in the universities as at the courts of princes, the houses of prosperous citizens, the papal curia, and the governmental headquarters of the republic.[11] The most celebrated court school of the period was that at Mantua, conducted by Vittorino da Feltre, the most famous of the humanistic schoolmasters, who represents a type of lay teacher for which the Italy of the fifteenth century is remarkable.[12] An able scholar, he was, like Guarino da Verona,[13] a practical teacher who labored to reduce the new studies to a system of teaching and to set the standards for this new kind of education of the young.

Vittorino de' Rambaldoni was born at Feltre, 1378, whence the surname by which he is best known. As noted above, he studied in the University of Padua. He attended the course of grammar and Latin letters given

---

[11] Ernest C. Moore, *The Story of Instruction* (New York: The Macmillan Company, 1938), II, 415.

[12] Thomas J. Shahan, *The Middle Ages* (New York: Benziger Bros., 1904), p. 404.

[13] *Cf.* W. H. Woodward, *Studies in Education during the Age of the Renaissance* (Cambridge: The University Press, 1906). Contains a chapter on Guarino da Verona.

by da Ravenna who was Petrarch's protégé and secretary. He devoted himself also to dialectic and philosophy. As a student he was obliged to support himself by tutoring. He also studied under Barzizza, who occupied the chair of rhetoric, and attended the lectures of Vergerio whose educational treatise, *De ingenuis moribus*, was being widely read. After receiving the doctorate he turned to mathematics under Pelacani da Parma and became a more successful teacher than his instructor. The same ardor for the study of Greek that took Vergerio from the doctor's chair at Padua to the student's bench at Florence, that drew Guarino, Aurispa, and Filelfo to Constantinople, and the Florentines to the lectures of Chrysoloras, finally carried Vittorino to Venice to attend the school of Guarino da Verona, who had lately returned to Italy after a five years' residence in Constantinople where he had learned Greek from Chrysoloras. At Venice he spent eighteen months studying Greek with Guarino, who was then considered the best Greek scholar in Italy. In exchange, Vittorino imparted to Guarino, it is believed, a finer knowledge of Latin. The two humanists formed a friendship which lasted throughout life.

Vittorino succeeded Barzizza in the chair of rhetoric at Padua in 1422 and, although a professor in the University, conducted a private school in his own household. There he received a limited number of students of the University and supervised their domestic life. After about a year, either being disgusted with the immorality of the city or unable to control the students, he resigned his chair and went to Venice where he organized a school. In that year, 1423, he was invited by Gian Francesco Gonzaga, Marquis of Mantua, to undertake the education of his children, three boys and a girl. Vittorino accepted the invitation with the understanding that he could conduct a school at the court and receive other students; and he established at Mantua the school with which his name is most familiarly associated. He remained in the service of the Marquis of Mantua for twenty-two years until his death in 1446.

A villa, formerly the recreation hall of the Gonzaghi, was transformed by him into an ideal schoolhouse. Because of its pleasant surroundings and the spirit that prevailed therein, it was called the "Casa Jocosa,"[14] or "Pleasant House." Alongside of it was the boarding house for the poor scholars, but all worked and played together. Vittorino endeavored to make the school as enjoyable as the ideal home, but all luxury was carefully excluded. Soft beds and silk hangings were done away with and the meals served were simple but substantial. Children of the nobility, sons of other humanists like Filelfo, Guarino, and Poggio, and poor children who showed an aptitude for learning were admitted to the classes. Eventually pupils came from the leading families of northern Italy, from Greece, from France, and from Germany.

Vittorino's system of education was based upon Guarino's translation of Plutarch's *De liberis educandis*, Quintilian's *De institutione oratoria*, and, in particular, the *De ingenuis moribus* of Vergerio. The thought in these treatises was assimilated by Vittorino but transfigured by his genius and originality. He was impressed

---

[14] Woodward calls the "Casa Giocosa" the great typical school of the humanities. *Cf.* W. H. Woodward, *Vittorino da Feltre and other Humanist Educators* (Cambridge: The University Press, 1897), p. 24. Burckhardt maintains that the schools of Vittorino and Guarino were unique of their kind. *Cf.* J. Burckhardt, *The Civilization of the Renaissance in Italy*. Translated by S. G. C. Middlemore (London: George G. Hurrop and Co., 1929), p. 213. Kane asserts that Vittorino's school had advantages which no ordinary school can expect to have. A single school like Vittorino's gives a fictitious character to the Renaissance. *Cf.* W. Kane, *An Essay Toward a History of Education* (Chicago: Loyola University Press, 1935), p. 209.

with the idea that a sound knowledge of literature and
language was essential to moral and spiritual formation;
that the two basic factors in the development of the complete man were Christianity and humanism.[15] Consequently, the instruction given in his school was of the
new humanist type, but thoroughly Christian in character
and spirit.

It was not merely a literary training, but embraced
the physical and moral requirements of a liberal education. Vittorino's academy was preeminently a preparatory or training school for life, as Monnier describes it,
"un institut de vie."[16] He preferred to receive the students when very young. Their characters and powers
of mind were then easily discernible; they had no prej-
udices and they had little to unlearn.

The age of the pupils seems to have varied widely[17]
and it appears that no child was refused on the grounds
of being too young. Although the fundamental branch
of instruction was letters, Latin and Greek did not constitute the entire curriculum of studies. Arithmetic,
geometry, algebra, logic, dialectics, ethics, astronomy,
history, music, and eloquence were all taught at Mantua
and frequently by special teachers; for as new departments of study developed, specially trained instructors in
logic and philosophy, masters in painting, music, dancing,
and riding, copyists and tutors, became associated with

---

[15] M. Jerrold, *Italy in the Renaissance* (London: Methuen and
Co., Ltd., 1927), pp. 76 f.
[16] R. Monnier, *Le Quattrocento* (Paris: Perrin et Cie., 1901), I,
241.
[17] The court schools received pupils very young and frequently
taught them until they were twenty-one years of age. The
matter covered was often more than that offered in the arts
course of the University. If a student wished to have a degree,
he went from the court school to the university; but, if he were
satisfied with a general course, he preferred the greater prestige
of being a pupil of a distinguished humanist at the head of a
court school.

the teaching staff. Vittorino did not favor large classes.
As his school increased in numbers he employed more
masters of whom some were Greeks who taught their
own language while they learned Latin and transcribed
Greek manuscripts. Vittorino himself taught for seven
or eight hours a day, holding class in the morning and
devoting the afternoon hours to particular pupils for
individual instruction.

A novel method of study and teaching resulted from
the humanistic conception of the value of classic literature. Latin no longer occupied the position of a preparatory study to dialectics and theology. It was studied
for its own intrinsic value, as a means to full mental
development and culture. The custom of exposing the
metaphorical, allegorical, and mystical meaning of a passage after the literal had been given disappeared when
the humanist proposed to ascertain, after acquiring the
literal sense and idea of the historical background, what
the passage without exaggeration or straining would
naturally signify. The history of the work under study
was to be given as vividly as possible. After a thorough
grasp of a selection, the author's characteristics were
pointed out, and the features of construction or diction
worthy of imitation were indicated. The method allowed
great freedom and elasticity in the treatment of an
author. It depended for success on the teacher's powers
of illustration and description. The Latin poets and
historians were read in this way. Vergil ranked first
among the poets. Each of the prose writers had his
special merit in style or manner. Vittorino was the first
to make a profound study of Livy, whose eloquence and
richness of diction he greatly admired. The pupils
learned from the first to converse in Latin and, as they
advanced, they were drilled in memorizing and reciting
intelligently portions of the classic authors and the
Church Fathers. Reading aloud was a particular feature

in the day's work; proper pronunciation was insisted upon; and much attention was given to clear instruction and right emphasis.

From the array of authors and the number of Greek scholars engaged at various times to teach at Mantua, the activity in studying Greek would seem to have been even greater than in Latin and the other branches. Perhaps the ardor with which the revival was undertaken is responsible for this impression. The rudiments were taught as in Latin. The historians Xenophon, Arrian, and Herodotus were the first authors read. "Homer and Demosthenes occupy a place corresponding to Vergil and Cicero in Latin." Aeschylus was Vittorino's favorite among the dramatists. St. Chrysostom, whose style placed him on a level with the great pagan orators, was translated as an exercise in Latin prose composition. Nowhere else in Italy, it is believed, was Greek so thoroughly and successfully taught.[18]

The aim of this study of letters was *eloquentia*—the ability to speak and to write Latin fluently. The art of composition, taught very early, tended to the formation of a good style in speaking and writing. The preliminary steps were to memorize certain formal phrases and to acquire from a study of selected passages a vocabulary and a sense of rhythm. Translations of Greek passages constituted the first exercises, and later original compositions on set forms were demanded. The advanced students could versify with facility.

Although intellectual training seems to have dominated, physical education was not neglected; nor was it provided merely for its good effect on the mind. Many of Vittorino's pupils were destined for a military life, and such a training was for them imperative. Apart from this fact, which really demanded consideration,

---

[18] Woodward, *Vittorino da Feltre and Other Humanist Educators,* p. 54.

Vittorino's ideal of culture—a harmonious development of all the faculties of mind and body—prescribed such a course. With the pupil's health he was always particularly concerned. The location of the school afforded excellent opportunities for exercise and games in the open air. Certain exercises were obligatory and were performed in all kinds of weather. Excellence in games was highly prized, but Vittorino's aim was to develop hardiness and power of endurance rather than mere athletic skill. All were directed in some form of exercise, chosen usually according to their needs, but, at times, according to their tastes. Vittorino taught here as elsewhere by example, and participated in the field games.

He was an exemplary Catholic layman, and as a teacher he strove to cultivate in his pupils all the virtues becoming the Christian gentleman. Every day had its regular religious exercises at which, like morning prayers and Mass, all assisted. He was a frequent communicant and desired his students to approach the Sacraments every month. He did not overlook the individual, but attained his success in overcoming faults and building up character by private direction and exhortation. His punishments were intended as remedies, and were not administered immediately upon the discovery of an offense.

Vittorino's great educational service was to adjust the new humanistic studies to a system of teaching, and to show how they could be taught without compromising the principles of Christianity. He insisted on pleasant surroundings, made study attractive, and by attention to individuals, more profitable. He developed a novel method of physical training, respecting the needs of the various pupils. He eminently succeeded with the education of Cecilia Gonzaga, who became one of the most cultured women of her time and ended her life as a nun. Vittorino has left us no written accounts of his work,

nor any educational treatises; and in this he has merited
the title of *Socrates*, a name by which he was often
called. What we know of him and his method, we owe
to his pupils.[19] Of his truly remarkable character
Symonds has written:

> Few lives of which there is any record in history are so
> praiseworthy as Vittorino's; few men have more nobly realized
> the idea of living for the highest objects of their age; few
> have succeeded in keeping themselves so wholly unspotted by
> the vices of the world around them.[20]

The Renaissance in Italy produced the pagan humanist
and the Catholic humanist. The aims of the paganizing
education of the Italian Renaissance were fame and
pleasure. The only immortality worthwhile was to live
in the memory of succeeding generations. A book
written by Lorenzo Valla about 1430 on pleasure represented the views of many leaders of the Renaissance.
In this work Valla held the position that enjoyment is
the sole aim of life and commended the ancients who
raised voluptuousness to a cult. The Christian educators of the period undertook to counteract the damage
done by the pagan humanists by insisting that the revival
of classical learning was not to obscure the antagonism
existing between the pagan and Christian conception of
life.

The Revival of Learning aimed at replacing the
medieval forms of the Latin language by the classical
literary form. Consequently, the humanists of the
Renaissance destroyed the living Latin language and
prepared the way for further growth of the vernaculars.
In the course of time the spirit of the Italian Revivalists

---

[19] For an account of the famous humanists and scholars, states-
men and prelates whom he prepared for their careers, *Cf.* A.
Rosmini, *Idea dell' ottimo precettore nella vita e disciplina di
Vittorino da Feltre* (Milan: Gio Silvestri, 1845).

[20] Symonds, *op. cit.*, p. 216.

was lost sight of and Latin grammar instead of Latin literature became the all important study in the schools with the result that Latin became a dead language. The ideal of the classical scholar as the only educated man placed the learner above the doer; overemphasized the power of literature over the mass of mankind; and failed to adjust school work to the development of the child.[21] The Revival of Learning in Italy had pretty well run its course before it had any noteworthy effect upon the education of the rest of Europe.

FOR FURTHER STUDY

Baudrillart, A., *The Catholic Church; the Renaissance and Protestantism*. Translated by Mrs. Philip Gibbs. London: K. Paul, French, Trübner and Co., 1908.

Burckhardt, J., *The Civilization of the Renaissance in Italy*. London: George G. Harrop and Co., 1929.

Castiglione, Count Baldesar, *The Book of the Courtier*. Translated by Leonard E. Opdycke. New York: Horace Liveright, 1929.

Cust, R. H., *The Life of Benvenuto Cellini*. A translation. London: The Navarre Society Limited, 1927. 2 vols.

Gebhart, E., *Les Origines de la Renaissance en Italie*. Paris: Hachette et Cie., 1879.

Gragg, F. A., *Latin Writings of the Italian Humanists*. New York: Charles Scribner's Sons, 1927.

Hutton, Edward, *Giovanni Boccaccio*. New York: John Lane Company, 1910.

Jerrold, M., *Italy in the Renaissance*. London: Methuen and Co., Ltd., 1927.

Lanciani, R., *The Golden Days of the Renaissance in Rome*. Boston: Houghton, Mifflin Co., 1906.

Monnier, P., *Le Quattrocento*. Paris: Perrin et Cie., 1901. 2 vols.

Moore, Ernest C., *The Story of Instruction*. New York: The Macmillan Company, 1938. Vol. II

---

[21] *Cf.* Robert H. Quick, *Educational Reformers* (New York: D. Appleton and Company, 1907), pp. 10-21.

Moore, Edward, *Studies in Dante*. Oxford: Clarendon Press, 1896-1917.

Muntz, E., *Les Precurseurs de la Renaissance*. Paris: J. Rouam, 1882.

————, *La Renaissance en Italie et en France a l'Epoque de Charles VIII*. Paris: Firmin-Didot *et al.*, 1885.

Muratori, L., *Rerum Italicarum scriptores*. Citta di Castello: Coi Tipi Della Casa Editrice S. Lapi, 1900-.

Quick, R. H., *Educational Reformers*. New York: D. Appleton and Co., 1907.

Robinson, J. H., and H. W. Rolfe, *Petrarch: the First Modern Scholar and Man of Letters*. New York: G. P. Putnam's Sons, 1909.

Rosmini, C., *Idea dell'ottimo precettore nella vita e disciplina di Vittorino da Feltre*. Milan: Gio Silvestri, 1845.

Sandys, John, E., *A History of Classical Scholarship*. Cambridge: The University Press, 1908. Vol. II.

————, *Harvard Lectures on the Revival of Learning*. Cambridge: The University Press, 1905.

Santayanna, S. G., *Two Renaissance Educators: Alberti and Piccolomini*. Boston: Meador Publishing Company, 1930.

Shahan, Thomas J., *The Middle Ages*. New York: Benziger Bros., 1904.

Scaife, W. B., *Florentine Life during the Renaissance*. Baltimore: The Johns Hopkins Press, 1893.

Symonds, J. A., *Renaissance in Italy; The Age of the Despots*. New York: Henry Holt and Company, 1881.

————, *The Revival of Learning*. New York: Charles Scribner's Sons, 1912.

Taylor, H. O., *Classical Heritage of the Middle Ages*. New York: The Macmillan Co., 1901.

Voigt, George, *Die Wiederbelebung des classichen Altertums oder das erste Jahrhundert des Humanismus*. Berlin: Georg Reimer, 1880. Vols. I and II.

Whitcomb, M. A., *A Literary Source-Book of the Renaissance*. Philadelphia: The University of Pennsylvania, 1903.

Woodward, W. H., *Vittorino da Feltre and Other Humanist Educators*. Cambridge: The University Press, 1905.

————, *Studies in Education during the Age of the Renaissance*. Cambridge: The University Press, 1906.

CHAPTER XIX

RENAISSANCE IN OTHER COUNTRIES

Italian schools and scholars were largely responsible for the formation of those who introduced the Renaissance movement in the countries outside of Italy. The first humanistic teachers of France and Spain came directly under Italian influences; those of Germany and England were students in Italian schools, especially the universities. The earliest patrons of the Renaissance in these countries were statesmen and churchmen who, having lived or traveled in Italy, became followers of humanism and its enthusiastic propagators.

Early humanistic influences in France can be discerned from the time of Petrarch's visit to Paris in 1361. His companion while there was Pierre Bersuire (†1362), a French priest who translated all the books of Livy for King John the Good (John II, 1316-22). Under Charles the Wise (Charles V, 1364-80) many of the classics were translated into French as, for instance, some works of Aristotle by Nicholas Oresme (†1382), chaplain to Charles V; *De senectute,* and *De amicitia* of Cicero, by Laurent de Premierfait (†1418). The first humanist of note, *Jean de Montreuil* (1354-1418), a papal secretary, for a time connected with the courts of the dukes of Burgundy and Orleans, and ultimately chancellor to Charles VI, was a student and admirer of Petrarch. He was also a friend of Leonardo Bruni and spent some time in Rome as an envoy of the king. His friend, Nicholas de Clemanges (1360-1440), taught the rhetoric of Cicero and Aristotle in the schools of Paris. The latter spent twelve years as papal secretary at Avignon, and later in life resumed his lectures at Paris. Many of the classics which then were imperfectly known in Italy, such as Cicero's *De oratore* and *Pro Archia*, were familiar to him.[1]

The influence of the University of Paris is exemplified in the textbooks prescribed for the academic course. "In the fourteenth century they included authors such as Vergil, Ovid, Juvenal, Terence, with Sallust and Livy, as well as Cicero, Seneca and Quintilian."[2] We have already noted the familiarity of Gerson (†1429), Chancellor of the University, with the ancient authors.

Although the Council of Vienne (1311) had decreed the appointment of two professors of Greek at Paris, the first to hold office was Gregorio Tifernas, a native of Città di Castello, Italy,[3] who had lived in Greece and taught the language at Naples. He lectured there for four years and was followed in 1476 by George Hermonymus of Sparta, the instructor of Erasmus and Budé. The Italian, Aleander, who came to Paris in 1508, lectured also on Greek and perhaps Hebrew. He was chosen Rector of the University in 1512, became librarian of the Vatican in 1517, and was later elevated to the rank of cardinal.

The art of printing furthered the movement in France and the North generally, and consequently the work of the copyist must not be considered the important factor it was in Italy. The first book printed in France (1470), curiously enough, was the *Letters* of Gasparino de Barzizza, one of the early Italian humanistic scholars.

The humanistic movement began in earnest in France in the sixteenth century. The most distinguished of the French humanists was *Guillaume Budé (Gulielmus Budaeus* 1467-1540), a fellow-student of Erasmus and Vives. Under his leadership an intensive interest in the study of Greek was developed among the humanists

---

[1] Sandys, *History of Classical Scholarship*, II, 167.
[2] *Ibid.*, p. 166.
[3] The ancient name of the city was Tifernum Tiberinum.

of Western Europe. Budé first studied law at Orleans but, like Leonardo Bruni d'Arezzo, turned later to letters. "He taught himself Greek, and read widely in Latin."[4] Apparently he learned little from Hermonymus. As secretary to Louis XII he went to Rome on diplomatic missions during the pontificates of Julius II and Leo X. His work on Roman coinage, *De asse et partibus ejus,* which was nine years in preparation, won for him a universal reputation for learning. The *Commentarii linguae graecae,* a vast collection of solid material, dictionary, criticism, and syntax in one, "established his fame as the first Greek scholar in Europe."[5] Besides philological studies he wrote *De studio litterarum recte et commode instituendo,* in which his views on classical learning are briefly set forth. Through his influence with Francis I was founded the Corporation of Royal Readers for the study of the classics and Hebrew, which afterward became the Collège de France.

Budé's chief educational treatise appeared in French bearing the title *De l'institution du Prince* (*On the Education of a Prince*). This was dedicated to the young king Francis I and, like the earlier treatises *de regimine principum,* embodies Budé's ideal of training the young ruler. He would have the prince become a student of philology, learned in Greek and Latin, widely read in history, both for his own complete education and appreciation of literature and for the patronage he should bestow upon scholars. Budé attacked the scholastics and the methods of the University of Paris, in which he desired letters to enjoy chairs as well established as those of philosophy and theology. He was engaged in bitter controversies and for many years was suspected of Calvinistic beliefs. This was disproved after his death.

---

[4] Woodward, *Studies in Education during the Age of the Renaissance,* p. 130.
[5] *Loc. cit.*

Mathurin Cordier (1479-1564), or Marturinus Cor-
derius, was a disciple of Calvin and after teaching some
years in Paris and Bordeaux joined his master in the
schools of Geneva. Cordier produced a work on Latin
inflections, *De corrupti sermonis emendatione libellus,*
and one on Latin conversation, *Colloquia,* both of which
were used in France and Switzerland. His activity indicates the attention given to the classics at the Collège
de Guyenne in Bordeaux. The course in this school extended over ten years of classical studies with two additional years of philosophy. Ordinarily the boy entered
the school at the age of six and completed the course
when he was eighteen. Latin, religion, reading and
writing in French were taught in the first six classes;
Greek, rhetoric, and mathematics were then added.
During the two-year course of philosophy, Greek and
mathematics were continued together with the study of
science. This college and the other schools with which
Cordier was identified were representative of those of
France in the sixteenth century.

In Spain

The first notable humanist in Spain, *Antonio of Lebrija*
(Antonius Nebrissensis, 1444-1522), spent twenty years
in Italy before teaching the humanities as professor at
Seville. He taught there several years and was afterward
connected with the Universities of Salamanca and Alcalá.
He published grammars of Latin, Greek, and Hebrew:
his *Introductiones Latinae* was the first Latin grammar
of note in Spain.[6] Lebrija was opposed by some of the
older teachers of his country, especially by Amiguet, the
instructor of Vives. He won over many Spanish scholars
to the cause of humanism, so that in the early sixteenth
century, especially in Salamanca, there were numerous
professors and distinguished patrons like Cardinal

---

[6] Sandys, *op. cit.,* II, 157.

Ximenes, founder of a college at Alcalá. Portugal also produced scholars and writers associated with the movement, among whom were Resende, historian and poet; the bishop Osorio, called the Cicero of Portugal; and Alvarez, the Jesuit, author of a Latin grammar long used in the schools of his order. Attention will be directed later on to a Spanish humanist whose influence was especially felt in England and Northern Europe.

In Northern Europe

The Brethren of the Common Life, an association of priests and laymen founded by Gerard Groote[7] (1340-84) at Deventer, Holland, should be noted as important factors in the spread of humanistic studies in the Netherlands and Germany. The members lived in community and chose teaching as one of their chief duties. The mysticism of Groote and the early Brethren showed itself in their educational systems, which before the Renaissance was not different on the academic side from that of the other medieval schools. The Brethren and their pupils, however, embraced the humanistic movement and were among the most influential agents in its propagation in the North. Their schools were elementary and secondary, and in the latter a classical training was given. Some famous pupils were Thomas à Kempis, Erasmus, Gabriel Biel, and Pope Adrian VI. Two of

---

[7] About 1380 he was ordained deacon and was licensed to preach throughout the diocese of Utrecht. His sermons in the vernacular attracted a large group of young men whom he directed in living sincerely Christian lives. A little band of these became his fellow workers. He encouraged them to study and to copy manuscripts for their support. Eventually they pooled their earnings from copying manuscripts and lived in common. Gradually a permanent organization was effected without vows, but pledged to practice poverty, chastity, and obedience according to each one's conditions of life. Groote contemplated organizing his clerics into a community of Canons Regular but he died in the pestilence and it was left to his successor, Florentius Radewyn, to realize this plan two years later.

their pupils were especially active in the Renaissance in Germany, *John Wessel* (1420-89) and *Rudolf Agricola.* The former, who was a native of Groningen, Holland, studied with the Brethren at Deventer. He learned Greek at Cologne from Greek monks who were then the guests of the Dominican convent in that city. He also pursued the humanities at Rome and Paris, and in the latter place, as teacher and student, he spent altogether about sixteen years. With Agricola and Reuchlin he shared the honor of introducing humanism in Germany and of expanding the curriculum of the schools of the Brethren. Wessel learned Hebrew as an aid to his spiritual studies.

Rudolf Agricola of Groningen (1443-85), who latinized his Dutch surname of Huysmann and thus showed how thoroughly he was imbued with the new spirit, studied in the Universities of Louvain, Paris, and Ferarra. He spent at least seven years in Italy, and upon his return to the North had a reputation for proficiency in Latin, Greek, French, and Italian. He accepted a lectureship at the University of Heidelberg, and sought like the best of humanists in Italy to maintain his Christian spirit and faith while pursuing the new studies. In elementary education he strongly advocated a careful moral formation and the study of the vernacular. Although a fervid humanist, he advocated composition in the vernacular before Latin writing and placed clearness above elegance in cultivating a good style. He wrote much on educational subjects—especially in his letters. His most famous pedagogical work was *De studio formando (On the Regulation of Study)*, which had a great influence on German education and especially on the schools of the Brethren of the Common Life.[8]

Alexander Hegius (1438-98), a native of Heeck, West-

---

[8] *Cf.* George, Ihm, *Der Humanist Rudolf Agricola, sein Leben und seine Schriften* (Paderborn: F. Schoningh, 1893).

phalia, was a pupil of Agricola, although ten years his senior. "When forty years of age," he said, "I came to young Agricola, from whom I have learned all I know or that others think I know." Through Hegius, who is thought to have been a member of the Brethren of the Common Life and in his advanced years a priest, Agricola's influence was carried into the schools. The work of Hegius was that of the practical schoolmaster who, in thorough sympathy with humanistic studies, influenced the movement by training some of the early humanistic educators, e.g., Rudolf von Langen, Murmellius, Dringenberg, and Erasmus. He conducted the school of Deventer for almost thirty years. At times he had as many as two thousand pupils in attendance; he improved the textbooks, and introduced new ones more suitable to the humanistic methods. The course followed at Deventer was imitated in many places and remained in use long after the death of Hegius.

Rudolf von Langen (1439-1519), as rector of the cathedral school of Münster, made that institution a center for humanistic studies which produced a number of famous teachers. *John Murmellius* (1480-1517) was vice-rector of this school at Münster under von Langen and contributed much to its fame as a teacher and writer. His *Enchiridion scholasticorum* was a serviceable manual for teachers and pupils. He wrote many textbooks, some of which were used until recent times. He was a successful rector in Altmaar and Deventer. His aim in education is summed up in his saying: "The ultimate purpose of study can be no other than the knowledge and worship of God."

Under Ludwig Dringenberg, rector of the school of Schlettstadt, were trained two famous priests and educators: Johann Geiler von Kaisersberg, the great preacher of Strassburg and a real force for moral education, and *Jacob Wimpheling* (1450-1528), the rector of Heidelberg. The latter merited the title *Preceptor Germaniae,* *(Preceptor of Germany).* He, too, upheld the Christian principle in learning and expounded it in his writings. *A Guide to German Youth* (1497), which discusses school methods, qualifications of teachers, and the religious aspect of education, is the "earliest systematic treatise on education by a German scholar."[9] *Youth,* written in 1500, treats especially of the moral basis of education. The *Compendium of German History* was written for use in the school where it proved very serviceable. His saying illustrates his view of religion and virtue in education: "What does it profit us if all our learning be without noble purpose, all our industry without piety, all our knowledge without love of our neighbor, all our intelligence without humility, all our study without the formation of character?" He is considered one of the chief influences in the German humanistic movement.

Johann Reuchlin (1455-1522), the granduncle of Melanchthon, was born at Pforzheim, in the Black Forest. His father was employed at the Dominican convent and there young Reuchlin received his earliest education. He studied the humanities at the University of Paris and, although he pursued a course in law and obtained his degree, he chose teaching as a profession. The esteem in which he was held as a scholar and humanist was well merited, for he contributed to the movement by collecting many Greek and Hebrew manuscripts and by publishing a Hebrew grammar and dictionary, the first brought out by a Western scholar; he also compiled a Latin lexicon and Greek textbooks, some of which were long in use in Germany. Reuchlin, who adopted Melanchthon, gave the latter his early humanistic training. In his declining years he was deeply grieved by Melanchthon's defection from the Church.

---

[9] Paul Monroe, *Textbook in the History of Education* (New York: The Macmillan Company, 1909), p. 378.

Desiderius Erasmus (1466-1536), of Rotterdam, Holland, the most famous of the humanists of northern Europe, was the son of Gerard of Gouda and Margaretha Rogers, whose union was not sanctioned by the Church.[10] Called Erasmus at birth, he later chose Desiderius, the Latin equivalent of Erasmus.[11] As noted above, he came while a student at Deventer under the influence of Hegius and also Agricola. An orphan at thirteen, he was placed by his guardians in the monastery school of the Brethren of the Common Life at Bois-le-Duc. In 1482 he entered the monastery of Emmaus at Stein near Gouda, a candidate for the Augustinian Order. While he was not really fitted for monastic life because he was neurasthenic and hypersensitive, he became a religious in 1488 and was ordained a priest in 1492, being then well content and pleased with the choice he had made. He then wrote *De contemptu mundi* (*On Contempt of the World*), and, as Woodward says, he left no contemporary record of the discontent of which he later complained.[12] He had leisure to cultivate his literary and scholarly tastes.

Erasmus was dispensed from the cloistral obligations by the bishop of Cambrai, who intended to make him his secretary on account of his exceptional linguistic talents, and was sent to Paris to continue the study of theology. Erasmus, however, devoted himself chiefly to the classics, and while pursuing these studies and

[10] This social disability may have influenced him in becoming a monk. Because he was illegitimate, the bishop of Utrecht who ordained him a priest must have gotten for him a dispensation from the law of the Church which barred illegitimate sons from the priesthood and from holding ecclesiastical offices and benefices. He was further dispensed by Pope Julius II and received a complete dispensation from Leo X in 1517.

[11] Erasmus is the Greek translation of the Dutch, Geert, the English of which is Gerard, meaning well beloved.

[12] W. H. Woodward, *Desiderius Erasmus Concerning the Aim and Method of Education* (Cambridge: The University Press, 1904), p. 6.

associating with humanists developed an antipathy for scholastic theology and methods then in the highest favor at the University. He taught Latin privately and had among his students some young Englishmen who rendered him no little assistance then and later in life. He accompanied one of these, Lord Mountjoy, to England in 1499, and on the visit made the acquaintance of More, Colet, and Warham, who were to be his patrons and lifelong friends. It is believed that following the advice of Colet he devoted himself more assiduously to the study of the Scriptures and historical theology. Returning to Paris, he continued his studies and produced the *Adagia,* selections from the classics. In 1502 he appeared at Louvain. A lectureship was offered him in rhetoric which he declined in order to be free for study and writing. He visited London again in 1505, leaving in 1506 for a journey to Italy, chiefly to obtain instruction in Greek. He received the doctorate in theology at Turin and made a stay of almost a year at Bologna. Aldus Manutius, one of the most celebrated printers of Europe, induced him to settle in Venice and bring out another edition of the *Adagia.* There Erasmus entered the society of the best native Greek scholars then in Italy, and he profited by his intimate relations with Aldus. His famous journey to Rome took place in 1509 and there he was accorded a reception by the cardinals which highly pleased him.

The five years spent in England (1509-1514) mark the most productive part of his literary career from the educational viewpoint. On this visit Erasmus was made a professor of Cambridge; he also taught Greek privately. Then appeared the *Moriae encomium (Praise of Folly),* a bitter satire on the times, and one of the most widely read books of the day; the *De ratione studii (On the Method of Study),* written for Colet, who was organizing St. Paul's school; and *De copia rerum et verborum,* on Latin composition. He revised the elementary Latin textbook of the head-master, Lily, a work which went through many editions in Erasmus' lifetime and still survives in a modified form in the present Eton Latin Grammar.[13] He also rendered into Latin the Greek Grammar of Theodore Gaza.

In 1516 Erasmus accepted the patronage of Archduke Charles, later Emperor Charles V, becoming one of his councilors at a fixed salary. From that time onward he was much in demand and received flattering invitations from princes and patrons to take up his residence in Paris, Vienna, and again in England. Erasmus, however, desired to be free for literary work and travel. He made his home in Basle, where he could write at leisure and attend to the publication of his books. Froben, one of the celebrated early printers and publishers, gave his works wide circulation. With the exception of a short sojourn in Freiburg, Germany, whither he fled to avoid the violence of the reformers and to be in Catholic surroundings, Erasmus passed the rest of his life at Basle. Here was published the *Colloquiorum formulae (Colloquies)*, a book intended to supply formulae for elegant conversational style, which the University of Paris condemned because of its unfitness for general reading. It was, nevertheless, widely read. At Basle were also published the treatise on *Christian Matrimony (Institutio Christiani matrimonii)*, which contains a chapter on the training of children; and his best known educational treatise, *De pueris statim ac liberaliter instituendis (On the Liberal Education of Children from Their Earliest Years)*, 1529.

Erasmus was about to take a journey to the Netherlands when stricken with his last illness. He died in

---

[13] *Ibid.,* p. 21.

communion with the Church and was buried with honors from the Cathedral of Basle.[14]

Owing largely to the trials of his youth and a physical malady from which he suffered most of his life, Erasmus was of an unhappy disposition. By his peculiarities he annoyed and severely tried his best friends. Unstable and changeable, he was more than once accused of duplicity. His tastes, however, were literary and his habits peaceful, and this may to some extent account for the charges of weakness and cowardice so often made against him. With all his shortcomings, and they were many, he won and kept friends of the type of Saint Thomas More and Pope Paul III,[15] who evidently saw in him more than the brilliant humanist and scholar and could overlook his foibles. His relation to the reformers throws light on his character.

By his bitter criticism of the Church and things ecclesiastical Erasmus prepared the way for the Reformation.[16] In his commentaries on the New Testament, he advocated the exercise of private judgment and expressed views contrary to the teaching of the Church. He sympathized with Luther at the beginning of the revolt and always opposed the Bull of Excommunication. When the Reformation was well advanced, he advocated a compromise with Luther, or a settlement of the troubles by a court of arbitration. When appealed to for support by the reformers he, however, claimed to maintain a neutral attitude. They charged him with duplicity, but Erasmus asserted that the reform he advocated was

---

[14] The cathedral by this time because of Protestant action had been stripped of most of its Catholic furnishings. *Cf.* J. J. Mangan, *Life, Character, and Influence of Erasmus of Rotterdam* (New York: The Macmillan Company, 1927), II, 406 f.

[15] Paul III offered him the cardinalate which he refused.

[16] His *Praise of Folly, Adagia*, and *Colloquies* attacked medieval learning, the religious orders, Catholic doctrine and practices, and weakened the respect of many minds for the authority of the Church.

to be preached to the learned, not to the ignorant; that it was to respect the hierarchy and especially the Pope; and to take place within the Church and not outside of it.

However opinions may vary regarding the character of Erasmus, his position as a humanist remains unchallenged. He was undoubtedly the leading man of letters of his time, and can well be taken as representing the Renaissance literary spirit in its good and bad aspects.[17] There is no doubt of the serious educational bearing of many of his writings, although it is also true they received more attention than others of the period which were of higher educational value, because of the author's antiecclesiastical attitude. He contributed to the furtherance of humanism by editing many of the ancient classics and writings of the Fathers and through his *Colloquies* and *Praise of Folly* which were read in the schools.[18]

---

[17] Joseph Sauer, "Erasmus," *The Catholic Encyclopedia* (New York: The Encyclopedia Press, Inc., 1913). V, 514.

[18] Woodward's *Desiderius Erasmus concerning the Aim and Method of Education* contains English translations of *De ratione studii* and *De pueris statim ac liberaliter instituendis*. Other educational treatises of Erasmus are *Dialogus Ciceronianus* in which he ridiculed the narrow tendencies of humanism which as early as the first half of the sixteenth century confined all work in the school to the study of the writings of Cicero and advocated all conversation and all writing in Ciceronian phrase. The new learning in less than two hundred years resulted in a change from Aristotelianism to Ciceronianism. In his *De civilitate morum puerilium (On Courtesy of Manners in Boys)* Erasmus wished the youthful mind to learn thoroughly the liberal arts and to be accustomed from its earliest years to the rudiments of good manners. His educational ideal in this treatise resembles that of Vittorino da Feltre. His *Institutum hominis Christiani* repeated many of the views expressed in his *Enchiridion militis Christiani*. His *Institutio principis Christiani* emphasized devotion of the ruler to the interest of his people and the promotion of peace. *Cf.* D. Reichling, *Ausgewählte pädagogische Schriften des Desiderius Erasmus* (Freiburg: Herder, 1896); Richard Becker, *Die Ansichten des Erasmus über die Erziehung und den ersten Unterricht der Kinder* (Leipzig: Druck von C. Grumback, 1890).

Erasmus was a thorough humanist in the sense that he believed the classics to be the basis of a liberal education, an aid rather than a hindrance to Christian training. He found much in antiquity besides letters, which he aimed to restore to the world of his own day. His ideal involved "a universal language—Latin, a universal church, a uniform standard of culture, and perpetual peace."[19] He disliked the vernaculars, refusing to learn Italian or English when in the countries where they were spoken, for he believed that in the restored classics were to be found the important elements then needed in Christian society for the reign of culture. They were to become effective through the education of the young.

His *De pueris* is chiefly devoted to the early training of the child. In this treatise he discusses the first steps in the physical, mental, and moral development of children. He dwells upon the importance of home influence and the unceasing care of parents concerning the systematic instruction of their children which he would have begin in the seventh year, under competent and carefully selected teachers, in the home or in the town school. The teacher's office is to discern the pupil's capacity, his special aptitudes, and to apply a method accordingly. In his *De ratione studii* he asserts that thought and expression form the twofold material of instruction.

All knowledge falls into one of two divisions: The knowledge of "truth" and the knowledge of "words": and if the former is first in importance the latter is acquired first in order of time. They are not to be commended who, in their anxiety to increase their store of truth, neglect the necessary art of expressing them.[20]

---

[19] W. H. Woodward, *Studies in Education during the Age of the Renaissance* (Cambridge: The University Press, 1906), p. 113.
[20] *De ratione studii. Cf.* Woodward, *Desiderius Erasmus concerning the Aim and Method of Education,* p. 162.

Instruction begins with object teaching; the child's vocabulary is derived from the familiar things about him; conversation is the first means of expression, and a fuller knowledge of words comes from learning ancient stories, historical and mythical, from descriptions of animal and plant life, all of which should be illustrated by pictures.

The letters of the alphabet were to be taught by pictures, by letter-shaped biscuits, and by ivory tablets; the first reading lessons were to be interesting in themselves and attractive to the child; writing was also to be taught pleasantly, "per lusum," by way of play. Erasmus outlined in *De ratione studii* the reading for his school. His *Colloquies* was in frequent use as a reader. He gave a definite place to all prose writers and poets in his curriculum. Like most of the humanists, he urged a special study of the *Letters* of Cicero. Grammar was taught in accordance with the advance of the students in the reading of authors, and in the art of expression. It was a means of progress in either direction, and was not studied merely for its own value. Erasmus recommended the *Rudimenta* of Nicholas Perotti, the pupil of Vittorino da Feltre. The ancient authors were the models of composition in all the accepted forms; in fact, education is Latin scholarship. History, arithmetic, music, astronomy, and dialectic are regarded as necessary subjects, but are subordinate to letters.

For all children he desired a sound moral and religious formation. This was to be aimed at from the beginning and assiduously pursued by parents and teachers. The manner of training he advocated for this end was that commonly used by the earlier humanists.

Erasmus included the education of girls in his plan, but not as elaborately nor as systematically as another Renaissance educator, Juan Luis Vives, whom we shall later consider. It is felt that Erasmus based his theory on the earlier treatise of Vives and on conditions prevalent in Italy, which were superior in this respect to those of northern Europe. His argument was that woman should be prepared for her place in society as daughter, wife, and mother, and that refinement and culture were indispensable in the mother who is charged with the duty of rearing children.

It must be remarked in connection with the influence of Erasmus that his position in the literary world lent peculiar force to his views. Being a great publicist and the most widely read author of his day, his views, whether original with him or not, were extensively circulated and read.[21] In the troubled time which followed his death, his bitter criticism of the monks and monastic schools attracted more attention to his writings from those outside the Church than they perhaps would otherwise have received.

The distinguished Catholic scholar of the Renaissance and the foremost educator of the Reformation period was *Juan Luis Vives*, a contemporary of Erasmus. He was born at Valentia, Spain, of a noble but impoverished family in that eventful year in world history, 1492. His early education was received under Jerome Amiguet, notable for his opposition to the humanist, Antonio de Lebrija, and to the humanistic movement generally—a man who, in our view, should be considered as behind his time rather than in advance of it. Vives then shared

---

[21] Mangan estimates that there were around five thousand editions of all the writings of Erasmus, and a total publication of some two million copies. *Cf.* Mangan, *op. cit.,* II, 395. The Council of Trent placed on the *Index librorum prohibitorum* several of Erasmus' works including the *Colloquies* and *Praise of Folly.* Pope Leo XIII, in 1897, removed the ban on all his writings. A complete edition of the works of Erasmus to which a sketch of his life was added was issued by Beatus Rhenanus in nine volumes at Basle, 1540-41. An edition of all his works was also published by Jean LeClerc in ten volumes at Leyden, 1703-06. P. S. Allen, the foremost authority on Erasmus, has edited in seven volumes the *Opus epistolarum Des Erasmi Roterdami* at Oxford, 1906-28.

the views of his master and, at the age of fifteen, wrote a book against Lebrija. This work is unfortunately lost. It would be a precious relic of the early and perhaps enthusiastic views which he later abandoned. Vives also studied law in Valentia. At the age of eighteen, he entered the University of Paris, where he won distinction as a student of letters and philosophy, especially dialectics. During his stay in Paris, he began to look more favorably upon the new studies and to be attracted to the cause of the humanists. Later, at the University of Louvain, when he came into contact with Erasmus and other distinguished humanists, he embraced the movement and became a noble example of the Catholic scholar of the Renaissance. At the completion of his studies, Vives went to Bruges, where there was a large Spanish population, and made his permanent residence there. His activities as a writer and teacher took him again to Paris, to Louvain, and to England; but Bruges he considered his home.

Vives embraced the work of teaching as a profession. In Louvain he had obtained, perhaps at the recommendation of Erasmus, a distinguished pupil in William of Croy, the youthful bishop of Cambrai, and later Cardinal Archbishop of Toledo. His associates at that famous seat of learning included the most notable scholars of the time, among them, Erasmus, Martin van Dorp, and Adrian Dedel, who afterwards ascended the papal throne as Adrian VI. Vives could then be classified with the humanists. Erasmus had received him enthusiastically at Louvain and had proclaimed him a great philosopher and a savant of incomparable powers as a speaker and a writer. He knew no one with whom he could compare Vives for his powers of expression.

Vives, then only twenty-six years of age, was really a prolific writer. Spiritual works like his *Meditations on the Seven Penitential Psalms,*[22] and on the *Passion of Christ,*[23] written most probably for his pupil, had been followed by treatises on the *De senectute* of Cicero,[24] and on the *Bucolics* and *Georgics* of Vergil.[25] In 1518, besides a philosophical treatise on man, *Fabula de homine,*[26] appeared his treatise on the beginnings of philosophy—*De initiis, sectis, et laudibus philosophiae,*[27] the earliest history of philosophy ever written in Latin. But the most startling of his writings, which attracted universal attention, was the *Liber in pseudo-dialecticos,*[28] in which he attacked the dialecticians, or the scholastics, and took definite issue with them on the study of philosophy and letters. He visited Paris shortly after publishing the work and, it is believed, then made the acquaintance of Budé, whose name appears so frequently in his writings in connection with the study of Greek.

Upon his return to Louvain, Vives accepted, in addition to his tutorial work, a professorship in the University. His subjects were law, philosophy, and letters, and we have evidence from the writings of Erasmus and other scholars of the period that he attracted great numbers of the learned to his courses. In this twofold capacity of tutor and professor he continued until after the death of Cardinal Croy in 1521, when, broken in health as a result of his constant application to study and teaching, he was forced to retire to Bruges. The

---

[22] *In septem psalmos penitentiales meditationes.* Opera, Basel edition, 1555, II, 147-192. The references here are made to this edition. The best edition of his works is that of Gregorio Majans y Siscar, published at Valentia, 1782-90.

[23] *De Passione Christi meditatio, ibid.,* pp. 193-198.

[24] *Anima senis, sive praelectio in librum de senectute Ciceronis, ibid.,* pp. 15-20.

[25] *Interpretatio allegorica in Bucolica Virgilii; Praelectio in Georgica Virgilii.* I, 640-679; 680-685.

[26] *Ibid.,* II, 269-272.

[27] *Ibid.,* pp. 4-14.

[28] *Ibid.,* I, pp. 272-286.

sting of poverty added to his sufferings, and when convalescing he was in need of a patron to enable him to continue his literary work. He hoped to interest King Henry VIII of England and thereby obtain a pension from him. Through the services of Thomas More, who greatly admired his writings, and Cardinal Wolsey he eventually succeeded in interesting the English court if not the king personally.

In 1523 Vives wrote *De institutione feminae Christianae*[29] *(On the Instruction of a Christian Woman)*, which, dedicated to Queen Catherine of England, brought him directly into favor at the court. This educational treatise was one of the most popular books of the century. Before the year 1584, it had appeared in three French, two Spanish, and two German translations. It was translated into English by Richard Hyrde about 1540, and is therefore one of our earliest educational documents on the education of girls. Vives was in that same year invited to England, where he acted in the double capacity or office of professor and tutor—professor at Oxford, and tutor at the court to the Princess Mary.

The career of Vives in England was brilliant indeed. He was esteemed as the most learned humanist of the time, whose lectures it was fashionable to attend. It is recorded that the king and queen were more than once present at them. Oxford honored him with the degree of Doctor of Law. At the court he was much in demand because of his scholarship and literary standing. Perhaps the affection of Catherine, and her pride in having a distinguished countryman near her, may have accounted for much of this popularity. At any rate, Vives became her counselor and thus acquired a knowledge of her

---

[29] In this treatise Vives asserts that no limits should be set to the learning of women any more than to that of men. A woman should be concerned with such knowledge as she will later use in improving the moral conditions of herself and others.

domestic trials not shared by others. In the light of the subsequent sorrows which came to the noble Queen, can we not say that there was more than educational significance attached to his little treatise, *De officio mariti* [30] *(On the Duty and Office of a Husband)*, which was written at this time, when the most conspicuous husband of the realm was sorely in need of Christian direction? This little work was translated into English in 1550 by Thomas Paynel.

On account of his interest in the matter of the divorce between Henry and Catherine, Vives incurred the displeasure of the king, was banished from the court, and escaped with a comparatively light punishment for that time—imprisonment for six weeks. When liberated, he hastened to Bruges, and although Catherine later solicited his assistance at the trial, Vives refused to return to England. He did not believe that a defence of Catherine's cause would avail anything. It is worthy of note that a remarkable book by Vives, *De subventione pauperum* [31] *(On Relief of the Poor)*, was dedicated to the municipality of Bruges In that work we have Vives' idea on the organization of public charities, an exposition on which was based, so it is believed, the English system of caring for the poor. [32] While in England he had written two short educational treatises under the title *De ratione studii puerilis*, [33] one dedicated to Catherine of Aragon, and intended for Princess Mary,

---

[30] *Opera*, II, 595-647.

[31] *Ibid.*, pp. 890-922.

[32] Dr. Lange, Barnard's *American Journal of Education*, XXVII, 342.

[33] *Opera*, I, 1-12. These treatises outline a complete system of studies for the boy and girl. While he recognized that the education of girls must obviously be different from that of the boys, he maintained that it was of equal importance. He suggested the use of notebooks as an aid in the learning process so that study might be an active affair and not mere passive absorbing of what was read.

and the other addressed to Charles Mountjoy, a pupil of Vives and son of one of his benefactors. They treat the question of study for the boy and girl respectively. To this time also belong his legal treatise, *De consultatione*,[34] and the translations of two orations of Isocrates. The collection of pious admonitions and adages which he called the *Bodyguard of the Soul (Satellitium animae)*,[35] and also the *Introductio ad sapientiam*,[36] which was translated into English by Sir R. Moryson in 1540 under the title, *Introduction to Wysdome from Vives*, were written during a vacation spent in Bruges.

Upon his final return to Bruges after the troubles of court life, Vives' industry as a writer did not diminish. He was again unfortunately in want; and, had not friends in England and on the Continent come to his aid, would have lacked the barest necessities of life. Among the numerous productions of this period which cover the field of theological, philosophical, and legal studies, and some of which, especially the theological, were remarkable in a layman, is to be found his great educational work, *De disciplinis*.[37] On this one work alone the claims of Vives as an educator might be safely based. It is a masterful exposition of the educational conditions of the time and an embodiment of the views of a real reformer of the Reformation period. In conjunction with the treatises *On the Method of Study, On the Instruction of a Christian Woman, On the Office and Duty of a Husband*, the *Introduction to Wisdom*, and other treatises on special phases of educational work, or on special subjects like the study of language, philos-

---

[34] *Ibid.*, pp. 154-178.
[35] *Ibid.*, II, 96-110.
[36] *Ibid.*, pp. 70-94.
[37] Ibid., I, 324-639. Foster Watson's *Vives on Education* (Cambridge: The University Press, 1913), contains a translation of the five books of *De disciplinis tradendis* (On the Transmission of Learning).

ophy, etc., this work, *De disciplinis,* affords us a real thesaurus of pedagogical wisdom. It is divided into two principal parts: the first gives the many causes for the decline of the sciences: grammar, dialectics, rhetoric, etc.; while the second contains an exposition of the reforms necessary in the schools and the means for their accomplishment. The latter, which is constructive throughout, offers Vives' practical reflections on such important topics as the location of the school, the qualifications of teachers, the curriculum, methods to be employed, discipline, etc. We might select some of the important educational principles and ideas for which Vives stood, many of which were adopted by later educators and are often considered original with them.

Although Vives proposes to treat of education in the following order: "quae, quomodo, quatenus, a quibus, quo loco tradenda singula," he begins with the latter, the location of the school. It should be built, he says, on the outskirts of the city, but not on the boundaries of the kingdom where wars are frequent; in an airy place, not amid noisy surroundings, not on a public highway, nor again near the court. Its site should be attractive to the pupils themselves.

More important than the selection of a site for the school is the choice of the teachers. Learning alone should not suffice to determine fitness, but teaching skill, probity of life, and devotion to the calling should also be demanded. The teacher is not a seller of wares, *"nunquam bene traditur disciplina quae venditur."* He should not be avaricious, nor inordinately ambitious, thirsting for honors at the expense of his pupils. He should be paid a fixed salary, and should not be striving to attract the wealthier students so as to increase his emoluments. In all things he should be an example and model for the imitation of his pupils. Vives favored teaching under inspection before the candidate for the office was awarded his degree or license to teach, and he expected that the teacher should also possess the faculty of getting along well with others.

The material management of the school was to be confided to the students themselves, who would select the stewards from the student body and provide the supplies and the service. He believed that the food should be simple, nourishing, and of a kind easily procured.

Of the disputations so closely associated with the scholastic method he disapproved. The real purpose of the disputation, seeking truth, was, of course, good; but in his time this was not always the end in view. Too many strove for skill or mastery over others and not for the truth. *"Ingenium contra veritatem sumit arma."* Anything subversive of truth was unworthy of the Christian, and as far as his experience permitted him to judge, most of the disputants closed the disputation more stubborn in their beliefs, more callous in their contentions without becoming more learned or better morally.

The vernacular which is learned at home should be the language first used in the classroom. The teacher must be ready to correct mistakes, and see that the native tongue is spoken and written correctly. Like all of the humanists, he believed that Latin was the language of the cultured; but, while he was devoted to the ancient classics, he also desired that modern authors be read, as e.g., Erasmus, Sadoleto, Bembo, and Pico della Mirandola. He favored, as we know from his *De institutione feminae Christianae,* the reading of the modern authors in the vernacular, in Spanish, Italian, etc. Like the best of the humanists, he did not approve of the promiscuous reading either of the ancient or of the modern authors; only those with a wholesome moral tone were to be recommended. So, for example, he deprecated the reading of Ovid and Boccaccio.

The various other subjects of the curriculum, like

geography, mathematics, history, were treated by Vives with a spirit that is surprisingly modern. He shows the order in which they should be taught and recommends, for instance, a study of geography, not only for an understanding of the ancient authors as did many of the humanists, but especially for its value to the man of affairs from a commercial and practical viewpoint. History would broaden one's culture, and the moral effect of great biographies like those of Charlemagne and the Saints he did not fail to notice and commend.

If he demanded much of the teacher, his exactions from the parents for the careful moral training of the young were also many and minute. The home education was most significant for the whole life course. We have seen that he has included in his scheme the education of girls.[38] In their regard he insisted on training in the household arts, in cooking, spinning, and in the care of the sick. As an inspiration for their study of letters he calls to mind the noble example of cultured women of ancient times and of his own day and mentions the notable instances of Queen Catherine and the daughters of Thomas More among the ladies of England. The Christian woman was to be trained above all in the practice of virtue. In his plan of study written for the young princess, he says, "The way to live is not less to be cultivated than the way to learn"; and, if he recommended general culture for the young woman, he especially desired that she possess that refinement which the reading of the New Testament, the Fathers, the Christian poets, and good books like the *Utopia* of Thomas More would bring.

---

[38] *Cf.* Foster Watson, *Vives and the Renaissance Education of Women* (New York: Longmans, Green, and Co., 1912). Partial translations are found in this work of *De institutione feminae Christianae; De ratione studii; Satellitium;* and Chapter III of the *De officio mariti.*

Vives advocated the use of the inductive method and in this anticipated Bacon by over fifty years. He therefore urged the cultivation of the power of observation and investigation. He respected the individual capacity of the pupils and insisted on self-activity. No students were to be forced to learn. Those who could not be induced to learn in his school he sent home lest they should waste their time. The doctrine of imitation is constantly referred to by him and used in his methods. He demanded meetings of teachers to plan the work of the students. He encouraged physical exercises and the care of health. Above all, he labored for the development of a sound Christian character by means of religious and moral training.[39]

The Catholic spirit pervades everything Vives produced. His profound knowledge of theology and the Sacred Scriptures, his love for the Church and veneration for ecclesiastical authority, his devotion to the cause of Catholic unity when it was so terribly assailed, his piety, are not less remarkable than his untiring and noble zeal in behalf of Christian education. In England he incurred the displeasure of Henry VIII and therefore was unacceptable as an educator to Protestant England. Because he was out of sympathy with the so-called Reformers, his name was not perpetuated by them. Numerous illustrations can be cited wherein educational writers and others borrowed ideas and whole passages from him.[40] Although his educational treatises are real bequests to modern pedagogy, his name remained unknown until his memory was revived in Spain, Germany, and England in the twentieth century. As has been truly said, "He founded no school, but the influence

---

[39] Cf. Walter A. Daly, *The Educational Psychology of J. L. Vives* (Washington, D. C.: The Catholic University of America, 1924).
[40] Cf. Foster Watson, *Vives on Education*, pp. 30 et sqq.

of his powerful mind had been clearly felt, although not always acknowledged by those who have profited by his writings."[41]

In England

Influences which contributed to the introduction of the Renaissance in England go back as far as *Chaucer*[42] (1328-1400), who visited Italy three times and was familiar with the works of Petrarch and Boccaccio. Chrysoloras and Poggio both were in England early in the fifteenth century; and many of the Englishmen attended the council of Basle, thereby coming into immediate contact with the Italian leaders of the Revival. In England, the first to render real service to the movement was Humphrey, Duke of Gloucester (1391-1447), who, in order to learn Latin thoroughly, employed Antonio Beccario of Verona, the disciple of Vittorino da Feltre, and who also encouraged the humanists D'Arezzo and Decembrio in their literary works. Another nobleman, John Tiptoft, Earl of Worcester (1427-70), who traveled extensively and studied at Padua and Rome, contributed to the movement. He was noted for his elegant style of speaking and writing, and translated the *De amicitia* of Cicero. Other Englishmen of note, students of Guarino da Varona at Ferrara or teachers in Italy who visited the celebrated humanist and ardently espoused the cause, were Andrew Holes, Reynold Chicheley, William Grey, John Free, John Flemming, and John Gunthorpe.[43]

The Benedictine, *William Selling*, after having longed

---

[41] Dr. Lange, *op. cit.*, p. 351.

[42] His *Troilus and Cressid*, and *Canterbury Tales* show the influence of Boccaccio's *Il Filostrato* and *Decameron*.

[43] Many of these leaders of the Renaissance in England were bishops and priests. *Cf.* C. Rosmini, *Vita a disciplina di Guarino Veronese e de' suoi discepoli* (Brescia: Bettoni, 1805-06); J. E. Sandys, *History of Classical Scholarship*, II, 222 ff.

for the privilege for many years, went to Italy with another monk, William Hadley, and studied for three years in Padua, Bologna, and Rome. He brought many manuscripts with him on his return. As Prior of Canterbury, he attracted attention for his scholarship and Latin oratory. A pupil of Selling, *Thomas Linacre* (1460-1524), also resorted to Italy. In the ten years passed there, Linacre studied medicine and the classics. He was privileged to be present at the instructions of Politian in the household of the Medici at Florence, and thus formed a lasting friendship with the future Pope Leo X. He held the office of royal physician to Henry VIII and enjoyed a lucrative practice among the nobility. In 1520, he resigned this office to become a priest. His endowments of chairs in Greek and medicine at Oxford and Cambridge, and his foundation of the Royal College of Physicians entitled him to rank among the notable patrons of learning. His translations from the Greek, especially of treatises of Galen, and his works on Latin grammar were of service in the schools. With Linacre are also to be grouped his friends and associates in the movement, viz., William Grocyn and William Latimer, teachers of Greek at Oxford, both of whom studied in Italy.

John Colet (1467-1519), Dean of St. Paul's, studied in France and Italy and returned to England a thorough humanist. He founded St. Paul's School, London, securing for it a large endowment. This school remained on its original site until 1884, when it was transferred to Hammersmith. By this foundation, by his preparation of the statutes [44] which have often been reprinted, and by his organization of the curriculum and teaching staff,

---

[44] The statutes indicate that the boys were admitted free at about seven or eight years of age. The course of study embraced eight classes or "forms." The only academic requirement for admission was the ability to read and write.

Colet merited a place among the promoters of humanism in England. William Lily was appointed headmaster under him and published a Latin grammar which was widely used in the sixteenth and seventeenth centuries.

St. Thomas More[45] (1478-1535), chancellor of England under Henry VIII and friend of many of the foregoing scholars and humanists like Vives and Erasmus, was largely responsible for the spread of humanism in England. He upheld the best elements of the literary Renaissance. His household has been described as a school, for there were entertained distinguished scholars; there learned discussions took place; and there his children were educated.[46] Of it Erasmus wrote:

You would say that in that place was Plato's academy. But I do the house injury in likening it to Plato's Academy. . . . I should rather call it a school, or university, of Christian religion. For there is none therein who does not study the branches of a liberal education. Their special care is piety and virtue.[47]

More's letters to his children and their instructors best express his educational views. "What doth the fame of being a great scholar bring us, if it be severed from virtue, other than a notorious and famous infamy?" he wrote to one of the teachers. He strongly favored the education of women, and his own daughters were among the most cultured of their time. In this respect his biographer writes:

And thus you may conjecture how learned his daughters were, to whom, for this respect, Erasmus dedicated his Com-

---

[45] Canonized by Pius XI in 1936.

[46] Cf. Foster Watson, *Vives and the Renaissance Education of Women* (New York: Longmans, Green, and Company. 1912). Contains a chapter on "The School of Sir Thomas More" taken from the *Life of Sir Thomas More* by Cresacre More ([Louvain]: [*n. n.*], 1631).

[47] Undated letter to John Faber. Quoted in Watson, *op. cit.*, p. 175.

mentary upon Ovid *de Nuce*. Lewis Vives also writeth great commendations of this school of Sir Thomas More's in his book to Queen Catherine of England.[48]

The earliest humanistic treatise in England was the *Governour* of *Sir Thomas Elyot* (1490-1546), a lawyer and clerk of the Council under Henry VIII, who acted as agent of the king at the court of Charles V in the divorce proceedings. The treatise reproduces the ideas of the Italian humanists more fully than any other English production of the period.[49] It expresses similar views on the care of the child from earliest infancy, particularly in regard to virtue, the selection of nurse, tutor, and master. Before being placed under the master, the child must be taught to speak Latin by the tutor, being able to tell the names of the familiar things about him, the parts of the body, garments, etc. He is to have regular recreation, physical exercise, and games. Music is to be taught early and Greek as a subject comes before Latin, the latter having been begun by conversation. If it has not been learned then, both are studied together. Like Erasmus, he approved of only a little grammar in the beginning. After the first steps were learned, easy authors were read; in Greek, Aesop's Fables. The matter was chosen to suit the moral needs of the child. Elyot maintained that after translation the lesson should be learned by heart, giving thereby undue value to memory. His idea of the teacher is interesting, for he would have him be (1) a Latinist, widely read in all branches of Latin literature; (2) a musician, to teach the subject, music, and to appreciate the beauties of

---

[48] Quoted in Watson, *op. cit.*, pp. 186 f., from Cresacre More's *Life of Sir Thomas More*.

[49] The ideas in this treatise were gotten by Elyot from his association with More, Erasmus, Linacre, Warham, Fisher, Grocyn and other humanists in the house of More at Chelsea. Elyot, out of fear of Henry VIII, repudiated his religion as well as his friendship for his fellow Catholics.

poetry; (3) an astrologist, to understand the allusions to the heavenly bodies found in poetry and prose; (4) a philosopher, to teach moral philosophy and train to good conduct. The treatise had a real influence on English educators, especially Ascham, whom we shall consider later on.[50]

Elyot also compiled a Latin-English dictionary, the first of its kind published. A little known but significant work was his *Defense of Good Women*, written probably in 1536, one of the numerous treatises of the period in praise of learning, culture, and virtue in women. It is probably the first imitation in English of the Platonic dialogue, and is further interesting since it deals with "one example among us, as well of fortitude, as of all other virtues"—an allusion to the discarded Queen, Catherine of Aragon, for whom, it seems, the book was intended. It bears no dedication, however, since such a testimonial of regard would probably have met with royal disapproval. Elyot is properly grouped with Vives, Hyrde, and Sir Thomas More among the advocates of higher education for women and supporters of Catherine's cause.[51]

In *Roger Ascham* (1515-68), humanism saw a more practical application to the schools. Much of his life was devoted to teaching. At Cambridge he taught Greek, both in his student days and later as lecturer, and he contributed largely to the firm establishment of Greek in that university. He was the tutor of Princess Elizabeth. As secretary of the English embassy to Ger-

---

[50] S. S. Laurie, *Educational Opinion from the Renaissance* (Cambridge: The University Press, 1903), p. 38. *Cf.* Woodward, *Education during the Age of the Renaissance*, pp. 268 ff.

[51] *Cf.* Watson, *Vives and the Renaissance Education of Women.* Contains the first reprint of Hyrde's treatise on the education of women which was written as an introduction to the translation of Erasmus' treatise on the Lord's Prayer, by Margaret Roper, daughter of Sir Thomas More.

many, he learned of the theories of Sturm, although he did not meet the latter while there. On his return, he held the office of Latin Secretary to the court under Edward VI, Philip, Mary, and Elizabeth. His prominence in public life, as with so many of the humanists, gave weight and influence to his views, which undoubtedly favored the advance of classical studies. His educational work, the *Scholemaster*, did not appear until after his death (1570). It is especially noteworthy for its treatment of the method of study. Ascham repeats many of the educational views of Elyot and the Italian humanists, but in the method of teaching Latin and Greek he had positive views of his own and practical methods to advocate.

The *Scholemaster* consists of two books, the first on "The Bringing-up of Youth" and the second on "The Ready Way to the Latin Tongue." In the second, his procedure is outlined. After a slight knowledge of the noun and verb, the pupil takes the author in hand, for example, the *Letters* of Cicero. The teacher outlines the occasion and the subject matter of the letter, construes it into English and makes the meaning clear to the child, then parses it perfectly. A short time afterward the child translates and parses the passage, being sure of its entire meaning. He then takes a notebook and writes his translation without receiving help from anyone. After an hour he translates the English rendition back into Latin in another notebook. IIis Latin rendering is then compared by the teacher with the original and resemblances or differences pointed out. The pupil was to be warmly commended for the good features of his translation. "For I assure you," Ascham says, "there is no such whetstone to sharpen a good wit, and encourage a will to learning, as is praise." The rules and grammatical constructions were indicated by the pupil after the translation. He was allowed to use his grammar when translating, and taught to follow the method for Greek as well as Latin, although he could also render the Greek into Latin instead of English. Technical grammar was thus learned in the language itself and in the practice of the art of expression; in this respect Ascham resembled Erasmus and other humanists. His method of the double translation and use of note-books can be traced to Vives.[52] He made the student use three notebooks: one each for the translation, the retranslation, and the classification of phrases and forms of speech, metaphors, etc.

Ascham also believed in imitation, and especially repetition. He would have lessons repeated until thoroughly mastered. In discipline, he distinguished be-tween intellectual and moral failures. For the first, gentleness was to accomplish more than severity, and a love for learning more than fear of the teacher. Dislike for study he attributed to the teacher rather than to the child. He tolerated the use of the rod only for moral offenses. In his knowledge of boy nature and his clas-sification of the different kinds of boys, Ascham reminds us of Vergerio. The *Scholemaster* contains little on physical training, but Ascham's other work, *Toxophilus*, on archery, advocates physical exercises and recreation. In the former book he insisted on the importance of a good constitution; but, as Laurie says, his exercises are more for pastime than for development.

Although the general humanistic movement was furthered by the interest of a distinguished teacher like Ascham, the methods of the schools, even in Cambridge, were not seriously affected. The *Scholemaster*, however, subsequently came to be more highly regarded. Dr. Samuel Johnson said of it: "It contains the best advice that was ever given for the study of languages." Ascham,

---

[52] *Cf.* Watson, *Vives on Education*, pp. 113 f.

unfortunately, often displays his Protestant bias when speaking of the monks or of Catholic Italy.

FOR FURTHER STUDY

Allen, P. S., *The Age of Erasmus*. Oxford: The University Press, 1914.

Bonilla ÿ San Martin, Adolfo, *Luis Vives y la filosofía del Renacimiento*. Madrid: Imp. de L. Rubio, 1903.

Cannon, M. A., *The Education of Women during the Renaissance*. Washington, D. C.: The Catholic University of America, 1916.

Chevalier, Ulysse, *Repertoire des sources historiques du Moyen Age*. Bio-Bibliographie, 2 vols., Paris, 1905-07; Topo-Bibliographie, 2 vols., Montbeliard, 1894-1903.

Classiques de l'historie de France au Moyen Age. L. Halphen, editeur. Paris, 1944 *et sqq.*

Daly, W. A., *The Educational Psychology of J. L. Vives*. Washington, D. C.: The Catholic University of America, 1924.

Drummond, R. B., *Erasmus, his Life and Character as Shown in his Correspondence and Works*. London: Smith, Elder, and Co., 1873. 2 vols.

Einstein, L., *The Italian Renaissance in England*. New York: Columbia University Press, 1902.

Emerton, E., *Desiderius Erasmus of Rotterdam*. New York: G. P. Putnam's Sons, 1899.

Grube, K., *Gerhard Groote und seine Stiftungen*. Cologne: Bachem, 1883.

Hentsch, A. A., *De la litterature didactique du Moyen Age s'addressant specialement aux femmes*. Halle: A. Coueslant, 1903.

Histoire litteraire de la France. Paris, 1862. Vol. 24.

Hollis, Christopher, *Thomas More*. New York: Sheed and Ward, 1934.

Hoppe, Gerhard, *Die Psychologie des Juan Luis Vives*. Berlin: Mayer und Muller, 1901.

Hyma, A., *The Christian Renaissance*. Grand Rapids, Michigan: The Reformed Press, 1924.

Kane, W., *An Essay Toward a History of Education*. Chicago: Loyola University Press, 1935.

Kettlewell, J., *Thomas à Kempis and the Brothers of the Common Life*. London: Kegan Paul, 1882.

Laurie, S. S., *Educational Opinion from the Renaissance*. Cambridge: The University Press, 1903.

Mangan, J. J., *Life, Character, and Influence of Erasmus of Rotterdam Derived from a Study of his Works*. New York: The Macmillan Company, 1927. 2 vols.

Marique, P. J., *History of Christian Education*. New York: Fordham University Press, 1926. Vol. II.

Monroe, Paul, *Text-book in the History of Education*. New York: The Macmillan Company, 1909.

More, Cresacre, *Life of Sir Thomas More*. [Louvain]: 1631.

Namêche, A. J., *Memoire sur la vie et les écrits de J. L. Vives*. Brussels: M. Hayez, 1841.

Nève, F., *La Renaissance en Belgique*. Louvain: C. Peeters, 1890.

Pade, Roman, *Die Affektenlehre des J. L. Vives*. Munster: Aschendorff, 1893.

Quick, R. H., *Educational Reformers*. New York: D. Appleton Co., 1907.

Rosmini, C., *Vita e discipline di Guarino Veronese e de' suoi discepoli*. Brescia: Bettoni, 1805-06.

Sandys, J. E., *A History of Classical Scholarship*. Cambridge: The University Press, 1908. Vol. II.

Sargent, D., *Thomas More*. New York: Sheed and Ward, 1936.

Stone, J. M., *Reformation and Renaissance, 1377-1610*. New York: Dutton, 1904.

Watson, Foster, *Vives on Education*. Cambridge: The University Press, 1913.

——————, *Tudor Schoolboy Life*. London: J. M. Dent and Co., 1908.

——————, *Vives and the Renaissance Education of Women*. New York: Longmans, Green, and Company, 1912.

Woodward, W. H., *Desiderius Erasmus concerning the Aim and Method of Education*. Cambridge: Cambridge University Press, 1904.

——————, *Studies in Education during the Renaissance*. Cambridg · Cambridge University Press, 1906.

SYNOPSIS OF THE REFORMATION

Germany

1. REVOLT AGAINST THE CHURCH AND ECCLESIAS-
   TICAL AUTHORITY
   - (a) Schools disorganized and in many places closed
   - (b) Destructive effect very noticeable in the universities
2. OTHER NOTABLE EFFECTS OF THE REFORMA-
   TION
   - (a) State support for the maintenance of schools
   - (b) Adherents of the new faith instructed in reading so
     they might exercise their privilege of private judgment
   - (c) Bible disseminated more widely in the vernacular
3. MARTIN LUTHER (1483-1546)
   - (a) Work primarily of religious nature and incidentally
     educational
   - (b) Taught justification through faith
   - (c) Letter to the burgomasters and councilors of all the
     cities of Germany in behalf of Christian schools is the
     first Reformation document on education
   - (d) Sermons, German Bible, Catechism, Fables of Aesop—
     all had educational influence
4. PHILIP MELANCHTHON (1497-1560)
   - (a) Exponent of Protestant doctrine and founder of
     Protestant theology
   - (b) Identified with the foundation of Protestant schools
     and universities of central and southern Germany
   - (c) Furthered humanism by his manuals and guides for
     various school subjects and especially by his Latin
     and Greek grammars
5. JOHANN BUGENHAGEN (1485-1558)
   - (a) Organizer of schools in North Germany according to
     Lutheran ideals
   - (b) Brunswick Church Code suggests plans for a Latin
     school of three classes and a German elementary
     school
6. JOHANN BRENZ (1499-1570)
   - (a) Author of widely used Catechism ranking next in in-
     fluence to Luther's
   - (b) Devised school plan for Württemberg

379

7. VALENTIN ICKELSAMER (1500-1541)
   (a) Protagonist of the vernacular in the schools
   (b) Author of a German grammar and first exponent of the phonetic method for reading
8. VALENTIN TROTZENDORF (1490-1556)
   (a) Organized a Latin school at Goldberg
   (b) Latin emphasized in the school; little attention given to the vernacular; Hebrew also taught
   (c) Exercises in the school were clear and practical with repetition frequent
   (d) Honor system in the school successful during administration of Trotzendorf
9. JOHANN STURM (1507-1589)
   (a) Thorough humanist
   (b) Latin school at Strassburg is the prototype of the modern German gymnasium
   (c) *De litterarum ludis recte aperiendis (The Right Way of Opening Schools of Literature) and Classicae epistolae (Classical Letters)* contain his educational views and explain his course and methods
   (d) Determined largely the character of the humanistic schools in northern Europe
10. MICHAEL NEANDER (1525-1595)
    (a) Rector of Protestant Latin school at Ilfeld in the Hartz Mountains
    (b) Course of studies in his school more liberal than current humanistic course; especial emphasis given to geography, physics, and natural history
11. ULRICH ZWINGLI (1484-1534)
    (a) Adopted system of justification by faith, similar to Luther's
    (b) *Christian Education of Youth* offered nothing new to the science or practice of education
12. JOHN CALVIN (1509-1564)
    (a) Commanded good style and addressed himself to the learned chiefly
    (b) Catechisms are of educational importance
    (c) Organized and taught in the College of Geneva which was similar to the humanistic schools of the North, but in which French was emphasized

13. MATHURIN CORDIER (1479-1564)
   (a) Associated with Calvin in educational work
   (b) Two humanistic treatises, *De corrupti sermonis emendatione libellus* and *Colloquia*, aimed to establish purity of style and to supply correct forms in Latin conversation

England

1. SEPARATION OF ENGLAND FROM CATHOLIC UNITY UNDER HENRY VIII
   (a) Suppression of monasteries
   (b) Between 1536-46, 600 monasteries, 90 colleges, 2,300 free chapels, 100 hospitals suppressed
   (c) Wholesale destruction of schools and colleges wrought
2. LEACH ON ENGLISH SCHOOLS AT THE REFORMATION
   (a) Three hundred grammar schools in existence when the Reformation took place
   (b) Seven classes of schools appear in records of the time —cathedral, monastic, collegiate, hospital, guild, chantry, independent
   (c) Poll-tax returns of 1377 show that of forty-two towns all but one had its grammar school
   (d) Chantries Act of 1545 struck at all schools which were strictly ecclesiastical foundations
3. OTHER EFFECTS OF THE REFORMATION
   (a) Many colleges at Oxford and Cambridge universities closed
   (b) Absolute extinction of any systematic education for women during a long period of time
   (c) Deterioration in all grades of education from university downward
   (d) Catholics resorted to the Continent for their education

Ireland

1. THE REFORMATION UNDER HENRY VIII STRIPPED THE ALREADY WEAKENED COUNTRY OF ITS EDUCATIONAL INSTITUTIONS
   (a) Inroads of Danes in the eighth century followed by Norman invasion in the twelfth

2. PENAL LAWS
   - (a) Catholics forbidden to educate their children at home or abroad
   - (b) Catholic child sent abroad for education forfeited for life all his goods and lands
   - (c) Those who conspired in his education received same penalties

3. CATHOLIC EDUCATION
   - (a) Irish schools and colleges established at university centers outside of Protestant countries
   - (b) Precarious training in the Hedge School
   - (c) Ireland allowed to maintain schools at home at end of 18th century

CHAPTER XX

THE REFORMATION

In Germany

The Reformation of the sixteenth century, which was primarily a religious [1] and social movement, had an immediate and serious effect on education. A sudden revolt against the Church and ecclesiastical authority, it struck a severe blow at the educational institutions then everywhere flourishing, with the result that schools were disorganized and in many places closed; the people lost interest in education and, as we know from the complaints of Luther and Melanchthon, refused to send their children to the schools; learning itself seemed to be threatened. As Paulsen, the Protestant historian, says:

The first effect of these events on the educational institutions was destructive; the old schools and universities were so bound up with the Church in all respects—socially, legally and economically—that they could not but be involved in its downfall. The mere cessation of the prospects of clerical livings was bound to exercise a deterrent influence in regard to school and university studies. Then followed the Peasants' War, with its unmerciful devastation on both sides; and thus it came about that the ten years between 1525 and 1535 resulted in a depression of learning and education which is without parallel in history. The figures of attendance at the universities were reduced to one quarter of their former amount, and the same was probably the case with the schools, so that Erasmus could exclaim: "Wherever Luther prevails, the cause of literature and learning is lost."[2]

---

[1] It did not keep a religious character for long in the Germanies or in England; it became political. In protestant Germany, the ruler's religion was declared to be that of his subjects. The Latin formula which expresed this new policy was *Cuius regio, eius religio*. With the adoption of this principle, the international character of the universities was destroyed.

[2] F. Paulsen, *German Education, Past and Present*. Translated by T. Lorenz (New York: Charles Scribner's Sons, 1908), p. 54.

Nowhere was the effect more noticeable than in the universities;[3] these higher institutions were practically depopulated. Janssen has furnished statistics for many of them, as well as for the lower schools. Cologne, for example, which usually had at the close of the Middle Ages about 2,000 students, in 1516 had 370; in 1521, 251; and in 1534, only 54; Erfurt, Luther's university, enrolled in 1521, 311; and in 1524, 34; Rostock, which usually had about 300 students, enrolled in 1525, 15; Vienna matriculated in 1519, 661; in 1532, one of the Reformation years, 12 students. The ancient University of Prague, which in the fifteenth century enrolled thousands of students, was left with 8 professors and 30 students in 1550.[4]

Some other notable effects of the Reformation were to obtain the support of the State for the maintenance of schools, since the Church of the Reformers was unable to maintain them; to endeavor to instruct all adherents of the new faith in reading, that they might exercise their privilege of private judgment, and to disseminate the Bible more widely in the vernacular. It cannot be concluded, however, that the Reformation, as has often been asserted, first established public schools; for there were more free schools and better provision for elementary education before the Reformation than for a century afterward; nor can it be con-

---

[3] The grammar schools and elementary schools also suffered severely, but not to the extent that the universities did, because they were not directly involved in religious controversy. Because the endowments upon which these lower schools depended were confiscated, and because parents were not interested in training that did not lead to materialistic gain, so great damage was done to the grammar and elementary schools as to call forth Luther's two pamphlets on education. *Cf.* Kane, *An Essay Toward a History of Education*, p. 227.

[4] *Cf.* J. Janssen, *History of the German People at the Close of the Middle Ages*. Translated by A. M. Christie and M. A. Mitchell (London: K. Paul, Trench, Trübner and Co., Ltd., 1896-1910), I, 93; III, 355.

cluded that the Reformation first brought out the Bible in the vernacular, for in Germany alone there were at least twenty editions before that of Luther.

The number of translations both of single books of the Old and New Testaments, as well as of the complete Bible, was indeed very great. We have evidence of twenty-two editions of the Psalms with German translations up to 1509, and twenty-five German versions of the Gospels and Epistles up to 1518. Between this period and the separation of the Churches at least fourteen complete editions of the Bible were published in High German, and five in Low German dialect.[5]

The Reformers

Martin Luther (1483-1546) was born at Eisleben, the son of a miner. During his childhood the family moved to Mansfeld and there his school life began. His father was then prosperous. Luther studied the humanities at Magdeburg and Eisenach, and in his eighteenth year entered the University of Erfurt intending to study law. Although this was a humanistic center, Luther did not go deeply into the new studies. In fact, he never became a humanist. He entered the monastery of the Hermits of St. Augustine in Erfurt in 1505. What his motives were in doing so is a much debated question. His own accounts of incidents in early life are very conflicting and misleading, and were undoubtedly colored by his later experiences. An unhappy home life and fear of death he spoke of as the chief reasons. "When I was terror-stricken and overwhelmed by the fear of impending death, I made an involuntary and forced vow"; so he wrote years later when telling his father the reasons for his defection from the Church.

Ordained a priest in 1507, Luther was the following year appointed a teacher of philosophy in Wittenberg. He continued his theological studies and in 1509 was

---

[5] *Ibid.*, I, 56.

recalled to Erfurt. His visit to Rome in 1511, perhaps as the representative of houses of his order, did not weaken his faith. After his return from Rome, his advance in the order was rapid. In 1512, he received the doctorate in theology and in the same year was named subprior of his monastery. In 1513, he lectured on the Bible. In 1515, an administrative appointment as district vicar increased his duties and took him more into the world of affairs. He continued his lectures on the Scriptures; but from this time onward, with the increasing distractions of a busy office and the irregular performance of his religious exercises, Luther's spiritual condition became much disturbed. Morbid, scrupulous, he was unable to study and went to extremes in the practice of penances and mortifications. He disregarded the monastic regulations and the admonitions of his confessor and found no comfort in the Sacraments. From this position, where he depended on himself alone, or his penances and good works, for his salvation, he went finally to the other extreme in which he made all depend upon God. Man, he held, could be saved by faith alone. The merits of Christ supply for every sin and defect and are applied to man through faith—justification through faith. This and other heretical doctrines Luther engaged to defend when, on October 31, 1517, he posted on the church door at Wittenberg his ninety-five theses. They were soon recognized as directed not only against indulgences but against the penitential system of the Church.

In the disorder which followed the revolt, when religious agitation came to mean political rebellion, and when even the Reformers deplored the condition of society, Luther clearly saw the need of schools to supplant those previously maintained by the Church. He appealed to the civil authorities. His letter to the Burgomasters and Councilors of all the cities of Germany in behalf of Christian schools (1524) is regarded as the first Reformation document on education.[6] These officials were to be convinced of their duty to build and maintain schools and libraries, since those of the former regime had now been destroyed. The letter begins thus:

> First of all, we see how the schools are deteriorating throughout Germany. The humanities are becoming weak, the monasteries are declining, and, as Isaiah says, "the grass withereth, the flower fadeth, because the spirit of the Lord bloweth upon it," through the Gospel. For through the word of God the unchristian and sensual character of these institutions is becoming known. And because selfish parents see they can no longer place their children upon the bounty of monasteries and cathedrals, they refuse to educate them. "Why should we educate our children," they say, "if they are not to become priests, monks, and nuns, and thus earn a support?"

He urges education for the spiritual benefits to be realized, especially in the understanding of Scripture and also for the support of the civil power.

> Even if there were no soul, as I have already said, and men did not need schools and the languages for the sake of Christianity and the Scriptures, still for the establishment of the best schools everywhere, both for boys and girls, this consideration is of itself sufficient, namely, that society, for the maintenance of civil order and the proper regulation of the household, needs accomplished and well trained men and women. No such men are to come from boys, and such women from girls; hence it is necessary that boys and girls be properly taught and brought up.

He complains of the years spent in learning in the monastic schools and says:

---

[6] The importance of this letter in the history of education has been greatly exaggerated. It is a vigorous plea for the founding of schools, but it is a misinterpretation of Luther's views in this letter to credit him with the creation of popular elementary schools. *Cf.* Eby and Arrowood, *The Development of Modern Education* (New York: Prentice-Hall, Inc., 1935), p. 99.

My idea is that boys should spend an hour or two a day in school; and the rest of the time work at home, learn some trade and do whatever is desired, so that study and work may go on together, while the children are young and can attend to both. . . . In like manner, a girl has time at home; for she sleeps, dances and plays away more than that. . . .

But the brightest pupils, who give promise of becoming accomplished teachers, preachers and workers, should be kept longer at school, or set apart wholly for study, as we read of the holy martyrs, who brought up St. Agnes, St. Agatha, St. Lucian, and others.

In Luther's sermons there are many references to the instruction of the young, as for instance in his discourse on the duty of keeping children at school (1530), and also on the dignity of the teacher and respect due to him. He held the teacher next in honor to the preacher and strove to restore the office to the high estimation in which it was held before the Reformation. His German Bible and his catechisms, and the Fables of Aesop, which he published, were all of educational influence. Luther did not, however, devise any new school, elementary or secondary; his work was primarily of a religious nature and incidentally educational. That the schools which he and his associates endeavored to establish were similar in curriculum and management to those of the humanistic period will appear from a view of the educational work of the other so-called Reformers.

Philip Melanchthon was a much more effective educator than Luther. Born in 1497, the son of a sword-cutler of Bretton in the Palatinate, and a grandnephew of Reuchlin, he seemed "predisposed, as it were, for humanistic and Greek studies." He had the advantage of a private tutor at his home for his elementary training. For a considerable time he lived with his grandmother, the sister of Reuchlin, and there came under the influence of that humanistic scholar. At the latter's suggestion he adopted the name Melanchthon, the Greek equivalent of his family name, Schwarzerd. Melanchthon entered the University of Heidelberg at the age of thirteen. He obtained the bachelor's degree in 1511, but was refused the master's the following year on account of his youth. At the University of Tübingen, in 1513, he broadened his studies by courses in astronomy, astrology, mathematics, law, and medicine; and, in 1514, at the age of seventeen, won the master's degree and was appointed an instructor in Latin classics. Four years later, upon the recommendation of Reuchlin, he was received into the University of Wittenberg as a professor of Greek. Reuchlin said of him: "I know of no one among the Germans who is superior to him save only Erasmus Roterdamus, and he is a Dutchman." In his opening address, Melanchthon proclaimed himself a humanist; and under most promising auspices began a teaching career in Wittenberg which was to last forty-two years. There he first came into close relationship with Luther and was won over by the latter to the study of theology. He became a bachelor of theology and finally a teacher of that subject. It is somewhat curious to note that when giving the two courses in the University, the theological and the classical, he complained of the small number in the latter class, whereas his theological courses were very popular and attended by as many as fifteen hundred students.

Although he never took the doctorate in theology, Melanchthon became the great exponent of the evangelical doctrine and the founder of Protestant theology. The defender of Luther in numerous controversies, he differed from the latter on many points and often rejected his doctrines. Desirous of unity and peace, he advocated moderation, and for this was accused of weakness. He was not highly esteemed by the radical Protestants of the early Reformation. In the Augsburg Confession, he endeavored to prove that Protestants, in spite of the new doctrines, had a right to be considered as members of the Catholic Church. He sought the reunion of Protestants with the Church, but insisted upon the validity of Protestant doctrine. While he believed in justification by faith, he claimed good works were required for ethical reasons. He was never ordained a minister of the new faith, but on Sundays he was accustomed to expound the Gospel in Latin to the groups of students who lived with him.

By nature religious, scholarly, and peace-loving, Melanchthon never entirely lost his affection for the Church. He did not sanction the denunciation of pope and bishop; and, in the face of strong opposition, he remained faithful to his principles after the death of Luther. He possessed unquestionable ability as a teacher, scholar, and educational organizer, and he was identified more than any other man of his time with the foundation of Protestant schools and universities.[7] From Wittenberg he furnished schoolmasters and advised local authorities on questions connected with the schools. He carried on an extensive correspondence with German cities on the matter, but he dealt chiefly with the Latin school and not the common school in our present understanding of the term. Melanchthon's textbooks had an important influence in Protestant Germany; his *Loci communes* was the textbook in evangelical theology, and, with his writings on theological study and commentaries on the Scriptures, was widely circulated. Manuals and guides for various school subjects, and especially his Latin and Greek grammars, furthered humanism in Protestant schools.

---

[7] He organized three university foundations: Marburg in 1527; Koenigsburg in 1544; Jena in 1548; and founded a gymnasium at Nuremberg on humanistic lines. His *Book of Visitation* was made the basis of the school reorganization in Saxony; it advocated a system of Latin schools somewhat similar to Sturm's gymnasium at Strassburg.

Johann Bugenhagen (1485-1558), a native of Pomerania, and sometimes known as Pomeranus or Dr. Pommer, was a prominent teacher associated with the Reform movement. After his defection from the Church he became a pastor and professor at Wittenberg, and was a close friend and colaborer of Luther. He possessed literary ability and wrote many works, including a history of Pomerania. He assisted Luther in his translation of the Bible. The *Brunswick Church Code* (*Braunschweiger Kirchenordnung*), in which he laid the plans for a Latin school of three classes and a German elementary school, is an example of his contributions to the educational side of the Reformation. He endeavored to encourage schoolmistresses to take up service in the schools as servants of the state.

Johann Brenz (1499-1570) was a canon of the Church before joining the Protestant ranks. He became famous as a preacher in Stuttgart, the capital of Württemberg, and as a theologian, for he took a prominent part in the Protestant Conferences and in the compilation of the Confessions. His Catechism ranked in influence next to Luther's, and his school code for Württemberg was, like Bugenhagen's, influential in the Protestant states. He devised a plan, certainly not an original one, to provide for a Latin school in the city, or populous community, and an elementary school in which the sexton or sacristan was appointed to teach reading, writing, catechism, and church music.

Valentin Ickelsamer (1500-1541?), about whose early life little is known, was a distinguished German writer, at one time the antagonist of Luther but in the end a Protestant, who rendered a real service in directing more attention to the use of the vernacular in the schools. He was the author of a German grammar and is considered the first exponent of the phonetic method for reading.

Valentin Trotzendorf (1490-1556), whose family name

was Friedland, was known through life as Trotzendorf, after his native place, a small village in Silesia near Görlitz. His parents were peasants and they sent him for his early education to the monks in Görlitz. He studied for a time in Leipzic and later was a school teacher in Görlitz. When twenty-five years of age, he went to Wittenberg to attend the classes of Melanchthon and there spent five years. Afterward he organized at Goldberg the Latin school with which he was connected for twenty-five years. To this school, mainly, is due his reputation as an educator. The curriculum was humanistic, Latin being the fundamental study and the vernacular receiving little attention. Besides the usual humanistic studies, Hebrew was also taught, while religion, it is said, was the soul of his school and of all instruction. In method he maintained that rules should be few and short, exercises clear and practical, and repetitions frequent. The remarkable feature of his work was that the honor system prevailed to control discipline, and the students governed the school. They formed a kind of school republic, in which all were obliged to profess the Lutheran doctrines and obey the laws established for the school. The officers were elected by the students with Trotzendorf as the perpetual dictator. The oeconomi or stewards, and the ephors or overseers, supervised all household and domestic affairs; the quaestors had jurisdiction over the studies and maintained academic discipline. The student senate tried all delinquents, who were obliged to defend themselves in well-constructed Latin discourses. The system worked fairly well during the dictatorship of Trotzendorf, but was not so successful afterwards.

The prototype of the modern German gymnasium is seen in the Latin school of *Johann Sturm* (1507-89), who by training and taste was a thorough humanist.

He studied under the Brethren of Common Life at Liège, was a pupil of Wimpheling, and began to teach privately while a student at the universities of Louvain and Paris. In 1537, he went to Strassburg to take charge of the Latin school, where he remained for forty years. Under his direction the school became one of the most famous of the time.[8] His writings gained wide attention and attracted students even from foreign countries. In 1538, he published *The Right Way of Opening Schools of Literature (De litterarum ludis recte aperiendis)*, and in 1565 his *Classical Letters (Classicae epistolae)*, which were addressed to teachers and explained his course and methods. He maintained an extensive correspondence with educators in other countries, like Ascham in England, and with school authorities in Germany.

Sturm's school was essentially a Latin or classical school with the same avowed purpose as the school of the Renaissance. It is notable for its organization and its methods.[9] The students were divided into ten classes, which pursued a definite plan of study.[10] The boy was

---

[8] Sturm in his later years aspired to develop a university from the college of Strassburg which had been endowed by the emperor and empowered to grant academic degrees. The college consisted became a university under Emperor Ferdinand II, in 1621. At Strassburg, Sturm became a Lutheran and because he opposed the of a course of public lectures following completion of the gymnasium; it did not thrive during Sturm's lifetime but eventually claims of the dominant party among the Lutherans he was deposed as head of the school.

[9] Sturm accepted the educational world of his day. He drew ideas from the schools of the Brethren of Common Life, from Louvain, and from the school of Trotzendorf. His system of dividing each class into *decuriae* with a *decurion* in charge was very likely taken from Trotzendorf. The educational aim of his school: piety, knowledge, and eloquence, was the same as that of the schools of the Brethren.

[10] For many years the school had only eight classes in operation, although originally ten classes were projected.

received at seven years of age. In the first year, the tenth class, he learned reading and writing, Latin declensions and conjugations, and the catechism in Latin or German. Greek was not begun until the sixth class, and, although geography, mathematics, and Hebrew were taught, little attention was paid to other than the humanistic studies. The subjects were arranged to meet the capacities of the students as Sturm saw them. He made all teaching clear and definite, exacting from the student only a little at a time, but assured by frequent review that it was thoroughly known. He used the double translation advocated by Ascham in England. It is thought by many that he was the first to use the intensive and cursory methods together for the reading of a Latin author.[11]

Sturm's influence was very great in Germany and other Protestant countries. He gained a wide reputation through his school and was highly esteemed by the nobility and ruling powers of Europe, some of whom bestowed pensions upon him. He trained many teachers and his ideas on the management of a Latin school were carried by them to all parts of Europe. Furthermore, many educators imitated both his organization and his methods, and thus his ideas played a large part in determining the character of the humanistic schools in Northern Europe.[12]

Sturm's school has survived in the modern gymnasi-

---

[11] Quick, *Educational Reformers,* p. 32.

[12] Sturm is most often cited as the source from which the Jesuits borrowed. No doubt Sturm's curriculum was regarded by the Jesuits as the best curriculum of the day, but it is very probable that Sturm and the Jesuits both drew from common sources, notably the Brethren of the Common Life. *Cf.* William McGucken, *The Jesuits and Education* (New York: The Bruce Publishing Company, 1932), pp. 23 ff.; R. Schwickerath, *Jesuit Education* (St. Louis, Mo.: B. Herder, 1904), pp. 125-29.

um.[13] It should be noted here that the *Fürstenschulen* (Princes' Schools) bore a more striking resemblance to the humanistic schools of Italy than did Sturm's school. These were established by noblemen, sometimes in connection with the courts, for the training of young men for public careers. They were supported by the endowments of the confiscated monasteries, and were never very numerous; whereas the gymnasien were usually maintained by the municipalities. Some famous *Fürstenschulen* were those of Meissen (1543), Pforta (1543), Grimma (1550), and Rossleben (1554).

One of the less famous rectors of Protestant Latin schools was *Michael Neander* (1525-95), whose family name was Neumann, but who, like his master, Melanchthon, adopted the Greek equivalent. He was for twenty-five years rector of the cloistral school of Ilfeld in the Hartz mountains, one of the Protestant schools supported by the income of an old cloistral foundation. His was a successful secondary school, more on the plan of the modern gymnasium and college than many which were established after Sturm's model. His students made a good impression at the universities. He laid especial emphasis in his course on geography, physics, and natural history and wrote textbooks on these subjects. Like a number of the Protestant schoolmasters, and Luther and Melanchthon before them, he did not accept the scientific discoveries of Copernicus (1473-1543).

Ulrich Zwingli (1484-1534), the Swiss Reformer, was a humanist and friend of Erasmus. As a priest in Einsie-

---

[13] The German gymnasium remained practically as Sturm left it until the middle of the eighteenth century, when a new revival of classicism took place in Germany which made Greek instead of Latin the study of main interest. Gradually the sciences, the modern languages, and the vernacular have been given more attention, but the classics remained down to the Hitler regime the central subjects.

deln and Zurich, he preached freely against the doctrines and practices of the Church, especially against indulgences, pilgrimages, and devotion to the Blessed Virgin. He adopted a system similar to Luther's in respect to justification by faith and scriptural interpretation but different in regard to the Eucharist, for he denied absolutely the truth of the Real Presence. In his scheme of reform, which depended largely on the civil power, he endeavored to improve the schools in the Protestant centers especially for the preparation of ministers of the new belief. His work in Latin on training the young (1523; rendered into German, 1524) was a moral rather than an educational treatise and was intended for children living in good circumstances. In it he contended education should give a greater knowledge of God through the study of nature or the works of men, and the studies he recommended were humanistic. He spoke favorably of physical culture, of industrial training for those who needed it, and of the cultivation of the social virtues. The treatise made no new contribution to the science or practice of education.[14]

John Calvin (1509-64), the son of a lawyer of Noyon, Picardy, France, received minor orders in the Catholic Church and as a cleric held some benefices. He took no solemn vows, and his training was chiefly in law and letters. Commanding a good style, he addressed himself as a reform writer chiefly to the learned.[15] Of his

---

[14] The treatise was first written in Latin, in 1523, under the title, *Praeceptiones pauculae quo pacto ingenui adolescentes formandi sunt*. It was published in German, the following year: *Leerbiechlein wie man die Knaben christlich unterwezen und erziehen soll*. An English translation, entitled *Christian Education of Youth*, has been made by A. Reichenbach (Collegeville, Pa.: Thompson Bros., 1899).

[15] Calvin was a scholar. He wrote classical Latin and excellent French. His *Institutio religionis Christianae* is a compendium of his religious teachings; it contains the doctrine of predestination and demands simplicity of Church ritual and organization.

writings, the catechisms may be considered of some educational importance. His claim as an educator is chiefly based on the influence of the college of Geneva, which he organized and in which he taught. This differed little from the humanistic schools of the North; it was, with other colleges in Switzerland, the model of Calvinistic schools elsewhere.[16] *Mathurin Cordier* (1479-1564), the French Huguenot associated with Calvin in the Swiss colleges, was undoubtedly a humanist both in his writings and educational undertakings.[17] Two humanistic treatises were produced by Cordier, viz., *De corrupti sermonis emendatione libellus* and *Colloquia;* the first to correct faulty diction and establish purity of style, and the second to supply correct forms in Latin conversation.

In England

The separation of England from Catholic unity under Henry VIII brought about another educational revolution. One of the first acts of the king in his programme of reform was the suppression in 1536 of the smaller monasteries, when 376 houses were closed and their properties confiscated. The regal act then spoke of the larger monasteries as "great, honorable, and solemn monasteries of this realm wherein, thanks be to God, religion is right well kept and observed." In a few years they too had come into his hands by suppression, dissolution, or surrender; and it is estimated that approximately eight thousand religious persons were thereby

---

[16] The Collège de la Rive at Geneva differed from the usual type of humanistic school in the attention that was given to the study of French. From Geneva where Calvin was commonly called the "Genevan Pope" Calvinism spread throughout Europe and to the American colonies. In France, the Calvinists were known as Huguenots; in Scotland, Presbyterians; in England and American colonies, Puritans.

[17] *Cf.*, p. 348; also Woodward, *Education during the Renaissance,* pp. 154 ff.

expelled from their homes, while probably more than ten times that number of people, who were their dependents or otherwise obtained their livings in their service, were left without support.[18] Graves maintains that within ten years Henry had suppressed "600 monasteries, 90 colleges, 2300 free chapels, and 100 hospitals." Very little of the annual income of 150,000 pounds, which was derived from the endowments of these institutions, was spent for education, higher or secondary, to atone for the wholesale destruction of schools and colleges.[19] Of Henry's son it has been truly said:

Never was a greater reputation more easily gained and less deserved than that of King Edward VI as a founder of schools. . . . To thoroughly appreciate how very little Edward VI or his father really did for education, we have first to realize the extraordinary antiquity of many of our existing schools. Grammar schools, instead of being comparatively modern, post-Reformation inventions, are among our most ancient institutions, some of them far older than the Lord Mayor of London or the House of Commons.[20]

According to Leach, the records investigated by him reveal that nearly 200 Grammar Schools (and the Schools of Winchester and Eton are included in the term Grammar Schools) existed in England before the reign of Edward VI, which were, for the most part, abolished or crippled under him. It will appear, however, that these records are defective. They are only the survivors of a much larger host which have been lost in the storms of the past, and drowned in the seas of destruction. They do not give, they could not from their nature give, a complete account of all the Grammar Schools then existing in England. Such an account is probably irrecoverable. The materials for it do not exist. Enough,

[18] F. A. Gasquet, *Henry VIII and the English Monasteries* (London: J. Hodges, 1895), II, 323.
[19] F. P. Graves, *History of Education during the Middle Ages* (New York: The Macmillan Company, 1910), p. 195.
[20] A. F. Leach, *English Schools at the Reformation* (Westminster: A. Constable, 1896), p. 5.

however, can be gathered from other sources of information to permit the assertion to be confidently made that these 200 schools do not represent anything like all the Grammar Schools which existed in, or shortly before, the reign of Edward VI. Three hundred is a moderate estimate of the number in the year 1535, when the floods of the great revolution, which is called the Reformation, were let loose. Most of them were swept away either under Henry or his son; or, if not swept away, plundered and damaged.[21]

In the records of the time seven classes of schools appear, viz., schools connected with cathedral churches, with monasteries, with collegiate churches or colleges, with hospitals, with guilds, with chantries, and lastly, independent schools. The Chantries Act of 1545 struck all but those which were not strictly ecclesiastical foundations, and the loss to England in schools and libraries was irreparable. There was not even in 1865 as ample provision in schools in proportion to population. Leach has computed that the grammar schools, apart from the primary schools, numbered in 1546 about 300 among two and one half million people, or one school for every 8,300 people whereas there was one for every 23,000 in 1865.

From a study of the poll-tax returns of 1377 he draws the following conclusions:

In the Poll-Tax returns of 1377, forty-two towns are given. . . . They had a total population of 166,000 . . . with the possible exception of Dartmouth, with its 949 people, every one of these towns had its Grammar School. . . . As regards the numbers attending these schools, wherever numbers are mentioned they are surprising for their magnitude.[22]

It is interesting to note the large number of free grammar schools and the provision made in them for poor scholars. These were not mere elementary schools,

---

[21] *Ibid.*, p. 5.
[22] *Ibid.*, p. 100.

for they had adopted the humanistic curriculum and were the models after which subsequent grammar schools in England and America were organized.

The universities of Oxford and Cambridge were affected by the revolt in a manner similar to the universities of Germany.[23] Many of the colleges were closed because the monastic endowments on which they were supported were confiscated, and the number of students declined. In this regard Magevney has written:

Of the three hundred Halls and schools which have been built in and about Oxford alone, all, with the exception of eight, were dissolved and their revenues appropriated by the time Henry's programme of educational reform was finished.[24]

Facilities for the education of women so abundant before the convents were suppressed now disappeared. "The destruction of these religious houses by Henry was the absolute extinction of any systematic education for women during a long period."[25] All classes from the nobility to the poor were affected; the former in more than one instance remonstrated with the king. The work of the nuns in their cloisters has been described by an eye-witness to their occupations at a Wiltshire convent.

"There," says John Aubrey, "the young maids were brought up (not at Hakney Larum Schools, etc., to learn pride and wantonness, but) at the nunneries, where they had examples of piety, and humility, and modesty, and obedience to imitate and to practice. Here they learned needlework, the art of

---

[23] At Oxford there were 108 graduates in 1535; in the following year the number of graduates dropped to 44. The average number of graduates a year for the six years between 1542-1548 was 32 at Cambridge and 28 at Oxford. In 1561 the doctor's degree was not conferred by any of the faculties at Oxford. Cf. Kane, An Essay Toward a History of Education, pp. 226 f.

[24] E. Magevney, The Reformation and Education (New York: The Cathedral Library Association, 1903), p. 34.

[25] Gasquet, op. cit., II, 221.

confectionery, surgery (for anciently there were no apothe-caries or surgeons—the gentlewomen did cure their poor neighbours: their hands are now too fine), physics, writing, drawing, etc. . . . This, concludes the author, was a fine way of breeding up young women, who were led more by example than precept; and a good retirement for widows and grave single women to a civil, virtuous and holy life."[26]

Not only girls but boys also were educated by the nuns as is clear from many of the regulations imposed upon convents by the bishops. All were not, of course, board-ing scholars.[27] To the nuns many distinguished Church-men owed their early education.

The immediate effect of the Reformation was con-sequently disastrous to education.

Deterioration was felt in all grades of education from the university downwards. "The rise in rents," says Latimer, "prevented the yeoman sending his son to school." Most of the schools at this time were closed, without any provision being made for a substitute.[28]

Bishop Latimer, who repudiated the Catholic Faith under Henry, makes the following remarks in a sermon on the sad condition of the schools:

Truly, it is a pitiful thing to see the schools so neglected; every true Christian ought to lament the same . . . to consider what hath been plucked from abbeys, colleges, and chantries, it is marvel no more to be bestowed upon this holy office of salvation. It may well be said by us that the Lord complain-eth by His prophet. . . . "My house ye have deserted, and ye run everyone to his own house.". . . Schools are not main-tained; scholars have not exhibitions. . . . Very few there be that help poor scholars. . . . It would pity a man's heart to hear that, that I hear of the state of Cambridge; what it is in Oxford I cannot tell. . . . I think there be at this day ten

---

[26] *Ibid.*, p. 224.
[27] Eckenstein, *Women under Monasticism*, p. 378,
[28] Gasquet, *op. cit.*, p. 520.

thousand students less than were within these twenty years and fewer preachers.[29]

Catholics were then compelled to resort to the Continent for their education. The English colleges at Douai, Rome, and Valladolid had for their object the training of the clergy. Not until the foundation of St. Omer, near Calais, France, in 1592, by Father Robert Parsons, S.J., was there an English college for the laity. This continued its noble work until 1762 when it was removed to Bruges. Stonyhurst college, opened about 1794, was the lineal descendent of St. Omer's as the first Catholic college for young English laymen after the Reformation.[30]

In Ireland

The course of the Reformation in Ireland was to strip the already weakened country of its educational institutions. The inroads of the Danes, begun at the end of the eighth century with the pillaging of monasteries and the burning of libraries, lasted for over two hundred years, and Ireland had not recovered from them even in the twelfth century when the Norman invasions ensued with their consequent depredations and confiscations. Whether wholly or partially under English control, Ireland did not regain her former prestige in the realm of learning. Occasionally her monasteries gave promise of again flourishing. The Dominicans and the Franciscans were established there in the early thirteenth century, but learning and the arts of peace could not well thrive in a country so racked by feuds and wars. The destruction begun by the Danes was completed by the Protestants of the Reformation.

It was not long before the penal laws forbade Catholics, who were the majority in Ireland, to educate their

<hr/>

[29] *Ibid.,* p. 520.
[30] *Cf.* P. Guilday, *The English Catholic Refugees on the Continent* (New York: Longmans, Green, and Co., 1914), vol. I.

children either at home or abroad. Protestants could not instruct Catholics. The child sent abroad for education could never afterward sue in law or equity, or receive any legacy or gift, but forfeited for life all of his goods and lands. Those who conspired in his education were also guilty and received the same penalties. In spite of all this, however, students were sent abroad for the education denied them at home; and at the university centers outside of the Protestant countries, Irish schools and colleges were eventually established, as at Louvain, Antwerp, Lille, Douai, Bordeaux, Toulouse, Rouen, Nantes, Paris, Salamanca, Seville, Madrid, Compostela, Lisbon, Alcalà, Coimbra, Prague, and Rome.

When the penal laws were severest and a price was placed upon the head of a teacher, the Irish boy received a precarious training in the Hedge School. "Still crouching neath the sheltering hedge or stretched on mountain fern, the teacher and his pupils met, feloniously to learn."

Not until the end of the eighteenth century, when the penal laws were relaxed, was any relief felt and Ireland allowed the right of maintaining schools at home.

FOR FURTHER STUDY

Audin, J. M. V., *Histoire de la vie, des ouvrages, et des doctrines du Calvin.* Paris: Maison, 1841. 2 vols. Translated by J. McGill. Baltimore: John Murphy, [*n. d.*]

Baudrillart, A., *The Catholic Church; the Renaissance and Protestantism.* Translated by Mrs. Philip Gibbs. London: K. Paul, Trench, Trübner and Company, 1908.

Belloc, H., *How the Reformation Happened.* New York: R. M. McBride and Company, 1928.

Cambridge Modern History. London: The Macmillan Company, 1904. Vol. II.

Cramer, F., *Geschichte der Erziehung und des Unterrichts in den Niederlanden während bis Mittelalters.* Stralsund: C. Hingst, 1843.

Denifle, H. S., *Luther and Lutherdom*. Translated by R. Volz. Somerset, Ohio: Torch Press, 1917.

Doumergue, E., *Jean Calvin, les hommes et les choses de son temps*. Lausanne: G. Bridel et Cie., 1899-1927. 7 vols.

Gairdner, J., *Letters and Papers Foreign and Domestic of the Reign of Henry VIII*. London: His Majesty's Stationery Office, 1883-98. Vols. 8-16.

Gasquet, F. A., *Henry VIII and the English Monasteries*. London: J. Hodges, 1890. 2 vols.

——————, *The Eve of the Reformation*. New York: G. P. Putnam's Sons, 1900.

Grisar, H., *Luther*. Translated by E. M. Lamond. St. Louis: B. Herder, 1913-17. 6 vols.

Guilday, P., *The English Refugees on the Continent*. New York: Longmans, Green, and Company, 1914. 2 vols.

Hartfelder, K., *Philip Melanchthon, Praeceptor Germaniae*. Berlin: A Hoffman, 1889.

Hume, E. M., *The Renaissance, the Protestant Revolution and the Catholic Reformation*. New York: The Century Co., 1915.

Imbart de la Tour, P., *Les Origines de la Reforme*. Paris: Hachette et Cie, 1905-14. 3 vols.

Janssen, J., *History of the German People at the close of the Middle Ages*. Translated by A. M. Christie and M. A. Mitchell. London: K. Paul, Trench, Trübner and Company, 1896-1910. 16 vols.

Kidd, J. B., *Documents Illustrative of the Continental Reformation*. Oxford: Clarendon Press, 1911.

Köstlin, J., *Martin Luther, sein Leben und seine Schriften*. Revised in the 5th edition by G. Kawerau. Berlin: A. Duncker, 1903. 2 vols.

Kuckelhahn, L., *Johannes Sturm, Strassburgs ersten Schulrektor*. Leipzig: J. F. Hartknoch, 1872.

Laas, E., *Die Paedagogik des Johann Sturm, historisch und kritisch beleuchtet*. Berlin: Weidmann, 1872.

Leach, A. F., *English Schools at the Reformation*. Westminster: A. Constable and Company, 1896.

Magevney, E., *The Reformation and Education*. New York: The Cathedral Library Association, 1903.

Maritain, J., *Three Reformers*. London: Sheed and Ward, 1928.

Murray, R. H., *Erasmus and Luther*. London: Society for Promoting Christian Knowledge, 1920.

Paulsen, F., *German Education, Past and Present*. Translated by T. Lorenz. New York: Charles Scribner's Sons, 1908.

Quick, R. H., *Educational Reformers*. New York: D. Appleton Co., 1907.

Ruccius, Walter M., *John Bugenhagen Pomeranus*. Philadelphia: The United Lutheran Publication House, 1916.

Schapiro, J. S., *Social Reform and the Reformation*. New York: Columbia University, 1909.

Stebbing, H., *The Reformation*. London: Brown, Green, and Longmann, 1836-37. 2 vols.

Sturm, L., *Valentin Trotzendorf und die Lateinische Schule zu Goldberg*. Goldberg: Verlag von K. Obst, 1888.

Taylor, H. O., *Thought and Expression in the Sixteenth Century*. New York: The Macmillan Co., 1920.

Warfield, B., *Calvin and Calvinism*. Oxford: University Press, 1931.

Watson, F., *The English Grammar Schools to 1660*. Cambridge: University Press, 1908.

SYNOPSIS OF THE CATHOLIC REACTION

1. COMMISSION OF REFORM APPOINTED 1537 BY POPE PAUL III
   (a) Cardinal Reginald Pole and Cardinal Jacopo Sadoleto, distinguished prelates devoted to the interests of the the school
   (b) Report of commission basis of many of the reforms of the Council of Trent
2. ECUMENICAL COUNCIL OF TRENT (1545-1563)
   (a) Standard established for the training of the clergy throughout the world
   (b) Parish school reopened where it had declined
   (c) Religious orders founded for instruction of the young to be encouraged
3. PROVINCIAL COUNCILS AND DIOCESAN SYNODS
   (a) Tridentine law accepted in diocesan statutes
   (b) Seminaries multiplied, colleges opened, free schools made accessible to the poor
   (c) Councils and synods of 16th century decree that there be a school in every parish
4. RELIGIOUS ORDERS
   (a) Older religious orders renew their educational efforts
   (b) Younger orders and congregations come into existence under the auspices of the Church—Theatines, Somaschi, Ursulines, Piarists, Fathers of Christian Doctrine
   (c) The Society of Jesus adopted the education of boys as one of its chief aims

CHAPTER XXI

THE CATHOLIC REACTION

The appointment of the Commission of Reform in 1537 by Pope Paul III was a fitting beginning of the Catholic Counter Reformation. Some of the distinguished prelates of the Commission were devoted to the interests of the schools, as for instance, Cardinal Reginald Pole, who had manifested his solicitude for them in England and especially in Oxford, and Cardinal Jacopo Sadoleto, the author of a notable educational treatise: *De liberis recte instituendis liber*[1] (1533). The latter, who had been papal secretary under Leo X, was a famous humanist and a correspondent of Erasmus. The treatise gives a beautiful exposition of a Christian and humanistic education and is of special note for its advocacy of compulsory education by the state. From churchmen like Sadoleto and Pole might naturally be expected the reform in the schools urged by the Commission. They condemned the heretical and impious teaching in the public school, especially of Italy, and the holding of so many public disputations; they urged the bishops to supervise more carefully the printing of books and to prohibit the reading of such works as the *Colloquies* of Erasmus in the schools. Their report was the basis of many of the reforms of the great Ecumenical Council of Trent, held from 1545-1563.[2]

The Council restored the ancient discipline for the

---

[1] *Cf.* Karl A. Kopp, *Ueber die richtige Erziehung der Kinder von Jacob Sadolet* (Freiburg: Herder, 1904). The *De liberis recte instituendis* has been translated into English, with an introduction by E. T. Campagnac and K. Forbes, under the title *Sadoleto on Education* (Oxford: H. Milford, 1916). *Opera omnia* of Sadoleto have been published in 4 vols. (Verona: Joannis Alberti Tumermani, 1737-35.)

[2] The princes who had profited politically by the Revolt did not favor the efforts of the Council. Even the Catholic rulers, Emperor Charles V of the German states and Francis I of France,

training of the clergy. The cathedral school or seminary being regarded as the best means for correcting abuses that had crept in since the rise of the universities, it was decreed that every diocese should have its own seminary for the preparation of ecclesiastical students. Regulations were also made regarding the courses and the qualifications of the teachers. There was universal satisfaction over the adoption of this decree, since a standard was thereby established for the training of the clergy throughout the world. The Council also made regulations to safeguard the teaching in universities by requiring all masters to engage upon oath to teach the Catholic faith according to the canons of the Council. Other phases of education, such as the instruction of the faithful by preaching and by the printed word, and the Sunday School, were subjects of legislation during the many sessions of the Council. The parish school [3] was to be reopened wherever it had declined; the religious orders founded for the instruction of the young were to be encouraged.

Provincial councils and diocesan synods throughout the Christian world enacted similar laws for their jurisdictions and designated more particularly how the injunctions were to be carried out. Thus we see in many instances the very words of the Tridentine law accepted in diocesan statutes, especially regarding the religious instruction of the people. St. Charles Borromeo (†1584) in Italy established diocesan seminaries and

---

viewed the purpose of the Council in the light of their political schemes; the latter forbade the French bishops to attend it. The first session of the Council had four archbishops, twenty-one bishops, and five general superiors of religious orders; the twenty-fifth and final session had four cardinal legates of the Pope, two cardinals, three patriarchs, twenty-five archbishops, one hundred and sixty-eight bishops, seven abbots, and seven general superiors of religious orders.

[3] *Cf.*, Fifth Session.

colleges. The Venerable Bartholomew of the Martyrs (Bartholomew of Braga, †1590) carried out the designs of the Council in Portugal; Cardinal Pole endeavored to do so in England. Seminaries were multiplied, colleges opened, and free schools made accessible to the poor.

France offers an excellent example of this activity, for there the Church was not subjected to such persecution as was encountered in England and Germany. Particular councils apply the Tridentine law according to the wants of their respective dioceses. Nearly all the provincial councils and diocesan synods of the sixteenth century deal with the question of the schools and decree that there be a school in every parish.[4] A decree of the Council of Cambrai, held in 1565, under the presidency of the archbishop and with the bishops of Tournai, Arras, Saint Omer, and Namur, is as follows:

They will be careful to restore, or to keep up, Christian schools to instruct children in the rudiments of religion. There is to be a schoolmaster for the instruction of youth in every parish. The boys are to be kept separate from the girls as much as possible. The masters will only read to their scholars books approved by the Bishops. The pastor, the chaplains, or the schoolmasters will teach the catechism to the children every Sunday after Vespers. The pastors will enquire every month into the progress of the children and will do their utmost to inspire them with the fear and love of God from their tenderest years. The rural deans will visit these little schools once a month, or at least once a year, and will report to the Ordinary concerning the method of instructing youth employed by each master.[5]

It was during the period of the Catholic Counter Reformation that one of the most complete treatises on

---

[4] A Ravalet, *Blessed John Baptist de la Salle* (Tours: Alfred Mame and Sons, 1888), p. 36.
[5] *Ibid.*, p. 37; *Cf.* Mansi, *Collectio Con.*, Vol. XXXIII, 1396.

the education of children appeared under the title *Dell'*
educatione cristiana dei figliuoli by *Cardinal Silvio*
Antoniano. Written at the request of St. Charles
Borromeo, the treatise was first published in 1584. As it
was intended as a book for the people, it was written in
Italian instead of the customary Latin. Pope Pius XI
in his Papal Encyclical, *Christian Education of Youth*,
refers to it as the "golden treatise" and speaks of its
author as the "holy and learned Cardinal to whom the
cause of Christian education is greatly indebted."[6]

The treatise consists of three books of which book
II is a splendid manual of Christian doctrine. Book I
points out the importance of the physical training of the
child; while book III is an exposition of the author's
theory of education. It aims to prepare man for his
place in society as a Christian gentleman and to direct
him to his supernatural destiny. The importance of the
preschool years of the child, a sympathetic understanding of child psychology, vocational guidance and
direct training for citizenship, all of which are important
matters in modern education, are fundamental concepts
in the educational theories of Antoniano.[7]

The prescriptions of the Council of Trent convinced
the churchmen of the period that before they could hope
to bring about religious reforms they must first reform
education. Accordingly, new fervor entered into the
older religious orders, and while they responded to the
appeal for renewed activity younger orders and congregations came into existence under the auspices of the
Church. Some of these, like the Theatines,[8] founded by

---

[6] Pope Pius XI, *Christian Education of Youth* (Washington,
D. C.: National Catholic Welfare Conference, 1926), p. 21.

[7] *Cf.* Sister Mary Lauretana Zanfagna, C.D.P., *Educational
Theories and Principles of Cardinal Silvio Antoniano* (Washington, D. C.: The Catholic University of America, 1940), p. 125.

[8] Popularly called from Theate, a city in southern Italy, where
they originated.

St. Cajetan in 1524, and the Somaschi,[9] or the Congregation of Somasca, Italy, founded by St. Jerome Aemilian in 1532, undertook the management of seminaries and colleges for the clergy and the laity. The Society of Jesus adopted the education of boys as one of its chief aims and the services of this great Order to the cause of religion and learning during the Counter Reformation were almost inestimable.

The Society of Jesus

St. Ignatius of Loyola, the founder of the Society of Jesus, was born in 1491 of a noble Spanish family. Although clerical tonsure was conferred upon him in youth, he chose to follow a military career. He was seriously injured while defending the citadel of Pamplona during an attack by the French, and as a result was confined to his bed for many months. During the period of convalescence, lacking other books, he read the lives of Christ and the Saints, and a spiritual transformation took place. He chose now to be a soldier of Christ and to imitate the Saints in their penances. Shortly afterward (1522) he

went forth a knight as ever, but not on an expedition terminating as before. An evening and a night spent in the monastery of Montserrat, as once before he had passed a vigil of arms, when dubbed a chevalier by the King of Navarré; a morning begun with the Holy Sacrifice attended and Holy Communion received, opened to him a new era; and he went forth, bound now by a new oath of fealty to the service of the King of Heaven.[10]

After a retreat of about a year spent in Manresa, Loyola traveled as a pilgrim to the Holy Land, endur-

---

[9] Their Motherhouse was at Somasca (Venice), whence the name.

[10] T. Hughes, *Loyola and the Educational System of the Jesuits* (New York: Charles Scribner's Sons, 1892), p. 20.

ing poverty and exposure, persecution and hardships of
every sort. When he returned, having already conceived
in general outline the idea of his future work,[11] he
undertook the study of Latin in Barcelona. After two
years he was able to enter the University of Alcalà.
Persecution drove him to Salamanca, but there, too,
he was harshly criticized for his views and religious
zeal and was even cast into prison. Convinced that
learning was necessary for the fulfillment of his plans,
he then (1528) went to Paris to follow courses in the
University. He completed the arts course and obtained
the master's degree in 1535. He had in the meantime
studied theology, for he received the licentiate in 1534.
In all, Loyola spent eleven years in study from the time
of his entrance into the school of Barcelona, and when
he left Paris he was a man forty-four years of age.

In the University of Paris he found the six staunch
companions who formed with him the nucleus of the
Society of Jesus. They were St. Peter Faber, a Genevan
Savoyard; St. Francis Xavier of Navarre; James
Laynez, Alphonsus Salmeron and Nicholas Bobadilla of
Spain; and Simon Rodriguez of Portugal. On August 15,
1534, they assembled in the church of the Blessed Virgin
at Montmartre, Paris, and desiring to imitate the life
of Christ bound themselves by vow to the practice of
poverty and chastity. They also vowed to go to the
Holy Land upon the completion of their studies, or, if
prevented in that, to go to Rome and place themselves
at the disposal of the Holy Father for whatsoever
services he might assign them. At the appointed time
they appeared in Rome, being unable to go to the Holy
Land on account of the troubled conditions existing

---

[11] R. Schwickerath, *Jesuit Education: Its History and Principles
in the Light of Modern Educational Problems* (St. Louis: B.
Herder Company, 1904), p. 56.

there. They sought the approval of the Holy See for
the new society and obtained it in 1540.

St. Ignatius called the little group the Company of
Jesus, thereby indicating both the social and military
aspects of the organization. The title, Society of Jesus,
came from the Latin form, *Societas Jesu,* given in the
papal bull of approval. The term Jesuits, at first one of
reproach applied as early as the fifteenth century to
those who used the Holy Name of Jesus too frequently,
was later adopted by the friends and members of the
Society and accepted in its good sense. The aim of
the Society of Jesus is well expressed in its motto:
Omnia ad majorem Dei gloriam—All for the greater
glory of God. The Society differed from the older orders
in making education one of its chief purposes, and in
this sense it was the first teaching order. Its primary
object was not to combat Protestantism.

It was the first intention of Ignatius to convert Palestine.
Frustrated in this plan, he chose Italy, Spain, Portugal as the
field of labor for himself and his companions. There he endeavored to reform the morals of the people and to encourage
the practice of works of charity.[12]

The Constitution of the Order, prepared by St. Ignatius before his death and granted papal approbation,
enumerated among the objects of the Society: teaching
catechism to children and the ignorant, instructing youth
in schools and colleges, and lecturing on philosophy and
theology in the universities. The original constitution
consists of ten parts. The fourth and longest part treats
of studies and the administration of colleges, the preparation of the teachers, etc. It contained a promise of
another document to appear later which would deal
specifically with the method and order of studies. "This
is the express warrant contained in the Constitution for

---

[12] Schwickerath, *op. cit.,* p. 78.

the *Ratio studiorum,* or System of Studies in the Society of Jesus." [13]

With the rapid spread of the Society and the increase in the number of colleges, the need was felt of a more uniform treatment of studies throughout the world. Members of the Order in Spain had devised plans of study, some of which served as the basis of the plan officially accepted for the whole Society. During the generalship of Father Claudius Aquaviva, 1581-1615, this official plan, the *Ratio studiorum,* was prepared. In 1584, the General appointed a committee of six Fathers taken from different provinces and nations, who after nine months' consultation and collaboration produced a tentative plan. This was submitted by the General to the Provincials of the Order for the criticism of the teachers under their jurisdiction. The Provincial was required to appoint at least five men well qualified in point of learning and judgment to examine and criticize the plan. A second plan followed in 1591 after most careful revision of the first by the General and the Fathers of every province of the Order. The Provincials reported on the revised plan at the General Congregation in Rome (1593-94), and further improvement was made. In 1599, fifteen years after the first plan was undertaken and after long examination and experiment in the schools, the final plan of studies appeared bearing the title, *Ratio atque institutio studiorum Societatis Jesu, (Method and System of Studies of the Society of Jesus).* [14]

The *Ratio studiorum* of 1599 was a practical method or system of teaching. It was not a treatise on methods,

---

[13] Hughes, *op. cit.,* p. 56.

[14] Cf. G. M. Pachtler, *Ratio studiorum et institutiones scholasticae Societatis Jesu per Germanian olim vigentes* (Berlin: Hofmann, 1887-94). 4 vols. These are vols. II, V, IX, and XVI of *Monumenta Germaniae paedagogica,* edited by Dr. Karl Kehrbach.

nor a discussion of them; such matters had been gone over and settled before the *Ratio* was adopted in its final form. It was "a code of laws, a collection of rules for different officials, in whose hands lies the government of a college, and for the teachers of the various classes."[15] It was the authoritative plan of studies until the suppression of the Order in 1773; and in the revised *Ratio* of 1832, following the restoration of the Order (1814), its essentials and fundamental principles remained unchanged although more provision was made for the study of the vernacular, history, and the natural sciences.[16] Under distinct heads it treats of (1) the duties of administrative officers, i.e., the Provincial, Rector, Prefect of Studies; (2) the professors of the higher faculties of the universities and seminaries where Sacred Scripture, theology, canon law, and similar professional subjects were taught; (3) the professors of the faculty of arts or philosophy; (4) the professors of the humanities—under the two latter will be found the rules for the college and high school teachers.[17]

The government of a college lies with the Rector assisted by the Prefect of Studies and the Prefect of

---

[15] Schwickerath, *op. cit.,* p. 114.

[16] The revised *Ratio* is known as Roothaan's *Ratio.* It never secured the approval of a General Congregation. In America there has been considerable deviation from it. McGucken points out that the parochial school, contact with secular colleges, relations with educational associations, need of adaptation to American needs, and requirements of standardizing agencies are influences that have played a part in the shaping of Jesuit educational policy in this country. *Cf.* W. J. McGucken, *The Jesuits and Education,* (Milwaukee: Bruce Co., 1932), pp. 135-45. The *Ratio* for lower schools has been translated into English in McGucken's, *The Jesuits and Education;* and a complete translation of the *Ratio* and Part IV of the Constitutions is given in E. A. Fitzpatrick, *St. Ignatius and the Ratio Studiorum* (New York: McGraw Hill Book Co., 1933).

[17] For two Ratios of 1599 and 1832 *Cf.* Pachtler, *op. cit.,* II 225 ff.

Discipline. He is required to supervise the class work. While having wide authority, he must follow the laws made for him, and regularly consult with his council. The Provincial also is bound to visit the colleges at least once a year. All the teachers must see him privately; and they may place before him any difficulties they have had with the Rector. The Prefect of Studies is naturally responsible for the quality of the teaching. He visits every class at least once in two weeks and is always accessible to teachers for consultation and direction. A similar task in the supervision of conduct falls to the care of the Prefect of Discipline.

The curriculum, apart from the university and professional studies, consisted of the *Studia inferiora* or Lower Studies, and the arts course, or philosophy. The former, or the humanities, had five classes, sometimes six, determined by advance or progress in classical studies. The course is essentially humanistic; other branches enter into it as completing the classical studies. The Prefect of Studies is instructed

to distribute History, Geography, the elements of Mathematics and whatever else is usually taught in these classes, in such a manner that each Master can satisfactorily and conveniently finish the matter assigned to him.

The classes are designated as follows: 1. Lower Grammar: for the rudiments of Latin and Greek, the reading of easy selections. 2. Middle Grammar; where "the aim is knowledge, though not entire, of all grammar;" another portion of the Greek grammar, selected readings from Cicero, *Commentaries* of Caesar, and easy poems of Ovid; in Greek: the Fables of Aesop, selected dialogues of Lucian and *Table* of Cebes.[18] 3. Upper Grammar: grammar completed in Latin; all of the rudiments in Greek grammar. Readings: Cicero, *De*

---

[18] Hughes, *op. cit.*, p. 271.

amicitia and *De senectute;* selections from Ovid, Catullus, Tibullus, and *Eclogues* of Vergil; in Greek, St. Chrysostom, Xenophon, and the like. 4. Humanities: the class which prepares for Rhetoric, daily study of Cicero, the historians, Caesar, Sallust, Livy, Curtius, and the poets, especially Vergil, with selections from Horace and others. In Greek, a study of the art of versification, and some composition in Greek; of prose authors, St. Chrysostom, St. Basil, Epistles of Plato, etc.; and of the poets, Homer, Phocylides, St. Gregory Nazianzus. 5. Rhetoric; the humanistic studies are completed as a preliminary to philosophy. A choice of authors may be permitted to perfect the student's style and powers of expression. In Greek, a fuller knowledge is given through the orators, historians, and poets. The list of authors includes St. Gregory Nazianzus, St. Basil, and St. Chrysostom.

As in the humanistic schools of the period, Latin took precedence over all other studies and the vernacular received less attention. This does not mean that the mother tongue was entirely neglected in the Jesuit schools, for the Fathers ordered its study and cultivated it themselves. For instance, as early as 1560 Father Jerome Nadal exhorted the Jesuits at Cologne, "to cultivate diligently the German language and to find out a method of teaching it; that they should also select pupils and teachers for this branch." [19]

The course in philosophy covered three years and included mathematics and the natural sciences. Such a course avoided the narrowness of a purely humanistic curriculum, and furthered that wider expansion of college work already noticeable in the schools of the Italian Renaissance.

---

[19] Schwickerath, *op. cit.,* p. 130.

Formal religious instructions took place once a week,[20] but all the means afforded by school work and by Catholic devotions and the Sacraments were used for the moral formation of the young. They were encouraged to acquire both learning and piety. The spirit of the discipline was not severe in the Jesuit schools; corporal punishment, for example, could not be inflicted by the teacher. It could be administered by the Prefect of Discipline. A benign firmness characterized the discipline of the classroom.

Among the most noteworthy features of the Jesuit system are the following:

I. The teacher was long and carefully trained. Selected in the first place for his qualifications as a religious novice, he underwent, after completing his classical studies, the course of two years in the novitiate. He then revised and extended his classical studies for two years from the standpoint of the teacher, and afterward pursued the Arts Course of three years, including philosophy and mathematics. He was then qualified to enter the classroom and to teach grammar and literature—this period, the "Regency," lasted about five years. Finally he followed a course in theology lasting four years, with another year of spiritual preparation before being professed. A fixed number of teachers was required for the grades of an institution and St. Ignatius had advised that invitations to establish colleges be refused when a full quota of teachers was not at hand.

II. The Jesuit schools were free. The poor who could undertake a higher education were welcome students.

III. The Jesuit schools were of the religious-humanistic type, the same as had been in Europe for more than a century previous to the founding of the Jesuit Order. Their educational aims were Christian character and

---

[20] *Ibid.*, p. 590.

humanistic culture, the same aims that had characterized the schools of the Renaissance in general. The Jesuits accepted the type of school education which was then prevailing and the curriculum then in vogue.[21] They labored to give a liberal training according to the concept of the time, to prepare young men for the professions and specialized courses. Characteristics of their method were: (a) the *praelectio*, or prelection, which meant in the lower grades an explanation of a passage in an author, and in the higher faculties, a lecture; this assured orderly and methodical procedure by all teachers; (b) discussions, reviews, contests, and consequent emulation, which were used as means of stimulation and interest; (c) assiduous cultivation of the powers of memory.

The Jesuit college had many features in common with the Latin schools of the period. St. Ignatius drew upon his own experience in the foundation and organization of colleges, and the Fathers who produced the *Ratio studiorum* profited by the educational practices as well as the theory of the time. It is incorrect to ascribe the source of the system to any individual educator as, for instance, to Vives or Sturm, or to a distinct institution like the humanistic school of the North. The first Jesuits were in possession of the educational inheritance of their day and they adapted it to the best advantage.[22] As a historian of the Society says:

It really looks as though some writers are determined to deny all originality to the Ratio Studiorum, if they are compelled to admit that it achieved great results. We frankly and willingly admit that the authors of the Ratio borrowed much from existing systems, it matters little whence and how much. We must, however, claim that their experience from 1540-1599, and their pains-taking efforts in drawing up the

[21] Kane, *op. cit.*, p. 209.
[22] *Cf.* McGucken, *op. cit.*, pp. 23-29.

Ratio, had a considerable share in the results that attended their system. Above all, what is most characteristic in the Jesuit system, the wonderful unity and organization, was not borrowed from any other system, but is the work of the framers of the Constitutions and of the Ratio Studiorum.[23]

The Society grew rapidly but was unable to meet all the demands for its services in the educational and missionary fields.[24] Bishops everywhere invited the Fathers to establish colleges in their dioceses and consequently within fifty years after the approval of the Order it had spread over the entire world, "from Europe to the Indies, from China and Japan in the East to Mexico and Brazil in the West. Wherever the Church was not actually persecuted, as in England, there sprang up educational institutions." In 1615, the Society conducted 373 colleges; in 1706, its colleges and universities numbered 769, and in 1756, 728, and the numbers of students attending were large. Rouen, France, had regularly 2,000; the College of Louis-le-Grand, Paris, usually enrolled between 1,800 and 3,000. Cologne began in 1558 with nearly 800, and Utrecht had 1,000. The total number of students in the seven hundred and more institutions of the Order before the suppression had been estimated as 210,000.[25] Through the suppression of the Order and the closing of its colleges and universities Catholic education and learning suffered greatly. The Society was formally restored in 1814 by Pope Pius VII and again empowered "to undertake the education of youth in the principles of the Catholic faith, to form

---

[23] Schwickerath, *op. cit.*, p. 142.

[24] The idea of a vast organization was foreign to the original purpose of St. Ignatius. He visualized a very select body of men, about sixty in number, university men, gifted, trained who would serve at the Pope's command. They were to sit in at the councils of kings, oppose the claims of heresiarchs, and by their learning and eloquence assure the leadership in the university centers. *Cf.* McGucken, *op. cit.*, p. 6.

[25] Schwickerath, *op. cit.*, p. 145.

them to good morals, and to direct colleges and seminaries." [26]

Teaching was again enthusiastically resumed. Colleges were opened in new fields, especially in England and her dependencies, and in the United States, and the cherished work of the Order, despite many hardships and trials, has been successfully prosecuted to the present time.

Other Teaching Orders

Special attention was paid during the Counter Reformation to the education of girls. The Benedictine convents of the North suffered much from the Reformation, and the Beguines of the Netherlands, who were often, like the Canonesses Regular, the teachers of girls in towns and villages, lost many of their establishments. None of these communities had for its primary purpose the education of girls, although many had undertaken the work extensively. The Order of St. Ursula, or the Ursulines, founded by *St. Angela Merici* (1474-1540), enjoyed this distinction in the history of education. The foundress, a native of Desenzano, a small village in Lombardy, Italy, was convinced that the greatest need of her time was the religious instruction of girls. She began the work modestly in her own home, gathering little girls about her for daily instruction in the elements of Christian Doctrine. She was successful from the beginning and in a short time was directing a number of zealous young women in the same occupation. An invitation from Brescia encouraged her to extend her operations, and there in 1535 with her chosen companions, twelve in all, St. Angela took her religious vows and became superioress of the community.[27]

---

[26] *Sollicitudo omnium ecclesiarum* of Pope Pius VII.

[27] The members were uncloistered religious women. St. Angela labored for forty years before she gained papal approval for her

The first Ursulines were encouraged by St. Charles Borromeo, who obtained for them the status of an order with enclosure, and they rapidly established themselves in Italy, Germany, and France. Their labors in all departments of female education have continued to the present. Reference might be made to their early educational establishments in Canada (1639) and the United States (1729). Their institution in Quebec is the oldest for the education of women in North America.

St. Joseph Calasanctius (†1648), a Spanish priest of noble family, opened in Rome in 1597 a free school for poor boys and girls. Encouraged by Pope Clement VIII in his undertaking, he won followers among the clergy and established the Order of Piarists whose schools spread into the cities of northern Italy, Austria, and Poland. During the eighteenth century they conducted many free elementary schools, as well as secondary or Latin schools.

The Fathers of Christian Doctrine (*Pères de la Doctrine Chrétienne*), founded in 1593 by a French priest, the Venerable César de Bus, for the religious education of the young, extended over France and Italy and eventually included among their activities the education of orphans and the blind.

FOR FURTHER STUDY

Adamson, John W., *Pioneers of Modern Education.* Cambridge: Cambridge University Press, 1905.

Campbell, Thomas, *The Jesuits.* New York: The Encyclopedia Press, 1921.

Corcoran, T., *Renatae litterae saeculo a Chr. XVI in scholis Societatis Jesu stabilitae.* Dublin: National University, 1927.

Donnelly, Francis P., *Principles of Jesuit Education in Practice.* New York: P. S. Kennedy & Sons, 1934.

---

congregation. The veil had always been symbolic of the cloistered nun and the Church was reluctant to grant permission for the founding of a community of uncloistered religious women.

Drane, A. T., *Christian Schools and Scholars*. London: Burns Oates and Washbourne, Lt., 1924.

Graves, F. P., *History of Education During the Middle Ages*. New York: The Macmillan Company, 1910.

Harvey, Martin P., *The Jesuits in History*. New York: The America Press, 1941.

Heimbucher, M., *Die Orden und Kongregationen der Katholischen Kirche*. Paderborn: F. Schöningh, 1907.

Hubert, J., *Die heilige Angela Merici*. Mainz: F. Kirchheim, 1891.

Hughes, T., *Loyola and the Educational System of the Jesuits*. New York: Charles Scribner's Sons, 1892.

Hyma, A., *The Christian Renaissance: A History of the "Devotio Moderna."* New York: The Century Co., 1925.

Kane, W., *An Essay Toward the History of Education*. Chicago: Loyola University Press, 1935.

Marique, P. J., *History of Christian Education*. New York: Fordham University Press, 1926. Vol. II.

Maurenbrecher, W., *Geschichte der Katholischen Reformation*. Noerdlingen: Bect, 1880.

McGucken, W., *The Jesuits and Education*. Milwaukee: The Bruce Publishing Company, 1932.

Monica, Sr. M., *Angela Merici and Her Teaching Idea*. New York: Longmans, Green, and Company, 1927.

Monumenta Germaniae paedagogica. Vols. II, V, IX, and XVI.

O'Reilly, B., *St. Angela Merici and the Ursulines*. New York: Pollard and Moss, 1880.

Pachtler, G., *Ratio studiorum et institutiones scholasticae Societatis Jesu per Germaniam olim vigentes*. Berlin: Hofmann, 1887-94. 4 vols.

Schwickerath, R., *Jesuit Education: Its History and Principles in the Light of Modern Educational Problems*. St. Louis: B. Herder Co., 1904.

Van Dyke, Paul, *Ignatius Loyola: The Founder of the Jesuits*. New York: Charles Scribner's Sons, 1926.

Ward, A. W., *The Counter-Reformation*. London: Longmans, Green, and Co., 1889.

SUMMARY OF RENAISSANCE AND REFORMATION PERIOD

The revival of ancient culture, although inaugurated as a movement in the fourteenth and fifteenth centuries, had its beginnings in the Middle Ages. Classical studies had never been entirely neglected in medieval schools. The Renaissance began in Italy and its course was determined by Italian scholars. Some of its notable patrons were the popes of the period. Educational theory as expounded by Italian writers, and educational practice as seen in the Renaissance schools, show the influence of Greek and Roman ideals on the education of Christian youth. The humanities were then successfully taught in the schools and became the chief elements in the curriculum which has survived until modern times.

Italy directly influenced the Renaissance movement in other countries, viz., France, Spain, Germany, and England. The Brethren of the Common Life were among the most noteworthy influences in the North. Some of their pupils were famous humanists, e.g., Erasmus. Vives, a Spaniard who lived mostly in the North, was the greatest educator of the period. The Renaissance in England was inspired by Italy, and the first educational treatises produced in England closely resembled those of the Italian Renaissance.

By the sixteenth century the educators of Western Europe in general were agreed that the humanities should be made the basis of a liberal education. However, through the slavish imitation of the writings of Cicero, the work of the schools became narrowly grammatical and linguistic. This decadent type of humanistic education eventually made Latin a dead language and reduced the new learning for the next four hundred years to a study of formal Latin grammar.

The first effects of the Reformation were destructive of schools and educational facilities. Higher education was especially affected. The unity of Europe was shattered; and the cosmopolitan character of the universities disappeared. The state exercised a rigorous control over university teaching in England, Scotland, and the Protestant German principalities. Luther and Melanchthon strove to reopen schools, but neither of them sought to establish a new type of elementary or secondary school.

In the secondary schools they really reproduced the Renaissance type. The famous schools of Trotzendorf, Sturm, and Neander were Latin schools. In England, the Reformation dealt a severe blow to the grammar schools and every type of school from the university downward, without supplying a substitute for what was confiscated or destroyed. Education practically ceased for Catholics in England and Ireland. In the Catholic Reaction, distinct measures in behalf of schools were adopted by the Council of Trent and provincial council. The older religious orders renewed their educational efforts and new orders, notably the Jesuits, entered the field.

Part IV

Modern Education

SYNOPSIS OF REALISM

1. REACTION FROM HUMANISM
    (a) Movement to counteract extreme aspect of the humanistic system of studies
    (b) Work of schools became formal and unreal for the man of affairs
    (c) Literary forms and words studied; ideas neglected; also, practical values in the subjects pursued neglected

2. HUMANISTIC REALISTS
    (a) Retained the humanities as the content of instruction
    (b) Advocated the study of ideas and training in judgment instead of literary or philological skill
    (c) Representatives are Rabelais, Montaigne, and Mulcaster

3. FRANÇOIS RABELAIS (1483-1553)
    (a) Realist, naturalist, humorist, humanist
    (b) Educational ideal is that of the Renaissance and similar to that of Erasmus
    (c) His educational ideas expressed in *Gargantua and Pantagruel*
    (d) Points out necessity of teaching through observation and through association of all instruction with practical life; value of physical training; gentleness in methods of discipline
    (e) Influenced later theorists—Montaigne, Locke, Fénelon, and Rousseau

4. MICHEL EYQUEM DE MONTAIGNE (1533-1592)
    (a) Essayist
    (b) *Pedantry* and *Education of Children* look to the practical purposes of study
    (c) Favored tutorial system over the class method of instruction
    (d) Critical of the school training of the time; complained that teachers attended too much to memorizing and not enough to thinking
    (e) Believed that the exercise of expression is one of the best indications of the pupil's progress

(f) Held that the vernacular should be studied before Latin or Greek on account of its real utility

(g) Approved of physical exercises in all games and pastimes of the period

(h) Urged the exposure of the young to the extremes of heat and cold, and to wind and sun

(i) Desired that the young be trained to virtue, but did not give the means for this moral training

(j) Offered many wholesome views on the practical side of training and influenced Locke and Rousseau

5. RICHARD MULCASTER (1531-1611)

(a) First headmaster of Merchant Taylors' School, London, for twenty-five years; directed St. Paul's School, London, for twelve years

(b) His *Elementarie* contains modern views on elementary education

(c) Appealed for the best teachers in the elementary classes

(d) Advocated giving a good knowledge of English before beginning Latin

(e) His *Positions* best expresses his views on physical training

(f) Maintained that girls should have almost the same training as boys

(g) The first to propose to England a college for the professional training of teachers

(h) Lacked an attractive style and his works were not widely read; his views were far in advance of his age, but had little effect on English schools; influenced later theorists

6. SENSE REALISTS

(a) Inaugurated the scientific movement in education

(b) Looked to nature and natural phenomena for the content of study and investigation

(c) Observed processes of nature for lessons in teaching

(d) Held that things in the objective order come before words; made sense perception a fundamental means to learning

7. FRANCIS BACON (1561-1626)
  (a) Rarely wrote directly on educational topics
  (b) Believed he had a mission to perform in behalf of science and learning
  (c) *Novum organum* (1620), *De augmentis scientiarum* (1623), *Sylva sylvarum* (1624) chiefly express his educational theories; *New Atlantis* and essays also show his educational views
  (d) Development of the inductive method is his great contribution to science and ultimately, through Ratke and Comenius, to education
  (e) Included education among the sciences to be studied; his principles were destined to be of far-reaching effect in the hands of later educators
8. WOLFGANG RATKE (1571-1635)
  (a) Most important educational ideas contained in his *Methodus institutionis nova,* published at Leipzig, 1617
  (b) Educational efforts failed due to contentiousness and lack of tact and administrative power
  (c) Influence slight on contemporaries; prepared way for Comenius
  (d) Shortcomings in his method—too much repetition, too much uniformity, and too great attention to the inductive process
  (e) Good points in his method—teaching in accordance with the child's nature; the use of the vernacular; thoroughness in what is studied; mildness in discipline
9. JOHN AMOS COMENIUS (1592-1671)
  (a) Pansophia or universal wisdom fundamental to his educational plan; his pansophic scheme in its literary aspect resembles the medieval attempt of Vincent of Beauvais and in its institutional equipment the Baconian pansophic university
  (b) *Didactica magna, Janua linguarum reserata, Vestibulum, Linguarum methodus novissima, Orbis sensualium pictus* reveal his educational theories and principles

      (c) Textbooks relied too much on information and did not consistently embody the principles of induction to which he subscribed

      (d) His principles adopted and elaborated by later upholders of sense training, correlation, and natural method

10. OTHER REALISTS AND THEORISTS

      (a) John Locke—in his theories of physical and religious training, a naturalist chiefly; in his conception of mental training, a rationalistic disciplinarian; in his treatment of the mind, a sense realist, speculatively; in practice his realism was humanistic

      (b) Archishop Fénelon—like Montaigne and Locke he was practical in his educational views; like Comenius he was a student and upholder of natural and psychological methods; because of his attention to child psychology and especially to curiosity and interest, he may be regarded as the forerunner of Herbart

11. JOHN LOCKE (1632-1704)

      (a) Ranks as the first of British empiricists; basic doctrine is all knowledge is acquired by experience

      (b) Educational views expressed in *Essay Concerning the Human Understanding* (1690); *Thoughts Concerning Education* (1693); *Conduct of the Understanding* (1706, posthumous)

      (c) First section of *Thoughts* devoted to physical training

      (d) Scheme of moral education admits the elements of divine revelation, but left it opened to the questioning of mere human reason; moral system was utilitarian and rationalistic, if not materialistic

      (e) In his description of the tutor the general character of mental training is presented; not a formal disciplinarian; insisted upon a curriculum embracing a wide range of subjects; rejected the idea that what is hard or difficult has special disciplinary value; recognized that the ability to reason upon any subject demands specific knowledge of the facts and of the specific technique involved

(f) Wrote for one class in English society, the gentry; his ideas were not intended for and not adopted in the schools; influenced English and American education especially in regard to the training process, the embodiment of the idea of discipline in education

12. FRANÇOIS DE SALIGNAC DE LA MOTHE FÉNELON (1651-1715)

(a) Educational writings—*Fables, Dialogues of the Dead, Adventures of Telemachus, Treatise on the Education of Girls* which ranks first among French educational classics

(b) Treats of elementary education in general and pleads for greater attention to the education of girls; views on training in infancy similar to those of the humanists and of Locke; from careful observation of children he advocated the use of gradual and indirect instruction, urged the value of leading over driving, and suggested practical devices for applying the principle of interest as a motive for education

(c) Suggests the modern normal school idea for religious and secular organizations devoted to training girls

(d) Believed that the education of girls should be different from that of boys; his general rule was to train girls according to their rank and station in life

CHAPTER XXII

REALISM

Realism, a reaction from Humanism, was that movement in the history of education which tended to counteract the ultra-literary or extreme aspect of the humanistic system. With the study of literary forms, of words, had arisen a neglect of ideas and the practical values in the subjects pursued; the work of the schools had become as formal and as unreal for the man of affairs as it ever had been in any of the older periods. The first phase of Realism offered a check to the extreme movement by recalling the real purpose of the study of the classics, by keeping in view the practical ends of training, and by substituting the study of ideas, training in judgment and power for literary or philological skill. These Realists retained the humanities as the content of instruction and are known as Humanistic Realists. They insisted that the work in Latin grammar be limited to the minimum requirement for the study and appreciation of literature. Emphasis was upon knowledge and that knowledge was to be gotten mainly from a wide reading of ancient literature, both sacred and secular. The ancients were not regarded as the only source of knowledge but were studied for the useful information which they could contribute in all branches of learning.[1]

The second phase of Realism begins with Bacon and undertakes to find in nature and natural phenomena the content of study and investigation. Instead of a reality found in books and experienced in human relationships,

---

[1] *Cf.* Paul Monroe, *Test-Book in the History of Education* (New York: The Macmillan Company, 1909), pp. 44 f; Eby and Arrowood, *Development of Modern Education* (New York: Prentice-Hall, Inc., 1935), p. 201.

the basic reality was to be found in the forces and laws of nature.[2] This phase of Realism, also known as Scientific Realism, inaugurated the scientific movement in education. The languages are used as tool subjects; and the curriculum is made pansophic with the hope that through the teaching of all knowledge a new social order would be constructed. The processes of nature are observed for their lessons in teaching; things in the objective order then come before words; and sense perception is made a fundamental means to learning. The exponents of this phase are the Sense Realists.

Humanistic Realists

François Rabelais (1483-1553), the celebrated French writer, has been variously styled realist, naturalist, humorist, or humanist. As an educational writer he seems most properly to come under the last classification for his ideal is that of the Renaissance and very similar to the one upheld by Erasmus.

Rabelais began his studies with the Benedictines of his native place, Chinon, in Touraine. He continued them under the Franciscans near Angers, became a member of the Order and was ordained to the priesthood. His life was very irregular and for the most part that of a wanderer. After leaving the monastery, for what reasons we are not certain, he became a medical student in Montpellier. Pope Paul III, at the instance of Cardinal Du Bellay, a friend and schoolfellow of Rabelais, absolved the ex-monk from the censures he had incurred and allowed him to practice medicine. He taught medicine at Lyons, and appeared afterward as a physician at Turin and Metz. As curé of Meudon he later resumed ecclesiastical duties, performing them seriously and regularly. He died in Paris.

---

[2] *Cf.* E. H. Wilde, *The Foundations of Modern Education* (New York: Farrar & Rinehart, 1936), p. 332.

Rabelais' educational ideas were expressed in his romances *Gargantua and Pantagruel*.[3] He depicts the older and the newer education in the training of Gargantua. His account is, of course, exaggerated and extravagant both in criticizing the old and in praising the new; yet, while it cannot in any sense be literally accepted, it must be viewed as an important satire on the education of the time.

Gargantua from three years upward until five was brought up and instructed in all convenient discipline by the commandment of his father, and spent that time like the other little children of the country, that is, in drinking, eating, and sleeping; in eating, sleeping, and drinking; and in sleeping, drinking, and eating.

About the end of his fifth year Grandgousier, his father, became convinced from a conversation with him that "his understanding did participate of some divinity" and that if he were well taught and had a fitting education he would attain to a supreme degree of wisdom. "Therefore will I commit him to some learned man to have him indoctrinated according to his capacity, and will spare no cost."

Presently they appointed him a great sophister-doctor, called Master Tubal Holofernes, who taught him his A B C so well, that he could say it by heart backward and about this he was five years and three months. Then read he to him *Donat, le Facet, Theodolet and Alanus in parabolis*. About this he was thirteen years, six months and two weeks ......
.... After that he read unto him the book *de Modis significandi* with the commentaries of Hurtbise, of Fasquin, . . . ; and herein he spent more than eighteen years and eleven months, and was so well versed in it that to try masteries in school disputes with his

---

[3] *Life of Gargantua and the Heroic Deeds of Pantagruel.* Translated by T. Urquhart and P. Motteux (New York: Boni and Liveright, 1933). 2 vols.

condisciples he would recite it by heart backward and did sometimes prove on his finger ends to his mother, *quod de modis significandi non erat scientia.*[4]

Thus Gargantua's education continued until his preceptor died and his father "got an old coughing fellow to teach him, named Master Jobelin Bride," by whose teaching Gargantua "became as wise as any we have ever since baked in an oven."

Finally his father perceived that Gargantua, although he studied hard, learned nothing, but "what is worse, grew thereby foolish, simple, doted and blockish" and when shown Eudemon, the pupil of the new schools, not yet twelve years old, was immediately in favor of a similar training for his son.

Rabelais gives a humorous description of the contrast between Eudemon and Gargantua:

The former with his cap in hand, a clear and open countenance, beautiful and ruddy lips, his eyes steady, and his looks fixed on Gargantua, with a youthful modesty, standing up straight on his feet, began very gracefully to commend him; first for his virtue and good manners; secondly for his knowledge; thirdly for his nobility; fourthly for his bodily accomplishments; and in the fifth place, most sweetly exhorted him to reverence his father with all due observancy, who was so careful to have him well brought up. . . . All this was by him delivered with such proper gestures, such distinct pronunciation, so pleasant a delivery, in such exquisite terms and so good Latin, that he seemed rather a Gracchus, a Cicero, an Aemilius of the time past than a youth of this age. But all the countenance that Gargantua kept was that he fell to crying like a cow, and cast down his face, hiding it with his cap, nor could they possibly draw one word from him, . . . Whereat his father was so grievously vexed that he would have killed Master Jobelin. . . .[5]

---

[4] *Ibid.,* I, 42-56.
[5] *Ibid.,* p. 59.

He then began a new method of study, so that he lost not any one hour in the day, but employed all his time in learning and honest knowledge. The tutor studied Gargantua and gradually changed his manner of life and study. The new training offers a perfect contrast to the old especially in the spirit in which it is given and received. The new teacher is intelligent and gentle; he instructs under favorable conditions, reviewing lessons with the pupil while playing and exercising; he directs the powers of observation at all times; and he gives interesting instruction even at meals in connection with the dishes, bread, wine, meats, fishes, herbs, etc. The pupil falls in love with arithmetic because of the pleasant beginning made with the subject, and so he remains throughout the higher courses in mathematics. At the close of the day the master reviewed with the pupil "what he had read, seen, learned, done and understood in the whole course of that day."

In a letter of Gargantua to his son, Pantagruel, we have a positive expression of Rabelais' views on the content of instruction, which like all of his writings is a mixture of jest and earnest.

Wherefore, my son, I admonish thee to employ thy youth to profit as well as thou canst, both in thy studies and in virtue. . . . I intend and will have it so that thou learn the languages perfectly; first of all, the Greek, as Quintilian will have it; secondly the Latin; and then the Hebrew, for the Holy Scripture sake; and then the Chaldee and Arabic likewise, and that thou frame thy style in Greek in imitation of Plato; and for the Latin after Cicero. Let there be no history which thou shalt not have ready in thy memory. . . . As for the civil law of that I would have thee to know the texts by heart, and then to confer them with philosophy.[6]

In matter of the knowledge of the works of nature he would have Pantagruel study that exactly; so that

----

[6] *Ibid.,* pp. 287 f.

there be no sea, river, nor fountain of which he does not know the fishes, so that of birds, trees and shrubs, herbs and flowers, metals and stores nothing will be hidden from him. He would have him in short become "an abyss and bottomless pit of knowledge, as well as a knight and defender of his house."[7]

There has been much discussion as to the purpose of Rabelais' writings. Undoubtedly he introduced much that was serious with the ridiculous, and while his descriptions are all overdrawn and exaggerated, he did point out the necessity of teaching through observation and through association of all instruction with practical life; also the value of physical training and of gentleness in methods of discipline. His views, which may be termed realistic as well as humanistic, influenced later theorists, especially Montaigne, Locke, Fénelon, and Rousseau.[8]

The successor of Rabelais among educational theorists was *Michel Eyquem, Seigneur de Montaigne*[9] (1533-

---

[7] This pansophic curriculum outlined by Rabelais was adopted by Milton in his tractate *Of Education* addressed to Master Samuel Hartlib. Milton did not favor the tutorial idea of Rabelais but suggested a single institution of learning which he called the Academy in which the entire education of the boy could be given instead of dividing it between the secondary school and the university. This scheme of education influenced the development of the academy in the American colonies; it replaced the Latin grammar school.

[8] Quick credits the writings of Rabelais with considerable educational purport. *Cf. Educational Reformers,* pp. 65 ff; Eby and Arrowood also claim that he exercised a powerful educational influence. *Cf. The Development of Modern Education,* pp. 208-13. Kane maintains that Rabelais' contribution to later educational thinkers was nothing but ribald and excremental humor; it is impossible to see how they could have made any educational use of it. *Cf. An Essay Toward A History of Education,* pp. 318 f.

[9] Also called a Social Realist because he advocated a practical education by which the versatile "man of the world" would be prepared to get along harmoniously with other people in all the activities of life,

92). Born at Périgord, near Bordeaux, the son of a landed proprietor, he received from his earliest years a systematic and well-planned training. His father evidently had his own ideas on the question of early training, or had the advantage of expert direction in the matter, for everything in connection with the child's rearing was carefully planned. The tutor, for example, although a German, and all others who came in contact with the child, were obliged to speak Latin with him. In the morning the child was awakened by the soft strains of music so that he would suffer no shock. This was characteristic of the mildness and care with which he was brought up.

When Montaigne entered the Collège de Guyenne at Bordeaux, then in his seventh year, he could speak Latin fluently. At thirteen he had completed the course and had in the meantime read widely. He then pursued a course in law; but an active career did not appeal to him and at the age of thirty-seven, when counselor of the Parliament of Bordeaux, he resigned his office and went into retirement. Toward the end of his life he was chosen Mayor of Bordeaux. It is quite generally agreed that Montaigne was not a great lawyer or a statesman, any more than he was a deep scholar and philosopher. Although skeptical and Pyrrhonistic in his philosophical views, he nevertheless always retained some attachment to religion and to the Church. He died, it is true, without receiving the Sacraments, but while Mass was being read at his request in the room where he lay.

Montaigne's position in educational history was won by his brilliant essays,[10] chiefly those on *Pedantry* and

---

[10] There are about ninety-nine in all. written in French, most of them brief and slightly pedantic. *Pedantry* and the *Education of Children* are directly concerned with education. In the English translation. the former covers about twelve pages and the latter, about thirty-six.

the *Education of Children*. Because he looked to the
practical purposes of study, he is known as a realist.
He endeavored to take what he considered a common-
sense view of everything, teaching that one should live
for all of life's enjoyments and should avoid all trouble
and sorrow.

His aim in education was to train the reason and
judgment so as to secure moderation of mind and the
practice of virtue, and to train the body to serve as
the ready instrument of the soul. Education was not to
develop mind and body separately, but together for
the whole man. He hoped to produce the cultured and
capable man of affairs.

Favoring the tutorial system or individual instruction
over the class method, he contrasted the results of the
school training of the time with his ideal. The teachers
then, he contended, gave the form of knowledge, or
learning, without being sure of the boy's understanding
or using what he learned. They attended too much to
memorizing and not enough to thinking.

I would have the tutor make the child examine and thoroughly sift all things, and harbour nothing in his head by
mere authority or upon trust ....
....
Who ever inquires of his pupil what he thinks of rhetoric, of
grammar, of this, or that sentence of Cicero? Our teachers
stick them full-feathered in our memories, and there establish
them like oracles, of which the very words and letters are the
substance of the thing. To know by heart only is not to
know at all; it is simply to keep what one has committed to
his memory. What a man knows directly, that will he dispose
of without turning to his book or looking to his pattern.[11]

The teacher was not to do all for the child but to
direct study, encouraging reflection and action upon

---

[11] *Education of Children.* Translated by L. E. Rector (New
York: D. Appleton and Company, 1899), pp. 31; 33.

what was learned. Exercise in expression is one of the best tests of the pupil's progress. The matter of instruction must be assimilated by the child or else he does not learn. "What is the good of having the stomach full of meat if it cannot nourish us?"

Montaigne also held that the vernacular should be studied before Latin or Greek on account of its real utility. Things come, however, before words.

Let our pupil be furnished with things—words will come only too fast; if they do not come readily, he will reach after them. I have heard some make excuses because they cannot express themselves, and pretend to have their heads full of a great many very fine things which for want of words they cannot bring out. . . . They do not know themselves what they are trying to say, and if you notice how they haggle and stammer, you will soon conclude their pretensions to learning are downright false. For my part I hold, and Socrates is positive in it, that whoever has in his mind a clear and vivid idea, will express it well enough in one way or another; and if he be dumb, by signs.[12]

Montaigne opposed the verbalism and the ultra-literary instruction associated with the later humanism. Thoughts came first; form and expression were later considerations. In history, lessons were to be drawn from an appreciation of the characters studied, the reason for certain happenings exacted rather than the memory of them. Dates were unimportant in comparison to the lessons in prudence and experience contained in history. This was, in fact, the main study in his scheme, the one most befitting a young gentleman, and was to be pursued with most attention. In all of the remaining subjects of the curriculum, he proposed a real purpose, namely, the utility of the study for the pupil's present needs. Mere learning of itself he condemned.

---

[12] *Ibid.,* p. 69.

"If the mind be not better disposed, if the judgment be not better settled, I would rather my student had spent his time at tennis, for at least his body would be in better health by that exercise."[13]

Montaigne thought parents were often too indulgent to children in not permitting them to suffer some hardships in order to develop their bodily powers for the strain of life. He approved of physical participation in all the gains and pastimes of the period such as riding, hunting, running, and jumping; and, keeping the training of the man in view, he advocated the exposure of the young to the extremes of heat and cold, and to wind and sun. He would wean the child from all effeminacy in eating, drinking, clothes, and lodging.

Montaigne desired pleasant surroundings in the classroom and a milder discipline than prevailed in the colleges he knew of.[14] "Where their profit is, there should also be their pleasure." He also desired that the young be trained to virtue but did not suggest the means for this moral training.[15] His writings, like those of his predecessor, Rabelais, widely read in his own time and

---

[13] *Pedantry.* Translated by L. E. Rector (New York: D. Appleton and Company, 1899), p. 96.

[14] Montaigne had little use for schools and colleges as agencies in education. He urged the use of a tutor just as Rabelais had done. Members of the French aristocracy who came under the influence of his social realism favored a school which should turn out a "gentleman" instead of a "pedant." Such schools were later set up under the name of academies. Richelieu was instrumental in establishing several. Their development in Germany was much more pronounced than in France. The sons of noblemen were withdrawn from the *gymnasien* and enrolled in the *Ritterakademie.*

[15] His moral training was an adaptation to the social customs of the gentleman ". . . . let a young man accustom himself to all nations and companies, even to debauching and excess, if he do so simply out of regard to the customs of a place. Let him be able to do everything, but love to do nothing but what is good . . . . Let the young man laugh, carouse, and debauch with his princes; . . ." *Cf.* Rector, *Education of Children,* p. 64.

ever since, are chiefly critical of the period. He offers, however, with his criticism many wholesome views on the practical side of training and some which were to have a profound influence on Locke and Rousseau.

In the Englishman *Richard Mulcaster* (1531-1611) were combined a schoolmaster of long experience and an educational writer whose views were far in advance of his age. He was born of poor parents in Cumberland, and received his education at Eton, Cambridge, and Oxford. He graduated from Oxford in 1556, and was then well versed in the classics and in Hebrew. When the Merchant Taylors' School, London, was founded, in 1560, Mulcaster was appointed the first headmaster, an office which he held for over twenty-five years. Queen Elizabeth conferred upon him the rectorship of Stanford Rivers, but he attended more to teaching than to clerical offices. The Merchant Taylors' School prospered under his direction. Because of trouble with the governors he resigned, and for twelve years directed St. Paul's School, London.

Mulcaster's conceited and haughty spirit showed itself in his writings. Although he wrote in English, he lacked an attractive style and for this reason his works were not read widely enough to be of great contemporary influence.[16] They possessed real value, nevertheless, for many of his ideas and theories have been adopted in the nineteenth century and put into practice. His first work appeared in 1581 bearing the title: *Positions wherein those Primitive Circumstances be examined, which are necessarie for the Training up of Children,*

---

[16] He regarded his own age as the golden age of English and proposed his own writings as the model to be followed in the writing of English. He had the boldness to criticize the English of Shakespeare. It is suspected that Shakespeare used him as the model for the schoolmaster whom he ridiculed in *Love's Labour's Lost.*

either for skill in their Booke or Health in their Bodie.
A later work (1582), *Elementarie which entreateth
chieflie of the right Writing of the English tung*, contains additional views on the beginnings of education.

Mulcaster had a very modern view of the importance
of elementary training. For this reason he wrote the
Elementarie. He did not fix the age at which school life
should begin; for this, he believed, depended upon the
individual. The beginning being the most important
phase of training, it was necessary to have the best
teachers for it, and hence these should be the best paid
of all. In the face of conditions which have prevailed
almost to the present time Mulcaster's views on this
point are remarkable. In appealing for the best teachers
in the elementary classes, he says:

The first master can deal but with a few, the next with
more, and so still upward as reason groweth on and receives
without forcing. It is the foundation well and soundly laid,
which makes all the upper building muster, with countenance
and continuance. If I were to strike the stroke as I am but
to give counsel, the first pains truly taken should in good
truth be most liberally recompensed; and less allowed still
upward, as the pains diminish and the ease increaseth. Whereat no master hath cause to repine, so he may have his children
well grounded in the Elementarie. Whose imperfection at this
day doth marvelously trouble both masters and scholars, so
that we can hardly do any good, nay, scantly tell how to place
the too too raw boys in any certain form, with hope to go
forward orderly, the ground-work of their entry being so rot-
ten underneath.[17]

Mulcaster advocated the use of English in the elementary classes and urged laying a good foundation in
it before beginning Latin. He maintained that our best
understanding is in our natural tongue and that all

---

[17] *Positions* (London: Longmans, Green, and Company, 1887)
pp. 223 f.

learning in foreign languages is understood by means of our own. In the *Elementarie* he writes:

> I honour foreign tongues, but wish my own to be partaker of their honour. Knowing them, I wish my own tongue to resemble their grace. I confess their furniture, and wish it were ours.[18]

In the elementary period, besides reading and writing he desired that singing, playing of a musical instrument, and drawing be taught.[19] Assuming that instruction begins at six, the child would profit most by a thorough fundamental training lasting until his twelfth year. In the higher or grammar school he would spend five years; but in regard to this curriculum Mulcaster did not differ essentially from the practice of the time. As already noted, he was a headmaster of two of London's most famous Latin schools. He discusses in greater detail than previous writers the physical aspect of training. A large part—fully one-third of the *Positions*—treats of games and exercises like dancing, running, leaping, swimming, wrestling, riding, hunting, and of physiology and the conservation of health.

In Mulcaster's plan girls should have almost the same training as boys, that is, cultural, literary, and musical. He pleads for this as for the maintenance of a venerable custom in his country which "hath made the maiden's train (education) her own approved travail." Another important appeal is that for the professional training of teachers. He is the first to have proposed to England, and to Cambridge in particular, the practical scheme of training teachers at the university, in a college especially designated for them.

---

[18] Quoted by Quick, *Educational Reformers*, p. 534.

[19] Arithmetic is not mentioned. It was not until the middle of the seventeenth century that this subject may be said to have won its place as the third of the three R's.

Why should not teachers be well provided for, to continue their whole life in the school, as Divines, Lawyers, Physicians do in their several professions? Thereby judgment, cunning, and discretion will grow in them; and masters would prove old men, and such as Xenophon setteth over children in the schooling of Cyrus.[20]

He urged his plea "that this trade requireth a particular college" first, because the education of children is the means to make or mar the whole fry of the nation; second, because of the number of children and of teachers; third, because of the necessity of the profession of teaching which cannot be spared; fourth, because of the nature and dignity of the science and art of teaching.

This schoolmaster would extend the facilities for education to all as their common right, but he would also restrict the number of the learned lest they become idle and seditious. Mulcaster's most notable contributions to the theory of his time were in behalf of elementary education, the use of the vernacular, the preparation of teachers, and the method of teaching which should respect the powers of the child and tend towards a symmetrical development physically and intellectually. His ideas had little effect on English schools, but later theorists were deeply influenced by them.

FOR FURTHER STUDY

Adamson, J. W., *Pioneers of Modern Education.* Cambridge: University Press, 1905.

Arnstädt, F. A., *François Rabelais und sein Traité d'Education mit besonderer Berucksichtigung der pädagogischen Grundsätze Montaigne's, Locke's und Rousseau's.* Leipzig: Siegismund & Volkening, 1877.

Barnard, H., *English Pedagogy.* Philadelphia: J. B. Lippincott & Co., 1862.

Bonnefon, P., *Montaigne, l'homme et l'oeuvre.* Paris: J. Rouam et Cie, 1893.

---

[20] *Positions,* p. 248.

Browning, O.. *Introduction to History of Educational Theories.* Kegan Paul, Trench & Co., 1881.

Collins, W. L., *Montaigne.* Philadelphia: J. B. Lippincott, 1879.

Laurie, S. S., *Educational Opinion from the Renaissance.* Cambridge: The University Press, 1903.

Mark, H., *Educational Theories in England.* London: S. Sonnenschein & Co., 1899.

Monroe, P., *Text-Book in the History of Education.* New York: The Macmillan Company, 1909.

Montaigne, M., *Essais.* Edited by J. V. Leclerc. Reprinted, Paris: Garnier, 1925.

————, *Essays.* Translated by Charles Cotton. Edited by W. C. Hazlitt. New York: Boni, 1923. 5 vols.

————, Essays. Translated by L. E. Rector. New York: D. Appleton & Co., 1899.

————, *Essays.* Translated by E. J. Trechmann. Oxford: University Press, 1927. 2 vols.

Mulcaster, R., *Elementarie.* Edited by E. T. Campagnac. Oxford: Oxford University Press, 1925.

————, *Positions.* London: Longmans, Green, and Company, 1887.

————, *Positions.* Edited by R. H. Quick, Syracuse: Bardeen, [n.d.].

Oliphant, J., *The Educational Writings of Richard Mulcaster.* Glasgow: J. Maclehose & Sons, 1903.

Plattard, J., *The Life of François Rabelais.* Translated by L. P. Roche. New York: A. A. Knopf, 1931.

Quick, R. H., *Educational Reformers.* New York: D. Appleton and Company, 1907.

Rabelais, F., *Oeuvres.* Edited by P. d'Espezel. Paris: à l'enseigne de la Cité des livres, 1930. 4 vols.

————, *Life of Gargantua and the Heroic Deeds of Pantagruel.* Translated by T. Urquhart and P. Motteux. New York: Boni and Liveright, 1933. 2 vols.

Watson, F., *Richard Mulcaster and his Elementarie.* London: Educational Times, 1893.

Wilds. E. H., *The Foundations of Modern Education.* New York: Farrar & Rinehart, 1936.

CHAPTER XXIII

REALISM (Continued)

Sense Realists

Francis Bacon (Lord Verulam) (1561-1626), another Englishman, claims attention here as an educational innovator. He was the son of Sir Nicholas Bacon, Lord Keeper of the Great Seal under Queen Elizabeth, and of Anne, the daughter of Sir Anthony Cooke, the renowned tutor of Edward VI. It is thought that his early education was received at home under tutors. He entered Trinity College, Cambridge, at the age of thirteen. Three years later he began the study of law but quickly discontinued it to become attached in some official way to the English embassy in Paris. "After he had passed the circle of the liberal arts," says his early biographer, "his father thought fit to frame and mould him for the arts of state." [1] Returning to England after his father's death, he resumed the study of law and was admitted to practice in 1582, being then twenty-one years of age. Two years later he was elected to Parliament and quickly won recognition for his ability as a speaker and writer. He made a close friend of Essex, the favorite of Queen Elizabeth, but did not succeed in gaining the royal favor and patronage as readily as he desired; for, as Rawley observed, though Elizabeth "cheered him with the bounty of her countenance, yet she never cheered him with the bounty of her hand." [2]

Bacon sued more successfully for advancement under James I. From Counsel Learned to His Majesty, he

---

[1] Dr. Rawley, *Life of Francis Bacon,* in *The Works of Francis Bacon,* collected and edited by Spedding, Ellis and Heath (New York: Hurd and Houghton, 1869), 1, 37.

[2] *Ibid.,* p. 40.

became in 1607 Solicitor General, and in 1613, Attorney General. In 1617 he was made Lord Keeper of the Great Seal, an office once held by his father, and in 1618 he rose to the rank of Lord High Chancellor with the title of Baron Verulam, becoming Viscount St. Albans in 1621. Accused at the height of a brilliant career of corruption and venality in having accepted bribes, Bacon confessed his guilt and was stripped of his offices by Parliament. Although allowed to retain his titles, he was declared incapable of holding thereafter any office, place, or employment in the State; neither could he appear in Court or Parliament. Bacon's remaining years were devoted to literary and scientific pursuits. While experimenting with the preservative qualities of snow he contracted a cold which resulted in his death.[3]

While a student at Cambridge, Bacon acquired a dislike for Aristotelian philosophy and the methods then prevalent in the schools; and even as a young man, when striving with all his energies for political preferment, he believed that he had a mission to perform in behalf of science and learning. As early as 1592 he wrote to his uncle, Lord Burleigh, that he had taken all knowledge to be his province, and that if he could purge the field of

two sorts of rovers, whereof the one with frivolous disputations, confutations and verbosities (the schoolmen), and the other with blind experiments and auricular traditions and impostures (unmethodical investigators, e.g. alchemists, astrologers, etc.), hath committed so many spoils, . . .

he hoped to bring in industrious and profitable in-

---

[3] The thought came to him that fresh meat might be preserved as well by snow as by salt. He stuffed with snow the body of a chicken which had been prepared for cooking; while so doing he suffered a chill and fell sick and died in three days. He lived long enough to know that his experiment was successful. Essentially, his process of preserving meat is the same as that of cold storage today.

ventions and discoveries. Whether one considered this
curiosity, or vainglory, or nature, he said, it was so fixed
in his mind that it could not be removed.

During a busy career he did not abandon this purpose,
and all his leisure was spent in study and writing. The
great work in which he hoped to execute his plan, but
which he did not live to complete, was the *Instauratio
magna* (the *Great Restoration* or *Renewal*), in the preface of which he says: "There is no other course left
but with better assistance to begin the work anew, and
raise or rebuild the sciences, arts and all human knowledge from a firm and solid basis." It consisted of three
parts: *The Dignity and Advancement of Learning*, a
defense, survey, and examination of the sciences, which
appeared in 1605; [4] *Novum organum (New Instrument)*,
a presentation of the rules and principles of his new
method, a study in deduction and induction (1620);
and the *Sylva sylvarum*, or *Natural History*, a product
of his last years. The remaining parts which entered
into his scheme were never completed.

Bacon's educational views are found in this work,
also in the *New Atlantis*, an unfinished Utopian fable,
wherein the pansophic university, "Solomon's House,"
is described; and in some of his numerous Essays,
especially *Of Parents and Children, Of Travel, of Custom and Education*, and *Of Studies*. He rarely wrote
directly on educational topics, and his views, although
attractively expressed, did not surpass the best educational thought of the Renaissance.

One of the chief services Bacon rendered to education was, as Laurie observes,

his including it among the sciences to be studied. It was

---

[4] In 1623 this work appeared translated into Latin with "several
enrichments and enlargements," under the title *De augmentis
scientiarum*.

called by him "tradition"—the handing down of the acquired intellectual possessions of mankind to those who are to be our successors.[5]

His development of the inductive method, however, must ever remain his great contribution to science and ultimately through his successors, Ratke and Comenius, to education. He did not invent induction, but

he gave to the world the Logic of induction and formulated the practice of Galilei and the premonitions of Da Vinci. He was, as Isaac Newton called him, "the great secretary of Nature and Science."[6]

The following aphorisms contained in the *Novum organum* refer to what has been called the scientific method:

I. Man, as the minister and interpreter of nature, does and understands as much as his observations on the order of nature, either with regard to things or the mind, permit him, and neither knows nor is capable of more.

IX. The sole cause and root of almost every defect in the sciences is this, that while we falsely admire and extol the powers of the human mind, we do not search for its real helps.

XIX. There are and can exist but two ways of investigating and discovering truth. The one hurries on rapidly from the senses and particulars to the most general axioms, and from them, as principles and their supposed indisputable truth, derives and discovers the intermediate axioms. This is the way now in use. The other constructs its axioms from the senses and particulars, by ascending particularly and gradually, till it finally arrives at the most general axioms, which is the true but unattempted way.

According to Bacon, the human race was to be re-educated on scientific lines; a new social order was to

---

[5] S. S. Laurie, *Educational Opinion from the Renaissance* (Cambridge: The University Press, 1903), p. 121.
[6] *Loc. cit.*

be brought about through the scientific investigation of natural phenomena by means of inductive reasoning. Science was to promote the improvement of the material conditions of life and make men better and happier. The dissemination of scientific knowledge by the schools would ultimately lead to the solution of all the problems that had perplexed mankind. In his plan of education, Bacon's fundamental thesis was that knowledge is power and that if men knew better they would do better. He did not reject divine revelation, but he denied it any part in his scheme of education, because all living was to be based upon scientific knowledge. The influence of Bacon in this regard is clearly discernible in educational theory during the past three hundred years.[7] While Bacon was not a master of induction, and while he underestimated deduction which had been or was again to be an instrument in the discovery of truth, his principles were destined to be of far-reaching effect in the hands of contemporary educators, especially Ratke and Comenius.

Wolfgang Ratke, or *Ratich* (from Ratichius, the Latinized form of his name), was born at Wilster, in Holstein, in 1571. He studied for the Lutheran ministry at Hamburg and the University of Rostock, but owing to a defect in speech which spoiled his preaching, he turned to educational work. While traveling in England, he became acquainted with the philosophy of Bacon and developed his educational plans in accordance with it. When forty years of age, he addressed a memorial to the Imperial Diet held at Frankfurt-on-Main, 1612, in which he placed before the princes a number of startling propositions, since famous as his educational claims. He declared that he was able first to teach young or old

---

[7] *Cf.* W. Kane, *An Essay Toward a History of Education,* pp. 321-25; Pierre J. Marique, *History of Christian Education,* II, 215.

Hebrew, Greek, and Latin, or other languages, in a very short time and without any difficulty; second, to establish schools in which all arts should be taught and extended; third, to introduce and peaceably establish throughout the German Empire a uniform speech, a uniform government, and a uniform religion.

The princes were so favorably impressed by his proposal that a committee was appointed to examine his scheme. They reported favorably on it, saying:

Ratichius has discovered the art of teaching according to Nature. By his method, languages will be quickly learned, so that we shall have time for science; and science will be learned even better still, as the natural system suits best with science, which is the study of Nature.

As a result, the town of Augsburg engaged Ratke and his assistant, Holweg, to apply the system to their schools. The scheme after one year met with the disapproval of the townspeople of Augsburg and Ratke left for other scenes of labor.

In an experimental school at Köthen, Ratke was given an excellent opportunity to prove his claims. Prince Lewis of Anhalt-Köthen, at the instance of his sister, Duchess Dorothy of Weimar, who had studied Hebrew under Ratke, authorized the organization of a band of teachers who were to be instructed by Ratke himself. They were sworn to secrecy regarding the new methods. Buildings for the model school were provided and about five hundred children were enrolled.[8] Ratke apparently lacked all power of administration and this experiment, like that of Augsburg, proved a failure.

---

[8] The school was a combination of elementary and secondary education and was organized on a six year plan. The vernacular was used in the first three classes; Latin was started in the fourth and Greek in the sixth. All other languages were to be approached through the medium of the vernacular. Arithmetic, singing, and religion were also included in the curriculum.

Furthermore, Ratke was thrown into prison by the enraged Prince Lewis, who believed he had been duped by an impostor. While in prison, Ratke signed a paper to the effect that he had attempted more than he was able to accomplish. A later experiment in Magdeburg met with similar results. Ratke received, however, an offer to reform the schools of Sweden, but a stroke of paralysis prevented his acceptance. He died in 1635.

Ratke's failures, it is generally admitted, were due to his lack of tact and of administrative power. He did not get along well with his assistants, and he fell into sectarian difficulties with the townspeople by whom he was engaged. Some of his ideas were nevertheless influential in shaping modern education. The most important are contained in the rules laid down in his work on method, *Methodus institutionis nova*, published at Leipzig, 1617, some of which follow:

1. In everything we should follow the order of nature. The natural sequence along which the human intelligence moves in acquiring knowledge must be studied, and instruction must be based on the knowledge of it.

2. One thing at a time.

3. The same thing should be often repeated.

4. First let the mother tongue be studied, and teach everything through the mother tongue, so that the learner's attention may not be diverted by language.

5. Everything without constraint. "Boys are often beaten for not having learned, but they would have learned had they been well taught."

6. Nothing may be learned by rote.

7. Uniformity in all things—in methods, books, discipline

8. The thing itself should come first, then whatever explains it, things before words.

9. Everything is to be learned through induction, by experience and investigation.

In Ratke's school, the Bible was used as a reader When the children knew the alphabet, *Genesis* was read and by a uniform method, the teacher reading the whole book first, then each chapter twice, before asking for trials by the children. Grammar was taught in connection with reading. A Latin author was read several times in a translation before being rendered into German. The task of translating was methodically performed and involved especially the rule on repetition.

Ratke exerted only a slight influence on his contemporaries. He prepared the way for Comenius, but to what extent modern education is indebted to him for his efforts concerning methods of teaching languages has not been satisfactorily determined. His admirers have maintained that he was consciously psychological in his methods and anticipated the main principles of modern pedagogy.[9] On the other hand, such claims in his behalf have been discredited because they have been regarded as ill-founded.[10] Although he had many shortcomings in respect to method, or, for instance, in requiring too much repetition, too much uniformity, and too great attention to the inductive process, he advocated (1) teaching in accordance with the child's nature; (2) the vernacular; (3) thoroughness in whatever is studied; and (4) mildness in discipline.

John Amos Comenius (Komensky), heir to the published theories of Ratke, was a more practical follower of Bacon. Both as a teacher and writer, he applied to education the new Baconian principles pertaining to the investigation of truth. Although he enjoyed international fame in his own day as an educational reformer, he was soon forgotten and for over two hundred years his works were almost entirely neglected.

[9] *Cf.* R. Quick, *Educational Reformers,* pp. 109-18; O. Browning. *Educational Theories* (London: Kegan Paul, Trench & Co., 1881), pp. 53-56.
[10] *Cf.* G. Krause, *Wolfgang Ratichius* (Leipzig: Dyk, 1872); J. W. Adamson, *Pioneers of Modern Education* (Cambridge: University Press, 1905).

Comenius was born in the village of Nivnitz, Moravia, in 1592, one hundred years after the birth of Vives. He lost both parents when very young, and his early education seems to have been irregular. He did not begin the study of Latin until his seventeenth year—a late start for a pupil of that period. With the intention of preparing for the ministry of the Protestant sect known as the Moravian Brethren, he pursued higher studies in various German cities, especially Herborn and Heidelberg. Upon his return to Moravia, he taught in one of the schools of the Brethren in Prerau. He was duly advanced to the ministry; but while he was a devout member of his communion, and as a bishop a capable leader of an exiled church, his chief activities were along educational lines. Before the age of twenty-five he published his first book on grammar, *Grammaticae facilioris praecepta*. He wrote much of a spiritual nature to support his coreligionists during the religious strife of the Thirty Years' War. When Protestants were expelled from Moravia in 1628 by imperial decree he took refuge in Poland, settling in Lissa. Here also, as in Fulneck, his former parochial charge, he taught school. This period was very productive in educational works. He then wrote the *Great Didactic (Didactica magna)*, which was to show "the art of readily and solidly teaching men all things," and his other more famous work, the one which won for him a European reputation, the *Janua linguarum, reserata*, or *Gate of Tongues Unlocked*. There, too, he began to dream of his pansophic scheme, or plan to impart all knowledge, which resembled in its literary aspect the medieval attempt of Vincent of Beauvais, and in its institutional equipment the Baconian pansophic university.

When his reputation as an educational reformer was established, Comenius received an invitation to reform the schools of Sweden, and after refusing this, was invited by the British Parliament to submit plans to England. He accepted the latter offer and his own account of his visit to England [11] is especially interesting in reference to his pansophic scheme.

. . . My people having consented to the journey, I came to London on the very day of the autumnal equinox (September 22, 1641) and there at last learned that I had been invited by the order of the Parliament. But as the Parliament, the King having gone to Scotland, was dismissed for a three months' recess, I was detained there through the winter, by my friends mustering what pansophic apparatus they could, though it was but slender. . . . The Parliament meanwhile, having reassembled, and our presence being known, I had orders to wait until they should have sufficient leisure from other business to appoint a commission of learned and wise men from their body for hearing us and considering the grounds of our design. They communicated also beforehand their thoughts of assigning to us some college with its revenues, whereby a certain number of learned and industrious men called from all nations might be honourably maintained, either for a time of years or in perpetuity. There was even named for the purpose The Savoy in London; Winchester College out of London was named; and again nearer the city, Chelsea College; inventories of which and of its revenues were communicated to us, so that nothing seemed more certain than that the design of the Great Verulam, concerning the opening somewhere of a Universal college, devoted to the advancement of the Sciences, could be carried out. But the rumour of the Insurrection in Ireland, and of the massacre in one night of more than 200,000 English and the sudden departure of the King from London and the plentiful signs of the bloody war about to break out disturbed these plans, and obliged me to hasten my return to my own people.[12]

---

[11] It is claimed that during his London visit the presidency of Harvard was offered him. *Cf.* Matthew Spinka, *John Amos Comenius* (Chicago: University of Chicago Press, 1943), pp. 84 ff.

[12] Cited in Quick, *Educational Reformers*, pp. 126 f.

Convinced that a reconstruction of the methods for language study was fundamental to all of his pansophic plans, Comenius devoted most of his time for some years to the preparation of textbooks, one of which was the *Methodus linguarum novissima.* Although as bishop he took a prominent part in the religious and political controversies of the period, he still continued his educational work and was for a time engaged in reforming the schools of Transylvania. Later on he directed a school of the Brethren at Saros-Patak. He lived again in Lissa, but was finally driven out by the Poles after the Swedish invasion, because he had publicly welcomed a Protestant enemy to the country. After further wandering, he settled in Amsterdam and there spent the last years of his life in teaching and writing. He died in 1671 at the age of seventy-nine.

Among the voluminous writings of Comenius, over forty treat of education. The *Didactica magna* is, however, the chief exposition of his principles and methods; the *Janua linguarum reserata,* the *Orbis sensualium pictus,* and the *Vestibulum* are the most famous of his textbooks.

Pansophia, or universal wisdom, is fundamental to Comenius' educational aim. It must be kept in mind for a proper understanding of his activities as an educator, for toward it all his didactic efforts tend. The following aphorisms were given forth by Comenius in explanation of it, i.e., of the manner in which this universal knowledge is to be obtained.[13]

1. Universal knowledge, so far as it can be obtained by man, has as its objects God, nature, and art.

2. A perfect knowledge of these three is to be sought.

3. The knowledge of things is perfect when it is full, true and ordered.

---

[13] M. W. Keating, *The Great Didactic of John Amos Comenius,* Part I (London: A. and C. Black, Ltd., 1921), pp. 33 ff.

4. Knowledge is true when things are apprehended as they exist in reality.

5. Things are apprehended in their essential nature when the manner in which they have come into existence is understood.

6. Each object comes into existence in accordance with its "idea," that is to say, in relation to a certain rational conception through which it can be what it is.

7. It follows that the rational conceptions of things are identical, and only differ in the form of their manifestation, existing in God as an Archetype, in nature as an Ectype, and in art as an Antitype.

8. Therefore the basis of producing as of apprehending all things is harmony.

9. The first requisite of harmony is that there should be nothing dissonant.

10. The second is that there should be nothing that is not consonant.

11. The third is that the infinite variety of sounds and concords should spring from a few fundamental ones, and should come into being by definite and regular processes of differentiation.

12. Therefore, if we know the fundamental conceptions and the modes of their differentiation, we shall know all things.

13. Such rational conceptions can be abstracted from phenomena by means of a certain method of induction, and must be posited as the norms of phenomenal existence.

14. These norms of truth must be abstracted from those objects whose nature is such that they cannot be otherwise, and which are at everyone's disposal for the purpose of making experiments, that is to say, from natural phenomena.

Man's ultimate end is eternal happiness with God and there are three stages in the preparation for eternity: to know oneself (and with oneself all things); to rule oneself and to direct oneself to God; or to express these things in three well-known words, erudition; virtue or seemly morals; and religion or piety. The seeds of these three are naturally implanted in us;

but the actual knowledge, virtue and piety are not so given. These must be acquired by prayer, by education, and by action. He gave no bad definition who said that man was a "teachable animal" and indeed it is only by a proper education that he can become a man.[14]

Comenius believed that the young of both sexes, both noble and ignoble, rich and poor, should be educated, and for this schools were necessary. "Let none be excluded unless God has denied him sense and intelligence."[15]

The basis of school reform must be exact order in all things. "The art of teaching, therefore, demands nothing more than the skillful arrangement of time, of the subjects taught, and of method."[16] The exact order of instruction must be borrowed from nature. "If we wish to find a remedy for the defects of nature, it is in nature herself that we must look for it, since it is certain that art can do nothing unless it imitate nature."[17]

Comenius drew up a number of these principles from nature and urged them as the basis of method. Nature observes a suitable time. Nature prepares the material before she begins to give it form. Nature chooses a fit subject to act upon, or first submits one to a suitable treatment in order to make it fit. In all the operations of nature, development is from within. Nature, in its formative process, begins with the universal and ends with the particular. Nature makes no leaps, but proceeds step by step. Nature carefully avoids obstacles and things likely to cause hurt.

He also gave a number of principles which were to assure facility in teaching and learning.

---

[14] M. W. Keatinge, *The Great Didactic of John Amos Comenius*, Part II (London: A. & C. Black, Ltd., 1923), p. 52.

[15] *Ibid.*, p. 67.

[16] *Ibid.*, p. 96.

[17] *Ibid.*, p. 98.

Following in the footsteps of nature we find that the process of education will be easy:

1. If it begin early, before the mind is corrupted;
2. If the mind be duly prepared to receive it;
3. If it proceed from the general to the particular;
4. And from what is easy to what is more difficult;
5. If the pupil be not overburdened by too many subjects;
6. And if progress be slow in every case;
7. If the intellect be forced to nothing to which its natural bent does not incline it, in accordance with its age and with the right method;
8. If everything be taught through the medium of the senses;
9. If the use of everything taught be continually kept in view;
10. If everything be taught according to one and the same method.

"These," said Comenius, "are the principles to be adopted if education is to be easy and pleasant."[18] He treated these and many other principles in order to show that nature should be imitated in educational method.

On the study of languages, Comenius also expressed significant views.

Now the necessary languages are these: the vernacular, for use at home, and the languages of adjoining countries, for the sake of holding intercourse with neighbors. . . . For the reading of serious books Latin is also advisable, as it is the common language of the learned ....
....
The study of languages, especially in youth, should be joined to that of objects, that our acquaintance with the objective world and with language, that is to say, our knowledge of facts and our power to express them, may progress side by side. For it is men that we are forming and not parrots.[19]

Words, he held, should not be learned apart from the

---

[18] *Ibid.*, p. 127.
[19] *Ibid.*, p. 203.

objects to which they refer, and his textbooks, the *Vestibulum* and *Janua,* were devised upon that plan.

Comenius divided school life into four periods of six years each: infancy, in the mother-school lasting until the age of six; childhood, in the vernacular school until the age of twelve; boyhood, in the Latin school, until the age of eighteen; youth, in the university, until the age of twenty-four. In the mother-school the children were to be instructed by the mother in correct speaking, in observation, and in their religion. Comenius wrote his *School of Infancy* for the instruction of parents and teachers in directing the education of this period. It appeared first in Bohemian and was subsequently translated into German, Polish, Latin, and English (1641).[20] In its piety, it resembles the writings of Gerson. The vernacular or elementary school of Comenius had these notable characteristics: it was intended for all children; it included reading and writing in the mother tongue, drawing, arithmetic, singing, civil government, history, geography, and the catechism. The Latin school differs from those of the period in that "the pupils should learn four languages (vernacular, Latin, Greek, and Hebrew), and acquire an encyclopaedic knowledge of the arts,[21] i.e., the seven liberal arts, being versed also in physics, geography, history, morals, and, to some extent, in theology. They would have a solid foundation for advanced courses in the university. In the latter, specialization in theology, medicince, law, etc., may hold, but those of exceptional talent should be urged to pursue all the branches of study that there may always be some men whose knowledge is encyclopaedic." [22]

The *Janua linguarum reserata,* the most famous of

---

[20] W. S. Monroe, *Comenius' School of Infancy* (Boston: D. C. Heath & Co., 1908), p. xi.

[21] Keatinge, *op. cit.,* Part II, p. 274.

[22] *Ibid.,* p. 282.

Comenius' textbooks, embodies the ideas of the reformer on the method of studying Latin. It contains about eight thousand common Latin words arranged so as to form one thousand sentences; on one side of the page appears a Latin phrase, and on the other, the same in the vernacular. Each word is used in its root-signification and, with the exception of the particles, occurs only once. Each of the one hundred sections, or chapters, deals with some topic taken from life, nature, the arts and sciences, and the virtues, such as trees, the parts of the body, arithmetic, friendship, temperance, etc. The boy learned the Latin word in association with the object, and became familiar by graded lessons with all the ordinary grammatical constructions. The success of the book was marvelous. It was translated into twelve European and four Oriental languages during the lifetime of Comenius.

It was not, however, an entirely original work. The idea had been suggested by *Bodin* (*Bodinus*, 1530-1596), but was never carried out by him,[23] while an Irish Jesuit, *William Bathe* [24] (*Bateus*, 1564-1614), then a teacher

---

[23] Keatinge, *op. cit.*, Part I, pp. 18 f.

[24] William Bathe, a native of Dublin, was the eldest son of John Bathe, Attorney General and Chancellor of the Exchequer in Ireland under Elizabeth, and Eleanor Preston, daughter of Jenico Preston, third Viscount Gormanston. He studied, as he tells us, "humanities in Ireland, philosophy at Oxford and Louvain and theology at Louvain." As a student he wrote *A Brief Introduction to the Art of Music* (London, 1584), to which he later added *A Brief Introduction to the Skill of Song* (London, 1600). He won the favor of Queen Elizabeth through his writings and musical skill. He entered the Jesuit noviceship at Tournai, completing his studies in Padua, where he was ordained priest in 1601. As the companion of Father Louis Manzoni, Apostolic Nuncio to Ireland, he went on a diplomatic mission to Spain and there spent the rest of his life. While a member of the staff of the Irish College at Salamanca, he produced in collaboration with other Irish Fathers of the Society the first *Janua linguarum*. For his influence on Comenius. *Cf.* Edward A. Pace, "Bathe and Comenius," *Catholic University Bulletin*, 13: 354-60, July, 1907.

at Salamanca, Spain, had already produced in 1611 a *Janua linguarum* from which Comenius borrowed more than the name. This pioneer work was intended to facilitate language study for missionaries in the mastery of foreign tongues, confessors, men advanced in years, students of grammar, teachers, men of affairs; for all those, in short, says the author, "who object to spending long years in the study of the litterae humaniores, all who wish to learn the nobler languages, Italian, Spanish, German, French."

The collection of sentences originally designed to be twelve hundred in number ran up to about 1,330, and the total number of words was about 5,300, making a book of 144 pages quarto. In the first edition only Latin and Spanish were used, while in later editions four and even eight languages were incorporated. The work appeared in England in a Latin and English version in 1615, and again in 1617 as *The Messe of Tongues, Latin, French, English, Hispanish, neatly served up together for a wholesome repast to the worthy curiosite of the studious*. The method was quickly applied to all of the modern tongues and had been adapted to eight languages before 1629. Comenius speaks of it in the preface to his *Janua* and again in the *Novissima linguarum methodus*, in the latter as the "elegans inventio Januae Linguarum Hibernica." He was disappointed with it as a *Janua* (gate, or introduction). It would not aid beginners, he said, because of the character of the words used. Nevertheless he adopted the same construction as his predecessor, using sentences pertaining more to objects than did those of Bathe. As a careful student of the two works has written:

An examination of typical portions of the Irish *Janua Linguarum* will show that its *sententiae morales* were in far closer conformity to true educational ideals than were the later if better known *sententiae reales* of Comenius. The former aimed at conveying sound ethical principles through words complete but not encyclopaedic in their range; the latter offered a systematized vocabulary for natural objects. It will be easy to form a judgment as to which of the two recedes from true reality into the dreary waste of mere verbal knowledge.[25]

The *Janua linguarum reserata* proved too difficult, however, for beginners and in order to meet their needs Comenius composed the *Vestibulum,* or *Entrance Hall,* to the *Janua.*[26] This employs about one thousand of the most common Latin words in 427 sentences. It, too, was successful, although never as popular as the *Janua.* He planned on writing two more textbooks in the Janual series, the one called the *Palatium* which was an expansion of the *Janua* following the same plan and treating of the same subjects in greater detail and giving more attention to grammar; and the *Thesaurus* which was to be a summary of the best in Latin literature and was to cover the subjects discussed in the *Janua.* Apparently these works never were completed. As a help to both the *Vestibulum* and the *Janua,* Comenius produced the *Orbis sensualium pictus (World of Sensible Things Pictured),* really a simplified and illustrated edition of the *Janua.* The objects in each picture are numbered and the numbers are affixed to individual words in the text so that the pupil may pick out in the picture the exact object to which the word refers. This work, the first pictured book written for children, went through numberless editions and was used extensively in the home and school.

The influence of Comenius on contemporary education was comparatively slight. His theories did not affect school administration or methods; and although his textbooks were widely disseminated they failed as instru-

---

[25] Timothy Corcoran, *Studies in the History of Classical Teaching* (London: Longmans, Green, & Co., 1911), p. xviii.

[26] *Januae linguarum reseratae vestibulum quo primus ad Latinam linguam aditus tirunculis paratur.*

ments of teaching. "Comenius immensely overestimated the importance of knowledge and the power of the human mind to acquire knowledge." [27] His textbooks were too condensed, did not admit of repetition with interest, relied too much on information and did not consistently embody the principles of induction to which he had otherwise subscribed. He endeavored, however, to formulate educational method along scientific lines, while retaining a religious purpose and aim; and in large measure he succeeded. Rousseau could propose many of the ideas of Comenius as novelties and Basedow could attract attention by applying his method of illustration and object teaching; while many of his principles were consciously or unconsciously adopted and elaborated by the later upholders of sense training, correlation, and natural method. His works were revived by German scholars in the middle of the nineteenth century.

FOR FURTHER STUDY

Adamson, J. W., *Pioneers of Modern Education*. Cambridge: University Press, 1905.

Altemoeller, W., editor, *Johann Amos Comenius' Didactica magna oder grosse Unterrichtslehre*. Paderborn: F. Schöningh, 1908.

Bardeen, C. W., *The Orbis pictus of John Amos Comenius*. Syracuse: C. W. Bardeen, 1887.

Barnard, H., *German Teachers and Educators*. Hartford: Brown and Gross, 1878.

Browning, O., *Educational Theories*. London: Kegan Paul, Trench, & Co., 1881.

Comenius, J. A., *J. A. Comenii Opera didactica omnia*. Amsterdam: C. Cunradus & G. A. Roy, 1657.

Eby and Arrowood, *The Development of Modern Education*. New York: Prentice-Hall, Inc., 1935.

---

[27] Quick, *Educational Reformers*, p. 168.

Hoffmeister, H. W., *Comenius und Pestalozzi als Begründer der Volksschule*. Leipzig: J. Klinkhardt, 1896.

Kane, W., *An Essay Toward A History Of Education*. Chicago: Loyola University Press, 1935.

Kayser, W., *Johann Amos Comenius; sein Leben und seine Werke*. Hannover-Linden: Manz & Lange, 1892.

Keatinge, M. W.. *Comenius*. New York: McGraw-Hill, 1931.

—————, *The Great Didactic of John Amos Comenius*. London: Adam and Charles Block, 1896. Reprinted Part I and II, 1921-23.

Krause, G., *Wolfgang Ratichius*. Leipzig: Dyk, 1872.

Kvascala, J., *Die pädogogische Reform des Comenius in Deutschland bis zum Ausgange des XVII. Jahrhunderts, Monumenta Germaniae paedagogica*. Vols. 26 and 32. Berlin: A. Hoffman & Co., 1903-04.

Laurie, S. S., *History of Educational Opinion from the Renaissance*. Cambridge: The University Press, 1903.

Lippert, F. A. M., *Johann Heinrich Alsted's pädagogisch-didaktische Reform Bestrebungen und ihr Einfluss auf J. A. Comenius*. Meissen: C. F. Klinkicht & Sohn, [n.d.].

Monroe, W. S., *Comenius' School of Infancy*. Boston: D. C. Heath, 1908.

—————, *Comenius and the Beginnings of Educational Reform*. New York: Charles Scribner's Sons. 1900.

Quick, R. H., *Educational Reformers*. New York: D. Appleton and Company, 1907.

Spedding, James, Robert E. Ellis, and Douglas D. Heath, editors. *The Works of Francis Bacon*. New York: Hurd and Houghton, 1869. 15 vols.

Spinka, Matthew, *John Amos Comenius*. Chicago: University of Chicago Press, 1943. Chap. IV.

Vogt, G., *Wolfgang Ratichius, der Vorganger des Amos Comenius*. Langensalza: Schulbuchhandlung von F. G. L. Gressler. 1894.

CHAPTER XXIV

REALISTS AND THEORISTS OF THE SEVENTEENTH CENTURY

John Locke (1632-1704) was born of Puritan parents at Wrington, near Bristol, England. At the age of twenty he entered Oxford and took up with avidity the study of philosophy, natural science, and medicine. His course was interrupted for a year to enable him to go as private secretary to Sir Walter Vane on a diplomatic mission to Germany. He returned afterward to Oxford and completed his studies, taking his B.A. degree in 1656, and his M.A. in 1658. In 1667 he became associated with Lord Ashley, afterward Earl of Shaftesbury, in the capacity of secretary, physician, and tutor of his son. Through this connection with Shaftesbury, at one time Lord Chancellor, he obtained important public offices; but when his patron fell from power and fled from England Locke sought refuge with him in Holland returning in 1689, after six years' absence. In 1693 he published his *Thoughts Concerning Education*. This, together with his great philosophical work, *Essay Concerning the Human Understanding*, and another essay on the *Conduct of the Understanding*, furnishes the reader with a comprehensive view of his ideas on the training of the young.

Locke's educational experience was limited to private teaching as tutor in the household of Lord Ashley and other noblemen. His first pupil, Lord Ashley's son, a sickly child, recovered under Locke's direction, afterward married and brought up seven children, the oldest of whom, a son, Locke also educated. His advice and direction, as a physician and tutor, were often sought

469

by parents. The *Thoughts Concerning Education* were originally letters to his friend Edward Clarke, of Chipley, in reference to the rearing of his son. The views there expressed refer exclusively to the training of the young gentleman, or noble child, and not to youth in general. "That most to be taken care of is the gentleman's calling. For if those of that rank are by their education once set right, they will quickly bring all the rest into order." [1]

In philosophy Locke ranks as the first of British empiricists whose basic doctrine was that all knowledge is acquired by experience. The mind is in the beginning according to him a blank sheet, *tabula rasa*. Experience through sensation, or the perception of external phenomena by means of the senses, and through reflection, or the perception of the internal phenomena, that is, of the activity of the understanding itself, is the source of all our ideas. Locke held to belief in a divine revelation, but he left it open to the questioning of mere human reason.[2] He applied to the study of mental processes the method advocated by Bacon for the study of natural phenomena. In education as well as in philosophy he held many views in common with Bacon, but he is much more truly the disciple of Montaigne. As the practical philosopher he taught that the boy must be reared physically and morally with great care and that his instruction be first related to concrete things. He is consequently to be classified with the sense realists.

Locke's educational aim is threefold: (1) vigor of body; (2) virtue of the soul, with its manifestation in good breeding; wisdom in conduct; (3) knowledge, or mental acquirements; but this latter is subordinate to health of body, virtue, and good breeding. To physical

---

[1] Epistle Dedicatory in *Thoughts Concerning Education.*
[2] *Essay Concerning Human Understanding*, Book IV, Ch. 18.

training the first sections of the *Thoughts* are devoted (1 to 29). He begins the work with the following:

A sound mind in a sound body, is a short, but full description of a happy state in this world; he that has these two, has little more to wish for, and he that wants either of them, will be but little the better for anything else. Men's happiness, or misery, is most part of their own making.

It seems but natural that Locke as the physician should first examine, and so minutely, this phase of training.

I imagine the minds of children, as easily turned, this or that way, as water itself; and though this be the principal part, and our main care be about the inside, yet the clay cottage is not to be neglected. I shall therefore begin with the case, and consider first the health of the body, as that which perhaps you may rather expect, from that study I have been thought more peculiarly to have applied myself to.[8]

For the preservation and improvement of a healthy "or at least not a sickly constitution in their children" he advises parents that children be not too warmly clothed even in winter; they should go bareheaded. Boys should learn to swim and run in the open air. He outlines their diet, forbids meat to small children, urges early retiring and rising, eight hours' sleep, and in short advises a care and training that always tends to develop hardiness.

His views on moral training may be summarized as follows: We should keep the body strong so that it may be able to execute and obey the orders of the mind. The next thing is

to set the mind right, that on all occasions it may be disposed to consent to nothing but what may be suitable to the duty and excellency of a rational creature. . . . I do not doubt . . . that the difference to be found in the manners and abilities of

---

[8] *Thoughts Concerning Education*, Sect. 2.

men is owing more to their education than to anything else.
. . . As the strength of the body lies chiefly in being able to
endure hardships so also does that of the mind. And the great
principle and foundation of all virtue and worth is placed in
this, that a man is able to deny himself his own desires, cross
his own inclinations, and purely follow what reason directs as
best, though the appetite lean the other way.[4]

Self-denial and self-control must early be learned.
Mind must be obedient to discipline and pliant to reason when at first it is most tender, most easy to be
bowed. Children should be used to submit their desires
and go without their longings, even from their cradles.
The first thing they should learn should be that they are
not to have anything because it pleases them, but because it is thought fit for them.

The formation of good habits is the main purpose in
early training. The authority of the parent or teacher
must be ever recognized by the child. Awe and fear give
first power over children's minds, love of friendship in
riper years will hold it. Severe punishments are of little
good. Praise and commendation are better. "Children
who have been most chastised seldom make the best
men."[5] Corporal punishment should rarely be applied
and only in cases of extremity. "On the other hand to
flatter children by rewards of things that are pleasant
to them is as carefully to be avoided."[6] Esteem and dis-
grace are proper instruments of discipline, when the
love of the one and fear of the other have been assiduously cultivated. The example of the parent or
teacher, and Locke agrees with Montaigne in preferring
the tutor or private instructor, is important here. "You
must do nothing before him which you would not have
him imitate."[7]

---

[4] *Ibid.*, Sects. 31-33.
[5] *Ibid.*, Sect. 43.
[6] *Ibid.*, Sect. 52.
[7] *Ibid.*, Sect. 71.

It is virtue then, direct virtue, which is the hard and valuable part to be aimed at in education; and not a forward pertness, or any little arts of shifting. All other considerations and accomplishments should give way, and be postponed, to this. This is the solid and substantial good, which tutors should not only read lectures and talk of; but the labour and art of education should furnish the mind with, and fasten there, and never cease, till the young man had a true relish for it, and placed his strength, his glory and his pleasure in it.[8]

Placing virtue first, Locke held it to be absolutely requisite to make the pupil "valued and beloved by others, acceptable or tolerable to himself. Without that, I think, he will be happy neither in this, nor the other world."[9] He would have him instructed in religion, and kept "constantly morning and evening to acts of devotion to God,"[10] as to the Maker, Preserver, and Benefactor of all. He should have a true notion of God, as of the independent supreme Being, Author and Maker of all things, from whom we receive all our good, who loves us, and gives us all things: and, consequent to this . . . a love and reverence of this supreme Being.[11]

The intellectual side of the young man's training, acording to Locke, is secondary to the moral. The boy needed not, as Comenius thought, to acquire universal knowledge. "The business of education," said Locke, "is not to make the young perfect in any one of the sciences, but so to open and dispose their minds as may best make them capable of any, when they shall apply themselves to it."[12] In his description of the tutor this is made clearer and the general character of the mental training exposed.

The great work of the governor is to fashion the carriage, and form the mind; to settle in his pupil good habits, and the

[8] *Ibid.*, Sect. 70.
[9] *Ibid.*, Sect. 135.
[10] *Ibid.*, Sect. 136.
[11] *Loc. cit.*
[12] *Ibid.*, Sect. 19.

principles of virtue and wisdom; to give him, by little and little, a view of mankind; and work him into a love and imitation of what is excellent and praiseworthy; and, in prosecution of it, to give him vigour, activity, and industry. The studies which he sets him upon are but, as it were, the exercises of his faculties, and employment of his time, to keep him from sauntering and idleness, to teach him application, and accustom him to take pains, and to give him some little taste of what his own industry must perfect. For who expects, that under a tutor a young gentleman should be an accomplished critic, orator, or logician; go to the bottom of metaphysics, natural philosophy, or mathematics; or be a master in history or chronology; though something of each of these is to be taught him; but it is only to open the door, that he may look in, and, as it were, begin an acquaintance, but not to dwell there: and a governor would be much blamed, that should keep his pupil too long, and lead him too far in most of them. But of good breeding, knowledge of the world, virtue, industry, and a love of reputation, he cannot have too much: and, if he have these, he will not long want what he needs or desires of the other.[13]

Mental power and activity Locke sought after rather than knowledge. "The right improvement and exercise of our reason," he says, "is the highest perfection that a man can attain to in this life." [14] Intellectual education is a formation of thought through exercise and discipline. If a man is to reason well "he must exercise his mind in observing the connection of ideas and following them in train." [15] Nothing does this better than mathematics which should be taught all those who have the time and opportunity, not so much to make them mathematicians as "to make them reasonable creatures."

I have mentioned mathematics as a way to settle in the mind a habit of reasoning closely, and in train; not that I think it necessary that all men should be deep mathematicians, but

---

[13] *Ibid.*, Sect. 94.
[14] *Ibid.*, Sect. 122.
[15] *Conduct of the Understanding,* Sect. 6.

that having got the way of reasoning, every single argument should be managed as a mathematical demonstration, the connection and dependence of ideas should be followed till the mind is brought to the source on which it bottoms and observes the coherence all along. . . .[16]

What Locke hopes for from the study of mathematics is not a mental power universally applicable to any and every situation, but rather the method, the way of reasoning and "the habit of reasoning closely and in train." [17] None of the things learned should ever be made a burden or imposed as a task,[18] because learning is to be pleasurable; elsewhere in the *Thoughts* and in the *Conduct of the Understanding* the necessity of discipline of mind is emphasized.

Few men are from their youth accustomed to strict reasoning, and to trace the dependence of any truth, in a long train of consequences, to its remotest principles and to observe its connection; and he that by frequent practice has not been used to this employment of his understanding, it is no wonder that he should not, when he is grown into years, be able to bring his mind to it, than that he should not be, on a sudden, able to grave or design, dance on ropes, or write a good hand, who has never practiced them.[19]

As an educational theorist, Locke is difficult to classify. He has been designated a humanist, a realist, and a utilitarian, and there are grounds for each classification. Though he advocated discipline of the mind, his educational theories do not warrant our classifying him as a formal disciplinarian. His discipline is specific; he rejected the theory of universal and undiminished transfer of training effect. He most closely resembles

---

[16] *Ibid.*, Sect. 7.
[17] *Cf.* Sr. Mary Louise Cuff, *The Educational Theory of John Locke* (Washington, D. C.: The Catholic Education Press, 1923), p. 126.
[18] *Thoughts Concerning Education*, Sect. 73.
[19] *Conduct of the Understanding*, Sect. 6.

Montaigne and, like the French philosopher, may be most safely called the realist, the philosophical writer aiming for a practical and concrete training for the young. Locke, however, wrote for one class in English society, the gentry; his ideas were not intended for and were not adopted in the schools. They nevertheless influenced English and American education, especially in regard to the training process, the embodiment of the idea of discipline in education, and they also affected Rousseau in the formulation of his "education according to nature."

The learned French writer and prelate, *Fénelon*, represents another phase of the reform movements of the seventeenth century, viz., that in behalf of the education of girls. François de Salignac de la Mothe Fénelon (1651-1715) was born at the Château de Fénelon, in Périgord, of an old, noble family. He received his early education under a tutor. After some time in the University of Cahors, which he entered at twelve, he went to the Collège du Plessis, Paris, and while there attended lectures on theology at the Sorbonne. An evidence of his early ability may be seen in the feat of preaching a successful sermon when fifteen years of age. He studied in the Seminary of St. Sulpice, then under the regency of M. Tronson, and was ordained a priest in 1675. At one time Fénelon felt called to missionary work in the far East or America. He joined the Sulpician community, and a few years after ordination was appointed director of the convent of New Catholics (Nouvelles-Catholiques), an institution which had been founded for the instruction and training of young women who were or contemplated becoming converts to the Catholic Church. This position called forth Fénelon's great powers as a preacher, instructor, and defender of the Faith. Although he has often been accused of sanctioning the use of force in convert making, Protestant writers today admit that he resorted to persuasion rather than compulsion. "When hearts are to be moved," he wrote, "force avails not. Conviction is the only real conversion." This characterized his missionary work among the Huguenots after the revocation of the Edict of Nantes by Louis XIV, when compulsory measures were employed to stamp out heresy and restore religious unity.

While attached to the convent of New Catholics, Fénelon wrote his *Traité de l'éducation des filles (Treatise on the Education of Girls)*, as a guide for the Duchess de Beauvilliers who had sought his advice on the training of her children. It was given a practical trial in the household of the duchess; and, when her husband, the Duke of Beauvilliers, became governor of the grandchildren of Louis XIV, he engaged Fénelon as tutor of the eldest, the Duke of Burgundy. The boy, described as passionate, self-willed, vindictive, and even cruel by nature, became under Fénelon's tutelage an amiable, humane, and conscientious prince. For his instruction were prepared Fénelon's *Fables, Dialogues des morts (Dialogues of the Dead)*, and *Aventures de Télémaque (Adventures of Telemachus)*, the latter affording lessons in government and illustrating matters pertaining to the education of a prince.

In 1695, Fénelon succeeded to the archbishopric of Cambrai, then one of the most important in France. His interest in education did not cease. Madame de Maintenon, the morganatic wife of Louis XVI, herself a writer of educational treatises,[20] frequently consulted him in regard to the administration of her school for girls at Saint-Cyr.

The Education of Girls contains much on the training of children, especially on the period of infancy, ap-

---

[20] *Letters and Conversations on the Education of Girls. Counsels to Young Women Who Enter Society.*

plicable to boys as well as to girls. Its general thesis is
that the education of women is as necessary for the good
of society as that of men.

> The weaker they are, the more important it is to strengthen
> them. Have they not duties to fulfill, and duties, too, that lie
> at the foundation of all human life? . . . .
> . . . .
> Virtue, moreover, is no less incumbent on women than on men;
> and, not to speak of the good or harm they may do to man-
> kind, women constitute half of the human race redeemed by
> the blood of Christ and destined to eternal life.[21]

Like the humanists of the Renaissance and his contemporary, Locke, Fénelon began training with infancy,
caring for the child's health by means of well-chosen
food and the regulations of a simple life. Some of his
notable directions were:

> Be content to form their character little by little as occasions
> naturally come up. . . . You should content yourself with
> following and assisting nature. . . . Children's curiosity is a
> natural bent that prepares the way for instruction; do not fail
> to avail yourself of it. . . . You ought never to be annoyed by
> their questions; they are the openings offered you by Nature
> herself to facilitate instruction; show that you take pleasure
> in them.[22]

Fénelon knew the value of imitation, the necessity of
good models, especially in conduct, and urged parents
and teachers to use exemplars as means of indirect instruction. "Often you need only, without saying a word,
to show them in another, what you wish them to do." [23]
Good persons were to be made attractive to children,
their amiable and exemplary traits pointed out, and
"above all their piety which is the source of all the

---

[21] Fénelon, *Education of Girls,* translated by K. Lupton (Boston: Ginn and Company, 1891), p. 12 f.

[22] *Ibid.,* p. 24 f.

[23] *Ibid.,* p. 27.

rest." [24] First instruction, and in fact, everything exacted of the young, was to be agreeable and pleasant.
Fénelon did not approve of the austerity of Locke. The
teacher must early win the affection of the children and
must deal compassionately with their weaknesses. "If
confidence and persuasion are not powerful enough,
authority will not fail to find its place." [25] In short, he
advocated a gentle and patient training.

On the intellectual side, he would have few formal
lessons for beginners; instruction should be largely
given through cheerful conversation. The art of reading
will be learned first in the vernacular; and, that it may
be a pleasant task, the books should contain short
stories beautifully illustrated. Experiencing pleasure in
it the children would learn to read quickly. All the
tediousness of child life Fénelon thought was in study,
all the enjoyment in amusements.

Let us then, try to change this arrangement; let us make
study agreeable, let us conceal it under the guise of liberty
and pleasure, let us allow children to break in upon their
studies sometimes with brief sallies of amusement. They need
these distractions to refresh their minds.[26]

He disapproved of overloading the memory, of burden-
some regulations, and of threats and punishments for
failures in study.

First among the notable elements in Fénelon's theory
was the use of stories for children—the fables, but not
heathen fables. "A girl will be fortunate," he says, "if
she remains in ignorance of those all her life, for they
are impure and full of impious absurdities." [27] Scriptural stories form a basis and vehicle for religious instruction. Facts connected with the life of Christ should

---

[24] *Ibid.*, p. 30.
[25] *Ibid.*, p. 33.
[26] *Ibid.*, p. 38.
[27] *Ibid.*, p. 49.

be presented as a concrete setting for instruction on the mysteries; the baptism of Christ, for example, might be described when telling children of the Trinity. Stories fill the imagination of childhood; in their recital are brought together the most pleasing and instructive pictures, descriptive of the historical course of religion. "Every means should be employed to lead children to find religion beautiful, attractive, and impressive, instead of which they ordinarily conceive of it as something gloomy and melancholy." [28] The first use of reason is to be turned "gently towards God." "Follow at first the method of Scripture: appeal vividly to their imaginations; set nothing before them that is not clothed with striking imagery." [29] Simple questions, comparisons, illustrations, observation by the children: all have their place in teaching the first principles of religion and the practices of the Church. In the chapters on religious instruction covering the Decalogue, Sacraments, and prayer, both as to content and method, Christ is the central figure. Wholesome reflections on the faults characteristic of girls, on beauty and adornments, lead to Fénelon's famous treatment of the special duties of a woman. He enumerates these duties as follows: the education of children, the boys up to a certain age, the girls until they are married or enter a convent; management of the household, regarding the conduct of servants, and expenditures. He maintains that these are not too limited occupations if the education of the young be faithfully discharged, and if management be really economical, for "there is a science of domestic service which is not insignificant." [30] Girls are to be assigned some household cares in order to develop in them a sense of responsibility, and give them the benefit of the

[28] *Ibid.*, p. 55.
[29] *Ibid.*, p. 58.
[30] *Ibid.*, p. 102.

mother's direction before they undertake the management of homes of their own.

Fénelon's general rule was to train girls according to their rank and station in life. He required them to learn reading, writing, grammar, arithmetic, in so far as needed by a mother for the instruction of her children and management of the home; some of the principles of law referring to wills, contracts, etc., the duties of landowners; ancient history and that of their own country; music, art and embroidery. Other modern languages should only be studied for their utilitarian value.

"It is not fair to expect that a good education can be conducted by a poor governess." [31] Fénelon discourses on the choice and preparation of one for the office, suggesting the modern normal school idea for "religious and secular organizations that devote themselves, according to their regulations, to training girls." [32]

Fénelon was far in advance of his day in his ideas for training girls; his book, which ranks first among French educational classics, is still widely read in the original and in translations; and *Télémaque*, the *Fables*, and *Dialogues* have not ceased to be popular as school texts. Fénelon, like Montaigne and Locke, was practical; like Comenius, a student and upholder of natural and psychological methods. Because of his attention to child psychology and especially to curiosity and interest, he may be regarded as the forerunner of Herbart.

FOR FURTHER STUDY

Locke

Adamson, J. W., editor, *The Educational Writings of John Locke.* Cambridge: University Press, 1912.

Bourne, H. R. Fox, *The Life of John Locke.* London: Henry S. King and Company, 1876. 2 vols.

---

[31] *Ibid.*, p. 116.
[32] *Ibid.*, p. 117 f.

Cuff, Sr. Mary Louise, *The Educational Theory of John Locke.*
Washington, D. C.: The Catholic Education Press, 1923.

Fowler, Thomas, *John Locke.* New York: Harper and Bros.,
1880.

Laurie, S. S., *Educational Opinion from the Renaissance.*
Cambridge: University Press, 1903.

Locke, John, *Essay Concerning Human Understanding,* 1690.

————, *Some Thoughts Concerning Education,* 1693.

————, *Conduct of the Understanding,* published 1706.

Quick, R. H., *Educational Reformers.* New York: D. Appleton
and Co., 1907.

————, editor, *Some Thoughts Concerning Education.*
Cambridge: University Press, 1913.

Thayer, V. T., *The Misinterpretation of Locke as a Formalist
in Educational Philosophy.* Madison: University of Wisconsin
Press, 1921.

Turner, W., *History of Philosophy.* Boston: Ginn and Co.,
1903.

Fénelon

Calvet, Jean, *La littérature religieuse de François de Sales a
Fénelon.* Paris: J. de Gigord, 1938.

Fénelon, F. de S., *Oeuvres.* Paris. Lefèvre, 1859, 5 vols.

————, *Fables.* Paris: Librairie Poussielgue Frères, 1879.

————, *Les Aventures de Télémaque.* Paris: Hachette
et Cie, 1927.

————, *The Spiritual Letters of Archbishop Fénelon.*
Translated by H. L. Sidney Lear. New York: Longmans, Green,
and Co., 1931.

————, *On the Education of Girls.* Translated by K. Lupton. Boston: Ginn and Company, 1891.

Hodgson, Geraldine, *Studies in French Education.* Cambridge:
University Press, 1908.

Munroe, J. P., *The Educational Ideal.* Boston: D. C. Heath
Co., 1895.

Schieffer, F. von, *Fénelon über die Erziehung der Mädchen.*
Sammlung der bedeutendsten pädagogischen Schriften. Paderborn: E. Schöningh, 1894.

SYNOPSIS OF RELIGIOUS ORGANIZATIONS OF THE SEVENTEENTH CENTURY

1. THE ORATORIANS
   - (a) The curriculum of their colleges embodied some notable details in respect to the vernacular, French, mathematics, the natural sciences, history, geography, correlated with history, and for which mural maps were employed
2. THE PORT-ROYALISTS
   - (a) *Petites écoles*
   - (b) Gentleness characterized the discipline; rivalry and emulation banished
   - (c) French emphasized; their readers were translations of simple Latin works
   - (d) The influence of their schools, though suppressed, was continued by the writings and especially the treatises and textbooks of their leaders
3. THE BROTHERS OF THE CHRISTIAN SCHOOLS
   - (a) Founded by St. John Baptist de la Salle (1651-1719)
   - (b) Claims of Saint de la Salle as an educator rest on the movement which he directed for the organization and improvement of free elementary instruction; established a teaching congregation which has become worldwide in its operations; opened the first normal school for training lay teachers; applied successfully the simultaneous method to teaching and conducting classes
4. OTHER CATHOLIC RELIGIOUS CONGREGATIONS OF MEN AND WOMEN DEVOTED TO EDUCATION
   - (a) Congregation of the Mission of St. Vincent de Paul
   - (b) The Sulpicians, Society of St. Sulpice
   - (c) The Sisters of Notre Dame, founded by St. Peter Fourier in 1598, introduced into America in 1657 as the Congregation of Notre Dame of Montreal
   - (d) The School Sisters of Notre Dame
   - (e) The English Ladies
   - (f) Institute of Mary
   - (g) The Visitandines

483

    (h) Daughters of the Presentation
    (i) The Sisters of the Presentation of the Blessed Virgin
    (j) The Sisters of Charity of St. Vincent de Paul
    (k) The Sisters of St. Joseph
    (l) Sisters of Mercy of St. Charles Borromeo

5. AUGUST HERMAN FRANCKE (1663-1727)
    (a) The representative of the Pietists in education
    (b) Organized the famous Francke foundations
    (c) His colleague, Semler, opened with him the first *Realschule*

CHAPTER XXV

RELIGIOUS ORGANIZATIONS OF THE SEVENTEENTH CENTURY

The *Oratorians* in France, founded by Cardinal de Bérulle in 1613, although not a teaching order, engaged extensively in educational work. They differed in organization from the Fathers of the Oratory founded at Rome by St. Philip Neri, in 1575, in that the various houses of the congregation were directed by a common superior general, whereas in Italy they were independent.[1] Bound to no other vows than those of the priesthood, the Oratorians sought as their aim sacerdotal perfection. They conducted diocesan seminaries and were diligent in observing the regulations of the Council of Trent. Juilly, founded in 1638, was the most famous of their colleges. The curriculum embodied some notable details in respect to, first, the vernacular, French, which was pursued until the fourth year, when Latin became obligatory; second, mathematics and the natural sciences, which received more attention than was usual in secondary schools; third, history, which embraced ancient and French history; fourth, geography, correlated with history, for the teaching of which mural maps were employed.

The management of the schools resembled that of the Jesuits in many respects, for example, in the mildness of the discipline; in allowing the same teacher to conduct the class throughout the course; and in having a course in philosophy, which, however, was not free, at times, from Cartesianism. After the suppression of the

---

[1] The English Oratorians founded by Cardinal Newman in 1847 are substantially the same as the Roman.

Jesuits, the Oratorians succeeded them in the control of many schools.

Every large congregation has given the world its quota of learned and saintly members. Among the Oratorians arose *Louis Thomassin* (*Thomassinus*, 1619-1695), one of the most learned men of his time, author of works on theology, history, ecclesiastical antiquities, and liturgy, who also treated of the methods of studying and teaching the humanities, philosophy, grammar and history.[2] *Bernard Lamy* (1640-1715), trained from boyhood by the Oratorians, a professor in the college of Vendôme and Juilly, and in his later years in Rouen, was the author of many Scriptural treatises, and also of a treatise on the sciences, *Entretiens sur les sciences* (1683), which dispels any doubt of the interest of the Oratorians in the exact and natural sciences.

The *Port-Royalists*, so-called because of their chief establishment, Port Royal des Champs in the valley of Chevreuse, near Versailles, lasted as a religious organization only twenty-four years, from 1637 until 1661, when they were suppressed by King Louis XIV. Their schools were not really opened until 1646. In that short time, however, they devised an educational plan which was unique in many respects. Their influence did not cease with their suppression, but was continued by the writings and especially the treatises and textbooks of their leaders.

The founder of the Port-Royalists, *Jean Duvergier de Hauranne* (1581-1643), Abbé of Saint-Cyran, was a friend and supporter of Cornelis Jansen, Bishop of Ypres (Jansenius, 1585-1638), whose work, *Augustinus*, published in 1640, fell under the ban of the Church. Saint-Cyran, as the founder was commonly known, made Port-

---

[2] *Cf. La méthode d'étudier et d'enseigner chrétiennement et solidement les lettres humaines par rapport aux lettres divines et aux écritures* (Paris: F. Muguet, 1681).

Royal the stronghold of Jansenism in France. To him the first "solitaires" owed their rigorism and the Little Schools, *petites écoles,* their inspiration. Although a lover of children and earnestly desirous of their salvation, he did not believe knowledge was good for all. "Sometimes," he said, "out of a hundred children not one ought to study." Nevertheless, he designated child training as one of the important works of his followers. In keeping with his Jansenistic views, he permitted only the docile children and those of good promise to enter the schools.

The classes in the Little Schools were small, five or six pupils being intrusted to a teacher who remained with them day and night. Gentleness characterized the discipline. The teacher was directed to bear with the children patiently; to pray God before correcting them, in order not to give way to ill temper; and to resort to corporal punishment only in the last extremity; in short "to speak little, bear much and pray still more." Rivalry and emulation were banished, with the result, as Pascal admitted, that the boys became indifferent. The effort was constantly made to render study more enjoyable than play.

The curriculum embodied some real innovations. Like the Oratorians, the Port-Royalists taught reading first in the vernacular, and they devised a system of phonics in place of the alphabetical method. Their readers were translations of simple Latin works. When the students approached the study of Latin, they already had some knowledge of the literature. They rendered Latin authors into French in order to avoid the word study of the classics then quite common. No definite provision was made for systematic physical training. Moral and religious formation remained the chief aim.

Some of the Port-Royal writers whose works were widely disseminated after the closing of the Little

Schools may be here mentioned. *Antoine Arnauld* (1612-1694), brother of Mère Angélique, a superioress of the Port-Royal Nuns, in his *Règlement des études (Regulation of Studies)*, which is often coupled with the *Traité des études of Rollin* (1661-1741), Rector of the University of Paris, gave an exposition of Port-Royal methods for the study of literature. The *Port Royal Logic* is attributed to him, also the *New Elements of Geometry*, in the preparation of which he was assisted by Nicole; he directed Lancelot in the production of the *Grammaire générale et raisonée*, or *Port Royal Grammar*. The latter also wrote *Nouvelle méthode pour apprendre facilement la langue Latin (New Method of Easily Learning the Latin Tongue)* (1644); a similar method book for Greek (1655) and the *Jardin des racines Grecques (Garden of Greek Roots)* (1657), noteworthy for a criticism of Comenius' *Janua linguarum*.

The book is filled with all sorts of unusual and difficult words, and the first chapters are of no assistance for those that follow, nor these for the last, because there is no word in one which is found in the others. . . . The Entrance to languages ought to be a short and easy method to lead us as quickly as possible to the reading the best written books.[3]

Nicole wrote on the training of a prince, *Vues générales pour bien élever un prince;* Coustel drew up *Rules of the Education of Children.* Mother Angélique, sister of Arnauld, who wrote the *Constitutions of the Monastery of Port-Royal du Sacrament*, and Sister Sainte-Euphemie (Jacqueline Pascal), younger sister of Pascal, who produced *The Regulations for Children*, show the application of the Port-Royal methods to the training of girls.

The Brothers of the Christian Schools owe their foun-

---

[3] Claude Lancelot. *Le jardin des racines Grecques* (Paris: Pierre le Petit, 1657), preface.

dation to *St. John Baptist de la Salle* (1651-1719), a doctor of theology and priest of the diocese of Rheims, France. From the time of his ordination, in 1678, he showed a deep interest in the welfare of the poor teachers of Rheims. His educational work dates from 1679, when Madame Maillefer sought his assistance in the establishment of a free school, which she intended to endow. De la Salle generously responded and with a lay teacher, Adrian Nyel, to aid him, opened the school. This undertaking drew him into another of a similar nature made possible by the generosity of Madame de Croyères. Through these engagements and his abiding love for the poor, Saint de la Salle came to know intimately the condition and needs of the struggling teachers. His sympathy prompted him to render them financial help, provide them with dwellings, and eventually to receive them into his household. From being merely their adviser and patron, he soon became, through a growing attachment to them, their spiritual father and superior.

In 1683, Saint de la Salle resigned his office as canon of the cathedral of Rheims, sold his patrimony, and distributed his fortune gradually and judiciously to the poor. He was then actually the superior of the teachers, although no permanent organization had been reached, and he intended to devote himself entirely to their welfare. Freed from all worldly attachments by voluntary poverty, he directed the humble community at home and in its spread to neighboring cities. At a retreat which he called in 1684, the elements of the rule were agreed upon, also the vows, and the distinctive garb to be worn by the Brothers. The vows were not then perpetual; they bound the Brothers to obedience for one year, and so they remained until 1694, when perpetual vows of obedience and stability in the Institute were required. When approved by the Holy See

(1725) the vows included chastity, poverty, obedience, stability in the Institute, and gratuitous teaching of the poor.

More than once during the first ten years the community had to struggle for its very existence, deaths and defections often depleting the ranks. In the meantime, however, de la Salle had inaugurated at Rheims two important institutions, viz., the novitiate, for training the members of the Institute, and the normal school (teachers' seminary), for training lay teachers for the country schools. The latter, the first normal school in history, originated to meet a peculiar demand. Pastors in the villages had been begging Saint de la Salle for teachers; but as their schools were small and they usually wanted only one teacher, he was unable to accommodate them. The rule of the Institute forbade the sending of a single brother to any school. The priests then sent young laymen from their parishes to be trained for the work by the Brothers. They lived apart from the Brothers, and received their education and support gratuitously. De la Salle thus successfully launched the first normal school for primary teachers, an institution which was destined to be officially adopted a century later by France, and is now everywhere regarded as an essential feature of an educational system.

Saint de la Salle personally opened the first schools of his Institute in Paris in 1688. Despite the opposition of the writing masters, primary teachers, and certain clerics, he successfully maintained his first foundation among the poor of the large parish of Saint Sulpice. While the primary schools were the first objects of his devotion, de la Salle stood ready to offer his Brothers for any educational service they could render. So in 1698 he opened his first boarding school at the request of the Archbishop of Paris, to educate the sons of the Catholic lords who accompanied the exiled James II to

France. Most of these boys were Irish, and their state in life demanded more advanced instruction than that of the elementary school. In Paris was also begun the work of reforming the wayward (1705), industrial training, and the Sunday School (1698). The latter, intended for young working men under twenty years of age, offered instruction in religion, also in reading, writing, arithmetic, geometry, and drawing. Its sessions lasted two hours, but the young men were also provided with wholesome recreation in Catholic surroundings.

With the extension of the activities of the Institute came persecution from civil and ecclesiastical authorities, and to the Founder innumerable personal trials. In 1702, due to a series of misrepresentations and calumnies, he was deposed by Cardinal de Noailles, but shortly afterward he was restored to power if not to office. The general chapter of 1717 gave the Institute permanent organization. De la Salle counselled the Brothers to elect his successor as superior general and, to his great satisfaction, the choice fell upon Brother Barthélemy. He desired that the Brothers, who by their Constitution were forbidden to become priests, should be governed by a member of the community. The Saint did not live to see his Institute approved by the Holy See. The bull of Benedict XIII, *In Apostolicae dignitatis solio*, constituting the community a religious congregation, appeared January 26, 1725, six years after his death (1719). He was canonized by Pope Leo XIII, May 24, 1900. At the time of his death, the Brothers numbered 274; their houses 27; and their pupils 9,885. When the French Revolution brought about its suppression, the Institute included 920 Brothers in 125 houses, enrolling some thirty-six thousand pupils.

The claims of Saint de la Salle as an educator rest securely on the movement which he directed for the organization and improvement of free elementary in-

struction, first, through the establishment of a teaching
congregation which has become worldwide in its operations; second, through the normal school; and, third,
through the application of the simultaneous method to
teaching and conducting classes.

In the elementary school, the special field of the
Brothers, the vernacular alone was used, and that education given in reading, writing, arithmetic, and religion
which was needed by poor children. In contrast to the
poorly managed and noisy primary schools of the time,
the Brothers' schools were orderly and quiet; the pupils
worked in silence, broken only by recitations, prayers,
and gentle voice of the teacher. The simultaneous method
assured proper grading of the children in classes and
orderly progress. The pupils were divided into groups
according to their capabilities, those of about the same
level receiving their instruction together. "The pupils
follow in the same lesson; they observe strict silence;
the master in correcting one, is correcting all; here is
the essence of the simultaneous method." [4] De la Salle
composed his *Management of Christian Schools (Con-
duite des écoles chrétiennes)*, published after his death,
to explain all the details of the method. "Later works
on the same subject," wrote Matthew Arnold, "have
little improved the precepts, while they entirely lack the
unction." [5] The teacher in consequence had both the
matter and method of his teaching indicated. Industry
and neatness in the pupils' work were demanded.
Especial care was shown for penmanship.

All school work proceeded in a spirit of prayer. At
stated times in study and class periods a student broke
the silence to recall the presence of God. In addition to

---

[4] Brother Azarias, *Essays Educational* (Chicago: D. H. McBride
& Co., 1896), p. 231.

[5] Matthew Arnold, *The Popular Education of France* (London:
Longmans, Green, and Roberts, 1861), p. 15.

regular instruction from the Catechism, the rules required training in religious exercises, attendance at Mass, reception of the Sacraments, and the practice of a devout life. Saint de la Salle composed in the form of readers *The Duties of a Christian* and *The Rules of Politeness*, which contain instruction on the truths of faith and on polite behavior. His directions, in short, covered the entire field of the teachers' work—recitation, study, recreation; they regulated method and management even to the extent of prescribing minutely when and how punishments should be inflicted. It is true that the details seem excessive and calculated to curtail all initiative on the part of the teachers. They would be annoying for teachers today, but in de la Salle's time, when lack of order was prevalent in the elementary schools, special details of method and procedure were deemed necessary to secure the results at which the Saint aimed.

The simultaneous method, which de la Salle placed on a working basis, was a distinct contribution to the art of teaching and management. For many elements of this method he was indebted to his predecessors. Saint Peter Fourier (1565-1640), founder of the Congregation of Notre Dame, had sketched it in the *Constitutions* of his Congregation; Comenius (1592-1671) touched upon it in the *Great Didactic*,[6] Bishop de Nesmond of Bayeux (1629-1715) in his *Plan of Instruction and Education for Primary Schools* assigned to the same bench children of the same capacity occupied with the same subject; Father Charles Demia (†1689), founder of the Brethren of St. Charles, expressed similar ideas in his *Rules for the Schools of the City and Diocese of Rouen*. De la Salle, however, reduced to a workable and practical method, "what Blessed Peter Fourier touched, what Komensky (Comenius) and Mgr. de Nesmond, and Charles Demia had glimmerings of"[7]—a method which

---

[6] Azarias, *op. cit.*, p. 219.
[7] *Ibid.*, p. 230 f.

has been at the basis of primary school procedure ever since.

Another contribution, and according to many a greater one than the preceding, was the normal school for teachers. The novitiates of religious communities, and obviously those of teaching orders, had been training schools for teachers; but nowhere had schools for training laymen been in operation although, as already noted, Mulcaster had advocated them in England. When M. de Chennevières, a priest, petitioned Louis XIV for them in France (1686), de la Salle's Seminary for Schoolmasters was already in existence. In 1699, he opened one in Paris; and although his schools did not long survive him they were the models after which the primary normal schools of France were formed in 1861. Before de la Salle's death (1719) the institution had been adopted in Brussels by Des Roches (1687) and in Halle through the efforts of Francke. Of its spread into Austria something will be noted later.[8]

Other Catholic religious congregations of men and women founded in the seventeenth century and devoted to education may be briefly noted here. The Vincentians or Lazarists, properly called the Congregation of the Mission of St. Vincent de Paul, were founded at Paris in 1625 by St. Vincent de Paul, for the purpose of conducting missions and charitable works, including education. The Sulpicians (Society of Saint Sulpice), founded at Paris in 1642 by Jean Jacques Olier, a priest, for the training of teachers and directors of ecclesiastical seminaries, grew into a numerous and potent community. At the time of the suppression of religious orders in France (1900) they controlled there twenty-six large diocesan and provincial seminaries. They came as missionaries to Canada in 1657.

---

[8] *Cf.* p. 511.

The communities of women founded in this century were more numerous than those of men, especially in France. The Sisters of Notre Dame, now a large teaching body in the Church, were founded by St. Peter Fourier in 1598 for the education of poor girls. They were introduced into America in 1657 with some modifications by Marguerite Bourgeoys, who is venerated as the founder of the Congregation of Notre Dame of Montreal. The School Sisters of Notre Dame, a branch of the congregation founded by St. Peter Fourier, controlled in the seventeenth century many convent schools in Germany. The English Ladies, founded 1609, in France, by Mary Ward, and suppressed by the Church in 1630, were succeeded as a religious body by the Institute of Mary, established at Munich, Bavaria, for the maintenance of convent schools and the care of orphans. In 1669 they opened a house at Hammersmith, London, and at the close of the century their institutions were flourishing in Bavaria, Italy, France, and England. The Visitation Nuns (Visitandines), founded 1610, in France, by St. Jane Frances de Chantal and St. Francis de Sales, undertook among their earliest works the education of girls. The Presentation Sisters, or Daughters of the Presentation, as they were first called, founded 1627 by Nicholas Sanguin, Bishop of Senlis, France, for the education of poor girls, did not survive the French Revolution. The Sisters of the Presentation of the Blessed Virgin appeared in 1684, a foundation of the Venerable Marie Poussepin, at Sainville, France, for the work of teaching and the care of the sick. The Sisters of Charity of St. Vincent de Paul, founded 1633, in Paris, by St. Vincent de Paul, for charitable works, engaged in instructing the poor. The Sisters of St. Joseph, founded 1650 at Le Puy, France, by Jean Paul Medaille, a Jesuit, like the Sisters of Mercy of St. Charles Borromeo (Borromean Sisters), were the forerunners of large associations bearing the same name and identified with Catholic schools in many countries.

August Hermann Francke (1663-1727), the representative of the Pietists in education, studied in preparation for the ministry at the universities of Erfurt, Kiel, and Leipzig. He taught at Leipzig after receiving the master's degree (1685). The Bible club which he there organized attracted the attention of Spener, Court preacher at Dresden and leader of the Pietistic movement. In 1687, Francke was located at Hamburg. It was there he opened the elementary school which formed the basis of his later educational activities. Again a professor at Leipzig in 1689, his unorthodox views on the Scriptures brought him into conflict with the conservative professors, and he was forced to leave. He was treated even less kindly by the Protestant clergy in Erfurt where he had accepted a pastorate; they drove him from the city. He then became professor of Greek and Oriental languages at the newly founded University of Halle, through the influence of Spener, holding at the time the pastorate of Glaucha, a suburb of Halle. There he remained for the rest of his life, thirty-five years, zealously organizing the famous institutions which have survived to the present time as the Francke Foundations *(Franckesche Stiftungen)*.

Francke began his educational work by opening a poor or charity school in his own house and employing a needy university student as teacher. Before long, some citizens of Halle asked admission for their children and Francke was obliged to furnish new schoolrooms with division for these two classes of pupils. He accepted a fee from those who could afford it. From funds supplied by a friend he also established an orphan school in which the children were boarded. In the same year, 1695, three children of noble family were placed under his care to be educated. This formed the beginning of the *Paedogogium*, or Boarding School. In 1698 there were one hundred orphans and five hundred other children receiving instruction in his institutions. Generous benefactors then came forward to assist him with funds and colaborers rallied to his support. The printing press of the orphanage and the apothecary proved sources of revenue. In 1705 his establishment included eight school classes, with eight hundred scholars, among whom were one hundred and twenty-five orphans, and sixty-seven teachers; the *Paedogogium*, with seventy scholars and seventeen teachers; a seminary for teachers, supporting seventy-five persons gratuitously; a Widow's House; and Oriental college. The boarding school for girls, opened in 1698, was closed seven years later. At the time of his death there was furthermore a Latin school for the children of the city and the brighter boys of the orphanage. The elementary school of the orphans was then distinct from the burghers' school, or that attended by children of the city. Buildings had been erected through the gifts of benefactors and the earnings of the establishment, which then included a printing press, a bookstore, and a paper mill. There were over seventeen hundred children, boys and girls, in the elementary schools, four hundred in the Latin school, and two hundred and fifty boarded at a free table.

Francke's religious and practical aim in education can be seen in these foundations and in his writings. Always deeply religious as the Pietist, he strove both to train children to virtue and to prepare them for their callings in life. The religious purpose is exposed in his *Short and Simple Instruction for Leading Children to True Piety and Christian Wisdom*,[9] in which he treats of the method of religious instruction; his real or practical purpose may be seen in his *Organization and Training*

---

[9] *Kurzer und einfältiger Unterricht wie die Kinder zur wahren Gottseligkeit und christlichen Klugheit anzuführen sind.*

Method in the Orphan Schools [10] and his *Directions for Inspectors of Schools.* [11]

In his own time and afterward Francke's institutions wielded a great influence in Germany, in regard to, first, the education and care of orphans; second, the training of teachers, for his training school was reproduced in most of the Protestant states; and third, the emphasis on the practical or real subjects in elementary and secondary education. In the burgher school the vernacular alone was used and practical instruction given in arithmetic, geography, and the useful arts; in the secondary, German, French, and mathematics were offered as well as the classics. His colleague, Semler, opened in association with him the first *Realschule,* or secondary non-classical school, and his disciple Hecker inaugurated this institution in Berlin.

FOR FURTHER STUDY

Adamson, J. W., *Pioneers of Modern Education.* Cambridge: University Press, 1905.

Annales de l'Institut des Frères Écoles Chrétiennes (1679-1719). Paris: Poussielgue, 1883.

Azarias, Brother, *Essays Educational.* Chicago: D. H. McBride & Co., 1896.

Barnard, H., *German Teachers and Educators.* Hartford: Brown and Gross, 1878.

Barnard, H. C., *The Little Schools of Port Royal.* Cambridge: University Press, 1913.

————, *The French Tradition in Education.* Cambridge: University Press, 1922.

Blain, Jean, *Vie de M. Jean-Baptiste de la Salle.* Rouen: Mame et Fils, 1733.

Cadet, Felix, *Port Royal Education.* Translated by A. H. Jones. New York: Charles Scribner's Sons, 1898.

Carré, G., *Les Pédagogues de Port Royal.* Paris: Hachette et Cie, 1887.

---

[10] *Ordnung und Lehrart der Waisenhaus-Schulen.*
[11] *Instruction des Inspectoris Scholarum.*

——————, *L'Enseignement secondaire à Troyes du Moyen Age à la Révolution.* Paris: Hachette et Cie, 1888.

Currier, C. W., *History of Religious Orders.* New York: Murphy & McCarthy, 1894.

De La Salle, St. Jean-Baptiste, *The Management of Schools.* Translated by Christian Brothers. New York: De La Salle Institute, 1887.

——————, *The Rules for Politeness and Christian Civility.* Translated by Christian Brothers. New York: New York Catholic Protectory, 1884.

——————, *The Duties of the Christian.* Translated by Christian Brothers. New York: New York Catholic Protectory, 1882.

Dempsey, Martin, *John Baptist De La Salle.* Milwaukee: Bruce Publishing Co., 1940.

Guibert, J., *Life and Virtues of St. John Baptist de la Salle.* Translated by Christian Brothers. Tours: Alfred Mame et Fils, 1912.

Hamel, C., *Histoire de l'Abbaye et du Collège de Juilly.* Paris: J. Gervais, 1888.

Heimbucher, Max, *Die Orden und Kongregationen der Katholischen Kirche.* Paderborn: F. Schöningh, 1933-34.

Hélyot, P., *Histoire des ordres monastiques, religieux,* etc., Guingamp: B. Jollivet, 1838.

Marique, P. J., *History of Christian Education.* Vol. II. New York: Fordham University Press, 1926.

Prunel, J., *La Renaissance Catholique en France au dix-septième Siècle.* Paris: Desclée de Brouwer & Cie, 1921.

Ravelet, Armand, *Blessed John Baptist de la Salle.* Translated by K. O'Meara. Tours: Alfred Mame et Fils, 1888.

Rigault, George, *Histoire générale de l'Institut des Frères des Écoles Chrétiennes.* Paris: Librairie Plon, 1937.

Wilson, R. F. Mrs., *The Christian Brothers, Their Origin and Their Work.* London: Kegan Paul, Trench Co., 1883.

SYNOPSIS OF EDUCATIONAL REACTIONS IN THE EIGHTEENTH CENTURY

1. THE ENCYCLOPEDISTS IN FRANCE
   - (a) Promised a universal Enlightenment
   - (b) Attacked prevalent systems of thought and government, revealed religion, and the groundwork of morality
   - (c) Voltaire represented the revolt among the educated classes.

2. JEAN JACQUES ROUSSEAU (1712-1778)
   - (a) Champion of the revolt as it extended to the masses of the people
   - (b) *Social Contract* burned both in Paris and Geneva
   - (c) *Emile, or Concerning Education* condemned by Catholics and Protestants alike; in it Naturalism in education found its great exponent
   - (d) Educational opinions called attention to the study of the child, his natural abilities and tastes, and the necessity of accommodating instruction and training to him and of awaiting natural development

3. JOHANN BERNARD BASEDOW (1723-1790)
   - (a) Applied many of the naturalists' theories in his Philanthropinum
   - (b) His *Elementary Book* aimed to give the child a knowledge of words and things, of nature, of natural religion, of social duties, etc.
   - (c) Joachim Heinrich Campe, his successor, established a Philanthropinum at Hamburg; Christian Gotthilf Salzmann established another at Schnefenthal; similar institutions were opened in many parts of Germany and had a favorable influence on industrial, agricultural, and primary education

4. RELIGIOUS INFLUENCES OF THE EIGHTEENTH CENTURY
   - (a) Protestant and Catholic circles undertook to counteract the current naturalism in education
   - (b) August Hermann Niemeyer, leader of the Pietists
   - (c) Franz von Fürstenberg, foremost among the Catholic reformers of Germany
   - (d) Johann Ignaz von Felbiger empowered by Empress Maria Teresa to reform educational conditions in Silesia and Austria

CHAPTER XXVI

THE EIGHTEENTH CENTURY

Naturalism and Education

The Eighteenth Century, like the one preceding, brought with it a series of reactions. The empiricism of Locke became a materialistic rationalism and skepticism with the Encyclopedists in France. Reason, enthroned and empowered to explain all things, promised a universal Enlightenment. The Illuminati, however, remained few in number, and their chief delight was found in attacking prevalent systems of thought and government, the Church and all revealed religion, and the groundwork of morality. In Voltaire [1] appeared the representative of the revolt as it was confined to the educated classes; in Rousseau, the champion and voice as it extended to the masses of the people and prepared the way for the terrible upheaval of the Revolution.

Jean Jacques Rousseau (1712-1778) was the son of a watchmaker of Geneva, Switzerland. Due to the early

---

[1] Voltaire and the Encyclopedists were intellectual aristocrats with little interest in the common people. They sought to test everything by the universal criterion of common sense and to make everything rational or reasonable. Against this artificial outlook, a reaction set in which, under the leadership of Rousseau, has left its traces in modern thought and life. To him right feeling was as important as right thinking. He maintained that the emotions had been lost sight of while philosophers were concerned only with the intellect. Rousseau had seen and felt the suffering of the poor. The indifference with which educated men had regarded it was due he claimed to science and learning which seemed to have made men only more selfish. Cf., Harold Höffding, *A History of Modern Philosophy*, translated by B. E. Meyers (London: The Macmillan Company, 1900), vol. I: William H. Hudson, *Rousseau and Naturalism in Life and Thought* (New York: Charles Scribner's Sons, 1903).

death of his mother, his upbringing by his father and an indulgent aunt was most irregular. He contracted many vicious habits in his boyhood. Although he acquired a taste for reading and read extensively with his father, his mental discipline was as lax as his moral. He spent two years in the care of a clergyman at Bossey, near Geneva, with little improvement in his moral character. He did acquire a greater love for the beauties of nature. A punishment, however, inflicted for one of his offenses made him morbid and dejected. As an apprentice to an attorney and later to an engraver, he was unable to succeed; one discharged him for negligence, the other he left because of harsh treatment. He then ran away from home, beginning the vagabond life which he followed for almost the rest of his days. At Borney, France, he found a friend in the Catholic bishop, who out of pity tried to provide some systematic training for him at the hands of Madame de Warens, a recent convert. She sent him to Turin where he embraced the Catholic faith. He did not remain long there, but after some years of wandering returned to accept again the hospitality of his benefactress. She obtained appointments for him in all of which Rousseau demonstrated a consistently unstable and unreliable character. In 1741 he appeared in Paris, supporting himself by copying music and occasional employments. He attracted notice in literary circles by his extreme views and the boldness of his style. As secretary of the French Embassy at Venice, he continued to lead the same immoral life as formerly. After two years he had quarreled with his superior officers and lost his position. In Paris again, he took up his abode with an ignorant girl, Thérèse Levasseur, with whom he lived for twenty years before marrying her. Five children were born of their illicit union, all of whom the father placed in a foundling asylum.

Association with Diderot, D'Alembert, and the Encyclopedists brought Rousseau into some connection with the literary lights of Paris. When he won the literary prize offered by the Academy of Dijon for the best essay on "Whether the progress of the arts and sciences has tended to the purification of manners and morals," he found himself famous. He had taken the negative side and produced an essay as brilliant as it was daring. He also wrote on music, attracting attention by his novel theories and views. Some of his articles appeared in the Encyclopedia.[2]

During a visit to Geneva, Rousseau renounced the Catholic belief and returned to Protestantism. It is noteworthy that his *Social Contract (Contrat Social)*, voicing his views on social equality, was burned both in Paris and Geneva. In 1762 he produced his famous educational work *Émile, or Concerning Education*, which was condemned by the archbishop of Paris and publicly burned. In it Naturalism in education found its great exponent. Because of the influence of the work on modern education, through Basedow and Pestalozzi in Germany and Spencer in England, its chief views will be here summarized.

Written in answer to the inquiries of Madame de Chenonceaux, *Émile* is an educational romance. It does not attempt to describe a system of education but to trace nature's course of development. Its ideas would not generally be practicable today, but on almost every page Rousseau suggests a newer study of child nature and touches upon principles which are now at the basis of educational methods. Despite its falsities, sophistries, oddities, and theories long outlived, *Émile* is in part at least worthy of study. In its five books, Rousseau treats first of the training of early infancy, or education of

---

[2] *Encyclopédie, ou Dictionnaire raissoné des sciences, des arts et des métiers.* Paris, 1751-80.

Émile to the age of five, when he has learned to talk; second, his childhood from the age of five to twelve; third, his boyhood, from twelve to fifteen; fourth, adolescence from fifteen to twenty, when he is ready for marriage; and fifth, of Sophie, his wife, and her education. "Émile, . . . is humanity personified, in the natural condition of childhood; a tutor teaches this child of nature naturally."[3]

Rousseau in the beginning states some general principles of his naturalistic theory.

Everything is good as it comes from the hands of the Author of Nature; but everything degenerates in the hands of man. . . . We are born weak; we have need of strength; we are born destitute of everything; we have need of assistance; we are born stupid; we have need of judgment. All that we have not at birth, but which we need when we are grown, is given us by education.[4]

Education is derived from three sources, namely, from nature, from men, and from things.

The internal development of our faculties and organs is the education of nature; the use which we learn to make of this development is the education of men; while the acquisition of personal experience from the objects that affect us is the education of things.[5]

These sources Rousseau makes teachers.

The pupil in whom their different lessons are at variance is badly educated, and will never be in harmony with himself; while he in whom they all agree, in whom they all tend to the same end—he alone moves toward his destiny and consistently lives; he alone is well educated.[6]

Since the education of nature is independent of man, the other two must be directed towards it. The natural

---

[3] Henry Barnard, "Jean Jacques Rousseau," *Barnard's American Journal of Education*, V, 469.

[4] Jean Jacques Rousseau, *Émile*, translated by William N. Payne (New York: D. Appleton and Co., 1906), pp. 1 f.

[5] *Ibid.*, p. 2.

[6] *Ibid.*, p. 3.

man is complete in himself, the numerical unit, the absolute whole, who is related only to himself or to his fellow man, whereas civilized man is but a fractional unit that is dependent on its denominator, and whose value consists in its relation to the whole, which is the social organization.

Good social organizations are those which are the best able to make man unnatural, and to take from him his absolute existence in order to give him one which is relative, and to transport the one into the common unity. . . .[7]

There is consequently a conflict between the individual and the social purpose in education.

In the first period, that of infancy, Émile's education is chiefly physical. The mother is teacher and the rule given here is:

Observe nature, and follow the route which she traces for you. She is ever exciting children to activity; she hardens the constitution by trials of every sort; she teaches them at an early hour what suffering and pain are.[8]

The growing body is not to be restrained in any way. Without overtaxing its strength it is to be hardened to seasons and climates; to hunger, thirst, and fatigue. The child must be healthy, for Rousseau said, "I would not assume charge of a sickly and debilitated child, was he to live eighty years." [9] He should have a vigorous body, acquired in the open air of the country and by frequent bathing.

From five to twelve Émile's education is almost entirely a negative one.

It consists not at all in teaching virtue or truth, but in shielding the heart from vice, and the mind from error. If you could do nothing and allow nothing to be done; if you could bring your pupil sound and robust to the age of twelve years without his being able to distinguish his right hand from

---

[7] *Ibid.*, pp. 5 f.
[8] *Ibid.*, p. 13.
[9] *Ibid.*, p. 22.

his left—from your very first lesson the eyes of his understanding would be open to reason. Without prejudice and without habit, he would have nothing in him which could counteract the effect of your endeavors. . . . Take the very reverse of the current practice, and you will almost always do right.[10]

The only moral training at this time proper for children is a preventive one. The opportunities for wrongdoing are to be forestalled. Rousseau does not believe in original sin; children, he says, have no natural propensity to evil. They become bad when the seeds of evil have been sown by others in their hearts.

They learn much now through things, not books, for instance, simple facts of geography; and the method is that of observation. Reading can wait until the eleventh or twelfth year. Émile in his twelfth year must scarcely know what a book is. Physical exercise continues during this period and the training is chiefly that of the senses through systematic observation and experience.

In the third period, from the age of twelve to fifteen, Émile has a natural curiosity and eagerness to learn. Objects and ideas, not words, are his teachers. He must learn everything himself, using his own reason and experience and not relying upon the authority of others. He discovers his powers. Geography he studies in his immediate neighborhood; he makes simple beginnings of the natural sciences. He learns only the useful and understands the usefulness of his knowledge to his present well-being.[11] Rousseau prescribes only one book for Émile's reading; *Robinson Crusoe* should constitute his whole library, for this book alone truly depicts a situation where all the natural needs of man are exhibited, and where the means of providing for these needs are successively developed.[12] · Émile must also

---

[10] *Ibid.*, pp. 59 f.
[11] *Ibid.*, pp. 136-38.
[12] *Ibid.*, pp. 163 f.

learn a trade, that of carpenter, for example, to be independent of changes in fortune. He will then think better of workmen.[13]

From fifteen to twenty Émile is conducted through the period when selfishness changes to self-esteem as he comes into contact with men. He now learns history, an aid to his great study, men.[14] He is taught no religion, but Rousseau will have him put in a condition to be able to choose one for himself. Finally, in the fifth book Émile is given a wife, Sophie. Her training has been ordered to fit her for companionship with Émile. It represents the education of Rousseau's ideal woman and is purely relative to that of man. Woman, he believed, was constituted to please man.[15]

Émile was condemned by the Archbishop of Paris because of the abominable doctrine it taught.

... calculated to overthrow natural law, and to destroy the foundations of the Christian religion; establishing maxims contrary to Gospel morality; having a tendency to disturb the peace of empires, to stir up subjects to revolt against their sovereign; as containing a great number of propositions respectively false, scandalous, full of hatred towards the Church and her ministers, lessening respect due to Holy Scripture and the tradition of the Church, erroneous, impious, blasphemous, and heretical.[16]

As noted above, the book was also condemned by the Protestants of Geneva. Purely naturalistic and therefore unacceptable to Christians, it abounds in contradictions and sophistries. Although its influence in the domain of school education has been more good than

---

[13] *Ibid.,* pp. 177-83.
[14] *Ibid.,* pp. 213-17.
[15] *Ibid.,* p. 260.
[16] *"Mandement de Monseigneur L'Archevêque de Beaumont de Paris portant condamnation d'un livre qui a pour titre: Émile, ou De L'Education par J. J. Rousseau, citoyen de Genève,"* *Oeuvres de J. J. Rousseau* (Paris: Lefèvre, 1819-20), X, 158.

bad,[17] pedagogically it is defective in purpose, having only temporal existence in view; it is one-sided, accepting only the utilitarian, and neglecting the aesthetic, cultural, and moral. Yet, among so much error there was some truth. Rousseau, like Comenius, called attention to the study of the child, his natural abilities and tastes, and the necessity of accommodating instruction and training to him and of awaiting natural development. His criticism served many useful purposes and in spite of his chicanery and paradoxes many of his views were successfully applied by Basedow, Pestalozzi, and other educators.

Rousseau's educational influence was first felt outside of his own country. *Johann Bernard Basedow* (1723-90), a representative of the German "Enlightenment," applied many of the naturalist's theories in his Philanthropinum. Basedow was born in Hamburg, the son of a wigmaker. His youth, like Rousseau's, was a stormy one. He ran away from home because of his father's severity towards him, returning upon the latter's entreaties. As a student he wrote many poems and supported himself at times by their sale. He studied theology at Leipzig, intending to enter the Lutheran ministry. Instead, he became a tutor to a noble family in Holstein. With these children Basedow attempted to use newer methods of teaching, following the principles of Locke and Comenius. The theological writings he produced as professor of ethics at the Danish Academy of Soroe, and also while teaching in the gymnasium of Altona, were roundly attacked as heretical and rationalistic by the Protestant clergy. His reputation suffered as a result. After reading *Émile*, he resolved to devote himself to educational reform. In 1768, through his *Address upon Schools, Studies, and Their Influence upon the Public*

---

[17] *Cf.* W. Kane, *An Essay Toward A History of Education,* pp. 343 f.

Weal, he sought the aid of the benevolent and rich for the publication of an elaborate elementary work, the first step in his reform. Before it appeared (1774) Basedow wrote his *Book of Methods* [18] for parents and teachers.

The *Elementary Book,*[19] consisting of four volumes, was a kind of encyclopedia for the young. Accompanying it was a book of one hundred plates illustrating the subjects treated. It aspired to be an interesting reading book and aimed to give the child a knowledge of words and things, of nature, of natural religion, of social duties, of commerce, etc. It was in the form of a dialogue and its plan resembled the *Orbis pictus* of Comenius. It was intended, in short, to contain all the young should learn; but Basedow soon realized he had outlined too much and afterward revised it.

In 1774, the year the *Elementary Book* appeared, Basedow, aided by the generosity of many patrons and especially of Prince Leopold of Anhalt-Dessau, opened at Dessau the institution in which his reforms were carried out, the Philanthropinum. His aim was to give a general or cosmopolitan education, one suitable to youth of any country. The wealthy were required to pay a fee and were designated especially for this training; the poor were prepared for teaching. Supposedly nonsectarian and encouraging the child to follow the belief of its parents, the Philanthropinum actually gave instruction in a natural and rationalistic religion. Among its characteristics may be noted a careful physical training through daily exercise and simplicity in dress and living; a utilitarian standard in determining the choice of studies; a system of rewards; insistence on obedience to rules; instruction in regard to sexual behavior.

---

[18] *Methodenbuch für Väter und Mütter der Familien und Völker.*

[19] *Elementarwerk.*

All students, wealthy and poor, were taught handiwork or a trade. Part of their recreation was spent at manual work. Much of the study too was done at play. Latin received more attention than Rousseau would favor; German and French were also studied. The method of learning a language through conversation, drawing and games, and practical instruction in geography, mathematics and nature study were commendable and would have been approved by Rousseau. He would not have sanctioned the compulsory obedience, the rewards, or the prominence given to Latin.

The institution promised great results, but Basedow lacked administrative ability. He quarreled with the teachers and eventually failed in raising the necessary funds. He resigned in 1776 and tried many callings until his death in 1790. The institution lasted only until 1793. *Joachim Heinrich Campe* (1746-1818), his successor, wrote on education, but is best known for his *Robinson Crusoe Junior (Robinson der jüngere)*. He established a Philanthropinum at Hamburg. *Christian Gotthilf Salzmann* (1744-1811), once a teacher at the Dessau Philanthropinum, established another at Schnefenthal which has survived to the present time. Similar institutions were opened in many parts of Germany and had a favorable influence on industrial, agricultural, and primary education.

Religious Influences of the Eighteenth Century

During this century there arose in both Protestant and Catholic circles vigorous religious movements to counteract the current naturalism in education. Although the Pietists had fallen into a formalism which threatened the existence of their foundations in the first half of the century, they were saved from extinction by the reforms of the great-grandson of Francke, *August Hermann Niemeyer* (1754-1828). Among the Protestants were to be found many followers of Basedow and their opposition to rationalism and naturalism was neither so potent nor so consistent as that presented by the Catholics. The Church then produced some statesmen and leaders whose influence educationally extended far beyond their respective domains. Foremost among the Catholic reformers of Germany should rank *Franz von Furstenberg* (1729-1810) vicar-general and minister of education of the diocese of Münster, whose school ordinances gave new life to the whole educational system over which he was placed. He began with the reform of the gymnasium, introducing more modern subjects and giving greater prominence to German, the natural sciences, and mathematics. He also improved facilities for the education of the clergy, and it was through his efforts that the University of Münster really started on its career. The normal school founded by him and over which he placed the well-known educator and priest, Bernard Overberg, became the model of other training schools in Catholic centers.[20]

To the Augustinian abbot, *Johann Ignaz von Felbiger* (1724-1788), was due the reform of educational conditions in Silesia and Austria. As abbot of Sagan in Silesia, Felbiger became interested in the schools near his monastery. He realized that their deplorable condition was due chiefly to the unskilled and untrained teachers in charge. Encouraged by the government of Silesia, he issued a series of ordinances; but he accomplished his best results when, after a visit to Berlin and an inspection of the schools of the Pietists, Hähn and Hecker, he introduced their newer methods and system of training teachers in his own country. He adopted the tabular and alphabetical methods devised by Hähn, opened a college or training school for teachers, and published

---

[20] *Cf.* J. Esch, *Franz von Fürstenberg, sein Leben und seine Schriften* (Freiburg: Herder, 1891).

many textbooks, notably a new Catechism. He attracted wide attention by the success of his plans.

The Empress Maria Teresa called Felbiger to Austria in 1774 to become the general minister of education for all the German schools of her domains. His first work was to draw up an ordinance designating elementary schools for all cities and villages, and secondary schools or *Gymnasien* for the cities. In the latter, besides Latin and German, history, geography, higher mathematics, and even surveying were offered. In every province he opened a normal school which was actually a combination of *Real Gymnasium* and training school for teachers. The plan also included girls' schools providing instruction in the domestic arts.

Felbiger's methods of organization and his textbooks were adopted in many parts of Germany and even in St. Petersburg. His work aroused wide enthusiasm but also considerable jealousy. Joseph II, who did not espouse his cause, removed him from Vienna and limited his educational endeavors to Hungary. Before he withdrew from Austria, however, Felbiger's influence had called into existence or shaped anew 3,933 schools.[21] The great abbot deserves to rank high as an educational organizer and administrator. Frederick the Great recognized his ability by requesting him in 1765 to draw up the Ordinances for Catholic schools in Silesia and the county of Glatz. Although he wrote much on education, he contributed little to pedagogical science. The tabular method, or use of tables presenting subjects in their various divisions which could be displayed in the classrooms, was a help in maintaining discipline; and the alphabetical method, or use of initials for recalling words, assisted in training memory and was a stimulus to curiosity and interest. As teaching devices both were,

---

[21] C. Krieg, *Lehrbuch der Pädogogik* (Paderborn: Ferdinand Schönigh, 1905), p. 221.

however, too mechanical to be of permanent utility. They promised more than they really accomplished. Felbiger's writings for teachers, particularly the *Method Book*,[22] sanctioned the class method especially in recitations, encouraged the practice of questioning, and secured a certain degree of uniformity in the methods of the many teachers who were prepared in his schools.

FOR FURTHER STUDY

Barnard, H. C., *German Teachers and Educators*. Hartford: Brown and Gross, 1878.

————, "Felbiger," *American Journal of Education*. Vol IX.

Boyd, W., *The Educational Theory of Jean Jacques Rousseau*. Longmans, Green, & Co., 1911.

Davidson, T., *Rousseau and Education according to Nature*. New York: Charles Scribner's Sons, 1898.

Eby and Arrowood, *The Development of Modern Education*. New York: Prentice-Hall, Inc. 1935.

Foxley, B., translator, *Emile: or, Education*. New York: E. P. Dutton & Co., 1911.

Grand-Carteret, J., *J. J. Rousseau jugé par les Français d'aujourd'hui*. Paris: Pertin et Cie, 1890.

Höffding, H., *Jean Jacques Rousseau and his Philosophy*. London: Oxford University Press, 1930.

Hudson, W. H., *Rousseau and Naturalism in Life and Thought*, New York: Charles Scribner's Sons, 1903.

Kane, W., *An Essay Toward A History of Education*. Chicago: Loyola University Press, 1935.

Lang, O. H. *Basedow, His Life and Work*. New York: E. L. Kellogg & Co., 1891.

MacDonald, Mrs. Fredericka, *J. J. Rousseau*. 2 vols. London: Chapman and Hall, Ltd., 1906.

Maritain, J., *Three Reformers*. London: Sheed and Ward, 1928.

Morley, J., *Rousseau*, 2 vols. London: The Macmillan Company, 1891.

————, *Rousseau and his Era*. London: The Macmillan Co., 1923.

---

[22] *Methodenbuch für Lehrer der deutschen Schulen.*

Oeuvres complètes de J. J. Rousseau, Paris: Musset-Pathy, Editeurs, 1823.

O'Connell, G., *Naturalism in American Education.* Washington, D. C.: The Catholic University of America, 1936.

Panholzer, J., *Johann Ignaz von Felbiger's Methodenbuch.* Freiburg: Herder, 1892.

Payne, William, translator, *Rousseau's Émile.* New York: D. Appleton and Company, 1906.

Quick, R. H., *Educational Reformers.* New York: D. Appleton and Company. 1907.

Reynaud, L., *Histoire générale de l'influence française en Allemagne.* Paris: Hatchette et Cie, 1915.

Texte, Joseph, *J. J. Rousseau and the Cosmopolitan Spirit in Literature.* Translated by J. W. Matthews. New York: The Macmillan Co., 1899.

Volkmer, Franz, *Johann Ignaz von Felbiger und seine Schulreform.* Habelschwerdt: I. Franke, 1890.

Walther, E. G., *Die Grundzuge der Pädagogie Ignaz von Felbiger.* Leipzig: Dr. Seele, 1903.

SYNOPSIS OF THE PSYCHOLOGISTS AND OTHER THEORISTS OF THE NINETEENTH CENTURY

JOHANN HEINRICH PESTALOZZI (1746-1827)

EDUCATION IS DEVELOPMENT

Johann Friedrich Herbart (1776-1841)	Friedrich Wilhelm Froebel (1782-1852)
(a) development from without	(a) development from within
(b) business of the teacher	(b) the pupil is the active agent
(c) doctrine of interest	(c) principle of self-activity
(d) doctrine of apperception	(d) principle of social participation

METHODIZERS

ANTONIO ROSMINI-SERBATI—Views on pupil activity are noteworthy; fundamental principles for early training closely resemble those of Froebel

JOSEPH JACOTOT—Asserted the principle of thoroughness in learning; touched upon correlation and coordination of all learning; methods too mechanical, unduly burdening the memory

HERBERT SPENCER
CHAMPION OF THE SCIENCES IN THE MODERN CURRICULUM

(a) What Knowledge is of Most Worth? ⎫ Essays
(b) Intellectual Education ⎪ published
(c) Moral Education ⎬ later in
(d) Physical Education ⎭ book form with the title, *Education*

CHAPTER XXVII

THE NINETEENTH CENTURY

That the Naturalism of Rousseau had a real effect on the Psychological Movement of the nineteenth century will be seen from the study of the first phase of that movement, Pestalozzianism. Education according to nature will become education by development. The general direction of the movement will be seen in Pestalozzi, the scientific formulation of its principles in Herbart, and the application to the early training of the child in Froebel. Father Rosmini and Jacotot represent the aims, and, in a measure, the achievements of the century in the field of methods. The Italian priest because of the philosophical basis of his work deserves to rank with Herbart and Froebel as the expounder of many of the principles on which modern elementary education rests. Herbert Spencer, finally, may be taken as the vigorous champion of the scientific studies.

The Psychologists [1]

Johann Heinrich Pestalozzi (1746-1827), an educator whose field of influence was world-wide, displayed in boyhood and youth many of the characteristics that marked him as the mature man. He was born at Zurich, Switzerland, the son of a physician. Deprived of his father at the age of five, he was reared by his mother

---

[1] Pestalozzi, Herbart, and Frobel were three outstanding figures in the field of education in the nineteenth century. The years through which they lived were marked by the Industrial Revolution in England, and, on the continent, by the French Revolution and the Napoleonic Wars. In our own country the Declaration of Independence was proclaimed and the American Revolution was fought to establish our independence. These three educators were natural products of their age which was characterized by democratic aspirations and by a craving of the human spirit for greater achievement and self-realization.

and a devoted maid servant, Babeli, who had promised Pestalozzi's father on his deathbed that she would not desert his wife and little family. Although poor, Pestalozzi's mother had resolved to provide a good education for her children. Johann, the eldest son, was kept much indoors under her care and deprived of contact with other boys. When he entered the public school he was puny and delicate, shy and awkward. He showed no talents and was dubbed by his companions "Harry Oddity of Foolborough." His unselfishness, however, gained their good will.[2]

From his tenth year Pestalozzi spent part of his vacations with his grandfather, then pastor of Höngg, a village near Zurich. There he learned to love nature and to sympathize with the lot of the peasants. He accompanied his grandfather on his visits to the poor, and perhaps in this way first conceived the desire to enter the ministry. After completing his secondary studies, he pursued courses in theology. One attempt at preaching convinced him of his unfitness for a clerical calling, and believing that he could still ameliorate the condition of the poor he turned to law. As a student he associated with the Swiss Reform Party, became an active member of the Helvetian Society, and contributed to their journal the *Memorial (Der Erinnerer)*, which was suppressed because of its criticism of the government. Pestalozzi and other writers were more than once imprisoned for their views. During these student years the reading of *Émile* and the *Social Contract* had made him an ardent disciple of Rousseau and had aroused in him a hatred of civilization and cities. Realizing after one of the elections that he could not raise the condition of the peasants through his services as a lawyer, and being

---

[2] Roger De Guimps, *Pestalozzi: His Life and Works*. Translated by J. Russell (New York: D. Appleton Company, 1902), p. 6.

advised by his physician to live in the country, Pestalozzi became a farmer.

In 1769 he married Anna Schulthess whom he had known from his childhood in Zurich, and that same year began his experiments in farming at Neuhof, near Birr, in the canton of Aarhau. He had been studying farming methods for a year with the result that he became an agricultural visionary. He tried vegetable and madder raising. After five years his venture proved a failure. A son had in the meantime been born to him, and it was in this child's early training that the great educator first began the work which shortly afterward he adopted as the means for elevating the peasant and poor classes. Basing his methods on Rousseau's theory, he soon modified the naturalist's principles by his own observations and experience. The journal kept by Pestalozzi of his child's progress, *A Father's Journal,* shows the gradual development of the principle which he later formulated as the essence of his educational method. Gratified by his child's progress, Pestalozzi was inspired to resume his efforts in behalf of the peasants, but this time through their education. The kind of training he considered proper for their regeneration may be seen in the school he opened at Neuhof.

In 1774, the farm project having failed, Pestalozzi received into his house twenty-five poor children. He took up cotton-spinning as a means of livelihood and put the children to light tasks in this industry and in the field. Had it not been for a public appeal for support, this enterprise would soon have failed. Donations enabled him to increase the number of children so that at one time it reached eighty. The children improved physically under his care and enjoyed their instruction, which was given in connection with their work and chiefly by conversation. Pestalozzi would not teach the child to read until he knew how to talk. He conversed constantly on subjects connected with everyday life and made the children repeat passages from the Bible until they knew them by heart.[3] At the proper time he would teach them reading, writing, and simple arithmetic. The boys learned farming, the girls sewing and household arts, and both cotton-spinning. There were twenty-one girls and sixteen boys in the house in 1778 according to Pestalozzi's account for the year. He was then assisted in managing the establishment by a Fräulein Spindler of Strassburg; a master to teach weaving and two skilled weavers; a mistress to teach spinning and two spinners; a man to assist the weavers and teach reading; two men and two women who were employed on the land.[4] In 1780, owing to Pestalozzi's lack of administrative ability, the school had to be closed and the children sent away.

Pestalozzi was able to keep his house, but years of poverty were in store for him. Encouraged by Iselin, in whose paper, *Ephemerides,* Pestalozzi's appeals had been published, he wrote the *Evening Hours of a Hermit,* a collection of aphorisms on the improvement of the people's lot by education, which attracted little attention. Pestalozzi was not discouraged. In suffering, he believed, he came to know better than ever before the miseries of the poor. He supported himself by writing. In 1781 he wrote *Leonard and Gertrude, A Book for the People,* a story of Swiss peasant life which was immediately popular and has since become an educational classic. Without appearing to teach, the author found a pleasant and simple way of placing his educational ideas before the world. The lesson of the story was not generally understood and Pestalozzi wrote continuations of it in 1783, 1785, and 1787, none of which was as well received as the first part. *Christopher and Eliza*

---

[3] De Guimps, *op. cit.,* p. 54.
[4] *Ibid.,* p. 62.

(1782), a second book for the people, was intended to point out the lessons of *Leonard and Gertrude*. During this period of great literary productivity, Pestalozzi published the *Swiss Journal*, a weekly paper which lasted only one year. Nothing then appeared from his pen until 1797 when he wrote, at the suggestion of Fichte, the obscure work entitled: *An Inquiry into the Course of Nature in the Development of the Human Race*.

In 1798, when the city of Stanz was taken by the French, Pestalozzi, who sympathized with the new government, was asked to take charge of the children made destitute by the war. A confiscated Ursuline convent was turned over to him. He had no assistants except a woman servant. Forty children were taken in and indescribable confusion prevailed. All were housed at first in one room, and Pestalozzi was nurse as well as teacher for many of them. The number increased eventually to eighty. The people, being Catholics, were distrustful of the new government and of the teacher, a Protestant.

Pestalozzi made some of the older pupils assist in teaching. He aimed first to win their affection and build up a common love among them, a family spirit which he believed should exist in every educational establishment.

I knew no other order, method or art, but that which resulted naturally from my children's conviction of my love for them, nor did I care to know any other. Thus I subordinated the instruction of my children to a higher aim, which was to arouse and strengthen their best sentiments by the relations of every-day life as they existed between themselves and me. ... I tried to connect study with manual labor, the school with the workshop, and make one thing of them.[5]

His aim was, he said, so to simplify the means of instruction that it should be quite possible for even the most ordinary man to teach his children himself; "thus schools would gradually almost cease to be necessary, so

---

[5] *Ibid.*, p. 166.

far as the first elements are concerned." Despite the
distrust of many and the adverse criticism of those who
visited his school, Pestalozzi wrote:

You will hardly believe that it was the Capuchin friars and
the nuns of the convent that showed the greatest sympathy
with my work. Few people except Truttman took any active
interest in it. Those from whom I had hoped most were too
deeply engrossed with their high political affairs to think of
our little institution as having the least degree of importance.[*]

The convent became a military hospital during the same
year and the school was abandoned. Pestalozzi retired
to the mountains to rest and recuperate, hoping to return and resume the work.

Unable to return to Stanz, Pestalozzi offered his services as a teacher in Burgdorf, in the canton of Berne.
After teaching in the elementary schools, he was appointed master of the higher school. He eventually
succeeded Fischer as head of the training school for
teachers in the castle of Burgdorf. With the assistance
of his first co-worker, Krüssi, who had already aided
him in the management of an elementary school, and
other devoted disciples, he made Burgdorf notable for
its experiments which proved quite successful. Teachers
from foreign countries came to study his methods. Here
Pestalozzi produced, in 1801, *How Gertrude Teaches
Her Children,* an attempt to show mothers how they can
teach their children themselves. Then also appeared *The
Mother's Book, The A B C of Intuition, The Intuitive
Teaching of Number Relations, The Natural Schoolmaster,* and other books on methods. During the disturbed political situation of 1804, the castle was taken
over by the town of Burgdorf for municipal purposes,
and Pestalozzi was again deprived of his school.

In 1804 he found a new location in a convent at

---

[*] *Ibid.,* p. 71

Münchenbuchsee near Bern, and, at the request of his teachers, entrusted the management of the school to his friend, Emmanuel Fellenberg,[7] who was then head of an agricultural institution nearby. The arrangement did not work successfully; it proved humiliating to Pestalozzi and he left to open another institution at Yverdun. In a year his former assistants and many of the pupils were glad to rejoin him. Here from 1805 to 1810 he achieved greater success than in any of his previous undertakings. The number of pupils and teachers became larger than in Burgdorf. He then really had an efficient staff of co-workers many of whom had been his former pupils, men capable both of applying his methods and of supplying for his inability on the side of administration. The work at Yverdun became that of an institution rather than of an individual man. When the Emperor Frederick William determined to reform elementary education in Prussia, seventeen young men were sent to Yverdun to spend three years in preparation for their work. Blochmann, a former pupil of Pestalozzi, propagated his methods in Saxony, and Denmark and Holland also sent students and teachers to Yverdun.

Parents then came from different countries to place their children in the institution. Due to the multiplication of activities and the daily influx of visitors, the order of work suffered; disagreements arose among the teachers. Finally, Pestalozzi was induced to invite a government inspection of the institution. The report of

---

[7] His institutions at Hofwyl, Switzerland, were famous in the first half of the nineteenth century. He was attracted to Pestalozzi's educational ideas concerning industrial training, but insisted that religion was an essential part of education. His program of manual labor in education affected for a time the schools of England and the United States. *Cf.* Thomas Jordan, "Philip Emmanuel Fellenberg: Catholic Educator and Philanthropist" (unpublished Master's dissertation, The Catholic University of America, Washington, D. C., 1939).

the inspectors, prepared by Père Girard,[8] a Catholic priest, was unfavorable especially in regard to the practical results discernible in the children's work. Joseph Schmidt, a Catholic, who brought considerable fame to the school as a teacher of arithmetic and author of *Exercises on Numbers,* was implicated in the troubles and in 1810 was obliged to leave. In 1815 the teachers voted to recall him. A strong-willed man, he evidently possessed administrative power, and it is significant that during his absence the management of the school became extremely bad. Although he exercised a great influence on Pestalozzi afterward, he could not hold the teachers together. By 1817 most of the oldest assistants had left Yverdun. The institution continued until 1825. It represents Pestalozzi's greatest educational undertaking, for it embraced elementary and higher, or classical courses, industrial training for boys and girls, and the preparation of teachers. He started one more school for the poor at Clindy with the aid of funds which were raised by subscriptions and largely through the efforts of Schmidt. This school was later transferred to Yverdun. Pestalozzi spent the last three years of his life with his grandson at Neuhof, where he died in 1827.

It has been seen that Pestalozzi found in education the means he desired for social reform, for the betterment of the poor. In making it a practical agency, he endeavored to place it on a scientific basis. "I want to psychologize education," he once said. In all his writings, however, there is no clear statement of the principles of his theory or method. *How Gertrude Teaches*

---

[8] Jean Baptiste Girard was a Franciscan educator who admired the educational efforts of Pestalozzi; he accepted Pestalozzi's theory of harmonious development, but disagreed with him on his overemphasis of the intellectual at the expense of the moral and religious aspects of education. For a summary of Girard's report on Pestalozzi's Institute, *Cf.* Andrew Maas, *Père Girard, Swiss Educational Reformer* (New York: Joseph F. Wagner Ic., 1931).

Her Children is the nearest approach to a definite exposition of his teaching plan. It well represents his idea that the teaching process should be made simple and effectual even in the hands of uninstructed parents, especially mothers. One thing always remained clear and that was Pestalozzi's life purpose, namely, to bring education within the reach of all, even the poorest and the lowliest. The principles and details of his method were the result of a life spent in patient experimentation. Although he disavowed having fixed or absolute modes of procedure, and although he instructed his disciples to continue as he had with experiments and further study of the child, certain fundamental principles became firmly established in his theory.[9] It is to their formulation and application by Pestalozzi and his followers that modern pedagogy owes much of its progress. One of his biographers, Morf, has drawn up the principal ideas of his theory and practice as expounded in *How Gertrude Teaches Her Children*. They are as follows:

1. Instruction must be based on the learner's own observation or experience (*Anschauung*, rendered as "intuition" and also "apperception" by some commentators).

2. What the learner experiences or observes must be connected with language.

3. The time for learning is not the time for judging, nor the time for criticism.

4. In every department instruction must begin with the simplest elements, and starting from these must be carried on step by step according to the development of

---

[9] Pestalozzi's contribution to the progress of education. it is claimed, lay in the genius with which he applied Rousseau's fundamental principles of naturalism to actual schoolroom practice. The particular ideas for which Pestalozzi himself stands are: the uplift of the masses by means of education; educational experimentation; industrial training; kindly discipline; objective teaching; and the analytical method. *Cf.* Ross L. Finney, *A Brief History of the American Public School* (New York: The Macmillan Company, 1925), pp. 70-82.

the child, that is, it must be brought into psychological sequence.

5. At each point the instructor shall not go forward till that part of the subject has become the proper intellectual possession of the learner.

6. Instruction must follow the path of development, not the path of lecturing, teaching, or telling.

7. To the educator the individuality of the child must be sacred.

8. Not the acquisition of knowledge or skill is the main object of elementary instruction, but the development and strengthening of the powers of the mind.

9. With knowledge must come power; with information, skill.

10. Intercourse between teacher and pupil, and school discipline especially, must be based on and controlled by love.

11. Instruction shall be subordinate to the aim of education.

12. The ground of moral religious bringing-up lies in the relation of mother and child.[10]

With this review of Pestalozzi's life and summary of his principles, the following features of his work and theory may be noted:

1. He showed education to be a development. His teacher becomes the director and minister, drawing out in accordance with nature's laws the unfolding powers of the child.

2. Development being from within, the child is to be trained to self-activity, to the exercise and use of his powers. All instruction is based on his experience, or observation, or intuition, that is, on what he already knows, and by such a method as to prepare him for further knowledge.

3. Sense training is a necessary condition of his proper

---

[10] *Cf.* Quick, *Educational Reformers,* p. 368.

development. Pestalozzi and his assistants, following Rousseau, elaborated this phase. Sense perception was the starting point in instruction, just as the idea was the end or aim. Things, the objects of sensation, come before words, the concrete before the abstract, not so much for a knowledge of the things themselves as for the training of the child in observation. Ideas or concepts are acquired by a graduated process. From vague sense impressions of an object the mind evolves a value or meaning. From "a swimming sea of sense impressions" some one thing is perceived, a distinct idea. Further and more detailed observation is required to make the idea clear. By analysis and comparison with other objects, its essential qualities become known—the idea is then definite. This progress or development of ideas, Pestalozzi said, is accomplished by Number, Form, and Language, that is, by investigating how many kinds of objects appear in consciousness; distinguishing their forms or outlines; and repeating what they are called, by a sound or word.

4. Training must be symmetrical at all stages, i.e., it must be a training of the whole being, moral, intellectual, and physical.

5. The spirit of the school is the home spirit, love in the teacher engendering confidence in the pupil.

Pestalozzi's religion has been the subject of much discussion. His Christianity has even been questioned. This is, indeed, one of the weak points in his system. He maintained that religion is an emotion and cannot be taught. Just, as in the case of the intellectual and practical powers, it is the art of pedagogy to seek the beginning elements, so in dealing with the moral-religious nature the original emotions which have grown out of dependence upon the mother must be transferred to mankind first and then to God Himself.[11] His faith was

---

[11] Eby and Arrowood, *Development of Modern Education*, pp. 658 f.

severely shaken by Rousseau and while he ever wrote and spoke reverently of God, and of the beliefs of Protestants and Catholics alike, he gave up his Christian belief for the vague Deism then popular; and there is little positive Christian doctrine evident in his writings or school work.[12] One of his pupils has written:

> Pestalozzi proved himself a Christian by his actions, his whole life, his ardent and universal charity; he never attacked any of the Christian dogmas, but neither did he ever make any clear and formal profession of them.[13]

In departing from the Calvinism of his early youth, Pestalozzi unfortunately seems to have fallen victim to a naturalism similar to that of the Philanthropinists.

Pestalozzi's failures were due to lack of ability as an administrator; his shortcomings and inconsistencies, to dependence upon his own experience and ignorance of the theories of his predecessors in educational work. Once he declared he had not read a book in thirty years. Nevertheless his influence was greater than that of any other modern educator. It extended over almost all Europe and the United States.[14] It has already been

---

[12] On the other hand he is regarded as neither schoolman nor educator but a master of charity. The practice of Christian love for neighbor determined his vocation. So earnest was he as an apostle of love for the children of the poor that he is ranked with St. Francis. St. Vincent de Paul. and Don Bosco. *Cf.* De Hovre-Jordan, *Philosophy and Education* (New York: Benziger Bros.. 1931), p. 211.

[13] De Guimps, *op. cit.,* p. 399.

[14] Pestalozzianism had much to do with the spread of naturalism in American education. What was only theory with Rousseau was reduced to practice by Pestalozzi. From 1800 on, and notably after 1850-60, Pestalozzianism emphasized the study of the child's physical environment, of real things. Between 1820 and 1860 a voluminous literature on Pestalozzianism appeared in America. The sixties and seventies were the great period of Pestalozzian influence in this country. *Cf.* Geoffrey O'Connell. *Naturalism in American Education* (Washington, D. C.: The Catholic University of America, 1936), pp. 58 ff.

noted that Prussia adopted his system and all Germany was eventually affected. A modified Pestalozzianism was introduced in England, while Joseph Neef opened the first Pestalozzian school in Philadelphia in 1808[15] Elementary education for all as their natural right was his leading bequest to posterity. The further extension of his influence to philanthropic institutions, to the care of orphans, is also noteworthy. He gave a new meaning to the educative process, that of development, and thereby started the Psychological Movement of modern times. His theories and methods of experimentation have been the basis and inspiration of later investigators and have influenced special methods in many directions —in adjusting instruction to the needs of the child, in emphasizing object-teaching, motor-activity, and correlation.

FOR FURTHER STUDY

Anderson, L. F., *Pestalozzi.* New York: McGraw-Hill, 1931.

Barnard, H., *American Journal of Education.* Vols. 3, 4, 7, 30, 31.

—————, *Pestalozzi and Pestalozzianism.* New York: F. C. Brownell, 1862.

Biber, E., *Henry Pestalozzi and his Plan of Education.* London: J. Souter, 1831.

Channing, Eva, translator, *Leonard and Gertrude.* Boston: Heath Co., 1885.

[15] Neef, an Alsatian, had studied for the priesthood before he went to Yverdun and became interested in Pestalozzi's method of teaching. He served as one of his teachers later at Burgdorf. He became a liberal in religion and opposed dogmatic religious instruction in the schools. He also organized schools at Louisville, Kentucky, and attempted to make New Harmony, Indiana, another Yverdun. He conducted schools in Cincinnati and Steubenville and spent the last twenty years of his life in writing at New Harmony. He died in 1854. *Cf.* W. S. Monroe, *History of the Pestalozzian Movement in the United States* (Syracuse: C. W. Bardeen, 1907).

De Guimps, Roger, *Pestalozzi: His Life and Work,* translated by J. Russell. New York: D. Appleton & Co., 1895.

Finney, Ross, *A Brief History of the American Public School.* New York: The Macmillan Co., 1925.

Gebhardt, B., *Die Einführung der Pestalozzischen Methode in Preuszen.* Berlin: R. Gaertner, 1896.

Green, J. A., *The Educational Ideas of Pestalozzi.* London: University Tutorial Press, Ltd., 1911.

————, *Life and Work of Pestalozzi.* University Tutorial Press, Ltd., 1913.

————, *Pestalozzi's Educational Writings.* London: Longmans, Green, and Co., 1912.

Greaves, J. P., *Letters on the Early Education of the Child.* London: Sherwood, Gilbert, and Piper, 1827.

Guillaume, J., *Pestalozzi; Étude biographique.* Paris: Hachette et Cie, 1890.

Holland, Lucy, and Francis Turner, translators, *How Gertrude Teaches Her Children.* Syracuse: C. W. Bardeen, 1894.

Israel, Augustus, *Pestalozzi-Biographie;* and *Die Schriften und Briefe Pestalozzi.* Monumenta Germaniae pedagogica, vols. 25, 29. Berlin: A. Hoffman, 1903.

Jullien, M. A., *Exposé de la méthode d'éducation de Pestalozzi.* Paris: L. Hachette, 1842.

Hérrison, F., *Pestalozzi, élève de J. J. Rousseau.* Paris: C. Delagrave, 1886.

Krüsi, Hermann, Jr., *Pestalozzi: His Life, Work and Influence.* New York: American Book Company, 1875.

Monroe, W. S., *History of the Pestalozzian Movement in the United States.* Syracuse: C. W. Bardeen, 1907.

Morf, H., *Zur Biographie Pestalozzi's.* 3 vols. Winterthur: Bleuler-Hausheer and Company, 1868-1889.

Parker, S. C., *The History of Modern Elementary Education.* Boston: Ginn and Company, 1912.

Pinloche, A., *Pestalozzi and the Foundation of the Modern Elementary School.* New York: Charles Scribner's Sons, 1901.

Quick, Robert H., *Essays on Educational Reformers.* New York: D. Appleton and Co., 1907.

Seyffarth, L. W., *Pestalozzi's sämmtliche Werke.* Liegnitz: C. Seyffarth, 1899-1902.

CHAPTER XXVIII

THE NINETEENTH CENTURY (Continued)

The Psychologists (Continued)

Johann Friedrich Herbart, who was to furnish the real psychological basis for Pestalozzi's methods, was born in Oldenburg, Germany, in 1776. His father was a lawyer and his mother a woman of more than ordinary ability. As a boy, Herbart displayed unusual talent and an aptitude for philosophy. He began the study of logic at eleven. After completing the course in the gymnasium of his native town, he studied philosophy at the University of Jena, coming under the influence of Fichte. Although he spent three years under the idealistic philosopher, Herbart did not subscribe to his views. As a student he produced some remarkable essays in criticism of the Idealism of Fichte and Schelling, outlining even then the basic principles of the system of philosophy he was later to develop.

In 1796, after three years spent in university study, Herbart accepted the office of tutor in the family of the Governor of Interlaken, Switzerland. His charges were three boys, aged eight, ten, and fourteen, and it was through their systematic instruction that he acquired the practical experience upon which was afterward constructed his pedagogical theory. By agreement with the father of the children he wrote bimonthly reports of their progress. Only five of these, unfortunately, have been preserved, but they suffice to show that the philosophical, humanistic, and mathematical studies which he had cultivated in Jena all contributed to the development of his ideas of method. While minutely observing and experimenting with his pupils, Herbart became acquainted with Pestalozzi. He visited the institute at Burgdorf (1799), and was won over to the man and his work. During that same year Herbart left Switzerland for Bremen, and, intending to prepare for a university professorship, resumed his philosophical studies. He spent two years there and produced the essays which inaugurated the scientific formulation of Pestalozzi's ideas, viz., *Pestalozzi's latest work "How Gertrude Teaches Her Children,"*[1] and *Pestalozzi's Idea of an A B C of Observation.*[2] In the latter, mathematics is given prominence as a means of training in observation. In 1802 Herbart, then dependent on friends for his support, secured an instructorship in the University of Göttingen. There he received the doctorate and won such success as a teacher of pedagogy and ethics that in 1805 the University of Heidelberg offered him a full professorship in philosophy. This he declined. To the Göttingen period belong *The Moral Revelation of the World as the Chief Function of Education,*[3] in which he demonstrates the moral values to be attached to all phases of the child's training; *Standpoint for Judging Pestalozzi's Method of Instruction;*[4] *Science of Education;*[5] and treatises on metaphysics, logic, and practical philosophy.

Herbart's reputation may be gauged by the flattering invitation he received in 1809 to fill the chair of philosophy at Königsberg, made famous by Kant who had died four years before. There as professor of philosophy

---

[1] *Pestalozzi's neueste Schrift: Wie Gertrud ihre Kinder lehrt* (1802).

[2] *Pestalozzi's Idee eines A B C der Anschauung* (1802).

[3] *Ueber die ästhetische Darstellung der Welt als Hauptgeschäft der Erziehung* (1804).

[4] *Standpunkt der Beurteilung der Pestalozzischen Unterrichts-Methode* (1804).

[5] *Allgemeine Pädagogik* (1806). English translation by Henry M. and Emmie Felkin. Boston: D. C. Heath, 1902.

and pedagogy he did his best work. Through his efforts
a teacher's seminary was opened in 1810 and in connection with it a model or practice school limited to twenty
pupils. Young men who were preparing to be superintendents, inspectors, and principals taught there under
the observation of the professors of pedagogy while at
the same time they followed university courses. Herbart
lectured on education in the University and taught
mathematics in the practice school. In his ambitious endeavor to succeed Hegel in the chair of philosophy at
Berlin, he incurred the displeasure of governmental
officials and lost his professorship in Königsberg.
Göttingen welcomed him back in 1833. There he lectured until two days before his death in 1841. During
the Königsberg period Herbart wrote many philosophical works, including his *System of Philosophy* and *Textbook of Psychology*. While at Göttingen he published
the *Outlines of Pedagogical Lectures* which later
appeared as *Outlines of General Pedagogy* (1841), the
work which best describes his system.[6]

Herbart based education upon ethics and psychology;[7]
the former as pointing out the aim and the latter the
means.

The term virtue expresses the whole purpose of education.
Virtue is the idea of inner freedom which has developed into

---

[6] *Umriss der allgemeinen Pädagogik.* English version: *Outlines
of Educational Doctrine.* Translated by A. F. Lange (New York:
The Macmillan Company, 1901).

[7] His psychology was founded on a threefold basis: metaphysics,
mathematics, and experience. He borrowed from Leibnitz the
notion of the monad and asserted that the soul, like other sub-
stances, is a monad; but it is superior to the myriad other
monads with which it is in eternal interaction. The soul is
called the mind so far as it conceives; and the heart so far as
it feels or desires. All actions arise from what he called the
"circle of thought" made up of ideas, interests, desires, volitions,
conduct. According to his thesis feeling and willing are secondary functions derived from ideation or thought.

an abiding actuality in an individual. Whence, as inner freedom is a relation between insight and volition, a double task
is at once set before the teacher. It becomes his business to
make actual each of these factors separately, in order that
later a permanent relationship may result.[8]

Virtue or morality is then the end of education and
this is dependent upon "volition" and "insight," that is,
upon voluntary action in accordance with the intuition
or knowledge of the individual. A full or complete
knowledge is in consequence the ground or support of
virtue. Instruction therefore is the chief means in education, as morality is the aim. The teacher's office is to
develop both factors, insight and will, so that a permanent and harmonious relation will be established between
them. He must first know his pupil.

Now, in order to gain an adequate knowledge of each pupil's
capacity for education, observation is necessary—observation
both of his thought masses and of his physical nature. The
study of the latter includes that of temperament, especially
with reference to emotional susceptibility. Instruction in the
sense of mere information-giving contains no guarantee whatever that it will materially counteract faults and influence
existing groups of ideas that are independent of the imparted
information.[9]

Herbart usually discusses education under the head-
ings of Government, Instruction, and Training (Discipline).[10] From the preceding remarks it may be assumed that he emphasized the second as the chief means
of education. Government deals with the present condition of the child, instruction and training with the future.
Government provides a favorable arrangement, good
order, etc., for the child's instruction and training. It
seeks to make the child obedient, to keep him employed,

---

[8] *Outlines of Educational Doctrine*, p. 7.
[9] *Ibid.*, pp. 22 f.
[10] *Cf.* Charles De Garmo, *Herbart and the Herbartians* (London: William Heinemann, 1895), pp. 83-98.

and with activities that are, if possible, instructive, although not necessarily on the intellectual side. Instruction has for its end, virtue; and training, which is a will-training, ultimately depends upon instruction, since willing depends upon knowing.[11]

Man's worth does not, it is true, lie in his knowing, but in his willing. But there is no such thing as an independent faculty of will. Volition has its roots in thought; not, indeed, in the details one knows, but certainly in the combination and total effect of the acquired ideas.[12]

While Herbart made training aim to develop moral character, he especially emphasized instruction as resulting in insight on which will depends. The present treatment will be chiefly concerned with his ideas on this phase of education.

The ultimate purpose of instruction, virtue, can only be attained according to Herbart by another and a nearer aim, that is, many-sidedness of interest. Through the development of this now famous doctrine of interest and its associated ideas Herbart made one of the great advances of modern education.

The word interest stands in general for that kind of mental activity which it is the business of instruction to incite. Mere information does not suffice; for this we think of as a supply or store of facts, which a person might possess or lack, and still remain the same being. But he who lays hold of his information and reaches out for more, takes an interest in it. Since, however, this mental activity is varied, we need to add that further determination supplied by the term many-sidedness.[13]

This latter term distinguishes the true from one-sided or scattering interest. Many-sidedness of interest cannot

---

[11] This assertion is in agreement with the Baconian principle that "Knowledge is power."

[12] *Outlines of Educational Doctrine*, p. 40.

[13] *Ibid.*, p. 44.

be brought about quickly, for a store of ideas must first be obtained, their unification and assimilation realized, and this by an alternation of concentration (absorption) and reflection.

The business of instruction is to form the person on many sides, and accordingly to avoid a distracting or dissipating effect. And instruction has successfully avoided this in the case of one who with ease surveys his well-arranged knowledge in all its unifying relations and holds it together as his very own.[14]

Attention then, as concentration or reflection, becomes an essential factor in producing interest. Herbart distinguishes between involuntary (spontaneous) and voluntary attention. The former might be primitive or apperceiving: primitive, which depends upon the strength of the sense impression; apperceiving, which presupposes primitive, and "takes place through the reproduction of previously acquired ideas and their union with the new element."[15] The essentials of the first or primitive attention are: "strength of sense-impression, economy of receptivity, avoidance of harmful antithesis of existing ideas, and delay until the aroused ideas have recovered their equilibrium";[16] the elements of the second, apperceiving, are shown in the development of the doctrine of apperception which was greatly extended by later members of the Herbartian school.

Ideas arise from experience and social intercourse. Instruction supplements acquired knowledge by supplying the proper presentations to the mind; it presumes as foundations the ideas derived from experience and social intercourse. Should they be wanting, an effort must be made to establish them, for all new knowledge is to be united with the mental content, with the ideas already

[14] *Ibid.*, p. 49.
[15] *Ibid.*, p. 63.
[16] *Ibid.*, p. 66.

possessed. Otherwise voluntary attention is resorted to by the teacher. The knowledge already possessed by the pupil constitutes his apperceiving mass, i.e., the body of ideas by means of which he assimilates new ones.

Herbart accordingly classified interests as follows: I. Those arising from knowledge which are: 1. empirical, from sense experience; 2. speculative, from speculation as to the nature of the object; 3. aesthetic, from a contemplation of its beauty. II. Those arising from association as: 1. sympathetic ideas or relating to other individuals; 2. social, relating to the social body or community; and 3. religious, relating to one's destiny. In instruction, all these interests are to be energetically awakened and unfolded. Herbart would have none developed to the exclusion of others lest interest be one-sided.

The practical question as to the manner of arousing these interests gave rise to Herbart's method of instruction. "Interest depends partly, it is true, on native capacity which the school cannot create, but it depends also on the subject matter of instruction." [17]   This subject matter, arranged so as to produce many-sidedness, was chosen in accordance with the two main kinds of interest. Dividing the subjects of instruction into the historical and the scientific, as they included, on the one side, history, literature, and language, or, on the other, mathematics, and the natural sciences, he would have all teaching be educative, that is, instruction having an ethical bearing, or influence on character.[18] This was based

on the idea that, not school discipline alone, but also school.

---

[17] *Ibid.*, p. 126.

[18] Developing character in young persons was mainly a matter of building up within them certain approved interests. Education, according to Herbart, should build up in young persons an interest in the interests of civilized society. *Cf.* R. Finney, *A Brief History of the American Public School,* pp. 86 ff.

instruction in the common branches should be of service to the child in moral and especially in social growth. The studies help to reveal to him his place and function in the world, they form his disposition toward men and things, they give him insight into ethical relations.[19]

In the process of instruction first comes the presentation of the idea to the child in language adapted to the subject matter and the child's mental state. The method is then both analytical and synthetical, the teacher requiring the pupil to analyze his percepts and assisting him in forming a synthesis of them. The quality of attention attained and sustained is of importance here, in particular the attention mentioned above as concentration and reflection. For the successful treatment of a subject in view of interest and apperception Herbart then outlined certain formal steps in method which have been amplified and extended by his followers. These formal steps of method were: (a) clearness, (b) association, (c) system, (d) method: clearness in the presentation of the facts or elements to be mastered; association of the facts with one another, and with other related facts previously acquired, in order that assimilation, or apperception, may be adequately complete; system, the organization and unification of the ideas acquired; method, the application of what is assimilated in exercises demanding self-activity. At present these steps are designated as follows: (a) preparation, (b) presentation, (c) association or comparison, (d) systematization or generalization, and (e) application.[20]

Herbart's contribution to educational science consists chiefly in his formulation of psychological principles as

---

[19] *Outlines of Educational Doctrine,* footnote, p. 98.

[20] These steps have become known as the five formal steps of the inductive-deductive teaching technique. This teaching technique is limited to logically-organized subject matter, such as the sciences, languages, history, and geography. *Cf.* Cubberly and Eells, *An Introduction to the Study of Education* (New York: Houghton Mifflin Co., 1933), pp. 266 f.

a basis of method. What Pestalozzi learned through experience or sympathetic insight he endeavored to place on a scientific basis in accordance with his psychological views; he strove, indeed, to justify method by psychology. With his doctrine of interest and apperception [21] he unified educational processes and inspired the fruitful efforts of his followers in behalf of correlation and coordination of studies. He demonstrated the value of the practice school for teachers and inaugurated a movement which, in spite of some grave excesses, has done much for the improvement of methods of teaching.[22] While he had the secondary school in mind, his views have been especially applied to elementary school work. In their application, however, many of his ideas or suggestions have suffered from a too literal interpretation on the part of Herbartians. To cite an instance, *Tuiskon Ziller* (1817-1883) of Leipzig, while drawing up the curriculum in accordance with the Herbartian idea of arranging study material in the order in which it has developed historically, went to the extent of elaborating the culture epoch theory.[23] Maintaining that the individual's development is parallel to that of the race, he held that his cultural interests are best satisfied by the productions of the race in the epoch similar to the one through which he is passing. The theory, always subject to the most materialistic interpretation, was for some time widely received but was never consistently applied to educational methods.

---

[21] The term is rarely used in present-day works on psychology. In place of "apperceptive mass," the terms "mental set" and "pattern" are commonly used.

[22] The Herbartian influence in this country was chiefly between 1889-1902.

[23] This theory is related to the theory of evolution. It maintains that each individual in his own personal growth has passed through the same stages that the race as a whole has passed in the course of its evolution. This theory was basic to the pedagogy of Rousseau, Pestalozzi, and Froebel.

Herbartians like *Karl Volkmar Stoy* (1815-1885) and *Wilhelm Rein* (1847-1929) made Jena a great center for the training of teachers and the propagation of the views of their school. From Jena the influence has spread to all Germany and foreign countries, notably the United States, where normal schools in the latter part of the nineteenth century were especially affected. Textbooks and courses of study have also shown the influence in the greater use of historical and literary material adapted to the mental states of children.

It should be noted in connection with Herbart's contribution to educational science that his psychology was not metaphysically sound and could not but produce untoward results if consistently applied. He rejected the idea of distinct mental faculties and left practically no place for free will, for he taught that voluntary action really depends on and is the inevitable result of the dominating idea or body of ideas. Although he made virtue the end of instruction, he practically assumed it to be an acquisition of the intellect and not of the will. Instruction also surpassed discipline; and interest, as an aim in successful teaching, was attained at the cost of effort and mental training. Finally, his aim, virtue and morality, although ethical was really self-culture,[24] the limitations of which, for the Christian, were sufficiently demonstrated in many of his followers.

FOR FURTHER STUDY

Adams, John, *The Herbartian Psychology Applied to Education.* Boston: D. C. Heath Co., 1897.

Cole, P. R., *Herbart and Froebel.* New York: Columbia University, 1907.

---

[24] To the term moral character he gave a social significance; it implied the ideals and habits that make one a desirable member of the social group. His aim of education is the same as the "social efficiency" aim in American pedagogy. *Cf.* Finney, *op. cit.,* p. 266.

Compayré, Gabriel, *Herbart and Education by Instruction.* New York: Crowell, 1907.

Darroch, J., *Herbart, and the Herbartian Theory of Education; a Criticism.* New York: Longmans, Green, and Company, 1903.

De Garmo, Charles, *Herbart and the Herbartians.* New York: Charles Scribner's Sons, 1895.

————, *Outlines of Educational Doctrine.* New York: The Macmillan Company, 1901.

Felkin, H., and E., *Herbart's Lectures and Letters on Education.* Syracuse: C. W. Bardeen, 1898.

————, *Herbart's Science of Education.* Boston: D. C. Heath, 1902.

Finney, Ross, L., *A Brief History of the American Public School.* New York: The Macmillan Company, 1925.

Lange, A. F., *Herbart's Outlines of Educational Doctrine.* New York: The Macmillan Company, 1901.

McMurray, C. A., *The Elements of General Method Based on the Principles of Herbart.* Bloomington, Illinois: Public-School Publishing Co., 1892.

Parker, S. C., *The History of Modern Elementary Education.* Boston: Ginn and Company, 1912.

Ribot, T. A., *German Psychology of To-day.* New York: Charles Scribner's Sons, 1886.

Smith, M. K., *Herbart's Text-Book in Psychology.* New York: D. Appleton Co., 1891.

Van Liew, C. C., *Life of Herbart and Development of his Pedagogical Doctrines.* London: S. Sonnenschein & Co., 1893.

Willmann, Otto, *Johann Friedrich Herbart's pädagogische Schriften.* 2 vols. Leipzig: A. W. Zickfeldt, 1913.

————, *Didaktik,* 2 vols. Braunschweig: F. Vieweg und Sohn, 1894-95. Translated under the title *Science of Education* by Felix M. Kirsch, O. M. Cap., from the fifth German edition. Beatty, Pa.: Archabbey Press, 1930, 2nd edition. Vol. I, 28 sqq. et passim.

Wolff, J. J., *Johann Friedrich Herbart's pädagogische Schriften.* Paderborn: F. Schöningh, 1891-95.

CHAPTER XXIX

THE NINETEENTH CENTURY (Continued)

The Psychologists and Other Theorists

Friedrich Wilhelm Froebel, pupil of Pestalozzi and author of another phase of the Psychological Movement, was born in 1782 at Oberweissbach, a village in Thuringia. His father, a Lutheran minister with a number of village churches under his charge, could scarcely afford to give his children a liberal education. Friedrich, after some instruction from his father, went first to the girls' division of the village school. At ten his maternal uncle, the pastor of Stadt-Ilm, took him in charge and sent him to the town school. As a boy he displayed no especial talent. When fifteen, he was apprenticed to a forester. In the two succeeding years he studied botany and mathematics but mostly in private, for he received little attention from his master. In 1799, an errand to Jena, where his brother was a student, gave Froebel an opportunity to attend university lectures for part of the year. He returned the following year, but before its close had the unhappy experience of spending nine weeks in the university jail because of an unpaid debt of about twenty-five dollars. After his father's death in 1802, he wandered about Germany in one occupation and another for about four years. At Frankfurt, where he had taken up the study of architecture, he met Grüner, head teacher of the training school, a former pupil of Pestalozzi, who persuaded him to become a teacher. With his first class Froebel felt he had found his calling and decided to make teaching his life work. He first met Pestalozzi at Yverdun in 1805. A visit of two weeks which he spent there inspecting the institute made him resolve to return for a longer stay.

Froebel taught in the model school of Frankfurt for two years, applying what he could of Pestalozzi's method in language and arithmetic. He was very successful with geography. In order to have more time for his own mental improvement he gave up school work for tutoring. His pupils, three boys, were given over completely to his charge. In 1808, when much experimenting with methods of teaching had convinced him of his limitations as a teacher, he brought his pupils to Yverdun. There, as he said, he remained as "teacher, and scholar, educator and pupil." From close observation of the work and association with Pestalozzi he learned the strength and the weakness of the new system. In the teaching he missed a certain "satisfying of the human being, the essence of the subject." "Pestalozzi's views," he said, "were very universal, and, as experience taught, only awakening to those already grounded in the right." [1]

Like many other students Froebel served as a volunteer in the war with France. In the same battalion were Langenthal and Middendorff, afterward his associates in educational work. When peace was declared he returned to Berlin and, in 1813, obtained the position of assistant in the museum of mineralogy. [2]

In 1816 upon the death of his brother, the pastor of Griesheim, Froebel undertook to tutor the latter's children and thereby returned to his favorite calling. He opened school in the parish house of Griesheim where he undertook the education also of two nephews sent him by another brother. Middendorff soon joined him as an assistant. When the pupils increased in number he was

---

[1] Letter to Duke of Meiningen. *Cf. Barnard's American Journal of Education*, XXX. 665.

[2] Froebel worked under Professor Weiss at the University of Berlin who was celebrated for research in mineralogy and natural history. The early nineteenth century witnessed a forward movement in the various sciences. Philology, chemistry, physics, and geology had made remarkable progress. Froebel studied in all these fields together with mathematics.

obliged to secure a farm at Keilhau where Langenthal also joined him. He succeeded admirably with the school until 1829 when local opposition forced him to leave. While in Keilhau, Froebel wrote the *Education of Man,* an exposition of the theory on which the school was conducted.

From 1831 until 1835 Froebel carried on his work in Switzerland, succeeding best in the school of Burgdorf. The pupils there were orphans from four to six years of age, and Froebel engaged to educate them and train teachers at the same time. Upon the death of his wife, he returned to Germany and at Blankenburg opened the institution for small children, the first to be known by the name of the "kindergarten." From an educational viewpoint the Blankenburg school was a great success; distinguished visitors frequented it and teachers came to learn of the new methods. As a financial enterprise, however, it failed, and after eight years Froebel was obliged to give it up. Some five years spent in lecturing to mothers and women teachers won him many enthusiastic supporters, and kindergartens were opened in several large cities. Froebel suffered a severe blow in 1851 when the government of Prussia, apparently confounding his views with those of his nephew, the socialist, forbade the establishment of kindergartens because of their socialistic and irreligious tendencies.[3] The founder died the following year, 1852.

---

[3] His nephew, Karl Froebel, was a teacher in Zurich. It is clear from *Die Opposition,* published by Karl Heinzen in 1846 at Mannheim, Germany, that Karl Froebel was a radical. In this work Heinzen proposed to publish the *Teutscher Emigranten-Almanach* and requested like-minded radical writers to submit articles for publication. Among the radicals who had already promised their cooperation he mentions Karl Froebel. Heinzen later settled down in the United States and established a journal *Der Pionier* which was published until 1879 at Boston. The articles in this journal were of an extremely radical character. Froebel's kindergarten was imbued with the democratic spirit. Bismarck had just come into power; all forms of democratic as-

Froebel's educational theory rests upon religious concepts. It was profoundly affected by the idealism of Schelling and Fichte and the naturalism of Rousseau. Many of his expressions appear to have a tinge of pantheism. Froebel maintained, however, that in theory and practice he strove for the realization of Christian ideals. The groundwork of his theory of education is the Law of Unity which underlies all things. This is universal, eternal. "In all things there lives and reigns an eternal law" manifested to those of faith with equal clearness and distinctness "in nature (the external), in the spirit (the internal), and in life which unites the two." This law is based on eternal Unity, God, Who is the source of all things, for all things live and have their being through Him. It is the destiny and life-work of all things to unfold their essence, hence their divine being, and, therefore, the Divine Unity itself—to reveal God in their external and transient being; and it is the special destiny of man, as an intelligent and rational being, to become fully, vividly, and clearly conscious of his essence, of the divine effluence in him, and, therefore, of God.[4]

---

pirations were suppressed. The kindergarten was suppressed by edict of the Prussian government on the absurd charge of being atheistic.

[4] The word in German, coined to express this conception of Divine Unity, is *Gliedganzes*. Every object in the universe is at once a unity of itself and at the same time a part of some more comprehensive entity. For example, the finger is a unity when considered by itself, but at the same time it is part of the hand; the hand in turn is a unity in and of itself, but it is part of the arm, and so on. The entire universe is a living organism, the unity of which is God. *Cf.* Eby and Arrowood, *The Development of Modern Education,* p. 799. Froebel believed in the divinity of everything. His pantheistic views led him to defend the "divine" goodness of each human being and this basic principle became the foundation of his educational theory that education should be passive as regards all interference with free self-activity. *Cf.* W. Kane, *An Essay Toward A History of Education,* p. 458.

Education consists in leading man, as a thinking, intelligent being, growing into self-consciousness, to a pure and unsullied, conscious and free representation of the inner law of Divine Unity, and in teaching him ways and means thereto.[5]

Education with such a function must be "originally and in its first principles, passive, following (only guarding and protecting) not prescriptive, categorical, interfering." [6] The operation of the Divine Unity is necessarily good and should not be disturbed. Again Froebel says: "In view of the original soundness and wholeness of man, all arbitrary (active), prescriptive and categorical, interfering education in instruction and training must, of necessity, annihilate, hinder, and destroy." [7] The divine principle demands and requires free self-activity and self-determination on the part of man. Teaching or education becomes active and mandatory when natural development has been marred. The development is furthermore to be continuous, the child manifesting a degree of self-activity proper to his stage of development. "The child, the boy, man, indeed, should know no other endeavor but to be at every stage of development wholly what this stage calls for." His development is to be at once complete and continuous, not respecting any sharp limits or definite subdivisions between the stages of infancy, boyhood, youth, etc. Activity is furthermore to be productive; first activity of the senses, as the formative impulse, then through play, building, modeling as a preparation for future industry, diligence, and productive activity.[8] Lessons come through and by work, through and from life. Such learning is much more beneficial and developing than that coming from a ver-

---

[5] *The Education of Man.* Translated by W. N. Heilmann (New York: D. Appleton and Company, 1887), p. 2.
[6] *Ibid.,* p. 7.
[7] *Ibid.,* p. 9.
[8] *Ibid.,* p. 34.

bal exchange of ideas. It is a learning through self-expression.

Froebel wrote of education in the stages of infancy, early childhood, boyhood, and youth. Because of the fame of the kindergarten, his theory on the training of early childhood is best known. His views, nevertheless, on the other stages were not less significant. It will be possible to give only an outline of them here.

Froebel held that the infant's environment should be pure and in every way wholesome in order that its earliest impressions might be the best. Even in infancy, the seeds of piety may be planted and chiefly by the example of the parents. The child's learning he described as an absorption, or an endeavor to make internal what it perceives by the senses, the external. Its activity means the use, employment, exercise of the body, senses, etc. Infancy has passed when the child begins to express outwardly what is within him. His expression should be like his perception, correct. He should designate things in their true relations, rightly, distinctly, clearly. Expression commences with speech, and especially in play, which is the highest point of human development in the child stage, for it is the free expression of the child's inner being.[9] It is the source of all good, according to Froebel, and was methodically used by him in the kindergarten. The instinct to draw was encouraged and directed as a mode of expression, and this really constituted the first formal teaching.[10]

Boyhood Froebel characterizes as the stage of acquisition. Here instruction predominates, just as guidance did in the earlier period, and the purpose is to give firmness of will, "so as to realize and practice genuine humanity." It is presumed that the boy has acquired a good disposition in childhood. His activity at this stage always has an end in view; he anticipates a certain re-

----

[9] *Ibid.*, pp. 54f.
[10] *Ibid.*, pp. 77-80.

sult in his games, and develops individual power. His curiosity and questioning are to be turned to educational ends. He then, for instance, craves to know the past, how present things originated; he loves tales, etc., and history. Among other forms of expression, he delights especially in singing. Whatever faults he may have acquired are due to an incomplete or faulty development, to a positive interference by teachers or parents with the natural unfolding of his powers. Like Rousseau, Froebel would not attribute them to any original depravity in the child; many faults he attributed to thoughtlessness.[11]

In the scholar or pupil stage Froebel treats of the school, whose office is

to render the scholar fully conscious of the nature and inner life of things and of himself, to teach him to know the inner relations of things to one another, to the human being, to the scholar, and to the living source and conscious unity of all things—to God.[12]

The boy when entering school leaves behind the outward view of things and begins to acquire an inner or intellectual view. An intelligent consciousness hovers over and between the outer world and the scholar, mediates between the two, and imparts to them mutual understanding. The child's faith and hope in learning are to be heightened by the skilled teacher who rejoices in vivacity and uses it for developing and quickening his power. School subjects are determined by a knowledge of the nature and requirements of the boy's development. The school is to lead the boy to the threefold, yet in itself one, knowledge—"to the knowledge of himself in all his relations, and thus to the knowledge of man as such; to the knowledge of God, . . . and to the knowledge of nature and the outer world."[13] It is in

---

[11] *Ibid.*, pp. 119-127.
[12] *Ibid.*, p. 128.
[13] *Ibid.*, p. 138.

striking conformity with his whole theory that Froebel treats religion as the first subject of the curriculum, and as presenting and pointing out "the ways and means by which the desire to live in true unity with God may be gratified, and by which this unity, if impaired, may be restored." [14] To live in accordance with this knowledge is Christian religion, Froebel holds. He believed that first of all and above all the school should instruct for and in this religion.

The kindergarten as the concrete embodiment of his ideas on early training is his great bequest to posterity. It represents the best of Froebel's labors. In it self-activity of the kind described above was stimulated and directed, and play was organized to satisfy both the child's interests and the ends of the educative process. The exercises trained the child to correct observation and expression. As Pestalozzi emphasized the former, so Froebel laid stress on the latter. His theory demanded it and in practice it was secured in the form of gesture or bodily movement, song, language, and construction, or graphic representation.

Froebel spent the last fifteen years of his life in perfecting the songs and other materials for the kindergarten.[15] The "Gifts" consisted of six woolen balls of different colors, the sphere, the cube, and the cylinder. They were used to acquaint the child with various materials, colors, form, and dimensions—the basis of number and mathematical work; the "Occupations" were the activities in construction with paper, clay, wood, and similar materials—the basis of manual training and creative work. Froebel made little, if any, distinction between the "Gifts" and "Occupations"; both were

---

[14] *Ibid.*, p. 141.

[15] *Mutter-und Kose-Lieder* (Mother and Play Songs). *Cf.* H. Eliot and S. Blow, *Mottoes and Commentaries of Friedrich Froebel's Mother Play* (New York: D. Appleton and Company, 1896).

coordinate activities. Since his time, however, the distinction has been marked because of a tendency to extol the "Occupations" over the "Gifts."

The kindergarten project spread quickly over Europe.[16] The Baroness von Bülow, a devoted pupil of Froebel, labored unceasingly for twenty years by pen and voice to further the movement. The first kindergarten in the United States was opened by Mrs. Schurz, about 1855, in Watertown, Wisconsin; the earliest ones for English-speaking children were those established in Boston about 1860 through the efforts of Elizabeth P. Peabody. Maria Bölte, who had studied with Froebel's widow in Hamburg, inaugurated the movement in New York in 1872. In a few years not only were private kindergartens widely flourishing in the United States, but many cities had adopted the institution as an organic part of their elementary school systems. A notable example was St. Louis, where in 1873, through the efforts of Dr. W. T. Harris and Miss Susan E. Blow, the city undertook the management of twelve kindergartens.

Although Froebel's psychological methods were applied only in the kindergarten, his ideas on self-activity and development, like Pestalozzi's "observation" and

---

[16] The materials and methods employed in the Montessori system are little more than a development of the kindergarten. Born at Rome, 1870, Maria Montessori was the first woman physician graduated from the University of Rome; she afterwards became director of the State Orthophrenic School in Rome. Her success in the teaching of feeble-minded children led her to apply her methods to the training of normal children between the ages of three and seven. She holds that nature is fundamentally good; demands complete freedom for the child; and advocates "auto-education." Critics of her method which is outlined in her book, *The Montessori Method,* translated by A. E. George (New York: Frederick A. Stokes, 1912), maintain that her didactic materials devised for the training of the senses are better suited to mental defectives than to normal children; they also are of the opinion that her methods lack the social motive. and do not develop the imagination and feelings.

Herbart's "interest," have profoundly affected all subsequent educational practices. No successful method
today disregards them, or the principle of expression
which he elaborated. Froebel's devotion to the idea of
development, however, carried him into the naturalism
of Rousseau, although he always professed his adherence
to Christian beliefs and ideals. As mentioned before,
he did not accept the doctrine of original sin, holding
that the child's early faults came from without, by interference with his natural development. He also accepted
with Herbart the underlying principle of the culture
epoch theory.

Contemporaneously with Froebel an Italian priest had
formulated a theory of education which remarkably resembled that of the German reformer. *Antonio Rosmini-Serbati* (1797-1855), the founder of the Institute
of Charity, and one of the deepest thinkers of modern
times, was born of noble parents at Rovereto in the
Austrian Tyrol. His early education was received in
his native city. At the age of twenty he entered the
University of Padua where he studied three years. Ordained a priest in 1821, he was the following year made
a doctor of theology and canon law by the University
of Padua. During the early years of his priesthood
he conceived a plan for the reconstruction of philosophy
with the aim of making it more than ever before the
servant of revealed truth. Pope Pius VII encouraged
him in the project.

In 1823, Rosmini founded at Domodossola the Institute of Charity, a religious community whose members
are known in Italy as the Rosminians and in England
as the Fathers of Charity. That he took a conspicuous
part in civil and ecclesiastical affairs is evidenced by
his appointment as the envoy of King Charles Albert
of Piedmont to the Pope to enlist the latter's support
against Austria, and by his nomination by the Pope as
Minister of Public Instruction, an office which he de-

clined to accept. Rosmini's most notable achievements were, however, in the field of philosophy and education.[17] Although forty propositions taken from his works were condemned by the Inquisition in 1887, Father Rosmini's piety and religious zeal were never questioned by the Holy See. He was devoted to the education of the young and the members of the Institute which he founded have consistently maintained his spirit in their scholastic activities. Never a large community, they now have colleges and religious houses in Italy, England, and the United States.

Rosmini's chief educational treatise, *The Ruling Principle of Method Applied to Education (Del principio supremo della metodica)* is but a fragment of a work intended to embrace five books and to furnish a method for the whole educative process. The two completed books contain, however, the fundamental principles for early training and these so closely resemble Froebel's that we may say with Rosmini's translator that the kindergarten system worked out by Froebel

in entire ignorance of Rosmini, and under conditions of birth, education, circumstances, so widely different, is yet the complete application, to every detail of infant education, of Rosmini's principles, or rather of the principles common to both, because both had arrived at them by the same road—the profound study of human nature.[18]

The reformers differ, however, on the nature of the religious knowledge to be acquired by the child.

Rosmini's purpose, briefly stated, was to find out the ruling or basic principle whence is derived the whole method of teaching. His problem was thus expressed:

---

[17] For a list of his philosophical works *Cf.* Thomas Davidson, *The Philosophical System of Antonio Rosmini-Serbati* (London: Kegan Paul, Trench-Trübner, 1882).

[18] Rosmini-Serbati, *The Ruling Principle of Method Applied to Education,* translated by Mrs. William Grey (Boston: D. C. Heath and Co., 1893), p. viii.

How shall we find the sure rule by which the teacher of youth shall know what things he must begin with, and which should follow, so that the child who hears him may be led on, by gradations always duly adapted to his power, from what he knows to what he does not know and has yet to be taught?[19]

The child is to be led by easy steps in the natural order of development. The general law he discovers is "A thought is that which becomes the matter, or provides the matter of another thought."[20]   A second thought cannot possibly arise until the first has arisen and provided the matter needed for it.   Hence, the whole sum of thoughts which have occurred or can occur to the human mind may be distributed and classified in divers orders: first, thoughts whose matter is not derived from antecedent thoughts; second, thoughts which take their matter from thoughts of the first order, and from those only; third, thoughts which take their matter from thoughts of the second order, and so on for the various series of orders.

The ruling principle of method he then defines as follows:

Present to the mind of the child (and this applies to man in general), first, the objects which belong to the first order of cognitions; then those which belong to the second order; then those which belong to the third, and so on successively, taking care never to lead the child to a cognition of the second order without having ascertained that his mind has grasped those of the first order relative to it, and the same with regard to cognitions of the third, fourth, and other higher orders.[21]

Rosmini explains the cognitions proper to each order, including in the first, observation, perceptions, association of perceptions, and ideas. He further explains the activities corresponding to each order, following always

---

[19] *Ibid.*, p. 11.
[20] *Ibid.*, p. 38.
[21] *Ibid.*, p. 40.

the principle that the process of teaching is determined
by the needs of the growing child. In early childhood,
he urged mothers to attend to the training of feeling and
will rather than of reason. The child should be filled
with good will towards others, an affection which springs
up naturally if an atmosphere of joyousness be maintained in its mind.

Language is the stimulus which "impels and helps the
human mind to attain cognitions of the second order."[22]
It produces reflection on earlier cognitions and enables
the child to perceive the relations existing among them
and makes classification possible.

Cognitions of the third order are reached through synthetic judgments, and those of the fourth chiefly through
analytical judgments. Rosmini's work is a treatise in
psychology on these points. His views on activity are
noteworthy. He maintains that the child at every age
must act. He requires that activity which is natural
to the child as a means of development and this should
be physical, intellectual, and moral. He not only treats
of spontaneous activity but attempts to define its laws.
In this connection he considers play which he believes
could be used in developing intelligence if the teacher
knew how to take advantage of it. "It will become in
his hands a real and delightful method of instruction.[23]

Rosmini also advocated the use of pictures in teaching. He planned to write a picture book and began one
for teaching the alphabet which was to be used in the
schools of the Rosminians and the Sisters of Providence.
In the *Ruling Principle of Method* he indicates the matter of instruction and especially for moral and religious
training. His influence as an educator has been chiefly
confined to Italy, and the schools conducted elsewhere

---

[22] *Ibid.,* p. 89.
[23] *Ibid.,* p. 197.

by the Institute of Charity, and the daughters of Charity, or Sisters of Providence.[24]

Rosmini, as we have seen, sought a fundamental principle of method for all teaching. Just before his time, *Joseph Jacotot* (1770-1840), a French educator, had wrestled with the problem of method and attained some success. Jacotot began his teaching career at the age of nineteen as professor of classical literature in the college of Dijon, his native place. He successively taught "the method of sciences," ancient languages, mathematics, and Roman law. As a professor, he attracted wide and favorable attention. Obliged for political reasons to leave France, he became professor of French language and literature at the University of Louvain. This was in 1818.

Jacotot's first students knew no French, and it was his attempt to enable them to learn the language quickly that resulted in his famous method. He furnished the students with copies of Fénelon's *Télémaque*, having both the French text and Dutch translation. They were required to memorize some French sentences daily, but only after having compared them with the Dutch and grasped their full meaning. They learned French chiefly by their own efforts, and the success of the method seems undeniable. Jacotot was encouraged to

---

[24] The pedagogy of the schools of the Salesians, a Society named after St. Francis de Sales, its patron saint, has much in common with the educational principles of Rosmini and Froebel. The Institute founded by Saint Don Bosco in 1859 has houses in Europe, Asia, and the two Americas. The primary object of the congregation is the training of boys, especially for the trades; secondary schools and seminaries are also conducted by its members. The method of education advocated by Don Bosco is called the preventive method. This method is cultivated and followed by the Salesians in all their institutions. The preventive method is founded upon reason, religion, and benevolence. *Cf.* Carola E. Koft-Seitz, *Don Bosco as an Educator* (Washington, D. C.: The Catholic University of America, 1926).

formulate the principles on a large scale, as the basis of a universal method for the acquisition of all knowledge. He returned later to France and devoted himself to writing and furthering. his plans for the intellectual emancipation of humanity.

The principles and axioms of Jacotot's method were set forth in paradoxical form in his work *L'Enseigne-ment universel* (Louvain, 1822). Those which best represent his theory and contain the basic elements of his method were the following: "All men are equally capable of learning," a fallacy even greater than the next, which was apparently based on his own experience, viz., "Everyone can teach; and moreover, can teach what he himself does not know," and as a corollary, "Everyone can be his own instructor." Perhaps the most famous of the paradoxes was "All is in All" *(Tout est dans tout)*, the implication being that all knowledge is so related or connected that to know one thing well is to have the starting point or means of understanding all. He prescribed in consequence that the student should know something thoroughly and refer everything to that. The student of language undertook first to master a model book. Jacotot prescribed Fénelon's *Télémaque* and while he insisted on the memorizing of six books, this was not mere verbal memorizing. The student was required to show that he understood everything committed to memory and that he grasped the spirit of the author. This involved constant repetition so that he would forget nothing. "We are learned," said he, "not so far as we have learned, but only so far as we remember."[25]

Jacotot's influence was never great in France. He found more adherents and admirers in Germany, and many among English writers. While his axioms are paradoxical and will not stand analysis, and his methods

---

[25] Quoted by Quick, *Educational Reformers*, pp. 429 f.

mechanical, unduly burdening the memory, his insistence on thoroughness in learning is sound; likewise his emphasis on correlation and coordination of all knowledge. His exercises in comparison and verification aroused pupil interest and individual effort.

Herbert Spencer (1820-1903), the English philosopher and the apostle of Agnosticism, entered the educational field in a controversial spirit with his essay *What Knowledge is of Most Worth?* In this and three succeeding essays on intellectual, moral, and physical education he championed the right of scientific studies to a place in the modern curriculum. These essays were afterward published in a book form with the title, *Education* (New York, 1861). Spencer attacked the question of the relative values of the studies of his time and vigorously opposed the preeminence enjoyed by the humanities.

Spencer defined education as a preparation for complete living. The important question in determining the curriculum is not whether such or such knowledge is of worth, but what is its relative worth?

... Before there can be a rational curriculum, we must settle which thing it most concerns us to know; or to use a word of Bacon's, now unfortunately obsolete—we must determine the relative values of knowledges.[26]

To this end he made utility the measure of values, that is, the practical bearing of the subject upon some phase of life.

How to live?—that is the essential question for us. Not how to live in the mere material sense only, but in the widest sense. The general problem which comprehends every special problem is—the right ruling of conduct in all directions under all circumstances ... how to use all our faculties to the greatest advantage of ourselves and others—how to live completely?

---

[26] Herbert Spencer, *Education: Intellectual, Moral, and Physical* (New York: D. Appleton and Co., 1866), p. 29.

And this being the great thing needful for us to learn, is, by consequence, the great thing which education has to teach. To prepare us for complete living is the function which education has to discharge; and the only rational mode of judging of any educational course is, to judge in what degree it discharges such function.[27]

Complete living is the end to be achieved. The subjects and methods of instruction are to be chosen with deliberate reference to this end. Their selection is to be determined, not by the fashion of the time, nor the opinion of a parent, but by their respective values in relation to the end in view. Spencer classified in the order of their importance the chief activities of life as follows:

1. Those activities which directly minister to self-preservation; 2. those activities which, by securing the necessaries of life, indirectly minister to self-preservation; 3. those activities which have for their end the rearing and discipline of offspring; 4. those activities which are involved in the maintenance of proper social and political relations; 5. those miscellaneous activities which make up the leisure part of life, devoted to the gratification of the tastes and feelings.[28]

The educational values are similarly estimated, so that, according to Spencer,

the rational order of subordination is: that education which prepares for direct self-preservation; that which prepares for indirect self-preservation; that which prepares for parenthood; that which prepares for citizenship; that which prepares for the miscellaneous refinements of life.[29]

The ideal of education is complete preparation in all these divisions, but since this is humanly impossible the aim should be to maintain a due proportion between

---

[27] *Ibid.*, pp. 14 f.

[28] *Ibid.*, p. 16. The educational opinions of most of our American educators have been shaped in large measure in relation to the five departments of living as outlined by Spencer.

[29] *Ibid.*, pp. 18 f.

the degrees of preparation in each, giving attention to all, the greatest attention where "the value is greatest, less where the value is less, least where the value is least."

Upon examination, Spencer finds that the scientific studies are fundamental and of most worth as a preparation for the chief activities: for direct self-preservation, or the maintenance of life and health; for that indirect self-preservation which we call gaining a livelihood; for the due discharge of parental functions; for that interpretation of rational life, past and present, without which the citizen cannot regulate his conduct; for the most perfect production and highest enjoyment of art in all its forms; and for the purposes of discipline, intellectual, moral, religious. In the essays on intellectual, moral, and physical education he aimed at reforming the curricula and methods of the schools. On intellectual training, he upheld many principles of the psychologists, as for instance, the cultivation of the powers of observation, object teaching, learning through self-instruction and in a pleasurable manner; on moral training, while not touching the religious, he also shared views with Rousseau in advocating that the child should learn naturally, from the natural consequences of his acts, and in opposing artificial punishments; on physical training, he differed from Locke in not approving of the hardening process since many children were "hardened" out of the world. He believed that the regimen of the nursery and the school should conform to the established truths of modern science. "It is time that the benefits which our sheep and oxen have for years past derived from the investigations of the laboratory should be participated in by our children."[30] In this spirit he treated diet, exercise, clothing, and the excellence of health.

Spencer's educational essays were widely read in Eng-

---

[30] *Ibid.*, p. 213.

lish-speaking countries, and it is believed they helped to secure for the sciences their present position in the modern curriculum. Many of his views could not stand critical analysis, and like those of Herbart failed of wide acceptance. The philosopher's evolutionary, utilitarian, and agnostic theories were not absent from his educational writings.

FOR FURTHER STUDY

Froebel

Barnard, Henry, *Kindergarten and Child Culture Papers.* Hartford: American Journal of Education, 1884.

Bowen, H. C., *Froebel and Education through Self-activity.* New York: Charles Scribner's Sons, 1897.

Cole, P. R., *Herbart and Froebel.* New York: Teachers College, Columbia University, 1907.

Eliot, H., and S. Blow, *Mottoes and Commentaries of Friedrich Froebel's Mother Play.* New York: D. Appleton Co., 1896

Froebel, F. W., *Autobiography.* Translated by E. Michaelis and H. K. Moore. Syracuse: C. W. Bardeen, 1889.

―――――, *Education of Man.* Translated by W. N. Hailmann. New York: D. Appleton Co., 1887.

―――――, *Pedagogics of the Kindergarten.* Translated by Josephine Jarvis. New York: D. Appleton Co., 1900.

―――――, *Education by Development.* Translated by Josephine Jarvis. New York: D. Appleton Co., 1903.

Guillaume, J., "Froebel," *Dictionnaire de pédagogie et d'instruction primaire,* I, i, 1117-31.

Herford, W. H., *The Student's Froebel.* Boston: D. C. Heath Co., 1900.

Hughes, J. L., *Froebel's Educational Laws.* New York: D. Appleton Co., 1898.

Kilpatrick, W. H., *Froebel's Kindergarten Principles Critically Examined.* New York: The Macmillan Company, 1916.

Lange, W., editor, *Froebel's gesammelte pädagogische Schriften.* Berlin: T. C. F. Enslin, 1861-62. 3 vols.

MacVannel, J. A., *The Educational Theories of Herbart and Froebel.* New York: Columbia University Press, 1906.

Snider, D. J., *The Life of Frederick Froebel, Founder of the Kindergarten.* Chicago: Sigma Publishing Company, 1900.

Vanderwalker, N. C., *The Kindergarten in American Education.* New York: The Macmillan Co., 1908.

Rosmini

Davidson, Thomas, *The Philosophical System of Antonio Rosmini-Serbati.* London: Kegan Paul, Trench-Trübner, 1882.

Lockhart, W., *Life of Antonio Rosmini-Serbati.* London: Kegan Paul, French, and Company, 1886. 2 Vols.

Rosmini, Antonio Serbati, *The Ruling Principle of Method Applied to Education.* Translated by Mrs. William Grey. Boston: D. C. Heath Company, 1893.

Bredestege, Francis J., "The Educational Philosophy of Antonio Rosmini-Serbati," (unpublished doctoral dissertation, The University of Cincinnati, 1932).

Jacotot

Jacotot, Joseph, *Enseignement universel.* Louvain: H. de Pauw, 1822.

Payne, J., *Lectures on the History of Education.* London: Longmans, Green, and Company, 1892.

Perez, Bernard, "Jacotot," *Dictionnaire de pédagogie et d'instruction primaire.* II, i, 1399-1405.

Quick, R. H., *Educational Reformers.* New York: D. Appleton Co., 1907.

Spencer

Compayré, G., *Herbert Spencer and Scientific Education.* Translated by Marie E. Findlay. New York: Thomas Y. Crowell and Co., 1907.

De Hovre-Jordan, *Philosophy and Education.* New York: Benziger Bros., 1931.

Laurie, S. S., *Educational Opinion from the Renaissance.* Cambridge: The University Press, 1903.

Macpherson, H., *Spencer and Spencerism.* New York: Doubleday, 1900.

Spencer, Herbert, *Education; Intellectual, Moral and Physical.* New York: D. Appleton and Company, 1866.

Ward, J., *Naturalism and Agnosticism.* London: A. & C. Black, 1903.

SYNOPSIS OF RECENT DEVELOPMENTS IN AMERICAN EDUCATION

1. INFLUENCE OF PESTALOZZI, HERBART, FROEBEL, AND SPENCER
   - (a) Objective teaching and oral expression introduced in elementary school subjects
   - (b) Expansion of history courses in the elementary curriculum: United States history and general history
   - (c) Increased recognition of the value of standard literature
   - (d) Extensive application of the pedagogical principles: self-activity and social participation
   - (e) Inclusion of the exact sciences in the curricula of schools and colleges
   - (f) Rapid changes in American school practice in the light of the needs of democracy justified largely by Froebelian philosophy
2. FRANCIS W. PARKER (1837-1902)
   - (a) First great American disciple of Froebel
   - (b) Most influential advocate of self-expression in educational theory and practice during the nineties
3. WILLIAM T. HARRIS (1835-1909)
   - (a) Distinguished school administrator of past century
   - (b) Advocated best school practices of the time
   - (c) U. S. Commissioner of Education (1889-1906)
4. WILLIAM JAMES (1842-1910)
   - (a) The father of modern educational psychology
   - (b) The *Principles of Psychology* published in 1890
   - (c) *Talks to Teachers on Psychology* (1899)
   - (d) Exerted powerful influence upon American educational theory and practice
5. G. STANLEY HALL (1844-1924)
   - (a) Pupil of James
   - (b) Attempted to trace the history of mental life
   - (c) *Adolescence* (1904)
   - (d) Weakness of his educational conclusions seen in his questionnaire method used in securing data on child life and his belief in the recapitulation theory

6. JOHN DEWEY (1859-   )
  (a) Leader in socialized education
  (b) *Democracy and Education* (1916) may be considered his most important educational work
  (c) Deprecates the traditional type of school; the child must learn by doing
  (d) Influence on education has been world-wide
  (e) Social philosophy is naturalistic; has marked concern for individualization and socialization, but neglects idealization
  (f) To Dewey and other "Molders of the American Mind" is traceable in large measure current thinking in educational circles

7. EDWARD L. THORNDIKE (1874-   )
  (a) Father of the statistical movement in education
  (b) *Mental and Social Measurements* (1904) presents the details of the statistical method
  (c) He and his pupils devised scales for the scientific measurement of the results of instruction

8. EARLY CONTRIBUTORS TO EDUCATIONAL MEASUREMENT
  (a) James McKeen Cattell
  (b) Francis Galton
  (c) Binet and Simon
  (d) William Stern
  (e) Frederick Kühlmann
  (f) Lewis M. Terman

9. FORMS OF EDUCATIONAL MEASUREMENT
  (a) Scales
  (b) Intelligence tests
  (c) Standard tests
  (d) Achievement tests

10. HIGHER LEARNING IN AMERICA
  (a) The status of the Liberal Arts College
  (b) Criticisms of Hutchins concerning American programs of general education and University courses of study
  (c) Adler's condemnation of the philosophy of education of many American professors
  (d) The Harvard Report

11. THOMAS E. SHIELDS (1862-1921)
    (a) Catholic priest and distinguished educator
    (b) The Shields Method: religion is the core; projects
        are organized on the basis of active doing
    (c) The Catholic University Campus School exemplifies
        the principles of the Shields theory of education

CHAPTER XXX

RECENT DEVELOPMENTS IN AMERICAN EDUCATION

The educational theories and principles of Pestalozzi, Herbart, Froebel, and Spencer have greatly influenced education in America. Pestalozzian methods introduced objective teaching and oral expression into all subjects of the elementary school. Through the activities of the Herbartians, history courses were expanded in the elementary curriculum and included not only United States history but general history also; to the Herbartian influence was also due in part the increased recognition of the value of standard literature. The application of the pedagogical principles of Froebel, self-activity and social participation, has been extended far beyond primary school education. Spencer was perhaps the most influential educational writer in stimulating a demand that the exact sciences, because of their importance to life, be included in the curricula of schools and colleges. The rapid changes occurring in American school practice in the light of the needs of democracy may be explained and justified largely by the Froebelian philosophy.

The first great American disciple of Froebel was *Francis W. Parker* (1837-1902). He advocated training in all forms of expression, such as gesture, voice, speech, music, construction, modeling, drawing, painting, and writing; and reorganized the entire elementary course in the schools that he controlled starting from the standpoint of the child. Much of his work was accomplished at the Cook County Normal School in Chicago, Illinois. He continued his work at the University of Chicago and teachers came from all parts of the country to be trained by him. During the nineties he was the most influential

564

advocate of self-expression in both theory and practice. Contemporaneous with Parker was *William T. Harris* (1835-1909), who was one of the foremost school administrators of the past century. Through his philosophic and psychological study of educational problems he defended the schools as social institutions and advocated the best school practices of the times. Harris served as Superintendent of Schools of St. Louis from 1867 to 1880 and as United States Commissioner of Education from 1889 to 1906.

At about this time *William James* (1842-1910), who is regarded as the "father of modern educational psychology," labored to promote the empirical and experimental approach to the subject of education. His "biological point of view"—that man is primarily a behaving organism—supported the claim of the disciples of Froebel that motor expression was fundamental to physical and mental growth.[1] As a trained physician, he maintained the interdependence of the mental and physical life. In his philosophical views he was highly pragmatic.

For thirty-five years James taught on the staff of Harvard University. He was first an instructor of physiology and anatomy, and later a professor of psychology and of philosophy. A prolific writer in the fields of philosophy, psychology, and education, he favored the experimental approach to truth and held that we should settle our problems by experimentation. *Principles of Psychology* published by him in 1890 and *Talks to Teachers on Psychology* (1899) exerted a powerful influence upon American educational theory and practice. In his *Principles of Psychology* he has emphasized the importance of the early development of individual and class habits in the teaching process for

---

[1] William H. Burton, *Introduction to Education* (New York: D. Appleton-Century Company, 1934), p. 250.

the purpose of producing a more integrated society. "Habit" he maintained "is the enormous fly-wheel of society, its most precious conservative agent." His doctrine of habit was basically individualistic. He believed that the purpose of education is the organization of acquired habits in the individual with a view of promoting his personal well-being.

A distinguished pupil of James was *G. Stanley Hall* (1844-1924), much of whose educational thinking was the outgrowth of Froebel's philosophy. Born at Ashfield, Massachusetts, he came of a family of unusual culture and intellectual superiority. Hall studied under the many noted university men of Germany, including the great Wilhelm Wundt, at Leipzig, and also under the most distinguished teachers of America. His comprehensive education included specialization and study in theology, philosophy, psychology, physiology, anthropology, biology, anatomy, and neurology.

In 1880 Hall made his famous study of the *Contents of Children's Minds on Entering School.* Eight years later he was appointed President of Clark University, meanwhile having taught psychology and pedagogy at Johns Hopkins University. Under his direction, Clark University became the acknowledged center for the study of genetic psychology. Hall's educational theories are expressed in some fourteen volumes, notable among which are his two-volume study *Adolescence, Educational Problems,* and *Youth, Its Education, Regimen and Hygiene.* He also wrote numerous articles dealing with the scientific study of child nature and development in *The Pedagogical Seminary,* the publication of which he began in 1891. The articles together with the vast number of investigations made by the students under his direction at Clark University deeply influenced the attitudes of educators and teachers in regard to school methods and curricula.

Hall agreed with the educational reformers of the nineteenth century that the aim of education was the development of the child's own nature, activities, capabilities, and interests. He based his educational views upon the principles of biological evolution. Just as Darwin had attempted to trace the history of physical life, so Hall had attempted to trace the history of mental life. He believed that mental life and physical life are always parallel; that mind and body have evolved together; that there is "no psychosis without neurosis." So completely did the evolutionary theory enter into Hall's thinking that he was convinced that it is equally true of mental life as well as the physical that "ontogeny repeats phylogeny."

According to Hall, the business of the teacher is to see to it that education facilitates natural evolution; the individual must be made a suitable instrument in the upward climb of the race. This point of view urges the development of the individual child as an end in itself; loses sight of the social function of education; and disregards entirely the Christian ideal of training. Hall maintained that educational development proceeds in distinct stages: infancy, childhood, youth, adolescence. This theory was an influential factor in bringing about the establishment of the Kindergarten-Primary Unit, the Junior High School, and the Junior College in the American school system so as to make the passing of the child from one school to another more in keeping with the changes in his psychological nature. The weakness of Hall's educational principles is seen from the fact that he used the questionnaire method extensively in securing data on child life, which is regarded as not sufficiently accurate for scientific purposes, and based his views on the recapitulation theory which has been largely discredited.[2]

---

[2] Eby and Arrowood, *The Development of Modern Education* (New York: Prentice-Hall, Inc., 1935), pp. 855.

Most educators of today consider the ultimate aim of education as social rather than individualistic. Modern education has become socialized in all its implications and purposes. In the present-day conception of education, sociological objectives and socializing techniques have come to be emphasized as the result in large part of the educational work and writings of *John Dewey* (1859-   ). The educational principles of Dewey are fundamentally Froebelian. Froebel advocated self-activity and social participation for psychological reasons, because they quicken the learning process; Dewey advocates them because he recognizes in them the means of social salvation in the new social life into which we are entering.[3] Dewey's pioneer venture in socialized education was made at the University of Chicago where he conducted an experimental school between 1896 and 1903. Here he succeeded Francis W. Parker as head of the school of education. From 1904 until recently he has been professor of philosophy at Columbia University; in connection with his work as professor of philosophy, he has expounded his pedagogical theories.

Dewey has made many contributions to American philosophical and educational thought. *The Philosophy of Dewey*, 1928, selected and edited by Joseph Ratner of Columbia University gives a comprehensive outline of the total range of Dewey's philosophy. The following are his chief works on education: *My Pedagogic Creed*, 1887; *The School and Society*, 1889; *The Educational Situation*, 1902; *The Child and the Curriculum*, 1902; *Moral Principles in Education*, 1913; *Schools of To-morrow* (with his daughter, Evelyn), 1916; *Democracy and Education*, 1916; *Sources of a Science of Education*, 1929.

Dewey is a pragmatist; he believes that the test of

---

[3] Ross L. Finney, *A Brief History of the American Public School* (New York: The Macmillan Company, 1925), p. 269.

any theory is whether it will work. He does not admit fixed principles. The only principle he subscribes to is the principle of change. In the universe "change is omnipresent," constant in function, not constant in existence, and without final ends and forms.[4] In accordance with this view he has elaborated the instrumental theory of intelligence. Mind is the effective instrument by which man has raised himself above the other creatures. In the process of biological evolution, mind and intelligence have evolved in a purely natural way. The activity of human organisms in meeting the varied and practical and social situations of life explains this evolution. Life, therefore, must be regarded as a series of problematic situations in which the intellect strives to solve the problem and make the adjustment. Social life is likewise a series of problematic situations; and since in a democracy it is the people who must solve the social problems involved in living together, it is obvious that citizens must be trained as problem solvers.

In view of the changing American life, Dewey deprecates the traditional type of school. The activity of the new schools is to supplant the passivity of the traditional school. The educative process must, for both psychological and sociological reasons, consist of a series of problems that are within the normal experience of the child. The child must learn by doing. He should be given something to do that involves self-activity and interest, not something to learn. The doing demands thinking and learning naturally results. The teacher's part in conformity with the self-activity curriculum is to keep out of relation with the pupil as much as possible. The child leads in activity; the teacher furnishes "the environment which stimulates responses and directs the learner's course." The educative process must be

---

[4] John Dewey, *Reconstruction in Philosophy* (New York: Henry Holt and Company, 1920), pp. 61, 69.

also a practice in cooperative social activity. The school should be life; not a preparation for life. Social life should be interpreted to the child through school life which must be a natural social life, in a sort of miniature society. Dewey insists that the educative process must be extended to include a liberal education for all. In a democracy citizens must not only have the problem-solving attitude; they must be prepared to participate in all the knowledge and arts of civilization.

Dewey's influence upon education has been world-wide. China, Japan, Turkey, and Russia have been affected by his philosophic thinking and educational reforms. Kerschensteiner and Lietz in Germany, Findlay in England, Claparède and Demolins in France, and Decroly in Belgium acknowledge their indebtedness to him. In America he is quite properly regarded as Progressive Education's "patron saint."[5] Partly as a result of Dewey's work several progressive schools have been established in the United States. Among these are: The School of Organic Education in Fairhope, Alabama (1907); the Park School in Baltimore (1912); the Phoebe Ann Thorne School of Bryn Mawr College (1913); the City and Country School in New York City (1913); the Walden School in New York City (1914); the Oak Lane Country Day School in Philadelphia (1916); the Lincoln School of Teachers College, Columbia University (1917); the Moraine Park School in Dayton, Ohio (1917); the Chevy Chase Country School in Washington, D. C. (1919); the Beaver Country Day School in Brookline, Massachusetts (1921); and the John Dewey School in Hollywood (1930).[6] While the introduction of the activity program

---

[5] Sister Mary Ruth Sandifer, R.S.M., *American Lay Opinion of the Progressive School* (Washington, D. C.: The Catholic University of America, 1943), p. 5.

[6] Frank, P. Graves, *A Student's History of Education* (New York: The Macmillan Company, 1936), p. 540.

into the public schools has been gradual, some public school systems, such as the schools of Roslyn, Long Island; Santa Monica, California; and Houston, Texas, have adopted the new methods in their entirety. Experimental curricula have been established in several well known colleges: Black Mountain College, North Carolina; Sarah Lawrence College, New York; Bennington and Goddard colleges, Vermont; and Antioch College, Ohio.[7]

Dewey has made noteworthy contributions to educational practice by his devotion to method, but the shortcomings of his fundamental philosophical principles are apparent to the Christian teacher and educator. Dewey does not believe in God nor in any religion; he rejects Revelation and the supernatural. His social philosophy aims to build a man-centered not God-centered society. His system of education makes the school child-centered rather than Christ-centered. Dewey objects to any indoctrination; yet his whole philosophy of education is concerned with indoctrinating the young with his ideas of life and society. In the midst of change he fails to realize that some reality remains unchanged and that ultimate reality is the personal God who, according to the Eternal Law, rules all creatures and directs them to their final end which is Himself. His ideal of life is but a partial account of life. In his regard for the success of democracy, he has a marked concern for individualization and socialization but neglects the idealization which a full view of the world and of life brings to men.[8]

Dewey has had many disciples, including William H.

---

[7] Sister Mary Ruth, *op. cit.*, p. 7.
[8] James H. O. Hara, *The Limitations of the Educational Theory of John Dewey* (Washington, D. C.; The Catholic University of America, 1929), p. 103.

Kilpatrick,[9] John L. Childs, George S. Counts,[10] Harold Rugg, and Boyd H. Bode. Among the educators who disagree with the educational tenets of Dewey may be mentioned Charles H. Judd, David Snedden,[11] Edward L. Thorndike, Ernest Horn, Werrett W. Charters,[12] and Franklin Bobbitt. More conservative contemporary educators who respect the traditional values in American education and regard Dewey's educational position as radical are Herman H. Horne, Henry C. Morrison,[13] William C. Bagley,[14] Ellwood P. Cubberly, Thomas H. Briggs, and Ross L. Finney.[35] Current thinking in educational circles is traceable in large degree to the writings of Dewey and these contemporary educators.[16]

While Dewey was engaged in improving educational methods, *Edward L. Thorndike* (1874-   ) of Columbia University was concerned with the application of exact scientific measurement to the results of teaching. His aim has been to construct a science of education. There

---

[9] *Cf.* Bro. Jaìme Andrés Paez, "An Evaluation of the Educational Philosophy of William Heard Kilpatrick" (unpublished Master's dissertation, The Catholic University of America. 1944).

[10] *Cf.* Sr. M. Chrysostom Durnin, "The Educational Philosophy of George S. Counts" (unpublished Master's dissertation, The Catholic University of America, 1940).

[11] *Cf.* Sr. Alice Marie O'Neil, "A Critical Evaluation of the Educational Philosophy of David Snedden" (unpublished Master's dissertation, The Catholic University of America, 1941).

[12] *Cf.* Frederick O. Hughes, "An Inquiry into the Educational Theory of Werrett W. Charters" (unpublished Master's dissertation. The Catholic University of America, 1942).

[13] *Cf.* Sr. Jane Frances O'Hara, "The Educational Philosophy and Methodology of Henry Clinton Morrison" (unpublished Master's dissertation, The Catholic University of America, 1939).

[14] *Cf.* Sr. Mary Marguerite Cartwright, "The Educational Philosophy of William Chandler Bagley" (unpublished Master's dissertation, the Catholic University of America, 1937).

[15] *Cf.* Mary Donoghue, "The Educational Philosophy of Ross Lee Finney" (unpublished Master's dissertation, The Catholic University of America, 1944).

[16] *Cf.* Norman Woelfel, *Molders of the American Mind* (New York: Columbia University Press, 1933).

is little in his science of education that agrees with the Christian ideal of life. Naturalistic evolution is the basis of his explanation of man, society, and the universe.[17] It is the source of his educational psychology which in turn forms his educational ideal. On this foundation he has formulated new ideas on original nature, individual differences, and laws of learning. He has concluded that human mental life has developed as a mediation between stimulus and reaction. S-R bonds constitute the basis of all learning.[18]

Although Thorndike may rightly be called the father of the statistical movement in education, he was not the first to undertake scientific measurement of the results of instruction. This important work was begun in the United States by *J. M. Rice* who in 1897 published the results of an investigation in the field of spelling carried on over a period of sixteen months. Rice attempted to show what instruction in spelling had accomplished, what might reasonably be demanded in the subject, and the extent to which efficiency was affected by factors such as time spent on spelling, age, maturity, home environment, and nationality.

Thorndike began his monumental contributions to the field of educational psychology with the publication of his *Educational Psychology* in 1902. In this work he maintained that a quantitative description of individual differences and of the factors conditioning them is essential to an adequate understanding of educational theory and practice. Two years later the details of the method were presented in his *Mental and Social Measurements*. Subsequently he urged that scales should

---

[17] *Cf.* Geoffrey O'Connell, *Naturalism in American Education* (Washington, D. C.: The Catholic University of America, 1936), pp. 140-63.

[18] *Cf.* Walter A. Pax, *A Critical Study of Thorndike's Theory and Laws of Learning* (Washington, D. C.: The Catholic University of America, 1938).

be devised for measuring variations in ability and changes due to maturity and instruction. Thorndike himself constructed his Handwriting Scale in 1910; it was improved on by more refined scales in the field prepared under the direction of Ayres, Freeman, and Starch. Similar measurements of this kind have been the Hillegas Composition Scale, the Trabue Language Scale, the Woody Fundamentals of Arithmetic Scale, the Thorndike-McCall Reading Scale, the Ayres Scale in Reading, the Ayres-Buckingham Scale in Spelling, the Iowa Spelling Scale, the Hahn Scales in history and in geography, the Van Wagenen Scale for English Literature, and the Odell Scales for scoring essay tests.[19]

The educational efforts made in the direction of the quantitative measurement of school achievement have been supplemented by scales for measuring intellectual ability. In 1890 *James McKeen Cattell* who was associated with Francis Galton of England proposed a group of tests designed to measure the higher thought processes themselves. It remained, however, for a French psychologist, *Alfred Binet,* to devise a type of mental testing which led to our present mental tests. Binet in 1905 published a group of tests with a view to combining the results of all into one composite score which would serve as an index of the individual's intelligence. Three years later the Binet-Simon scale was published in which the tests were arranged in groups suitable to the various ages from three to thirteen years inclusive. A revision of this scale was later made in 1911. It did not occur to Binet that the ratio of the individual's mental age divided by his chronological age might be used as an index of his ability. It was left to William Stern and Frederick Kühlmann to make this suggestion. To this

---

[19] Graves, *op. cit.,* pp. 543 f.; Good, Barr, Scates, *The Methodology of Educational Research* (New York: D. Appleton-Century Co., 1936), p. 417.

concept was given the name, mental quotient. Lewis M. Terman, who is the author of the Stanford Revision of the Binet-Simon tests, later adopted the concept; multiplied the ratio by 100 to clear of decimal fractions, and applied to it the term intelligence quotient or I. Q. Terman's book, *The Measurement of Intelligence*, stimulated the movement of intelligence testing in this country. During the first World War, the Army Alpha group intelligence scale was constructed for classifying the soldiers for vocational work and for officer-training and revealed the possibilities of measuring the intelligence of large groups at one time. Since then similar group tests, notably the National, Terman, Haggerty, Kühlmann-Anderson, and Otis, have been constructed to measure the intelligence of pupils on the elementary, secondary, and college levels.[20]

Another form of educational measurement has been the standard tests for the various school subjects; they have partially replaced the traditional examinations. In this objective standard of measurement four closely related values have been distinguished: the comparative, the diagnostic, the corrective, and the incentive values. Among the most widely known are the arithmetic tests worked out by S. A. Courtis, the Monroe Test in Spelling, the Monroe Test in Arithmetic, the Freeman Test in Handwriting, the Charters Test in Language, the Briggs Test on English Form, the Pressey Test in English Composition, the Hotz Test in Algebra, the Witham Test in Geography, the Gregory Test in American History, the Gray tests in Reading, the Minnick tests in Geography, the Iowa Physics tests, and the Handschin tests in Modern Languages.[21] A frequently used combination of tests devised to determine the effectiveness of instruc-

[20] Elmer H. Wilds, *The Foundations of Modern Education* (New York: Farrar and Rhinehart, 1936), pp. 512 f.
[21] Graves, *op. cit.*, p. 544.

tion in a school as a whole or a pupil's average standing is the Stanford Achievement Test. Achievement and intelligence tests, singly and combined, have served teachers and educators in classification and promotion of pupils, in educational and vocational guidance, and in school surveys.

In the field of higher learning the curriculum of the Liberal Arts College has undergone marked changes. The elective system inaugurated by Charles W. Eliot (1834-1926), president of Harvard University, has made serious inroads upon the time-honored course of studies. Certain educators feel that the Liberal Arts College has served its purpose and must give way to a new organization of studies which better answer the demands of the times. On the other hand, the Liberal Arts College has many staunch defenders which indicates that it will be preserved.[22] In this regard President Hutchins of Chicago University has declared that the overemphasis on the empirical sciences to the detriment of the classics and the liberal arts is due to an erroneous notion of progress. Education has been made to yield to contemporary movements in society, regardless how superficial. In preparing youth for further political, social, and economic changes, educators have undertaken to decide what changes are desirable and then set about to educate them not merely to anticipate such changes but actually to take part in bringing them about.[23] The Report of the Harvard Committee on the objectives of a general education in a free society observes that there is an increasing amount of diversification among the liberal colleges, so much so that it is often difficult for a student who has transferred from one college to another to carry

---

[22] *Cf.* E. K. Rand, "Bring Back the Liberal Arts," *The Atlantic Monthly,* 171:79-85, June, 1943.
[23] Robert Maynard Hutchins, *The Higher Learning in America* (New Haven: Yale University Press, 1936), pp. 65 f.

on work of the kind earlier begun. The committee recommends a shifting of emphasis from special to general education. In its scheme of proposed courses at Harvard College three areas of learning are advocated: the humanities, the social sciences, mathematics and science. The Report maintains that the primary concern of the college is the individual, while the primary concern of the university is the advancement of learning, yet both concerns are inseparable and indispensable.[24] Apropos of higher learning Hutchins decries the lack of unity and coordination of knowledge in our American universities. He points out that the medieval university had a principle of unity; it was theology. Without theology or metaphysics a unified university cannot exist. Without them there is no intelligible basis for the study even of natural science. If the world presents itself to the student as a mass of meaningless data, then the pursuit of truth for its own sake becomes the indiscriminate accumulation of data. Scientific and technological advance must be directed by reason; true prosperity includes external goods but does not overlook those of the soul; true liberty can exist only in a society rationally ordered.[25]

A deplorable fact in the many profound changes that have taken place in the conduct of education is that the aims of education underlying modern educational theories make no mention of religion and express no concern for preparation for an eternal destiny. An analysis of the educational opinions of many of our prominent leaders in American education has revealed that they ignore God, the supernatural, the Ten Commandments, the eternal moral law, the soul, immortality

---

[24] *General Education in a Free Society, Report of the Harvard Committee* (Cambridge: Harvard University Press, 1945), pp. 180; 204-30.

[25] Hutchins, *op. cit.*, pp. 96, 99, 119.

—everything in fact which is above and beyond the empirical realm of existence.

In view of this, Mortimer Adler of the University of Chicago has declared, with respect to the crisis of Democracy, that we have less to fear from the totalitarian powers than from our professors.

It is they who have made American education what it is, both in content and method: in content, an introduction of positivism and naturalism; in method, an exhibition of anarchic individualism masquerading as the democratic manner. . . . the culture which is formed by such education cannot support what democracy we have against interior decay.[26]

The aim of modern education is primarily materialistic. Naturalistic philosophy controls education, stressing almost exclusively the equipment and training of the mind. According to the Educational Policies Commission, a basic principle underlying education for democracy in the United States is that the public schools must be secular schools.[27] Modern education disregards spiritual values—values which are universal and which by faith are considered eternal.[28] As a result of this,

---

[26] Mortimer J. Adler, "God and the Professors." A paper read at the Conference of Science, Philosophy and Religion. New York. 1940.

[27] Educational Policies Commission, *The Structure and Administration of Education in American Democracy* (Washington, D. C.: N.E.A., 1938), p. 123. *Cf.* William Sheehan, "A Critical Evaluation of the Interrelation of Democracy and Education according to the Educational Policies Commission" (unpublished Master's dissertation, The Catholic University of America, 1944).

[28] The recent report of the committee of ten appointed by President Seymour of Yale University to study the role that religion should play in a university warns against moral and intellectual anarchy and recommends that Yale take the lead in providing wholesome religious life for the student body. The committee urges that Yale, together with other colleges and universities, re-evaluate the role that religion can play on the campus and in the life of the students. The colleges and universities of the country must foster the development of students that they may become responsible bearers of spiritual values. *Cf. New York Times,* August 5, 1945.

Mr. Adolf A. Berle, formerly Assistant Secretary of State, has declared: "The world at this moment is not looking for another great scientist. It is looking, instead, for a great saint."

FOR FURTHER STUDY

Ames, E. S., *et al.*, *Essays in Honor of John Dewey, on the Occasion of His Seventieth Birthday.* New York: Henry Holt Co., 1929.

Brown, J. N., *Educational Implications of Four Current Conceptions of Human Nature. A Comparative Study.* Washington, D. C.: The Catholic University of America, 1940.

Dewey, John, *Democracy and Education, An Introduction to the Philosophy of Education.* New York: The Macmillan Co., 1933.

Eby and Arrowood, *The Development of Modern Education.* New York: Prentice-Hall, Inc., 1935.

Finney, Ross L., *A Brief History of the American Public School.* New York: The Macmillan Co., 1925.

General Education in a Free Society, Report of the Harvard Committee. Cambridge: Harvard University Press, 1945.

Graves, Frank P., *A Student's History of Education.* New York: The Macmillan Co., 1936.

Hall, G. Stanley, *Adolescence; Its Psychology and Its Relation to Physiology, Anthropology, Sociology, Sex, Crime, Religion and Education.* New York: D. Appleton Co., 1904. 2 vols.

Hutchins, Robert M., *The Higher Learning in America.* New Haven: Yale University Press, 1936.

James, William, *Pragmatism.* New York: Longmans, Green, and Co., 1926.

Monroe, Paul, *Founding of the American Public School System.* New York: The Macmillan Co., 1940.

O'Connell, Geoffrey, *Naturalism in American Education.* Washington, D. C.: The Catholic University of America, 1936.

O'Hara, James, *The Limitations of the Educational Theory of John Dewey.* Washington, D. C.: The Catholic University of America, 1929.

Partridge, G. E., *Genetic Philosophy of Education.* New York: Sturgis and Walton Co., 1912.

Raby, Sr. Joseph Mary, *A Critical Study of the New Education*. Washington, D. C.: The Catholic University of America, 1932.

Ratner, Joseph, *Philosophy of Dewey*. New York: Henry Holt Co., 1928.

Roche, P. J., "The Social Ideas of John Dewey." Unpublished Master's dissertation, Washington, D. C.: The Catholic University of America, 1940.

————, *Democracy in the Light of Four Current Educational Philosophies*. Washington, D. C.: The Catholic University of America, 1942.

Sandifer, Sr. Mary Ruth, *American Lay Opinion of the Progressive School*. Washington, D. C.: The Catholic University of America, 1943.

Thorndike, Edward L., *Educational Psychology*. New York: Lemcke and Buechner, 1902.

————, *Introduction to the Theory of Mental and Social Measurements*. New York: The Science Press, 1904.

Wilds, Elmer, H., *The Foundations of Modern Education*. New York: Farrar and Rinehart, 1943.

Wilson, Louis N., *Granville Stanley Hall*. New York: G. E. Stechert and Company, 1914.

Woelful, Norman, *Molders of the American Mind*. New York: Columbia University Press, 1933.

CHAPTER XXXI

RECENT DEVELOPMENTS IN AMERICAN EDUCATION (Continued)

No Catholic educator was more keenly aware of the subversive influence of the materialistic and naturalistic philosophy current in educational theory at the beginning of the twentieth century than was Dr. Shields, of the Catholic University of America. *Very Reverend Thomas Edward Shields* was born at Mendota, near St. Paul, Minnesota, May 9, 1862. He attended the one-room village school which he entered at the age of six years, and made reasonable progress in the fundamental school subjects during the first three years of his schooling. Due to wrong methods of teaching and an abnormally rapid physical growth, he was unable to read the selections in the advanced reader, developed a hesitant, stumbling manner of speech, and consequently was kept home from school and put to work on the farm. His nerve energy must have been all used in building up his physical frame, because at thirteen he was able to do a man's work in nearly every kind of farm employment.[1]

Realizing that he was timid and unlike other boys, and seeing him marvel at young people around him who could talk plainly and readily, his parents sent him back to school in the hope that he might learn to read the papers and know something of what was happening beyond his immediate environment. Unfortunately, the kindly understanding, the encouragement and careful teaching which would have awakened the slumbering intelligence of this singularly gifted, but strangely retarded youth were lacking in the teacher who took him in hand

---

[1] Thomas E. Shields, *The Making and Unmaking of a Dullard* (Washington, D. C.: The Catholic Education Press, 1921), p. 96.

only to employ the harsh and impatient methods which were usual at the time in dealing with the backward pupil. As a result his old hatred of the classroom soon revived and after a few weeks he was taken away from school and again put to work on the farm. He made no further attempt to read, and even forgot how to write his name.[2]

In the beginning of his fifteenth year the mental life of young Shields began to reawaken. He realized that he was regarded as a hopeless dullard, but his work on the farm was his salvation. His success in ploughing, hoeing, making straight furrows, measuring and estimating spatial relationships encouraged him and made him feel a sense of self-respect. The improvement of a grindstone produced in him the first realization of his own mental power, while the invention of a grubbing machine had far-reaching effects in developing his mind and character. If he could not read or speak properly, he at least understood something about mechanics. Self-reliance now took the place of uncertainty and an undaunted self-confidence took possession of him and remained with him throughout the rest of his life.

Doctor Shields tells us that he learned to read because of his interest in an unfinished story which he could not get anyone to read aloud to him. He undertook to read for himself by studying each letter and pronouncing each syllable. This experience developed the habit of pronouncing each syllable aloud as his eye rested on it and led to a locked synergy between the movements of the eye and the movements of the vocal organs which often proved detrimental in reading and singing.[3] Because he was hungry for knowledge, reading became a fundamental necessity. In the spring of 1879 Mrs. Southworth's novel, *Ishmael or In the Depths,* and its

---

[2] *Ibid.,* pp. 102-104.
[3] *Ibid.,* pp. 275 ff.

sequel, *Self-Raised or From the Depths,* fell into his hands and he successfully read both of them. Of these works he later wrote:

I saw myself reflected in Ishmael; he was a companion in misery. Hand in hand with him I climbed, step by step, up out of the gloom into the sunshine of hope. . . . It was possible to come up out of the depths! . . . I resolved with a resolution in which all the energies of my whole being were concentrated, that I would rise from the condition in which I had lived for years. . . . No difficulty would have daunted me in that moment of exaltation.[4]

The idea of studying for the priesthood now took hold of Doctor Shields, and his family gave him financial assistance with which to defray the expenses of private tutoring. He applied himself assiduously to classical studies, and his mind, untrammelled by formalism and memory loads, developed remarkably. In 1882 he entered St. Francis College, Milwaukee, as a sophomore where he passed all his courses quite successfully and showed especial talent in the various branches of mathematics. Three years later he entered the Seminary of St. Thomas Aquinas at St. Paul and here pursued courses for two years in philosophy, ethics, and the physical sciences; and for four years in theology, Scripture, Church history, and canon law. While in the seminary he indulged his talent for invention by devising a filing system for the accumulation of information under the title of *Index Omnium.* He was ordained to the priesthood by Archbishop Ireland in 1891 and was assigned as curate to the cathedral of St. Paul. Later he entered St. Mary's Seminary, Baltimore, and there received a Master's degree. Graduate work in the department of biology of Johns Hopkins University was next undertaken, and here he completed the courses prescribed for the Doctorate in Philosophy, which was conferred on him in June, 1895.

---

[4] *Ibid.,* pp. 286 f.

His doctoral dissertation, *The Effects of Odours, Irritant Vapours, and Mental Work upon the Blood Flow,* was published in the first volume of *The Journal of Experimental Medicine,* which was founded in 1896 for the publication of original work in the medical sciences with a view to aiding materially the advancement of scientific medicine which was developing rapidly in the United States. Doctor Shields' laborious researches, however, were not for biology itself, but that biology might give him a scientific basis for the theory of Catholic education which he was later to espouse and bring to a successful issue.

After teaching biology in St. Paul Seminary and enriching his experience in the priesthood through the exercise of parochial duties in the city of St. Paul, Dr. Shields joined the faculty of the Catholic University in 1902 as instructor in physiological psychology. During the years 1904 to 1909 the Department of Education at the University was organized and Dr. Shields was raised to the rank of professor of physiological psychology and education. The National Catholic Educational Association was meanwhile founded and in all its activities Dr. Shields was prominent. Correspondence courses prepared by him for the preparation of religious teachers throughout the country, and his "Notes on Education" which he contributed to the *Catholic University Bulletin* from 1907 to 1910 indicated very clearly his deep concern for the cause of Catholic education in the United States. In 1911, in conjunction with Doctor Edward A. Pace of the University staff, he rendered further service to the promotion of Catholic education by founding the *Catholic Educational Review,* an educational periodical which has since served as a vehicle for the dissemination of some of the best ideas in Catholic educational theory and practice.

A notable advance towards the professional training of our teaching sisters was made when the first Summer

School was opened at the Catholic University (1911). In this movement Right Reverend Thomas J. Shahan, Rector of the University, and Dr. Pace were most active, but Dr. Shields was the enthusiastic driving force. In October of the same year the formal opening of the Catholic Sisters College, Brookland, D. C., followed and at last the goal for which Dr. Shields had striven was realized. In a very special manner this foundation was his project. He was appointed first Dean and continued in office until his death. Realizing that through the Sisters College the needed relationship and coordination between the Catholic University and the Catholic school system could be more easily effected, he proposed a plan and prescribed the conditions for affiliation of colleges and high schools with the University which was approved by the Board of Trustees of the University in 1912.

The duties of Dr. Shields were manifold. The Catholic Education Press, organized in 1910 for the publication of his own books and of the texts his colleagues were preparing, demanded his personal supervision. The success which he achieved as the organizing and directing head of the Sisters College could hardly have been duplicated by any other Catholic educator of his generation. His lectures at the University and at Trinity College, the courses which he conducted at the Sisters College, the completion of his textbooks, his numerous contributions to periodicals and educational associations, his painstaking efforts towards the development of a system of Catholic elementary education of which religion should form the center, and in which the cultural subjects of music and art should find a recognized place, all received his customary attention.

Years of intense labor, however, weakened his health; he developed a heart ailment, and though it was apparent to his friends and colleagues that his condition was precarious, he continued to work with his usual eagerness in the hope that he might accomplish much more of his self-appointed task. On February 2, 1921, he lectured at the Sisters College for the last time. A severe attack of influenza incapacitated him and twelve days later he passed to his eternal reward. He was buried in Mount Olivet Cemetery, Washington, D. C.; but in recognition of his noble services to the Sisters College, his remains were exhumed and laid to rest in a mausoleum on the College campus on November 13, 1928.

Dr. Shields wrote various educational essays, the influence of which was due in no small measure to their remarkable timeliness. His first pedagogical contributions which were not published, "The Teaching of Religion" [5] and "Twenty-Five Lessons in the Psychology of Education," [6] were sources of instruction in the Catholic correspondence school conducted for sisters from 1905 to 1910, and also in extension courses, conferences, and teachers' institutes. It is estimated that over six thousand students derived assistance from these two treatises.[7] *The Education of Our Girls* (1907) written in dialogue form is a keen psychological analysis of the problem and a plea for the higher education of women in a school or college for women; the alleged advantage of coeducation is shown to be outweighed by its disadvantages. *The Making and the Unmaking of a Dullard* (1909), also written in dialogue form, was dedicated "in loving sympathy to the misunderstood children who are reached the stone of discouragement instead of the bread of hope." This book is a distinct contribution to the literature on atypical children, and is one of

---

[5] Preserved with his other writings in the Mullen Library of The Catholic University.

[6] *Loc. cit.*

[7] Sister Mary Callista McConville, "The Development of the Professional Training of Teachers for the Catholic Schools in the United States" (unpublished Master's dissertation, The University of Maine, Orono, Maine, 1933), p. 67.

the pioneers in this field, appearing as it did about the same time as the famous Binet tests.[8] *The Catholic Education Series of Textbooks* represents his greatest efforts as an author. Begun in 1908 with *Religion First Book*, they included, within ten years, four distinct books in Religion and three Readers, the latter correlated and associated in method with the books in Religion. In connection with this series he published in 1912 *The Teachers Manual of Primary Methods* which is a detailed analysis of the content of the first four texts, together with a discussion of the method involved and the aims which the series of texts sought to attain. *Philosophy of Education* (1917) is perhaps the author's most learned work. In it he contrasts the philosophy of the Catholic Church and its aims in education with current educational literature animated by a philosophy of education wholly at variance with Catholic ideas and ideals. For many years it enjoyed the distinction of being the only exposition of fundamental educational problems from a Catholic viewpoint. Although certain chapters have obvious limitations and there is a lack of clear distinction between curriculum and course of study in the chapter dealing with "curriculum," nevertheless the work has solid worth as a whole and maintains a place in the front rank of literature on educational theory.

Doctor Shields taught that the child comes into the world with a definite body of instinctive tendencies. Among them are certain ones which if permitted to develop along native lines would lead to the formation of an undesirable member of society. Five of these must be given careful attention by the teacher in the first grade: reliance upon parents for love, nourishment, protection, remedy, and models for imitative activity. It

---

[8] Pierre J. Marique, "Thomas Edward Shields, Apostle of Progress in Education," *Thought*, 2:367-69, December, 1927.

is the duty of the Christian educator to transform these tendencies into their opposites. The child must be taught to love as well as to expect love, to give as well as to take, to protect the weak, to help the needy, and to edify others by leading an upright life. He must also be taught to develop towards God the five-fold attitude which he maintains towards his parents. God is the source of love, food, protection against temptation, deliverance from evil, and the model for imitative activities.

Apart from the operation of divine grace, the child's social inheritance which is at least five-fold enables the teacher to accomplish this transformation. These inheritances are—Science, by means of which the child learns to adjust himself to the physical world in which he lives; Letters, by means of which the child learns the results of the experience of the race under the divine precepts which were given man to direct him; Institutions which the child must learn to respect, because through human institutions such as home, church, school, state, all the higher aims in life are attainable; Aesthetics, which inspire the soul of the child to respond to beauty in all its forms, thus raising the child above the level of the brute; Religion, which teaches him that if he is to merit eternal life, he must learn to know God, to love Him, and to serve Him. God must be found as the center of all unity for the world at large and for the child's own life; in this way only can the pupil develop normally as a social and ethical being and as a child of God.[9]

Religion, then, must be the core of all instruction. The purpose of religious training is not really to give knowledge of God, but to consecrate human life. Religious truths must illumine and unify all the subjects taught in school. Religion must transform the child's

---

[9] Thomas E. Shields, *Teachers Manual of Primary Methods* (Washington, D. C.: The Catholic Education Press, 1912), pp. 104 ff.

entire mental life, and guide his conduct in all the situations of life. The truths that are to become vital in the life of a child must be presented in a manner suited to the child's plan of mental development. Abstract formulations, therefore, should be avoided.[10] It is an erroneous belief that most rote memory work should be done during the earliest school years. Intellectual life does not fall into sharply differentiated periods. Perception, imagination, memory, judgment, reasoning are always at work in every stage of development, though not all with the same evidence of efficiency.

In his theory and method of education, Dr. Shields was influenced by the educators of the modern period, and in a special manner by Pestalozzi, Herbart, and Froebel. His educational psychology is essentially Froebelian, and his whole method in elementary education is influenced by his scientific studies in biology. In his *First Book* of the *Catholic Education Series* the order observed is not regarded as psychologically sound. The domestic story should precede the nature story. Had Doctor Shields lived he would no doubt have made the necessary revision and adjustment in this respect. The Catholic University Campus School, located near the Sisters College, Brookland, D. C., is an experimental center for the Shields Method of elementary education. An essential part of the method consists of the projects organized on the basis of active doing. The child is led to think in religion by getting him to think in all that he does.

FOR FURTHER STUDY

Johnson, George W., "Thomas Edward Shields," *Catholic Historical Review,* 8:582-85, January, 1929.

---

[10] Thomas E. Shields, "Method of Teaching Religion," *The Catholic Educational Association Bulletin,* 5:204-207, November, 1908.

Marique, Pierre J., "Thomas Edward Shields, Apostle of Progress in Education," *Thought*, 2:367-69, December, 1927.

O'Connor, Sr. M. Augustine, "The Influence of Very Reverend Doctor Thomas E. Shields on Catholic Education in the United States." Unpublished Master's dissertation, The Catholic University of America, Washington, D. C., 1941.

Shields, Thomas E., *The Education of Our Girls*. New York: Benziger Brothers, 1907.

——————, *The Making and Unmaking of a Dullard*. Washington, D. C.: The Catholic Education Press, 1909.

——————, *Catholic Education Series*. Washington, D. C.: The Catholic Education Press, 1908-18.

——————, *Teacher's Manual of Primary Methods*. Washington, D. C.: The Catholic Education Press, 1912.

——————, *Philosophy of Education*. Washington, D. C.: The Catholic Education Press, 1917.

Ward, Justine B., "The Life of Thomas E. Shields," *The Catholic Educational Review*, 19:200-22, April, 1921.

——————, "Music Restored to the People," *The Catholic Educational Review*, 19:277-84, April, 1921.

SYNOPSIS OF MODERN SCHOOL SYSTEMS

1. RISE OF STATE SYSTEMS
    (a) Passage of compulsory attendance laws
    (b) Regulation of teachers' requirements
    (c) Government grants
    (d) Legal separation of church and state
2. THE SCHOOL SYSTEM OF GERMANY
    (a) Prussia has been more or less the model in the evolution of German school education.
    (b) The elementary school, *Volksschule*, is divided into two sections, the lower, *Grundschule*, of four years, and the upper, *Volksschule*, also of four years.
    (c) Most of the secondary schools, *Gymnasien*, have been converted into *Deutsche Oberschulen*. Other forms of secondary schools are *Aufbauschulen*, *National-politische Institute*, and *Adolf Hitler Schulen*. Secondary schools for girls are *Studienanstalten*, the work of which is based upon the fundamental course given in the *Lyzeum*. Other types of girls' secondary schools are *Frauenschulen*, *Oberlyzeums*, and *Aufbauschulen*.
    (d) The twenty-five universities are exclusively state institutions and are coeducational. Higher instruction of a practical and technological character is given in *Hochschulen*.
    (e) The *Einheitsschule* or common system of education has been advocated since the establishment of the Republic in Germany. This system aims to replace the horizontal system by a vertical system of schools organized on a functional basis adapted to various abilities.
3. THE SCHOOL SYSTEM OF FRANCE
    (a) The present national system of France dates from the Revolution which began the modern program of secularization.
    (b) The elementary school system consists of primary and higher primary schools. In addition to the elementary schools, maternal schools and infant classes

591

are provided. Beyond the higher primary school are trade schools, adult courses, and continuation schools.
   (c) Secondary education is obtained in the *lycées* or *collèges;* education in state secondary schools is tuition-free. The seven-year course of study entitles the student to take the *baccalauréat* or examination for university entrance.
   (d) Eighteen universities at present exist; private faculties or departments of universities are tolerated, although they may not grant degrees.
   (e) The movement in favor of the *école unique* or unitary system of education favors a closer articulation of the *lycées* and *collèges* with the common elementary school and asserts the right of every individual to education appropriate to his abilities.
4. THE SCHOOL SYSTEM OF SPAIN
   (a) The Golden Age of Spanish education was from 1474 to 1621.
   (b) Modern system of education is not so centralized as it is in France or Germany.
   (c) Public schools have been inadequate; local authorities have recognized many private schools and supported them from public funds.
   (d) Secondary education is provided in the *institutos* and the *colegios*. The education of girls has been supplied for the most part by teaching Sisterhoods. Two-thirds of total secondary school enrollment is in private secondary schools. Under the Franco government reform of secondary education has been undertaken based on a sense of tradition.
   (e) There are twelve national universities, some of which like Salamanca, Valencia, and Valladolid were founded in the Middle Ages. University education is coeducational. Students in private universities take examinations annually set by state authorities; only national universities grant degrees.
5. THE SCHOOL SYSTEM OF ENGLAND
   (a) The Forster Act of 1870 was the basic law for the direction of education in England.

(b) Education Act of 1902 admitted the voluntary schools to a share in the local rates as well as in the state grants.

(c) The Junior School, Central School, and Senior School constitute the elementary system of education; a wide range of part-time education, general and vocational, has been established on a voluntary basis.

(d) The several types of secondary schools are the Public Schools, the Grammar Schools for Boys, the High Schools for Girls, the Municipal or County Secondary Schools, usually coeducational, and private adventure schools conducted by a headmaster for personal profit. Catholics have famous secondary schools and colleges, notably Stonyhurst.

(e) Oxford and Cambridge share the patronage for advanced studies with younger institutions of university grade located in manufacturing and commercial centers and devoted to technical and scientific instruction; no higher education up to the present is entirely supported and controlled by the state.

6. THE SCHOOL SYSTEM OF THE UNITED STATES

(a) Early schools of New World modeled after those of European countries from which the first settlers came.

(b) Mission schools of Spanish Franciscans in Florida and New Mexico were first elementary schools in present territory of United States.

(c) Common characteristic of schools in different colonies was their relation to the church of the colony.

(d) The Massachusetts type of school is that from which it is believed the modern common school takes its origin.

(e) The period of most rapid and extensive development of state systems is marked by the activities of Horace Mann.

(f) Henry Barnard wielded a wide influence from the literary viewpoint on the development of state systems of education.

(g) During the second half of the nineteenth century high schools formed an integral part of public school systems.

    (h) State universities have had their greatest expansion since the middle of the nineteenth century; denominational colleges and universities have been in existence from colonial times.

    (i) The Catholic school system had its origin in the Maryland colony.

    (j) The Catholic elementary schools are organized in diocesan systems. Secondary schools, embracing parish high schools, academies, and preparatory schools, flourish throughout the country. A significant advance in Catholic higher education began with the establishment of the Catholic University of America at Washington.

CHAPTER XXXII

DEVELOPMENT OF MODERN SCHOOL SYSTEMS

The nineteenth century, so productive of educational theories and reforms, was also the period of the greatest development of state systems of education. Pestalozzianism and the Psychological Movement generally had awakened widespread interest in universal education. Individual philanthropists and charitable societies undertook to meet the educational needs of the poor; the Church, wherever free to do so, enlisted the services of her teaching organizations some of whom were especially devoted to gratuitous instruction. State activity in regard to schools was due to a variety of causes, some very notable factors being the passage of compulsory attendance laws, the regulation of teachers' requirements, government grants, and the legal separation of church and state.

The development of educational systems in foreign countries, especially Germany, France, and England, has proved suggestive in the organization of the school system in the United States; yet in none of these countries is the system the same as in America. In the European system, for all students beyond the age of eight to ten years the schools branch into schools for the leaders and schools for the masses. In the United States, an "educational ladder" has been set up in keeping with the democratic principles of the nation. An appreciation of these modern school systems is best derived from a survey of their gradual development to their present form in accordance with the genius and social organization of the people concerned.

The earliest and most effective of modern state systems of education is that of Germany. Previous to World War I the government of the German Empire was a constitutional monarchy. At the end of the War in 1918 a Republican form of government was established. The Republic continued until 1934 when Hitler, who had become the leader of the Nazi Party and chancellor under Von Hindenberg, was by law made president of the German Reich. The Nazi Party was opposed to a republican form of government and set up a totalitarian state. Under Hitler and his cabinet all Germany has been unified.[1]

In pre-Republican days Prussia, the largest of the states, was to a greater or lesser extent the model of German school organization. Although compulsory education laws were passed in some of the Thuringian states in the seventeenth century, the beginnings of general and compulsory education in Prussia date from the reign of Frederick William I (1713-1740). The friend and patron of Francke, he made school attendance obligatory by rescripts issued in 1716 and 1717, and encouraged the better preparation of teachers. His successor, Frederick the Great (1740-1786), promulgated General School Regulations in 1763 in which it was stipulated that compulsory school attendance should begin at the latest at the fifth and last until the fourteenth year. Parents were subject to fine for an infringement of the law. The Regulations made provision for the support of schools through systematic taxation, for the compensation of teachers, and for supervision by the local and state authorities.

Like his father, Frederick is supposed to have raised the standard for the preparation of teachers, but it is well known that he ordered superannuated soldiers to be appointed schoolmasters. As Paulsen says:

---

[1] Unification Act in 1933 and the law of 1934, which transferred all powers of the state to the Reich, included those powers formerly exercised by the states in educational matters. *Cf.* Henry L. Smith, *Comparative Education* (Bloomington, Indiana: Educational Publications, 1941), p. 155.

No professional education for teachers in the proper sense was yet in existence. Normal schools or training colleges (*Lehrer-Seminare*) were only just appearing here and there above the horizon; the Prussian orphanages founded at Königsberg, Züllichau, Stettin, etc., after the model of Halle, and later on, Hecker's "Realschule" offered facilities of this kind within small limits.[2]

The first real normal school was not opened until 1778, at Halberstadt. Efficient ministers had, however, been appointed and centralization begun. A central administration board was formed in 1787 through the efforts of Baron von Zedlitz, minister of public instruction under Frederick the Great. Through this and subsequent legislation (1794) the state obtained full powers over all schools. In the nineteenth century, the era of the development of the primary school as a state institution, Prussia led the way, as Paulsen declares, "for better or for worse in the domain of education."[3] Under Wilhelm von Humboldt (1767-1835) the educational ministry was organized and national education took the direction which it has maintained with few variations throughout the century. The University of Berlin, founded in 1810 largely through his efforts and representing a new ideal in higher education, namely, the furtherance of the sciences by original research, affected the other universities either newly founded or reorganized.

All of the German universities, twenty-five in number, are exclusively state institutions. Since the Nazi Revolution of 1933 the government of higher institutions has been concentrated in the Rector, responsible to the Reich Minister for Higher Education. The old division into faculty, senate, and dean has survived, but these offices have lost their administrative autonomy and serve

---

[2] F. Paulsen, *German Education, Past and Present*. Translated by T. Lorenz (New York: Charles Scribner's Sons, 1908), p. 140.
[3] *Ibid.*, p. 181.

solely in advisory capacities.[4] The universities have traditionally been limited to the four faculties of philosophy, theology, medicine, and law. The faculty of philosophy has included letters and science. The need for higher instruction of a practical and technological character has been met by the establishment of special *Hochschulen* wherein engineering, forestry, agriculture, veterinary medicine, commerce, graphic and plastic arts, music, and pharmacy are taught; and teacher training is given. In 1935, there were ten technical *Hochschulen,* twelve philosophical-theological *Hochschulen,* and sixteen teacher training *Hochschulen.*[5]

The secondary school first in vogue was the *Gymnasium,* or classical school, whose curriculum showed the effect of the new humanistic movement of the early nineteenth century. In opposition to this purely classical school, there arose the semi-classical or *Real-Gymnasium* adapted to modern requirements in respect to the study of the vernacular and science. Then later appeared the *Oberrealschule* or non-classical school, in which modern languages, mathematics and natural sciences constituted the curriculum. These schools gave nine-year courses. Parallel to these three, developed six-year schools known as *Progymnasium, Realprogymnasium,* and *Realschule.* At present the nine-year secondary school has been shortened to an eight-year school.[6] Most of the *Gymnasien* have been converted into *Deutsche Oberschulen.* The curriculum of the latter consists largely of German and mathematics; in some, a year of Latin. Another form of secondary school is the *Aufbauschule* which gives a six-year course following either that of the upper *Oberrealschule* or that of the *Deutsche Oberschule* and bringing the pupil up to standard required for admission to the university. Other types of secondary schools are

---

[4] Smith, *op. cit.,* p. 192.
[5] *Loc. cit.*
[6] *Ibid.,* p. 179.

the *Nationalpolitische Institute* and the *Adolf Hitler Schulen.*

Secondary schools for girls parallel the *Gymnasien* and *Realgymnasien* and are known as *Studienanstalten.* The work of these schools is based upon the fundamental course given in the *Lyzeum* and many continue in the *Oberlyzeum* whose curriculum is that of an *Oberrealschule* or in a *Frauenschule* which has a home-arts curriculum. In addition, there are an *Oberlyzeum,* of a more academic type, and also *Aufbauschulen* for girls making it possible for them to prepare for the universities.

Education in the secondary schools is not free; however, a number of scholarships are given to gifted pupils and there is also available a small percentage of maintenance grants. Separate schools are maintained for boys and girls; only in exceptional cases is coeducation permitted.

The elementary school, *Volksschule,* provides for the education of children during the period of compulsory attendance, from the age of six to fourteen.[7] It is divided into two sections, the lower or *Grundschule* of four years, and the upper, also of four years. The *Grundschule* is the foundation school in which all children regardless of class distinction are required to attend unless they are enrolled in private schools or educated at home under exceptional conditions.[8] Pupils of superior ability may complete the course of the *Grundschule* in three years. Physical education is an important part of the elementary school program. One afternoon weekly must be spent in group gymnastics. Only thirteen per cent of the elementary schools in Germany are fully organized with a separate class for each year; one-third of the schools have one room and a single teacher.[9] Separate

---

[7] I. L. Kandel, *Comparative Education* (Boston: Houghton Mifflin Company, 1933), p. 437.
[8] *Ibid.,* p. 435.
[9] *Loc. cit.*

schools are as a rule maintained for the sexes and women are not allowed to teach boys. Further education for graduates of the elementary school may be obtained in the continuation and vocational schools.

Pupils who have completed the *Grundschule* may be admitted to a *Mittelschule,* which is established in a locality unable to maintain a recognized secondary school. The aim of the middle school is to prepare boys for business and administrative positions in commerce, forestry, and agriculture; and to train girls in domestic science. The course is parallel to that of the first six years of a secondary school and qualifies pupils for entrance to the last three years of a full secondary school. The middle school is better equipped than the elementary school, charges a moderate fee, and has smaller classes with teachers who are specialists in particular subjects or who hold special certificates for teaching in the middle school. Mixed classes may be taught by men or women, although separate schools or departments must be established for boys and girls when this is possible.

Due to democratic idealism which brought about the establishment of the Republic in Germany, the *Einheitsschule* or common system of education has been advocated. This system would replace the horizontal system of one school for the classes and one for the masses by the vertical system of schools organized on a functional basis adapted to various abilities.[10] Nowhere has the *Einheitsschule* been realized, but efforts have been made to attain unity of purpose and ideal rather than unity of form by uniting various institutional types in an organic system of education.

France

While the national school system of France is of very recent origin, it would be a mistake to suppose that

[10] *Ibid.,* p. 63

popular education in that country dates from its inception. That educational institutions were numerous in the Middle Ages, and especially before the French Revolution, and that they were adequate to the needs of the time has been well substantiated by modern historical research. The work of Père Allain, *L'Instruction primaire en France avant la Révolution* (Paris, 1881), offers abundant testimony to the generous provision made by Church and municipality for elementary instruction. His work is but one of many similar studies undertaken for the various provinces and dioceses of France. Reference has already been made to some of them in connection with the later medieval schools.[11]

The present national system owes much by way of precedent to the Revolution, which by its frenzied attacks upon the properties of the Church may be said to have begun the modern program of secularization. The Constitutional Convention of 1793 dissolved the existing educational system including the historic University of Paris, the colleges, and secondary schools. Its measures of reform, however expressive of the goodwill of the legislators, were not carried into effect. Napoleon I in his scheme of organization compressed all of the higher institutions, the universities, *lycées* and *collèges*, into one corporate body called the University of France. He did not attempt to organize elementary education.

The *Loi Guizot* (Guizot's law) of 1833, passed during the reign of Louis Philippe and providing a school for each commune, is regarded as the first general and effective step ever taken towards the realization of a state system. Elementary education did not become compulsory until 1882.[12]

The *Loi Guizot* gave the Church liberty to establish

---

[11] *Cf.* pp. 300-307.
[12] Kandel, *op. cit.*, p. 404.

her own elementary schools. It was not until the *Loi Falloux* was passed by the Second Republic in 1850 that the same concession was made for secondary education. After the fall of Louis Philippe in the revolution of 1848, the Catholics of France who numbered then a majority of the population fought under the leadership of Dupanloup chiefly for *enseignement libre* for higher education. Accordingly, the *Loi Falloux* granted the Church permission to have her own primary and secondary schools with little state control, made the *curé,* among others, supervisor of moral instruction in state schools, and led to a later concession by which the approval of books concerning religion was referred to the proper religious authorities.[13]

The policy of the Third Republic, ostensibly one of secularization, was actually anti-religious and especially anti-Catholic. During its régime religion was gradually eliminated from the curriculum, textbooks, and all instruction; the religious orders and congregations, the devoted teachers of France for centuries, were expelled from the schools by a series of laws which began in 1886 and culminated in 1904 when "the teaching of every grade and every kind" was forbidden in France to religious congregations. After the First World War, however, due to the heroic examples of patriotism shown by Catholic priests and religious on the battlefield, the laws against Catholic schools were not rigidly enforced. In 1941, through the efforts of Marshal Pétain, these anticlerical statutes were repealed.

Many changes have taken place in the organization of education in France since World War I. The elementary schools supply instruction during the compulsory attendance period, from six to fourteen.[14]   Higher

---

[13] Clarence E. Elwell, *The Influence of the Enlightenment on the Catholic Theory of Religious Education in France 1750-1850* (Cambridge: Harvard University Press, 1944), pp. 177 f.

[14] Smith, *op. cit.,* p. 86.

primary schools are provided to supplement the work of the lower with more advanced courses in mathematics, bookkeeping, literature, and also manual and industrial training. In these superior primary schools sometimes, for economy, the sexes are taught together. There is offered in many places where the locality is financially unable to establish a higher primary school, a supplementary course (*cours complémentaire*) which is two years in length, under the same administration, and similar to the higher primary courses. Beyond the higher primary schools are trade schools, adult courses, and part-time or continuation schools. There are in addition to the elementary schools the *écoles maternelles,* or mother schools, for children from two to five years of age; and the *classes enfantines* or infant classes, which are intermediate between the *écoles maternelles* and the elementary schools.

Secondary education may be obtained in the *lycées* or *collèges.* Formerly, these secondary schools usually had their own primary classes, but the law of 1937 ordered that pupils who seek admission to the secondary schools must have completed satisfactorily the first six years of the seven-year primary school.[15] The primary schools are thus regarded as "education of the first level," and the secondary schools as "education of the second level." The *lycée* is a national school, located usually in the capital of a department, whereas the *collège* is communal and is maintained by the municipality and the state. The student who completes the seven-year course of the *lycée* or the *collège* is entitled to take the *baccalaureat* or examination for university entrance. In 1930 a law was passed that all education in all state secondary schools should be tuition-free. Tuition fees have been abolished in *lycées* and *collèges* since 1933.[16]

---

[15] *Ibid.,* p. 87.
[16] *Ibid.,* p. 86.

The requirements for teachers in the *lycées* are more exacting than for those in the *collèges*. In order to teach in the *collège*, the teacher must have taken the *licence*, which is granted by a university faculty after two years of work beyond the obtaining of the *baccalaureat* from a secondary school. To become a full professor in the *lycée*, the teacher must obtain the *agrégé*, which is really not a degree, but a title conferred by the state on the basis of a special examination given by a special board.

When Napoleon I organized the University of France he divided the country into twenty-seven academies, each to have a faculty of letters and science. Other authorized faculties were medicine, law, and theology. The government, however, granted scanty support to these faculties. Their professors were chiefly taken from the neighboring *lycées;* and, although degrees were conferred, few faculties had the standing of universities. The law of 1896 revived the universities; eighteen at present exist.[17] Private faculties or departments of universities are tolerated, although they may not grant degrees; they must submit their candidates for degrees to the state university examinations. Catholics have maintained seventeen well-known faculties of theology, law, medicine, letters, and the sciences at Paris, Marseilles, Angers, Lille, Lyons, and other large cities.

The French system differs from the German in that it is national. The supreme head is the Minister of National Education who is assisted in his duties by several committees, two of the most important of which are the Superior Council of Public Instruction and the Consulting Committee of Public Instruction. The former advises concerning the curricula, teaching methods, administrative and disciplinary matters, regulations concerning examinations and the awarding of the degrees, as well as supervision of private education; while the latter

---

[17] *Ibid.,* p. 128.

recommends promotions for personnel and appointments to vacancies.[18] The country is divided into seventeen areas to form the academic districts. Over each academic district is placed a rector, who is the president of the university in the district, charged with the administration of all instruction above the elementary primary education in the district in which he resides. The state, therefore, exercises a direct influence in all departments of instruction, and this is especially seen in the appointment of supervising inspectors and the conditions laid down for the approval of teachers in state and private schools. Holland, Belgium, Italy, and in certain respects Switzerland have shown the influence of France upon their state organization of schools.

Within recent years a strong movement has developed in France in favor of the decentralization control and of a unitary system known as the *école unique*. This scheme asserts the right of every individual to the best education appropriate to his abilities and advocates the abolition of the parallelism in the educational system and a closer articulation of the *lycées* and *collèges* with the common elementary school. As a result of this movement, the curricula of the elementary classes of the *lycées* and the primary schools have been unified; fees for day pupils in the secondary schools have been abolished; and a uniform system of awarding scholarships for secondary schools, post-graduate grades of the primary schools, and technical schools has been adopted.[19]

Spain

There is a lack of ready material on modern education in Spain and for this reason the subject of Spanish

---

[18] *Ibid.*, p. 78.
[19] A. E. Meyer, *The Development of Education in the Twentieth Century* (New York: Prentice-Hall, Inc., 1939), p. 312.

education is generally ignored by educational writers.[20] Spain's record in the history of education is a long and creditable one. Beginning with the period of Roman domination, Spanish education developed gradually until it rose to its greatest splendor during the period known as the Golden Age (1474-1621). In modern times the system of education as developed in Spain is not so centralized as that in France or Germany. The national government has left more control to local authorities. While schools are numerous, both public and private, the percentage of attendance is not high because the compulsory attendance law is not everywhere enforced. For an understanding of present conditions in Spain, it should be noted that there are few really large cities; the population is mostly rural, and the nation in comparison to former times is poor.

The law which regulated educational conditions until very recent years was that of 1857.[21] It centralized authority in a general director, appointed by the king, an advisory council, and a corps of inspectors; it recognized however, the provincial and local authorities and also the teaching orders; it made attendance compulsory from six to twelve years of age; and permitted parents to elect to send their children to the public or private schools.

As the public schools are inadequate, the local authorities have recognized many private schools and supported them from the public funds. The percentage of illiterates among the Spaniards has been and is yet very much exaggerated. The statistics of 1860 are often cited to indicate their number at 75 per cent of the popu-

[20] The most complete, although not impartial, work on Spanish education is *De la instruccion pública en España* in 3 vols. published at Madrid by Gil Y Zárate in 1855. Nothing substantial has since been written.

[21] John R. Perz, *Secondary Education in Spain* (Washington, D. C.: The Catholic University of America, 1934), p. 58.

lation. In 1900, with what figures were available, it was estimated that they numbered 30 per cent. These illiterates were, for the most part, persons from the upper age brackets.[22]

Secondary education is provided in the *institutos* and the *colegios*. The *institutos* are the national day schools; the *colegios* are boarding and day schools, supported largely by the local or municipal government. In spite of adverse conditions, the Jesuits, Augustinians, Piarists, Franciscans, Dominicans, and the orders that entered Spain during the second half of the nineteenth century, such as the Christian Brothers, the Brothers of the Sacred Heart, the Marist Fathers, the Marist Brothers, the Marianists, and the Salesians, have maintained secondary schools with buildings and school equipment superior to those of the state schools. These private secondary schools usually had more than two-thirds of the total secondary school enrollment.[23] Although the *institutos* have freely admitted girls, the education of girls has been supplied in large measure by the teaching Sisterhoods because Spanish parents do not favor coeducation. After the establishment of the Republic, April 14, 1931, the expulsion of the Jesuits followed, yet the majority of pupils attending the schools of the Society of Jesus entered the other private schools.

The Franco government, by means of new regulations for education issued from Burgos, September 20, 1938, has declared that the transformation of society in Spain and the intellectual and moral formation of its future leading classes must be achieved through a profound reform of secondary education based on a strong sense of tradition. The elements of Spanish tradition are enumerated: Christianity; Graeco-Roman culture; Spanish

[22] A. J. Shipman, "Spain of Today," *The Catholic World*, 91:809, September, 1910.
[23] Perz, *op. cit.*, p. 97.

humanism as found in its language, literature, and history; and the more recent developments in science and mathematics.[24] The framework of the new system of secondary education is a seven-year course which the student enters about his tenth year. At its completion, a state board administers a comprehensive examination and the successful candidates receive the A.B. degree and university status. The course contains the seven fundamental disciplines: religion, classics, Spanish tradition, world backgrounds, mathematics, science, and modern languages. Physical education, including singing and dancing, training in civics and patriotism, drawing, modeling, and visits to the art treasures of Spain, are also prescribed.[25]

The new law of Franco aims to organize a system of education calculated to achieve a balanced development of the human person. The system encourages private initiative and provides for the general inspection of both public and private schools. A provision of the law empowering the Minister of Education to suppress private institutions for "motives of common or public good" may easily lead to the arbitrary practices of an omnipotent state. Likewise, the emphasis on patriotic and military training, although commendable in itself, may easily conduce to the inculcation of inordinate nationalism.

Spain has been divided into university districts similar to the academic districts of France. There are twelve national universities, some of which like Salamanca, Valencia, and Valladolid date from the Middle Ages. University education is coeducational and it is estimated that in 1943 there was an increase of 12 per cent in the total attendance of men and women. The

---

[24] R. J. Henle, "Spain Remembers Its Origins; Educational Reform Under Franco," *The Catholic World*, 149:55, April, 1939.
[25] *Ibid.*, pp. 56 f.

Jesuits and the Augustinians conduct independent universities at Bilboa and Escorial. Students in the private universities are obliged to take oral and written examinations annually set by the state authorities. Only national universities grant degrees.

The rehabilitation of religious teaching in the Nationalists' schools has resulted in a great deal of unfair criticism from unfriendly contemporary observers who fail to realize how deeply rooted a religious tradition is in Spain and how six or seven years of secularization previous to the Franco administration had subjected many boys and girls now approaching adolescence to influences violently hostile to Catholicism and in fact to all forms of Christianity. If the program of religious training appears exaggerated to the modern educator, because he regards it as excessive insistence on ceremonies and observances, he should remember that to the defender of Spanish culture it is thoroughly Catholic and imperative.[26]

England

Elementary education in England until very recent times came almost entirely under the control of ecclesiastical or local authorities and charitable societies, rather than under the general government. The relation of the national government to the schools in the eighteenth century consisted chiefly in the granting of state funds for their erection and support wherever they were not otherwise provided for. Through the National Society representing the Anglican Church and the British and Foreign Society, also Protestant, grants were made in behalf of elementary education as early as 1832. In 1847 the first grant was made to Catholic elementary schools through the Catholic Poor School Committee;

[26] Edgar E. Peers, *Spain In Eclipse* (1937-1943), (London: Methuen and Co., Ltd., 1943), pp. 116 f.

since then Catholic secondary schools, colleges, and private schools have grown into a well organized system supported by the combined efforts of church and state.[27]

The British and Foreign Society and the National Society are of interest as the two organizations that fostered and perpetuated the monitorial system of Lancaster (1778-1832) and Bell (1753-1832). The former society espoused Lancaster's cause when he was engaged in conducting a school for the poor in London; and, like Lancaster, who was a Quaker, it opposed dogmatic religious instruction. The latter society, whose full title was "The National Society for Promoting the Education of the Poor in the Principles of the Established Church," represented the Anglican Church, and adopted the monitorial method as introduced by Andrew Bell, who as an army chaplain had seen it in use in the schools of India. The system, worked out independently by Lancaster and Bell, consisted in the employment of older pupils as monitors in instructing the younger who were arranged in groups or classes. The method enabled one teacher to supervise the work of a large school.

The basic law for the direction of education in England was that of 1870, the Forster Act, which provided among other things for the legal establishment of local or town boards as the governing bodies of schools, and for compulsory attendance at the option of the local government. It recognized the voluntary or denominational schools and entitled them to share in the state funds, reserving the right of governmental inspection.

Compulsory attendance laws became generally effective in 1876 and 1880; their enforcement, however, depended on the local authorities. Child labor laws did much towards establishing compulsory attendance; the

---

[27] Sister Mary John Broderick, *Catholic Schools in England* (Washington, D. C.: The Catholic University of America, 1936), p. 160.

act of 1893 made eleven years the minimum age for exemption from school attendance and that of 1899 raised the minimum from eleven to twelve years. The Education Act of 1936 provided for the raising of the compulsory school attendance age to fifteen, and empowered local education authorities to grant employment certificates only after the child had reached the age of fourteen.[28] In 1899 the creation of the Central Board of Education in place of the former Council on Education and other bodies then having jurisdiction over certain departments of education, resulted in a more unified system for the administration of state funds.

The Education Act of 1902 abolished local school boards and invested the county or borough council with jurisdiction over the schools. An exception was made in the case of large cities. This Act admitted the voluntary schools to a share in the local rates as well as in the state grants. They were to equip and maintain their own buildings and be subject to inspection by the school managers. In 1937 the enrollment in the voluntary schools was approximately one and two-thirds millions and in the elementary council schools 3,620,000.[29]

The four years of the Junior School complete the primary educational work of a majority of the children of England who attend free public schools. Children enter this school at the age of seven and remain until they are eleven. The brighter pupils then go to the secondary school, the next best to the central school, and the remainder, who are the majority, continue their education in the senior school. During recent years the secondary school movement has spread rapidly in England. Secondary education has been articulated with the elementary so as to meet the needs of the middle or poor classes of children. The several types of English secondary

[28] Smith, *op. cit.*, p. 12.
[29] *Ibid.*, p. 19.

schools are the Public Schools, the Grammar Schools for Boys, the High Schools for Girls, the Municipal or County Secondary Schools, usually coeducational, and private adventure schools conducted by a headmaster for personal profit. The Great Public Schools, Eton, Harrow, Rugby, Winchester, Westminster, Charterhouse, Merchant Taylors, Shrewsbury, and St. Paul's, are boarding schools attended by the wealthy. At the present time great concern is felt for the future of many of the traditional schools of England. Mounting war taxes have left parents unable to pay the fees ranging from $500 to $2,500 annually. Catholics have many famous secondary schools and colleges some of which, like Stonyhurst, can trace their origin back to penal times. A certain standard in secondary education has been effected by university and governmental examining bodies.

The older universities, Oxford and Cambridge, now divide the patronage for advanced studies with younger institutions of university grade which are located in large manufacturing cities, e.g., Birmingham, Bristol, Durham, Leeds, Liverpool, Manchester, London, Reading, and Sheffield.[30] These institutions, however, do their most extensive work in the technical and scientific field. Their development has been furthered by grants from Parliament since 1889.

The Fisher Act passed in 1918 prepared the way for the system of educational control and supervision which England had until 1944. The primary aim of this act was to broaden the educational opportunities for England's children. It provided for the establishment and maintenance of schools above the elementary level for the masses and for closer cooperation between national and local authorities.[31]

---

[30] Kandel, *op. cit.*, p. 104.
[31] Smith, *op. cit.*, p. 11.

The pamphlet of the Board of Education on the *New Prospect in Education,* issued in 1928, recommended some form of secondary education for all children above the age of eleven. Up to the age of fifteen, which was proposed as the upper limit of compulsory attendance, pupils were to attend a variety of schools according to their ability and bent which would prepare them for the life before them. The recommendations of this pamphlet would have been put into effect, had the School Attendance Bill which passed the House of Commons, but was rejected by the House of Lords in 1931, been enacted. As a result the reorganization of elementary and intermediate education was left to the judgment of local authorities.[32]

The characteristics of the English people and their philosophy of life are reflected in the organization and administration of their school system. The English have a conservative respect for tradition and an ingrained fear of bureaucratic control. The national government has undertaken to promote education through the distribution of annual grants for educational purposes and has determined certain minimum requirements for the receiving of such grants. Such control as has been provided has dealt with the larger aspects of educational organization and administration; has been characterized by stimulus and consultation; and has encouraged variety, flexibility, individual and local initiative.

---

[32] Kandel, *op. cit.,* pp. 385 f. On April 1, 1945, in accordance with the Education Act (1944), the old division of education is replaced by a system of public education in three progressive stages: primary, secondary, and further education. The educational process is regarded as a continuous one and all children will be offered a full-time secondary education. The compulsory school age will be raised ultimately to 16. *Cf. Education In Britain* (British Information Services, Washington, D. C., 1945), p. 9.

FOR FURTHER STUDY

General

Abel, James F., *Bulletins and Pamphlets on Foreign School Systems*. United States Office of Education, Washington, D. C.

Annual Reports of the United States Commissioner of Education.

Kandel, I. L., *Comparative Education*. Boston: Houghton Mifflin Co., 1933.

Meyer, A. E., *The Development of Education in the Twentieth Century*. New York: Prentice-Hall, Inc., 1939.

Monroe, Paul, *Essays in Comparative Education*. New York: Columbia University, 1927.

Roman, F. W., *The New Education in Europe*. New York: E. P. Dutton Co., 1930.

Smith, H. L., *Comparative Education*. Bloomington, Indiana: Educational Publications, 1941.

Germany

Alexander, T. and B. Parker, *The New Education in the German Republic*. New York: John Day and Company, Inc., 1929.

Hartshorne, Edward Y., *The German Universities and National Socialism*. Cambridge: Harvard University Press, 1937.

Hoover, Calvin B., *Germany Enters the Third Reich*. New York: The Macmillan Co., 1934.

Kandel, I. and L. Alexander, *Reorganization of Education in Prussia*. New York: Teachers' College, Columbia University, 1927.

Kerschensteiner, George, *Begriff der Arbeitsschule*. Leipzig: B. G. Teubner, 1925.

Lexis, Wilhelm, *Das Unterrichtswesen im Deutschen Reich*. Berlin: G. Fisher, 1904. 4 vols. Translated in part by G. J. Tamson, as *A General View of the History and Organization of Public Education in the German Empire*. Berlin: A. Ascher and Company, 1904.

Paulsen, F., *German Education, Past and Present*. Translated by T. Lorenz. New York: Charles Scribner's Sons, 1908.

Lindegren, A. M., *Education in Germany. U. S. Office of Education, Bulletin 1938, No. 15*.

France

Abel, James F., *A Study of the Requirements for the Degrees of Bachelier, License-dès-Lettres, and Agrégation Granted by Secondary Schools and Universities in France.* United States Office of Education, Foreign Education Circular No. 11, Washington, D. C.: July, 1928.

Autin, Albert, *L'École unique.* Paris: Felix Alcan, 1933.

Buisson, F. and F. E. Farrington, *French Educational Ideals.* New York: World Book Co. 1919.

Farrington, F. E., *French Secondary Schools.* New York: Longmans, Green, and Co., 1910.

————, *The Public Primary School System of France.* New York: Teachers' College, Columbia University, 1906.

Hayes, Carlton J., *France, A Nation of Patriots.* New York: Columbia University Press, 1930.

Kandel, I., *The Reform of Secondary Education in France.* New York: Teachers College, 1924.

Richard, C., *L'Enseignement en France.* Paris: Librairie Armand Colin, 1925.

Spain

Altamira y Creven, Rafael, *Historia de España y de la civilizacion Española.* 4 vols. 3rd ed. Barcelona: Gili, 1913-14.

Fuente, Vicente de la, *Historia de las universidades, colegios y demas establecimientos de ensenanza en Espana.* 4 vols. Madrid: Impr. de Gomez Fuentenebro, 1884-89.

Gil y Zarate, Antonio, *De la instruccion publica en España.* 3 vols. Madrid: Imprenta del Colegio de Surdo-Mudos, 1855.

Peers, E. Allison, *Spain in Eclipse.* London: Methuen and Company, 1943.

Perz, John R., *Secondary Education in Spain.* Washington, D. C.: The Catholic University of America, 1934.

Problemas de la nueva organizacion de España. Barcelona: Universidad de Barcelona, 1939.

Sanchez, Evergisto B., "The Schools in Spain." Unpublished Master's dissertation, The Catholic University of America, Washington, D. C.: 1926.

Tarre, Manuel, *La Reforma de la segunda ensenanza.* Barcelona: Miguel Casals, 1930.

————, *Los colegios de la Compania de Jesus.* Valencia: Renovacion Tipografica, 1927.

Turgnets, Juan, *Origines de la Revolucion Española.* 2nd ed. Barcelona: Editorial Vilamela. 1932.

Ward, G. H. B., *The Truth about Spain.* London: Cassell Company, 1911.

Zabala, y Lera, Pio, *Historia de España y de la civilizacion Española.* 2 vols. Barcelona: Editorial Liturgica Española sucesor de Juan Gili, 1930.

England

Adamson, John W., *Outline of English Education.* Cambridge: University Press, 1925.

Balfour, Graham, *The Educational Systems of Great Britain and Ireland.* Oxford: Clarendon Press, 1903.

Barnes, Arthur, *The Catholic Schools of England.* London: William and Nogate, 1929.

Barker, Ernest, *Universities in Great Britain.* London: Student Christian Movement Press, 1931.

Birchenenough, Charles, *History of Elementary Education in England and Wales.* London: W. C. Cline, 1925.

Broderick, Sister Mary John, *Catholic Schools in England.* Washington, D. C.: The Catholic University of America, 1936.

Darwin, Bernard, *The English Public School.* London: Longmans, Green, and Company, 1929.

Holman, Henry, *English National Education.* London: Blackie and Son, 1898.

Matthews, Roderic, *Post-Primary Education in England.* Philadelphia: University of Pennsylvania, 1932.

Norwood, Cyril, *The English Traditions of Education.* London: John Murray, 1929.

Smith, F., *History of English Elementary Education.* London: University of London Press, Hodder, 1931.

Wilson, J. Dover, *The Schools of England.* London: Sidgwick and Jackson, Ltd., 1928.

CHAPTER XXXIII

DEVELOPMENT OF MODERN SCHOOL SYSTEMS
(Continued)

The United States

With the exception of the mission schools for Indians, the early schools of the New World were modeled after those of the European countries from which the first settlers came. The mission schools as established by the Spanish Franciscans in Florida and New Mexico were in existence in 1629, "four years before the establishment of the oldest school in the thirteen eastern colonies."[1] They were, consequently, in the order of their foundation, the first elementary schools in the present territory of the United States. The most common characteristic of the schools in the different colonies was their relation to the church of the colony. In Protestant settlements, like New Netherlands, Massachusetts, and Pennsylvania, the teacher was connected by custom or agreement with the church, and in the Catholic settlements of the Spaniards and French, priests were teachers.

In the colonial period may be distinguished certain general types to which the schools of all the colonies as a rule conformed. The oldest of the colonies, Virginia, for example, resembled the mother country in her indifference to elementary education. The planters could employ private teachers or send their children abroad, and the poor in consequence suffered. The government's first concern there was in behalf of Latin or secondary schools. The College of William and Mary, founded in 1693, was well endowed before any systematic education

---

[1] J. A. Burns. *The Catholic School System in the United States* (New York: Benziger Bros., 1908), p. 39. *Cf.* Report of United States Commissioner of Education, 1903, I, 555.

of the poor outside of trades was provided. When schools were subsidized or permitted by the state, they were characterized as "poor" and were not well attended even by the poor. Maryland reproduced in like manner many of the customs of England. It is important to note in this connection that the Jesuits who accompanied the early settlers established the first Catholic school in the English-speaking colonies in 1640, at Newtown, with Ralph Crouch, a former novice, as schoolmaster.

Church schools represented the first educational endeavors of the Dutch colony in New York and the Quakers in Pennsylvania. The schoolmaster in New York resembled the parish clerk of the Old World, having duties to perform in the church as well as in the school. The various Protestant sects and the Catholics in Pennsylvania followed the plan of erecting parish schools. The Quakers opened a secondary school in Philadelphia in 1711.

The type represented by Massachusetts is that from which it is believed the modern common school takes its origin. It, too, in the beginning was a church or denominational school, for church and state were then united in a common purpose. The distinguishing and important feature of this type is that in 1642 and 1647 its establishment and support became a matter of law. In the latter year, every township of fifty householders was required to "appoint one within their town to teach all such children as shall resort to him to read and write," and where any town should increase the number of householders or families to one hundred, "they shall set up a grammar school, the master thereof being able to instruct youth . . . for the university." While in the beginning, just as in England, the school was supported by voluntary contributions, there gradually developed a system of assessment and in the first quarter of the eighteenth century the school was or could be supported by public funds. In the early years of statehood, divisions of each town were permitted to have their own school, district school, and a system began which, allowing great autonomy to the district, brought with it serious drawbacks to the development of efficient schools. New Hampshire, Maine and Connecticut followed generally the same lines of development.

In New York, after the English occupation, little was done for the organization of elementary education. In 1787, the University of the State of New York or Board of Regents was legally set up; but it was not until the early part of the nineteenth century that the basis of a state system was laid with the appointment (1812) of a state superintendent and the distribution of funds for partial support of elementary schools. School societies and the churches were then maintaining schools with the aid of occasional grants from the state.

In all the states established after the adoption of the constitution, the Federal government by a wise provision reserved the equivalent of two townships and one section in every township to be used as an educational endowment.

The period of the most rapid and extensive development of state systems is marked by the activities of *Horace Mann* (1796-1859), who as Secretary of the Massachusetts State Board of Education brought the more or less scattered educational forces of the state into a system. Mann held the office for twelve years. Through his trips of inspection, counsel to town committees, organization of teachers' institutes, lectures, annual reports, and especially the organization of state normal schools, he improved educational conditions and raised the standard of instruction, not, however, without encountering opposition from many quarters. He antagonized the religious bodies by eliminating religious instruction. By his writings he acquainted Massachusetts and, of course, a wider field, with European systems and methods, particularly the Pestalozzian, which he had personally investigated.[2]

From the literary viewpoint, *Henry Barnard* (1811-1900), Secretary of the Connecticut Board of Education and afterward the first United States Commissioner of Education, wielded a still wider influence. Besides notable reports as Secretary in Connecticut and later in Rhode Island, he published the *Connecticut Common School Journal* and the *Rhode Island School Journal,* and as Superintendent in Connecticut (1855) that great collection of historical and biographical material, Barnard's *American Journal of Education,* one of the most valuable educational works in the English language. He became United States Commissioner of Education in 1867, and organized the Bureau of Education to serve as an office of information and advice to the schools of the country.

The influence of Mann and Barnard was especially seen in the appointment of superintendents by various states, greater centralization of school administration, the further establishment of normal schools, and the rise of an educational literature. Perhaps, too, the substitution of town high schools for the private academies or grammar schools may be attributed as much to Mann's influence as to any other cause.

Until the middle of the nineteenth century secondary schools, or academies, as they were called, were founded by the churches and by individuals. They usually offered the classical course of the Latin grammar school. When these schools were taken over by the towns, or founded by them, and known as high schools, the modern subjects, especially science, received more attention.

---

[2] *Cf.* Thomas Moran, "The Influence of Horace Mann on American Education" (unpublished Master's dissertation, The Catholic University of America, 1926).

During the second half of the nineteenth century they developed rapidly and now form an integral part of public school systems.[3]

Higher education was first provided by the colleges, and these, like Harvard (1636) and Yale (1701), were the foundations of religious bodies. Although often maintained through the united action of church and state, they were not state institutions. Before the Revolution, all were conducted for religious purposes. Their organization and curriculum were chiefly determined by the standards of the English colleges. Many were engaged in graduate and professional work before assuming the title of universities. State universities have had their greatest expansion since the middle of the nineteenth century. They are now to be found in all except five states. Denominational colleges and universities have also continued to flourish; many, however, of the so-called universities, owing to the confused notion of the scope of a college or university, do little advanced or graduate work; their courses should be more strictly classified as collegiate. Because there is no generally accepted line of demarcation between university and college, it is impossible to designate the number of American universities. The Association of American Universities "composed of institutions on the North American continent engaged in giving advanced or graduate instruction" included thirty-four institutions in 1941, of which fifteen were state universities.

Education is administered in the United States by the individual states and not by the Federal government. In this it resembles the German system. The free

---

[3] In 1874, the decision in the Kalamazoo Case established the principle that the high school is an essential part of the common school system. Equality of educational opportunity was guaranteed to every boy and girl irrespective of creed or social status. *Cf.* Kandel, *Comparative Education,* p. 79.

elementary schools, with courses of eight years, care for the period during which attendance is compulsory;[4] the high school course of four years supplements the elementary and prepares for college entrance.[5] Higher instruction may then be obtained in many of the states in universities which are owned and controlled by the commonwealth.

The failure of the state to provide religious instruction and training in the elementary and secondary schools explains the establishment of independent systems and private institutions, which are supported by religious bodies or by endowments. The Catholic school system, the largest and most extensive of all, had its origin in colonial times. The growth of its elementary schools has been commensurate with that of the Church itself. Dr. Burns, the historian of the Catholic school system, says of this period:

As a matter of fact, the foundation of the Catholic parish-school system in the United States dates from the early years of the Maryland colony. It represents, therefore, a development covering a period of over 250 years. Broadly speaking, we can distinguish two great periods in its development—the first, extending down to the Revolution, and the second, from that epoch-making event to our own day. The salient feature of its growth throughout the whole time is its dependence upon the growth of the Church in general. A direct relation existed

---

[4] Compulsory attendance ages vary in the different states, but the attendance is generally compulsory between the ages of seven and sixteen. *Cf.* Smith, *Comparative Education,* p. 476.

[5] During the past two decades there has been a remarkable growth of the Junior College. This growth has been largely in the South and West. It has not yet been satisfactorily determined whether the Junior College is to be classified as an added two years to the high school or as the first and second years of the college level. The latter classification is favored by most educators. The ever-increasing demands made upon the four-year colleges to meet higher standards have forced many such schools to reduce their course to two years. *Cf.* W. C. Eells, *The Junior College* (Boston: Houghton Mifflin Company, 1931).

between the development of the Church and the development of Catholic schools. We can see the proof of the existence of this relation during the first period in the fact that wherever Catholic settlements were formed and Catholic life reached any degree of maturity Catholic schools were set up and a corresponding educational development took place. In settlements where Catholic life was weak or short-lived, either no schools were established, or those that were had only a short or desultory existence. In the post-Revolutionary period the relation is even more clearly illustrated.[6]

In the early days of the Republic they were opened as free schools in large cities like Baltimore and New York wherever the parish funds allowed.

The bishops discussed the parish school in the First Synod of Baltimore, in 1791; and in the First Provincial Council of Baltimore, in 1829, they decreed as follows:

Since it is evident that very many of the young, the children of Catholic parents, especially the poor, have been exposed and are still exposed, in many places of this province, to great danger of the loss of faith or the corruption of morals, on account of the lack of such teachers as could safely be intrusted with so great an office, we judge it absolutely necessary that schools should be established in which the young may be taught the principles of faith and morality while being instructed in letters.[7]

For a struggling Catholic population it was a tremendous problem to provide schools as well as churches, and one of the chief difficulties was to obtain Catholic teachers. The introduction of the teaching orders met this demand; and during the immigration period, when thousands of Catholics came to America from Europe, Ireland, and Germany especially, the Sisters and Brothers were engaged for the work of the elementary schools. At the time of the Second Plenary Council of

---

[6] Burns, *op. cit.*, p. 14.
[7] *Cf. Conciliorum provincialium et plenarii Baltimorensium decreta* (Baltimore: John Murphy, 1853), Decretum 33.

Baltimore, in 1866, despite the difficulty of obtaining all the teachers necessary, the bishops were exhorted by the council as follows:

We exhort the bishops, and in view of the great evils which usually result from the defective education of youth, we beseech them through the bowels of the mercy of God to see that schools be established in connection with all of the churches of the dioceses; and, if it be necessary and circumstances permit, to provide from the revenues of the Church to which the school is attached, for the support of competent teachers.[8]

In the Second Provincial Council of Cincinnati, held in 1858 (the province of Cincinnati extended at that time from the Alleghanies to the Mississippi), it was decreed:

It is the judgment of the Fathers that all pastors are bound, under pain of mortal sin, to provide a Catholic school in every parish or congregation subject to them, where this can be done; and in order that each Ordinary may know what are the parishes in which the obligation exists, they decree that the Tridentine Law, s. xxii, c. ix, is to be practically enforced, by which the rectors of churches are required each year to render an exact account to their Ordinaries of all the revenues accruing to their churches in any way, which they therefore strictly enjoin as to be observed by the aforesaid rectors.[9]

In 1875 the Congregation of the Propaganda, then in charge of American affairs, issued an "Instruction to the Bishops of the United States concerning the Public Schools," in which the Catholics, both for their own sake and the vital interests of the American Republic, were directed to establish their own schools. The Instruction read:

All are agreed that there is nothing so needed to this end as the establishment of Catholic schools in every place—and

---

[8] *Ibid.,* Decretum 13.
[9] *Cf. Acta et decreta Sacrorum Conciliorum recentiorum collectio Lacensis* (Friburgi Brisgoviae: Herder and Company, 1875), iii, col. 209.

schools in no way inferior to the public ones. Every effort, then, must be directed toward starting Catholic schools where they are not, and, where they are, toward enlarging them and providing them with better accommodations and equipment until they have nothing to suffer, as regards teachers or equipment, by comparison with the public schools.[10]

The next important ecclesiastical law for this country was promulgated by the Third Plenary Council of Baltimore, 1884, which has been the directing force during the period of the greatest development of the parish schools. Therein Catholic parents were not only exhorted to send their children to Catholic schools, but commanded to do so.

Therefore we not only exhort Catholic parents with paternal love, but we also command them with all of the authority in our power, to procure for their beloved offspring, given to them by God, reborn in Christ in baptism, and destined for heaven, a truly Christian and Catholic education, and to defend and safeguard them from the dangers of an education merely secular during the entire period of childhood and youth; and therefore to send them to parish schools or others truly Catholic, unless perchance the Ordinary, in a particular case, should judge that it might be permitted otherwise.[11]

Due allowance was made for those parents who for a sufficient cause did not send their children to the parish schools. A decree of far-reaching importance was the following:

Near each church, where it does not yet exist, a parish school is to be erected within two years from the promulgation of this council, and is to be maintained "in perpetuum," unless the bishop, on account of grave difficulties, judge that a postponement be allowed. . . . All Catholic parents are bound to send their children to the parish schools, unless either at

---

[10] *Cf. Concilii plenarii Baltimorensis tertii, acta et decreta* (Baltimore: John Murphy, 1886), p. 280.
[11] *Ibid.,* Decretum 196.

home or in other Catholic schools they may sufficiently provide for the Christian education of their children, or unless it be lawful to send them to other schools on account of a sufficient cause, approved by the bishop, and with opportune cautions and remedies. As to what is a Catholic school, it is left to the judgment of the Ordinary to define.[12]

This council, furthermore, by its decrees touching upon the supervision of the schools by the pastor, the training of teachers in the normal schools of their novitiates, the certification of teachers, both religious and secular, laid the foundation for that development in organization and administration which in the past half century has been remarkable.

The parish or elementary schools are organized in diocesan systems. Their administration in some dioceses is confided to a school board consisting of priests of the diocese appointed by the bishop, and of which the bishop is chairman.[13] In many dioceses the chief officer of administration is the diocesan superintendent. Of the 118 dioceses of the United States, 107 have school superintendents. The supervision of schools is under the direction of the school superintendent assisted by community supervisors. In 1945 the parochial elementary schools numbered 7,493 with their pupils 2,029,012.

Secondary schools, embracing parish high schools, academies, and preparatory schools, conducted usually by members of the teaching orders, have reached the number of 2,361; and colleges and universities, 210. A significant advance in higher education began with the establishment in 1889 of the Catholic University of America at Washington. Inaugurated as a graduate

---

[12] *Ibid.*, Decreta 196, 199.
[13] *Cf.* Arthur M. Leary, "The Place, Function, and Present Status of Diocesan School Boards" (unpublished Master's dissertation, The Catholic University of America, Washington, D. C., 1944).

school in theology, it now includes Schools of Philosophy, Civil Law, Canon Law, Architecture and Engineering, Social Sciences, Arts and Sciences, Nursing Education, and Social Work; and also a College of Arts and Sciences. Through its affiliated institutions it extends its influence throughout the country.

FOR FURTHER STUDY

Annual Reports of the United States Commissioner of Education.

Bowler, Sr. M. Mariella, *A History of Catholic Colleges for Women in the United States of America.* Washington, D. C.: The Catholic University of America, 1933.

Brown, Elmer E., *The Making of Our Middle Schools.* New York: Longmans, Green, and Company, 1902.

Burns, J. A., *The Catholic School System in the United States: Its Principles, Origin and Development.* New York: Benziger Bros., 1908.

————, *The Growth and Development of the Catholic School System in the United States.* New York: Benziger Bros., 1912.

Burns, J. A., and B. J. Kohlbrenner, *A History of Catholic Education in the United States.* New York: Benziger Bros., 1937.

Cassidy, Frank P., *Catholic College Foundations and Development in the United States (1677-1850).* Washington, D. C.: The Catholic University of America, 1924.

Confrey, Burton, *Secularism in American Education.* Washington, D. C.: The Catholic University of America, 1931.

Cubberly, E. P., *Public Education in the United States.* Boston: Houghton Mifflin Co., 1934.

Dexter, E. G., *History of Education in the United States.* New York: The Macmillan Co., 1904.

Erbacher, Sebastian A., *Catholic Higher Education for Men in the United States, 1850-1866.* Washington, D. C.: The Catholic University of America, 1931.

Goebel, Edmund J., *A Study of Secondary Education During the Colonial Period Up to the First Plenary Council of Baltimore, 1852.* New York: Benziger Bros., 1937.

Hinsdale, B. A., *Horace Mann and the Common School Revival.* New York: Charles Scribner's Sons, 1898.

Kandel, I. L., *Comparative Education.* Boston: Houghton Mifflin Co., 1933.

Meyer, A. E., *The Development of Education in the Twentieth Century.* New York: Prentice-Hall, Inc., 1939.

Prose, Sr. M. Redempta, *The Liberal Arts Ideal in Catholic Colleges for Women in the United States.* Washington, D. C.: The Catholic University of America, 1943.

Smith, H. L., *Comparative Education.* Bloomington, Indiana: Educational Publications, 1941.

Thwing, Charles F., *A History of Higher Education in America.* New York: D. Appleton and Company, 1906.

Wilson, L. M., and I. L. Kandel, *Introduction to the Study of American Education.* New York: Thomas Nelson and Sons, 1934.

Woody, Thomas, *A History of Women's Education in the United States.* Lancaster, Pennsylvania: Science Press, 1929.

SUMMARY OF MODERN EDUCATION

The first reaction from humanism retained the humanistic content of instruction, and its representatives, Rabelais, Montaigne, and Mulcaster, were known as Humanistic Realists. They sought to counteract the extreme tendencies of the Renaissance and in education aimed at a practical preparation for public life. They were followed by the Sense Realists who found in nature and the objective order both the content and method of instruction. The inductive method of Bacon was to become with Ratke and Comenius the method of teaching. More practical results were derived from the theories of later innovators, Locke in England and Fénelon in France.

In the seventeenth century the religious organizations, Oratorians, Port-Royalists, Brothers of Christian Schools, and the Pietists, were especially active. The work of the Brothers in France and the Pietists in Germany, particularly in regard to elementary schools and the training of teachers, deserves special attention. There were also many religious communities engaged in the education of women.

The eighteenth century saw the rise of naturalism owing to the spread of Rousseau's theories in France and those of the Philanthropinists in Germany. Catholics presented a strong counteracting influence. A notable ecclesiastic of the century was Felbiger. That the psychological movement of the nineteenth century owed something to the naturalistic movement which preceded it was seen in Pestalozzi, its first exponent. Herbart defined the principles of modern educational psychology and gave the world the doctrine of interest and apperception. Froebel organized the kindergarten as the embodiment of his psychological theories and as the special means of developing spontaneous activity. Father Rosmini contributed noteworthy views on method, and Jacotot labored conspicuously in the same field. Herbert Spencer presented an important plea in behalf of scientific studies.

In the latter part of the nineteenth century influential educators in the United States were Harris, Parker, James, and G. Stanley Hall. In recent times John Dewey has been the central figure in American education and the chief advocate of the activity school. Edward L. Thorndike has been prominent in the application of the scientific principles of statistics to education and has stimulated a movement for measuring educational achievement and intelligence itself through scales and tests. A deplorable fact in present-day European and American education is the almost exclusive emphasis on the training and equipment of the mind. The Catholic educator in this country who has labored more than any other in the defense of spiritual values in a sound Christian education is Reverend Thomas E. Shields.

The nineteenth century witnessed the greatest development of modern systems of education, especially in Germany, France, England, Spain, and the United States.

INDEX

Aachen, Council of, 223, 287

ABC shooters, 304

Abelard, Peter, 255f.

Abraham, 62

Academies, 619

Academy (Athens), 101, 124

Accusations Against Julian, St. Gregory of Nazianzus, 180

Adam of St. Victor, 287

Adler, Mortimer, 578

Adrian VI, Pope, 349, 361

Aemilian, Jerome, St., 411

Aeschines, 109, 110

Aeschylus, 105f.

Aesop, 101, 227, 373, 388

Agricola, Rudolf, 350, 351

Ahriman, 52

Ahura Mazda, 52

Alberti, Leon Battista, 325, 331

Albertus Magnus, St., 193, 260, 261, 263, 266, 291

Alcalá, University of, 348, 403

Alcuin, 220, 229, 230 sqq.; his writings, 240; educational influence, 241

Aldhelm, 239

Aleander, 346

Alexander of Hales, 256, 289

Alexander of Macedon, 124

Alexander of Villedieu, 229, 281

Alexander the Great, 24, 37f., 47, 49, 59, 76, 108, 129

Alexandria. University of, 130, 131, 145, 146

Alfarabi, 249

Alfred the Great, King, 194; educational revival in England, 225ff.; educational achievements, 227

Alkendi, 249

Allain, Abbé, 301, 600

Alvarez, Manoel, 349

Ambrose, St., 184f.; writings, 185; influence of orations and sermons, 185, 188, 189, 209, 210, 239, 328

Amiguet, Jerome, 348, 360

Ancient education, summary of, 156ff.

Andronicus, Livius, 140

Anselm of Canterbury, 255

Anthony, St., 210

Anthusa, St., 216

Antoniano, Cardinal Silvio, 410

Antonio of Lebrija, 348f., 360

Apollodorus, 105

Apologeticum, Tertillian's, 183

Apologies, St. Justin Martyr, 174

Appolonia, University of, 146

Aquila, 176

Arabs, 5, 248ff.

Arezzo, University of, 277

Aristophanes, 106f.

Aristotle, 88, 113, 124ff., 131; pupil of Plato, 124; school of Peripatetics, 124f.; his works, 125; his educational scheme, 125; theory of the state, 125f.;

views on virtue, 126; educational theories, 126ff.; compared with Socrates and Plato, 128; influence on Scholastics, 129; 194

Artaxerxes, 49

Artaxerxes III, 49

Aryans, 35f., 46, 83

Ascham, Roger, 374ff.; method of double translation, 375; 394

Ashurbanipal, 64

Association of American Universities, 621

Assyrians, 64ff.; secret of their supremacy, 64f.; development of roads, 65; achievements in architecture, painting and sculpture, 65ff.; libraries, 67; educational training, 68

Athanasius, St., 210, 239

Athenaeum, 146

Athenian education, ideal of, 99; support of teachers, 100; the pedagogue, 100; schoolrooms, 100; methods of teaching the three R's, 100f.; higher schools, 102; moral training, 102f.; criticism of, 110f.; period of transition, 111

Athens, 94-131; limited nature of its democracy, 95f.; position of women, 96f.; fashion in clothes, 97f.; the Athenian house, 98f.; art of, 103ff.; famous painters, 105; dramatists, 105f.; development of comedy, 106f.; poetry and prose literature, 107; orators, 108ff.

Athens, University of, 130, 131, 145

Augustine, St., 188ff.; works of educational value, 189f.; opinions on use of secular learning, 191f.; 209, 210, 229, 255, 286, 292, 328

Augustine, St. (England), 210

Augustinians, 607

Aurispa, 336

Averroës, 249

Avesta, 46, 52, 53

Avicenna, 249, 282

Baal (Moloch), 72

Babylonians, 46, 58-64; sources of history, 59; education of the priestly class and higher laity, 63; education of the scribe, 63; writing materials, 63; information concerning schools, 63f.

Bacon, Francis, 434, 449 sqq.; his educational theories and influence, 453f.

Bacon, Roger, 260, 289f.; important educational works, 290

Bagley, William C., 572

Baliol College, 284

Baltasar, 62

Barbaro, Francesco, 325, 332

Barnard, Henry, 620

Bartholomew of Braga, 409

Barzizza, Gasparino, 323, 336, 346

Basedow, Johann Bernard, 508ff.; his *Elementary Book,* 509; 511

Basil the Great, St., 177ff.; Rule for Monks, 177; treatise on study of pagan literature, 178f.; 209, 216, 239

Bathe, William, 464ff.

Beccario, Antonio, 370

Bede, Venerable, 212, 215, 227, 230, 239

Behistan Mountain, 54

Bel, chief Babylonian god, 59

Bell, Andrew, 43

Bellerophon, 85

Bembo, Cardinal Pietro, 367

Benedict of Aniane, St., 223

Berle, Adolf A., 579

Bernard, St., 254, 256

Benedict, St., Rule of, 197, 210f., 213

Benedictines, 210 sqq.

Berosus, 58, 59

Bersuire, Pierre, 345

Berthold of Ratisbon, 289

Biel, Gabriel, 349

Binet, Alfred, 574

Blochmann, Karl, 522

Blow, Susan E., 549

Board of Regents, 619

Bobbitt, Franklin, 572

Boccaccio, 322f., 367, 370

Bode, Boyd H., 572

Bodin, 464

Boethius, St., 192ff.; first of the Scholastics, 192f.; treatises on Quadrivium, 193; influence of his *Consolation of Philoso-phy,* 193ff.; 227, 229, 230, 231, 239, 246, 253, 281, 295, 320

Bologna, University of, 231, 274, 275, 276, 277, 278, 279, 282, 289, 306, 371

Bölte, Maria, 549

Bonaventure, St., 263, 266, 289

Boniface, St., 212

Borromeo, Charles, St., 408, 410, 422

Bosco Don, St., 554

Boxer Uprising, 15

Brenz, Johann, 391

Brethren of the Common Life, 349ff., 393, 424

Brahma, 37, 40

Brahmanism, 40, 44

Brahmans, 36, 41, 43, 44

Bridget, St., 287

Briggs, Thomas H., 572

Brothers of the Sacred Heart, 607

Buddha, his teachings, 41f.

Buddhism, 19, 20, 38, 41

Buddhists, 7

Budé, Guillaume, 346; most distinguished French humanist, 346f.; chief educational treatise *On the Education of a Prince,* 347; 362

Bugenhagen, Johann, 391

Burns, James A., 622

Cadmus, 85

Caesar, 146, 321

Cambyses, 47

Caesarius of Arles, St., 209

Cajetan, St., 411

Calasanctius, Joseph, St., 422

Calvin, John, 348, 396f.

Cambridge, University of, 277, 284, 289, 371

Campe, Joachim Heinrich, 510

Canonesses Regular, 287f.

Canons of St. Victor (Victorines), 287

Canons Regular, 286f.

Capella, Martianus, 229

Cassian, John, St., 197, 210

Cassiodorus, 195ff.; monastic writings, 195f.; "the father of literary monasticism," 196f.; influence on early Benedictine schools, 197; his program of studies for monks, 198; 229, 239

Catacheses, St. Cyril of Jerusalem, 176f.

Catechetical schools, 169ff.

Catechumenal schools, 169

Catechumenate, 171

Catherine of Aragon, Queen, 368, 373, 374

Catholic secondary schools in U. S. (1945), 626

Catholic University of America, 626f.

Cato, Marcus, 151

Cattell, James, 574

Catullus, 146, 194

Chaldea, 59; observations of Chaldeans in astronomy, 62f.

Champollion, Jean Français, 31

Chandragupta, 38

Charlemagne, 205, 218-24; coronation as Emperor of the West, 219; capitularies on education, 220ff.; influence on reorganization of monastic and cathedral schools, 222ff.; 234, 239

Charles V, King of France, 345

Charles V, Roman Emperor, 355, 373

Charles VI, King, 345

Charters, Werrett W., 572

Chaucer, 194, 370

Cheops, 28

Chesterton, Gilbert, 261

Chicheley, Reynold, 370

Childs, John L., 572

China, Great Wall, 5f.; most common religion, 7; Catholics, 7; Protestant communicants, 7; language, 8f.; printing, 9f.; oldest educational system, 12; origin of competitive examinations, 12; elementary schools, 13f.; secondary and higher schools, 14; educational degrees, 13f.; education on Western lines, 14f.; latest school organization and curriculum, 15f.; curriculum of modern educational system, 15f.; estimate of ancient education, 16

Chinese classics and commentaries, 8

Chivalry, 234 sqq.; educational training of knight, 235f.; ceremony of knighting and vow of candidate, 236; influence on European civilization and culture, 236

Christian Brothers, 489f., 607

Christian Doctrine, The Fathers of, 422

Christian Doctrine, St. Augustine's, 190ff.

Christian education, early, 164-71

Christian education, summary of, 308

Chrodogang, Bishop of Metz, 207, 286

Chrysostom, John, St., 180ff.; writings, 180f.; opinion of public schools, 181; educational theories and principles, 182; views on study of pagan literature, 183; 216, 239

Chrysoloras, Emmanuel, 323f., 336, 370

Church, Fathers of, 173-92; interest in education, 173; 328, 339, 368

Cicero, 146, 147, 149, 185 192, 194, 230, 239, 246, 321, 323, 334, 345, 346, 349, 370, 424

City of God, St. Augustine's, 189

Cleisthenes I, 88, 95

Clement IV, Pope, 289, 290

Clement VIII, Pope, 422

Clement of Alexandria, 170, 174f.

Cleopatra, 24

Cluny, Monastery of, its educational influence, 254

Colet, John, 371f.

Collège de France, 347

Collège des Dix-Huit, 283

College of William and Mary, 617

Colonna, Aegidius, 263, 292

Columbanus, St., 212

Comenius, John Amos, 456 sqq.; the *Great Didactic*, 459-62; views on the study of languages, 462; the *Janua linguarum reserata*, 463f.; influence on contemporary education, 466f.; 493, 508

Commission of Reform (1537), 407

Community supervisors, 626

Confessions, St. Augustine's, 189

Confucius, 7, 8, 10, 35

Congregation of the Propaganda, instruction of, to the American Bishops (1875), 625

Consolation of Philosophy, Boethius', 193ff.

Constantine, Emperor, 184, 205

Constantine the African, 274

Constantinople, University of, 146

Copernicus, 395

Cordier, Mathurin, 348, 397

Counts, George S., 572

Ctesiphon, 110

Cubberley, Ellwood P., 572

Cyaxeres, 46

Cyprian, St., 428

Cyril of Jerusalem, St., 176f.

Cyropaedia, Xenophon's, 55

Cyrus the Great, 46, 50

DaFeltre, Vittorino, 323, 328, 332; 335 sqq.; school at Mantua, 337; basis of his system of education, 337f; curriculum of his school, 338f.; methods of teaching, 339f.; aim of studies, 340; views on physical training, 340f.; views on moral training, 341; estimate of educational service, 341f.; 370

Da Gama, Vasco, 38

D'Alembert, Jean, 503

Damasus, Pope, 186

Daniel the Prophet, 62

Dante, 129, 289, 320f., 322

Da Parma, Pelacani, 336

D'Arezzo, Leonardo Bruni, 325, 328f., 345, 347, 370

Darius III, 49

Darius Hystaspes, 47

Da Ravenna, Giovanni Conversino, 323, 336

"Dark Ages," 205

Da Verona, Guarino, 323, 325, 334, 335, 336, 337, 370

De Bérulle, Cardinal, 485

De Bus, César, 422

De catechizandis rudibus, St. Augustine's, 190

Decembrio, 370

De Clemanges, Nicholas, 345

De disciplinis, Vives', 366ff.

De la Ramée, 270

De la Salle, John Baptist, St., 489 sqq.; claims as an educator, 491f.; application of the simultaneous method to teaching, 493; first normal school for lay teachers, 494

De liberis, Sadoleto's, 407

De liberis educandis, Cato's, 141

De liberis educandis, St. John Chrysostom's, 182

Delisle, Leopold-Victor, 300

De magistro, St. Augustine's, 190

De magistro, St. Thomas', 264f.

De Merton, Walter, 284

Demia, Charles, 493

De Montreuil, Jean, 345

De Morgan, Persian excavations of, 60

Demosthenes, 109, 110, 131, 149

De Nesmond, Bishop, 493

Denis the Carthusian, 263, 297

De officiis ministrorum, St. Ambrose's, 185

De Premierfait, Laurent, 345

De principiis, Origen's, 176

De pueris, Erasmus', 358f.

Dewey, John, 568ff.; his views on the self-activity program, 569f.; his world-wide influence on education, 570; the shortcomings of his philosophical principles, 571

Diderot, Denis, 503

Dialogue, St. Justin Martyr, 174

Didaskaleion, 99, 102, 116

Diocesan school board, 626

Diocesan superintendent, 626

Diodorus of Sicily, 108

Dionysius of Halicarnasus, 108

Divinae institutiones, Lactantius', 184

Dominic, St., 290

Dominicans, 290ff., 402, 607

Dominici, Cardinal John, 291, 325, 329

Donatus, 185, 229, 239, 281
Dörpfeld, Wilhelm, 86
Douai, English college at, 402; Irish college at, 403
Dravidians, 36
Dringenberg, Ludwig, 351
Du Bellay, Cardinal, 435
De Perron, Anquetil, 53f.
Duns Scotus, 263, 266, 289
Dunstan, St., 228

Edgar, King, 227f.
Education, domestic, early Christian, 216
Education of Children, Montaigne's, 441ff.
Education of Man, Froebel's, 545ff.
Educational Policies Commission, 578
Education, Spencer's, 556
Edward VI, 375
Egypt, chief sources of its history, 23; chronology of its ancient history, 23f.; classes of people, 24ff.; development of arts and sciences, 26ff.; the scribe, 27; literature, *Ptahhetep*, oldest book in the world, 29; *The Book of the Dead* or Bible of the Egyptians, 29; elementary education in, 31f.; handwriting, 31; training of the priests, 32
Elementarie, Mulcaster's, 445
Eliot, Charles W., 576
Émile, Rousseau's, 503-7; condemnation by Archbishop of Paris, 507; its influence, 507f.

Emmelia, St., 216
England, education in, 609-13; Forster Act, 610; Education Act of 1902, 611; Fisher Act, 612; Education Act of 1944, 613; elementary school system, 611; types of secondary schools, 612; universities, 612; characteristics of the English people and their philosophy of life in relation to school systems, 613
Englebert, 293
English Ladies (Mary Ward, Foundress), 495
Episcopal or Cathedral School, 205f.; advanced curriculum in schools of Gaul, 206f.; Cathedral School of York, 207; two departments (inner and outer), 223; notable schools in France, England, Germany, 224f.
Eramus, Desiderius, 253, 346, 349; 353-60; at Paris, 353f.; at Rome, 354; in England, 354f.; at Basle, 355f.; relation to the Reformation, 356; position as humanist, 357; view on vernaculars, 358; opinion on education of girls, 359f.; estimate of his influence, 360; 361, 367, 372, 373, 395, 407, 424
Eriugena, John Scotus, 244f.; educational activities, 245
Euclid, 231, 281
Eugenius II, Pope, school decrees of (853), 225

Elyot, Thomas, Sir, 373f.
Ephesus, University of, 146
Ethics, Aristotle's, 125, 129
Etymologies, St. Isidore's, 199f.
Euripides, 106, 194
Eusebius, 177
Evelyn, John, 182

Fables, Aesop's, 227, 373, 388
Felbiger, Johann Ignaz von, 511ff.
Fellenberg, Emmanuel, 522
Fénelon, François de Salignac, 439, 476 sqq.; *Treatise on the Education of Girls*, 477ff.; general rule for training girls, 481
Ferrara, University of, 332, 350
Fichte, Johann, 530, 544
Filelfo, Francesco, 323, 336
Finney, Ross L., 572
First Provincial Council of Baltimore, 623
First Synod of Baltimore, 623
Flemming, John, 370
Florence, University of, 323, 324
Fortunatianus, 230
Fourier, Peter, St., 493
France, education in, 600-605; *Loi Guizot*, 601f.; *Loi Falloux*, 602; elementary education, 602f.; secondary education, 603f.; higher education, 604; *école unique*, 605
Francis I, King, 347
Francis of Assisi, St., 288
Franciscans, 288ff., 402, 607, 617
Francke, August Hermann, 496ff.

Frederick I (Barbarossa), 278
Free, John, 370
Froebel, Friedrich Wilhelm, 516, 541-50; his educational theory and the Law of Unity, 544; his principle of self-activity, 545f.; his principle of social participation, 547; his views on religion in the curriculum, 548; his ideas on early training in the kindergarten, 548f.; his influence, 550; 564, 589
Froebel, Karl, 543
Fulgentius, 239
Furstenberg, Franz von, 511
Fürstenschulen (Princes' Schools), 395

Galen, 282, 371
Gall, St., 212; architect's plan of monastery of, 223; the lost Quintilian found in monastery of, 334
Gamala, Joshua b., 80
Gargantua and Pantagruel, Rabelais', 436ff.
Gaudentius, 186
Gaumata, 47
Gautama, 41
Gerbert, 231, 234, 246ff.; as a mathematician, 247; educational accomplishments, 247f.
Germany, education in, 595-600; universities and *Hochschulen*, 597f.; secondary schools, 598f.; elementary school system, 599f.; the *Einheitsschule*, 600

George of Trebizond, 323

Gerson, Jean, 293ff.; educational tracts, 294ff.; views on formation of a portable library, 295; 301, 346

Ghandi, Mahatma, 39

Giacomino of Verona, 289

Girard, Jean Baptiste, 523

Gilbert, St., 287

Gonzaga, Cecilia, 341

Gozaga, Gian Francesco, 336

Gorgias, 112

Governour, Elyot's, 373f.

Gratian, 275

Graves, Frank P., 398

Greek education, 83-134; later period of, 129ff.; different opinions concerning, 131

Gregory IX, Pope, 277, 278, 282

Gregory the Great, Pope, St., 169, 208, 211, 227, 239

Gregory of Nazianzus, St., 177, 179f., 209, 216

Gregory of Nissa, St., 177, 179

Gregory Thaumaturgus, his description of Origen's school, 170f.; 175

Grey, William, 370

Grocyn, William, 371

Groote, Gerard, 349

Guarino, Battista, 325, 332

Gunthorpe, John

Hadley, William, 371

Hähn, Johann, 511

Hall, G. Stanley, 566ff.

Hammurabi, his famous Code of Laws, 60f.

Harris, William T., 549, 565

Harvard College, 548, 621

Hebrews, 30, 33; education of, 72-81; religious belief, 73; periods of Jewish history, 73-76; education of children, 77ff.; education of priests, 77ff.; schools of the prophets, 77f.; education of scribe, 78f.; origin of synagogue, 79; organization of academies, 80; the Bible, gift to mankind, 80; education of women, 81; estimate of educational achievements, 81

Hecker, Julius, 511, 597

Hedge School, 403

Hegel, 532

Hegius, Alexander, 350f.

Heidelberg, University of, 350, 352, 388

Helenes, 83; branches of, 87

Henry VIII, King, 369, 371, 372, 373, 397; suppression of monasteries, 397f.; and the Chantries Act (1545), 399; effects of his revolt on Oxford and Cambridge, 400; his destruction of systematic education of women, 400f.

Herbart, Johann Friedrich, 481, 516, 530-39; three-fold basis of his psychology, 532; his doctrine of interest, 534ff.; his doctrine of apperception, 537; his four formal steps, 537; contribution to educational science, 538; 564

Hermes, 102

Hermonymus, George, 346, 347

Herodotus, 23, 26, 28, 46, 58, 85, 107, 108

Herrad, Abbess, 234

Hesiod, 101, 144

Hexapla, Origen's, 176

Hilary of Arles, St., 239

Hildegard, St., 233

Hincmar, Archbishop, 225

Hindus, 39f., 46; religion of, 39f.

Hippias, 112

Hippocrates, 282

Holes, Andrew, 370

Homer, 26, 86, 99, 101, 144, 150, 194, 321

Honoratus, St., 210

Horace, 142, 144, 146, 194, 239, 321

Horn, Ernest, 572

Horne, Herman H., 572

How Gertrude Teaches Her Children, Pestalozzi's, 523ff.

Hugh of St. Victor, 255, 257f., 258, 262, 287, 297

Humphrey, Duke of Gloucester, 370

Hutchins, Robert Maynard, 576, 577

Hyrde, Richard, 363, 374

Ickelsamer, Valentin, 391

Iliad, 86, 87, 101

India, caste system, 36f.; religious and national life, 39; idea of transmigration of souls, 40; sacred writings, 42; elementary schools, 43; collegiate institutions (Parishads), 43f.; modern education, 44

Innocent VIII, Pope, 267

Ireland, Danish invasion of, and effects, 402; Norman invasion of, and educational destruction, 402; penal laws against Catholic education, 402f.; precarious training in the Hedge School, 403

Irnerius, 274

Ismail, 50

Isidore, St., 198ff.; educational achievements, 199; educational writings, 199f.; his influence on the European mind, 200, 229, 281f.

Israelites, 68

Institutiones, Cassidorus', 197

Isocrates, 109

Jacotot, Joseph, 516, 554-56

James, William, 565f.

Japan, education in, 18-22; language, 20; introduction of Christianity, 21; percentage of Christians, 21; development of modern school system, 21f.

Jason, 85

Jerome, St., 185ff.; his Latin Vulgate, 186; education of girls, 186ff.; 216, 239, 328

Jesuits, see Society of Jesus

Jesus Christ, teaching of, 164-68; His teaching Church, 168-71

John II, King, 345

Johnson, Samuel, 376

Joly, Claude, 302

Judaeus, Isaac, 282

Judd, Charles H., 572

Julian the Apostate, 155
Julius II, Pope, 347
Justin Martyr, St., 173f.
Justinian, Emperor, 147
Juvenal, 147, 194, 346
Juvencus, 239

Kant, 531
Khordan Avesta, 53
Khufu, 28
Kilpatrick, William H., 572
Kublai Kahn, 6
Kühlmann, Frederick, 574
Kshatriyas, 36

Lactantius Firmianus, 183f.; attitude toward pagan learning, 184; 328
Lamy, Bernard, 486
Lanfranc, 255
Lao-tse, 7ff.
Lateran, Third Council of, 299f.; Fourth Council of, 300
Latimer, Hugh, his sermon on sad condition of English schools after Reformation, 401f.
Latimer, William, 371
Laws, Plato's, 123
Leach, A. F., concerning English schools at the Reformation, 398ff.
Leander, Bishop of Seville, 198
L'Enseignement universel, Jacotot's, 555
Leo III, Pope, St., 219
Leo X, Pope, 325. 347, 371, 407
Leo XIII, Pope, 291
Leonard and Gertrude, Pestalozzi's, 519

Liberal Arts College, changes in its curriculum, 576f.
Letter to Gaudentius, St. Jerome's, 186
Letter to Laeta, St. Jerome's, 186ff.
Liber de viris illustribus, Saint Jerome's, 186
Lily, William, 372
Linacre, Thomas, 371
Livy, 146, 295, 321, 339, 345, 346
Locke, John, 439, 469 sqq.; views on physical training, 471; views on moral training, 471ff.; views on intellectual training, 473ff.; educational opinions and theory of transfer of training, 475
Lombard, Peter, 280
Louis IX, King, 258, 263, 283
Louis XII, King, 347
Louvain, University of, 350, 361, 393
Loyola, Ignatius, St., 411ff.
Lucan, 144, 194, 239
Lucretius, 146
Luther, Martin, 383; doctrine of justification through faith, 386; advocated state control of schools, 387; education of boys and girls, 388; work primarily religious, 388; 391, 395, 424
Lyceum, 102, 124
Lycurgus. 26, 90
Lysias, 109

Magi, 57
Mahabharata, 43

Manchu dynasty, 6
Manetho, 23
Manetti, Gianozzo, 325
Mann, Horace, 619f.
Manu, Code of, 42f.
Marco Polo, 6, 18
Marianists, 607
Marist Brothers, 607
Marist Fathers, 607
Marseilles, University of, 146
Martin of Deume, St., 210
Martin of Tours, St., 210
Maur, St., 210, 211
Maurus, Rhabanus, 223, 229, 242 sqq.; his writings, 243; educational influence, 244
Maurya dynasty, 38
Medes, 46
Medieval education, summary of, 308f.
Meiji, Emperor, 19
Melanchthon, Philip, 352, 383, 388ff.; founder of Protestant theology, 389; educational influence, 390; 395, 424
Mencius, 8
Merchant Taylors' School, 306, 444
Merici, Angela, St., 421
Middle Ages, period of, 204
Milton, 439
Ming dynasty, 6, 10
Minos, King of Crete, 85
Mitylene, University of, 146
Monasticism, eremetical and cenobitical forms, 209f.; influence of St. Benedict, 210
Monastic School, 209; early schools of Gaul and Ireland,

214f.; seven liberal arts curriculum, 215; discipline of students, 215; two departments (externs and interns), 215; notable schools in France, Germany, England, 224f.; fuller development of, 228
Modern education, summary of, 627f.
Mohammedans, 40, 49; their influence on medieval education, 248 sqq.; contributions to Europe, 250
Montanists, 183
Moses, 26
Monica, St., 332
Monnier, R., 338
Montaigne, 439 sqq.; 481
Montessori, Maria, 549
Montpellier, University of, 274, 279
More, Thomas, St., 356, 368, 372ff., 374
Morrison, Henry C., 572
Mulcaster, Richard, 444ff.
Murmellius, John, 351
Muses, 102

Nabuchodonosor, 61
Naples, University of, 277
Naturalism, 501 sqq.
Neander, Michael, 395, 425
Neef, Joseph, 528
Neri, St. Philip, 485
Nestorians, 7
Nicholas V, Pope, 324
Niemeyer, August Hermann, 510
Nonna, St., 216

Odyssey, 86, 87; translation into Latin, 140

Oratio catechetica magna, St. Gregory of Nyssa, 179

Oratorians, 485; the curriculum of their College of Juilly

Origen, 170f., 175f.

Oresme, Nicholas, 345

Orosius, 227, 239

Osmania University, 44

Osorio, Bishop, 349

Outlines of General Pedagogy, Herbarts', 532ff.

Overberg, Bernard, 511

Ovid, 146, 194, 321, 346, 367, 373

Oxford, University of, 276f., 282, 283, 284, 289, 371

Pachomius, St., 209

Padua, University of, 277, 321, 323, 324, 335, 346, 370, 371

Palaestra, 99, 101, 102, 116

Palencia, University of, 277

Palmieri, Matteo, 325, 331

Pantaenus, 170

Pariahs or untouchables, 36, 37

Paris, University of, 274, 275, 276, 278, 279, 282, 283, 284, 289, 292, 293, 347, 350, 352, 393, 403

Parish Schools, 207f.; decrees of Council of Vaison and Ecumenical Council of Constantinople concerning them, 208; ecclesiastical law of England (ninth and tenth centuries) regarding them, 227f.; Tridentine laws in regard to them, 408

Parker, Francis W., 563f.

Parochial elementary schools in U. S. (1945), 626

Parsees, 50, 53

Parsons, Robert, 402

Paul III, Pope, 356, 407, 435

Paulsen, Friedrich, 303, 383

Pavia, University of, 324

Peabody, Elizabeth P., 549

Pedantry, Montaigne's, 440ff.

Perseus, 85

Pergamum, University of, 131, 146

Pericles, Age of, 88, 104, 107

Perneb, tomb of, 28

Perotti, Nicholas, 325, 359

Pegasus, 85

Persia, satraps, 50f.; fundamental religious beliefs, 52; religious literature, 52; system of writing, 54; elementary school training, 55f.; higher education, 56; position of woman, 56; estimate of ancient education, 56

Pestalozzi, Johann Heinrich, 508, 516-28; educational activities at Neuhof, 518f.; educational efforts at Stanz, 519f.; educational work at Burgdorf, 521; educational achievements at Yverdun, 522f.; summary of his principles, 525f.; his religion, 526f.; causes of his failures, 527; his influence, 527f.; 531, 541, 549, 564, 589

Pestalozzianism and naturalism, 527

Petrarch, 321f., 334, 336, 345, 370

Pharisees, origin of, 79

Pharaoh, 23, 24, 47

Phidias, 104, 147

Philanthropinum, Basedow's, 508f.

Philip IV (The Fair), 292, 302

Phoenicians, 68ff.; extensive sea trade, 69; chief cities, 69; colonization, 69f.; formation of alphabet, 70ff.; literature of, 72; shortcomings of educational training, 72

Piarists, 422, 607

Piccolomini, Aeneas Sylvius, see Pius II, Pope

Pico della Mirandola, 267, 367

Pietists, 510

Pius II, Pope (Aeneas Sylvius), 263, 324, 325, 329f.

Pius XI, Pope, 410

Plato, 26, 30, 92, 102, 113, 120ff.; relation to Socrates, 121; his ideal state, 121; his writings, 122; emphasis on quadrivium and theory of "formal discipline," 123; mature views, political and educational, 123; philosophical teachings, 123f.; importance of his theory of education, 124; 194, 321

Pliny, 147, 239

Plutarch, 108, 334, 337

Poggio, 334, 370

Pole, Cardinal Reginald, 407, 409

Polentone, Secco, 325

Politics, Aristotle's, 125, 129

Polybius, 108

Porphyry, 192, 229, 246

Port-Royalists, 486; their petites écoles, 487; the curriculum of their schools, 487; some Port-Royal writers and their works, 488

Positions, Mulcaster's, 444f.

Praxiteles, 147

Presentation Sisters, 495

Priscian, 229, 239, 281

Prodicus, 112

Protagoras, 112

Pseudo-Dionysius, 245

Psychological Movement, 516, 595

Ptolemies, 24, 131

Ptolemy, Claudius, 231, 281

Punishment, corporal, 330f., 333

Pythagoras, 26, 113ff.

Queen Victoria, Empress of India, 39

Quintilian, 147, 148ff.; educational views: learning the alphabet, 148; first steps in writing, 148; cultivation of memory, 148; principles of emulation and imitation, 148; opinion on corporal punishment, 148f.; the teacher and his pupils, 149; choice of books, 149f.; favored classroom instruction, 150; ethical purpose of orator's training, 151; 230; discovery of complete copy of his De institutione oratoria, 334; 346

Rabelais, François, 270, 435ff.

Ramayana, 43

Rawlinson, Henry, Sir, 54

Rashdall, Hastings, 274, 284

Ratke, Wolfgang, 453 sqq.; his model school, 454; extent to which modern education is indebted to him, 456

Realism, 434 sqq.

Realists, humanistic, 435 sqq.

Realists, Sense, 449 sqq.

Reformation, character of, 383; effects of on education in Germany, 384; and the Bible, 385; in Switzerland, 395ff.; in England, 397-402; in Ireland, 402f.

Reformation, Catholic Counter, 407 sqq.

Reformation, summary of, 424f.

Rein, Wilhelm, 583

Remigius of Auxerre, 229

Renaissance of twelfth century, 254

Renaissance in Italy, 319-43; character of, 319; opportunities for scholars, 325; treatises on education, 325-35; similarity of subject matter in educational treatises, 333f.; influence of Quintilian on educational ideas, 334; outstanding feature of these early treatises, 334f.; education of Florentine women, 331f.; pagan humanists, 342; in France, 345-48; in Spain, 348f.; in Northern Europe, 349-70; in England, 370-77

Renaissance, summary of, 424

Report of the Harvard Committee, 576f.

Republic, Plato's, 122

Resende, 349

Retractions, St. Augustine's, 189

Reuchlin, Johann, 350, 352, 388

Revival of Learning, 319; influence on the Latin language, 342f.

Rhodes, University of, 131, 146

Ricci, Matteo, 7

Rice, J. M., 573

Richelieu, 443

Ritterakademie, 443

Rig Veda, 42

Roman citizen, compared to Greek citizen, 137f.

Roman education, 135-55; three general periods of, 135; ideal of, 138; types of schools, 143ff.; best exposition of theory of, 147f.; place of religion in, 153; decline of, 154f.

Roman Empire, causes of its fall, 137

Roman law, 147

Roman literature, Golden Age of, 146; Silver Age of, 146f.

Roman social system, 152; position of woman, 152f.

Rome, University of, 131, 325, 350, 370, 371, 403

Rosetta Stone, 31

Rosmini-Serbati, Antonio, 516, 550-54; his ruling principle of method, 552

Rousseau, Jean Jacques, 439, 501-8, 526, 527, 544, 547

Rugg, Harold, 572

Rule for Monks, St. Isidore's, 200

Sacrificial Veda, 42

Sadoleto, Cardinal Jacopo, 367, 407

Saducees, origin of, 79

Saint-Cryan, Abbé of (Jean Duvergier de Hauranne), 486

Salamanca, University of, 277, 348, 403

Salerno, University of, 231, 274

Salesians, pedagogy of their schools, 554; 607

Sallust, 146, 346

Salzmann, Christian Gotthilf, 510

Sama Veda, 42

Sanskrit, 37

Sassanid Empire, 49

Schelling, Friedrich. 530, 544

Schliemann, Heinrich, 86

Schmidt, Joseph, 523

Scholars, Wandering, 303f.

Scholastic Movement, 231; its educational scheme, 268; period of decay and decline, 269

Scholasticism, 253-70; in the twelfth century, 255ff.; in the thirteenth and fourteenth centuries, 258ff.

Scholemaster, Ascham's, 375f.

School at Bec, 255

School Sisters of Notre Dame, 495

Schools, types of (later Middle Ages), 302 sqq: burgh, 302; town, 302f.; venture, 303; chantry, 304f.; guild, 305ff.

Scriptorium, 196, 212

Scythians, 46

Second Plenary Council of Baltimore, 624

Second Provincial Council of Cincinnati, 624

Sedulius, 239

Seleucus, 38, 49

Selling, William, 370f.

Semitic peoples, 58-81

Seneca, 147, 194, 295, 321, 346

Sennacherib, 64

Septuagint, 76, 176

Seven liberal arts, 228-31; trivium, 228ff.; quadrivium, 230ff.

Shalmaneser, 64

Shakespeare, 320

Shields, Thomas Edward, 581-89; his theory of education, 587ff.; the Shields Method and The Catholic University Campus School, 589

Shintoism, 20

Sisters of Charity of St. Vincent de Paul, 495

Sisters of Mercy of St. Charles Borromeo, 495

Sisters of Notre Dame, 495

Sisters of the Presentation of the Blessed Virgin, 495

Sisters of St. Joseph, 495

Smerdis, the Usurper, 47

Smyrna, University of, 146

Snedden, David, 572

Social Contract, Rousseau's, 503

Society of Jesus, 7, 411-21; Constitution of the Order, 413f.; *Ratio Studiorum,* 414ff.; noteworthy features of Jesuit educational system, 418f.; growth of Society and development of schools, 420f.; 425, 607, 609

Socrates, 113, 117, 118, 120, 121, 128, 131; refutation of teaching of sophists, 118f.; methods of teaching, 119; religious beliefs, 120; educational achievements, 120; 321

Solon, 26, 99

Somasca, Congregation of, 411

Song Schools, 208f.; Pope Gregory the Great and Schola Cantorum at Rome, 208; curriculum of schools, 208

Sophists, 111ff.; their educational influence, 112f.; 116f.

Sophocles, 86, 107

Sorbonne, College of, 283

Spain, education in, 605-9; percentage of illiterates, 606f.; secondary education, 607; university education, 608f.; the new law of Franco, 608

Sparta, 88, 89ff.; organization of city, 89; government, 90; system of education, 90ff; discipline of boys, 93; education of women, 93f.; criticism of educational system, 94

Speculum majus of Vincent of Beauvais, 259-262

Spencer, Herbert, 516, 556ff.; his definition of education, 556; his influence, 558f.; 564

St. Omer's, Calais, France, 402

St. Paul's School, 444

Statius, 144, 239

Stern, William, 574

Stonyhurst College, 402

Stoy, Karl Volkmar, 538

Stromata, Clement of Alexandria, 175

Sturm, Johann, organization of his Latin school at Strassburg, 393f.; educational influence, 394; and the German gymnasium, 395; 425

Sudras, 36, 37

Suetonius, 147, 295

Sulpicians (Society of St. Sulpice), 494

Sumerians, 59f.

Sunday School, 408

Symmachus, 176

Symonds, J. A., 335, 342

Tacitus, 147

Talmud, 79, 80

Taoism, 11

Tarsus, University of, 146

Temple of Jerusalem, 70

Terence, 346

Terman, Lewis M., 575

Tertullian, 182f.

Tertullianists, 183

The Pedagogue, Clement of Alexandria, 174f.

Teutonic peoples and reshaping of Europe, 204

Theatines, 410f.

Theodoric, 192

Theodotion, 176

Theognis, 101

Theodulf of Orleans, Bishop, his decree regarding free elementary education for poor, 222; 225

Thibaut, King of Navarre, 263

Third Order of St. Francis, 288f.

Third Plenary Council of Baltimore, 625

Thomas, Saint, apostle of India and the East, 7

Thomas à Kempis, 349

Thomas Aquinas, St., 193, 256, 263, 264f., 266, 267, 282, 291

Thomas of Cantimpré, 292

Thomassin, Louis, 486

Thorndike, Edward L., 572ff.

Thucydides, 107

Tibullus, 194

Torah (Law), 79, 80

Tifernas, Gregorio, 346

Tiptoft, John, 370

Toulouse, University of, 277, 282, 403

Trent, Council of, 407ff.; regulations of, concerning seminaries, universities, Sunday school, parish school, 408; 425

Tribonian, 147

Trojan War, 86

Trotzendorf, Valentin, 391f., 425

Trypho, 174

Tschu-li, educational principles of, 11f.

Tübingen, University of, 389

Tutankhamen, tomb of, 29

Twelve Tables, Laws of, 139

United States, education in, 617-27; origin of modern common school, 617f.; academies, 620f.; the development of the high school, 621; the Kalamazoo Case, 621; higher education, 621; the Junior College, 622; the Catholic school system, 622-27

Universities, medieval, 273 sqq.: general causes of their rise, 273f.; origin of name, 275f.; "student universities," 276; "master universities," 276; charters, 277; privileges, 278; faculties, 278f.; entrance requirements, 279; degrees, 279f.; methods of teaching, 280f.; content of studies and texts, 281f.; influence on medieval culture and modern institutions, 282f.; enrollment, 282f.; colleges, 283f.; achievements of, 284f.

Ursuline, 421

Vaisyas, 36

Valentinian I, 184

Valerius Maximus, 295

Valla, Lorenzo, 342

Valladolid, University of, 277, 402

Van Dorp, Martin, 361

Vatican Library, 324

Vedas, sacred writings of Hindus, 42, 43

Vendidad, 53

Vegio, Maffeo, 325, 330f.; views on training of women, 331

Vergerio, Pier Paolo, 323, 325; idea of a liberal education, 326; analysis of his treatise, *On Noble Character,* 327f.; influence of treatise, 328; 334, 335, 336, 337

Vergil, 144, 146, 150, 194, 229, 239, 321, 339, 340, 346

Vicenza, University of, 277

Victor, St., 210; School of, 287

Victorinus, 185, 239

Vienne, Council of, 346

Vincent of Beauvais, 258ff.; his treatise, *On the Instruction of Princes,* 263; 282, 291

Vincentians (Congregation of the Mission of St. Vincent de Paul), 494

Visitation Nuns (Visitandines), 495

Vives, Juan Luis, 346, 348, 359, 360-70; career in England, 363ff.; views on the teacher, 366f.; opinion on the disputations in the schools, 367; emphasis on use of the vernacular, 367; modern treatment of curriculum in general, 367f.; suggestions concerning education of women, 368; as an educational psychologist, 369; estimate of his educational activities, 369; 372, 374, 424

Voltaire (François Marie Arouet), 501

Von Bülow, Baroness, 549

Von Kaisersberg, Johann Geiler, 351

Von Langen, Rudolph, 351

Wessel, John, 350

William of Champeaux, 256, 287

William of Croy, Cardinal Archbishop, 361

William of Occam, 254, 263, 266, 289

William of Tournai, 291

Wimpheling, Jacob, 351, 393

Wittenberg, University of, 385, 389, 391

Women, education of in Middle Ages, 231 sqq.: skilled copyists, 232; instructed in useful and household arts, 232; higher instruction in seven liberal arts, 233; learned women, 233f.

Xavier, Francis, St., 21

Xenophon, 46, 49, 55, 108

Xerxes, 48

Ximenes, Cardinal, 349

Yale University, 621; report of its committee of ten, 578

Zarathustra, 51

Zend-Avesta, 46, 49, 53, 54

Zeuxis, 105

Ziller, Tuiskon, 538

Zoroaster, 49, 51

Zwingli, Ulrich, 395f.